PRENTICE HALL FINANCE SERIES

Personal Finance
Keown, *Personal Finance: Turning Money into Wealth, Second Edition*
Trivoli, *Personal Portfolio Management: Fundamentals & Strategies*
Winger/Frasca, *Personal Finance: An Integrated Planning Approach, Fifth Edition*

Investments/Portfolio Management
Alexander/Sharpe/Bailey, *Fundamentals of Investments, Third Edition*
Fabozzi, *Investment Management, Second Edition*
Fischer/Jordan, *Security Analysis and Portfolio Management, Sixth Edition*
Francis/Ibbotson, *Investments: A Global Perspective*
Haugen, *Modern Investment Theory, Fifth Edition*
Haugen, *The New Finance*
Haugen, *The Beast on Wall Street*
Haugen, *The Inefficient Stock Market, Second Edition*
Holden, *Spreadsheet Modeling: A Book and CD-ROM Series* (Available in Graduate and Undergraduate Versions)
Sharpe/Alexander/Bailey, *Investments, Sixth Edition*
Taggart, *Quantitative Analysis for Investment Management*
Winger/Frasca, *Investments, Third Edition*

Options/Futures/Derivatives
Hull, *Fundamentals of Futures and Options Markets, Fourth Edition*
Hull, *Options, Futures, and Other Derivatives, Fourth Edition*

Risk Management/Financial Engineering
Mason/Merton/Perold/Tufano, *Cases in Financial Engineering*

Fixed Income Securities
Handa, *FinCoach: Fixed Income* (software)

Bond Markets
Fabozzi, *Bond Markets, Analysis and Strategies, Fourth Edition*

Corporate Finance/Survey of Finance/Financial Economics
Bodie/Merton, *Finance*
Emery/Finnerty/Stowe, *Principles of Financial Management*
Emery/Finnerty, *Corporate Financial Management*
Gallagher/Andrew, *Financial Management: Principles and Practices, Second Edition*
Keown/Martin/Petty/Scott, *Financial Management, Ninth Edition*
Keown/Martin/Petty/Scott, *Foundations of Finance: The Logic and Practice of Financial Management, Third Edition*
Mathis, *Corporate Finance Live: A Web-based Math Tutorial*
Shapiro/Balbirer, *Modern Corporate Finance: A Multidisciplinary Approach to Value Creation*
Van Horne, *Financial Management and Policy, Twelfth Edition*
Van Horne/Wachowicz, *Fundamentals of Financial Management, Eleventh Edition*

International Finance
Baker, *International Finance: Management, Markets, and Institutions*
Click/Coval, *The Theory and Practice of International Financial Management*
Grabbe, *International Financial Markets, Third Edition*
Rivera-Batiz/Rivera-Batiz, *International Finance and Open Economy Macroeconomics, Second Edition*

Capital Budgeting
Aggarwal, *Capital Budgeting Under Uncertainty*
Bierman/Smidt, *The Capital Budgeting Decision, Eighth Edition*

The Theory and Practice of International Financial Management

The Theory and Practice of International Financial Management

❖ ❖ ❖

REID W. CLICK

GEORGE WASHINGTON UNIVERSITY

JOSHUA D. COVAL

UNIVERSITY OF MICHIGAN

Prentice
Hall

UPPER SADDLE RIVER, NEW JERSEY 07458

Click, Reid W.
   The theory and practice of international financial management /
     Reid W. Click, Joshua D. Coval.
     p. cm.
   Includes bibliographical references and index.
   ISBN 0-13-020457-9
     1. International finance.   I. Coval, Joshua D.   II. Title.
   HG3881 .C5814 2001
   332′.042—dc21   00-065284

Senior Editor: Maureen Riopelle
Editor-in-Chief: P. J. Boardman
Managing Editor (Editorial): Gladys Soto
Assistant Editor: Cheryl Clayton
Editorial Assistant: Melanie Olsen
Media Project Manager: Bill Minick
Marketing Manager: Joshua P. McClary
Marketing Assistant: Lauren Tarino
Manager, Production: Gail Steier de Acevedo
Production Editor: Maureen Wilson
Permissions Coordinator: Suzanne Grappi
Associate Director, Manufacturing: Vincent Scelta
Manufacturing Buyer: Natacha St. Hill Moore
Cover Design: Bruce Kenselaar
Cover Illustration/Photo: Reza Estakhrian/Stone
Full-Service Project Management: BookMasters, Inc.
Printer/Binder: Maple Vail

Credits and acknowledgments borrowed from other sources and reproduced, with permission, in this textbook appear on appropriate page within text.

10 9 8 7 6 5 4 3 2 1
ISBN 0-13-020457-9

BRIEF CONTENTS

CONTENTS

The field of international financial management addresses financial decisions facing corporate managers regarding trade and investment across national borders. As firms become increasingly involved in the global economy, issues in international financial management become more important. Simultaneously, events taking place on the international financial stage—from trade disputes to currency crises—make the issues more intriguing. As a result of the additional attention to international financial management, new approaches to the issues have been developed over the past decade. These new approaches are characterized by high analytical rigor, substantial attention to empirical evidence, and integration of functional areas (including finance, economics, strategy, and accounting/taxation). Most importantly, however, the new approaches are designed to establish decision processes that can be applied in various situations and under changing circumstances.

This book captures the newfound importance and excitement of international financial management, and highlights the new approaches in the field. It is the result of designing our own courses in international financial management to be rigorous and timeless, as well as practical, interesting, and relevant for the students. The book covers the theoretical foundations of international financial decisions, but also contains extensive applications of the theory to financial practice. This combination has been quite rewarding for us and for our classes, and we are sure that you will find the structure rewarding as well—whether you are the instructor or the student.

We are grateful to three editors who helped us develop this book. At Prentice Hall, Paul Donnelly was the Finance Editor who did all the work to get us a publishing contract, and Maureen Riopelle was the Finance Editor who did all the work to get the book finished. Libby Rubenstein, the Developmental Editor, read every sentence of the manuscript and provided extensive corrections and suggestions for improvement.

Those who have also reviewed this text include Jorge L. Urrutia, Loyola University Chicago; Youngho Lee, School of Business, Howard University; Joseph E. Finnerty, University of Illinois; Mark Eaker, University of Virginia; Geert Bakaert, Columbia University; Amar Gande, Vanderbilt University, Owen Graduate School of Management; Christopher T. Stivers, University of Georgia, Terry College of Business; Andrea L. DeMaskey, Villanova University; Stanley Heyn, St. Mary's College; Balasundram Maniam, Sam Houston State University; Michael W. Carter, University of Arkansas–Fayetteville; and Owen Gregory, University of Illinois at Chicago.

THE ESSENCE OF THIS BOOK

The Theory and Practice of International Financial Management provides a streamlined, consistent framework of principles that form the basis of decisions in this field. Although there are already many books on international financial management,[1] we were motivated to write this one because we found that nearly all of the existing books fail to provide adequate analytical foundations. In contrast, this book is more rigorous than most other books because it presumes a familiarity with many ideas that form the basis of modern business curriculums. In recognition of the fact that the world is changing faster than textbooks can convey, this book also contains less institutional detail than most textbooks, as many specific facts are likely to be outdated by the time you read this preface.

In addition to presenting the theory of international financial management, however, and despite the lack of ever-changing institutional detail, this book contains a significant focus on applications of the theory to managerial decisions. Students are typically more motivated to study theory when they see its practical applications, so we present the practice of international financial management alongside the theory. Although the specific examples may no longer be current, and while students will be confronted by completely different situations in their professional careers, the applications here are nonetheless valuable because they highlight the use of relevant theory rather than the details of the applications themselves. Because the challenges of operating in an interdependent and competitive global marketplace are constantly changing, providing principles and analytical concepts is far more useful than providing institutional facts and specific advice. The main objective of this book is thus to help students develop critical thinking skills regarding the theory and practice of international financial management.

THE READER

Like a workman's toolkit that holds the mechanical implements necessary to confront a wide variety of repair jobs, this book is a toolkit that holds the intellectual principles necessary to confront a wide variety of managerial decisions. These principles come from many different fields, including accounting, taxation, corporate finance, statistics, economics, international finance, marketing, management, production, strategy, and a few other areas of business. In this regard, the book is much more than a finance text. In fact, it is a particularly economic approach to international financial management, providing applications of international macroeconomics to the microeconomic theory of the firm.

In studying the theory and practice of international financial management, some knowledge of accounting, taxation, corporate finance, statistics, economics, international finance, marketing, management, production, strategy, and other areas of business will be helpful, but is not required because we explain the main concepts when we introduce them. We designed this book to integrate relevant concepts from all of these areas, however, so we do not put much effort into reinventing any particular concept. The intended audience thus consists of MBA and advanced undergraduate students who have substantially completed the required courses in their programs. For readers needing more background information, we provide citations to materials explaining the concepts throughout, with particular attention to practitioner-oriented resources.[2] By focusing on basic principles and integrating concepts from many areas, this book establishes a broad framework in which international financial decisions in corporate enterprises are readily analyzed.

Globalization of business and economics curricula has produced a generation of students and managers with a deeper understanding of the international environment than previously presumed, and this book uses that understanding as a base for additional development. It will soon be clear that a fundamental understanding of capital flows, exchange rates, financial risk, and the parity theorems of international finance provides powerful insights to the theory and practice of international financial management. In many schools, these topics are covered in core courses required for the degree, either through a separate course explicitly designed to introduce issues in the world economy or through international components in functional courses ranging from finance and accounting to strategy. In this regard, international financial management is most appropriately studied after an introduction to such topics. Students may additionally benefit from a preliminary course on either international finance or international financial markets. For example, a course in international finance covering the macroeconomics of balance of payments adjustments, exchange rate determination, the effects of government or central bank intervention in the foreign exchange markets, and the history of the international monetary system will provide a solid background for the examination of international financial management.[3] Similarly, a course on international financial markets covering spot and forward foreign exchange markets, futures and options on foreign exchange, offshore ("Eurocurrency") markets for deposits and borrowing, long-term bank lending, and international bond and stock markets will also provide a solid background.[4] A previous course on international finance or international financial markets is not an absolute prerequisite, however, because we review the main concepts from international finance and international financial markets when we introduce them, although again we do not put much effort into reinventing any particular concept.

A GUIDE TO MANAGEMENT ACTIVITIES

This book is short, especially for a textbook. In fact, it is something akin to a libretto ("little book"), which serves as a guide to operatic activities that unfold on the theater stage, except that this "little book" serves as a guide to management activities that unfold on the international financial stage. As the book's focus is on providing the basic principles which together make a toolkit for analysis, it is necessarily short, presenting a concise, compact approach to issues in international financial management. Because of this streamlined presentation, we have had particularly good results using the book as the core of a course supplemented with practitioner articles, academic articles, current news reports, and a wide variety of case studies tailored to the audience. We provide citations to some of these supplemental materials throughout the text for anyone needing more specific information, and instructors will undoubtedly add some of their favorites.

The tools and principles we develop in this little book are also developed through a variety of pedagogical techniques: diagrammatic models, statistical summaries, numerical examples, mathematical formulas, small case studies in boxes paralleling the analytical development, and extended spreadsheet examples, to name a few. For each topic we take up, we have chosen the presentation technique most suitable for that issue. Whenever possible, we examine the topic from more than one perspective, using more than one pedagogical technique. The result is a diverse textbook in which variety keeps the material interesting while simultaneously recounting a consistent, compelling, and comprehensive story. At the end of each chapter, we include 10–15 questions for review so that students can test their comprehension of the material. For the instructor we provide a Solutions Manual to serve as an answer guide to those text review questions. Also included in the manual are lecture notes to be used by the instructor for class preparation. We provide advanced technical material in "Tools for Analysis" appendices at the ends of most chapters for students who want to study some elements of the material in more precise detail, perhaps because they intend to pursue a career in international financial management. Our accompanying Web site will serve as another helpful tool for students who wish to expand on their study sessions. This Web site is available to download at www.prenhall.com/financecenter.

OVERVIEW OF THE BOOK

The material in this book is organized into four parts containing twelve chapters. Broadly speaking, the core of the material on financial management in multinational corporations is in Parts II and III. Part II focuses on the main foreign investment decisions: deciding whether to undertake a foreign project based on capital budgeting analysis, deciding how to finance the foreign investment once the decision to undertake the project is made, and deciding on a foreign investment strategy that is profitable. We introduce these issues early in the book because they represent the most fundamental decisions in international financial management required to get foreign projects up and running.

Part III then focuses on the traditional issues of foreign exchange risk for foreign investments once they have been made: measuring foreign exchange exposure, evaluating foreign exchange risk, and implementing hedging and operating techniques to reduce foreign exchange risk. This material covers the ongoing financial concerns associated with foreign investments, and is an integral part of foreign project analysis.

Before getting to this core material in Parts II and III, however, Part I provides analytical material on international capital flows and international parity propositions which is used in the analysis of foreign investment decisions and foreign exchange risk. At the end of the book, to wrap up the main analysis, Part IV examines two special topics in international financial management: international taxation and political risk.

Part I introduces international macroeconomic concepts in two chapters. Chapter 1 focuses on international investment and capital flows in general, analyzing portfolio investment and bank lending as well as investment in foreign projects by multinational corporations, known as direct foreign investment. We organize the discussion around models of international capital flows, differences between foreign and domestic investments, and real interest parity. Chapter 2 examines international parity propositions which we subsequently use throughout the rest of the book: purchasing power parity, uncovered interest parity, covered interest parity, and the unbiased forward rate hypothesis.

Part II begins the focus on the practice of international financial management by considering what it takes for a firm to get a foreign project going. Chapters 3 and 4 examine the evaluation of foreign projects (international capital budgeting) and the financing of international projects, respectively. These chapters concentrate on the fundamental choice between centralizing financial decisions in multinational corporations at the headquarters level or decentralizing them to the level of foreign subsidiaries. This framework of centralization versus decentralization is one of the chief paradigms in the traditional literature—perhaps even folklore—of international financial management. Chapter 5 synthesizes the foreign project evaluation and financing issues by considering the broader perspective of foreign investment strategy.

Part III then considers international financial management once a project is operating. In five chapters, it examines the impact of exchange rate changes on various firms and the management policies that can be used to mitigate the effects. The material ranges from foreign exchange exposure (Chapters 6 and 7), through foreign exchange risk analysis (Chapter 8), to hedging or operationally managing foreign exchange risk (Chapters 9 and 10). More specifically, Chapter 6 examines the impact that exchange rate changes have on the translation of financial statements and contractual transactions, and Chapter 7 examines the impact on the ongoing economic activity of the firm. These chapters focus on what the company has exposed to exchange rate changes—or measures of what the company has at stake. The former chapter is an analysis of nominal exchange rate changes and the accounting process, while the latter chapter is an analysis of real exchange rate changes and cash flows. Chapter 8 then presents an analysis of the risk associated with the exposure to exchange rate changes. The methodology in this chapter uses the statistical standard deviation of exchange rate changes as a measure of risk, and covariances and correlations among currencies for portfolios of multiple exposures. Chapter 9 pursues some financial tools for hedging the foreign exchange risk using foreign currency forwards, money markets, futures, and options. The final chapter in this part, Chapter 10, is an overview of motivations and strategies for managing foreign exchange risk. This chapter draws together much of the analysis on exposure, risk, and hedging contained in Chapters 6–9.

Part IV examines multinational firms' interactions with different governments. Two key areas have been the subject of considerable research: international taxation and political risk. Chapter 11 looks at the theoretical public policy aspects of international taxation and analyzes international tax management within firms. This chapter considers accounting techniques and transaction management decisions designed to reduce the tax burden of multinational firms. Chapter 12 presents the public policy foundations of political risk, and follows up with political risk assessment and management decisions within firms. This chapter examines political risk much like any other risk facing business, and reconsiders the capital budgeting decision in the presence of political risk.

THEMES OF THE BOOK

Foreign investments are distinguished from domestic investments not only by location, but also by currency, applicable interest rates, and governmental jurisdiction. The main reason that international financial management merits its own field of study is because national borders are not irrelevant: dealing with multiple currencies, interest rates, and governments creates a whole new dimension of financial complexity. However, this would not be the case if currencies and interest rates continuously behaved according to international parity conditions and if governments never got involved in cross-border financial transactions. Indeed, under these circumstances, international financial management would be nearly identical to domestic financial management and remaining distinctions would be trivial.

The major questions in international financial management thus center around the degree to which international parity propositions hold and to which there is government intervention. The questions boil down to whether the world is characterized by complete integration of capital markets into a global capital market in which parity propositions hold and government intervention is minimal, or whether instead the world is characterized by segmentation into individual national capital markets across which parity propositions do not hold and governments intervene extensively.

If there is an integrated global capital market, financial managers will all be on a level playing field competing against each other for investment projects and market financing, and will typically find that risk management is not a beneficial activity. If there are segmented national capital markets, financial managers will find different advantages in different locations and will search for unusually profitable investment projects and unusually inexpensive financing, and will find risk management more rewarding.

This integration-versus-segmentation paradigm provides the over-arching theme to the book, which is that global capital market integration makes international financial management easier, but that national capital market segmentation makes international financial management more valuable. We thus initially approach decisions from the perspective of integrated capital markets, then reconsider the decisions from the perspective of segmented capital markets.

We develop the over-arching theme—that global capital market integration makes international financial management easier, but that national capital market segmentation makes international financial management more valuable—via four sub-themes throughout the remainder of the book. Typically, one new sub-theme is developed in each part, and is then extended to later parts. Three of the sub-themes derive from the parity propositions of international finance. Although some familiarity with the parity propositions will be helpful, they are introduced in Chapters 1 and 2 with the expectation that some readers will be encountering them for the first time and others will require a thorough review.

The first sub-theme is that there is an equilibrium level of international investment which generally equates real interest rates across countries. This concept, known as real interest parity, is introduced in Part I as the theoretical foundation for analyzing international capital flows. Whether real interest parity holds depends on whether international capital markets are perfectly integrated or are at least partially segmented, so this sub-theme is directly related to the over-arching theme. Whether or not there are deviations from equilibrium in international investment levels is a critical facet in Part II when considering the impact of international differences in real interest rates on capital budgeting and financing decisions. Segmentation and deviations from equilibrium also provide the motivation for some theories of direct foreign investment examined in Chapter 5 on foreign investment strategy. We also extend the concepts in Part IV, examining the effects of taxes and political risk on the levels of international investment and real interest rates. Hence, this first theme is carried throughout the book.

The second sub-theme is that the choice between centralizing or decentralizing various financial management decisions within a multinational firm should be based on the relationship between nominal interest rate differentials and the expected nominal exchange rate change. Application of this relationship, known as uncovered interest parity, provides the topics of Part II. We examine international capital budgeting and the cost of capital with respect to the uncovered interest parity condition, and show centralization-versus-decentralization to pertain to both the location of decision making and the methodology of capital budgeting used. We also examine international financing with respect to uncovered interest parity, in the same centralization-versus-decentralization framework. However, the importance of the centralization-versus-decentralization framework is tied to the integration-versus-segmentation theme. For both the capital budgeting and financing discussions, integration of capital markets implies that the choice of centralization versus decentralization is largely irrelevant because the different perspectives lead to identical conclusions. On the flip side, segmentation of capital markets implies that the choice between centralization and decentralization is important because the choice affects the outcome of the decision.

The third major sub-theme is that analysis of the impact of exchange rate changes and methods to mitigate these effects should be based on inflation-adjusted exchange rate changes, rather than on purely nominal changes. This is an application of the purchasing power parity proposition. We begin Part III with a critical examination of the effects of nominal exchange rate changes on financial statement translations and contractual transactions, and follow this examination with an economic interpretation of the effects of inflation-adjusted exchange rate changes on the ongoing activities of the firm. The analysis of risk explicitly compares and contrasts nominal and real measures of risk. The balance of Part III examines the way hedging decisions should be made based on inflation-adjusted exchange rate changes, which includes an analysis of pricing nominal financial instruments, short-term transactions management, and longer-term operating strategies for coping with exchange risk. As with the first two sub-themes, this one is directly related to the integration-versus-segmentation framework. If markets are integrated, purchasing power parity is more likely to hold, so exposure and risk are lower, and hedging is less beneficial although it is also less costly. If markets are segmented, purchasing power parity is less likely to hold, so exposure and risk are more serious, and hedging is more beneficial although it might be more costly.

The fourth sub-theme is that government policies influence international financial management—probably even more than they influence domestic financial management. Some of these policies relate to taxation of corporate income, and others give rise to additional uncertainties in the form of political risk. These topics are taken up in Part IV of the book, and again relate to the integration-versus-segmentation paradigm. If policies are trivial, capital markets will approach complete integration, and the impact of government policy on international financial decisions will be minor. If government policies are more intrusive, capital markets will be segmented, and the impact of government policy on international financial decisions will be important. With this kind of segmentation, corporate financial management in response to the policies is more valuable, and in Part IV, we consider methods to manage tax burdens and political risk.

Taken together, these themes provide guidance for all the international financial management issues addressed in this book. Each of the four parts of this book begins with a short introduction that briefly reviews the previous chapters and themes, and previews the upcoming chapters and themes. In each of these introductions, the reader is encouraged to think about the overview of the book—the proverbial forest—rather than focus on the individual chapters—or the individual trees. By providing these frequent overviews, the subject matter of the book becomes less confusing and more intellectually rewarding.

❖ REFERENCES

Eiteman, David K., Arthur I. Stonehill, and Michael H. Moffett. *Multinational Business Finance*, eighth edition, Addison-Wesley, 1998.

Giddy, Ian. *Global Financial Markets*, D.C. Heath and Company, 1994.

Grabbe, J. Orlin. *International Financial Markets*, third edition, Prentice Hall, 1996.

Kim, Suk H., and Seung H. Kim. *Global Corporate Finance: Text and Cases*, fourth edition, Blackwell Publishers, 1999.

Krugman, Paul R., and Maurice Obstfeld. *International Economics: Theory and Policy*, fourth edition, Addison-Wesley, 1997.

Levi, Maurice D. *International Finance: The Markets and Financial Management of Multinational Business*, McGraw-Hill, third edition, 1996.

Levich, Richard M. *International Financial Markets: Prices and Policies*, Irwin/McGraw-Hill, 1998.

Madura, Jeff. *International Financial Management*, sixth edition, South-Western Publishing Company, 1999.

Obstfeld, Maurice, and Kenneth Rogoff. *Foundations of International Macroeconomics*, MIT Press, 1996.

O'Brien, Thomas J. *Global Financial Management*, John Wiley & Sons, 1996.

Sercu, Piet, and Raman Uppal. *International Financial Markets and the Firm*, South-Western, 1995.

Shapiro, Alan. *Multinational Financial Management*, sixth edition, John Wiley & Sons, 1999.

❖ ENDNOTES

1. Some of the most popular textbooks in the field are Eiteman, Stonehill, and Moffett (1998), Shapiro (1999), Kim and Kim (1999), and Madura (1999). More specialized books include Levi (1996), Sercu and Uppal (1995), and O'Brien (1996).

2. These materials include citations to practitioner journals as well as citations to books for general audiences and relevant introductory textbooks.

3. Two of the finest sources for information on international finance are the second half of Krugman and Obstfeld (1997), chapters 12–23, and Obstfeld and Rogoff (1996).

4. The most noteworthy books on international financial markets are Giddy (1994), Grabbe (1996), and Levich (1998). Sercu and Uppal (1995) is also primarily about international financial markets.

THE THEORY AND PRACTICE OF
INTERNATIONAL FINANCIAL MANAGEMENT

INTERNATIONAL MACROECONOMIC CONCEPTS

International financial management requires a solid understanding of issues in the global macroeconomic environment. The two chapters in this part provide a general introduction to these macroeconomic issues and the theoretical concepts behind them. In particular, the chapters provide the foundation for analyzing foreign investment decisions by multinational corporations based on analyses of international capital flows and relationships among macroeconomic variables. Both of these topics are examined here in a framework comparing integrated capital markets and macroeconomies to segmented capital markets and macroeconomies, which provides insights regarding the nature of international capital flows and international parity propositions that are later applied to financial decisions in multinationals.

Chapter 1, "International Capital Flows," examines all kinds of international capital flows, but particularly the direct foreign investment flows attributed to multinational corporations. The analysis introduces trade in financial assets based on the international balance of payments and briefly considers models of international investment related to real interest rates and diversification. If capital markets and macroeconomies are integrated, international capital flows will achieve equilibrium related to return and risk. If, on the other hand, capital markets and macroeconomies are segmented, international capital flows will not achieve the same equilibrium, and this absence of equilibrium will have significant implications for international business. One section of the chapter therefore details the main factors which distinguish foreign investment from domestic investment in preparation for a more thorough discussion of international capital mobility.

The chapter also contains a brief examination of data on the U.S. international investment position, which puts many insights of the international investment models into perspective. This section examines salient features of the patterns of international capital flows, principally the emergence of the United States as both the world's largest debtor country and the world's largest host country for direct foreign investment. On the whole, the chapter is fairly broad—examining international capital flows in the spirit of macroeconomic theory—to provide an overview of the financial environment in which multinationals operate.

Chapter 2, "International Parity Propositions," contains a careful discussion of a number of theorems which relate macroeconomic variables—such as interest rates, inflation rates, and exchange rate changes—across countries. In particular, we examine the theoretical macroeconomic concepts of purchasing power parity, uncovered interest parity, covered interest parity, and the unbiased forward rate hypothesis. The approach is highly empirical, both in terms of presenting some basic data on the macroeconomic variables and measuring the relationships among them, and in terms of surveying published empirical literature on the parity propositions. If capital markets and macroeconomies are integrated, the parity propositions will generally hold. If capital markets and macroeconomies are segmented, there will be deviations from the parity propositions and, once again, this will have significant implications for international business. Hence, these theoretical parity propositions are subsequently used as analytical tools which aid in the evaluation and management of a multinational's foreign subsidiary.

The material in this part is standard material in the field of international macroeconomics, and these two chapters are but small pieces of a much broader literature. Textbooks in international economics develop the issues surrounding international capital flows and international parity propositions in much greater depth. The presentation here is necessarily streamlined to focus on the main insights that explain and help managers make decisions regarding foreign investments. Further study of international macroeconomic concepts is certainly desirable, and in fact highly recommended, particularly with respect to exchange rate determination and the linkages among macroeconomic variables across borders. For more, see Krugman and Obstfeld (1997), Chapters 12–23; Obstfeld and Rogoff (1996); or any other textbook on international economics or international macroeconomics.

❖ REFERENCES

Krugman, Paul R., and Maurice Obstfeld, *International Economics: Theory and Policy*, fourth edition, Addison-Wesley, 1997.

Obstfeld, Maurice, and Kenneth Rogoff, *Foundations of International Macroeconomics*, MIT Press, 1996.

CHAPTER 1

INTERNATIONAL CAPITAL FLOWS

CHAPTER OBJECTIVES
AFTER READING THIS CHAPTER YOU SHOULD BE ABLE TO:

❖ Understand international capital flows in the balance of payments accounts.

❖ Explain the benefits of international capital flows in terms of rates of return and diversification of risks.

❖ Describe salient features of the U.S. international investment position.

❖ Identify differences between foreign and domestic investment having to do with multiple currencies and exchange rates, multiple interest rates, differences in corporate income tax rates, and political risk.

❖ Conceptually analyze the international capital market in terms of a continuum from nationally segmented capital markets to a perfectly integrated global capital market, and provide reasons for imperfect capital mobility.

❖ Benchmark capital market equilibrium using the real interest parity condition.

This chapter provides an overview of the issues discussed in the rest of this book by presenting an international macroeconomic context in which to address international financial management. It first introduces the various forms of international investment: direct foreign investment, portfolio investment, and intermediated invest-ment. The first section examines the aggregate international capital flows, along with in-ternational trade flows, in the balance of payments accounts, including decomposition of capital flows into the various forms of international investment. The second section explains some theoretical models of international capital flows to provide reasons for international capital flows. The third section examines some empirical features of the U.S. international investment position to provide an understanding of the importance of the issues pursued in the rest of the book. The fourth section considers the factors which distinguish foreign investment from domestic investment—mainly the existence of multiple currencies and multiple governments, two factors that provide the basis for all the issues examined in the rest of this book—because without them, international fi-nancial management would be no different from domestic corporate finance. The fifth section draws together the models of international investment and differences between foreign and domestic investment in an examination of international capital mobility. This section introduces one of the main analytic frameworks applied throughout the book: the continuum from segmented national capital markets to perfectly integrated global capital markets. The sixth and final section examines various answers to a basic question related to the issue of whether international capital markets are segmented or integrated: Does real interest parity hold?

1.1   INTRODUCTION

International capital flows have increased dramatically over the past few decades and direct foreign investment (DFI) by multinational corporations (MNCs) has played an important role in the action. DFI is distinguished from other types of capital flows—portfolio investment and intermediated investment—in that the purchaser of the asset maintains operating control over the asset, such as when an MNC establishes a wholly-owned subsidiary in a foreign country. International portfolio investment has recently exploded, after a lengthy period of being ignored, as investors all over the world have attempted to capture high returns and diversify their domestic portfolios by buying stocks and bonds in both developed countries and emerging markets. International bank lending surged during the late 1970s and the early 1980s, and then dropped off as the international debt crisis emerged. Throughout all of this, however, DFI continued to climb all over the world. Substantial amounts of DFI have been inflows into the United States, as mergers with and acquisitions of U.S. companies by foreign capitalists occurred during the 1980s. Japanese firms established new subsidiaries in the United States, and these have come under scrutiny for competing aggressively against their American counterparts. Although the United States is still a major source country for worldwide direct foreign investment, providing over $1 trillion of capital, by most measures it is now the world's largest host country as well, hosting roughly $750 billion. It is thus no surprise that DFI has received a considerable amount of public attention lately. Although DFI is the focus of this book, it is best analyzed given an understand-ing of international capital flows in general. This chapter therefore sets the stage for all of the issues pursued throughout the rest of the book.

1.2   THE BALANCE OF PAYMENTS

International capital flows are reported along with international trade flows in each country's **balance of payments accounts,** a record of international transactions between domestic residents and the rest of the world. The two main parts of the balance of payments accounts are the **current account,** which records the value of exports and imports of goods and services, and the **capital account,** which records the value of asset sales and purchases. The nature of international investment is to place financial capital abroad in one period with the anticipation of receiving dividend or interest payments along with repayment of the capital in subsequent periods. The initial flow of capital is recorded in the capital account of the balance of payments as the purchase of a foreign asset. Receipts of interest and dividends are recorded in the current account of the balance of payments, because they are viewed as payments for the services of the capital. These payments, though, are recorded in a section of the current account separate from the value of imports and exports of goods and other services. As a result, the subaccount of the current account for imports and exports of goods and services is more specifically referred to as the **balance of trade**. When repayments of capital take place, the transactions are recorded in the capital account as sales of a foreign asset that thereby reverse the original transaction.

These recording concepts can be summarized by looking at the balance of payments equation for a country:

$$[(X - M) + (D^i - D^o) + UT] +$$
$$[(DFI^i + DFI^o) + (PI^i - PI^o) + (II^i - II^o) + OI] + OSB = 0.$$

where:

X	denotes exports of goods and services
M	denotes imports of goods and services
D^i	denotes dividends and interest received as income (inflows)
D^o	denotes dividends and interest paid as expenses (outflows)
UT	denotes net inflows of unilateral or unrequited transfers
DFI^i	denotes direct foreign investment inflows
DFI^o	denotes direct foreign investment outflows
PI^i	denotes portfolio investment inflows
PI^o	denotes portfolio investment outflows
II^i	denotes intermediated investment inflows
II°	denotes intermediated investment outflows
OI	denotes official investment
OSB	denotes the official settlements balance

The first term in brackets, $[(X - M) + (D^i - D^o) + UT]$, represents the current account balance. The first term in parentheses, $(X - M)$, is the balance of trade, or the net exports of goods and services. Net dividends and interest, $(D^i - D^o)$, and unilateral or unrequited transfers (gifts and aid for which no future repayment is expected), UT, are added to the balance of trade to form the current account. The second term in brackets, $[(DFI^i - DFI^o) + (PI^i - PI^o) + (II^i - II^o) + OI]$, represents the capital account balance, which will be explained in the next paragraph. The final term in the balance of payments equation, OSB, denotes the **official settlements balance,** which is the net sales or purchases of currency by the central bank in the foreign exchange market.

In the capital account of the balance of payments, there are the following four types of capital flows:

1. **Direct foreign investment (DFI)** is a long-term capital movement in which the owner of the asset has operating control over the investment. This type of capital flow generally consists of corporations setting up foreign branches or subsidiaries, or buying substantial shares in foreign firms. In U.S. statistics, ownership of 10 percent or more of the voting shares of a foreign firm constitutes DFI.
2. **Portfolio investment (PI)** is the purchases and sales of corporate stocks, corporate bonds, government bonds, or other bonds. This component of international investment has been growing rapidly and is the subject of much research. (For an introduction to international portfolio investment, see Solnik, 1996.)
3. **Intermediated investment (II)** is both short- and long-term lending and deposit-taking activity by financial intermediaries such as banks. This category, too, has been of great interest recently as banks have become heavily involved in international transactions. (For an introduction to international banking, see Aliber, 1984.)
4. **Official investment (OI)** represents government loans to foreigners, such as the U.S. government's loans to developing countries or to the World Bank.

There is additionally a miscellaneous category to accumulate transactions by non-banking firms.

When transactions between domestic residents and foreign residents occur, each one implies two offsetting entries in the balance of payments, and this double-entry system preserves a balance at zero. For example, suppose a U.S. corporation imports $1 million worth of Burgundy wine from France and pays for it by writing a check on its U.S. bank account. The U.S. import account (M) increases by $1 million to reflect the import of wine, thus decreasing the trade balance ($X - M$) by $1 million.

In addition, however, the French seller of wine deposits the check it received as payment in its bank account and the U.S. corporation effectively transfers part of its own bank account to the French vendor. This deposit transfer is an export of a U.S. asset, which gets recorded in the intermediated investment account of the balance of payments. The transfer can be interpreted as the purchase of a bank deposit by the French winemaker (using the check it received from the U.S. corporation) and the sale of a bank deposit by the U.S. corporation (as payment for the check).

As there is a sale of a U.S. asset, the payment for the wine enters the balance of payments as an inflow of intermediated investment, so II^i increases by $1 million. Note that the balance of payments indeed balances, because the $1 million increase in M, which is associated with a $1 million decrease in the current account, is balanced by a $1 million increase in II^i, which corresponds to a $1 million increase in the capital account. Although this is just one example of the many transactions that are recorded in the balance of payments, no matter how many or what kind of transactions take place, the balance of payments must sum up to zero because of the double-entry bookkeeping.

Some transactions in the balance of payments affect only the capital account, and can be interpreted as exchanges of assets. For example, suppose a U.S. MNC builds a new plant in Germany for $100 million and pays the German construction company by writing a check on its U.S. bank account. If the U.S. multinational maintains operating control of the plant, the investment is considered DFI. This is a purchase of a foreign asset, so the transaction will show up in the U.S. balance of payments as a $100 million increase in DFI^o, or an outflow of DFI. Because the U.S. MNC pays for the plant by writing a check on its bank account, the German construction company must deposit the check and thereby purchase the $100 million deposit that the MNC wishes to sell. This part of the transaction will show up in the U.S. balance of payments as a $100 million increase in II^i, or an inflow of intermediated investment. The $100 million outflow of DFI is offset by the $100 million inflow of intermediated investment, so the balance within the capital account remains at zero. Hence, the net effect of the transaction is simply to change the composition of assets the United States and the foreign country own without changing the total value of assets.

Once all transactions during a period are recorded, the accounts in the balance of payments may also be interpreted with respect to surpluses and deficits. For example, if the United States imports more goods and services than it exports, the trade balance will be negative, or in deficit. If dividends and unilateral transfers do not offset this, there will be a deficit in the current account. As the balance of payments must balance at zero, the current account deficit must be financed by a surplus in the capital account, in which capital inflows exceed capital outflows. This capital account surplus is accomplished by selling assets to and borrowing from foreigners.

Similarly, a surplus in the current account must be offset by a deficit in the capital account, which is accomplished by purchasing foreign assets and lending to foreigners. There may also be a small adjustment for central bank intervention through the official settlements balance. In reality, there is usually also a statistical discrepancy, reflecting the fact that gathering complete data is impossible.[1]

EXAMPLE 1.1

The U.S. balance of payments is reported by the Department of Commerce in the *Survey of Current Business*. In 1998, the United States was a net recipient of capital in the amount of $216.6 billion, which means that foreigners invested $216.6 billion more in the United States than Americans invested abroad. This is the balance of the capital account for the United States in 1998, which is a surplus, so:

$$[(DFI^i - DFI^o) + (PI^i - PI^o) + (II^i - II^o) + OI] = +\$216.6 \text{ billion.}$$

The United States paid a net amount of $12.2 billion in 1998 for the use of the net capital stock borrowed from foreigners to date, which is part of the current account. Combined with a balance of trade deficit of $164.3 billion, which means that imports exceed exports, and net transfers of gifts to foreigners of $43.5 billion, the current account balance is a deficit of $220.0 billion:

$$[(X - M) + (D^i - D^o) + UT] = [(-164.3) + (-12.2) - 43.5] = -\$220.0 \text{ billion.}$$

The official settlements balance was −6.8 billion, reflecting a cash outflow of U.S. dollars and a decrease in official reserve assets:

$$OSB = -\$6.8 \text{ billion.}$$

As the surplus on the capital account, the deficit in the current account, and the official settlements balance total $10.2 billion:

$$[(X - M) + (D^i - D^o) + UT] + [(DFI^i - DFI^o) + (PI^i - PI^o) + (II^i - II^o) + OI]$$
$$+ OSB = -\$220.0 \text{ billion} + \$216.6 \text{ billion} - \$6.8 \text{ billion} = -\$10.2 \text{ billion}$$

there is a statistical discrepancy reflecting the fact that net inflows of $10.2 billion have not been recorded.

DEBT-EQUITY SWAPS[2]

During the early 1970s, vast amounts of international intermediated investment took place as dollar-denominated loans from banks in the United States to the governments of developing countries in Latin America and Asia. In the early 1980s, the borrowers began experiencing difficulty repaying these debts, and many countries stopped making payments on the loans and negotiated to restructure the payment plans. Eventually, alternative ways of dealing with this debt crisis were developed in order to benefit both the debtor country and the lender bank. One of those alternatives was a **debt-equity swap** in which developing countries exchanged some of the intermediated investment for portfolio investment or direct foreign investment by converting debt into equity in local investments.

A debt-equity swap is typically arranged by a broker, such as an investment bank, for a firm wanting to make an equity investment in an indebted developing country which has established a swap program. The broker approaches banks which are interested in selling off some of their nonperforming developing country loans. The broker purchases the loans in U.S. dollars at a deep discount from face value. At this point, the bank agrees to accept cash to liquidate the loan.

As this is happening, the broker also approaches the developing country authorities to redeem this portion of their external dollar-denominated debt with local currency. The conversion from dollars into local currency typically also takes place at a discount from face value, although not at the same steep discount at which it originally traded because the debt is liquidated in the local currency rather than dollars. Of course, the government redeems the debt under the condition that the acquiring company invest the proceeds in a preapproved equity position in a local company or an expansion of a direct foreign investment.

By participating in the debt-equity swap, the company making the equity investment enjoys a discount over what it would otherwise have had to pay for the local currency, represented by the difference between the discount on the debt liqui-

dated by the developing country in the local currency and the discount on the debt liquidated by the bank in dollars (less a transaction fee to the broker).

Chile launched the first debt-equity swap program in 1985, and Chile's is still one of the biggest programs. The program gained attention in 1986 when Bankers Trust swapped approximately $60 million in debt for a 40 percent stake in a pension fund and a 97 percent stake in a life insurance company. There is another large program in Brazil, and there are currently programs operating in Argentina, Mexico, the Philippines, Uruguay, Venezuela, and several smaller countries. In Argentina, debt-equity swaps have often been matched with privatizations of state-owned enterprises, such as the telephone company, ENTEL, and the airline, Aerolinas Argentinas.

An example of a debt-equity swap is the 1988 deal by Coats-Viyella, a large European textile group, for expansion of textile plants in Rio Grande do Norte, a relatively underdeveloped area of Brazil. Coats purchased a nominal $4,924,623 face value of debt from its broker, international Dutch bank NMB, for $2,757,789, or 56 percent of face value. Coats was able to exchange the dollar debt for Brazilian cruzados at an exceptionally low discount of 0.5 percent from face value, netting $4,900,000 worth of cruzados. A month later, Coats purchased $5,000,000 of debt for $2,675,000, or about 54 percent of face value. Coats exchanged this dollar debt for Brazilian cruzados at a discount of 16 percent of face value, netting $4,200,000 worth of cruzados. When all was done, Coats paid $5,432,789 for Brazilian debt that it transformed into $9,100,000 worth of cruzados for equity investment. The effective discount on the cost of its funds was therefore 40.3 percent, minus brokerage fees and related costs.

Through the debt-equity swap, Brazil was able to reduce its debt burden and stimulate equity investment in the country, and the creditor banks were able to liquidate some of their nonperforming loans.

We can decompose the capital account surplus of $216.6 billion for the United States in 1998 into its basic components. The net inflow of *DFI* was $60.5 billion; the net inflow of portfolio investment was $178.0 billion; and the net inflow from intermediated investment was $15.8 billion. There was a net outflow of official investment, mostly sales of U.S. securities by foreign central banks, of $22.1 billion. A miscellaneous category of short-term capital flows by nonbank institutions, such as export companies, accounts for the remaining −$15.6 billion. Hence:

$$[(DFI^i - DFI^o) + (PI^i - PI^o) + (II^i - II^o) + OI + \text{miscellaneous}]$$
$$= \$60.5 \text{ billion} + \$178.0 \text{ billion} + \$15.8 \text{ billion} - \$22.1 \text{ billion} - \$15.6 \text{ billion}$$
$$= \$216.6 \text{ billion}.$$

1.3 MODELS OF INTERNATIONAL CAPITAL FLOWS

The balance of payments records international trade and international capital flows but does not explain reasons for the flows. In the field of international trade, the theory of comparative advantage suggests that countries will export goods and services which they are relatively efficient in producing and will import goods and services which other countries are relatively efficient in producing. Note that there is no role for international capital flows (other than, possibly, to finance the trade). In the field of international finance, international capital flows are modeled as investment decisions. Investors want to transfer productive resources such as steel or machinery to countries where the productivity of capital is highest to produce the greatest amount of output. Thus, the demand for capital may be different across countries, depending on the level of technology or labor skills available. In addition, savings and the capital stock are lower in some countries than in others, and these countries must borrow needed capital. Together, the demand for and the supply of capital suggest how much capital will be imported from abroad or exported to foreign countries.

Beyond this, part of the investment decision also involves motives to diversify risks by investing in a broad array of assets. Hence, there will also be international capital flows designed to seek diversification even if an equilibrium between the demand for capital and the supply of capital is achieved.

MODELS OF RISK-FREE RETURNS

Some of the simplest models of international capital flows examine the productivities and the quantities of capital in two countries. These models are of **risk-free returns,** in which there is no uncertainty about the rate of return on capital, so there is nothing to diversify. Here we summarize the main results of the models; at the end of this chapter "Tools for Analysis I" contains a more detailed development of two of these models. One of these is a purely static model, characterizing international capital flows as an optimum allocation of existing capital between two countries. It is often referred to as the "MacDougall model," in reference to the seminal development in MacDougall (1960). (For another summary, see Grubel, 1987.) A second model is an intertemporal model, recognizing that the quantity of capital available is chosen by optimizing behavior in which investment must be made one period in advance to have productive capital in the next period, and recognizing that capital may come from domestic sources or from abroad. (This is the type of intertemporal model frequently covered in international economics or macroeconomics.) We highlight four interrelated insights from these models below:

1. The models achieve an equilibrium real interest rate in each macroeconomy by setting the rate of return on capital equal to the cost of capital its owners require, or by setting the demand for capital represented by the marginal product of capital schedule equal to the supply of capital represented by past and present output not consumed. This equilibrium risk-free interest rate can be denoted as r in the home country and as r^* in the foreign country.

2. International capital flows are driven by differences in the risk-free real interest rates across countries. If $r < r^*$, then capital will flow out of the home country into the foreign country. Symmetrically, if $r > r^*$, capital will flow into the home country from the foreign country. The motivation for international capital flows is therefore to seek the highest real return. An international equilibrium is achieved when $r = r^*$, so there are no incentives to reallocate capital further. The proposition that $r = r^*$ is known as **real interest parity (RIP),** meaning that real interest rates should be identical across countries if capital is free to flow across borders.

3. The financial flows seeking the highest returns are associated with real, physical resource transfers, as indicated in the balance of payments accounts. When $r < r^*$ and there is a capital outflow from the home country that achieves real interest parity, this capital outflow is represented in the balance of payments as a deficit in the capital account (because outflows in any of the capital accounts increase). This is accompanied by a current account surplus, meaning that exports exceed imports, and this is how real, physical resources are transferred abroad.

4. The international capital flows and the accompanying transfer of real resources result in gains to both the capital exporter (asset purchaser or lender) and the capital importer (asset seller or borrower). As capital and resources are allocated to their most productive uses, total output in the two countries increases. The capital-exporting home country receives a higher rate of return on its foreign investment than it would domestically, so the home country is better off. Similarly, the capital-importing foreign country is able to produce more output with the additional capital, and it is better off even after paying dividends and interest to the home country for the use of their capital because there is production in excess of the payment to the home country. (Graphical and numerical examples in the section on "Tools for Analysis I" describe this dynamic further.) Hence, just as there are gains from international trade in goods and services, there are gains from international trade in assets.

All four of these conclusions are fairly intuitive, and are not controversial. We give further details of how the results are derived in "Tools for Analysis I" at the end of this chapter. We therefore take these conclusions as given and proceed to an additional reason for international capital flows.

MODELS OF RISK DIVERSIFICATION

The models described above consider r and r^* as risk-free real rates of return, but reality is characterized by various business risks associated with investments. Part of any investment decision involves an assessment of such risks. Suppose home and foreign investments both have uncertain returns, but investors know a distribution of possible rates of return. For example, suppose the distribution of returns for the investment in the home country is normal, in a statistical sense, with a mean of 12 percent (denoted as $E[r] = 12$ where E is the expectations operator) and a standard deviation of 5 percent (denoted as $\sigma = 5$). Figure 1-1 plots this distribution. The expected return is 12 percent, but the actual return might be higher or it might be lower with equal probability. From the properties of the normal distribution, the return will be between 7 percent and 17 percent (one standard deviation below and one standard deviation above 12 percent) 68 percent of the time. The return will be between 2 percent and 22 percent (two standard deviations below and above 12 percent) 95 percent of the time, and between −3 percent and 27 percent (three standard deviations) slightly less than 100 percent of the time.

Suppose that the distribution of returns for the investment in the foreign country is identical, or again normally distributed with a mean of 12 percent ($E[r^*] = 12$) and a standard deviation of 5 percent ($\sigma^* = 5$). An investor will likely be indifferent between the home and foreign investments because they are expected to have both the same return and the same risk. In fact, we can restate real interest parity to include these expectations as $E[r] = E[r^*]$. If the expected returns are not equal, capital will again flow from one country to another until the expected returns are equal. Once expected real interest parity is achieved, there is no obvious reason for further flows of international capital.

An important part of the investment decision is to not only compare the returns and risks of the different investments, but also to examine how the returns on the two investments are related. The relationship between the two investments may then produce an additional reason for international capital flows, although these additional capital flows will net out to zero. Suppose that claims (such as stocks or loans) on the home and the foreign investment are traded and that investors in both the home and foreign countries are able to purchase either or both of these claims. These investors could be portfolio managers selecting stocks, banks making international loans, or MNCs making capital budgeting decisions. Without specifying which, we simply refer to an investor making decisions. If both investments will always have the same actual return, implying that the return on the home project is high when the return on the foreign project is high and that the return on the home project is low when the return on the foreign project is low, the two investments are perfectly correlated. In this case, any investor is likely indifferent between the two projects.

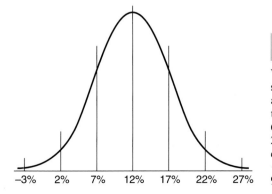

FIGURE 1-1 NORMAL DISTRIBUTION OF RATES OF RETURN

With a mean of 12 percent and standard deviation of 5 percentage points, the return will be between 7 percent and 17 percent 68 percent of the time, between 2 percent and 22 percent 95 percent of the time, and between −3 percent and 27 percent 99.7 percent of the time.

Suppose that the returns on the home and foreign investments are not correlated, or are statistically independent, so that the return on the home project is not related to the return on the foreign project. This independence of returns is often thought to be the case with respect to international investments because business cycles across countries are often not correlated. Investors recognize that returns on the two investments are not correlated and optimally construct a portfolio containing some of each investment. A portfolio of investments which spreads the risks of holding individual investments is referred to as a **diversified portfolio**. In our simple example, the optimum is to hold half of the portfolio in the home investment and half in the foreign investment. Note that the expected return on the portfolio is still 12 percent, because a weighted-average of returns on two investments with expected returns of 12 percent each is just 12 percent:

$$E[r_P] = (1/2)E[r] + (1/2)E[r^*] = (1/2)(12\%) + (1/2)(12\%) = 12\%$$

where $E[r_P]$ represents the expected return on the portfolio. When the returns on the two investments are independent and the portfolio is divided equally between the investments, the standard deviation of the portfolio follows the formula:

$$\sigma_P = \sqrt{(1/2)^2\sigma^2 + (1/2)^2\sigma^{*2}} = \sqrt{(1/2)^2(5)^2 + (1/2)^2(5)^2} = \sqrt{12.5} = 3.54$$

so the risk of the diversified portfolio is 3.54 percentage points, which is less than the risk of either undiversified portfolio at 5 percentage points. If investors are risk averse, they prefer the portfolio with a standard deviation of 3.54 percent over portfolios with standard deviations of 5 percent.

If investors in both the home and the foreign countries hold diversified portfolios, the home country will sell (or export) assets representing claims to the domestic investment and will buy (or import) an equal value of assets representing claims on the foreign investment. Similarly, the foreign country will sell assets representing claims to the foreign investment and will buy an equal value of assets representing claims on the home country investment. Hence, there is a reason for international capital flows even if capital is not always chasing the highest expected return, because there are benefits of international diversification. These benefits are associated with further gains from trade in assets, not because output increases but, instead, because the welfare of the portfolio owners increases. Although we have considered a very simple example in this section, the principle of portfolio diversification is completely generalizable. "Tools for Analysis II" at the end of this chapter considers the general case of portfolio optimization with home and foreign investments for any investment standard deviation and correlation.

The models of international capital flows which examine the productivity and the quantities of capital in two countries can be combined with the model of international capital flows seeking portfolio diversification to obtain a more complete description of international capital flows. In finance, most investment analysis in fact considers the return and the risk of investments together. Note that the models which examine demands for and supplies of capital do a very good job of explaining a one-way, or net, flow of capital associated with the capital account balance of a country, but cannot explain why there may be capital flows in both directions to achieve this net position. In other words, models of risk-free returns do not say anything about two-way flows or **cross-hauling,** the fact that most nations are both borrowers and lenders.

In contrast, the model of portfolio diversification with risky returns clearly provides a reason for capital flows in both directions, but basically does not change the net amount of capital flows (although a complete equilibrium, not examined here, could alter this). Together, these two models explain a lot about international capital flows, but they do not explain whether the capital flows will be in the form of DFI, portfolio investment, or intermediated investment. We simply note this for now, and come back to examine the issue in Chapter 5 when we discuss theories of DFI.

1.4 THE U.S. INTERNATIONAL INVESTMENT POSITION

A country's **balance of international assets and liabilities** depicts the aggregate amount of domestic-owned assets held abroad and foreign-owned assets held domestically, and thus the country's net international investment position. If we keep track of the capital flows that go through the capital account of the balance of payments in each year and total them up over time, we arrive at the balance of international assets and liabilities. Some revaluation of assets and liabilities is necessary to be completely accurate, but the principle behind establishing the balance of international assets and liabilities is to look at the capital stock rather than the periodic capital flows. In this section, we examine the accounts of the balance of international assets and liabilities, or the international investment position, of the United States.

Table 1-1 presents a T-account for the balance of international assets and liabilities for the United States as of 1998. U.S. assets abroad are listed on the left-hand side, and foreign assets in the U.S. are shown on the right-hand side. The column on the far right presents the net assets (U.S. assets abroad minus foreign assets in the United States). This exhibit raises several key points. First, the United States is a net debtor by $1.240 trillion; indeed, it is often said that America is the world's largest debtor country. Second, the United States is a very large net debtor in portfolio investments ($1.008 trillion) and government assets ($608 billion), and is a small debtor in intermediated investment ($3 billion). However, the country is a net creditor in direct foreign investment using current costs ($244 billion), as well as in the miscellaneous category ($135 billion). Third, cross-hauling exists in every category because the United States is both a creditor and a debtor in each account.

The T-account in Table 1-1 represents a snapshot in time, specifically the end of 1998. Of equal importance is a sense of how the United States got to the position in Table 1-1, which requires an analysis of time series data. For example, the United States has not always been a net debtor. During its early industrial development, it depended heavily on foreign capital, so the country was a debtor until World War I. By the end of World War I, however, the United States was a creditor. The country was a slowly growing creditor during the Depression, despite heavy capital flight from Europe, and remained a growing creditor throughout World War II and most of the postwar period. The United States was generally a growing creditor until about 1980, at which time large capital inflows began to reduce its net creditor position. With continuing capital inflows, the United States became a net debtor once again by 1986, and has been a growing debtor ever since. Figure 1-2 plots a time series of the recent 1976–1998 period; the

TABLE 1-1 International Investment Position of the United States, 1998 (billions of dollars)

U.S. Assets Abroad		%				Foreign Assets in the United States		%	Net
Direct Foreign Investment*	1123	23				Direct Foreign Investment*	879	14	244
Portfolio Investment	1969	40				Portfolio Investment	2977	48	−1008
of which: Bonds			562		955	of which: U.S. Treasury Bonds and Currency			
of which: Corporate Stocks			1407		901	of which: Other Bonds			
					1121	of which: Corporate Stocks			
Bank Lending	1014	20				Bank Deposits	1017	17	−3
Other Private Assets	596	12				Other Private Assets	461	7	135
Government Assets	228	5				Foreign Government Assets	836	14	−608
TOTAL	4930	100				TOTAL	6170	100	−1240

*at current cost

Source: based on data reported in Table 1 of Russell B. Scholl, "The International Investment Position of the United States at Yearend 1998," *Survey of Current Business*, July 1999, p. 44.

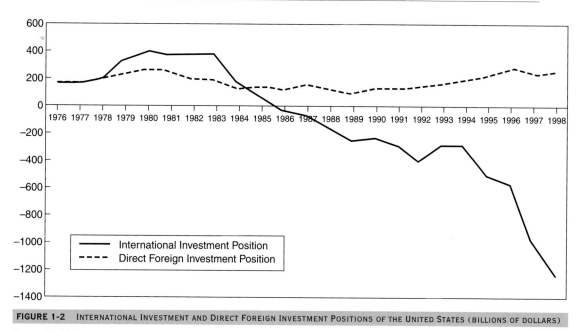

FIGURE 1-2 INTERNATIONAL INVESTMENT AND DIRECT FOREIGN INVESTMENT POSITIONS OF THE UNITED STATES (BILLIONS OF DOLLARS)

Source: U.S. Department of Commerce, *Survey of Current Business*, various issues.

reversal of the creditor position and the growing debtor status are evident in the line representing the net international investment position.

As the focus of this book is on direct foreign investment, a closer look at the data on U.S. DFI is in order. The broken line in Figure 1-2 plots the recent time series for the net DFI position. Note that the balance is always positive, reflecting the fact that the United States has traditionally been a major source or home country for DFI. Even despite recent capital inflows in the form of direct investment, making the United States the world's largest host country, the United States is a net creditor.

The valuation of direct foreign investment in Table 1-1 and Figure 1-2 uses estimates of the "current replacement cost" from the U.S. Department of Commerce. This is not the only valuation method available, however. In fact, direct foreign investment has traditionally been aggregated using the historical cost of the investment, or accounting book value, adjusted for valuation changes resulting from exchange rate changes. More recently, the Department of Commerce has also been estimating the market value of DFI by examining the ongoing value of the operation (in terms of cash flows as well as net asset value), in which case valuation changes reflect changes in the value of the business as well as exchange rate changes. Table 1-2 summarizes these three valuation methods for 1998 DFI. Using historical cost, the net DFI position is $168.809 billion. Moving to current cost, the net DFI position rises to $244.723 billion, reflecting revaluation of the U.S. direct investment abroad in excess of revaluation of foreign direct investment in the United States. This is due primarily to the fact that U.S. direct investment abroad is on average older than foreign direct investment in the United States, so there is more understatement in the value of U.S. assets abroad at historical cost. Finally, net DFI at market value is −$53.574 billion, suggesting that the ongoing operations of direct foreign investments in the United States are actually more valuable than U.S. direct foreign investments abroad.

TABLE 1-2   Alternative Direct Investment Position Estimates, 1997 and 1998 (millions of dollars)

Valuation Method	Position at Yearend 1997[r]	Changes in 1998 (decrease (−))			Position at Yearend 1998[p]
		Total	Capital Flows	Valuation Adjustments	
U.S. direct investment abroad:					
Historical cost	865,531	115,034	121,644	−6,610	980,565
Current cost	1,004,228	119,213	132,829	−13,616	1,123,441
Market value	1,784,494	356,034	132,829	223,205	2,140,528
Foreign direct investment in the United States:					
Historical cost	693,207	118,549	188,960	−70,411	811,756
Current cost	764,045	114,672	193,375	−78,703	878,718
Market value	1,642,365	551,737	193,375	358,362	2,194,102

[p]Preliminary.

[r]Revised.

Source: Sylvia E. Bargas and Rosaria Troia, "Direct Investment Positions for 1998: Country and Industry Detail," Table 1, *Survey of Current Business*, July 1999, p. 48. Reprinted by permission.

The valuation of direct foreign investment in Table 1-2 also reports the change in DFI from 1997 to 1998 attributable to new capital flows. For U.S. direct investment abroad, new capital flows amounted to $122 billion. This is a bit misleading, however, because $48 billion was not an outflow from the United States but rather earnings on DFI retained and reinvested abroad. Typically, over half of the capital flows of U.S. DFI in a given year is actually retained earnings, which do not really represent an outflow of money. This may be partially due to the fact that U.S. taxes on foreign income are deferred until the income is repatriated, so reinvestment of profits is encouraged. Furthermore, reinvestment also avoids any withholding taxes the foreign country may impose on profits taken out of the country. (These issues will be taken up again in Chapter 11.) For foreign direct investment in the United States, however, almost all the capital flow represents new money. In fact, the capital flow of inward DFI reported at $189 billion consists of $181 billion in actual capital inflows and reinvested earnings of just $8 billion.

Tables 1-3 and 1-4 present disaggregated data on direct foreign investment by industry and location or source. Both of these tables use data on historical costs because the estimates of current cost and market value are not made at disaggregated levels. Table 1-3 summarizes U.S. DFI abroad and Table 1-4 summarizes foreign DFI in the United States.

Table 1-3 demonstrates that most U.S. DFI is in developed countries. In fact, approximately 75 percent of all DFI abroad is in developed countries and only about 25 percent is in developing countries. This may seem unusual. Wouldn't we expect DFI to go from capital-rich countries to capital-poor countries? Not really. The theories of investment we examined suggest that capital goes where the marginal product of capital, or return to capital, is greatest. Developing countries do not always have the highest real rates of return, and the expected returns may be lower due to various risks.

From Table 1-3, we also note that manufacturing industries account for 40 percent of DFI. Most important in this category are chemicals, nonelectrical equipment, and transportation equipment. Service industries account for 31 percent of DFI abroad, the petroleum industry accounts for another 14 percent , and wholesale trade accounts for 10 percent.

Table 1-4 demonstrates that most of the DFI in the United States comes from developed countries. We see that 64 percent of DFI in the United States is from Europe, 21percent is from Japan, 7 percent is from Canada, and 5 percent is from Latin America. Of the total, 40 percent is in manufacturing, 30 percent in services, and 9 percent petroleum. What this table fails to indicate is the rapid expansion of DFI in the United States during the 1980s, especially by Japan, which has caused some controversy.

From a global standpoint, the analysis of the U.S. position covers most of the salient features of direct foreign investment. Data on worldwide stocks of DFI are difficult to find, but some data are available from the United Nations Centre on Transnational Corporations (UNCTC) in their *World Investment Report*. The global data confirm that the United States is the single most important source country and the single most important host country. In addition, roughly 75 percent of direct foreign investment is located in developed countries and about 25 percent is located in developing countries. For DFI in developing countries, U.S. DFI is relatively more important in Latin America, whereas Japanese DFI is relatively more important in Asia, and Western European DFI is relatively more important in Eastern Europe.

1.5 DIFFERENCES BETWEEN FOREIGN AND DOMESTIC INVESTMENT

Up to this point, discussion in this chapter has considered home investments and foreign investments differentiated exclusively by location. If this were the only concern, then international business would really be no different from domestic business—it would simply be done in multiple locations separated by irrelevant borders. When an investor considers a foreign investment, however, he immediately faces a number of complications not found in the domestic marketplace.

What then is different about foreign investment? On the financial front, multiple currencies and multiple interest rates complicate financial management. Equally important, the operating environment involves multiple legal systems, tax authorities, and government policies. In a nutshell, foreign investments must contend with a simple feature that has little impact in a domestic environment: international borders. Crossing an international border will generally result in a number of important consequences, and it is these consequences that motivate the analysis provided in the remainder of this book.

Most of the financial complications resulting from crossing an international border can be traced to two factors which have not yet been covered in this chapter: crossing a border means that (1) multiple currencies have to be used and (2) multiple governments can intervene. Multiple currencies imply that investors must worry about exchange rates and exchange rate changes as well as confront multiple interest rates and costs of capital. Multiple governments imply that investors must decipher multiple tax codes, as well as the way domestic and foreign tax codes interact, and must consider additional

TABLE 1-3   U.S. Direct Investment Position Abroad on a Historical-Cost Basis, 1998 (millions of dollars)

	All Industries	Petroleum	Manufacturing Total	Food and Kindred Products	Chemicals and Allied Products	Primary and Fabricated Metals
All countries	980,565	91,113	304,690	33,871	83,589	17,098
Canada	103,908	12,559	46,428	5,143	8,295	3,231
Europe	489,539	30,640	154,864	15,433	53,149	9,750
Austria	3,838	152	1,062	30	45	2
Belgium	18,920	156	8,969	1,012	5,390	189
Denmark	2,628	286	638	160	60	(D)
Finland	1,700	104	1,004	11	308	14
France	39,188	1,162	18,974	3,615	4,227	4,034
Germany	42,853	2,860	22,259	922	3,894	1,848
Greece	660	−75	91	−9	45	2
Ireland	15,936	(D)	8,090	669	3,184	177
Italy	14,638	(D)	8,559	406	2,267	137
Luxembourg	14,930	58	2,556	2	0	(D)
Netherlands	79,386	2,826	16,242	1,078	10,212	224
Norway	7,609	4,045	831	(D)	17	3
Portugal	1,474	(D)	335	113	114	−5
Spain	12,807	199	7,435	1,756	1,211	933
Sweden	6,053	79	3,359	18	1,496	6
Switzerland	37,616	15	5,508	47	2,859	217
Turkey	1,069	97	604	208	53	(D)
United Kingdom	178,648	15,603	46,436	4,371	17,345	1,658
Other	9,588	1,530	1,913	(D)	422	(D)
Latin America and Other Western Hemisphere	196,655	9,711	48,008	9,784	12,250	2,403
South America	73,290	6,967	30,325	4,590	7,690	1,898
Argentina	11,489	1,565	3,654	974	1,130	349
Brazil	37,802	1,825	22,292	2,472	5,524	1,324
Chile	9,132	18	845	162	294	39
Colombia	4,317	1,159	1,094	301	352	(D)
Ecuador	952	576	188	30	70	1
Peru	2,587	117	215	75	83	(D)
Venezuela	5,697	1,518	1,856	536	192	124
Other	1,315	192	183	40	43	0
Central America	56,387	1,407	15,188	5,156	2,444	483
Costa Rica	2,126	28	371	102	137	20
Guatemala	429	(D)	191	83	58	2
Honduras	186	(D)	190	184	2	(*)
Mexico	25,877	235	14,267	4,744	2,203	438
Panama	26,957	681	137	32	28	10
Other	812	293	32	10	16	13
Other Western Hemisphere	66,978	1,338	2,495	39	2,116	22
Bahamas	287	58	81	0	(D)	0
Barbados	1,077	82	5	0	0	0
Bermuda	41,076	(D)	(D)	0	0	0
Dominican Republic	535	(D)	390	22	22	0
Jamaica	2,105	(D)	144	−6	141	0
Netherlands Antilles	4,472	(*)	27	(D)	0	0
Trinidad and Tobago	1,054	697	49	(*)	5	(D)
United Kingdom Islands, Caribbean	15,713	308	1,628	0	(D)	(D)
Other	658	236	(D)	(D)	(D)	0

Industrial Machinery and Equipment	Electronic and Other Electric Equipment	Transportation Equipment	Other Manu-facturing	Wholesale Trade	Depository Institutions	Finance (Except Depository Institutions), Insurance, and Real Estate	Services	Other Industries
34,755	34,531	35,615	65,231	75,188	42,029	337,600	52,514	77,432
3,046	2,174	11,179	13,359	7,265	1,203	22,057	4,598	9,799
19,890	12,458	15,116	29,058	40,750	25,614	178,179	33,810	25,682
114	(D)	295	(D)	515	(D)	(D)	200	−38
472	361	538	1,007	2,716	321	5,262	1,684	−188
5	216	−8	(D)	(D)	(*)	(D)	34	54
(D)	(D)	(D)	48	302	20	(D)	67	(D)
2,358	974	676	3,089	2,587	2,385	7,778	4,570	1,729
3,887	585	7,106	4,038	2,759	1,510	11,022	1,905	537
0	9	3	41	92	166	126	59	50
185	1,529	15	2,332	332	(D)	6,638	305	(D)
2,201	928	715	1,905	2,725	334	774	1,082	(D)
9	4	0	(D)	(D)	289	11,596	84	(D)
993	1,860	348	1,526	9,446	(D)	42,838	6,985	(D)
168	7	15	(D)	303	(D)	1,881	290	(D)
(D)	(D)	37	9	397	239	261	98	(D)
90	863	1,453	1,128	1,470	2,124	694	475	411
316	52	(D)	(D)	224	(D)	782	1,009	(D)
578	609	403	797	7,831	3,695	18,446	1,651	469
0	−9	99	(D)	(D)	224	15	46	(D)
8,464	3,509	3,433	7,655	7,772	10,365	65,846	13,144	19,483
45	10	44	765	(D)	(D)	3,103	124	(D)
2,009	3,089	6,478	11,985	7,997	3,198	98,845	6,910	21,986
1,549	2,215	4,412	7,973	1,900	4,738	11,444	3,057	14,859
50	(*)	448	702	340	1,801	1,945	878	1,308
1,463	2,097	3,390	6,022	508	1,687	4,728	1,664	5,118
14	(D)	(D)	204	342	627	3,429	212	3,659
(D)	25	(D)	307	168	(D)	808	87	(D)
0	(D)	24	(D)	68	(D)	36	4	(D)
(*)	0	0	(D)	96	(D)	322	32	(D)
26	81	369	529	230	(D)	64	153	(D)
(D)	0	0	(D)	148	303	112	29	348
814	(D)	2,066	(D)	3,233	737	29,563	1,622	4,637
−17	(D)	0	(D)	(D)	0	(D)	(*)	(D)
0	0	0	48	26	5	(D)	5	(D)
0	0	0	3	2	5	29	0	(D)
831	569	2,066	3,415	1,092	591	4,206	1,108	4,378
0	0	0	68	(D)	118	25,145	501	(D)
0	−15	0	8	25	18	(D)	8	(D)
−354	(D)	0	(D)	2,884	−2,277	57,837	2,230	2,490
−3	0	0	(D)	150	−1,585	1,401	131	50
0	2	0	4	305	(D)	357	275	(D)
0	(D)	0	0	2,022	0	37,519	1,591	−15
0	0	0	316	(D)	58	(*)	20	(D)
0	0	0	9	(D)	11	6	39	1,660
0	0	0	(D)	43	5	4,400	−3	(*)
2	0	0	(D)	20	(D)	20	1	(D)
−352	(D)	0	19	92	−814	13,711	144	645
0	0	0	3	(*)	(D)	422	31	(D)

TABLE 1-3   (cont.)

	All Industries	Petroleum	*Manufacturing*			
			Total	Food and Kindred Products	Chemicals and Allied Products	Primary and Fabricated Metals
Africa	13,491	8,984	1,942	635	295	237
Egypt	1,955	1,423	435	(D)	32	7
Nigeria	1,925	1,696	56	(D)	20	−1
South Africa	2,363	(D)	864	139	193	(D)
Other	7,247	(D)	587	166	50	(D)
Middle East	10,599	3,010	2,383	75	−66	50
Israel	3,067	41	2,344	71	65	15
Saudi Arabi	4,209	270	149	14	(D)	20
United Arab Emirates	710	284	83	0	8	16
Other	2,613	2,415	−193	−9	(D)	0
Asia and Pacific	161,797	23,228	51,065	2,801	9,666	1,426
Australia	33,676	4,344	6,387	662	2,749	359
China	6,348	911	3,729	122	325	167
Hong Kong	20,802	600	3,122	4	348	282
India	1,480	190	256	−40	128	−110
Indonesia	6,932	4,610	197	16	131	8
Japan	38,153	4,496	14,224	528	2,608	365
Korea, Republic of	7,365	(D)	2,940	380	530	22
Malaysia	6,193	1,027	4,199	3	306	5
New Zealand	6,136	460	1,045	(D)	122	25
Philippines	3,192	283	1,634	440	477	33
Singapore	19,783	2,920	8,438	13	255	153
Taiwan	4,937	49	3,258	99	1,372	45
Thailand	5,721	1,579	1,633	109	334	70
Other	1,080	(D)	4	(D)	−19	2
International[1]	4,578	2,981	....	....	....	....
Addenda:						
Eastern Europe[2]	8,143	1,531	1,888	515	427	112
European Union (15)[3]	433,658	24,953	146,007	14,155	49,798	9,308
OPEC[4]	23,252	11,742	2,155	599	211	167

* Less than $500,000 (±).

D Suppressed to avoid disclosure of data of individual companies.

1. "International" consists of affiliates that have operations spanning more than one country and that are engaged in petroleum shipping, other water transportaiton, or offshore oil and gas drilling.

2. "Eastern Europe" comprises Albania, Armenia, Azerbaijan, Belarus, Bulgaria, Czech Republic, Estonia, Georgia, Hungary, Kazakhstan, Labria, Lithuania, Moldova, Poland, Romania, Russia, Slovakia, Tajikistan, Turkmenistan, Ukraine, and Uzbekistan.

3. The European Union (15) comprises Austria, Belgium, Denmark, Finland, France, Germany, Greece, Ireland, Italy, Luxembourg, Netherlands, Portugal, Spain, Sweden, and the United Kingdom.

4. OPEC is the Organization of Petroleum Exporting Countries. Its members are Algeria, Indonesia, Iran, Iraq, Kuwait, Libya, Nigeria, Qatar, Saudi Arabia, the United Arab Emirates, and Venezuela.

Source: Sylvia E. Bargas and Rosaria Troia, "Direct Investment Positions for 1998: Country and Industry Detail," Table 3.2, *Survey of Current Business,* July 1999, p. 57. Reprinted by permission.

Industrial Machinery and Equipment	Electronic and Other Electric Equipment	Transportation Equipment	Other Manufacturing	Wholesale Trade	Depository Institutions	Finance (Except Depository Institutions), Insurance, and Real Estate	Services	Other Industries
52	124	159	440	165	338	612	263	1,187
13	(D)	(D)	(*)	−48	163	0	43	−60
0	0	(D)	0	1	(D)	(D)	0	4
37	112	(D)	293	145	(D)	247	162	(D)
2	12	(D)	146	67	108	(D)	59	(D)
10	1,710	11	592	319	614	2,194	496	1,382
−11	1,709	5	490	91	0	386	(D)	(D)
(D)	1	5	51	105	(D)	1,533	280	(D)
3	0	0	55	122	(D)	(D)	137	(D)
(D)	0	(*)	−4	1	−44	(D)	(D)	(D)
9,747	14,975	2,672	9,777	18,692	10,862	35,714	6,438	15,798
586	173	581	1,278	2,057	2,595	8,347	2,198	7,748
463	1,472	175	1,005	372	127	771	31	407
167	1,230	29	1,062	5,054	1,637	5,007	1,009	4,373
227	78	−61	35	54	500	356	40	83
−17	35	(D)	(D)	(D)	186	171	53	(D)
3,588	2,043	1,724	3,368	4,948	539	12,318	1,415	212
288	558	128	1,034	(D)	2,251	38	446	−38
743	2,669	0	473	166	393	352	84	−27
15	35	0	(D)	274	(D)	3,169	60	(D)
16	483	0	184	172	288	627	187	2
2,747	4,763	106	401	3,245	727	3,769	681	4
280	1,191	(D)	(D)	368	614	337	163	148
648	243	24	205	1,508	486	351	42	122
−4	3	(D)	(D)	(D)	(D)	103	28	98
......	......	......	......	......	......	......	......	1,597
45	−12	44	757	264	313	2,845	41	1,260
19,100	11,841	14,555	27,250	32,324	20,190	154,733	31,699	23,751
24	117	312	725	474	(D)	2,125	685	(D)

political interventions which affect operations. There are other features which distinguish foreign investment from domestic investment, but these are less important with respect to international financial management than they are with respect to international business in general. Having to deal with multiple cultures, for example, has implications for employing labor, distributing goods and services in the marketplace, negotiating, and the like. As there are no direct effects on financial management, however, we do not consider them further here.

DEALING WITH MULTIPLE CURRENCIES: EXCHANGE RATES AND FOREIGN INTEREST RATES

A central issue facing an investor entering foreign markets is that the prices for goods, services, wages, and investment capital vary much more widely across borders than within them. In the domestic market, a firm certainly must contend with regional

TABLE 1-4   Foreign Direct Investment in the United States on a Historical-Cost Basis, 1998 (millions of dollars)

	All Industries	Petroleum	Manufacturing Total	Food and Kindred Products	Chemicals and Allied Products	Primary and Fabricated Metals
All countries	811,756	53,254	329,346	18,112	101,351	22,512
Canada	74,840	2,533	26,152	4,268	2,762	4,872
Europe	539,906	42,771	252,893	11,589	91,041	13,250
Austria	4,872	(D)	365	(D)	(D)	(D)
Belgium	9,577	(D)	4,232	2	3,187	(D)
Denmark	3,229	4	711	186	19	(*)
Finland	4,321	(D)	2,224	(D)	(D)	(D)
France	62,167	(D)	37,820	2,701	14,034	1,784
Germany	95,045	312	51,018	131	17,091	3,144
Ireland	13,227	739	4,874	734	(D)	(D)
Italy	3,830	(D)	907	−82	284	231
Liechtenstein	118	−2	(D)	1	0	−8
Luxembourg	20,214	0	(D)	206	(D)	508
Netherlands	96,904	11,505	35,109	−1,567	11,595	1,652
Norway	3,616	(D)	1,595	(D)	901	(D)
Spain	2,292	−3	714	19	8	(D)
Sweden	14,564	(D)	9,065	−2	803	595
Switzerland	54,011	252	26,310	2,577	16,189	564
United Kingdom	151,335	26,277	64,022	6,531	24,795	2,978
Other	584	3	128	47	−14	−2
Latin America and Other Western Hemisphere	32,210	4,072	4,329	350	1,229	448
South and Central America	11,916	−457	1,067	573	96	178
Brazil	609	(D)	−173	−14	(D)	(D)
Mexico	4,029	−9	887	588	−89	20
Panama	7,025	(D)	482	1	(D)	(D)
Venezuela	−333	(D)	−9	1	−13	(*)
Other	586	27	−120	−3	−72	3
Other Western Hemisphere	20,294	4,529	3,262	−222	1,133	270
Bahamas	2,141	(D)	131	(D)	1	(D)
Bermuda	2,674	207	552	−22	(D)	3
Netherlands Antilles	4,727	(D)	795	(D)	997	(D)
United Kingdom Islands, Caribbean	10,395	1,578	1,792	219	(D)	(D)
Other	357	(D)	−9	2	−11	4
Africa	884	−4	−90	(D)	(D)	(D)
South Africa	43	2	−88	(D)	−4	−1
Other	841	−6	−2	4	(D)	(D)
Middle East	7,831	1,061	966	(D)	(D)	(D)
Israel	2,459	−3	601	(D)	(D)	(D)
Kuwait	(D)	(D)	9	0	0	0
Lebanon	−19	0	(D)	0	(D)	0
Saudi Arabia	(D)	(D)	3	0	(*)	0
United Arab Emirates	57	−5	−3	0	−2	(*)
Other	414	−5	(D)	0	(D)	0

Machinery	Other Manufacturing	Wholesale Trade	Retail Trade	Depository Institutions	Finance (Except Depository Institutions)	Insurance	Real Estate	Services	Other Industries
59,260	128,112	96,261	18,778	44,785	50,858	80,378	44,436	50,252	43,409
5,467	8,783	5,098	1,039	2,569	7,130	7,861	9,064	2,488	10,786
41,591	95,423	43,554	14,479	26,725	18,914	65,745	14,303	36,463	24,059
148	107	485	(D)	(D)	(D)	1	5	(D)	3
(D)	654	1,018	935	(D)	306	1	51	1,489	(D)
174	332	2,010	8	(D)	(D)	−4	(D)	167	253
233	1,357	1,012	1	(D)	−46	(D)	3	3	(D)
10,184	9,118	1,972	515	3,851	5,545	4,886	(D)	3,018	3,251
7,095	23,556	12,405	2,520	5,712	1,741	9,657	3,547	5,924	2,209
378	1,584	1,980	(D)	(D)	−268	1,849	31	816	638
5	468	423	595	1,094	(D)	(D)	65	(D)	188
4	(D)	65	0	0	1	0	47	(D)	41
(D)	(D)	1,311	(D)	0	110	(D)	(D)	4,315	(D)
7,093	16,236	5,606	4,898	6,473	4,301	16,844	6,612	3,625	2,131
270	38	269	2	(D)	−9	2	40	(D)	170
10	(D)	154	84	1,135	−74	168	48	(D)	(D)
5,578	2,092	2,028	(D)	(D)	(D)	−6	744	2,036	333
1,854	5,126	2,579	183	(D)	2,478	17,112	211	2,341	(D)
7,709	22,009	10,099	3,894	3,210	1,957	14,265	1,801	12,058	13,752
36	61	137	(D)	243	19	(*)	1	(D)	2
296	2,004	1,858	897	3,526	4,859	5,356	4,105	1,472	1,736
−216	437	270	24	2,601	2,394	(D)	232	176	(D)
−102	8	−54	6	691	(D)	(D)	(D)	1	8
−55	423	495	6	70	2,000	2	85	174	320
−7	−2	−108	5	(D)	284	(D)	182	17	333
−2	6	−10	2	268	−1	6	(D)	(D)	(D)
−60	1	−52	6	(D)	(D)	30	2	(D)	−9
514	1,567	1,588	872	924	2,465	(D)	3,873	1,296	(D)
0	2	440	(D)	(D)	(D)	0	441	272	191
(D)	517	226	237	5	−66	204	644	173	493
(D)	184	(D)	(D)	(D)	85	0	255	−55	125
494	867	608	25	648	(D)	(D)	2,614	791	208
−1	−3	(D)	(D)	0	11	(D)	−80	116	(D)
−14	−292	21	17	47	432	0	116	234	111
−14	(D)	(D)	0	0	(D)	0	(D)	(D)	−1
(*)	(D)	(D)	17	47	(D)	0	(D)	(D)	112
522	246	131	392	931	216	0	3,728	125	280
165	236	129	(D)	819	(D)	0	(D)	46	284
0	9	3	0	(D)	(D)	0	3,657	(D)	−2
(D)	0	(*)	−2	0	0	0	(D)	0	(*)
1	2	−1	(D)	(D)	0	0	(D)	(D)	−8
−1	0	0	(D)	(D)	0	0	13	0	(D)
(D)	0	(*)	−3	48	0	0	37	8	(D)

TABLE 1-4   (cont.)

| | | | Manufacturing | | | |
	All Industries	Petroleum	Total	Food and Kindred Products	Chemicals and Allied Products	Primary and Fabricated Metals
Asia and Pacific	156,085	2,720	45,096	1,951	5,643	3,957
Australia	14,755	3,202	2,982	−68	135	1,164
Hong Kong	2,097	(D)	358	(D)	(*)	(D)
Japan	132,569	234	39,918	1,762	4,838	2,760
Korea, Republic of	285	(D)	27	(D)	55	−78
Malaysia	89	(D)	57	2	(*)	1
New Zealand	352	(*)	20	7	−1	(D)
Philippines	69	(*)	13	−2	(*)	0
Singapore	1,813	2	244	(D)	−34	(D)
Taiwan	3,120	−2	1,505	−1	911	3
Other	936	57	−28	(D)	−61	(D)
Addends:						
European Union (15)[1]	481,731	41,330	224,885	8,978	73,967	12,296
OPEC[2]	4,939	448	−24	1	−18	(*)

* Less than $500,000 (±).

D Suppressed to avoid disclosure of data of individual companies.

1. The European Union (15) comprises Austria, Belgium, Denmark, Finland, France, Germany, Greece, Ireland, Italy, Luxembourg, Netherlands, Portugal, Spain, Sweden, and the United Kingdom.

2. OPEC is the Organization of Petroleum Exporting Countries. Its members are Algeria, Indonesia, Iran, Iraq, Kuwait, Libya, Nigeria, Oatar, Saudi Arabia, the United Arab Emirates, and Venezuela.

Source: Sylvia E. Bargas and Rosaria Troia, "Direct Investment Positions for 1998: Country and Industry Detail," Table 4.2, *Survey of Current Business*, July 1999, p. 59. Reprinted by permission.

differences and fluctuations in prices for products, labor, and capital. Yet, as it turns out, these prices differ and fluctuate much more widely across borders. This is partly due to the fact that these prices are set in different currencies—currencies whose values fluctuate with respect to one another as well. Generally, an investor cannot consider price and currency fluctuations independently. In Chapter 2, we detail a number of international parity propositions that should hold between exchange rates and the prices for goods, services, labor, and investment capital in different countries. These parity propositions provide important guidance for how investors should establish foreign projects, and how they should contend with fluctuating cross-border prices and exchange rates in their ongoing projects.

Most cross-border transactions would not be possible without the ability to exchange currencies, because no single currency is an acceptable means of payment in all countries. The foreign exchange market serves to facilitate international transactions in this regard. The foreign exchange market is a collection of major financial institutions in world financial centers that are linked by an electronic trading network. Its main function is to match offers to purchase and sell various currencies. The prices at which these transactions are matched are known as **exchange rates,** simply the prices of one currency in terms of others. Each day, major newspapers include a listing of the prevailing exchange rates. Table 1-5 shows a listing of exchange rates published in the *Wall Street Journal*. The first two columns reflect the price of one unit of a given currency in dollar terms, or the dollar/foreign currency exchange rate. The second two columns re-

Machinery	Other Manufacturing	Wholesale Trade	Retail Trade	Depository Institutions	Finance (Except Depository Institutions)	Insurance	Real Estate	Services	Other Industries
11,395	21,949	45,598	1,954	10,988	19,307	1,416	13,101	9,469	6,436
472	1,278	−55	14	157	(D)	(D)	691	(D)	4,202
123	40	599	15	229	(D)	1	268	305	314
10,036	20,522	43,114	1,868	9,043	17,445	990	10,743	7,304	1,910
14	(D)	673	(D)	−39	(D)	(D)	45	15	2
43	11	16	0	(D)	(D)	0	3	207	−11
(*)	(D)	179	(D)	(D)	0	(D)	71	−4	47
15	(*)	−6	(*)	73	0	−6	−2	0	−3
199	20	287	4	117	−1	(*)	1,258	69	−146
497	95	558	(D)	720	125	(*)	45	53	(D)
−4	−46	254	6	672	2	2	−22	(D)	(D)
39,429	90,214	40,509	14,272	24,095	16,441	48,631	14,008	33,837	23,722
(*)	−7	−2	24	649	(D)	6	3,690	66	(D)

flect the price of one dollar in terms of a given currency, or the foreign currency/dollar exchange rate. Most of the listed prices are known as **spot exchange rates,** which are quotes for immediate exchanges of one currency for another. Some currencies, such as the British pound, Canadian dollar, French franc, German mark, Japanese yen, and Swiss franc, also contain listings of exchange rates for transactions that take place 30, 90, and 180 days into the future. These prices are known as **forward exchange rates,** which reflect prices at which parties today agree to exchange one currency for another at some specified time in the future.

Another important aspect of international financial markets is that prices for investment capital—represented by interest rates—are also set in local currency terms. Furthermore, they are not the real rates of return examined theoretically earlier, but are nominal rates of return combining an expected real rate of return and an expected rate of inflation. Interest rates are also determined in markets which trade obligations of varying quality and maturity.

In the United States, markets exist to trade obligations that range in quality from extremely high (such as government debt) to quite low (such as junk bonds). Maturities range from overnight deposits to 30-year treasury bonds. The returns that are paid on these obligations determine the country's various interest rates. In the United States, as well as in other countries, these returns are paid in local currency terms, producing a local currency rate of interest. Table 1-6 shows a variety of nominal interest rates for several currencies at different maturities. The first four interest rates are for **offshore deposits,** or currencies on deposit outside the country from which the currency originates. The last interest rate is the yield on long-term (approximately 10-year) government bonds. These are useful financial instruments because the deposits are identical in all respects except for the currency of denomination. As we can immediately see, the rates of return are far from identical across the different currencies: interest rates on Japanese yen are exceptionally low and interest rates on the U.S. dollar are somewhat high.

TABLE 1-5 Exchange Rates

CURRENCY TRADING

Thursday, June 24, 1999

EXCHANGE RATES

The New York foreign exchance mid-range rates below apply to trading among banks in amounts of $1 million and more, as quoted at 4 p.m. Eastern time by Telerate and other sources. Retail transactions provide fewer units of foreign currency per dollar. Rates for the 11 Euro currency countries are derived from the latest dollar-Euro rate using the exchange ratios set 1/1/99.

Country	U.S. $ Equiv.		Currency per U.S. $	
	Thu	Wed	Thu	Wed
Argentina (Peso)	1.0005	1.0005	.9995	.9995
Australia (Dollar)	.6592	.6576	1.5170	1.5207
Austria (Schilling)	.07569	.07509	13.212	13.317
Bahrain (Dinar)	2.6525	2.6525	.3770	.3770
Belgium (Franc)	.0258	.0256	38.7330	39.0400
Brazil (Real)	.5571	.5590	1.7950	1.7890
Britain (Pound)	1.5882	1.5805	.6296	.6327
1-month forward	1.5883	1.5806	.6296	.6327
3-months forward	1.5892	1.5813	.6292	.6324
6-months forward	1.5910	1.5833	.6285	.6316
Canada (Dollar)	.6793	.6792	1.4720	1.4723
1-month forward	.6796	.6794	1.4715	1.4718
3-months forward	.6800	.6799	1.4705	1.4708
6-months forward	.6806	.6806	1.4693	1.4693
Chile (Peso)	.001948	.001966	513.45	508.75
China (Renminbl)	.1208	.1208	8.2778	8.2784
Colombia (Peso)	.0005803	.0005848	1723.26	1710.03
Czech. Rep. (Koruna)				
Commercial rate	.02800	.02800	35.709	35.708
Denmark (Krone)	.1401	.1391	7.1395	7.1895
Ecuador (Sucre)				
Floating rate	.00008749	.00008493	11430.00	11775.00
Finland (Markka)	.1752	.1738	5.7088	5.7541
France (Franc)	.1588	.1575	6.2982	6.3482
1-month forward	.1591	.1579	6.2848	6.3345
3-months forward	.1598	.1586	6.2564	6.3057
6-months forward	.1609	.1597	6.2133	6.2623
Germany (Mark)	.5325	.5283	1.8779	1.8928
1-month forward	.5336	.5295	1.8739	1.887
3-months forward	.5361	.5319	1.8654	1.8801
6-months forward	.5398	.5356	1.8526	1.8672
Greece (Drachma)	.003210	.003187	311.52	313.77
Hong Kong (Dollar)	.1289	.1289	7.7579	7.7578
Hungary (Forint)	.004147	.004138	241.11	241.68
India (Rupee)	.02308	.02312	43.325	43.255
Indonesia (Rupiah)	.0001475	.0001482	6780.00	6750.00
Ireland (Punt)	1.3224	1.3120	.7562	.7622
Israel (Shekel)	.2430	.2431	4.1150	4.1130
Italy (Lira)	.0005379	.0005337	1859.12	1873.87

TABLE 1-5 (cont.)

Country	U.S. $ Equiv.		Currency per U.S. $	
	Thu	**Wed**	**Thu**	**Wed**
Japan (Yen)	.008199	.008200	121.97	121.95
1-month forward	.008234	0.8236	121.45	121.42
3-months forward	.008307	.008310	120.38	120.33
6-months forward	.008421	.008423	118.75	118.72
Jordan (Dinar)	1.4104	1.4104	.7090	.7090
Kuwait (Dinar)	3.2595	3.2637	.3068	.3064
Lebanon (Pound)	.0006631	.0006631	1508.00	1508.00
Malaysia (Ringgit)	.2632	.2632	3.8000	3.8000
Malta (Lira)	2.4691	2.4558	.4050	.4072
Mexico (Peso)				
Floating rate	.1055	.1063	9.4800	9.4050
Netherlands (Guilder)	.4726	.4689	2.1159	2.1327
New Zealand (Dollar)	.5375	.5344	1.8605	1.8713
Norway (Krone)	.1280	.1277	7.8103	7.8303
Pakistan (Rupee)	.01940	.01939	51.550	51.575
Peru (New Sol)	.2994	.2996	3.3405	3.3380
Philippines (Peso)	.02639	.02642	37.893	37.855
Poland (Zloty)	.2541	.2551	3.9355	3.9205
Portugal (Escudo)	.005195	.005154	192.49	194.02
Russia (Ruble) (a)	.04129	.04127	24.220	24.230
Saudi Arabia (Riyal)	.2666	.2666	3.7506	3.7506
Singapore (Dollar)	.5877	.5873	1.7015	1.7028
Slovak Rep. (Koruna)	.02298	.02279	43.522	43.872
South Africa (Rand)	.1650	.1663	6.0615	6.0150
South Korea (Won)	.0008638	.0008602	1157.70	1162.50
Spain (Peseta)	.006259	.006210	159.76	161.02
Sweden (Krona)	.1190	.1189	8.4003	8.4078
Switzerland (Franc)	.6515	.6470	1.5349	1.5457
1-month forward	.6537	.6492	1.5298	1.5404
3-months forward	.6583	.6539	1.5190	1.5294
6-months forward	.6653	.6609	1.5030	1.5132
Taiwan (Dollar)	.03091	.03091	32.353	32.348
Thailand (Baht)	.02723	.02723	36.730	36.730
Turkey (Lira)	.00000239	.00000239	417704.00	417758.00
United Arab (Dirham)	.2723	.2723	3.6729	3.6729
Uruguay (New Peso)				
Financial	.08797	.08808	11.368	11.353
Venezuela (Bolivar)	.001653	.001653	604.96	604.96
SDR	1.3349	1.3335	.7491	.7499
Euro	1.0415	1.0333	.9602	.9678

Special Drawing Rights (SDR) are based on exchange rates for the U.S., German, British, French, and Japanese currencies. *Source:* International Monetary Fund.

a-Russian Central Bank rate. Trading band lowered on 8/17/98. b-Government rate.

The Wall Street Journal daily foreign exchange data from 1996 forward may be purchased through the Readers' Reference Service (413) 592-3600.

Source: The Wall Street Journal, June 25, 1999, p. C17. Reprinted by permission.

TABLE 1-6   Interest Rates, June 1999 (percentage points)

	Offshore Deposits				Long-Term Government Bonds
	1-month	3-month	6-month	1-year	
U.S. (dollar)	5.14	5.22	5.42	5.72	6.31
Britain (pound)	5.03	5.09	5.14	5.33	5.16
Canada (dollar)	4.72	4.81	4.94	5.34	5.70
France (franc)	2.61	2.64	2.69	2.91	4.94
Germany (mark)	2.61	2.64	2.69	2.91	4.40
Japan (yen)	0.08	0.13	0.08	0.11	1.30
Switzerland (franc)	1.09	1.09	1.16	1.45	3.02

Sources: Offshore deposit rates are calculated as the midpoint of the range quoted in the *Financial Times*, June 25, 1999, p. 25 (France and Germany listed as Euro area). Yields on long-term government bonds are from *OECD Hot File: Key Economic Indicators, Weekly Update on the Internet*, July 30, 1999.

Although enormous sums of capital can move among these markets with the press of a computer key, nominal interest rates are usually quite different at a given point in time, and these differences have important consequences for an investor. For instance, in which currency should an investor hold cash reserves? In which currency should an investor borrow to finance an investment? Should interest rate differences influence where to locate the project? The international parity propositions developed in Chapter 2 will aid us in understanding such questions.

Because of multiple currencies, investors face additional challenges in evaluating foreign investments and confront additional risks due to uncertainties over interest rates, inflation rates, and exchange rate changes. A substantial portion of this book examines such challenges, particularly by applying international parity propositions to managerial decisions. Chapter 3 evaluates foreign projects with multiple currencies and multiple costs of capital, and Chapter 4 examines financing with multiple interest rates and the risk of exchange rate changes. Chapters 6–10 contain a complete analysis of **foreign exchange risk,** the risk resulting from uncertainty over exchange rate changes, through discussions of what the investment has exposed (or is at stake), what the risk associated with the exposure is, and how the risk may be hedged or managed.

DEALING WITH MULTIPLE GOVERNMENTS: INTERNATIONAL TAXES AND POLITICAL RISK

Upon entering the global arena, an investor must also contend with multiple tax systems and multiple rates of taxation. Table 1-7 illustrates that the marginal corporate income tax rates facing a multinational can vary widely across countries: at the low end Switzerland imposes taxes at a rate less than 10 percent, and at the high end Italy and Germany impose taxes at a rate more than 50 percent. Furthermore, there has been variation over time. One aspect not captured by Table 1-7 is that the tax base—the definition of taxable corporate income—also varies across countries, depending on what costs are deductible from revenues to arrive at taxable profits. Governments usually set tax rates as a function of domestic political considerations, but will sometimes treat foreign investors differently to the extent that they choose to encourage or discourage

TABLE 1-7   Marginal Corporate Income Tax Rates

Country	1981	1982	1983	1984	1985	1986	1987	1988	1989	1990	1991	1992
Australia[a]	.46	.46	.46	.46	.46	.49	.49	.39	.39	.39	.39	.39
Belgium[b]	.48	.45	.45	.45	.45	.45	.43	.43	.43	.41	.39	.39
Canada[c,d]	.483	.483	.472	.46	.483	.483	.464	.391	.391	.391	.391	.391
Denmark	.40	.40	.40	.40	.50	.50	.50	.50	.50	.40	.38	.38
France[e]	.50	.50	.50	.50	.50	.45	.45	.42	.39	.37	.34	.34
Germany[f]	.56	.56	.56	.56	.56	.56	.56	.56	.56	.50	.519	.519
Ireland[d]	.45	.50	.50	.50	.50	.50	.50	.47	.43	.43	.40	.40
Italy[c]	.363	.413	.413	.464	.464	.464	.464	.464	.464	.464	.478	.552
Japan[c,g]	.42	.42	.42	.433	.433	.433	.42	.42	.40	.375	.384	.384
Netherlands	.48	.48	.48	.43	.43	.42	.42	.42	.35	.35	.35	.35
New Zealand	.45	.45	.45	.45	.45	.48	.48	.28	.33	.33	.33	.33
Norway[h]	.508	.508	.508	.508	.508	.508	.508	.508	.508	.508	.508	.28
Spain	.33	.33	.35	.35	.35	.35	.35	.35	.35	.35	.35	.35
Sweden[i]	.58	.58	.58	.52	.52	.52	.52	.52	.52	.40	.30	.30
Switzerland[j]	.098	.098	.098	.098	.098	.098	.098	.098	.098	.098	.098	.098
United Kingdom	.52	.52	.52	.45	.40	.35	.35	.35	.35	.35	.33	.33
United States[c]	.46	.46	.46	.46	.46	.46	.40	.34	.34	.34	.34	.34

[a]Undistributed profits were taxed at the rate of .50 until an imputation system came into operation July 1987.

[b]Excess profits surtax at the rate of .04 applied until 1982.

[c]Additional corporate income tax levied by state and/or municipal government which is rebated or deductible at the federal level.

[d]Corporate income tax is levied at a lower rate on manufacturing firms.

[e]Split-rate system, which applied a higher tax rate to distributed profits, was in effect from 1989 until 1992.

[f]Distributed profits taxed at a lower rate of .36.

[g]Distributed profits were taxed at a .10 lower rate until 1988. In 1989, distributed profits were taxed at a .05 lower rate. The split-rate system was permanently abolished in 1990.

[h]Additional corporate income taxes were levied at the municipal level and for a "tax equalization fund" resulting in a combined rate of .23 which was not deductible from the federal rate of .278. Effective 1992, the federal corporate income tax was abolished, the municipal rate was lowered to .11, and the tax equalization fund rate was increased to .17.

[i]Additional corporate income tax levied at the municipal level, which was deductible at the federal level, was abolished in 1985.

[j]Federal, cantonal, and municipal corporate income taxes, which are typically partially deductible against one another, are levied at graduated rates based on the proportion of taxable profits to equity capital. Top federal rate reported.

Source: Jason G. Cummings, Trevor S. Harris, and Kevin A. Hassett, "Accounting Standards, Information Flow, and Firm Investment Behavior," in *The Effects of Taxation on Multinational Corporations*, edited by Martin Feldstein, James R. Hines, Jr., and R. Glenn Hubbard, University of Chicago Press, 1995, p. 195. Reprinted by permission.

DFI. As we shall develop more carefully in subsequent chapters, there are some methods with which investors can manage differences in tax rates.

One method of managing different tax rates involves the financing of foreign projects. If a firm uses internal funds in financing an overseas subsidiary, its decision about whether to use debt or equity is strongly affected by the tax rates in the respective countries. From the firm's perspective, the main distinction between debt and equity financing is that interest payments made by a debt-financed subsidiary are made from pretax profits. That is, interest payments on debt are transferred from the subsidiary to the parent prior to the determination of subsidiary profits. The interest is then income to the parent, and is taxed accordingly. Clearly, when the parent-country tax rate is lower than that of the subsidiary, the firm has incentives to finance with debt.

Conversely, the firm has incentives to finance with equity when the parent-country tax rate is higher than that of the subsidiary. This effectively puts profits (returns on equity) where the corporate income tax is lower, and the firm pays any residual tax liability to the home country government only when these profits are repatriated. An extension of this analysis to external financing implies that a firm has an incentive to arrange for the units located in high-tax countries to undertake a larger share of the external borrowing than units located in low-tax countries. The tax and financing problems of a multinational facing different tax rates represent important concerns for firms entering foreign markets, and are addressed in great detail in Chapter 4.

Differences in tax rates can also be managed through the ongoing operations of the multinational corporation. In particular, a multinational corporation has a number of tools at its disposal with which it can reduce its total tax payment. It may allocate some costs between subsidiaries and the parent, adjust the transfer prices of intermediate goods, and determine the timing of dividends to repatriate profits from the subsidiary to the parent. These issues, highlighting a significant difference between an international and a purely domestic operation and reflecting the optimal operation of a firm facing different tax rates, are discussed in Chapter 11.

A final consequence of operating in a foreign country is the introduction of **political risk,** the uncertainty about government intervention and policy changes that results from having to deal with various foreign governments. Most DFI, taking place among developed countries, faces little problem in this regard. However, increasing proportions of the world supply of investment funds are flowing to emerging economies—economies often with only limited experience with open and stable markets. These countries have traditionally imposed restrictions on international trade, capital flows, currency conversion, and other transactions. They have occasionally resorted to nationalizations and outright expropriations as well. Political risk has important consequences for a firm's decisions of where to locate subsidiaries and which projects to undertake. It also has direct effects on a company's operations, as there are often several ways in which a firm can react to and mitigate the impact of a changing political environment.

Table 1-8 displays a compendium of political risk ratings for most countries in the world from *Euromoney.* This particular evaluation is very narrowly defined to capture the riskiness of lending to foreign countries, or **country risk.** The overall country risk rankings for 180 countries are on a 100-point scale, on which Luxembourg emerges as the safest country at 98.48 and North Korea as the riskiest country at 1.28. The overall country risk ranking is based on weighted ratings in nine categories: political risk (25 percent), economic performance (25 percent), debt indicators (10 percent), debt in default or rescheduled (10 percent), credit ratings (10 percent), access to bank finance (5 percent), access to short-term finance (5 percent), access to capital markets (5 percent), and the discount on forfeiting (5 percent). Although 50 percent of the rating is based on the creditworthiness of the government, the political risk component captures a subjective judgment of political risk experts regarding the willingness to pay.

Table 1-8 demonstrates that a number of countries have significant country and political risks that must be factored into firms' financial decisions. Firms contemplating direct foreign investment need to be concerned about many more sources of political risk

TABLE 1-8 Country Risk Ratings

Mar 99	Sept 98	Country	Total Score 100	Political Risk 25	Economic Performance 25	Debt Indicators 10	Debt in Default or Rescheduled 10	Credit Ratings 10	Access to Bank Finance 5	Access to Short-Term Finance 5	Access to Capital Markets 5	Discount on Forfaiting 5
		Weighting:										
1	1	Luxembourg	98.48	24.28	25.00	10.00	10.00	10.00	5.00	5.00	5.00	4.20
2	6	Switzerland	98.36	24.88	23.85	10.00	10.00	10.00	5.00	5.00	5.00	4.63
3	8	Norway	95.43	23.96	21.90	10.00	10.00	10.00	5.00	5.00	5.00	4.57
4	2	United States	94.92	25.00	20.28	10.00	10.00	10.00	5.00	5.00	5.00	4.64
5	4	Netherlands	94.22	24.51	19.71	10.00	10.00	10.00	5.00	5.00	5.00	5.00
6	3	Germany	94.04	24.87	19.55	10.00	10.00	10.00	5.00	5.00	5.00	4.62
7	7	France	93.68	24.78	19.27	10.00	10.00	10.00	5.00	5.00	5.00	4.62
8	5	Austria	93.30	23.96	19.35	10.00	10.00	10.00	5.00	5.00	5.00	4.99
9	11	Denmark	93.24	23.32	20.96	10.00	10.00	9.38	5.00	5.00	5.00	4.59
10	13	Belgium	91.18	23.27	18.76	10.00	10.00	9.17	5.00	5.00	5.00	4.99
11	23	Japan	90.94	23.81	18.88	10.00	10.00	9.58	5.00	5.00	4.80	3.87
12	12	Finland	90.91	22.52	19.22	10.00	10.00	9.58	5.00	5.00	5.00	4.59
13	9	United Kingdom	90.87	24.72	16.52	10.00	10.00	10.00	5.00	5.00	5.00	4.63
14	14	Sweden	90.33	22.54	19.24	10.00	10.00	8.96	5.00	5.00	5.00	4.59
15	10	Ireland	90.12	22.66	17.69	10.00	10.00	9.79	5.00	5.00	5.00	4.97
16	15	Canada	90.09	23.48	17.72	10.00	10.00	8.96	5.00	5.00	5.00	4.93
17	21	Singapore	88.88	23.41	18.62	10.00	10.00	9.58	5.00	5.00	3.80	3.46
18	19	Australia	87.79	21.89	18.02	10.00	10.00	8.75	5.00	5.00	5.00	4.13
19	18	Italy	87.62	22.52	16.57	10.00	10.00	8.96	5.00	5.00	5.00	4.57
20	17	New Zealand	86.90	21.70	16.20	10.00	10.00	9.06	5.00	5.00	5.00	4.93
21	16	Spain	86.72	22.33	15.63	10.00	10.00	9.17	5.00	5.00	5.00	4.60
22	22	Iceland	84.47	20.22	17.30	10.00	10.00	7.81	5.00	5.00	5.00	4.13
23	20	Portugal	84.41	21.91	14.18	10.00	10.00	9.17	5.00	5.00	5.00	4.16
24	114	Bermuda	81.49	20.91	19.62	10.00	10.00	8.96	5.00	5.00	2.00	0.00
25	24	Taiwan	79.74	20.38	14.27	10.00	10.00	8.75	5.00	5.00	3.13	3.22
26	32	Hong Kong	76.73	18.68	15.75	10.00	10.00	6.88	5.00	4.29	3.30	2.84
27	27	Greece	75.87	18.04	13.84	10.00	10.00	5.31	5.00	5.00	5.00	3.67
28	25	Cyprus	75.39	18.00	12.72	10.00	10.00	7.19	5.00	4.29	5.00	3.19
29	28	United Arab Emirates	73.39	17.10	15.26	10.00	10.00	6.88	5.00	4.11	1.70	3.35
30	26	Malta	71.81	19.48	11.74	9.82	10.00	6.88	1.01	4.29	5.00	3.60
31	31	Israel	70.62	15.97	12.82	10.00	10.00	6.25	5.00	4.20	3.25	3.13
32	33	Slovenia	70.06	16.62	12.07	9.94	10.00	6.46	3.84	3.84	3.90	3.39

TABLE 1-8 (cont.)

Rank		Country	Total Score 100	Political Risk 25	Economic Performance 25	Debt Indicators 10	Debt in Default or Rescheduled 10	Credit Ratings 10	Access to Bank Finance 5	Access to Short-Term Finance 5	Access to Capital Markets 5	Discount on Forfaiting 5
Mar 99	Sept 98	Weighting:										
33	29	Kuwait	69.43	17.41	10.78	10.00	10.00	6.46	5.00	4.29	2.00	3.50
34	35	Qatar	68.76	15.32	13.32	10.00	10.00	5.00	5.00	4.29	2.33	3.50
35	84	Bahamas	68.17	17.95	12.69	10.00	10.00	6.25	5.00	4.29	2.00	0.00
36	34	Saudi Arabia	66.81	16.43	10.06	10.00	10.00	4.38	5.00	4.20	3.33	3.42
37	36	Bahrain	66.41	15.00	12.52	10.00	10.00	3.75	5.00	4.29	2.33	3.53
38	69	Brunei	66.20	18.81	15.86	10.00	10.00	0.00	5.00	4.29	2.25	0.00
39	39	Hungary	65.75	17.39	10.74	9.51	10.00	5.00	2.80	2.95	4.00	3.35
40	37	Oman	64.40	15.38	9.04	10.00	10.00	4.69	5.00	4.29	2.50	3.50
41	30	Chile	64.31	17.19	9.77	9.32	10.00	6.04	2.66	3.39	2.88	3.05
42	38	Poland	62.06	15.99	10.54	9.56	10.00	4.79	0.37	3.13	4.20	3.49
43	40	Czech Republic	61.96	16.58	9.97	9.65	10.00	5.83	0.50	3.13	3.80	2.50
44	42	South Korea	61.63	15.91	12.03	9.60	10.00	4.17	0.84	4.05	2.75	2.30
45	41	China	56.51	15.32	9.46	9.70	8.36	6.04	0.06	2.32	2.80	2.45
46	77	Mauritius	56.38	14.34	4.49	9.50	10.00	5.00	5.00	3.39	2.50	2.16
47	47	Mexico	55.18	13.35	9.27	9.46	10.00	3.13	1.27	3.21	3.00	2.49
48	44	Uruguay	54.67	12.38	8.97	9.37	10.00	4.38	0.18	4.11	2.67	2.62
49	54	Thailand	54.46	13.49	8.58	9.38	10.00	3.96	1.00	3.04	2.73	2.27
50	51	Estonia	54.38	12.52	9.09	9.92	10.00	5.42	0.62	2.46	2.63	1.73
51	43	Tunisia	54.25	14.55	7.59	9.35	10.00	4.38	0.06	3.30	1.67	3.35
52	66	Croatia	54.04	11.01	9.42	9.64	10.00	4.38	2.55	2.28	2.60	2.17
53	55	Philippines	54.00	13.22	8.57	9.52	10.00	3.75	0.91	3.21	2.88	1.93
54	49	Egypt	53.01	13.83	7.86	9.36	9.85	4.17	0.00	2.92	1.67	3.35
55	48	Argentina	52.90	12.09	9.64	8.42	10.00	2.92	0.81	4.02	2.90	2.10
56	50	South Africa	52.83	12.83	7.51	9.70	10.00	3.75	0.27	3.30	2.67	2.80
57	56	Morocco	52.17	13.20	7.23	9.20	10.00	3.44	0.10	3.13	2.67	3.22
58	53	Malaysia	51.66	12.75	8.49	9.71	10.00	3.96	2.00	3.24	1.50	0.00
59	45	Colombia	51.21	11.44	6.75	9.17	10.00	4.38	1.28	3.21	2.67	2.32
60	59	India	50.90	13.17	7.34	9.22	10.00	3.13	0.19	3.30	1.90	2.65
61	52	Botswana	50.85	15.23	9.13	10.00	10.00	0.00	0.00	3.39	0.75	2.36
62	57	Latvia	50.67	11.23	8.54	9.93	10.00	5.00	0.20	2.37	1.67	1.73
63	62	Lithuania	50.14	11.81	8.25	9.87	10.00	3.96	0.00	2.28	2.25	1.73
64	71	Panama	49.84	9.83	10.42	9.59	10.00	4.38	1.16	3.13	1.33	0.00
65	46	Trinidad & Tobago	48.91	11.91	8.97	9.65	10.00	3.75	0.00	.13	1.50	0.00
66	58	Slovak Republic	48.33	10.91	8.51	9.54	10.00	3.75	0.53	2.28	2.10	0.71

67	61	Turkey	48.25	11.29	7.90	9.27	10.00	1.67	1.69	3.13	2.25	1.07
68	63	Jordan	47.51	10.56	8.86	9.16	9.22	2.50	0.00	2.32	2.00	2.89
69	68	Lebanon	47.10	9.56	7.05	9.54	10.00	2.29	1.11	2.41	2.50	2.63
70	60	Costa Rica	46.08	11.11	7.86	9.63	10.00	3.44	0.00	3.04	1.00	0.00
71	72	Peru	44.08	8.86	7.81	8.57	9.24	2.81	0.75	2.68	1.33	2.02
72	80	Fiji	44.00	11.80	9.42	9.93	10.00	0.00	0.00	2.86	0.00	0.00
73	67	El Salvador	43.98	9.55	6.65	9.62	10.00	3.75	0.14	3.27	1.00	0.00
74	97	Barbados	43.08	13.73	10.86	0.00	10.00	3.75	0.00	3.75	1.00	0.00
75	79	Papua New Guinea	42.15	8.85	7.39	9.52	10.00	1.88	0.87	2.77	0.88	0.00
76	70	Brazil	41.74	8.77	5.96	8.75	9.96	1.46	1.48	3.13	1.30	0.93
77	73	Guatemala	41.19	8.18	7.10	9.51	10.00	3.13	0.00	2.95	0.33	0.00
78	81	Kazakhstan	40.68	8.54	6.25	9.75	10.00	2.50	0.81	1.83	1.00	0.00
79	83	Sri Lanka	40.58	9.24	6.92	9.44	10.00	0.00	0.00	2.86	2.13	0.00
80	64	Dominican Rep	40.53	9.05	8.26	9.72	9.12	1.88	0.00	2.50	0.00	0.00
81	65	Jamaica	40.42	7.93	5.02	9.40	10.00	2.50	0.62	2.95	2.00	0.00
82	76	Venezuela	40.33	7.96	5.93	9.40	10.00	1.88	0.53	2.77	1.88	0.00
83	75	Paraguay	39.36	8.36	5.79	9.77	10.00	1.88	0.12	2.95	0.50	0.00
84	99	Syria	38.36	6.53	9.28	8.32	10.00	0.00	0.00	1.37	1.00	1.87
85	78	Bolivia	38.34	7.24	7.27	8.38	8.35	2.19	1.24	2.68	1.00	0.00
86	85	Ghana	37.91	10.28	4.73	8.37	10.00	0.00	0.00	2.53	0.00	2.00
87	93	Bulgaria	37.87	6.85	6.30	9.17	10.00	1.46	0.09	1.83	1.50	0.67
88	88	Indonesia	36.37	6.52	5.71	9.02	10.00	0.42	2.25	1.96	0.50	0.00
89	82	Romania	36.28	7.76	4.85	9.52	10.00	0.83	0.47	1.83	0.75	0.27
90	95	Senegal	36.00	7.72	6.29	8.90	9.91	0.00	0.17	2.68	0.33	0.00
91	89	Iran	35.85	7.13	6.69	9.75	10.00	0.00	0.00	0.98	0.50	0.80
92	87	Vietnam	35.67	7.44	5.54	9.06	9.02	1.88	0.00	2.44	0.30	0.00
93	96	Bangladesh	35.42	7.17	6.27	9.00	10.00	0.00	0.00	2.86	0.13	0.00
94	131	Belize	35.07	9.42	—	9.41	10.00	3.13	0.00	2.95	0.17	0.00
95	91	Uganda	34.87	6.85	6.44	8.10	10.00	0.00	0.00	2.41	0.00	1.07
96	101	Guyana	34.74	5.75	8.42	8.64	10.00	0.00	0.00	1.43	0.50	0.00
97	98	Kenya	34.53	7.97	5.00	8.99	10.00	0.00	0.00	2.41	0.17	0.00
98	86	Ecuador	34.33	6.61	4.72	8.82	9.88	0.63	0.17	2.86	.67	0.00
99	94	Gabon	34.15	6.85	7.28	9.28	7.89	0.00	0.00	2.86	0.00	0.00
100	74	St Lucia	34.00	11.06	—	9.97	10.00	0.00	0.00	1.96	1.00	0.00
101	90	Zimbabwe	33.89	6.80	3.72	9.23	10.00	0.00	0.61	3.04	0.50	0.00
102	106	Nepal	33.81	6.69	5.05	9.22	10.00	0.00	0.00	2.68	0.17	0.00
103	145	Gambia	33.80	5.41	7.76	9.02	10.00	0.00	0.00	1.61	0.00	0.00
104	102	Honduras	33.67	5.84	5.45	8.99	9.35	1.25	0.83	1.79	0.17	0.00

TABLE 1-8 (cont.)

Rank Mar 99	Rank Sept 98		Total Score 100	Political Risk 25	Economic Performance 25	Debt Indicators 10	Debt in Default or Rescheduled 10	Credit Ratings 10	Access to Bank Finance 5	Access to Short-Term Finance 5	Access to Capital Markets 5	Discount on Forfaiting 5
		Weighting:	100	25	25	10	10	10	5	5	5	5
105	112	Burkina Faso	33.47	6.02	6.88	8.67	9.98	0.00	0.00	1.79	0.13	0.00
106	116	Azerbaijan	33.39	4.88	6.48	9.82	10.00	0.00	0.00	1.55	0.67	0.00
107	150	Seychelles	33.35	8.72	—	9.79	10.00	0.00	0.00	3.84	1.00	0.00
108	100	Mali	33.34	6.28	7.33	8.11	10.00	0.00	0.00	1.61	0.00	0.00
109	104	St Vincent	33.16	10.86	—	9.84	10.00	0.00	0.00	1.96	0.50	0.00
110	128	Krygyz Republic	32.86	5.41	7.12	9.36	9.91	0.00	0.00	0.89	0.17	0.00
111	125	Turkmenistan	32.63	5.18	5.61	8.91	10.00	0.94	0.00	1.83	0.17	0.00
112	140	Tonga	32.46	9.95	—	9.64	10.00	0.00	0.00	2.86	0.00	0.00
113	103	Algeria	32.02	6.70	6.56	9.08	7.83	0.00	0.00	1.85	0.00	0.00
114	138	Vanuatu	31.93	9.23	—	9.85	10.00	0.00	0.00	2.86	0.00	0.00
115	141	Maldives	31.38	8.48	—	9.76	10.00	0.00	0.00	2.77	0.38	0.00
116	139	Lesotho	31.05	8.41	—	9.52	10.00	0.00	0.00	3.13	0.00	0.00
117	142	Moldova	30.79	3.64	3.71	9.52	10.00	1.25	0.00	1.83	0.83	0.00
118	146	Solomon Islands	30.77	8.20	—	9.71	10.00	0.00	0.00	2.86	0.00	0.00
119	122	Togo	30.69	4.01	7.35	9.00	9.26	0.00	0.00	1.07	0.00	0.00
120	111	Mongolia	30.65	4.72	5.63	9.29	10.00	0.00	0.00	0.89	0.13	0.00
121	92	Côte d'Ivoire	30.63	8.37	6.47	8.36	5.20	0.00	0.20	1.88	0.17	0.00
122	148	Western Samoa	30.58	9.26	—	9.35	10.00	0.00	0.00	1.96	0.00	0.00
123	109	Grenada	30.14	7.46	—	10.00	10.00	0.00	0.00	2.68	0.00	0.00
124	123	Pakistan	30.11	4.50	5.11	8.82	10.00	0.00	0.38	0.89	0.40	0.00
125	147	Swaziland	29.94	7.06	—	9.85	10.00	0.00	0.00	3.04	0.00	0.00
126	118	Ukraine	29.85	3.17	4.05	9.76	10.00	0.63	0.16	1.83	0.25	0.00
127	105	Uzbekistan	29.78	6.23	6.83	9.71	4.80	0.00	0.05	1.83	0.33	0.00
128	132	Nigeria	29.72	3.37	4.85	9.25	10.00	0.00	0.00	1.25	1.00	0.00
129	124	Niger	29.69	4.88	5.98	7.70	9.52	0.00	0.00	1.61	0.00	0.00
130	110	Dominica	29.38	7.35	—	9.36	10.00	0.00	0.00	2.68	0.00	0.00
131	129	Malawi	28.75	5.44	3.69	8.36	10.00	0.00	0.00	1.25	0.00	0.00
132	107	Yemen	28.55	4.76	7.38	9.43	4.91	0.00	0.00	1.83	0.25	0.00
133	126	Guinea	28.42	3.28	7.06	7.85	9.33	0.00	0.00	0.89	0.00	0.00
134	151	Bhutan	28.14	5.69	—	9.66	10.00	0.00	0.00	2.80	0.00	0.00
135	121	Cameroon	27.86	5.26	5.43	8.25	6.95	0.00	0.06	1.79	0.13	0.00
136	108	Haiti	27.82	2.55	6.46	7.91	10.00	0.00	0.00	0.89	0.00	0.00

#	Rank	Country										
137	144	Belarus	27.69	2.35	3.83	9.95	10.00	0.00	0.00	0.89	0.67	0.00
138	149	Cape Verde	27.52	5.22	—	9.48	9.66	0.00	0.00	3.04	0.13	0.00
139	170	Tajikistan	27.43	4.04	3.52	9.46	9.40	0.00	0.00	0.89	0.13	0.00
140	157	Congo	27.10	2.80	5.66	8.26	9.49	0.00	0.00	0.89	0.00	0.00
141	134	Georgia	26.81	3.12	5.89	9.12	6.69	0.00	0.00	1.61	0.38	0.00
142	156	Macau	26.03	15.47	—	0.00	0.00	5.63	0.00	3.93	1.00	0.00
143	159	Cambodia	25.94	2.03	4.18	8.91	9.93	0.00	0.00	0.89	0.00	0.00
144	115	Benin	25.84	4.54	—	8.73	10.00	0.00	0.00	2.44	0.13	0.00
145	120	Tanzania	25.48	4.25	5.18	7.40	6.96	0.00	0.00	0.89	0.00	0.80
146	143	FYR Macedonia	25.33	4.56	8.19	9.40	0.00	0.16	0.00	2.19	0.50	0.33
147	136	Zambia	25.31	2.81	4.61	7.53	9.47	0.00	0.00	0.89	0.00	0.00
148	113	Ethiopia	25.31	4.13	4.46	5.65	9.70	0.00	0.00	1.37	0.00	0.00
149	164	Angola	25.22	1.66	4.19	8.73	9.73	0.00	0.00	0.89	0.00	0.00
150	154	Mozambique	23.99	3.40	5.20	5.06	9.35	0.09	0.00	0.89	0.00	0.00
151	119	Namibia	23.92	11.73	7.06	0.00	0.00	0.00	0.00	2.86	0.50	1.77
152	152	Laos	23.71	5.18	—	7.47	10.00	0.00	0.00	0.89	0.17	0.00
153	174	Djibouti	23.60	2.78	—	9.39	10.00	0.00	0.00	1.43	0.00	0.00
154	163	Mauritania	23.53	4.07	1.33	7.21	9.86	0.00	0.00	1.07	0.00	0.00
155	160	Equatorial Guinea	23.23	2.53	—	9.63	10.00	0.00	0.00	1.07	0.00	0.00
156	155	Nicaragua	23.20	3.05	2.52	7.06	7.72	1.25	0.00	1.43	0.17	0.00
157	133	Chad	22.85	3.70	—	8.36	9.72	0.00	0.00	1.07	0.00	0.00
158	130	Central African Rep	22.48	3.29	—	8.12	10.00	0.00	0.00	1.07	0.00	0.00
159	137	Armenia	21.22	2.98	—	9.36	6.82	0.00	0.00	0.89	1.17	0.00
160	159	Sudan	20.88	0.61	5.87	.51	10.00	0.00	0.00	0.89	0.00	0.00
161	127	Russia	20.86	3.02	3.67	9.46	2.09	0.14	0.31	1.96	0.20	0.00
162	117	Madagascar	20.14	3.89	4.38	7.58	3.22	0.00	0.00	1.07	0.00	0.00
163	166	Guinea-Bissau	20.06	2.57	4.34	2.35	9.91	0.00	0.00	0.89	0.00	0.00
164	171	Antigua & Barbuda	19.25	5.64	10.61	0.00	0.00	0.00	0.00	2.50	0.50	0.00
165	161	Rwanda	18.96	0.82	—	7.07	10.00	0.00	0.00	1.07	0.00	0.00
166	153	Myanmar	18.96	4.22	4.44	0.00	10.00	0.00	0.00	0.18	0.13	0.00
167	135	Albania	17.49	2.94	4.10	9.42	0.00	0.00	0.00	0.89	0.13	0.00
168	165	Dem Rep Congo	17.11	0.58	0.00	5.99	10.00	0.00	0.00	0.54	0.00	0.00
169	162	Libya	16.72	6.88	8.41	0.00	10.00	0.00	0.00	1.43	0.00	0.00
170	158	Sierra Leone	16.54	1.85	0.63	4.54	8.62	0.00	0.00	0.89	0.00	0.00
171	168	Yugoslavia	15.25	0.92	3.83	0.00	10.00	0.00	0.00	0.00	0.50	0.00
172	173	Somalia	14.54	0.59	3.05	0.00	10.00	0.00	0.00	0.89	0.00	0.00
173	172	Liberia	13.50	1.09	1.88	0.00	10.00	0.00	0.00	0.54	0.00	0.00
174	167	Surinam	13.37	4.13	8.19	0.00	0.00	0.00	0.00	0.89	0.17	0.00

TABLE 1-8 (cont.)

Rank Mar 99	Rank Sept 98		Total Score 100	Political Risk 25	Economic Performance 25	Debt Indicators 10	Debt in Default or Rescheduled 10	Credit Ratings 10	Access to Bank Finance 5	Access to Short-Term Finance 5	Access to Capital Markets 5	Discount on Forfaiting 5
		Weighting:										
175	176	Sao Tome & Principe	13.23	3.21	—	0.00	8.77	0.00	0.00	1.25	0.00	0.00
176	177	New Caledonia	12.96	11.53	—	0.00	0.00	0.00	0.00	1.43	0.00	0.00
177	175	Cuba	7.47	1.40	4.68	0.00	0.00	0.00	0.00	0.89	0.50	0.00
178	178	Iraq	4.65	0.31	3.81	0.00	0.00	0.00	0.00	0.54	0.00	0.00
179	180	Afghanistan	2.66	1.41	—	0.00	0.00	0.00	0.00	1.25	0.00	0.00
180	179	North Korea	1.28	0.00	0.26	0.00	0.00	0.00	0.00	0.89	0.13	0.00

Methodology for main ranking

To obtain the overall country risk score, *Euromoney* assigns a weighting to the nine categories listed below. The best underlying value per category achieves the full weighting (25, 10 or 5); the worst scores zero and all other values are calculated relative to these two. The formula used is the following: $A - (A/(B - C)) \times (D - C)$, where A = category weighting; B = lowest value* in range; C = highest value* in range, D = individual value.

* NB for Debt indicators and Debt in default, B and C are reversed in the formula: the lowest score receives the full weighting, the highest zero.

- **Political risk** (25% weighting): the risk of non-payment or non-servicing of payment for goods or services, loans, trade-related finance and dividends, and the non-repatriation of capital. Risk analysts give each country a score between 10 and zero—the higher, the better. This does not reflect the creditworthiness of individual counterparties.

- **Economic performance** (25%): based (1) on GNP* figures per capita and (2) on results of Euromoney poll of economic projections, where each country's score is obtained from average projections for 1999 and 2000. The sum of these two factors, equally weighted, makes up this column—the higher the result, the better.
  * GNP figures were unavailable for the following countries, so GDP data were used instead: Afghanistan, Bahrain, Brunei, Cuba, Djibouti, Iraq, North Korea, Kuwait, Liberia, Libya, Macau, Myanmar.

- **Debt indicators** (10%): calculated using these ratios from the World Bank's "Global development finance 1999": total debt stocks to GNP (A), debt service to exports (B); current account balance to GNP (C). Scores are calculated as follows: $A + (B \times 2) - (C \times 10)$. The lower this score, the better. Figures are for 1997. Because of lack of consistent economic data for OECD and rich oil-producing countries, these score the full weighting, except where they report debt figures to the IMF. Developing countries which do not report complete debt data get zero.

- **Debt in default or rescheduled** (10%): scores are based on the ratio of rescheduled debt to debt stocks, taken from the World Bank's "Global Development Finance 1999". The lower the ratio, the better. OECD and developing countries which do not report under the debtor reporting system (DRS) score 10 and zero respectively.

- **Credit ratings** (10%): nominal values are assigned to sovereign ratings from Moody's, Standard & Poor's and Fitch IBCA. The higher the average value, the better. Where there is no rating, countries score zero.

- **Access to bank finance** (5%): calculated from disbursements of private, long-term, unguaranteed loans as a percentage of GNP. The higher the result, the better. OECD and developing countries not reporting under the DRS score five and zero respectively. Source: the World Bank's "Global Development Finance 1999".

- **Access to short-term finance** (5%): takes into account OECD consensus groups (source: ECGD) and short-term cover available from the US Exim Bank and NCM UK. The higher the score, the better.

- **Access to capital markets** (5%): heads of debt syndicate and loan syndications rated each country's accessibility to international markets at the time of the survey. The higher the average rating out of 10, the better.

- **Discount on forfaiting** (5%): reflects the average maximum tenot for forfaiting and the average spread over riskless countries such as the US. The higher the score, the better. Countries where forfaiting is not available score zero. Data were supplied by Bank of America, Morgan Grenfell Trade Finance, Standard Bank and West Merchant Capital Markets.

If you have any comments about the country risk survey, please e-mail Rebecca Cicolecchia at rcicolecchia@euromoneyplc.com

Source: "In Search of a Safe Haven," *Euromoney*, March 1999, pp. 97–101. Reprinted by permission.

than just those captured in *Euromoney*'s evaluation of the riskiness of loans. For most developed economies, however, such risks are generally quite low. While political risk plays an important part in both the establishment and running of overseas operations, it applies to only a limited set of overseas investment opportunities, and thus we relegate its discussion to the end of the book in Chapter 12.

APPLICATION 1-2

THE ROLE OF CAPITAL FLOWS IN THE 1997 ASIAN CRISIS

During the second half of 1997, the world witnessed an unprecedented collapse in the currencies of Thailand, the Philippines, Indonesia, Malaysia, and Korea. By the end of the year, currencies had lost between 34 percent (the Malaysian ringgit) and 54 percent (the Indonesian rupia) of their start-of-year values. The swiftness and severity of the devaluations caught much of the world off-guard and led to a worldwide retrenchment in capital flows to emerging markets. Since then, much has been written about the crisis and a variety of explanations have been offered, ranging from widespread "moral hazard" problems in the countries' financial sectors to the prolonged economic sluggishness of Japan during the 1990s.

Even with little knowledge of the subtle aspects of the currency crisis, an examination of the balance of payments for various Southeast Asian countries offers substantial insights into the underpinnings of the crisis. During the early 1990s, virtually all countries in Southeast Asia experienced record inflows of foreign capital. Total net private capital inflows to the region increased from $20.5 billion at the beginning of the decade to $142 billion in 1996. The fast growing Asian "tigers" attracted substantial attention from foreign investors, who were eagerly seeking high returns for their portfolios. The capital took varying forms: foreign direct investment, portfolio investment, and bank loans.

As with most countries experiencing capital inflows, the Southeast Asian countries spent their surplus three ways: (1) they used it to finance consumption; (2) they used it to purchase machinery and other capital goods from abroad; and (3) they used it to build up foreign exchange reserve levels.

The first two expenditures appeared in the balance of payments as current account deficits while the third appeared as an increase in official reserve transactions. In the event that the capital flows reversed, countries amassing reserves could easily maintain their exchange rate. As foreign investors withdrew from the country, the domestic monetary authority would simply use its built-up reserves to meet their demand for foreign currency at the current exchange rate.

On the other hand, countries with large current account deficits, and therefore lower accumulations of reserves, would be forced to offset the sudden reversal in the capital account with an equivalent reversal in the current account. Net purchases of goods and services from abroad would need to rapidly convert into net exports of goods and services to other countries. At current prices (current exchange rates), such rapid reversals are generally impossible. Prices of exports need to be reduced to induce foreigners to increase their purchases. Likewise, prices of imports need to go up to discourage consumer purchases. In other words, the currency needs to depreciate.

A brief examination of current accounts during the 1990s and corresponding precrisis reserve levels demonstrates the linkage clearly. All countries whose currencies devalued in 1997 were those with high current account deficits during 1990s: Thailand, Malaysia, Philippines, Korea, and Indonesia. On the other hand, current account deficits for nondevaluing countries (China, Hong Kong, Taiwan, and Singapore) were near zero or positive. Corsetti, Pesenti, and Roubini (1999) demonstrate this link by comparing the current

APPLICATION 1-2 (cont.)

account as a percent of GDP to the exchange rate change during 1997:

Country	CA/GDP (1996)	Exchange Rate Change (1996–1997)
Korea	−4.82%	−52.6%
Indonesia	−3.30	−49.6
Malaysia	−3.73	−35.2
Philippines	−4.67	−34.4
Thailand	−8.51	−44.4
China	0.52	0.0
Hong Kong	−2.43	0.0
Singapore	16.26	−16.1
Taiwan	4.67	−15.9

This is not to say that current account deficits are inherently bad. Indeed, growing economies that are in need of foreign machinery and other capital goods to improve productivity often run substantial current account deficits. However, if the capital does not improve productivity and generate sufficient return to keep foreign investors happy, a reversal in the flow of capital is likely to occur. This is particularly likely if the flows of capital are portfolio or intermediated investment flows, which can more easily lead to rapid reversals. If this is the case, countries that are unprepared (in the form of built-up reserves) are likely to see their currencies depreciate significantly.

Indeed, for the devaluing countries investors saw little productivity gains to justify their investments. The OECD (1998) estimated that return on invested capital was below cost of capital for two-thirds of the Korean chaebol prior to the collapse of the Korean won. In other countries, investors experienced similar gains. Moreover, the capital flows themselves were highly reversible. Korea and Thailand financed 10 percent and 16 percent of current account deficit with long-term DFI. Corsetti, Pesenti, and Roubini (1999) estimate that the ratio of short-term liabilities to major foreign banks relative to reserves at the end of 1996 was 213 percent for Korea, 181 percent for Indonesia, 169 percent in Thailand, 77 percent for the Philippines, and 47 percent in Malaysia.

Although the causes and consequences of the Asian financial crisis of 1997 are multifaceted, the story told by the balance of payments offers a key lesson for emerging economies. When the promise of rapid economic growth leads to large capital inflows, either use the capital to improve productivity and deliver on the promise of growth, or be prepared to face the consequences should the capital retreat as rapidly as it arrived.

1.6   INTERNATIONAL CAPITAL MOBILITY

We have now considered foreign investments and domestic investments as differentiated by location, the use of multiple currencies, and the consequences of multiple governments. Together, these issues affect the degree of international capital mobility and point to one of the main analytical paradigms used in this book: the continuum from completely segmented national capital markets to a perfectly integrated global capital market. The models of international capital flows which examine, first, the risk-free real rate of return and second, the motivations for diversification, highlight the two extremes of segmentation and integration in international capital markets. At one extreme, the closed-economies autarky scenario before trade in assets is permitted to occur represents complete segmentation, where there are suboptimal allocations of capital and undiversified portfolios. At the other extreme, the optimal allocation of capital and complete diversification of portfolios achieved once trade in assets is permitted to take place represents the perfect integration of national capital markets into a global capital market, or perfect capital mobility. In reality, markets are neither completely segmented nor perfectly integrated, but are probably somewhere in between, reflecting imperfect capital mobility. There are several reasons for this, most of which demonstrate the types of issues we consider in the rest of this book.

EXCHANGE RATE RISK AND IMPERFECT CAPITAL MOBILITY

One reason for imperfect international capital mobility has to do with the fact discussed in the previous section that international investment must grapple with multiple currencies. Financial risk thus includes not only the business risk of the type considered in the model of portfolio diversification, but also foreign exchange risk. Furthermore, there is foreign interest rate and inflation risk. The reason multiple currencies may lead to partial segmentation of international capital markets is because investors usually value foreign investments in terms of their home currency and are averse to the risk of exchange rate changes which alter the home currency rate of return.

Even when free trade in assets is permitted, investors may not have an incentive to reach an optimum allocation because they have these additional risks associated with foreign investments: foreign interest rate risk in addition to domestic interest rate risk, foreign inflation risk in addition to domestic inflation risk, and the foreign exchange risk. More importantly, an investor in the foreign country values the same investment in the local currency and does not (typically) have the exchange risk (or the interest rate and inflation risk) of the other country.

All other things equal, home country investors may have a preference for home investments and foreign country investors may have a preference for foreign investments to avoid the cross-border risks. This is referred to as **home bias.** The way to think about this with respect to exchange rate risk is to consider what currency the cross-border financial instrument is denominated in. If the foreign country's currency is used, the lenders may require a higher real interest rate than they would if the claim were denominated in the home currency, because they are taking on exchange risk. If the lender's currency is used, the borrowers take on the exchange risk and the lenders may settle for a lower real interest rate than they would if the instrument were denominated in the borrower's currency. The spread between the home currency interest rate and the foreign currency interest rate due to the currency denomination of capital is a **risk premium for foreign exchange risk.** Note that this represents a deviation from real interest parity, as claims denominated in different currencies have different real rates of return: $r \neq r^*$.

Investors require a risk premium for holding claims denominated in anything other than their own currency, or debtors require a negative risk premium (a risk discount) for structuring liabilities in anything other than their own currency. The magnitude of the risk premium in this analysis would be determined by a schedule of the additional return the investors require to lend different amounts of capital internationally and a schedule of the additional return the borrowers are willing to pay for different amounts of foreign capital. These schedules depend on the risk aversion of lenders and borrowers, the risk characteristics of the currency (such as the standard deviation of the exchange rate), and the productivity of capital in the borrowing country. The result of this is that incomplete capital mobility leading to partial segmentation of national capital markets is caused by aversion to foreign risks and affects the net international investment position.[3]

Investors in both home and foreign countries are also likely to consider the benefits of portfolio diversification through international investment. Just as a foreign investment without foreign exchange risk (or foreign interest rate and inflation risk) may diversify a domestic portfolio, as we saw earlier, foreign investment with foreign exchange risk (and foreign interest rate and inflation risk, for that matter) may also diversify a domestic portfolio. Furthermore, some of the diversification may come not from the business risk of the project considered earlier, but directly from the exchange risk, foreign interest rate risk, or foreign inflation risk.

In this case, there are two components of the return on the foreign investment to the home country investor: the nominal rate of return on the investment denominated in the local currency (denoted R^*) and the rate of change of the exchange rate quoted in home currency units per unit of foreign currency (denoted X), which can be denoted as $(R^* + X)$. Hence, the standard deviation of the return on the foreign investment depends on the standard deviation of the return denominated in the local currency, the standard deviation of the exchange rate change, and any correlation between these two terms:

$$\sqrt{\sigma_{R^*}^2 + \sigma_X^2 + 2\rho\sigma_{R^*}\sigma_X}$$

where ρ is the correlation coefficient between R^* and X. Diversification would then be based on the standard deviation of the domestic investment, the standard deviation of the foreign investment denominated in the investor's home currency, and the correlation between these two. This can be formalized mathematically, although it is sufficiently complicated that we will not do it here.[4]

EXAMPLE 1.2

A U.S. portfolio investor holds shares of stock in a Dutch firm. The standard deviation of Dutch guilder returns on the stock is 9 percentage points. The standard deviation of percentage changes in the dollar/guilder exchange rate is 11 percentage points. The guilder return on the stock is mildly correlated with the percentage change in the exchange rate, with a correlation coefficient of 0.20. The standard deviation of the U.S. dollar-equivalent rate of return on the Dutch stock is thus:

$$\sqrt{\sigma_{R^*}^2 + \sigma_X^2 + 2\rho\sigma_{R^*}\sigma_X} = \sqrt{9^2 + 11^2 + 2(0.20)(9)(11)} = \sqrt{241.6} = 15.5$$

or 15.5 percentage points. Since 15.5 is greater than 11, the exchange risk adds to the underlying risk of the stock.

Using the above discussion of portfolio diversification, an alternative approach to the currency risk premium takes an integrated global capital market view of the world and attributes any premium only to the characteristics of the currency and its contribution to a diversified portfolio of investments. For example, whereas in the simple model with home bias you would need to "bribe" Americans with a risk premium to hold Chilean peso assets or liabilities, or Chileans to hold U.S. dollar assets or liabilities, in the portfolio model you would need to bribe everyone, Americans and Chileans alike, to hold peso assets and liabilities when the Chilean currency is riskier than the dollar and adds risk to a portfolio of investments. In this case, the risk premium will not have anything to do with whether the country is a net lender or a borrower; it will only be a function of the characteristics of the currency. It is possible, in fact, for the currency of the capital-exporting home country to be riskier than the currency of the capital-importing foreign country such that the exchange risk premium is on the home currency.

OTHER REASONS FOR IMPERFECT CAPITAL MOBILITY

Two additional reasons for imperfect capital mobility and home bias derive from the fact that international investment must grapple with multiple governments. First, governments may simply impose some capital controls, exchange controls, or other barriers to prevent capital inflows or capital outflows. However, governments often apply these controls selectively and do not prohibit all capital flows outright. As a result, markets are neither completely segmented nor completely integrated. Furthermore, even if barriers have not been imposed, there may be a possibility that such barriers will be introduced in the future, possibly even precluding the repatriation of the capital or the local return on the capital. This possibility of changes in government policy is the political risk faced by international investment, and this is a further disincentive to undertake a foreign investment. The foreign investment may thus require a **risk premium for political risk,** or a spread between the home return to capital and the foreign return to capital which compensates for political risk.

A second reason for partial segmentation has to do with taxation imposed by these governments. Taxes drive a wedge between the real rate of returns on an investment and the after-tax rate of return the investor receives. Internationally, taxes are imposed by both the government hosting the foreign investment and the home government, and this tax treatment can have an effect on capital flows leading to suboptimal allocations of capital and suboptimally diversified portfolios.

A final reason for imperfect international capital mobility and home bias is that there are other (noncurrency, nongovernment) barriers—such as transactions costs, costs of obtaining or translating information, monitoring costs complicated by distance, and the like—associated with foreign investments. Investors will only be willing to pay these additional costs if the rate of return on the investment is commensurately higher. Hence, as with other barriers, these can produce partially segmented national capital markets.

The reasons for imperfect capital mobility and home bias discussed here all imply that real interest parity, which we may generally expect to hold in a perfectly integrated global capital market, will not hold with partially segmented capital markets. Deviations from real interest parity will be of special interest as we apply financial theory to managerial decisions. As we will see in the next chapter, the concept of real interest parity is just the first of several international parity theorems that we will consider in this book. These additional parity theorems extend our investigation of rates of return to nominal interest rates which take account of the real interest rate and expected inflation. They also extend our investigation to include national differences in inflation rates and uncertainty over exchange rate changes. Like real interest parity, these additional parity conditions will generally hold in perfectly integrated capital markets, but will not hold in segmented capital markets.

We also apply these additional parity theorems to managerial decisions throughout this book. We will often begin an analysis from the standpoint of perfectly integrated markets, make a few points about the types of decisions that would be made under such circumstances, and then reexamine the analysis by considering segmentation of markets and the types of decisions which would be made in this situation. A main insight from the segmentation-versus-integration paradigm is that if capital markets are integrated, there are multiple ways of approaching a decision that produce the same result, but if national capital markets are segmented, the multiple ways of approaching a decision produce different results and methodology must be carefully analyzed.

1.7 DOES REAL INTEREST PARITY HOLD?

One way to examine international capital mobility is to test whether real interest parity holds. If capital markets are integrated, under most circumstances real interest parity will prevail. If capital markets are segmented, real interest parity is less likely to hold. Given the importance of the issue with respect to managerial decisions taken up in the rest of this book, we consider some of the empirical literature on real interest parity here.

Although simple and straightforward, the question of whether real interest parity holds is quite difficult to answer. One reason for this is that real interest rates are never actually observed—they must be constructed from nominal interest rates and inflation rates. As there are many interest rates and different ways to calculate inflation, choosing and preparing the data can affect the outcome of the test. Another reason is that construction of a real interest rate produces **ex post,** or after-the-fact, actual interest rates, and these may not be very good estimates of **ex ante,** or before-the-fact, expected real interest rates because of expectations errors. A final reason for difficulty answering the question is because no adjustment process is specified: on one hand, we could test whether real interest parity holds continuously, but on the other hand we may want to allow for short-run deviations from a long-run real interest parity equilibrium. In this case, the periodicity of the data (daily versus monthly versus quarterly versus annual, and so on) and time series characteristics (serial correlation) matter.

Empirical studies have traditionally tested whether real interest parity holds on short-run monthly data. The results overwhelmingly reject the real interest parity hypothesis; see, for example, Mishkin (1984), Mark (1985), and Cumby and Mishkin (1986). This brings us to the question of *why* real interest parity fails. For example, is it due to exchange risk? Unfortunately, these studies have been inconclusive in this respect.

One explanation for the failure of real interest parity is that there are constant shocks to the economy (e.g., to marginal products of capital or supplies of capital) so that within any month there are always high-interest-rate countries and low-interest-rate countries. However, macroeconomies would be expected to adjust to these shocks over time. Recently, studies which look at real interest parity over time suggest that deviations from short run real interest parity do tend to abate over time, such that real interest parity holds as a long-run proposition. Cavaglia (1992) shows that real interest differentials in Eurocurrency deposit rates for the period 1973–1987 are relatively short-lived and mean-reverting to zero. Kugler and Neusser (1993) show that deviations from real interest parity in Eurocurrency deposit rates for 1980–1991 are substantial in the short run, but disappear rather quickly as long run equilibrium is achieved within a short period of three to four months.

Although not everyone agrees with this conclusion, it seems that real interest parity does not hold continuously but does hold as a long-run proposition. One managerial implication of these results is that some decisions may be made one way in a short-run context (e.g., monthly) and another way in a longer-run context (e.g., annually).

❖ SUMMARY OF CHAPTER OBJECTIVES

1. Understand international capital flows in the balance of payments accounts.

International capital flows are recorded in the capital account of the balance of payments accounts. The three main categories of private capital flows are direct foreign investment (such as the investments of multinational corporations), portfolio investment (stocks and bonds), and intermediated investment (banking).

2. Explain the benefits of international capital flows in terms of rates of return and diversification of risks.

International capital flows allow capital to move from countries in which the real rate of return on capital is low into countries in which the real rate of return on capital is high. This reallocation of capital increases world output and makes both the owners of capital and the borrowers of capital better off. An equilibrium is reached when the real rate of return is the same in all locations because international capital flows cause rates of return to rise in the country where rates are initially low and fall in the country where rates are initially high. Furthermore, international capital flows serve to diversify the risks associated with uncertainty about the rates of return on capital when the rates of return are not perfectly correlated across countries.

3. Describe salient features of the U.S. international investment position.

The United States is a net debtor in terms of its international investment position, which means that foreign assets in the United States exceed U.S. assets abroad. The main source of the debtor position is portfolio investment, as the value of U.S. stocks and bonds held by foreigners is greater than the value of foreign stocks and bonds held by Americans. Prior to 1986, the United States was a net creditor in the international investment position, but since 1986, the country has been a growing debtor. With regard to direct foreign investments, the United States is usually acknowledged to be the world's largest source country as well as the world's largest host country. At the end of 1998, U.S. direct foreign investments abroad amounted to $1.123 trillion, and foreign direct investment in the United States amounted to $879 billion (both figures at current cost), making the United States a net creditor in the amount of $244 billion.

4. Identify differences between foreign and domestic investment having to do with multiple currencies and exchange rates, multiple interest rates, differences in corporate income tax rates, and political risk.

Foreign investments differ from domestic investments because: (1) the foreign investment must use a foreign currency and the domestic owner must convert the foreign currency into domestic currency using an exchange rate that varies, thus subjecting the owner to foreign exchange risk; (2) the foreign investment is affected by foreign interest rates which are not continuously at parity with domestic interest rates in either real or nominal terms; (3) the foreign investment is assessed foreign income taxes which are not identical to (and in fact may interact with) domestic income taxes assessed; and (4) the foreign investment is subject to government intervention by the host country (and sometimes the home country as well), thus subjecting the owner to political risk.

5. Conceptually analyze the international capital market in terms of a continuum from nationally segmented capital markets to a perfectly integrated global capital market, and provide reasons for imperfect capital mobility.

If international flows of capital are not possible, capital is segmented into separate national capital markets, and if international flows of capital occur without regard to borders, there is a single perfectly integrated global capital market. Between these two extremes is an intermediate range of imperfect capital mobility in which there is some international movement of capital without completely achieving perfect integration of national capital markets. Some reasons for imperfect capital mobility include: (1) capital owners' aversion to foreign exchange risk; (2) government restrictions on movement of capital or on exchange of currency; (3) capital owners' aversion to political risks which would affect the rate of return on the investment; and (4) transactions, information, and monitoring costs associated with operating in a foreign country.

6. Benchmark capital market equilibrium using the real interest parity condition.

The international capital market equilibrium in which the real rate of return on capital is the same in all locations is known as real interest parity. Because of changes in national capital markets and the reasons for imperfect capital mobility given above, real interest parity is not likely to hold at any particular moment in time. However, there will be a tendency for international capital flows to reduce deviations from real interest parity over time so that real interest parity would tend to hold as a long-run proposition. The real interest parity condition is thus a benchmark for capital market equilibrium, which suggests the nature of current deviations from long-run equilibrium.

❖ QUESTIONS FOR REVIEW

1. What are the components of the *capital account* in the balance of payments? What are the components of the *current account* in the balance of payments? Suppose you know that a certain country has a surplus on the capital account in its balance of payments; what does this imply about the current account? What does a surplus in the capital account mean?

2. How will the following transactions be reflected in the U.S. balance of payments?
   a. A U.S. MNC sells $5 million in automotive parts to a firm in Italy, receiving a check drawn on the Italian company's U.S. bank account.
   b. A Japanese corporation purchases a plant in the United States for $200 million, using the proceeds of a loan from a U.S. bank.

3. Why is there movement of capital across borders and what are the benefits of such capital movement?

4. Suppose an investor holds a portfolio consisting 50 percent of a home investment and 50 percent of a foreign investment. What is the standard deviation of the portfolio if the standard deviation of the home investment is 6 percentage points, the standard deviation of the foreign investment is 6 percentage points, and the returns on the two investments are statistically independent?

5. [Group Project] There is usually a lot of concern in any country when foreigners acquire a large share of domestic assets; Japanese acquisitions in the United States during the 1980s illustrate this point. In addition, there is concern when domestic capital is invested abroad; one complaint is that U.S. jobs are exported. Should

countries restrict capital inflows and/or capital outflows because of these concerns? Carefully analyze the benefits and costs of capital flows, focusing on direct foreign investment. What should public policy toward multinational corporations be, in both host countries and home countries?

6. [Group Project] What are the empirical characteristics of the stocks and flows of DFI between developed and developing countries? Why might these be of some concern?

7. Suppose an American is thinking about purchasing shares of stock in an Irish firm. The standard deviation of Irish punt returns on the stock is 7 percentage points and the standard deviation of percentage changes in the dollar/punt exchange rate is 10 percentage points. The Irish punt return on the stock is not correlated with the changes in the exchange rate. What is the standard deviation of the dollar-equivalent return on the Irish stock? Does exchange risk add to the underlying risk of the stock?

8. A portfolio investor holds shares of stock in an Italian firm. The standard deviation of Italian lira returns on the stock is 11 percentage points and the standard deviation of percentage changes in the dollar/lira exchange rate is 12 percentage points. The lira return on the stock is negatively correlated with the change in the exchange rate, with a correlation coefficient of -0.60. What is the standard deviation of the dollar-equivalent return on the Italian stock? Does exchange risk add to the stock's underlying risk?

9. [Class Discussion] Why is the issue of international capital mobility important in international financial management?

10. [Class Discussion] Does real interest parity hold?

TOOLS FOR ANALYSIS I
Models of Optimum International Investment

This section considers theoretical models of international capital flows which explain motivation for the capital flows, an optimized equilibrium, and benefits of the international trade in assets. The simplest models of international capital flows examine the productivity and the quantities of capital in two countries, although one of the two countries could be interpreted as "the rest of the world." One model is purely static, characterizing international capital flows as an optimizing allocation of existing capital between two countries. A second model is intertemporal, recognizing that the quantity of capital available is chosen by optimizing behavior in which investment must be made one period in advance to have productive capital in the next period, and recognizing that capital may come from domestic sources or from abroad. This section first considers the static model, often referred to as the MacDougall model in reference to the development in MacDougall (1960), and subsequently considers a simple version of the intertemporal model.

Although the two models sound very different, they are in fact quite similar and produce identical conclusions regarding the motivation for international capital flows, an international equilibrium, and the benefits of international asset trade.

THE MACDOUGALL MODEL OF INTERNATIONAL CAPITAL FLOWS

Given an aggregate supply or production function for the macroeconomy, we can easily derive a marginal product of capital schedule, MPK. This MPK schedule is downward sloping; as the quantity of capital invested increases, the marginal quantity of output produced declines because the quantity and quality of all other factors is held constant. Figure 1-3 presents an example of the downward-sloping MPK schedule, which represents the demand for capital in the macroeconomy.

If we assume that the price of capital is equal to the price of output, or that capital and output are

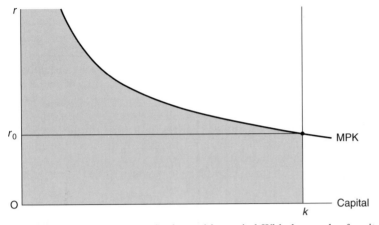

The MPK schedule represents the demand for capital. With the supply of capital fixed at k, the equilibrium interest rate is r_0. The shaded area under the MPK schedule to the left of k represents the economy's GDP.

FIGURE 1-3 THE MARGINAL PRODUCT OF CAPITAL AND THE SUPPLY OF CAPITAL

physically the same, the MPK schedule represents the rate of return on investment. As an example, a single unit of capital that is capable of producing one-fourth of a unit of itself during a certain time period would have MPK = 0.25, or a rate of return of 25 percent. The second unit of capital may be capable of producing one-fifth of a unit of itself during the period. so the MPK is 0.20 and the rate of return is 20 percent. We can therefore denote the real rate of return on investment as r, which is noted along the vertical axis in Figure 1-3. The MPK schedule represents the demand for capital because it indicates the quantity of capital that is desired by producers at each interest rate (which also represents the real cost of capital).

To simplify the model, the supply of capital in the economy is taken to be predetermined. In a sense, the stock of investment capital is simply the accumulated amount of unconsumed past income. For the country depicted in Figure 1-3, the quantity of capital is given as k. Using the vertical supply schedule and the downward-sloping MPK schedule, the intersection determines the real interest rate in the economy. In Figure 1-3, the real interest rate is r_0, and this represents the rate of return to capital, or what the users of capital must pay the suppliers of capital. Since the area underneath the MPK schedule represents total production, the macroeconomy's **gross domestic product (GDP)**, the aggregate value of all goods and services produced within a country, is the shaded area underneath the MPK schedule. If we were to subtract depreciation of capital from GDP, we would get net domestic prod-

uct. Although the model can be easily extended to account for depreciation of capital by drawing a net-of-depreciation MPK curve, we will keep the discussion simpler by focusing on gross values.

Now, consider a foreign country that has a different marginal product of capital schedule and a different supply of capital. Hence, this foreign country (most likely) has a different real interest rate. If these countries can trade assets with each other, capital will flow from the low-interest-rate country to the high-interest-rate country to obtain the highest return on investment available. The concept is illustrated in Figure 1-4. The MPK schedule of the first country, hereafter referred to as the home country, is exactly as shown in Figure 1-3, drawn from the origin O. The marginal product of capital schedule for the foreign country is denoted by adding an asterisk to MPK: MPK*. This MPK* schedule, however, is drawn from the O* origin on the right-hand side, where again the asterisk represents the foreign country. This construction simply rotates the usual MPK* schedule around the vertical axis 180 degrees. The length of the horizontal axis in Figure 1-4 represents the total quantity of capital available in the world, which is composed of k units in the home country (as drawn in Figure 1-3) plus k^* units of capital in the foreign country. The initial allocation of capital is at k, so the interest rate in the home country is r_0 and the interest rate in the foreign country is r_0^*.

If international capital flows are possible, there is an incentive to relocate capital from the home country

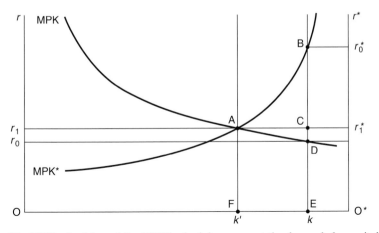

The MPK schedule and the MPK* schedule represent the demands for capital in the home and foreign countries from the origins O and O* respectively. The length of the horizontal axis represents the total quantity of capital available in the two economies and the initial allocation of capital is at k, so the interest rate in the home country is r_0 and the interest rate in the foreign country is r_0^*. The optimum allocation of capital is at k', where interest rates are equalized at $r_1 = r_1^*$, such that the distance kk' represents optimum international capital flows. The home country gains area ACD and the foreign country gains area ABC because of the international capital flows.

FIGURE 1-4 THE MACDOUGALL MODEL OF OPTIMUM INTERNATIONAL CAPITAL FLOWS

to the foreign country because the interest rate in the foreign country is higher. As capital flows out of the low-interest-rate country, becoming relatively more scarce, the interest rate edges upward. As capital enters the high-interest-rate country, thereby becoming more abundant, the interest rate edges downward. The optimal allocation of capital is at the intersection of the MPK schedule with the MPK* schedule, denoted by k', where the real return to capital is the same in the two countries. In Figure 1-4, when the optimum allocation of k' is achieved, $r_1 = r_1^*$. This means that the optimum international capital flow is represented by the distance between k' and k, which is the amount of capital owned by the home country that is invested in the foreign country. This allocation of capital comes about because capital will flow from the low-interest-rate country to the high-interest-rate country until the interest rates are equalized: $r = r^*$, which we have referred to as real interest parity.

The mechanism of transferring capital is a little more complex than is apparent. Typically, international capital flows take the form of trade in financial assets. For example, the home country might make a loan, buy stocks, or set up a direct foreign investment in the foreign country. This financial transaction does not yet involve a transfer of real, physical resources (such as

industrial machinery) across borders. However, the financial assets purchased by the home country and sold by the foreign country create a capital account deficit in the home country and a capital account surplus in the foreign country. From the discussion of the balance of payments in the chapter, we know that the capital account deficit is accompanied by a current account surplus in the home country, and that the capital account surplus is accompanied by a current account deficit in the foreign country. This is how the home country exports physical resources and the foreign country imports them. Hence, financial capital flows *are* associated with physical resource flows.

An analysis of the welfare effects resulting from international capital flows demonstrates that both countries are better off when trade in assets is permitted. Deploying additional capital in the foreign country clearly increases this country's GDP. Specifically, the GDP increases by the area underneath the MPK* schedule between the initial allocation of capital at k and the optimum international allocation of capital at k', which is represented by area ABEF. Because the home country gives up some capital, however, its GDP decreases by the area underneath its MPK schedule between the two allocations of capital, which is represented by area ADEF. It should be clear, however, that the area lost by the home country is smaller than the area gained by the foreign country so total world production actually increases by the triangular area ABD simply by reallocating capital.

For the use of the imported capital, the foreign country must pay the home country dividends or interest at the international equilibrium rate of interest, $r_1 = r_1^*$. The total interest bill is therefore the interest rate multiplied by the quantity of capital borrowed, and this is represented by area ACEF. For the home country, this is factor income from abroad that is added to GDP to get **gross national product (GNP)**, which is the aggregate value of all goods and services produced with factors from a specific country. This means that, although GDP in the home country declines by area ADEF, the addition of factor income ACEF results in a net increase in GNP of the triangular area ACD. Hence, the home country is better off when it lends capital to more productive countries. Similarly, even though the foreign country must pay the home country an interest bill of precisely ACEF, and this factor payment must be subtracted from the foreign country's GDP to find its GNP, the country is better off when permitted to borrow abroad because the increase in GDP is greater than the interest payment by the amount of the triangular area ABC. Hence, the total gains from international capital flows, shown by area ABD, are divided between the borrowing country (which benefits by the area ABC) and the lending country (which benefits by the area ACD). The diagram developed in Figure 1-4 is generally attributed to G.D.A. MacDougall, who first published a version in 1960; it has subsequently become known as "the MacDougall diagram."

EXAMPLE 1.3

Suppose the production function in one country, the home country, can be represented by the equation:

$$GDP = (1/2)k^{1/2}$$

which is a simple version of a Cobb-Douglas production function in which labor is fixed. For example, if $GDP = 0.10 \, k^{1/2} \, l^{1/2}$ and labor is fixed at $l = 25$ units, then $GDP = 0.10 \, k^{1/2} \, 25^{1/2} = 0.5 \, k^{1/2}$. With this production function, the MPK schedule is:

$$dGDP/dk = (1/4)k^{-1/2}$$

which is drawn in Figures 1-3 and 1-4. If the quantity of capital in the economy is exogenously given as $k = 21$ units, perhaps measured in trillions of dollars, then total output in the economy is

$GDP_0 = (1/2) \, 21^{1/2} = 2.291$, or \$2.291 trillion. The MPK at this quantity of capital is $(1/4)(21)^{1/2} = 0.055$, or \$0.055 trillion. Note that this corresponds to $r_0 = 5.5$ percent, because the last (marginal) trillion dollars of capital produces a return of \$0.055 trillion.

Suppose the production function in another country, the foreign country, can be represented by the equation:

$$GDP^* = (3/4)(k^*)^{1/3}$$

which is another simple version of a Cobb-Douglas production function in which labor is fixed. For example, if $GDP^* = 0.0878 \, (k^*)^{1/3} \, (l^*)^{2/3}$ and labor is again fixed at $l^* = 25$ units, $GDP^* = 0.0878 \, (k^*)^{1/3} \, 25^{2/3} = 0.75 \, (k^*)^{1/3}$. Comparing GDP^* with GDP, the coefficient 0.0878 suggests that the foreign country is less productive with capital and labor than the home country where the coefficient is 0.10. In addition, the exponent on capital (1/3) suggests that less of the total output of the foreign country accrues to capital owners than in the home country where the exponent on capital is (1/2). With this production function, the MPK schedule is:

$$dGDP^*/dk^* = (1/4)(k^*)^{-2/3}$$

and this is plotted on the right-hand axis in Figure 1-4. Suppose the foreign country has a relatively low quantity of capital; for example, $k^* = 3$ units, again measured in trillions of dollars. Total output in the economy is thus $GDP_0^* = (3/4)(3)^{1/3} = 1.082$, or \$1.082 trillion. At this level, the MPK* is $(1/4)(3)^{-2/3} = 0.120$, or \$0.120 trillion, which corresponds to $r_0^* = 12$ percent.

If trade in assets is permitted between the two countries, capital will flow from the home country, where the return is low, into the foreign country, where the return is high. As capital is exported from the home country, the MPK (or rate of return, r) increases, reflecting movement along the MPK schedule. As capital is imported into the foreign country, the MPK* (or rate of return, r^*) decreases, reflecting movement along the MPK* schedule. Equilibrium will occur when MPK = MPK* (or, equivalently, when $r = r^*$). Note that the total quantity of capital in these two countries is $k + k^* = 21 + 3 = \$24$ trillion. Hence, k must decrease by the same amount k^* increases to account for the total \$24 trillion of capital. Setting MPK equal to MPK* and substituting $(24 - k)$ for k^* reveals:

$$(1/4)(k)^{-1/2} = (1/4)(24 - k)^{-2/3}.$$

In this example, the intersection of MPK and MPK* occurs at $k = 16$, so $k^* = 8$. At this allocation, MPK $= (1/4)(16)^{-1/2} = 0.0625$ and MPK* $= (1/4)(8)^{-2/3} = 0.0625$, so real interest parity holds at 6.25 percent. Hence, the home country should optimally transfer $(21 - 16 =) \$5$ trillion of capital to the foreign country (so $3 + 5 = 8$).

The gains from trade in assets can be shown by looking at the GDP and GNP of both countries. With $16 trillion of capital in the home country, output is $GDP_1 = (1/2)(16)^{1/2} = \$2$ trillion. With $8 trillion of capital in the foreign country, output is $GDP_1^* = (3/4)(8)^{1/3} = \$1.5$ trillion. Note that GDP has declined from $GDP_0 = \$2.291$ trillion, but GDP* has increased from $GDP_0^* = \$1.082$ trillion. Furthermore, note that total output in the two countries has increased from $GDP_0 + GDP_0^* = 2.291 + 1.082 = \$3.373$ trillion to $GDP_1 + GDP_1^* = 2 + 1.5 = \$3.5$ trillion, or by $0.128 trillion. This increase in total GDP is a result only of reallocating capital between the two countries, as there is no increase in total capital. In exchange for loaning $5 trillion to the foreign country, the home country collects dividends and/or interest at a rate of 6.25 percent from the foreign country, for a total of $5(0.0625) = \$0.3125$ trillion. As these dividends and interest are the only international factor incomes, net factor income is $NFI_1 = 0.3125$ for the home country and $NFI_1^* = -0.3125$ for the foreign country. Thus, $GNP_1 = GDP_1 + NFI_1 = 2 + 0.3125 = \$2.3125$ trillion. Hence, home GNP has increased from $2.291 trillion. In addition, $GNP_1^* = GDP_1^* + NFI_1^* = 1.5 - 0.3125 = \$1.1875$ trillion, so foreign GNP has increased from $1.082 trillion. Both countries have therefore shared the world gains from reallocating capital. Table 1-9 summarizes these gains.

The MacDougall model is additionally useful in analyzing the effects of disturbances in the economy on interest rates and international capital flows. For example, technological improvement will shift the MPK upward and thereby raise interest rates at the given allocation of capital. The higher returns proceed to attract capital from abroad until the real interest parity condition holds and the new optimum allocation of capital is achieved. As another example, natural disasters such as earthquakes and hurricanes can cause shocks to the supply of capital. As these disasters destroy part of the capital stock, the horizontal axis of the MacDougall diagram shrinks. The MPK and MPK* schedules therefore move closer together. At the prevailing allocation of capital, interest rates in the country facing disaster rise and thereby attract capital from abroad. When the real interest parity condition holds, the world has reached the new optimal allocation of capital.

A SIMPLE INTERTEMPORAL MODEL OF INTERNATIONAL CAPITAL FLOWS

The MacDougall model is often thought to be deficient because it is static, or considers only one period of time. Recently, research has focused on intertemporal models of macroeconomics, international trade, and international finance to recognize two things. First, the quantity of capital in a country is chosen by optimizing behavior in which part of current GDP is not consumed and is instead invested in the capital stock and carried into the next period to produce next period's GDP. Second, capital account surpluses (reflected also as current account deficits) must be repaid in the future, with interest or dividends, by running trade account and current account surpluses (also producing a capital account deficit because of the repayment of principal). In this section, we consider a simple two-period model capable of incorporating these features. (Additional periods would unnecessarily complicate the model without altering its conclusions.) We refer to the two periods as period 1, for the current period, and period 2, for the next or future period.

TABLE 1-9 Example of Gains from International Trade in Assets in MacDougall Model (trillions of dollars)

Country	Before Trade		After Trade			
	Capital	GDP = GNP	Capital	GDP	NFI	GNP
Home	21	2.291	16	2.000	+0.3125	2.3125
Foreign	3	1.082	8	1.500	−0.3125	1.1875
TOTAL	24	3.373	24	3.500	0	3.5000

The behavior of capital is especially important in these intertemporal models. The capital stocks in the current period, k_1 and k_1^*, where subscripts now reflect time period 1, represent resources carried over from the previous period based on decisions made in that period. They can therefore be considered predetermined, as in the MacDougall model above. However, the capital stocks in the next period, k_2 and k_2^*, where subscripts reflect time period 2, are outcomes of decisions made in period 1, and modeling should appropriately take these capital stocks as choice variables rather than as given. A simple intertemporal model specifically sets $k_2 = k_1 + I_1$, where I_1 is investment during period 1. Similarly, $k_2^* = k_1^* + I_1^*$. There is no depreciation of capital in this model, which is consistent with our focus on gross rather than net output, although the model could easily be extended to incorporate depreciation.

The total wealth of the home country, representing the maximum it is able to consume, is the sum of current GDP and the current capital stock plus the discounted present value of the next period's GDP:

$$W = [\text{GDP}_1 + k_1] + [\text{GDP}_2]/[1 + r_{1,2}]$$

where $r_{1,2}$ is the real interest rate between period 1 and period 2. Note that the interest rate now explicitly recognizes the intertemporal nature of interest rates as the relative price of resources between periods 1 and 2. The interest rate must be consistent, in equilibrium, with the society's rate of time preference reflected in its utility function. As explained previously, the current GDP and next period's GDP are functions of the current capital stock (k_1) and next period's capital stock (k_2), respectively. Furthermore, k_2 represents the amount of period 1 resources explicitly carried into the future. As a result, wealth is the current GDP plus the current capital stock less the capital stock carried into the next period, plus the present discounted value of the sum of next period's GDP and the capital stock left over:

$$W = [\text{GDP}_1(k_1) + k_1 - k_2]$$
$$+ [\text{GDP}_2(k_2) + k_2]/[1 + r_{1,2}].$$

This also demonstrates that the resources consumed in period 1 are $[\text{GDP}_1(k_1) + k_1 - k_2]$ and the resources consumed in period 2 are $[\text{GDP}_2(k_2) + k_2]$.

If this economy is closed to international trade in assets, it will choose k_2 in period 1 to maximize its utility. If the utility function is represented by:

$$U = u(\text{GDP}_1(k_1) + k_1 - k_2)$$
$$+ \beta u(\text{GDP}_2(k_2) + k_2),$$

k_2 must satisfy:

$$\frac{dU}{dk_2} = \frac{du(\text{GDP}_1(k_1) + k_1 - k_2)}{dk_2}$$
$$+ \beta \frac{du(\text{GDP}_2(k_2) + k_2)}{dk_2} = 0$$

where β is the subjective discount rate reflecting the country's rate of time preference. There is also a similar condition for the foreign country closed to international trade in assets. (For simplicity, we are ignoring any uncertainty about the response of GDP_2 to changes in k_2; if there is uncertainty, the economy maximizes expected utility and the expectation would be recognized in the first-order condition.)

If international trade in assets is permitted, current resources can be carried into the next period either as domestic capital or as foreign capital. We represent this as a decomposition of k_2 into the two components:

$$k_2 = k_{D2} + k_{F2}$$

where the subscripts D and F represent domestic and foreign, respectively. This transfer of capital to the foreign country would be accomplished by making a loan, purchasing foreign stocks or bonds, or establishing a direct foreign investment in the foreign country, resulting in a capital account deficit for the home country and a capital account surplus for the foreign country in period 1. There is a corresponding current account surplus in the home country and a current account deficit in the foreign country as real resources flow from the home country to the foreign country. In period 2, these flows will be reversed: the home country will collect its capital from the foreign country, so the home country will have a capital account surplus and a current account deficit, and the foreign country will have a capital account deficit and a current account surplus. In addition, the foreign country will pay dividends or interest to the home country, making the home country's trade deficit and the foreign country's trade surplus even higher.

When the home country invests some capital abroad, GDP is a function of domestic capital only, but dividends and/or interest are earned on foreign capital in the next period. Hence, wealth is modified:

$$W = [\text{GDP}_1(k_1) + k_1 - k_{D2} - k_{F2}]$$
$$+ [\text{GDP}_2(k_{D2}) + k_{D2} + (1 + r_{1,2}^*)k_{F2}]/[1 + r_{1,2}]$$

so the amount of resources consumed in period 1 is $[\text{GDP}_1(k_1) + k_1 - k_{D2} - k_{F2}]$ and the amount of resources consumed in period 2 is $[GDP_2(k_{D2}) + k_{D2} + (1 + r_{1,2}^*)k_{F2}]$.

The situation in the foreign country reflects the transfer of resources from the home country in period 1 and the transfer of resources back to the home country in period 2. In addition, the foreign country internally carries resources from period 1 to period 2 by investing them in the capital stock for production in period 2. Hence, the foreign country's wealth is:

$$W^* = [GDP_1^*(k_1^*) + k_1^* + k_{F2} - k_2^*]$$
$$+ [GDP_2^*(k_2^*) + k_2^* - (1 + r_{1,2}^*)k_{F2}]/[1 + r_{1,2}^*]$$

so the amount of resources consumed in the foreign country in period 1 is $[GDP_1^*(k_1^*) + k_1^* + k_{F2} - k_2^*]$ and the amount of resources consumed in the foreign country in period 2 is $[GDP_2^*(k_2^*) + k_2^* - (1 + r_{1,2}^*)k_{F2}]$.

Each of the two countries chooses capital stocks to maximize its utility function. The home country selects k_{D2} to satisfy $dU/dk_{D2} = 0$ and k_{F2} to satisfy $dU/dk_{F2} = 0$. The foreign country selects k_2^* to satisfy $dU^*/dk_2^* = 0$ and k_{F2} to satisfy $dU^*/dk_{F2} = 0$. Hence, these four conditions can be solved to find the three unknown capital variables. This is difficult, so we proceed by considering a specific utility function and building on the production function used in the previous example.

EXAMPLE 1.4

Suppose the utility function for each country is a simple logarithmic function of the value of resources consumed. In the closed economies:

$$U = \ln(GDP_1(k_1) + k_1 - k_2)$$
$$+ \beta \ln(GDP_2(k_2) + k_2)$$
$$U^* = \ln(GDP_1^*(k_1^*) + k_1^* - k_2^*)$$
$$+ \beta^* \ln(GDP_2^*(k_2^*) + k_2^*)$$

Also assume that the production functions and the period 1 capital supplies are the same as those considered in the previous example for the MacDougall model:

$GDP = (1/2)\, k^{1/2}$	$GDP^* = (3/4)\, k^{*1/3}$
$MPK = (1/4)\, k^{-1/2}$	$MPK^* = (1/4)\, k^{*-2/3}$
$k_1 = 21$	$k_1^* = 3$
$GDP_1 = 2.291$	$GDP_1^* = 1.082$

Furthermore, suppose $\beta = \beta^* = 0.95$. For these utility functions and production functions, the optimization conditions are:

$$\frac{dU}{dk_2} = \frac{-1}{GDP_1 + k_1 - k_2} + \beta\,\frac{MPK_2 + 1}{GDP_2(k_2) + k_2} = 0$$

$$\frac{dU^*}{dk_2^*} = \frac{-1}{GDP_1^* + k_1^* - k_2^*}$$
$$+ \beta^*\,\frac{MPK_2^* + 1}{GDP_2^*(k_2^*) + k_2^*} = 0$$

Solving these equations determines that $k_2 = 10.952$ and $k_2^* = 1.727$. Hence, $GNP_2 = (1/2)(10.952)^{1/2} = 1.655$, and $MPK_2 = (1/4)(10.952)^{-1/2} = 0.0755$, $GNP_2^* = (3/4)(1.727)^{1/3} = 0.900$, and $MPK_2^* = (1/4)(1.727)^{-2/3} = 0.1737$. Each country's utility is:

$$U = \ln(2.291 + 21 - 10.952)$$
$$+ 95 \ln(1.655 + 10.952) = 4.920$$
$$U^* = \ln(1.082 + 3 - 1.727)$$
$$+ .95 \ln(0.900 + 1.727) = 1.774.$$

For reference, this information is summarized in Table 1-10.

If the two economies considered above are opened to international trade in assets, the optimizing conditions are:

$$\frac{dU}{dk_{D2}} = \frac{-1}{GDP_1 + k_1 - k_{D2} - k_{F2}}$$
$$+ \beta\,\frac{MPK_2 + 1}{GDP_2(k_{D2}) + k_{D2} + (1 + r_{1,2}^*)k_{F2}} = 0$$

$$\frac{dU}{dk_{F2}} = \frac{-1}{GDP_1 + k_1 - k_{D2} - k_{F2}}$$
$$+ \beta\,\frac{1 + r_{1,2}^*}{GDP_2(k_{D2}) + k_{D2} + (1 + r_{1,2}^*)k_{F2}} = 0$$

$$\frac{dU^*}{dk_2^*} = \frac{-1}{GDP_1^* + k_1^* + k_{F2} - k_2^*}$$
$$+ \beta^*\,\frac{MPK_2^* + 1}{GDP_2^*(k_2^*) + k_2^* - (1 + r_{1,2}^*)k_{F2}} = 0$$

$$\frac{dU^*}{dk_{F2}} = \frac{1}{GDP_1^* + k_1^* + k_{F2} - k_2^*}$$
$$+ \beta^*\,\frac{-(1 + r_{1,2}^*)}{GDP_2^*(k_2^*) + k_2^* - (1 + r_{1,2}^*)k_{F2}} = 0$$

and the solution to this system of equations is $k_{D2} = 7.895$, $k_{F2} = 3.120$, and $k_2^* = 4.710$. Hence, $GDP_2 = 1.405$, $MPK_2 = .089$, $GDP_2^* = 1.257$, and $MPK_2^* = .089$. Note that real interest parity holds at 8.9 percent. With $k_{F2} = 3.120$, the transfer of interest from the foreign country to the home country is 0.278. Utility in each country is:

$$U = \ln(2.291 + 21 - 7.895 - 3.120)$$
$$+ .95 \ln(1.405 + 7.895 + 1.089(3.120)) = 4.922$$

TABLE 1-10   Example of Gains from International Trade in Assets in Intertemporal Model

		Before Trade		
Country	*Capital*	*GDP*		*Utility*
Home	$k_2 = 10.952$	$GDP_2 = 1.655$		$U = 4.920$
Foreign	$k_2^* = 1.727$	$GDP_2^* = 0.900$		$U^* = 1.774$

		After Trade		
Country	*Capital*	*GDP*	*NFI*	*Utility*
Home	$k_{D2} = 7.895$	$GDP_2 = 1.405$	$NFI_2 = 0.278$	$U = 4.922$
	$k_{F2} = 3.120$			
Foreign	$k_2^* = 4.710$	$GDP_2^* = 1.257$	$NFI_2^* = -0.278$	$U^* = 1.810$
	$k_{F2} = 3.120$			

$$U^* = \ln(1.082 + 3 + 3.120 - 4.710)$$
$$+ \ .95 \ln(1.257 + 4.710 - 1.089(3.120)) = 1.810.$$

For reference, this information is also summarized in Table 1-10. Comparing the utilities before and after trade demonstrates that both countries have higher welfare after trade in assets is permitted.

The results of the intertemporal model reaffirm the results of the static MacDougall model. As with the MacDougall model, the transfer of capital from the home country to the foreign country increases world output, which is subsequently shared between the capital importing country and the capital exporting country, thus increasing welfare in both countries.

TOOLS FOR ANALYSIS II
Model of Optimum International Diversification

The chapter demonstrates that when home and foreign investments are not perfectly correlated there is a reduction in the standard deviation of a portfolio when investors are able to hold claims on both home and foreign investments. This section presents the general formula for selecting optimal portfolio weights. Let w, for weight, be the proportion of the portfolio held in the home investment and $(1 - w)$ be the proportion of the portfolio held in the foreign investment. The standard deviation of the portfolio consists of the standard deviations of the home and foreign investments (σ and σ^* respectively) and the correlation between the returns on the two investments (where ρ is the correlation coefficient):

$$\sigma_P = \sqrt{w^2\sigma^2 + (1 - w)^2\sigma^{*2} + 2w(1 - w)\rho\sigma\sigma^*}$$

The optimum weighting is found by taking the derivative of the variance of the portfolio, $(\sigma_P)^2$, with re-

spect to w and equating to 0. Subsequently solving for w, we find:

$$w = \frac{\sigma^{*2} - \rho\sigma\sigma^*}{\sigma^2 + \sigma^{*2} - 2\rho\sigma\sigma^*}$$

Although this equation is for only two investments, the intuition and methodology of finding optimal weightings generalizes to any number of investments. Note, however, that this formula assumes that the two investments still have the same expected return, so there is no trade-off between risk and return. Under such circumstances, portfolio investors will be interested in holding more of the investment with the lower standard deviation and less of the investment with the higher standard deviation. A full equilibrium then depends on the sizes of the two investments, and there may be resulting changes in the expected returns on the two investments depending on the sizes and the degree to which investors are willing to trade off risk and return.

EXAMPLE 1.5

Suppose a domestic and a foreign investment have the same expected return. However, the domestic investment has a standard deviation of 4 percentage points and the foreign investment has a standard deviation of 5 percentage points. Returns on the two assets are not perfectly correlated, and the correlation coefficient between the two assets is 0.50. From the formula above, the optimal weight is $w = (25 - 10)/(16 + 25 - 20) = 0.71$. Hence, the optimally diversified portfolio is for the investor to hold 71 percent of the portfolio in the home investment and 29 percent of the portfolio as the foreign investment. The investor is willing to hold some of the portfolio as the foreign investment, even though it has the same expected return as and a higher risk than the home investment, because it serves to diversify the portfolio. Note that this is the optimal portfolio regardless of whether the investor is located in the home country or the foreign country.

❖ ENDNOTES

1. For more discussion of the balance of payments, see Fieleke (1996).
2. Based on Business International Corporation, in conjunction with Shearson Lehman Hutton Inc., *The Debt-Equity Swap Handbook: Country Problems, Tax and Legal Issues, New Trends, and Corporate Case Studies*, November 1988.
3. For an extended intuitive discussion of exchange risk and a risk premium, see Kasman and Pigott (1988). For more on home bias in portfolio investments, including more reasons for home bias, see the survey of literature by Lewis (1999).
4. In addition, the ability to hedge the foreign exchange risk (for example, using forward contracts or other financial instruments that we consider in Chapter 9) allows the exchange rate changes to be separated from the return on the foreign currency return on the foreign investment in the portfolio diversification.

❖ REFERENCES

Aliber, Robert Z. "International Banking: A Survey," *Journal of Money, Credit, and Banking*, November 1984, Part II, pp. 661–678.

Bargas, Sylvia E., and Rosaria Troia. "Direct Investment Position for 1998: Country and Industry Detail," *Survey of Current Business*, July 1999, pp. 48–59.

Cavaglia, Stefano. "The Persistence of Real Interest Differentials: A Kalman Filtering Approach," *Journal of Monetary Economics*, June 1992, pp. 429–443.

Corsetti, Giancarlo, Paolo Pesenti, and Nouriel Roubini. "What Caused the Asian Currency and Financial Crisis?" *Japan and the World Economy*, October 1999, pp. 305–373.

Cumby, Robert E., and Frederic S. Mishkin. "The International Linkage of Real Interest Rates: The European-U.S. Connection," *Journal of International Money and Finance*, 1986, pp. 5–23.

Cummings, Jason G., Trevor S. Harris, and Kevin A. Hassett, "Accounting Standards, Information Flow, and Firm Investment Behavior," in *The Effects of Taxation on Multinational Corporations*, edited by Martin Feldstein, James R. Hines, Jr., and R. Glenn Hubbard, University of Chicago Press, 1995, pp. 181–213.

Fieleke, Norman S. *What Is the Balance of Payments?*, Federal Reserve Bank of Boston, Special Report No. 3, October 1996.

Grubel, Herbert G. "Foreign Investment," in *The New Palgrave: A Dictionary of Economics*, edited by J. Eatwell, M. Milgate, and P. Newman, MacMillan Publishing, 1987, pp. 403–405.

Kasman, Bruce, and Charles Pigott. "Interest Rate Divergences among the Major Industrial Nations," *Federal Reserve Bank of New York Quarterly Review*, Autumn 1988, pp. 28–44.

Kugler, P., and K. Neusser. "International Real Interest Rate Equalization: A Multivariate Time-Series Approach," *Journal of Applied Econometrics*, 1993, pp. 163–174.

Lewis, Karen K. "Trying to Explain the Home Bias in Equities and Consumption," *Journal of Economic Literature*, June 1999, pp. 571–608.

MacDougall, G.D.A. "The Benefits and Costs of Private Investment from Abroad," *Economic Record*, March 1960, pp. 13–35.

Mark, Nelson C. "A Note on International Real Interest Rate Differentials," *Review of Economics and Statistics*, 1985, pp. 681–684.

Mishkin, Frederic S. "Are Real Interest Rates Equal Across Countries? An Empirical Investigation of International Parity Conditions," *Journal of Finance*, December 1984, pp. 1345–1357.

Scholl, Russell B. "The International Investment Position of the United States in 1998," *Survey of Current Business*, July 1999, pp. 36–47.

Solnik, Bruno. *International Investments*, Addison-Wesley Publishing Co., third edition, 1996.

United Nations Center on Transnational Corporations. *World Investment Report*, 1994.

INTERNATIONAL PARITY PROPOSITIONS

CHAPTER OBJECTIVES
AFTER READING THIS CHAPTER YOU SHOULD BE ABLE TO:

❖ Distinguish between nominal exchange rate changes and real exchange rate changes using the concept of purchasing power parity.

❖ Describe empirical evidence both for and against the purchasing power parity proposition.

❖ Convert foreign nominal interest rates into the domestic-currency-equivalent nominal interest rates using the concept of uncovered interest parity.

❖ Describe empirical evidence both for and against the uncovered interest parity proposition.

❖ Determine the price of a forward contract on foreign exchange using the concept of covered interest parity, and calculate the forward premium or discount.

❖ Forecast future spot exchange rates using the unbiased forward rate hypothesis.

This chapter provides a number of tools, known as *international parity propositions,* that will facilitate our examination of foreign investment from a home country perspective. In particular, this chapter presents the parity propositions and some discussion of empirical evidence on them to illustrate the magnitude of their importance. In subsequent chapters, we focus on direct foreign investments, and we apply the parity theorems presented here to the various problems that a firm faces in the establishment and management of an overseas operation.

2.1   INTRODUCTION

As stressed in the previous chapter, an investor undertaking a foreign project must immediately cope with multiple currencies and multiple interest rates. A large portion of international financial management consists of handling the additional financial risk resulting from exchange rate changes, which is known as exchange risk. Although the exchange rate level on a particular day is important information, managers also need to know the paths of exchange rates over time. Figure 2-1 plots the time series of foreign exchange rates against the U.S. dollar for the currencies of major industrial countries over the period 1977 to 1998. Note that these currencies have fluctuated substantially, occasionally even changing more than 100 percent compared to their 1977 values. For comparison, Figure 2-2 plots the time series of exchange rates for traditionally highly inflationary Latin American currencies against the U.S. dollar. These currencies have fluctuated some, but have generally depreciated, and by as much as 2,500 percent compared to their 1977 values. Although these traditionally inflationary currencies in Latin America generally stabilized during the 1990s, high inflation is now characteristic of most nations in the Commonwealth of Independent States and in some other Eastern European countries (for which data are just now becoming available).

The level and the rate of change of the exchange rate are important building blocks in international financial management, as are interest rate and inflation rate differentials. Not surprisingly, these building blocks are interrelated—through the various international parity theorems we referred to before. Figure 2-3 presents a diagram of the main building blocks in international financial management, which are depicted in boxes, along with the names of the international parity theorems which relate the building

FIGURE 2-1   EXCHANGE RATES FOR MAJOR CURRENCIES

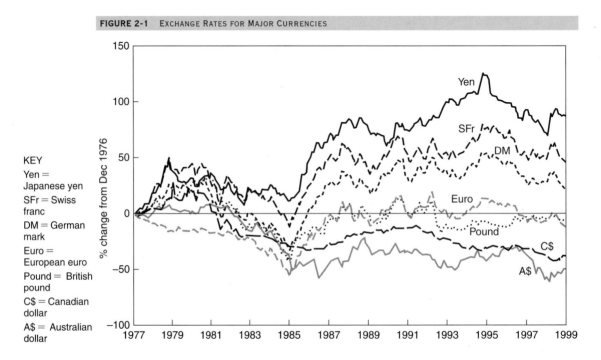

KEY

Yen = Japanese yen

SFr = Swiss franc

DM = German mark

Euro = European euro

Pound = British pound

C$ = Canadian dollar

A$ = Australian dollar

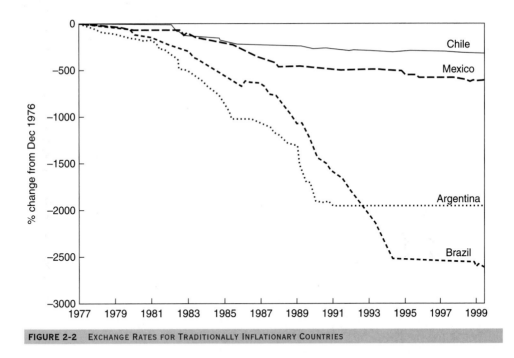

FIGURE 2-2 EXCHANGE RATES FOR TRADITIONALLY INFLATIONARY COUNTRIES

blocks to one another, shown between arrows linking the boxes. The exchange rate change appears at the top, and the interest rate differential is at the bottom. The inflation differential, usually considered an important contributor to both exchange rate changes and interest rate differentials, is on the left. The forward premium on the right is the percent by which the forward exchange rate varies from the spot exchange rate.

FIGURE 2-3 INTERNATIONAL PARITY PROPOSITIONS AND THEIR COMPONENTS

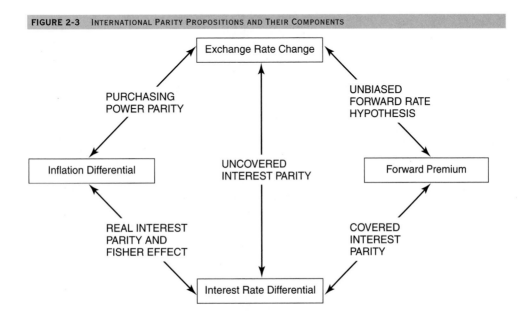

The link between the exchange rate change and the inflation differential is known as **purchasing power parity (PPP).** The link between the exchange rate change and the interest rate differential is referred to as **uncovered interest parity (UIP).** The link between the interest rate differential and the forward premium is known as **covered interest parity (CIP).** There is also a relationship between the expected exchange rate change and the premium on a forward contract, known as **the unbiased forward rate hypothesis.** The remaining link in Figure 2-3 is between the inflation differential and the interest rate differential, which will be briefly examined alongside uncovered interest parity when we reconsider real interest parity from Chapter 1 and the domestic Fisher effect relating nominal interest rates to real interest rates and the rate of inflation.[1]

2.2   PURCHASING POWER PARITY

To a large extent, when multinationals are concerned with changes in exchange rates, they are concerned with how these changes are linked to changes in currencies' purchasing power—or inflation. If, for example, the value of a subsidiary's currency drops by 50 percent, but inflation has caused the local-currency value of the subsidiary's assets and profits to simultaneously rise by 50 percent, the multinational has little cause for alarm. As a result, firms are interested primarily in real changes in exchange rates—those abstracting from inflation. This notion is clarified in a concept from international finance known as the purchasing power parity (PPP) proposition, which directly relates the exchange rate to the behavior of prices in two different countries. The purchasing power parity theorem is formulated in two different, though related, ways: the absolute version and the relative version

ABSOLUTE PURCHASING POWER PARITY

Absolute purchasing power parity is motivated by a basic idea known as the **law of one price,** which states that—in the absence of shipping costs, tariffs, and other frictions to international trade—identical goods should trade for the same real price in different countries. That is, when converted at the spot exchange rate into a common currency, the price of a homogeneous good (e.g., copper) will be identical across borders. If we construct a basket of consumption goods in two countries, the **absolute version of purchasing power parity** specifies that the exchange rate for any two currencies equals the relative own-currency price of the two baskets. In other words, it states that the law of one price holds between all goods in the two economies. In notational form:

$$S_t = P_t / P_t^*$$

where S_t is the nominal spot exchange rate in home currency units per foreign currency unit (e.g., U.S. dollars per pound), P_t is the home country price (in home currency) of a consumption basket, and P_t^* is the foreign country price (in foreign currency) of the same consumption basket.

From a simple transformation of the above equation, the real exchange rate is determined to be unity:

$$S_t[P_t^*/P_t] = 1.$$

As the exact price of a consumption basket is rarely known in two different countries, price indexes are often used in empirical work. This results in the construction of a real exchange rate index

$$S_t[P_t^*/P_t] = e_t$$

where e_t denotes the real exchange rate. The theory of purchasing power parity asserts that this real exchange rate is constant, although unknown. The real exchange rate can be directly calculated from known data on spot exchange rates and price indexes.

EXAMPLE 2.1

The spot exchange rate between the U.S. dollar and the U.K. pound was \$1.50/£ in 1995. The consumer price indexes (CPIs) in both the United States and the United Kingdom are set to a level of 100. Thus, the real exchange rate on a 1995 base was \$1.50/£. In 1996, the spot exchange rate was \$1.47/£. Also in 1996, the CPI in the U.S. was 103, and the CPI in the U.K. was 107. The real exchange rate in 1996 on a 1995 base was:

$$e_t = S_t[P_t^*/P_t] = 1.47[107/103] = \$1.527/£$$

and this can be compared to the 1995 value of \$1.50/£. Hence, although the UK£ depreciated in nominal terms from 1995 to 1996, it appreciated in real terms between the two years.

One difficulty in measuring PPP constructed from price indexes is that different countries use different baskets of goods to determine their price level. Countries will generally select baskets that reflect their tastes and needs—preferences that may vary widely across countries. Hence, even if the law of one price holds in each good, it may not hold overall for dissimilar consumption baskets. For this reason, it is sometimes useful to consider the PPP condition in its alternate, relative form.

RELATIVE PURCHASING POWER PARITY

The **relative version of purchasing power parity** implies that the rate of change of the exchange rate equals the difference between the inflation rates in the two countries. As the above equations hold at every point in time, we know that $S_t = P_t/P_t^*$ and $S_{t+n} = P_{t+n}/P_{t+n}^*$ when PPP holds. Taking the rates of change of each equation variable, the relative version of PPP is expressed as

$$\%\Delta S_{t,t+n} = \pi_{t,t+n} - \pi_{t,t+n}^*$$

where $\%\Delta S_{t,t+n}$ represents the percentage change in the exchange rate from point t to point $t + n$, $\pi_{t,t+n}$ denotes the inflation rate in the home country from point t to point $t + n$, and $\pi_{t,t+n}^*$ is similarly defined for the foreign country. Specific details of this transformation in continuous time are provided in "Tools for Analysis I" for readers interested in additional information, but here we intuitively accept the equation as given. If $\%\Delta S_{t,t+n}$ is positive, the foreign currency is appreciating and the home currency is depreciating. If $\%\Delta S_{t,t+n}$ is negative, the foreign currency is depreciating and the home currency is appreciating.

EXAMPLE 2.2

If the annual rate of inflation in the United States is 5 percent and the annual rate of inflation in Australia is 12 percent, the relative version of purchasing power parity asserts that the Australian dollar should be depreciating at an annual rate of 7 percent vis-à-vis the U.S. dollar:

$$\%\Delta S_{t,t+n} = \pi_{t,t+n} - \pi_{t,t+n}^* = 5\% - 12\% = -7\%$$

such that the spot exchange rate is decreasing at 7 percent per year.

Deviations from relative purchasing power parity can be expressed by an equation of the form

$$\phi_{t,t+n} = \%\Delta S_{t,t+n} - \pi_{t,t+n} + \pi^*_{t,t+n}$$

where $\phi_{t,t+n}$ is the deviation from purchasing power parity, which corresponds to the change in the real exchange rate. Again, the theory of purchasing power parity asserts that $\phi_{t,t+n}$ is zero. If $\phi_{t,t+n}$ is not zero, there are real changes in the exchange rate. If $\phi_{t,t+n}$ is positive, the foreign currency is appreciating in real terms. If $\phi_{t,t+n}$ is negative, the foreign currency is depreciating in real terms.

EXAMPLE 2.3

Reconsider the previous example in which the annual rate of inflation in the United States is 5 percent and the annual rate of inflation in Australia is 12 percent. If the nominal Australian dollar depreciates by 4 percent per year, purchasing power parity does not hold and there is a real exchange rate change:

$$\phi_{t,t+n} = \%\Delta S_{t,t+n} - \pi_{t,t+n} + \pi^*_{t,t+n} = -4\% - 5\% + 12\% = 3\%$$

such that the real value of the Australian dollar is appreciating at 3 percent per year.

As stated above, a multinational is generally concerned with deviations from purchasing power parity. Whether the firm benefits or suffers from a deviation in its subsidiaries' currency can differ widely from case to case. The outcome will depend on a number of factors, such as where the subsidiary's costs are located, in which currency sales are made, and so on. In Chapter 7, we closely examine the impact of deviations from PPP on various operational structures of multinationals.

APPLICATION 2-1

REAL EXCHANGE RATES AND THE 1997 ASIAN CRISIS

Chapter 1 noted that a key factor in bringing about the collapse of several Southeast Asian currencies in 1997 was the preceding tidal wave of capital inflows attracted by the prospect of rapid regional growth. The capital was expected to fund productivity improvements, which in turn would fuel the region's export engine. When this growth failed to materialize, capital retreated and exchange rates collapsed.

One clear way to see why the economies had difficulty improving productivity sufficiently to build their exports is to analyze the countries' real exchange rates. The real exchange rate is often used to measure a country's competitiveness, particularly relative to its competitors and the countries to which it exports. The real exchange rate provides a measure of how much production and consumption costs have changed over a period of time. Hence, it allows one to gauge how rapidly a given country's costs of producing exports have increased relative to those of its competitors or relative to the consumption costs in the country to which it plans to export.

Corsetti, Pesenti, and Roubini (1999) display the real exchange rate for nine Southeast Asian countries relative to the U.S. dollar:

Country	1991	1992	1993	1994	1995	1996
Korea	95.3	91.4	88.8	88.2	91.4	90.8
Indonesia	102.3	103.5	106.6	103.7	103.2	108.2

APPLICATION 2-1 (cont.)

Country	1991	1992	1993	1994	1995	1996
Malaysia	99.9	113.1	114.4	110.4	110.2	115.6
Philippines	3.4	115.9	105.4	120.9	118.6	126.0
Thailand	96.9	97.6	99.7	96.2	99.5	105.3
China	91.2	91.7	98.6	80.2	94.9	101.3
Hong Kong	104.2	108.8	116.3	114.8	116.3	126.2
Singapore	104.4	104.7	107.3	110.6	111.4	116.8
Taiwan	99.2	99.2	94.7	96.0	93.7	92.8

where the real exchange rate is calculated as $e_t = S_t [P_t^*/P_t]$ with 1990 = 100. Note that with the exception of the Korean won, all currencies that crashed in 1997 had experienced substantial real appreciation versus the U.S. dollar, indicating that a large part of why these countries failed to build their export sectors was the erosion in competitiveness of their currencies. In six years, the cost of producing a given quantity of exports for the U.S. market increased between 8 percent (in Thailand) and 26 percent (in the Philippines).

Singapore and Hong Kong also experienced real appreciations, but viewed in conjunction with these countries' current account balances, the appreciations were not sufficient to impair their abilities to export.

The erosion in competitiveness of the devaluing countries is even more pronounced when we take into account the markets to which they were exporting and the firms against which they were competing. Considering that many of the currencies were linked to the U.S. dollar and that the U.S. dollar appreciated significantly against the Japanese yen and the European currencies during the second half of 1995, the countries listed above likely had even greater difficulty exporting to Japan and Europe by 1997. Finally, relative to the Chinese yuan, which depreciated substantially during the first half of the 1990s, the devaluing countries' erosion in competitiveness was devastating. China, armed with an inexpensive currency (and therefore inexpensive production costs), captured large segments of export markets to the detriment of its Southeast Asian neighbors, including the steel market (at Korea's expense) and the apparel market (at the expense of Malaysia and Thailand).

2.3 THE EVIDENCE ON PPP

Figure 2-4 presents plots of real and nominal exchange rates for several currencies versus the U.S. dollar for the period 1977–1998. These plots suggest that the real exchange rate with respect to these currencies is not constant over time, so PPP does not hold continuously. Indeed, the deviations from absolute purchasing power parity were very large during the 1980s. Furthermore, the real exchange rates seem to track nominal exchange rates for industrial countries, suggesting that changes in nominal rates do not simply offset price changes. Such results are quite common for other periods and countries, and are not surprising given the difficulty in finding identical price indexes for different countries.

Turning to relative PPP, Figure 2-5 plots quarterly deviations from relative purchasing power parity for several countries against the U.S. dollar over the period

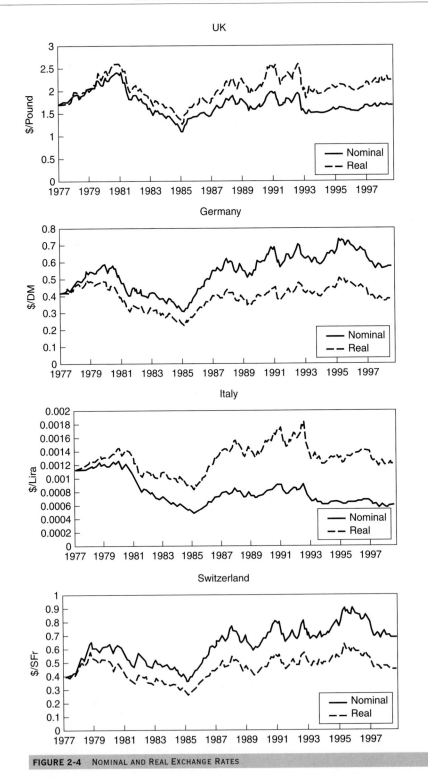

FIGURE 2-4　NOMINAL AND REAL EXCHANGE RATES

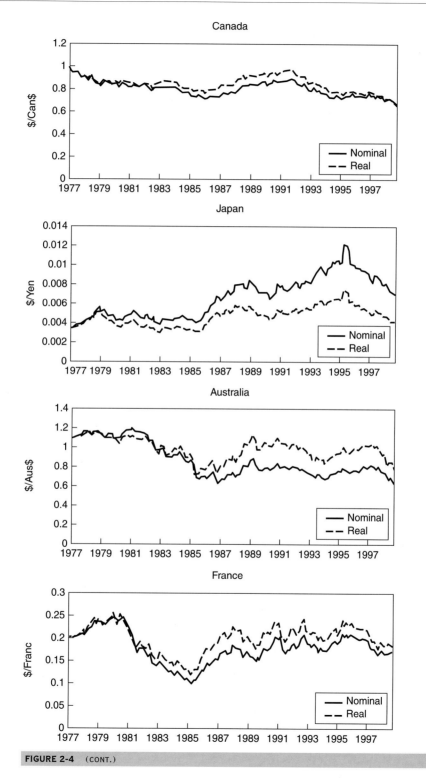

FIGURE 2-4 (CONT.)

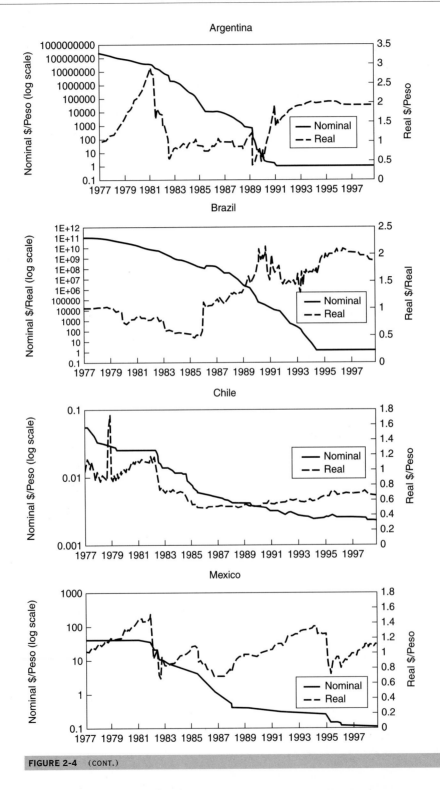

FIGURE 2-4 (CONT.)

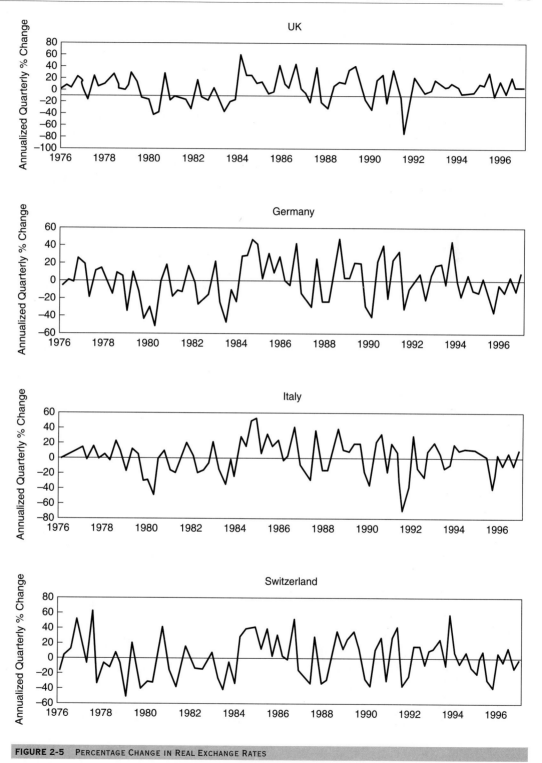

FIGURE 2-5 PERCENTAGE CHANGE IN REAL EXCHANGE RATES

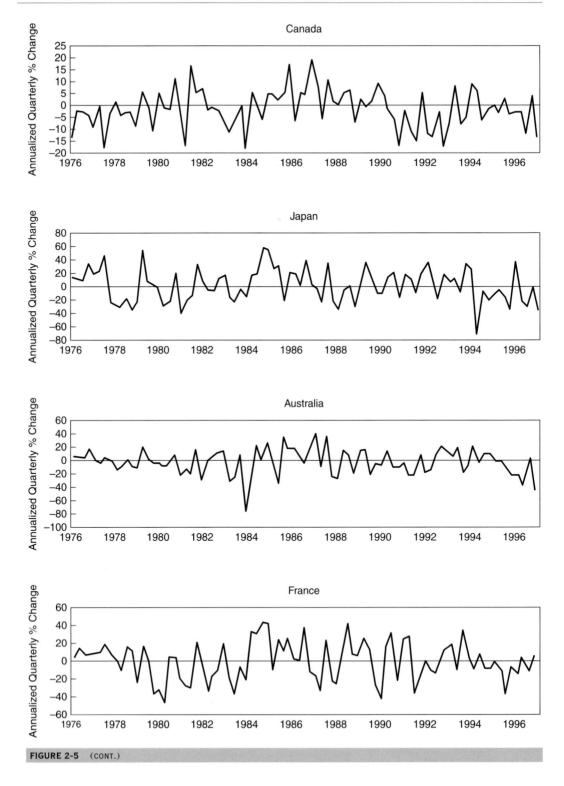

FIGURE 2-5 (CONT.)

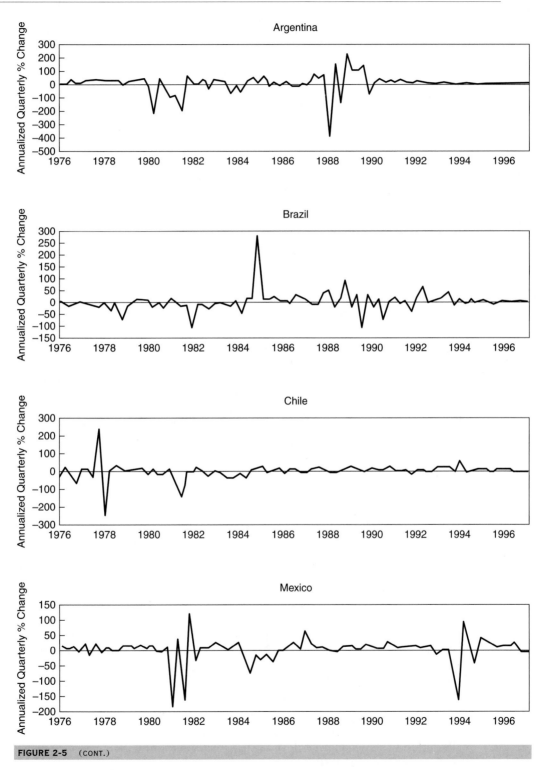

FIGURE 2-5   (CONT.)

1977–1998. These graphs suggest that the deviations from relative PPP can be very large at times. Yet, because the plots center around zero, the graphs also suggest that deviations may be offsetting over time. If this is the case, one interpretation would be that PPP does not hold in the short run, as we observe large deviations in any period. However, it may hold in the long run, as the period-to-period deviations offset one another and average out to zero when a sufficiently large number of periods is covered. When the deviation from PPP is positive, the foreign currency is appreciating in real terms and the U.S. dollar is depreciating. When the deviation is negative, the foreign currency is depreciating in real terms and the U.S. dollar is appreciating.

DEVIATIONS FROM RELATIVE PPP

Do periodic deviations from relative PPP tend to offset each other over time, or are some of the deviations permanent? Numerous studies, many using advanced econometric techniques, have found that currencies do indeed deviate quite widely and persistently from their relative parity levels; for example, see Froot and Rogoff (1995), Rogoff (1995), and Rogoff (1996) for surveys. A number of conditions may cause PPP to fail. It is certainly possible that the impacts of tariffs, shipping costs, and other frictions are not accurately captured in the price-index comparison because international trade in goods is not exactly arbitrage. Moreover, portions of the indexes may include substantial components that are not traded—known as **non-traded goods**—such as labor costs, marketing services, utilities, and so on. The relative price of these components may differ substantially and permanently across countries. A final possibility is that the law of one price is actually failing. Indeed, substantial evidence seems to suggest that easily tradable goods are not priced identically across borders.

Giovannini (1988), Engel (1993), Rogers and Jenkins (1995), and Gregorio and Wolf (1994) all find the law of one price to be grossly violated. A possible explanation for these findings is an ability of multinational firms to price discriminate by country due to market segmentation. If much of the indexes is comprised of products sold by monopolists with significant opportunities to charge different prices—prices which are set higher where demand is more inelastic—then failures in the law of one price may indeed be observed; see Feenstra and Kendall (1997) for a discussion of this literature. We take a closer look at this in Chapters 7 and 10, where we consider an ability to set different prices in different countries to be one of the strategic operating policies available to multinational firms.

Although there are short-run deviations from PPP, the emerging consensus among economists appears to be that exchange rates do indeed converge to parity levels in the very long run; see Wei and Parsley (1995), Flood and Taylor (1996), Froot and Rogoff (1995), and Rogoff (1995). Half-lives for deviations from PPP seem to be around four or five years—meaning that half of a deviation from PPP is reversed within four or five years—highlighting just how sluggishly real exchange rates do return to parity levels. Treating deviations from PPP as persistent over the immediate horizon, but as mean-reverting to zero over the long term, is appropriate for a multinational. Nonetheless, as we shall see in Chapters 7 and 8, short- and intermediate-run deviations from PPP are important sources of concern for firms operating internationally. Furthermore, as we discuss in Chapter 10, the management of short- and intermediate-run deviations from PPP must be designed to protect a firm's long-run position, which in turn must be consistent with long-run PPP.

THE BIG MAC INDEX[2]

Each year, *The Economist* publishes a list of Big Mac prices in various countries and compares the prices using the spot exchange rate to see whether the price of a Big Mac is the same everywhere. This has been informally referred to as the "Big Mac Index," and has been somewhat widely referenced because it is easy to understand. According to the law of one price or purchasing power parity, the ratio of the foreign price converted to dollars to the U.S. price should be 1.00. As the Big Mac cost in 1999 an average of $2.43 in the United States

(based on prices in New York, Chicago, San Francisco, and Atlanta), foreign prices converted to dollars should be $2.43 as well. Inevitably, the ratios are not identical to 1.00, and *The Economist* suggests that purchasing power parity does not hold. A relevant question is how close to 1.00 the price ratio should be to consider the ratio 1.00. Table 2-1 shows the prices of Big Macs in 31 foreign countries in 1999, along with the exchange rate and the ratio of the foreign price converted into dollars divided by the U.S. dollar price.

TABLE 2-1   Big Mac Prices and Exchange Rates

Country	(1) Big Mac Price	(2) Exchange Rate (per dollar)	(3) Price Ratio (col 1)/[(2.43)(col 2)]
United States	$2.43	——	——
Malaysia	M$ 4.52	M$ 3.80	0.489
China	Yuan 9.90	Yuan 8.28	0.492
Hungary	Froint 299	Froint 237	0.519
Hong Kong	HK$ 10.20	HK$ 7.75	0.542
Russia	Ruble 33.50	Ruble 24.70	0.558
Poland	Zloty 5.50	Zloty 3.98	0.569
South Africa	Rand 8.60	Rand 6.22	0.569
Thailand	Baht 52.00	Baht 37.60	0.569
France	Ffr 8.50	Ffr 6.10	0.573
Indonesia	Rupiah 14500	Rupiah 8725	0.684
Australia	A$ 2.65	A$ 1.59	0.686
Brazil	Real 2.92	Real 1.73	0.695
New Zealand	NZ$ 3.40	NZ$ 1.87	0.748
Singapore	S$ 3.20	S$ 1.73	0.761
Canada	C$ 2.99	C$ 1.51	0.815
Mexico	Peso 19.90	Peso 9.54	0.858
Taiwan	NT$ 70.00	NT$ 33.20	0.868
Spain	Pta 375	Pta 155	0.996
Japan	¥ 294	¥ 120	1.008
South Korea	Won 3000	Won 1218	1.014
Argentina	Peso 2.50	Peso 1.00	1.029
Italy	Lira 4500	Lira 1799	1.029
Chile	Peso 1258	Peso 484	1.070
Netherlands	Fl 5.45	Fl 2.05	1.094

TABLE 2-1 (cont.)

Country	(1) Big Mac Price	(2) Exchange Rate (per dollar)	(3) Price Ratio (col 1)/[(2.43)(col 2)]
Germany	DM 4.95	DM 1.82	1.119
Euro Area	€2.52	€0.93	1.120
Sweden	Skr 24.00	Skr 8.32	1.187
Britain	£1.90	£0.62	1.259
Israel	Shekel 13.90	Shekel 4.04	1.416
Denmark	Dkr 24.75	Dkr 6.91	1.474
Switzerland	Sfr 5.90	Sfr 1.48	1.641

Source: Columns (1) and (2) adapted from *The Economist,* "Big MacCurrencies," April 3, 1999, p. 66; column (3) based on authors' calculations.

Closer examination of the data in Table 2-1 suggests that the price ratios might indeed be 1.00. Note that the price ratios range from just under 0.50 to just over 1.50. The histogram in Figure 2-6 plots these price ratios. The average is 0.885 and the standard deviation is 0.312. If we consider the price ratios as random draws from a standard normal probability distribution, a relevant hypothesis is that the mean of the distribution is one. Using statistical hypothesis testing, we cannot reject the hypothesis that the mean is one at the 95 percent confidence level.

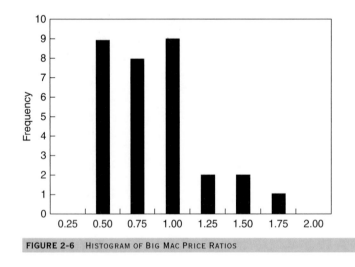

FIGURE 2-6 HISTOGRAM OF BIG MAC PRICE RATIOS

The test statistic is
$$(0.885494 - 1) \div (0.312326/\sqrt{31}) = -2.041$$
and the critical value is 2.045.

Hence, the observed price ratios can be considered as random draws from a standard normal distribution with a mean of 1.00, and we can infer that purchasing power parity holds pretty well on average. Further evidence presented in "Tools for Analysis II" at the end of this chapter suggests that purchasing power parity also holds over time during the period 1986–1997, and provides some explanation of remaining cross-country differences in prices.

2.4   UNCOVERED INTEREST PARITY

While the PPP condition applies to the cross-border pricing of goods and services, it has a close relative in the cross-border pricing of financial investments. **Uncovered interest parity (UIP),** sometimes also known as "Fisher Open," states generally that, lacking frictions in financial markets, the pricing of otherwise riskless financial investments—or, more precisely, the rate of return received on them—should be identical across borders. The frictions present in international financial markets are slightly different than those in goods markets. While there are likely to be few frictions in the form of costs to transferring capital across borders, markets for investment capital still include the frictions, causing the imperfect capital mobility described at the end of Chapter 1. Because the price received on an investment—the interest rate—is paid in the future, its receipt is associated with a degree of uncertainty. In international financial markets, looking at the equivalent domestic-currency return on an investment which pays interest in a foreign currency requires that exchange rate changes be added to the own-currency return. Uncertainty about the exchange rate change is the foreign exchange risk. There may also be some risk that the full return on the investment will not be received due to government intervention, which is political risk.

Uncovered interest parity requires that overseas returns be expected to equal domestic returns when converted at spot exchange rates. Denote annualized domestic and foreign nominal interest rates between time t and time $t + n$ as $R_{t,t+n}$ and $R^*_{t,t+n}$. The domestic-currency return on a foreign-currency investment will then be the foreign nominal rate of return plus the annualized percentage change in the exchange rate over the same period

$$R^*_{t,t+n} + a[\%\Delta S_{t,t+n}]$$

where the term a is an annualization factor. If n is six months, a is equal to two; if n is three months, a is equal to four; if n is one month, a is twelve; and so on. The domestic-currency return on a foreign investment expected *ex ante* is therefore

$$R^*_{t,t+n} + a\{E_t[\%\Delta S_{t,t+n}]\}$$

where E_t is the mathematical expectations operator for expectations at time t. To make investors in the marketplace indifferent between holding the foreign investment and the domestic investment, (the domestic-currency return expected on the foreign investment must equal the return of the domestic investment):

$$R^*_{t,t+n} + a\{E_t[\%\Delta S_{t,t+n}]\} = R_{t,t+n}.$$

Rewriting, it is clear that the nominal interest differential must reflect expected changes in the exchange rate and vice versa:

$$a\{E_t[\%\Delta S_{t,t+n}]\} = R_{t,t+n} - R^*_{t,t+n}.$$

The above expression equating the nominal interest differential and expected changes in the exchange rate is the condition for uncovered interest parity.

EXAMPLE 2.4

Suppose the nominal interest rate in the United States is 7 percent and in Japan it is 3 percent. Uncovered interest parity suggests that the market expects the U.S. dollar to depreciate against the Japanese yen at the rate of 4 percent per year:

$$a\{E_t[\%\Delta S_{t,t+n}]\} = R_{t,t+n} - R^*_{t,t+n} = 7\% - 3\% = 4\%.$$

Even if uncovered interest parity is expected to hold, that does not mean that it will hold. For studying the risk associated with monetary assets, managers are also interested in the unexpected or *ex post* deviations from uncovered interest parity:

$$\gamma_{t,t+n} = a[\%\Delta S_{t,t+n}] + R^*_{t,t+n} - R_{t,t+n}$$

where the exchange rate terms are no longer expected but actual values. These deviations, denoted by $\gamma_{t,t+n}$, represent the realized excess returns on foreign currency investments vis-à-vis the U.S. dollar returns.

EXAMPLE 2.5

Suppose that the nominal interest rate in the United States one year ago was 7 percent and the nominal interest rate in Japan was 3 percent. Uncovered interest parity suggested that the market expected the U.S. dollar to depreciate against the Japanese yen at the rate of 7 percent $-$ 3 percent $=$ 4 percent per year, but during the year the dollar actually appreciated against the yen by 2 percent. The *ex post* deviation from UIP is:

$$\gamma_{t,t+n} = a[\%\Delta S_{t,t+n}] + R^*_{t,t+n} - R_{t,t+n} = -2\% + 3\% - 7\% = -6\%$$

so there has been an excess return on the yen of -6 percent compared to the dollar, or an excess return on the dollar of 6 percent compared to the yen.

Further examination of this *ex post* deviation from UIP is warranted. First, consider that the nominal interest rate in each currency can be decomposed into a real interest rate and an inflation premium such that:

$$R_{t,t+n} = r_{t,t+n} + a\{E_t[\pi_{t,t+n}]\}$$
$$R^*_{t,t+n} = r^*_{t,t+n} + a\{E_t[\pi^*_{t,t+n}]\}$$

from the Fisher (Closed) proposition of macroeconomics. *Ex ante* annualized real rates of return are denoted with the lower-case r's and expected inflation rates are denoted with the second terms. Replacing the nominal interest rates with the summation of the real rates and expected inflation rates, the equation for *ex post* deviations from uncovered interest parity can be decomposed into:

$$\gamma_{t,t+n} = a[\%\Delta S_{t,t+n}] + r^*_{t,t+n} + a\{E_t[\pi^*_{t,t+n}]\} - r_{t,t+n} - a\{E_t[\pi_{t,t+n}]\}.$$

This equation will provide the rationale for focusing on the risk associated with real exchange rate movements rather than the risk associated with the other elements.

DEVIATIONS FROM UIP

We know that deviations from purchasing power parity relate the change in the exchange rate to actual inflation rates rather than to expected inflation rates. This suggests that we alter the above equation by adding and subtracting actual inflation rates. By regrouping the terms, we see that the *ex post* deviation from uncovered interest parity is decomposed into four components:

$$\gamma_{t,t+n} =$$

(1) $a\{\%\Delta S_{t,t+n} - \pi_{t,t+n} + \pi^*_{t,t+n}\}$

(2) $+\ a\{\pi_{t,t+n} - E_t[\pi_{t,t+n}]\}$

(3) $-\ a\{\pi^*_{t,t+n} - E_t[\pi^*_{t,t+n}]\}$

(4) $+\ \{r^*_{t,t+n} - r_{t,t+n}\}.$

These four components of *ex post* deviations from uncovered interest parity are, respectively, (1) deviations from PPP (the annualized version of $\phi_{t,t+n}$), (2) inflation surprises in the home country, (3) inflation surprises in the foreign country, and (4) deviations from *ex ante* real interest parity, which were introduced and discussed at length in Chapter 1. We will use this decomposition shortly to demonstrate that the first term, the deviation from PPP in line (1), is by far the most important element of deviations from UIP.

With respect to *ex post* deviations from UIP, an important issue is whether, or to what extent, the deviations from uncovered interest parity can be anticipated. In such a case, uncovered interest parity is not expected to hold *ex ante,* so an *ex ante* deviation can be defined:

$$\psi_{t,t+n} = a\{E_t[\%\Delta S_{t,t+n}]\} + R^*_{t,t+n} - R_{t,t+n}$$

where $\psi_{t,t+n}$ is the nonzero *ex ante* expected deviation from uncovered interest parity. After some rearrangement, the *ex post* deviation, $\gamma_{t,t+n}$, can be rewritten in terms which are known and unknown at time *t*:

$$\gamma_{t,t+n} =$$

(1) $a\{E_t[\%\Delta S_{t,t+n}] - E_t[\pi_{t,t+n}] + E_t[\pi^*_{t,t+n}]\}$

(2) $+\ r^*_{t,t+n} - r_{t,t+n}$

(3) $+\ a\{[\%\Delta S_{t,t+n}] - E_t[\%\Delta S_{t,t+n}]\}.$

The first term reflects any expected deviation from purchasing power parity. The second captures deviations from real interest parity. These two terms comprise the anticipated, or *ex ante,* deviations from uncovered interest parity, which we earlier referred to as $\psi_{t,t+n}$. The final term accounts for the unanticipated component in *ex post* deviations from uncovered interest parity—the annualized forecast errors in expected exchange rate changes, $\{[\%\Delta S_{t,t+n}] - E_t[\%\Delta S_{t,t+n}]\}$.

It is possible for lines (1) and (2) above to offset each other, which implies that there are no anticipated deviations from UIP, so *ex post* deviations are just forecast errors. If an investor in the home country is expecting a real depreciation of the foreign currency, for example, the real return required to induce him to invest or lend in the foreign country is correspondingly higher, but this is a deviation from real interest parity without being a deviation from UIP. Note that the expected depreciation of the real exchange rate provides a reason for deviations from real interest parity which we did not consider in Chapter 1.

To have anticipated deviations from UIP, lines (1) and (2) above must not offset each other. This is typically because there is a real interest differential $(r^*_{t,t+n} - r_{t,t+n})$

which is larger than an expected real exchange rate change. In most instances, in fact, the expected real exchange rate change may be zero (implying that purchasing power parity is expected to hold, so that deviations from PPP are completely unanticipated), and a real interest differential exists for some other reason. This puts the second term, the deviation from real interest parity, back into the limelight, as any deviation from real interest parity is also a deviation from UIP. Recall from Chapter 1 that the deviations from interest parity were predominantly attributed to imperfect capital mobility which resulted in partially segmented capital markets. One of the chief reasons for a deviation from real interest parity (covered in Chapter 1) is the foreign exchange risk involved in international investments, suggesting that investors may require a risk premium to be compensated for the exchange risk. Hence, an exchange risk premium is also a leading explanation for *ex ante* deviations from UIP.

Another reason for a deviation from real interest parity (also covered in Chapter 1) is market segmentation due to government-imposed barriers and/or the possibility of new government-imposed regulations of the investment and return on investment. Hence, a political risk premium is another possible explanation for *ex ante* deviations from UIP. To the extent that there are other explanations for the failure of real interest parity, there are also identical reasons for the failure of *ex ante* UIP.

CHARACTER OF UIP

Some inference about the long-run character of UIP can be made based on the same decomposition of the *ex post* deviation into the three components representing (1) deviations from PPP, (2) deviations from real interest parity, and (3) forecast errors. If PPP holds in the long run, as suggested in the previous section, then the first term averages to zero in the long run. If real interest parity holds in the long run, as suggested in Chapter 1, then the second term also averages to zero in the long run. Finally, if expectations are rational, such that market expectations do not have systematic mistakes, then the third term also averages to zero in the long run. Hence, all three terms average to zero in the long run, implying that UIP will hold in the long run. As we shall see, the extent of anticipated deviations from uncovered interest parity has significant consequences on a number of multinational decisions. Chapter 3 shows that *ex ante* deviations from UIP will cause a firm with capital budgeting centralized at the level of the parent to accept overseas projects more willingly. On the other hand, in Chapter 4 we find that if there are no predictable deviations from UIP, a firm will have incentives to decentralize their financing of subsidiaries to create a financial hedge.

The uncovered interest parity equation may also be examined in discrete time, for use when interest rates are quoted as simple rates of return (rather than compounded, particularly continuously compounded) and when levels of the current and expected exchange rates are important (rather than the exchange rate change). In discrete time, uncovered interest parity is expressed as:

$$E_t[S_{t+n}]/S_t = [1 + i_{t,t+n}]^{1/a}/[1 + i^*_{t,t+n}]^{1/a}$$

where $E_t[S_{t+n}]$ is the expected future spot exchange rate, $i_{t,t+n}$ is the home currency interest rate, and $i^*_{t,t+n}$ is the foreign currency interest rate.

EXAMPLE 2.6

The current spot exchange rate between the U.S. dollar and the German mark is \$0.56/DM. In London, the one-year offshore interest rate on dollars is 5.5 percent, and that on DM is 3.5 percent. From the discrete version of UIP, the spot exchange rate expected in one year is:

$$E_t[S_{t+n}] = [S_t][1 + i_{t,t+n}]^{1/a}/[1 + i^*_{t,t+n}]^{1/a} = [0.56][1 + 0.055]/[1 + 0.035] = 0.57.$$

2.5 THE EVIDENCE ON UIP

A firm doing business in international capital markets faces the possibility of experiencing *ex post* deviations from UIP. *Ex post* deviations from uncovered interest parity using national government interest rates are plotted in Figure 2-7 for several currencies against the dollar over the period 1977–1998. These deviations are also referred to as *ex post* excess returns because they represent the amount by which returns on the foreign deposit exceed returns on the domestic deposit. Clearly, these deviations can be of a very high magnitude at times. However, the plots seem to center around zero such that the periodic deviations from UIP may offset one another over several periods and average out to zero. This suggests that, although there are deviations from UIP in any period, such that UIP fails in the short run, UIP may hold as a long-run proposition.

An interesting comparison of the data in Figure 2-7 is with the plots of deviations from PPP we examined earlier in Figure 2-5. The plots, in fact, are quite similar. Figure 2-8 thus plots deviations from uncovered interest parity against deviations from PPP. There is undoubtedly a very high linear relationship between the two; in fact, the two series are almost perfectly correlated. The high correlations between deviations from purchasing power parity and uncovered interest parity mean that of the four components of *ex post* deviations from uncovered interest parity, the most important is the deviation from PPP. Inflation surprises represent inflation risk, and these are likely to be small in most countries, and zero on average. The *ex ante* real interest differential may exist, but this is also likely to be small. Focusing only on deviations from PPP is therefore not likely to seriously impair portfolio allocation decisions. This might not hold only for Mexico and other traditionally inflationary currencies. The correlation between deviations from PPP and deviations from UIP appears lower, reflecting high volatility of the nominal interest rate. Hence, concern for the standard deviation of the total return is warranted.

THE EMPIRICAL UIP LITERATURE

The empirical literature has focused on testing whether UIP holds *ex ante,* rather than simply *ex post* as examined in Figures 2-7 and 2-8. In general, this literature can be viewed as an attempt to model the equation above decomposing the *ex post* deviation from UIP into the three components of (1) expected deviations from PPP, (2) expected deviations from real interest parity, and (3) forecast errors. The first two components represent the total *ex ante* deviation from UIP, and are often taken together in empirical analysis (rather than being decomposed). A clear problem is that neither one of these is observed, so the sum cannot be easily calculated. The literature generally suggests that UIP most likely fails *ex ante*—that there are anticipated deviations from UIP.

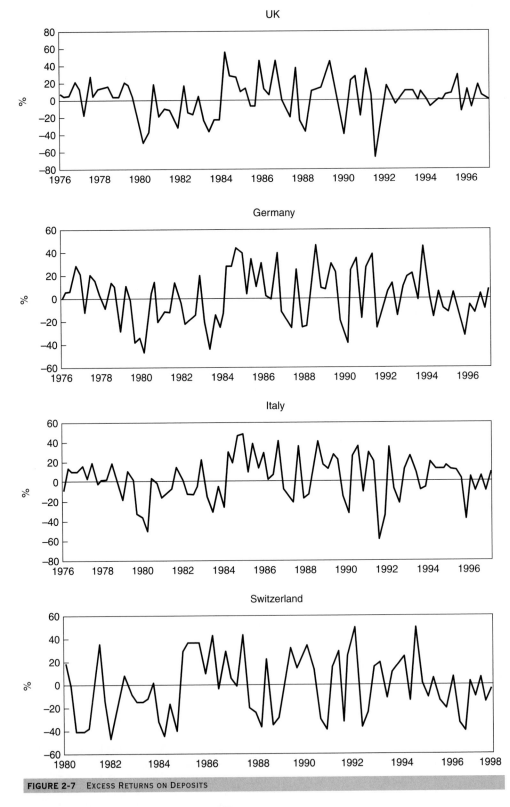

FIGURE 2-7 EXCESS RETURNS ON DEPOSITS

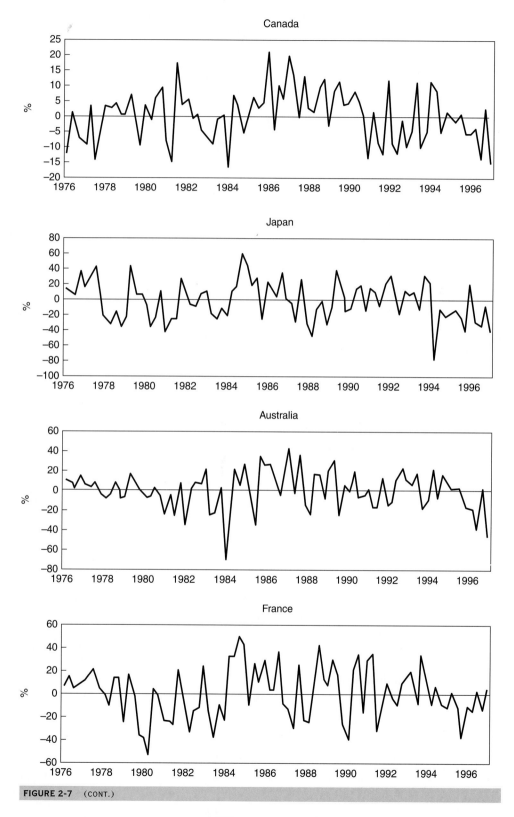

FIGURE 2-7 (CONT.)

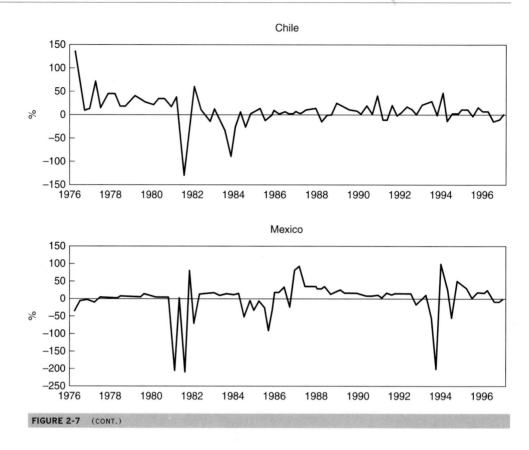

FIGURE 2-7   (CONT.)

Unfortunately, the literature has been much less successful in determining why there are anticipated deviations and how to anticipate them.

In the absence of a direct measure of expected future spot exchange rates, tests of UIP must formulate an additional hypothesis of expectations formation. The rational expectations hypothesis, which suggests that people do not make systematic forecast errors so deviations from UIP should be random, is typically adopted. The joint hypothesis of UIP and rational expectations is then examined by looking at the available data. In one of the seminal works in this area, Cumby and Obstfeld (1981) reject UIP (and the auxiliary rational expectations hypothesis) and suggest that the reason is because there is an *ex ante* risk premium which varies over time. Subsequent papers, such as the work of Frankel (1982) and Cumby (1988), attempting to model this time-varying risk premium have been inconclusive; the risk premium seems to exist, but does not seem to be easily related to economic fundamentals. Hence, the reason for the failure of *ex ante* UIP is unresolved.

In more extensive studies, such as those by Mishkin (1984) and Marston (1997), all three components (rather than just two) of the *ex post* deviation are considered. In this literature, the test is of the joint hypotheses of real interest parity, uncovered interest parity, and *ex ante* relative purchasing power parity, and the data typically reject the joint hypotheses. Once again, however, reasons are not determined. In response,

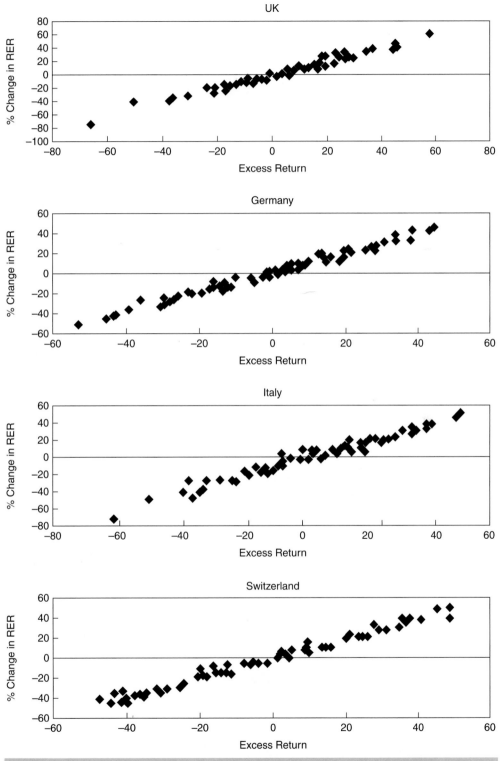

FIGURE 2-8 PERCENTAGE CHANGES IN REAL EXCHANGE RATES VERSUS EXCESS RETURNS ON DEPOSITS

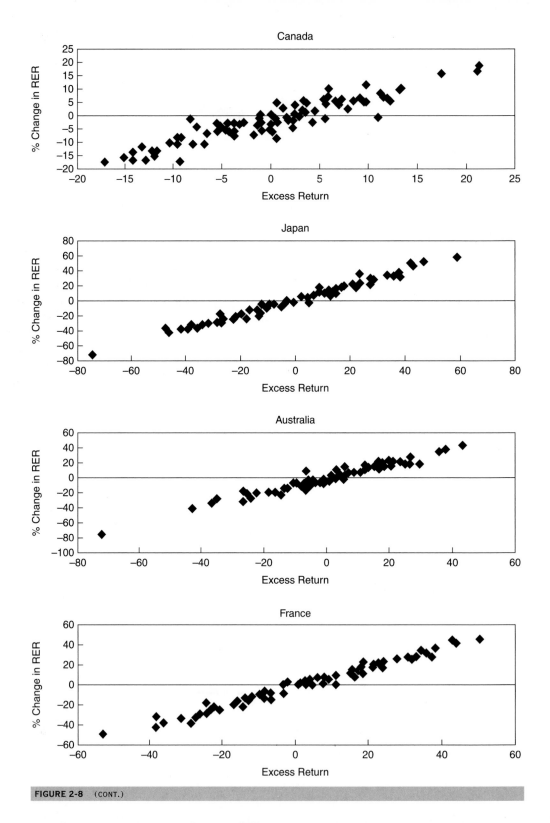

FIGURE 2-8 (CONT.)

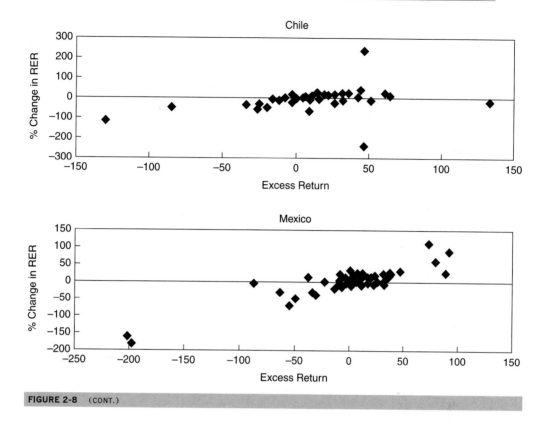

FIGURE 2-8   (CONT.)

economists do not necessarily believe that uncovered interest parity alone would be rejected. For example, Kasman and Pigott (1988) demonstrate that real interest rates in the United States were high during the 1983–84 period of dollar overvaluation because investors were expecting real devaluation of the dollar, and Cavaglia (1992) indicates that deviations from real interest parity indeed provide information about deviations of exchange rates from their long run values, which may explain the rejection of the three joint hypotheses.

In summary, the empirical literature on UIP is fairly inconclusive. We therefore approach topics related to UIP on two levels. First, we consider that UIP unambiguously fails *ex post* in the short run, giving managers reasons to manage the deviations. In addition, the implication here is that UIP holds in the long run, as the deviations average out to zero over a sufficiently large number of periods, possibly because it always holds *ex ante* in the short run anyway. Although this long-run parity has (somewhat curiously) not been addressed in the literature on UIP, it is often acknowledged (e.g., see Levich, 1998, pp. 145–147). Second, we consider what implications *ex ante* deviations that the managers know would have on decisions, although we often cannot specify where this *ex ante* knowledge originates. Perhaps surprisingly, this is also consistent with the notion that UIP holds in the long run because *ex ante* deviations might also average out to zero (e.g., a time-varying risk premium for foreign exchange risk may average out to zero over time) although this is not a requirement.

ARE THERE PROFITABLE DEVIATIONS FROM UIP?

In an introduction to the literature on UIP, Hopper (1994) focuses on three main reasons for deviations, and offers some conclusions on whether such deviations represent profitable opportunities for investors. To be profitable, the deviations must be recognized in advance so that managers can take advantage of them.

First, there is a "peso problem" in the data when the market expectations reflect the probability of an event, such as devaluation, that has not yet occurred. In the 1970s, the Mexican peso was pegged to the U.S. dollar, but it was widely expected that the government would devalue the peso sometime. Despite a fixed exchange rate, uncovered interest parity reflected expectations of the depreciation, and when devaluation did not take place there was an obvious deviation from UIP and the returns on Mexican bonds appeared high. Hence, even though expectations are rational, in finite samples of data the expectations may not be right on average and expectational errors may exhibit persistence when there is continuing expectation of a change. These kinds of statistical problems plague empirical studies of UIP.

Second, and in addition to the peso problem, expectations of exchange rate changes may simply be wrong on average if they do not properly account for all available information. In this sense, expectations are not perfectly rational. As evidence, some surveys of expectations in the foreign exchange market suggest that the participants may make biased predictions of future exchange rates.

Third, there may be a time-varying risk premium associated with the bonds and exchange rates used in the UIP condition. Because there is risk that the exchange rate will end up at something other than what market expectations predict, an investor holding a foreign bond must be compensated for bearing the risk. The problem is complicated by the fact that risk characteristics may change over time, giving rise to a time-varying risk premium.

Empirically, as Hopper (1994) points out, simple strategies of the investor holding foreign currency bonds carrying high interest rates seem to produce profits. Hence, high nominal interest rates are associated with high returns when compared to low nominal interest rates even when converted to a common currency! (This is also consistent with an assertion that high nominal interest rates reflect high real interest rates and should therefore yield high returns.) As Hopper considers, "Is the foreign exchange market inefficient? On the one hand, excess returns seem to result from following simple rules. On the other hand, the returns may be explained by a peso problem, the failure of rational expectations, or time-varying risk premia. It's possible that these phenomena may be present in the foreign exchange market, but the evidence is far from conclusive. Thus, at present, the best answer economists can give to the question of market inefficiency is—maybe.

"How can this help the investor or corporate treasurer? Economists may not be able to show investors how to make money in the foreign exchange market, but they do know enough to help investors avoid losing money. The insights gained by economists who study foreign exchange market efficiency can be used to assess proposed investment strategies. To see how, let us consider a final example.

"Suppose once again you are responsible for managing investments for your company. An investment consulting company approaches you with a proposition. The proposition involves not a simple filter rule, but rather a complex rule involving arcane mathematics. The consulting company shows that had their rule been followed during the past 10 years, a 20 percent average annual rate of return would have resulted. Moreover, clients who have actually used the rule over the past year have continued to earn a 20 percent annual rate of return. Should you use the rule? The analysis in this article suggests some questions that can guide your decision.

"First, what is the time-varying risk in following the strategy? After all, the complicated mathematics in the rule might merely be instructing the

APPLICATION 2-3 (cont.)

investor to invest in very risky assets at each point in time. If this were the case, it would not be surprising to find a large average return. But the return would be at the expense of assuming higher risk. Thus, the rule is valuable only if it earns returns above what it should earn when risk is accounted for. It's not enough, then, for the consulting company to claim a 20 percent average annual rate of return. The consulting company must show that the returns are above normal on a risk-adjusted basis, that is, the consulting company must have a plausible model of time-varying risk premia.

"Second, could a peso problem account for the rule's profitability? As we have seen, returns may appear to be available if investors expect an event that has not yet occurred. If a peso problem exists, an investor following a rule may make money before the event occurs but would lose it after the event occurs. Thus, if the market widely expects an event that has not yet occurred (such as a country withdrawing its currency from the European Exchange Rate Mechanism), a peso problem must be suspected when a technical trading rule seems to offer excess returns."

Source: Gregory P. Hopper, "Is the Foreign Exchange Market Inefficient?" *Federal Reserve Bank of Philadelphia Business Review,* May/June 1994, pp. 17–27.

2.6   COVERED INTEREST PARITY

The uncovered interest parity theorem discussed above established that in international financial markets, when looking at the domestic currency return on an investment that pays interest in a foreign currency, exchange rate changes must be added to the own-currency return. Another interest parity condition, **covered interest parity (CIP)** states that if we can remove currency risk, the same-currency return of two otherwise riskless assets (i.e., short-term cash deposits) should be identical. How can the currency risk be removed? Through a forward contract.

As briefly discussed in Chapter 1, a forward contract is an agreement between two parties to exchange a specific amount of one currency for another currency at a particular date in the future and at a specific exchange rate. The exchange rate that is quoted for transactions taking place in the future is called the **forward exchange rate.** Since they are quotes for transactions at different times, the quotations are not the same. The most common quotes are for 30-, 90-, and 180-day contracts. Banks make other contracts, such as longer-term contracts, available, but these are not traded as much so quotes are not published.[3] The use of forward contracts in hedging the ongoing transactions of a firm is discussed in detail in Chapter 9. Here, we use the forward contract to hedge exchange risk in the covered interest parity condition.

The CIP condition can be expressed in an equation that equates the n-period return on a domestic asset to the return on the equivalent, riskless foreign asset, purchased at the spot exchange rate and repatriated at the locked-in forward rate:

$$[1 + i_{t,t+n}]^{1/a} = [1 + i^*_{t,t+n}]^{1/a} F_{t,n}/S_t$$

where $i_{t,t+n}$ and $i^*_{t,t+n}$ represent the domestic and foreign (nominal, simple-interest) returns and $F_{t,n}$ and S_t represent the forward and spot exchange rates. The term a is again an annualization factor.

EXAMPLE 2.7

The current spot exchange rate between the U.S. dollar and the German mark is \$0.56/DM. In London, the one-year offshore interest rate on dollars is 5.5 percent, and that on DM is 3.5 percent. From CIP, the one-year forward rate must be

$$F_{t,n} = [S_t][1 + i_{t,t+n}]^{1/a}/[1 + i^*_{t,t+n}]^{1/a} = [0.56][1 + 0.055]/[1 + 0.035] = 0.57.$$

The covered interest parity theorem, in contrast to the uncovered interest parity theorem, is a riskless arbitrage condition because $i_{t,t+n}$, $i^*_{t,t+n}$, $F_{t,n}$, and S_t are all known at time t. Hence, it should be no surprise that CIP holds very well in practice, because arbitrage activity eliminates any deviation. Arbitragers who stand ready to make riskless profits thus enforce covered interest parity. Because of this, it is not surprising that empirically we seldom observe significant and lasting deviations from covered interest parity. From the standpoint of a multinational, covered interest parity should be treated as a condition that holds stringently. Empirical studies of covered interest parity have allowed for transactions costs, and have identified a zone surrounding the CIP condition in which deviations from CIP can occur without yielding any profit. The overwhelming conclusion from this literature is that CIP holds very well. See Thornton (1989) for an introduction and MacDonald and Taylor (1990) for a complete survey. Seminal research in the area includes Frenkel and Levich (1975), Frenkel and Levich (1977), Deardorff (1979), Bahmani-Oskooee and Das (1985), and Clinton (1988). More recently, Popper (1993) demonstrates that CIP holds in the markets for both long-term and short-term assets.

EXAMPLE 2.8

Consider the case in which the one-year-ahead dollar/DM forward rate is 0.72 and the current spot rate is 0.67. If the nominal dollar interest rate were 10 percent and the DM interest rate were 6 percent, then arbitragers could realize a riskless profit. To do so, they would borrow U.S. dollars at 10 percent, convert the dollars to DM at the spot exchange rate, earn 6 percent return on the DM during the year, convert the DM back to dollars at the precommitted forward rate at the end of the year, and repay the dollar loan with the proceeds. Such a transaction would yield a return per dollar of:

$$(1/0.67)(1.06)(0.72)/(1.10) = 1.0355$$

or 3.6 percent. This activity would continue until the DM appreciates vis-à-vis the U.S. dollar on the spot market (due to arbitragers' desire to purchase marks) and the DM depreciates on the forward market (due to arbitragers' demand to sell marks forward) enough to establish a spread between the two equivalent to the interest rate differential.

The annualized percentage difference between the forward rate and the spot rate is known as the **forward premium.** The absolute value of this quantity is called the **forward discount** if it is negative. If there is a forward premium on the currency, it is selling in the forward market at a higher price than the spot exchange rate. If there is a forward discount, the forward currency is selling for a lower price than the spot rate. Note that we may rewrite the covered interest parity equation as

$$F_{t,n}/S_t = [1 + i_{t,t+n}]^{1/a}/[1 + i^*_{t,t+n}]^{1/a}$$

and then, since $F_{t,n}/S_t = 1 + (F_{t,n} - S_t)/S_t$, we may rewrite it again as

$$[1 + (F_{t,n} - S_t)/S_t]^a = [1 + i_{t,t+n}]/[1 + i^*_{t,t+n}].$$

The term on the left-hand side is one plus the forward premium or discount. Note that Figure 2-3 specifies that covered interest parity is precisely a link between the forward premium and the interest rate differential. The term on the right-hand side is therefore the interest differential.

EXAMPLE 2.9

With respect to exchange rates between the U.S. dollar and the Swiss franc, a bank quotes a spot rate at \$0.8100/SwF and a six-month forward rate at \$.8284/SwF. It is also quoting interest rates on six-month deposits at 6.8 percent for dollars and 2.1 percent for francs. The forward premium on the Swiss franc is therefore:

$$[1 + (F_{t,n} - S_t)/S_t]^a = [1 + (.8284 - .8100)/.8100]^2 = 1.046$$

or 4.6 percent. The interest differential is:

$$[1 + i_{t,t+n}]/[1 + i^*_{t,t+n}] = 1.068/1.021 = 1.046$$

or 4.6 percent.

To find the approximate forward premium (or discount) on the foreign currency, more simply calculate:

$$a[F_{t,n} - S_t]/S_t.$$

The link between the forward premium and the interest differential can therefore be represented more simply by the approximation:

$$a[F_{t,n} - S_t]/S_t \approx i_{t,t+n} - i^*_{t,t+n}.$$

EXAMPLE 2.10

Using the data on the Swiss franc from the previous example, the approximate forward premium on the franc is:

$$a[F_{t,n} - S_t]/S_t = 2[0.8284 - 0.8100]/0.8100 = 0.045$$

or 4.5 percent. The interest differential is simply:

$$i_{t,t+n} - i^*_{t,t+n} = 6.8\% - 2.1\% = 4.7\%.$$

Both of these calculations, while not precise, are approximately the forward premium and interest rate differential just calculated.

Hence, covered interest parity also implies that the forward premium is equal to the interest rate differential. In fact, this formula holds exactly when continuous compounding is used. (Details are provided in "Tools for Analysis I" at the end of this chapter.) From these formulas, it should also be clear that if the foreign currency is at a forward premium, the home currency is at a forward discount of a similar magnitude. Symmetrically, if the foreign currency is at a forward discount, the home currency is at a forward premium of a similar magnitude. Note that covered interest parity implies that the forward premium (or discount) is equal to the periodic interest rate differential.

2.7   THE UNBIASED FORWARD RATE HYPOTHESIS

Not surprisingly, there is a close association between covered interest parity and uncovered interest parity. In discrete time, uncovered interest parity has been expressed as:

$$E_t[S_{t+n}]/S_t = [1 + i_{t,t+n}]^{1/a}/[1 + i^*_{t,t+n}]^{1/a}.$$

Note the similarity of this equation to the covered interest parity equation:

$$F_{t,n}/S_t = [1 + i_{t,t+n}]^{1/a}/[1 + i^*_{t,t+n}]^{1/a}.$$

If both covered interest parity and uncovered interest parity hold, then the forward exchange rate is an unbiased predictor of the future spot exchange rate, and this is known as **the unbiased forward rate hypothesis,** sometimes alternatively referred to as the **efficient markets hypothesis for foreign exchange.** Mathematically, the unbiased forward rate hypothesis is expressed as:

$$F_{t,n} = E_t[S_{t+n}]$$

based on the equations above.

EXAMPLE 2.11

The current spot exchange rate between the U.S. dollar and the German mark is \$0.56/DM. In London, the one-year offshore interest rate on dollars is 5.5 percent, and that on DM is 3.5 percent. From UIP, the spot exchange rate expected in one year is:

$$E_t[S_{t+n}] = [S_t][1 + i_{t,t+n}]^{1/a}/[1 + i^*_{t,t+n}]^{1/a} = [0.56][1 + 0.055]/[1 + 0.035] = 0.57.$$

From CIP, the one-year forward rate must be:

$$F_{t,n} = [S_t][1 + i_{t,t+n}]^{1/a}/[1 + i^*_{t,t+n}]^{1/a} = [0.56][1 + 0.055]/[1 + 0.035] = 0.57.$$

Hence, the spot exchange rate expected in one year can be taken to be the quoted forward rate:

$$E_t[S_{t+n}] = F_{t,n} = 0.57.$$

On the other hand, if there are *ex ante* anticipated deviations from UIP (of the type examined in the section above) at the same time that covered interest parity holds, then the forward rate will be a biased predictor of future spot exchange rates. Some observers would thus characterize the foreign exchange market as inefficient. Many empirical studies of UIP can therefore be put in the context of the unbiased forward rate hypothesis because CIP holds quite well. For a detailed survey, see Hodrick (1987).

❖ **SUMMARY OF CHAPTER OBJECTIVES**

   1. Distinguish between nominal exchange rate changes and real exchange rate changes using the concept of purchasing power parity.

A nominal exchange rate change is a change in the observed or quoted exchange rate. A real exchange rate change is the nominal exchange rate change adjusted for price changes in the two currencies, and this represents a deviation from relative purchasing power parity.

   2. Describe empirical evidence both for and against the purchasing power parity proposition.

Most empirical evidence suggests that purchasing power parity does not hold in the short run of a few years, but that there is a tendency toward purchasing power parity in a the long-run of several years or more.

   3. Convert foreign nominal interest rates into the domestic-currency-equivalent nominal interest rates using the concept of uncovered interest parity.

Foreign nominal interest rates can be converted into domestic-currency-equivalent nominal interest rates by simply adding a component for the expected percentage change in the exchange rate between the foreign currency and the domestic currency.

   4. Describe empirical evidence both for and against the uncovered interest parity proposition.

Empirical evidence on uncovered interest parity must recognize that *ex post* observations are used and that *ex ante* expectations cannot be observed. The difference between the two concepts is an expectations error. Most empirical evidence suggests that uncovered interest parity does not hold *ex post* in the short run of a few years, but that there is a tendency toward uncovered interest parity in a the long-run of several years or more.

   5. Determine the price of a forward contract on foreign exchange using the concept of covered interest parity, and calculate the forward premium or discount.

The price of a forward contract on foreign exchange is simply the spot rate adjusted for the interest rates in the two currencies. The forward premium or discount is simply the percentage difference between the spot and forward rates.

   6. Forecast future spot exchange rates using the unbiased forward rate hypothesis.

Under the unbiased forward rate hypothesis, the expected future spot rate is simply the forward rate for the identical time horizon, which is in turn the current spot rate adjusted for the interest rates in the two currencies.

❖ QUESTIONS FOR REVIEW

   1. [Class Discussion] There are many parity theorems in international finance.
      a. What is Purchasing Power Parity? Does Purchasing Power Parity hold?
      b. What is Uncovered Interest Parity? Does Uncovered Interest Parity hold?
   2. You are the treasurer of a U.S. multinational corporation with a subsidiary in Spain and you are concerned about the purchasing power of the Spanish peseta.
      a. Your expatriates in Spain tell you that the McDonald's Big Mac costs Pta375. You know that the Big Mac costs $2.43 in the United States. Given this information, what is the exchange rate at which the law of one price holds between the U.S. dollar and the Spanish peseta? Quote the exchange rate in terms of pesetas per dollar.
      b. The actual peseta/dollar exchange rate is Pta144/$. Is the peseta overvalued or undervalued as measured by the Law of One Price applied to the Big Mac? How much is the overvaluation or undervaluation (in percentage terms)?
      c. The actual exchange rate is still Pta144/$. The general level of inflation, as measured by the consumer price index, is 12 percent in Spain and 4 percent in the United States. If these rates of inflation continue for the next year, what will the exchange rate be if relative purchasing power parity holds?
      d. The actual exchange rate is still Pta144/$. The general level of inflation is still 12 percent in Spain and 4 percent in the United States. Suppose that one year from now the exchange rate is Pta 160/$. In real terms, has the peseta appreciated or depreciated? How much has the real appreciation/depreciation been (in percentage terms)?

3. You are the treasurer of a U.S. multinational corporation with operations all over the world. One subsidiary is located in Poznan, Poland. The exchange rate between the U.S. dollar and the Polish zloty was $0.30/zloty on January 1, 1997.

   a. If inflation in the United States was 4 percent and inflation in Poland was 16 percent during 1997, what was the exchange rate on January 1, 1998 if purchasing power parity held?

   b. If the risk-free interest rate on dollar deposits was 8 percent and the risk-free interest rate on zloty deposits was 18 percent on January 1, 1997, what was the uncovered interest parity forecast of the January 1, 1998 exchange rate?

4. You are the treasurer of a U.S. multinational corporation with operations all over the world. One subsidiary is located in Papua New Guinea and uses the local currency, the kina, which was at $0.75/kina on January 1, 1997.

   a. If the inflation rate in the United States was 5 percent and the inflation rate in Papua New Guinea was 3 percent, what was the exchange rate on January 1, 1998 if purchasing power parity held?

   b. Suppose that the corporation was not able to get a forward contract on the kina, but knew that one-year deposits on the kina paid 6 percent and that one-year deposits on U.S. dollars paid 8 percent on January 1, 1997. If covered interest parity held, what was the implied forward rate?

5. You are the treasurer of a U.S. multinational corporation with operations all over the world. Your staff provided you with the following information on financial markets in the United States and Beamish (off the coast of Erehwon) as of January 1, 1993.

	United States	Beamish
Inflation rate since January 1, 1992	10%	6%
1-year Eurocurrency deposit rate (through January 1, 1994)	14%	11%
Exchange rate:	U.S. $ 250/Beamish stout	

   a. You were not given the exchange rate for January 1, 1992. If purchasing power parity held between January 1, 1992 and January 1, 1993, what would the exchange rate have been on January 1, 1992?

   b. A member of your staff told you that the U.S. dollar experienced a 5 percent real appreciation against the Beamish stout. If this was the case, what was the exchange rate on January 1, 1992?

   c. You may have wanted to hedge a cash flow that would occur in one year, so you needed to know the forward exchange rate. Based on the information provided, what was the one-year forward exchange rate?

   d. Based on the information provided, what was the one-year forward discount or premium on the U.S. dollar? (Be sure to indicate discount or premium.)

6. The interest rate on one-year deposits denominated in U.S. dollars is 7 percent. The spot exchange rate between the Danish krone and the U.S. dollar is $0.2010/krone. The one-year forward rate quoted by a large bank is $0.2058/krone.

   a. What is the annualized forward premium or discount? Be sure to indicate whether it is a premium or discount on the krone or dollar.

   b. Based on this information, and assuming that covered interest parity holds, what is the implied interest rate on 1-year deposits denominated in Danish krone?

7. The spot exchange rate between the Danish krone and the U.S. dollar is $0.200/krone. The one-year forward rate quoted by a large U.S. bank is $0.210/krone. The interest rate on Danish krone deposits is 8 percent per year, and inflation in Denmark is (and is expected to be) 4 percent.

   a. What is the implied interest rate on U.S. dollar deposits if covered interest parity holds?

   b. What is the inflation rate in the United States expected to be if real interest parity holds?

8. The spot exchange rate between the Danish krone and the U.S. dollar is $0.210/krone. The one-year forward rate quoted by a large U.S. bank is $0.200/krone. The interest rate on Danish krone deposits is 11 percent per year, and inflation in Denmark is (and is expected to be) 7 percent.

   a. What is the implied interest rate on U.S. dollar deposits if covered interest parity holds?

   b. What is the inflation rate in the United States expected to be if real interest parity holds?

9. The spot exchange rate between the U.S. dollar and the German mark is $.5500/DM. The dollar deposit rate is 8 percent and the DM deposit rate is 4 percent.

   a. What is covered interest parity? What is the six-month forward rate if covered interest parity holds?

   b. What is the unbiased forward rate hypothesis? If the unbiased forward rate hypothesis holds, what do you expect the spot rate between the U.S. dollar and the German mark to be in six months?

10. [True or False] Indicate whether the statement is true or false and clearly explain why.

    a. The forward exchange rate is an unbiased predictor of the future spot exchange rate as long as there is no risk premium for holding assets denominated in one currency over the other.

    b. The forward exchange rate is an accurate predictor of the future spot exchange rate as long as there is no risk premium for holding assets denominated in one currency over the other.

11. [Group Project] Find the most recent listing of Big Mac prices in *The Economist*. In that listing, what currencies are overvalued and what currencies are undervalued? For the law of one price (or purchasing power parity) to hold, where should McDonald's lower the price of the Big Mac and where should McDonald's raise the price of the Big Mac? How does per capita income in each country affect the price of the Big Mac, and how might this affect your answer to the previous question?

TOOLS FOR ANALYSIS I
Continuous-Time Rates of Change in International Parity Theorems

This section provides details of continuous compounding and the continuous-time versions of the international parity theorems presented in the chapter, and links them more explicitly to simple compounding and the discrete-time versions often used in practice.

The relative version of PPP is computed from the absolute version. Because equations representing absolute purchasing power parity hold at every point in time, we know that $S_t = P_t/P_t^*$ and $S_{t+n} = P_{t+n}/P_{t+n}^*$. Taking the natural logarithms of each equation and subtracting the former from the latter, the relative version of PPP is expressed as

$$\% \Delta S_{t,t+n} = \pi_{t,t+n} + \pi_{t,t+n}^*$$

where

$$\% \Delta S_{t,t+n} = \ln S_{t+n} - \ln S_t$$
$$\pi_{t,t+n} = \ln P_{t+n} - \ln P_t$$
$$\pi_{t,t+n}^* = \ln P_{t+n}^* - \ln P_t^*$$

Deviations from relative purchasing power parity can be expressed as

$$\phi_{t,t+n} = \% \Delta S_{t,t+n} - \pi_{t,t+n} + \pi_{t,t+n}^*$$

where $\phi_{t,t+n}$ is the deviation from purchasing power parity, equivalent to the change in the real exchange rate, so $\phi_{t,t+n} = \ln e_{t+n} - \ln e_t$.

Relative PPP could alternatively be expressed in discrete time by dividing the absolute versions of PPP:

$$S_{t+n}/S_t = (P_{t+n}/P_t)/(P_{t+n}^*/P_t^*)$$

which is equivalently expressed as:

$$1 + \frac{S_{t+n} - S_t}{S_t} = \frac{1 + \dfrac{P_{t+n} - P_t}{P_t}}{1 + \dfrac{P_{t+n}^* - P_t^*}{P_t^*}}$$

and, using the simple notation from above, is equivalent to:

$$1 + \% \Delta S_{t,t+n} = \frac{1 + \pi_{t,t+n}}{1 + \pi_{t,t+n}^*}$$

which is approximately equal to:

$$\% \Delta S_{t,t+n} = \pi_{t,t+n} - \pi_{t,t+n}^*$$

exactly as above.

The continuous time version of UIP is:

$$a\{E_t[\% \Delta S_{t,t+n}]\} = R_{t,t+n} - R_{t,t+n}^*.$$

The discrete time version of UIP is:

$$E_t[S_{t+n}]/S_t = [1 + i_{t,t+n}]^{1/a}/[1 + i_{t,t+n}^*]^{1/a}$$

which can be rewritten as:

$$(E_t[S_{t+n}]/S_t)^a = [1 + i_{t,t+n}]/[1 + i_{t,t+n}^*i].$$

The discrete time version is thus equal to the continuous time version when $R_{t,t+n}$ is the continuously-compounding interest rate corresponding to the simple-compounding interest rate $i_{t,t+n}$, and similarly for the foreign interest rates. Specifically, note that:

$$a\{\ln(E_t[S_{t+n}]/S_t)\} = a\{E_t[\% \Delta S_{t,t+n}]\}$$
$$\ln[1 + i_{t,t+n}] = R_{t,t+n}$$
$$\ln[1 + i_{t,t+n}^*] = R_{t,t+n}^*$$

The CIP proposition can also be examined using both continuous compounding and simple compounding. The chapter presents the discrete time (simple compounding) version:

$$F_{t,n}/S_t = [1 + i_{t,t+n}]^{1/a}/[1 + i_{t,t+n}^*]^{1/a}$$

which was also rewritten to express the forward premium on the left-hand side:

$$[1 + (F_{t,n} - S_t)/S_t]^a = [1 + i_{t,t+n}]/[1 + i_{t,t+n}^*].$$

In continuous time, the corresponding expression for covered interest parity is:

$$(a)[\ln(F_{t,n}) - \ln(S_t)] = R_{t,t+n} - R_{t,t+n}^*$$

where, as above, $R_{t,t+n}$ is the continuously compounded interest rate on the domestic currency equal to $\ln[1 + i_{t,t+n}]$ and similarly for the foreign interest rates. Note that in continuous time the forward premium (discount) is precisely:

$$a[\ln F_{t,n} - \ln S_t].$$

TOOLS FOR ANALYSIS II

Statistical Inference and Big Mac Parity

Since its inception in 1986, *The Economist's* annual comparison of international Big Mac prices and exchange rates has gained attention from both the general public and economists. *The Economist* typically suggests that the purchasing power parity (PPP) theory of exchange rates is wrong because Big Mac prices are not identical across countries once converted to a common currency. This view has become the conventional wisdom because readership is substantial and the information is reprinted in a considerable number of textbooks on international economics and international business. Recently, Pakko and Pollard (1996), Cumby (1996), and Rogoff (1996) adopted the same view.

This note presents a contrarian view that Big Mac prices actually conform well to PPP, particularly in the time series dimension, and that country-specific deviations are explained by nontraded inputs rather than by misalignments of exchange rates. This section is based closely on Click (1996), although it is also a significant extension of it. A similar analysis is contained in Ong (1997).

The law of one price applied to the Big Mac is often interpreted as a test of PPP: $P_{it}^*/P_t = S_{it}$ where P_{it}^* is the price of a Big Mac in foreign currency i in year t, P_t is the price of a Big Mac in the United States in year t, and S_{it} is the exchange rate (foreign currency i per dollar) in year t. Algebraic manipulation implies that $P_{it}^*/(P_t\,S_{it}) = 1$ and $\ln(P_{it}^*/(P_t\,S_{it})) = 0$ if PPP holds. One simple test of PPP is whether, on average, the percentage deviation from PPP is zero: that is, whether $\ln(P_{it}^*/(P_t\,S_{it})) = 0$. Table 2-2 summarizes the deviations from PPP and reports tests of the hypothesis that deviations from PPP average zero for various years or countries based on the annual coverage in *The Economist*. Using 256 observations over the period 1986 to 1997 for 37 countries[4], the average of $\ln(P_{it}^*/(P_t\,S_{it}))$ is 0.054, or 5.4 percent, which seems to be a relatively small magnitude given the conventional wisdom. The standard deviation is 0.362, perhaps validating the conventional wisdom that there are some wild deviations from PPP. The standard error of the estimate of the mean is $0.362/\sqrt{256} = 0.023$; hence, the t-test for the hypothesis that the average is zero is 2.405, which is large enough to reject at the 5 percent significance level but not at the 1 percent level. PPP therefore does not hold on average when a 5 percent confidence level is used.

On an annual basis, however, 10 of the 12 years of data cannot reject the hypothesis that the average is zero at the 5 percent level; the exceptions are 1987 and 1992.

On a country-by-country basis, rejections are much more prevalent: only six of thirty-three countries cannot reject the hypothesis that the average is zero at the 5 percent level. At first glance, then, the rejection of PPP appears to be weak, and furthermore appears to be due to persistent cross-sectional differences rather than to misalignments in any given period. Positive (negative) deviations from PPP imply that the Big Mac is more (less) expensive in the foreign country than in the United States.

An important question is *why* the data indicate that PPP does not hold. In a logarithmic regression of the price ratio onto the exchange rate,

$$\ln(P_{it}^*/P_t) = \beta_0 + \beta_1 \ln(S_{it}) + \varepsilon_{it}.$$

PPP implies that $\beta_0 = 0$ and $\beta_1 = 1$ jointly.[5] The typical, loose explanation for the failure of PPP is that prices are set without regard to exchange rates, which might imply either that prices are set at different base levels ($\beta_0 \neq 0$) or, more likely, that prices do not change as exchange rates change ($\beta_1 = 0$), or possibly both. Next, we investigate which proposition explains the failure of PPP.

A logarithmic plot of the Big Mac price ratio against the exchange rate, presented in Figure 2-9, suggests that a line should fit at a 45-degree angle through the origin. Table 2-3 reports regressions from three models: (1) simple pooling, (2) country- and time-specific fixed effects, and (3) country- and time-specific random effects. Note that, in contrast to the work in Click (1996), the fixed effects and random effects models have been augmented to include time components to more fully address temporal variation. Cumby (1996) points out that "some shocks are likely to affect all exchange rates relative to the U.S. dollar (p. 5)," so these effects should be removed to ensure that errors are uncorrelated across countries. In addition, the Durbin-Watson test statistic for serial correlation in the residuals is reported in Table 2-3.[6]

Equations 1–3 in Table 2-3 use data for 1986 to 1997 and 37 countries, while equations 4–6 use data for 1986 to 1995 and 35 countries[7] as a test for robustness (and in anticipation of an upcoming extension). Note

TABLE 2-2 Summary of Percentage Deviations from PPP for Big Mac Prices Calculated as $\ln(P^*_{it}/(P_t S_{it}))$

Year or Country	N	Mean	Standard Deviation	t-test Mean = 0
1986	13	0.072	0.311	0.839
1987	8	0.330	0.211	4.424**
1988	16	−0.089	0.359	−0.994
1989	17	0.035	0.414	0.353
1990	17	0.064	0.369	0.713
1991	18	0.107	0.347	1.309
1992	21	0.166	0.361	2.110*
1993	23	0.111	0.356	1.494
1994	30	0.004	0.354	0.055
1995	31	0.074	0.414	1.001
1996	31	0.028	0.365	0.430
1997	31	−0.038	0.321	0.663
Argentina	6	0.309	0.166	4.567**
Australia	11	−0.254	0.114	−7.382**
Austria	4	0.317	0.175	3.626*
Belgium	12	0.297	0.120	8.553**
Brazil	6	0.024	0.254	0.266
Canada	11	−0.128	0.102	−4.149**
Chile	4	0.048	0.086	1.108
China	6	−0.682	0.141	−11.881**
Czech Republic	4	−0.260	0.051	−10.134**
Denmark	11	0.585	0.097	19.964**
France	12	0.375	0.094	13.843**
Germany	12	0.211	0.103	7.106**
Greece	1	0.071		
Hong Kong	11	−0.668	0.096	−23.116**
Hungary	7	−0.371	0.094	−10.462**
Indonesia	1	−0.283		
Ireland	8	−0.028	0.088	−0.890
Israel	3	0.281	0.053	9.131**
Italy	11	0.242	0.116	6.913**
Japan	11	0.290	0.207	4.639**
Malaysia	5	−0.476	0.054	−19.577**
Mexico	5	−0.132	0.155	−1.917
Netherlands	12	0.237	0.087	9.506**
New Zealand	3	−0.137	0.052	−4.527*
Poland	4	−0.507	0.037	−27.285**
Portugal	1	0.095		
Singapore	10	−0.216	0.230	−2.969*
South Africa	2	−0.340	0.031	−15.464**
South Korea	9	0.269	0.136	5.942**
Spain	11	0.203	0.107	6.275**

TABLE 2-2 (cont.)

Year or Country	N	Mean	Standard Deviation	t-test Mean = 0
Sweden	11	0.460	0.132	11.568**
Switzerland	5	0.623	0.131	10.596**
Taiwan	4	0.034	0.035	1.978
Thailand	5	−0.213	0.053	−9.009**
United Kingdom	12	0.130	0.119	3.796**
Venezuela	1	0.247		
Yugoslavia	4	−0.467	0.370	−2.523
ALL	**256**	**0.054**	**0.362**	**2.405***

*significant at 5% level; **significant at 1% level

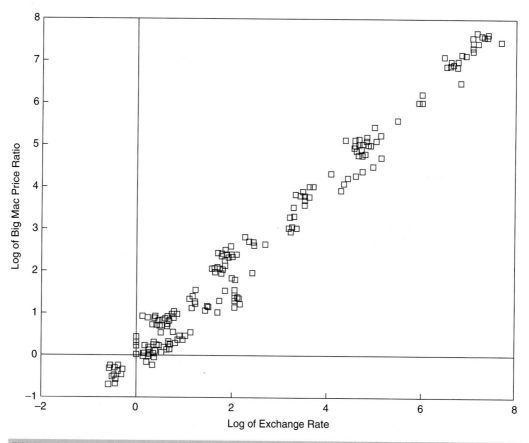

FIGURE 2-9 BIG MAC PRICE RATIO VERSUS EXCHANGE RATE

TABLE 2-3 Big Mac Prices as a Function of Exchange Rates and Per Capita Incomes Estimation of
$\ln(P^{*}_{it}/P_t) = \beta_0 + \beta_1 \ln(S_{it}) + \beta_2 \ln(YPC^{*}_{it}/YPC_t) + \epsilon_{it}$

	Estimation	Sample	β_0	β_1	β_2	N	Adj. R^2	SSR	D-W	Test $\beta_1 = 1$	Test $\beta_0 = 0$ and $\beta_1 = 1$
1	Pooled	1986–1997 37 countries	0.009 (.032)	1.019** (.010)		256	0.98	32.84	0.36	$F_{1,254} = 3.750$	$F_{2,254} = 4.798^{**}$
2	Fixed Effects	1986–1997 37 countries		0.995** (.019)		256	1.00	2.80	1.76	$F_{1,207} = 0.059$	
3	Random Effects	1986–1997 37 countries	0.102 (.097)	0.980** (.015)		256	0.94	3.33	1.60	$F_{1,254} = 1.832$	$F_{2,254} = 1.095$
4	Pooled	1986–1995 35 countries	0.019 (.038)	1.024** (.011)		191	0.98	25.29	0.51	$F_{1,189} = 4.299^{**}$	$F_{2,189} = 6.080^{**}$
5	Fixed Effects	1986–1995 35 countries		0.953** (.022)		191	1.00	1.96	2.06	$F_{1,146} = 4.665^{*}$	
6	Random Effects	1986–1995 35 countries		0.957** (.017)		191	0.94	2.43	1.98	$F_{1,189} = 6.441^{*}$	$F_{2,189} = 3.520^{*}$
7	Pooled	1986–1995 35 countries	0.171* (.103)	1.042** (.010)	0.250** (.025)	191	0.98	16.54	0.59	$F_{1,188} = 19.355^{**}$	$F_{2,188} = 45.671^{**}$
8	Fixed Effects	1986–1995 35 countries	0.150** (.033)	0.956** (.022)	0.166* (.096)	191	1.00	1.92	2.10	$F_{1,145} = 4.113^{*}$	
9	Random Effects	1986–1995 35 countries	0.206* (.099)	0.987** (.017)	0.146** (.033)	191	0.95	2.25	2.08	$F_{1,188} = 0.564$	$F_{2,188} = 2.158$

standard errors in parentheses; *significant at 5% level; **significant at 1% level that all equations have high explanatory content; the adjusted R^2 ranges from 0.94 to 1.00. The simple pooled models suggest that we reject the joint hypothesis that $\beta_0 = 0$ and $\beta_1 = 1$, although the separate hypotheses that $\beta_0 = 0$ and $\beta_1 = 1$ cannot be rejected at the 1 percent level. However, the Durbin-Watson statistic indicates that the residuals from this equation are serially correlated, so the results should be interpreted with caution. (Not surprisingly, visual inspection of the residuals reveals that the serial correlation is due to country effects which produce strings of errors with nonzero means.)

The fixed effects models (which reject the hypotheses that all country intercepts are identical and that all time intercepts are identical) cannot reject the hypothesis that $\beta_1 = 1$ at the 1 percent level (although one of the two equations rejects this hypothesis at the 5 percent level). In addition, the random effects models (which put the country- and time-specific effects in the error term) cannot reject the joint hypothesis that $\beta_0 = 0$ and $\beta_1 = 1$ at the 1 percent level (although one of the two equations rejects the joint hypothesis at the 5 percent level). Furthermore, the Durbin-Watson statistics from these regressions suggest that the residuals are not serially correlated.

Taken together, the results in equations 1–6 in Table 2-3 suggest that the apparent failure of PPP is again weak once country-specific and time-specific effects are accounted for, either in fixed effects or random effects models. In particular, the country effects are the most important, based on a comparison of models with and without time effects (not reported). Furthermore, the models suggest that a 1 percent change in the exchange rate is associated with a 1 percent change in the ratio of Big Mac prices, or that PPP holds well in the time-series dimension. In the terminology of the exchange rate pass-through literature, this represents complete pass-through of exchange rate changes to goods prices. (For more on the link between PPP and exchange rate pass-through, see Goldberg and Knetter, 1997.)

The most likely explanation for country effects is that the prices of some nontraded inputs (such as labor, utilities, and rent) for the Big Mac vary across countries. The Balassa-Samuelson effect suggests that prices of nontraded goods and services will be higher in highly productive, high-income countries, and this may explain deviations from PPP (see the references in Froot and Rogoff, 1995). A simple regression of thirty-five country averages of $\ln(P_{it}^*/(P_t\, S_{it}))$, denoted $\ln(P_{i\cdot}^*/(P_\cdot\, S_{i\cdot}))$, onto country averages of rela-

tive per capita income, $\ln(YPC_{i\cdot}^*/YPC_\cdot)$, using income data from the *World Development Report*[8] confirms this:

$$\ln(P_{i\cdot}^*/P_\cdot S_{i\cdot})) = 0.245 + 0.214\ln(YPC_{i\cdot}^*/YPC_\cdot)$$
$$\qquad\qquad (.065)\quad (.043)$$

$$\text{adjusted } R^2 = 0.41$$

The data points and the regression line are plotted in Figure 2-10. Note that the United States is revealed to be unusually inexpensive: the intercept suggests that the price of a Big Mac is 25 percent more expensive in a foreign country with a similar per capita income. The slope coefficient reveals that a 1 percent increase (decrease) in foreign per capita income relative to U.S. per capita income increases (decreases) the price of a Big Mac by 0.21 percent, revealing that high-income countries are high-price countries, reflecting the Balassa-Samuelson effect. Equations 7–9 in Table 2-3 proceed to augment the basic regressions by including the logarithmic ratio of foreign per capita income to U.S. per capita income. The pooled regression suggests that the price of a Big Mac is indeed higher where per capita income is higher. The equation still rejects the joint hypothesis that $\beta_0 = 0$ and $\beta_1 = 1$, and now also rejects the separate hypotheses that $\beta_0 = 0$ and $\beta_1 = 1$. In the presence of the relative per capita income variable, the intercept now captures the relatively high price of the Big Mac in a country with per capita income similar to that in the United States, so the joint hypothesis is somewhat less applicable.

The fixed effects model suggests that, once the country effects are accounted for, the time series of income does not add much to the regression (although the coefficient is statistically significant at the 5 percent level). Furthermore, the hypothesis that $\beta_1 = 1$ cannot be rejected at the 1 percent level. The random effects model suggests that the income ratio adds explanatory value. Again, the hypothesis that $\beta_1 = 1$ cannot be rejected, and, in addition, the joint hypothesis that $\beta_0 = 0$ and $\beta_1 = 1$ cannot be rejected.

Taken together, regressions 7–9 in Table 2-3 suggest that the income ratio contains cross-section information (largely captured by separate intercepts in the fixed effects model) but relatively little time-series information. Hence, country-specific deviations from PPP are probably explained by the Balassa-Samuelson effect: the Big Mac simply costs more where income is higher, although the Big Mac is unusually inexpensive in the United States. Equation 9 specifically suggests that: (1) the price of a Big Mac is 21 percent more

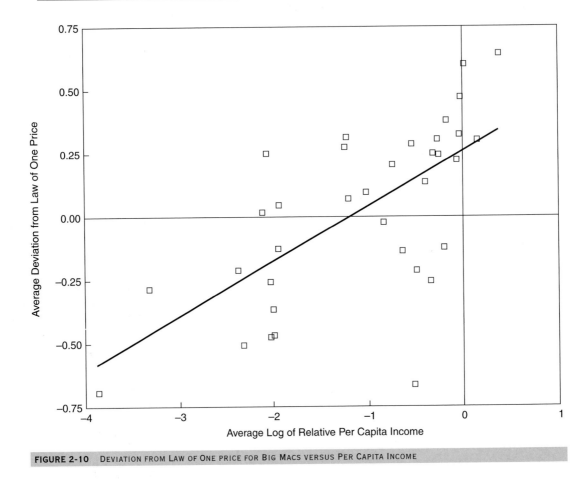

FIGURE 2-10 DEVIATION FROM LAW OF ONE PRICE FOR BIG MACS VERSUS PER CAPITA INCOME

expensive in a foreign country with per capita income similar to U.S. per capita income; (2) a 1 percent difference in foreign per capita income relative to U.S. per capita income alters the price of a Big Mac by 0.15 percent; and (3) a 1 percent change in the exchange rate is associated with complete pass-through as a 1 percent change in the ratio of Big Mac prices.

In conclusion, the statistical analysis we present here demonstrates that PPP holds very well for Big Mac prices, quite the opposite of the conventional

view. In particular, PPP holds well in the time series dimension because a 1 percent change in the exchange rate is associated with a 1 percent increase in the ratio of Big Mac prices. Cross-country differences that remain are typically ascribed to differences in per capita income, as suggested by the Balassa-Samuelson effect, rather than to misalignments of exchange rates. The Big Mac simply costs more where income is higher, although it is also unusually inexpensive in the United States.

❖ ENDNOTES

1. For a more detailed survey of these parity theorems, see MacDonald and Taylor (1990). For more on empirical characteristics of exchange rates along with models of exchange rate determination and the role of international parity theorems, see Levich (1985). For an advanced survey of recent econometric work on parity theorems and models of exchange rate determination, see Baillie and McMahon (1989).

2. Based on "Big MacCurrencies," *The Economist,* April 3, 1999, p. 66.

3. For an extended discussion of long-dated forward exchange contracts, see Handjinicolaou (1990).

4. The data set consists of all Big Mac price and exchange rate data reported in *The Economist.* The exceptions are data for Russia, which we have omitted due to variation in the type of exchange rate reported (commercial rate, market rate), and the 1986 observation for Brazil as an outlier due to currency reform. The data set has been compiled from various issues (September 6, 1986, p. 77. January 17, 1987, p. 68. April 2, 1988, p. 66. April 15, 1989, p. 86. May 5, 1990, p. 92. April 13, 1991, p. 78. April 18, 1992, p. 81. April 17, 1993, p. 79. April 9, 1994, p. 88. April 15, 1995, p. 74. April 27, 1996, p. 82. April 12, 1997, p. 71.)

5. This specification is chosen because P_{it}^* and P_t are likely to be measured with more error than S_{it}, so $\ln(P_{it}^*/P_t)$ is the appropriate dependent variable. In fact, changes in the U.S. Big Mac price reported (originally, the price in Washington, then subsequently, the price in New York, and finally, since 1989, the average of prices in New York, Chicago, San Francisco, and Atlanta) even introduces measurement error. Furthermore, S_{it} is almost definitely exogenous with respect to Big Mac prices, and thus is the appropriate independent variable. We also examined some estimates separating P_{it}^* and P_t

(by using $\ln(P_{it}^*)$ as the dependent variable and $\ln(P_t)$ as an independent variable), a typical test of the law of one price as outlined in Goldberg and Knetter (1997), but the results were poor because P_t does not vary across foreign countries (obviously) and does not have much temporal variation (aside from reporting changes) either.

6. Cumby (1996) addresses time series properties more thoroughly. He demonstrates that, based on unit root tests for thirteen countries, the deviations from PPP are transitory (rather than permanent). He then sets out to measure the rate of convergence to PPP. Once adjusting for country effects in a fixed effects model, he reports that the "half-life of deviations from Big Mac parity appear to be about 1 year (p. 12)," which is quite short.

7. Taiwan and South Africa drop out completely, and the 1991 observation for Yugoslavia drops out.

8. The data are GNP per capita in U.S. dollars calculated according to the World Bank Atlas method, which reduces the influence of currency fluctuations by converting foreign-currency-denominated income at the average of a country's exchange rate for that year and its exchange rates for the two preceding years, after adjusting them for differences in relative inflation between the country and the United States. The data are available only through 1995, and are not available at all for Taiwan.

❖ REFERENCES

Bahmani-Oskooee, Mohsen, and Satya P. Das. "Transaction Costs and the Interest Parity Theorem," *Journal of Political Economy,* August 1985, pp. 793–799.

Baillie, Richard, and Patrick McMahon. *The Foreign Exchange Market: Theory and Econometric Evidence,* Cambridge University Press, 1989.

Cavaglia, Stefano. "The Persistence of Real Interest Differentials: A Kalman Filtering Approach," *Journal of Monetary Economics,* June 1992, pp. 429–443.

Click, Reid W. "Contrarian MacParity," *Economics Letters,* November 1996, pp. 201–204.

Clinton, Kevin. "Transactions Costs and Covered Interest Arbitrage: Theory and Evidence," *Journal of Political Economy,* April 1988, pp. 358–370.

Corsetti, Giancarlo, Paolo Pesenti, and Nouriel Roubini. "What Caused the Asian Currency and Financial Crisis?" *Japan and the World Economy,* October 1999, pp. 305–373.

Cumby, Robert E. "Is it Risk? Explaining Deviations from Uncovered Interest Parity" *Journal of Monetary Economics,* 1988, pp. 279–299.

Cumby, Robert E., and Maurice Obstfeld. "A Note on Exchange-Rate Expectations and Nominal Interest Differentials: A Test of the Fisher Hypothesis," *Journal of Finance,* June 1981, pp. 697–703.

Cumby, Robert E. "Forecasting Exchange Rates and Relative Prices with the Hamburger Standard: Is What You Want What You Get with McParity?" National Bureau of Economic Research Working Paper Number 5675, July 1996.

Deardorff, Alan V. "One-Way Arbitrage and its Implications for the Foreign Exchange Markets," *Journal of Political Economy,* April 1979, pp. 351–364.

Engel, Charles. "Real Exchange Rates and Relative Prices: An Empirical Investigation," *Journal of Monetary Economics,* August 1993, pp. 35–50.

Feenstra, Robert C., and Jon D. Kendall. "Pass-through of Exchange Rates and Purchasing Power Parity," *Journal of International Economics,* 1997, pp. 237–261.

Flood, Robert, and Mark P. Taylor. "Exchange Rate Economics: What's Wrong with the Conventional Approach?" in *The Microstructure of Foreign Exchange Markets,* edited by Jeffrey A. Frankel, G. Galli, and Alberto Giovannini, University of Chicago Press, 1996.

Frankel, Jeffrey A. "In Search of the Exchange Risk Premium: A Six-Currency Test Assuming Mean-Variance Optimization," *Journal of International Money and Finance,* December 1982, pp. 255–274.

Frenkel, Jacob A., and Richard M. Levich. "Covered Interest Arbitrage: Unexploited Profits?" *Journal of Political Economy,* April 1975, pp. 325–338.

Frenkel, Jacob A., and Richard M. Levich. "Transaction Costs and Interest Arbitrage: Tranquil and Turbulent Periods," *Journal of Political Economy,* December 1977, pp. 1209–1226.

Froot, Kenneth A., and Kenneth Rogoff. "Perspectives on PPP and Long-Run Real Exchange Rates," Chapter 32 of *Handbook of International Economics,* volume 3, edited by Gene M. Grossman and Kenneth Rogoff, North Holland Press, 1995, pp. 1647–1688.

Giovannini, Alberto. "Exchange Rates and Traded Goods Prices," *Journal of International Economics,* February 1988, pp. 45–68.

Goldberg, Pinelopi Koujianou, and Michael M. Knetter. "Goods Prices and Exchange Rates: What Have We Learned?" *Journal of Economic Literature,* 1997, pp. 1243–1272.

Gregorio, Jose de and Holger C. Wolf. "Terms of Trade, Productivity, and the Real Exchange Rate," National Bureau of Economic Research Working Paper No. 4807, June 1994.

Handjinicolaou, George. "The Forward Foreign Exchange Market: An Alternative for Hedging Currency Risks," Chapter 13 of *The Handbook of Currency and Interest Rate Risk Management,* edited by Robert J. Schwartz and Clifford W. Smith, Jr., New York Institute of Finance, 1990, pp. 13-1–13-38.

Hodrick, Robert J. *The Empirical Evidence on the Efficiency of Forward and Futures Foreign Exchange Markets,* Harwood Academic Publishers, 1987.

Hopper, Gregory P. "Is the Foreign Exchange Market Inefficient?" *Federal Reserve Bank of Philadelphia Business Review,* May/June 1994, pp. 17–27.

Kasman, Bruce, and Charles Pigott. "Interest Rate Divergences among the Major Industrial Nations," *Federal Reserve Bank of New York Quarterly Review,* Autumn 1988, pp. 28–44.

Levich, Richard M. "Empirical Studies of Exchange Rates: Price Behavior, Rate Determination, and Market Efficiency," Chapter 19 in *Handbook of International Economics,* Volume 2, edited by Ronald W. Jones and Peter B. Kenen, North-Holland, 1985, pp. 979–1040.

Levich, Richard M. *International Financial Markets,* Irwin/McGraw-Hill, 1998.

MacDonald, Ronald, and Mark P. Taylor. "International Parity Conditions," in *Private Behavior and Government Policy in Interdependent Economies,* edited by A.S. Courakis and M.P. Taylor, Clarendon Press, 1990, pp. 19–52.

Marston, Richard C. "Tests of Three Parity Conditions: Distinguishing Risk Premia and Systematic Forecast Errors," *Journal of International Money and Finance,* 1997, pp. 285–303.

Mishkin, Frederic S. "Are Real Interest Rates Equal Across Countries? An Empirical Investigation of International Parity Conditions," *Journal of Finance,* December 1984, pp. 1345–1357.

Ong, Li Lian. "Burgernomics: The Economics of the Big Mac Standard," *Journal of International Money and Finance,* 1997, pp. 865–878.

Pakko, Michael R., and Patricia S. Pollard. "For Here or To Go? Purchasing Power Parity and the Big Mac," *Federal Reserve Bank of St. Louis Review,* January/February 1996, pp. 3–21.

Popper, Helen. "Long-Term Covered Interest Parity: Evidence from Currency Swaps," *Journal of International Money and Finance,* 1993, pp. 439–448.

Rogers, John H., and Michael Jenkins. "Haircuts or Hysteresis? Sources of Movements in Real Exchange Rates," *Journal of International Economics,* May 1995, pp. 339–360.

Rogoff, Kenneth. "What Remains of Purchasing Power Parity?" New York University Working Paper, March 1995.

Rogoff, Kenneth. "The Purchasing Power Parity Puzzle," *Journal of Economic Literature,* 1996, pp. 647–668.

Thornton, Daniel L. "Tests of Covered Interest Parity," *Federal Reserve Bank of St. Louis Review,* July–August 1989, pp. 55–66.

Wei, Shang-Jin, and David C. Parsley. "Purchasing Power Disparity During the Floating Rate Period: Exchange Rate Volatility, Trade Barriers, and Other Culprits," National Bureau of Economic Research Working Paper No. 5032, February 1995.

GOING GLOBAL: UNDERTAKING FOREIGN INVESTMENT PROJECTS

Having provided an understanding of the international macro-economy in Part I, we now more closely examine direct foreign investment decisions. Launching foreign projects is the very heart of multinational financial activities, so the three chapters in this part address the issues that make evaluating, financing, and understanding foreign projects different from domestic projects. To examine these issues, we introduce an organizing framework in which decisions could be aggregated and centralized at the level of the parent (home office) or a supranational regional headquarters, or alternatively decentralized to the level of the subsidiary. This framework is well established in the study of multinational corporations, and is broadly applied to marketing, production, and financial functions in international business; for example, see Aliber (1993) for a clear exposition, or Gates and Egelhoff (1986) for empirical evidence.

In this book, the centralization-versus-decentralization framework is applied to international financial management. The two major decisions concerning a foreign investment project—project evaluation and financing—are examined in this part using a centralization-versus-decentralization framework, and Part III subsequently considers foreign exchange exposure, risk, and hedging in the same framework.

The concept of centralization-versus-decentralization is linked to the issue of integration versus segmentation of capital markets discussed in Part I. The theme of this part of the book is that the choice between centralizing and decentralizing financial management decisions should be based on uncovered interest parity (the relationship between nominal interest rate differentials and the expected nominal exchange rate change), and the integration or segmentation of financial markets indicates whether uncovered interest parity holds. If uncovered interest parity holds, foreign project evaluation and international project financing decisions are comparatively straightforward. If uncovered interest parity does not hold, the deviations from uncovered interest parity have more complex implications for these decisions.

Chapter 3, "International Capital Budgeting," confronts project evaluation and the capital budgeting decision of a multinational corporation. The main rules for evaluating competing projects are presented in a particularly global context. In international capital budgeting, the centralization-versus-decentralization framework pertains to the level at which, and the methodology by which, new projects are evaluated. Centralized capital budgeting is undertaken by firms that convert expected local currency cash flows into home currency cash flows, and then discount the cash flows using the domestic cost of capital. Decentralized capital budgeting is undertaken by firms that discount the local currency cash flows using some local cost of capital, and then convert this present value into home currency units at the prevailing exchange rate. The chapter examines reasons why these two methods for international capital budgeting might produce different results, and what the implications for the firm's international capital budgeting decisions are. The reasons for differences are related to interest differentials, but also to differences in project-specific risk premia in the costs of equity capital in the two currencies and to effects of foreign exchange exposure on the project's expected cash flows. The multinational needs to consider all these issues when deciding whether to centralize or decentralize its international capital budgeting decisions.

Chapter 4, "Financing International Projects," examines the financing decisions for an overseas project, and how such decisions are integrated with the firm's financing decisions as a whole. In international financing, the centralization-versus-decentralization framework pertains predominantly to the choice of denominating debt in the home currency at the home interest rate or in the local currency at the local interest rate, but also to whether the debt is issued by the parent or by the subsidiary. The centralized solution is to have the parent borrow in the home country's currency where the firm might enjoy preferential access to capital markets. The decentralized solution is to have subsidiaries borrow in foreign currencies to create cash outflows denominated in the currencies in which the cash inflows (revenues) occur—which reduces risk because inflows and outflows are matched. The chapter considers these issues after addressing broader issues which pave the way for the discussion of debt, such as the value of debt when interest payments are tax deductible from corporate income, the topic of financing the multinational corporation as a whole versus financing the subsidiary, and the optimal level of debt financing versus equity financing.

Chapter 5, "Foreign Investment Strategy," synthesizes the two chapters on international capital budgeting and financing international projects by considering the sources of corporate profits and a corporation's international business. This chapter moves away from the centralization-versus-decentralization paradigm to provide a synthesis of the issues relating to project evaluation and financing in the context of international business strategy. The approach is based on the theory of economic rent, a return on capital in excess of the return required by shareholders, which specifies that positive present value originates in a firm's comparative advantage in the use of resources. The chapter applies this approach specifically to international business, first by looking at modes of international business—ranging from export/import operations through license/franchise agreements and joint ventures, to wholly-owned direct foreign investment—and next by more thoroughly examining major theories of direct foreign investment. In addition, the chapter considers the value of real options, or strategic opportunities to expand a project when conditions are favorable or contract a project when conditions are unfavorable.

The topics considered in Part II are the "big picture" topics in international financial management regarding the essence of any multinational corporation. To the extent that they are all extensions of decisions in domestic financial management, considerable discussion centers around the issues that make foreign projects different from domestic projects. This means that not much effort is dedicated to reviews of domestic capital budgeting, financing, or investment strategy before diving into the international counterparts of these topics. For background, see Brealey and Myers (1992) or Grinblatt and Titman (1998).

❖ REFERENCES

Aliber, Robert Z. *The Multinational Paradigm,* MIT Press, 1993.

Brealey, Richard A., and Stewart C. Myers. *Principles of Corporate Finance,* McGraw-Hill, 1992.

Gates, Stephen R., and William G. Egelhoff. "Centralization in Headquarters-Subsidiary Relationships," *Journal of International Business Studies,* Summer 1986, pp. 71–92.

Grinblatt, Mark, and Sheridan Titman. *Financial Markets and Corporate Strategy,* Irwin/McGraw-Hill, 1998.

INTERNATIONAL CAPITAL BUDGETING

CHAPTER OBJECTIVES
AFTER READING THIS CHAPTER YOU SHOULD BE ABLE TO:

❖ Value a foreign project using two methods of international capital budgeting.

❖ Calculate the cost of capital for a foreign project and explain cost of capital parity.

❖ Value a foreign project in the presence of segmented capital markets.

❖ Explain the concept of foreign exchange exposure and how exposure affects international capital budgeting.

❖ Understand how projects relate to one another and affect the firm's overall risk.

This chapter consists of six sections. The first introduces the two methods of international capital budgeting and illustrates them using a simple example. The second closely examines the cost of capital for a project assuming that international capital markets are perfectly integrated into a single global capital market, and illustrates the derivation of the costs of capital used in the first section. The third section reexamines capital budgeting and the cost of capital in the presence of international capital market segmentation and illustrates some implications for international investment using the same example used in the first and second sections. The fourth section briefly reconsiders international capital budgeting when the local currency cash flows depend on the level of the exchange rate, and the final sections briefly consider portfolio diversification theory applied to capital projects and the nature of international capital budgeting.

3.1   INTRODUCTION

This chapter examines the valuation of foreign projects. Firms decide what investment projects they should undertake based on the project's expected cash flows discounted by the **cost of capital,** the rate of return required by the owners of capital. If a project has a positive net present value, the firm should undertake it because it increases the firm's overall value. If a project has a negative net present value, the firm should not undertake it because it decreases the firm's value. The activity of allocating the firm's financial capital to investment projects is called **capital budgeting,** a technique which ensures that equity capital is directed toward the projects in which it is the most productive.[1]

International capital budgeting differs from domestic capital budgeting in two main ways. First, costs and revenues are incurred in a foreign currency, although the firm is ultimately concerned with home-currency-equivalent cash flows. Second, there are two relevant discount rates, a domestic rate and a foreign rate. In other words, the project has a cost of capital in each country or currency, where the cost of capital is the sum of the risk-free nominal interest rate and a risk premium that reflects the project's riskiness. This chapter examines two methods of evaluating international projects given these two differences in the economic environment. It also introduces a framework of analysis within which the two methods can be addressed: a centralization-versus-decentralization paradigm. The currency and cost of capital issues that distinguish foreign projects from domestic ones take center stage in this chapter because they are the most fundamental issues. Later in the book, in Chapter 12, we extend the analysis to include political considerations arising from the fact that the project is undertaken in a different governmental jurisdiction.

3.2   TWO METHODS OF INTERNATIONAL CAPITAL BUDGETING

There are two different procedures for evaluating international projects. Table 3-1 outlines the steps involved in both methods. They both focus on nominal values of cash flows, exchange rates, and costs of capital as opposed to real values, although there are two similar procedures for projects evaluated in real terms. We focus on nominal values because these are the ones most typically projected in reality.

The first method of evaluating foreign projects, generally called **decentralized capital budgeting,** discounts local currency cash flows at the foreign cost of capital and then converts the net present value into home currency units at the prevailing spot exchange rate. In mathematical notation, decentralized capital budgeting is represented by

$$PV = \left[\sum_{t=0}^{n} \frac{E_0[CF_t]}{(1 + COC^*)^t} \right] S_0$$

TABLE 3-1 Methods of International Capital Budgeting		
Step	**Decentralized**	**Centralized**
1	Forecast cash flows in local currency	Forecast cash flows in local currency
2	Discount cash flows using the foreign costs of capital	Convert cash flows into home currency using forecasts of the exchange rate
3	Convert to home currency at the prevailing spot exchange rate	Discount cash flows using the domestic cost of capital

where PV is present value, $E_0[CF_t]$ is the expected cash flow denominated in the local currency, COC^* is the cost of capital in the local currency, and S_0 is the current exchange rate. For simplicity, this formula assumes that the cost of capital is constant, implying that the term structure is flat.[2]

The second method of evaluating foreign projects, called **centralized capital budgeting,** converts all local currency cash flows into the home currency, then discounts the cash flows at the domestic cost of capital. In mathematical notation, centralized capital budgeting is represented by

$$PV = \sum_{t=0}^{n} \frac{E_0[CF_t S_t]}{(1 + COC)^t}$$

where COC is the cost of capital in the home currency, S_t is the exchange rate in period t, and all other variables are as previously defined. Again, the formula assumes the cost of capital is constant.

Note that centralization and decentralization here refer to the method of analyzing a project, rather than to the location of decision-making, but that there is a parallel between the two. If the headquarters office undertakes the analysis, there will be a tendency to convert local currency cash flows into the home currency, then discount at the domestic cost of capital; hence, the term "centralization" is appropriate. If the subsidiaries undertake the capital budgeting analysis, there will be a tendency to discount local currency cash flows at the local cost of capital and then convert to home currency units for reporting to the parent; hence, the term "decentralized" is appropriate.

Both methods of international capital budgeting begin by estimating the project's local currency cash flows. In estimating the cash flows over a long horizon, the firm should make projections based on long-run comparative and competitive advantages vis-à-vis the market or industry, whether the project is domestic or foreign. In international capital budgeting, a firm evaluating a foreign production site or entering a new foreign market should base the estimated future cash flows over a long horizon on long-run purchasing power parity exchange rates, rather than on what might be a current, short-run deviation from the competitive equilibrium or from the purchasing power parity exchange rate. Together, these bases ensure that the firm undertakes projects that are profitable, and therefore sensible, in the long run.

Projected cash flows should always represent incremental cash flows to the firm. In other words, the firm wants to figure the value to the parent, rather than simply the value of the project. If a new subsidiary reduces exports from the parent, for example, the project's revenues should be adjusted downward to reflect this. As always, money already spent is usually an unrecoverable sunk cost and should therefore be excluded.

Similarly, anything in the project associated with an opportunity cost, such as use of company property which would otherwise be rented out, must be included. However, costs which are not otherwise opportunity costs should be excluded. For example, if the new subsidiary pays a license fee to the parent that is not otherwise an opportunity cost (that is, if the license fee would not be received by the parent if the subsidiary were not established), the costs of the project should be adjusted downward to reflect this. If there are government limits on the amount of profits that can be repatriated, there will be a further distinction between the cash flows to the parent and the cash flows to the project. The project is probably worth less, but this depends on the nature of the limits to repatriation. We take up this final issue again in Chapter 12, under the topic of political risk, so we do not examine it further here.

The estimated cash flows must also be net of tax payments. This, in reality, is more difficult than it sounds. One issue firms face is that corporate taxes are not based on cash flows, but on accounting profits, which differ from cash flows for many reasons, including depreciation of physical assets over their useful lives and accruals of some current assets and liabilities. An issue arising in the international context is that taxes must be paid to two national governments, the host government and the home government. Additional problems arise because the amount of taxes a firm pays generally depends on the amount of profits repatriated. We take up this topic in Chapter 11, so we will postpone the details until then.

Table 3-1 also specifies that, once cash flows are estimated in local currency units, the firm must decide whether to decentralize or centralize capital budgeting. This decision is much more difficult than it appears. The decentralized capital budgeting method requires the foreign cost of capital, which is not usually readily available to the firm. Although the firm may have very good information concerning the domestic cost of capital from the domestic financial markets in which it operates or from its history of projects undertaken, that knowledge is not directly applicable to the foreign environment. Unless the company has extensive operations in the foreign country under consideration, it is hard to judge exactly what the required rate of return on the firm's capital, placed in the foreign country for the given project, is.

The alternative, centralized capital budgeting, is not any easier, though. With this method, the firm faces converting estimated future foreign currency flows into home currency units. This conversion requires forecasts of the future exchange rates, which are certainly not easy to formulate. The conversion will be even more difficult if the estimated local currency cash flows depend on the estimated exchange rate.[3]

Hence, the choice of decentralized or centralized capital budgeting partially depends on the relative expertise the firm has in determining a foreign cost of capital or future exchange rates. As it turns out, the method of capital budgeting chosen is irrelevant if (1) national capital markets are integrated into a single global capital market, and (2) local currency cash flows are independent of the exchange rate. We illustrate this point in the next section through the use of an example.

VALUING A FOREIGN PROJECT

Consider a simple three-year project that a U.S. multinational, which we will refer to as Victor Enterprises, is contemplating in Switzerland. From Table 3-1, it is clear that the first step in any capital budgeting problem is to estimate the cash flows associated with the project. Suppose the project requires a SFr 20 million initial investment outlay to purchase equipment which can be depreciated over the life of the project. Table 3-2 presents Victor Enterprises' estimates of incremental revenues and operating expenses, calculation of income taxes accounting for depreciation, and the final calculation of cash flows. By way of summary, the estimated cash flows are:

STEP 1

Year	SFr Cash Flows
0	−20m
1	10m
2	12m
3	15m

Victor Enterprises decides to calculate the project's present value using both the decentralized and centralized methods, assuming that the project is completely financed with equity. To do the present value calculation, Victor Enterprises needs estimates of the project's all-equity costs of capital. It knows the risk-free rate of return in each country, but needs to add a risk premium for the specific project. With the help of an international investment banking firm, Victor Enterprises concludes that the cost of capital relevant for the project is 17 percent in U.S. dollars and 26.36 percent in Swiss francs. We discuss determining the cost of capital in great detail in the next section of this chapter, in which the precise derivation of these figures is explained. For now, the firm takes the information as given.

Implementing the decentralized technique first, Victor Enterprises discounts cash flows using the foreign cost of capital:

STEP 2

$$PV = -20,000,000 + 10,000,000/1.2636 + 12,000,000/1.2636^2 + 15,000,000/1.2636^3$$
$$= \text{SFr } 2,864,150$$

At the same time, Victor Enterprises determines that the current exchange rate between the U.S. dollar and the Swiss franc is U.S.\$ 0.80/SFr. It therefore figures:

STEP 3

SFr 2,864,150[\$0.80/SFr] = U.S.\$ 2,291,320

TABLE 3-2   Victor Enterprises: Estimated Cash Flows for Swiss Project (Swiss francs)

Year	0	1	2	3
Revenues		50,000,000	55,000,000	60,000,000
Expenses		38,205,128	40,128,205	40,512,820
Depreciation		6,666,667	6,666,667	6,666,666
Taxable Income (Revenues minus Expenses and Depreciation)		5,128,205	8,205,128	12,820,514
Income Tax @ 35%		1,794,872	2,871,795	4,487,180
After-Tax Income		3,333,333	5,333,333	8,333,334
Depreciation		6,666,667	6,666,667	6,666,666
After-Tax Cash Flows (After-Tax Income plus Depreciation)	−20,000,000	10,000,000	12,000,000	15,000,000

so the project carries a net positive present value and the firm is interested in undertaking it.

To implement the centralized method of capital budgeting, Victor Enterprises must convert cash flows into the home currency using a forecast of the exchange rate. As well-developed financial markets exist for both the U.S. dollar and the Swiss franc, the firm decides to use the nominal risk-free interest rate differential to determine expected future spot exchange rates. Victor Enterprises determines that the risk-free rate of return on U.S. Treasury bills is 10 percent, and the risk-free rate of return on Swiss francs is 18.8 percent. Furthermore, the firm assumes that the term structure of interest rates is flat in both countries. Hence, based on the uncovered interest parity (UIP) theory discussed in Chapter 2, applied in discrete time for simple interest rates, the forecasts of the $/SFr exchange rate are:

STEP 2

Year	Expected Exchange Rate
0	0.80
1	$0.80 \, [1.10/1.188] = .7407$
2	$0.80 \, [1.10/1.188]^2 = .6859$
3	$0.80 \, [1.10/1.188]^3 = .6351$

Using the centralized method, then, Victor Enterprises figures the values of the cash flows in U.S. dollars:

Year	U.S.$ Cash Flows
0	SFr −20,000,000 [.80] = U.S.$ −16,000,000
1	SFr 10,000,000 [.7407] = U.S.$ 7,407,407
2	SFr 12,000,000 [.6859] = U.S.$ 8,230,453
3	SFr 15,000,000 [.6351] = U.S.$ 9,525,987

and then the present value:

STEP 3

$$PV = -16,000,000 + 7,407,407/1.17 + 8,230,453/1.17^2 + 9,525,987/1.17^3$$
$$= \text{U.S.\$ } 2,291,320$$

which is positive so the firm is still interested in undertaking the project.

Comparing the decentralized and centralized capital budgeting methods, Victor Enterprises realizes that the two methods produce the same present value. The reason this occurs becomes clear once we compare all the foreign and domestic variables. In the risk-free interest rates, the Swiss franc has a discrete-time premium of 8 percent over the U.S. dollar: $(1.10)(1.08) = 1.188$. This means that the expected depreciation of the Swiss franc, found through the UIP equation, is approximately 8 percent per year. Similarly, the costs of capital reflect this simple premium: $(1.17)(1.08) = 1.2636$. In other words, the cost of capital figures reflect the same interest differential. Hence, given that all variables conform to this premium, it is not surprising that the two capital budgeting methods yield the same result.

SUMMARY OF INTERNATIONAL CAPITAL BUDGETING

The methods of international capital budgeting have been developed here for the case of a perfectly integrated international capital market. By using the spread between foreign and domestic interest rates to derive a forecast of the exchange rate, we are implying that we expect uncovered interest parity to hold *ex ante*. By preserving this spread (between the foreign and domestic interest rates) in the foreign and domestic costs of capital for the project, we are also forcing a counterpart of UIP applied to the cost of capital to hold in international equity markets. This proposition has been loosely acknowledged in international finance, but has not been rigorously studied. To our knowledge, there is no term used to describe the proposition.

We here refer to the proposition that the spread between foreign and domestic costs of capital reflects expectations of exchange rate changes as **cost of capital parity,** and examine it further in the next section. The main result of this section is that, as long as there is an integrated international capital market, it does not matter whether the firm uses the decentralized method or the centralized method to evaluate an international project when cash flows are independent of the exchange rate. If the calculations are carried out correctly, the results are identical.

Before continuing, it is worth noting that there are several other forecasting methods a firm may use in Step 2 of centralized capital budgeting. For example, the firm may use the random walk hypothesis, in which the current exchange rate is viewed as the expected value of the future exchange rate. The firm may also use long-run or purchasing power parity equilibrium estimates. Finally, the firm may use judgment or econometric models to forecast exchange rates. Depending on the manager's view of the market, each of these is a reasonable forecasting choice. However, use of these alternative forecasts either implies that we do not expect UIP to hold, or that managers resort to them for lack of a better way of forecasting.

By and large, an interest rate differential is the best indicator of the market's expectation of future exchange rate changes if capital markets are perfectly integrated. Recall from Chapter 2 that the interest rate differential is used to calculate a forward exchange rate according to the covered interest parity (CIP) equation, and that when UIP and CIP both hold, the forward exchange rate is an unbiased predictor of the future spot exchange rate. If the firm's exchange rate forecast is different from the market's expectations, it can speculate through the financial markets, such as with forward contracts; it does not need a capital investment project to do so. However, in a later section we examine international capital budgeting when national capital markets are segmented and UIP does not hold, so we defer further consideration of these issues.

It is also worth noting that the two methods of international capital budgeting presented here are identical if the firm decides to hedge the expected values of the cash flows in the forward market. This is relevant for firms concerned about the *ex post* deviations from UIP. If forward contracts are available and the covered interest parity theorem holds, the actual forward exchange rates become the future spot rates relevant to the firm.[4] We will examine techniques for hedging in greater detail in Chapters 8–10, where we will also address the issue of determining the appropriate amount of the hedge.

Hedging is also relevant for a firm that may be tempted to use one of the aforementioned alternative exchange rate forecasts. For example, if a multinational corporation forecasts that the Swiss franc will be weaker than the consensus UIP forecast implies, the company can hedge against the adverse effects of a weaker Swiss franc, so that the company's differing forecasts do not affect the capital budgeting decision.

3.3 THE COST OF CAPITAL AND COST OF CAPITAL PARITY

A firm's cost of capital for a project is made up of the nominal risk-free interest rate (almost universally taken to be the interest rate on government bonds) and a project-specific risk premium. The project-specific risk premium reflects the fact that the riskiness of the company's activities leads to its cost of capital being higher than the interest rate on government debt. Because nominal risk-free interest rates are different across countries, we know that the multinational corporation is faced with two costs of capital for the same project. The nominal risk-free interest rates are different across countries largely because there are inflation differences across countries, as discussed in Chapter 2. The more important focus, however, is on how the firm comes up with the risk premium for the project.

In the theory of finance, the cost of capital is usually calculated from the Capital Asset Pricing Model (CAPM) and knowledge of the project's beta (β).[5] Consider the CAPM equation:

$$COC_{t,t+n} = R_{t,t+n} + \beta[R^M_{t,t+n} - R_{t,t+n}]$$

where $COC_{t,t+n}$ is the cost of capital, or the required rate of return on equity for the project, $R_{t,t+n}$ is the nominal return on a risk-free asset (i.e., the treasury-bill rate), $R^M_{t,t+n}$ is the required return on the market portfolio consisting of all risky projects (usually measured by a stock market index), and β is the project-specific beta. The term in brackets, $[R^M_{t,t+n} - R_{t,t+n}]$, is referred to as the **equity premium.** The **beta** is a measure of the systematic, or nondiversifiable, risk of the project, $\beta = \text{cov}[COC_{t,t+n}, R^M_{t,t+n}]/\text{var}[R^M_{t,t+n}]$. The beta is essentially a measure of the degree to which the returns on a particular project correlate with the returns in the market; it follows that the average beta is unity. From this formula and knowledge of the risk-free interest rate, the required market return, and the project beta, the firm is able to calculate the project's cost of capital.

In the capital budgeting problem for Victor Enterprises analyzed above, the cost of capital was given as 17 percent in U.S. dollars and 26.36 percent in Swiss francs. The underlying calculations were suppressed, but were developed from the Capital Asset Pricing Model. Recall that the risk-free interest rate in the United States is 10 percent and the risk-free interest rate in Switzerland is 18.8 percent for this example, which reflects an 8 percent discrete-time differential. The required market return in U.S. dollars is now assumed to be 15 percent and the required market return in Swiss francs is similarly assumed to be 24.2 percent, which we will discuss shortly, but reflects the same 8 percent discrete-time spread we started with: $(1.15)(1.08) = 1.242$. The beta for the project is assumed to be 1.4, implying that the project is riskier than the average project in the marketplace. Hence, the discrete-time costs of capital are:

$$COC_{t,t+n} = .10 + 1.4[.15 - .10] = .17$$
$$COC^*_{t,t+n} = .188 + 1.4[.242 - .188] = .2636$$

from the Capital Asset Pricing Model. Note that these preserve the same proportional differences between the domestic and foreign costs of capital that prevailed between the domestic and foreign risk-free interest rates: $1.2636/1.17 = 1.188/1.10 = 1.08$. However, note that the risk premia themselves are not exactly the same—$1.4[.15 - .10] = .07$ and $1.4[.242 - .188] = .0756$—but only because this version of the CAPM is actually a discrete-time approximation to a proposition that holds exactly in continuous time.[6]

CALCULATING THE COST OF CAPITAL

The next questions are, of course, how to determine the rate of return required on the market portfolio and how to determine the beta for a specific project. In a perfectly integrated international capital market, the market portfolio of concern is a weighted-average portfolio of all the projects in the world, or a **world market portfolio.** The required market return might then be inferred from the past behavior of an index of all the stocks in the world and current economic conditions (e.g., bond yields). This is merely the international counterpart to the domestic CAPMs often studied in the United States to determine the domestic cost of capital.

Determining the project beta is similarly substantially the same as determining the beta for a domestic project. One idea might be to look at the history of similar projects to assess their risk levels. If the project is of similar risk to the average project the firm selects, another possibility is to estimate beta by unleveraging the stock price beta. One final alternative, of course, is to make a best guess based on management's interpretation of the situation. The twin problems of determining the required market return and the project beta are not substantially different in an integrated international capital market from the problems in determining the required market return and the project beta in a perfect domestic market. We do not therefore take up the topic further here; the interested reader can refer to any textbook on corporate finance.

The essence of this section is that, in an integrated international capital market producing one world market portfolio, differences in the cost of capital across countries reflect only expected exchange rate changes. If this were not the case, international capital flows would drive down the current price of equity in the low-cost-of-capital country (thereby increasing the rate of return) and drive up the current price of equity in the high-cost-of-capital country (decreasing the rate of return) in the manner described in Chapter 1. The resulting equilibrium proposition is clearly a counterpart of the uncovered interest parity theorem applied to the cost of capital rather than to interest rates; for this reason we earlier referred to the property as cost of capital parity. An expression for cost of capital parity is thus:

$$COC_{t,t+n} - COC^*_{t,t+n} = a\{E_t[\%\Delta S_{t,t+n}]\}$$

where a is again an annualization factor, and the expression is similar to the expression for UIP developed in Chapter 2:

$$R_{t,t+n} - R^*_{t,t+n} = a\{E_t[\%\Delta S_{t,t+n}]\}$$

except that cost of capital parity pertains to costs of capital and uncovered interest parity pertains to interest rates.

Substituting using the CAPM equation, we find:

$$R_{t,t+n} + \beta[R^M_{t,t+n} - R_{t,t+n}] - R^*_{t,t+n} - \beta^*[R^{M*}_{t,t+n} - R^*_{t,t+n}] = a\{E_t[\%\Delta S_{t,t+n}]\}.$$

If uncovered interest parity holds *ex ante* in a perfectly integrated international capital market, we can subtract the UIP identity from the cost of capital parity equation to obtain the result that:

$$\beta[R_{t,t+n}^{M} - R_{t,t+n}] = \beta^*[R_{t,t+n}^{M*} - R_{t,t+n}^*]$$

which demonstrates that the cost is the same in different international capital markets when the project risk premium is the same in the different countries or currencies.

The finding that the project risk premium is the same in both currencies is an intuitively appealing result. The best way to think about this is to regard the market returns, $R_{t,t+n}^{M}$ and $R_{t,t+n}^{M*}$, as the returns on a world market portfolio, simply denominated in different currencies such that:

$$R_{t,t+n}^{M} - R_{t,t+n}^{M*} = a\{E_t[\%\Delta S_{t,t+n}]\}$$

This can be interpreted as an equation for **market returns parity,** or the proposition that the spread between foreign and domestic required market returns reflects expectations of exchange rate changes, which (like cost of capital parity) has also been loosely acknowledged in international finance but does not have an established name. If both UIP and market returns parity hold, subtracting the UIP identity from the market returns parity identity yields:

$$R_{t,t+n}^{M} - R_{t,t+n} = R_{t,t+n}^{M*} - R_{t,t+n}^*$$

in an integrated international capital market. By looking at this and the above result that the risk premium is the same in both currencies,

$$\beta[R_{t,t+n}^{M} - R_{t,t+n}] = \beta^*[R_{t,t+n}^{M*} - R_{t,t+n}^*],$$

we see that $\beta = \beta^*$. In other words, an integrated international capital market implies that the project beta is the same whether using the domestic-currency estimate of the world market returns or the foreign-currency estimate of the world market returns, because the project is evaluated against the same world market portfolio simply denominated in two different currencies.

APPLICATION 3-1

THE JAPANESE ADVANTAGE
IN THE COST OF CAPITAL

During the late 1980s and early 1990s, considerable attention was given to the proposition that the cost of capital in the United States was higher than the cost of capital in Japan, thus putting U.S. corporations at a disadvantage globally. One study by McCauley and Zimmer (1989) estimated that the cost of equity capital in the United States was three to four percentage points higher than the cost of equity capital in Japan over the period 1977 to 1988. A survey by Poterba (1991) points out that researchers have in fact found a lower cost of capital in Japan using a variety of methodologies. Another survey by Frankel (1991) concludes that the cost of capital was lower in Japan throughout the

APPLICATION 3-1 (cont.)

1970s and 1980s, but goes on to suggest that the differential disappeared in the early 1990s.

If there is a cost of capital disparity, a logical question is why the disparity could persist for so long, over two decades. The most popular explanation is that markets are not integrated internationally, so equity capital does not flow easily from low-cost countries into high-cost countries. Japan ended up with a cost of capital advantage because of the high domestic savings rate; the United States is well known to have a low domestic savings rate by comparison. With a large pool of savings, equilibrium interest rates and costs of capital would be lower in Japan. Poterba (1991) suggests that Japanese investors prefer to purchase equity in Japanese companies, even if returns are higher on U.S. equities. One reason for this is that Japa-

nese investors are probably less informed about U.S. equities than they are about Japanese equities. On the corporate side, U.S. firms may face constraints on their ability to issue equity in Japan to take advantage of the lower cost of capital. In fact, "Japanese investors may convey low-cost capital to Japanese firms but not to U.S. firms traded in Tokyo (whose shares are primarily traded and priced in New York)" (p. 27). However, Frankel (1991) suggests that the reason why the cost of capital differential disappeared in the early 1990s was because financial liberalization permitted arbitrage to occur. As foreign corporations have been permitted to borrow capital in Japan, and as Japanese investors have purchased more foreign equities, the costs of capital in the United States and Japan have moved much closer together.

3.4   INTERNATIONAL CAPITAL BUDGETING WITH SEGMENTED CAPITAL MARKETS

Although an integrated international capital market is desirable from a global economic standpoint, and the assumption of international capital market integration is convenient for capital budgeting analysis, there is a high likelihood that international equity markets are in reality nationally segmented. There are sometimes explicit government barriers to cross-border equity flows, and there are nearly always institutional constraints or informational asymmetries. Furthermore, there may be a risk premium associated with foreign exchange risk.

In this section, we therefore look at deviations from cost of capital parity that may occur because of capital market segmentation. This national segmentation of capital markets provides reasons why the centralized and decentralized methods of international capital budgeting may produce different net present values for the same project. The first subsection examines deviations from cost of capital parity that result only from deviations from UIP. Hence, it demonstrates that when bond markets are segmented, so are the equity markets. The second subsection examines deviations that result from differing project risk premia across countries when UIP holds. This second category therefore captures the case of an integrated international bond market but internationally segmented equity markets. The major conclusion from the analysis that follows is that centralized capital budgeting makes more sense than decentralized capital budgeting in a world with capital market segmentation, because the firm's equity capital is likely to come from the home country's equity markets.

EX ANTE DEVIATIONS FROM UNCOVERED INTEREST PARITY

Nominal risk-free interest rates are different across countries not only because of differing inflation rates, but also because deviations from real interest parity of the nature addressed in Chapter 2 may exist that reflect capital market segmentation. The result is that there may be deviations from uncovered interest parity expected *ex ante*. Due to barriers to capital movement or a risk premium on foreign exchange, for example, one currency may be expected to have a higher real return than another, which implies that the forward rate is then a biased predictor of the spot rate. In this situation the firm will want to adjust the capital budgeting analysis to yield different results.

It is important to note that all the firm's equity capital generally comes from the same place: the home country's equity market. Although there are some examples of multinational corporations raising capital outside their home countries, these are relatively rare and are not treated in this section. The implication of firms raising capital abroad is that arbitrage is occurring across equity markets. As the practice becomes more common, the world will move toward a perfectly integrated international capital market, and capital budgeting analysis will focus on the case of an integrated international capital market addressed in the first two sections of this chapter. Hence, the assumption that all capital is raised in a firm's home country is reasonable given the nature of market segmentation; when the assumption is not true, markets become completely integrated and the analysis in this section is irrelevant.

It is already becoming clear that a firm should use centralized capital budgeting to evaluate a foreign project because it needs to repay capital, with appropriate returns, in the currency of the market which is supplying the capital. The cost of capital for the firm undertaking the project is clearly determined in the domestic capital market, and this is therefore the relevant discount rate on the project. If the foreign project is expected to adequately compensate the owners of capital, it should be undertaken. The opposite, of course, is also true: If the foreign project is not expected to adequately compensate the owners of capital, it should not be undertaken.

In implementing the centralized capital budgeting method, *ex ante* deviations from UIP must be taken into account in the exchange rate forecast. If there is an interest premium on the foreign currency, the implication of centralized capital budgeting is that the multinational firm does not need to include the interest premium in capital budgeting decisions. This means that the firm is taking advantage of profitable deviations from UIP. Similarly, however, if there is an interest discount on the foreign currency, the firm must not include the interest discount in capital budgeting because it needs to compensate investors in the high-interest-rate country (the home country) who are supplying the capital.

Continuing our previously cited capital budgeting example for Victor Enterprises for *ex ante* deviations from UIP, assume that the Swiss franc interest rate contains a premium. Of the 18.8 percent interest rate, suppose that 2.8 percentage points represents the risk premium, such that the interest rate without the premium would be 16 percent. This means that the market does not expect the Swiss franc to depreciate as much as the interest rate differential suggests. The modified exchange rate forecasts would therefore reflect the difference between interest rates of 10 percent in the United States and 16 percent in Switzerland as follows:

Year	Expected Exchange Rate
0	0.80
1	$0.80\,[1.10/1.16] = .7586$
2	$0.80\,[1.10/1.16]^2 = .7194$
3	$0.80\,[1.10/1.16]^3 = .6822$

These rates are higher than what was previously forecast, reflecting expectations of a more valuable Swiss franc. Using centralized capital budgeting, the value of the project is determined to be:

$$PV = (-20{,}000{,}000)(.80) + (10{,}000{,}000)(.7586)/1.17$$
$$+ (12{,}000{,}000)(.7194)/1.17^2 + (15{,}000{,}000)(.6822)/1.17^3$$
$$= \$3{,}179{,}322$$

and this is higher than \$2,291,320 by \$888,002. The conclusion here is that, if the U.S. firm is centralizing capital budgeting and is prepared to take advantage of deviations from UIP, the Swiss project will be worth more. Because Victor Enterprises is headquartered in a low-interest-rate country, it has a cost of capital advantage.

We can conclude from this example that, if there are *ex ante* deviations from uncovered interest parity such that the foreign currency carries a higher interest rate than the home currency, a company centralizing capital budgeting will accept more projects abroad than it would if UIP held *ex ante*. A company would behave in this fashion because the profitable deviations from UIP are incorporated into the exchange rate forecast under the centralized capital budgeting method. Similarly, if the foreign currency carries a lower interest rate than the home currency, a company centralizing capital budgeting will accept fewer projects abroad than it would if UIP held, because the unprofitable deviations from UIP are incorporated into the exchange rate forecast under the centralized capital budgeting method.

Note that the preference here is to adjust the expected future spot exchange rate in centralized capital budgeting rather than to adjust the cost of capital in the decentralized counterpart. Local managers are familiar with the local environment and see risk-free nominal interest rates and local risk premia on projects. They do not find it obvious to adjust the cost of capital to reflect deviations from UIP vis-à-vis the home country. Any adjustment would therefore be fairly abstract, and may confuse the analysts rather than aid them.

If the managers or owners of a firm are sufficiently risk averse, they may consider hedging the cash flows associated with the foreign project if this is possible. Although we examine hedging in Part III, we point out here that in this case the forward rates are the relevant future spot exchange rates for the firm. Any deviations from uncovered interest parity become irrelevant because covered interest parity is the appropriate benchmark. The analysis reverts to the case of a hedged project as addressed in the section on capital market integration on page 110, and the method of capital budgeting used therefore becomes unimportant. If the foreign currency is associated with an interest premium, the company is not exploiting profitable deviations from UIP. Conversely, if the foreign currency is associated with an interest discount, the company is spared the additional cost of unprofitable deviations from UIP. This is, in fact, the inducement to locate the relatively high-cost domestic capital in the foreign country.

THE EXCHANGE RISK THEORY OF DFI

One theory explaining direct foreign investment (DFI) is Aliber's (1970) exchange risk theory. The main idea is that exchange rate changes which alter the domestic currency value of a foreign investment create a home bias in portfolio investment and intermediated investment by risk-averse investors. As a result, portfolio investors and financial intermediaries who manage capital require a premium on interest rates and returns in countries with certain weak or volatile currencies to invest there. In other words, they need compensation to overcome their home bias. Real interest parity and uncovered interest parity therefore do not hold when left up to portfolio investors and financial intermediaries. In this situation, flows of portfolio and intermediated investment are inadequate, so further investment opportunities exist for DFI. The door to the country is thus left open for direct investment to seek higher returns abroad as a substitute for portfolio investment and intermediated investment in the presence of exchange risk. With DFI, the investor maintains management control of the enterprise and can structure operations to reduce the risks from currency fluctuations. This means that direct foreign investments do not require as great a premium for holding exchange risk as otherwise similar intermediated investments or portfolio investments. With intermediated and portfolio investment, there is no ability to structure operations to reduce the risks from currency fluctuations, and the investment is therefore exposed to more exchange risk.

With knowledge of capital budgeting techniques, an example can be developed to show the ownership implications of the exchange risk theory. Consider the project in Switzerland that we examined in the case of *ex ante* deviations from uncovered interest parity. Further, assume that the evaluation of the cash flows is the same regardless of the firm or nationality of the firm valuing the project; this puts all the emphasis on the denominator in the present value calculation. Because the exchange risk premium results in deviations from uncovered interest parity, firms located in the two countries have different costs of capital and will therefore calculate different present values.

Suppose the project is being auctioned to the highest bidder and the U.S. firm is competing against a Swiss firm in the bidding. How much is the U.S. firm willing to pay for the project? If it centralizes capital budgeting, it is willing to pay the $3,179,322 previously calculated, which is equivalent to SFr 3,974,153, because the U.S. firm enjoys a relatively low cost of capital. How much is the Swiss firm willing to pay for the same project? The answer is the SFr 2,864,150 calculated earlier, because it must use the higher Swiss cost of capital. The U.S. firm centralizing capital budgeting is therefore willing to bid more for the project than the Swiss firm, and will end up owning the project.

In this example, the U.S. firm has a cost of capital advantage because the Swiss franc interest rate contains an exchange risk premium. Capital will therefore flow from the low cost-of-capital country into the high cost-of-capital country, but only in the form of DFI rather than as portfolio or intermediated investment.

DIFFERING PROJECT RISK PREMIA

In the analysis of *ex ante* deviations from UIP in the subsection above, the market portfolio is still taken to be a world market portfolio (with returns simply expressed in different currencies) and the domestic and foreign betas are still identical. This means that the project risk premium over the risk-free interest rate is the same in both currencies. A generalization of deviations from cost of capital parity, however, logically incorporates market segmentation that allows the required return on the market portfolio and the project beta to differ across countries. In fact, even if UIP holds in international capital markets, cost of capital parity will be violated if the required market return and the project beta are different across countries. These conditions effectively allow bond markets and intermediated markets to be integrated and conform to UIP while simultaneously allowing segmentation of equity markets.

Because all of a firm's capital comes from its home country's equity markets, cost of capital analysis in the presence of segmented equity markets requires U.S. firms to use a U.S. market index, thereby again imposing centralized capital budgeting. Similarly, Swiss firms would use a Swiss market index, thereby imposing centralization on them as well. Returns market parity is likely to be violated in segmented capital markets, although it may not be violated if both markets are driven by similar exogenous events. The beta for the project will therefore most likely be different across countries, depending on how the project's returns covary with the returns on the different market portfolios. It would not be appropriate to let the U.S. firms determine the project risk premium by using the Swiss market index, because the U.S. firms raise equity capital in the United States and this equity is priced vis-à-vis other U.S. issues. Hence, an additional reason explaining international ownership patterns arises from the differing project risk premia that firms from different countries assign to the same project.

To continue the example of Victor Enterprises' project in Switzerland, now assume that UIP holds *ex ante* but that cost of capital parity is still violated. If this is the case, the project risk premium must be different across countries. The risk-free interest rate in the United States is still 10 percent and the risk-free interest rate in Switzerland is still 18.8 percent as before. With equity market segmentation, the U.S. firm evaluates the foreign project risk premium in centralized capital budgeting with respect to the U.S. stock market. We now assume that the required rate of return on the U.S. market portfolio is 14 percent rather than the 15 percent considered earlier. Hence, the U.S. is a lower cost of capital country on average. The capital budgeting department estimates that the beta for the project vis-à-vis the U.S. stock market is 1.2 rather than the 1.4 considered earlier. For example, perhaps the project is still considered riskier than the average project being undertaken, but serves to diversify the U.S. market portfolio better than it diversifies the world market portfolio because it is undertaken in Switzerland rather than the United States. Thus, the cost of capital is lower than the 17 percent considered earlier:

$$COC_{t,t+n} = .10 + 1.2[.14 - .10] = .148$$

or 14.8 percent. Using this in the present value calculation yields a net present value of:

$$
\begin{aligned}
PV = & (-20,000,000)(.80) + (10,000,000)(.7407)/1.148 \\
& + (12,000,000)(.6859)/1.148^2 + (15,000,000)(.6351)/1.148^3 \\
= & \ \$2,993,837
\end{aligned}
$$

which is higher than $2,291,320 because the firm clearly has a lower cost of capital.

The alternative method of evaluating this project, decentralized capital budgeting, would be to evaluate the risk premium with respect to the Swiss stock market. We now assume that the Swiss market has a required return of 25 percent in Swiss francs, rather than the 24.2 percent considered earlier, so Switzerland is a high cost of capital country on average. Assume that the beta for the project vis-à-vis the Swiss stock market is 1.6 rather than the 1.4 considered earlier. For example, the project is still considered riskier than average and does not diversify the Swiss market portfolio very well because it is like many other projects in Switzerland. Thus, the cost of capital is higher than the 26.36 percent considered earlier:

$$COC^*_{t,t+n} = .188 + 1.6[.25 - .188] = .2872$$

and this yields a net present value of:

$$PV = 0.80[-20,000,000 + 10,000,000/1.2872$$
$$+ 12,000,000/1.2872^2 + 15,000,000/1.2872^3]$$
$$= \$1,635,612$$

which is lower than $2,291,320 because the firm has a higher Swiss franc cost of capital. As all the capital of the U.S. firm is raised in America, the centralized capital budgeting method illustrated in the paragraph above is the sensible one to use. Decentralized capital budgeting is not sensible if there are differing project risk premia required across countries, but is provided here for purposes of comparison. Indeed, the 28.72 percent cost of capital is appropriate for a Swiss firm.

APPLICATION 3-3

INTERNATIONAL CAPITAL MARKET INTEGRATION AND THE COST OF CAPITAL AT NESTLÉ

In a world of segmented capital markets converging toward global integration, a firm needs to evaluate its cost of capital against the appropriate benchmark. Stulz (1995) points out that globalization of capital markets is most likely lowering the cost of capital because the risk of a security can be shared among more investors. The Swiss multinational corporation Nestlé, for example, apparently faces a lower cost of capital when shares of the firm are evaluated against a world market portfolio than when shares are evaluated against the Swiss stock market.

According to Stulz (1995), beta estimates for Nestlé using the Swiss stock market as the relevant market portfolio are approximately 0.90. The average return on the Swiss stock market (from 1925 to 1993) was 9.8 percent and the average return on Swiss bonds (over the same period) was 4.5 percent. Hence, Nestlé's cost of capital is:

$$4.5 + 0.90(9.8 - 4.5) \approx 9.2\%.$$

Note that the equity premium—the required rate of return on the market portfolio in excess of the risk-free return—is 5.3 percent.

Evaluated against world market portfolios, however, beta estimates for Nestlé are appproximately 0.60, or just two-thirds of the beta evaluated against the Swiss market. Assuming that the required equity premium is 5.4 percent, slightly more than the equity premium on the Swiss stock market (for extensive discussion of this, see Stulz, 1995, pp. 36–37), Nestlés cost of capital is:

$$4.5 + 0.60(5.4) \approx 7.7\%,$$

which is 1.5 percentage points below the cost of capital estimated using the Swiss CAPM. As Stulz (1995) says (p. 30), "If an overseas company's stock price has a much weaker correlation with worldwide stocks than with its own domestic market, the firm may be significantly overstating its own cost of capital (and thus undervaluing its shares)."

APPLICATION 3-3 (cont.)

The effect of globalization on Nestlé's cost of capital is additionally interesting because Nestlé has liberalized its policy regarding ownership of shares. Nestlé previously had a class of shares restricted to ownership by Swiss nationals and a class of shares not restricted to Swiss ownership which were therefore globally held. The unrestricted shares traded at nearly twice the price of the restricted shares, implying that the cost of capital for shares restricted to Swiss investors exceeded the cost of capital for the unrestricted shares. Stulz (1995) estimates that when the cost of capital on the unrestricted shares was 10 percent, the cost of capital on the restricted shares was 18 percent. In 1988, Nestlé removed the restrictions on foreign ownership of its Swiss shares. The prices of the two classes of shares nearly converged through adjustment which led the value of the formerly restricted shares to increase by 36 percent and that of the unrestricted shares to decrease 25 percent. Stulz (1995) reports that the "net effect on the total equity capitalization of Nestlé was an increase of 10% which is consistent with a significant decrease in its overall costs of capital (p. 33)." (For more on the removal of ownership restrictions on Nestlé's Swiss shares, also see Loderer and Jacobs, 1995.)

Source: Rene M. Stulz, "Globalization of Capital Markets and the Cost of Capital: The Case of Nestlé," *Bank of America Journal of Applied Corporate Finance,* Fall 1995, pp. 30–38.

Once again, sufficiently risk averse owners or managers will consider hedging the cash flows on the foreign project. If UIP holds, there will be no effect on the capital budgeting problem because the values of expected future spot exchange rates will be unaltered, and, of course, there is no reason to alter the cost of capital. In this case, even risk aversion will not prevent equity capital from flowing from the low-cost-of-capital country to the high-cost-of-capital country.

APPLICATION 3-4

BETAS OF FOREIGN PROJECTS COMPARED TO BETAS OF DOMESTIC PROJECTS

The issue of differing betas as a result of comparing a project to different (i.e., domestic and foreign) market indexes raises a related question from a purely domestic standpoint: how do betas on foreign projects compare to betas on domestic projects? This question is relevant for MNCs choosing between two locations—one domestic and one foreign—for a specific project. On one hand, the additional risks of foreign projects may be interpreted as undiversifiable and therefore raise the systematic risk (which is explained more thoroughly in what follows), suggesting that the beta on a foreign project is greater than the beta on an otherwise similar domestic project, $\beta^F > \beta^D$. On the other hand, foreign projects may now diversify previously undiversifiable systematic risk and therefore reduce it, suggesting $\beta^F < \beta^D$.

Bartov, Bodner, and Kaul (1996) recently examined the effect of exchange risk on MNCs' stocks using the breakdown of the Bretton-Woods fixed-exchange-rate system as a natural experiment. They show that the increase in exchange rate

APPLICATION 3-4 (cont.)

volatility caused by the breakdown of Bretton-Woods was accompanied by increases in total and systematic risk of all stocks, but particularly for stocks of MNCs. Their explanation is that the additional foreign exchange risk significantly increased the total risk of MNCs' stocks, and that the foreign exchange risk was perceived, at least partially, as undiversifiable. They cite previous literature that reports a positive correlation between dollar risk premia on money market investments in foreign currencies and the risk premium on the U.S. equity market as supporting evidence.

The results in Bartov, Bodner, and Kaul (1996) are striking because the traditional literature emphasizes the benefits of multinational diversification in reducing risk. This literature suggests that MNC stocks should be less correlated with the domestic market portfolio and therefore diversify

previously undiversifiable systematic risk. For example, Fatemi (1984) reports lower standard deviations of monthly returns for MNCs than for DCs, together with lower betas. In an examination of MNCs, Agmon and Lessard (1977) demonstrate that the degree of multinationality is important because the returns of firms with proportionately more sales from foreign operations are less correlated with domestic market returns and are more correlated with foreign market returns.

Hence, there is no clear answer in the literature to tell us whether $\beta^F > \beta^D$ or $\beta^F < \beta^D$. The answer might depend on the specific project being considered, and possibly on the specific firm undertaking the project. As the literature does not currently provide a definitive answer, managers are required once again to exercise their judgment in selecting the relevant beta for the project analysis.

3.5   INTERNATIONAL CAPITAL BUDGETING AND FOREIGN EXCHANGE EXPOSURE

An additional reason for a difference in the present values calculated using the centralized and decentralized capital budgeting techniques for the same project arises when the local currency cash flows depend on the level of the exchange rate, a phenomenon known as **foreign exchange exposure.** In decentralized capital budgeting, the local currency cash flows are forecast and discounted without explicit consideration of the exchange rate. In fact, the only exchange rate needed is the spot exchange rate applied to the local currency present value at the end of the analysis. Hence, decentralized capital budgeting implicitly overlooks the dependence of local cash flows on the exchange rate.

In centralized capital budgeting, home currency cash flows are forecast, which requires forecasts of the local currency cash flows and the future exchange rates together. This means that any dependence of local currency cash flows on the exchange rate, known as covariation between the local currency cash flows and the future exchange rates, can be explicitly taken into account. This covariation is called foreign exchange exposure because the cash flows are exposed to exchange rate changes. We introduce this concept here, in the context of international capital budgeting, but discuss it in much greater detail in Chapters 6 and 7.

The issue behind foreign exchange exposure is that local currency cash flows may depend on the level of the exchange rate. Up to now, capital budgeting has considered the simple case in which local currency cash flow projections are independent of exchange rate projections, so $E[CF_t S_t] = E[CF_t] \times E[S_t]$ where CF_t is the local currency cash flow and S_t is the exchange rate. In the presence of foreign exchange exposure, such that local currency cash flows and exchange rates are not independent, the covariation between the cash flows and the exchange rate must be accounted for: $E[CF_t S_t] = E[CF_t] \times E[S_t] + \text{cov}[CF_t, S_t]$. The existence of foreign exchange exposure in a project strengthens the case for centralized capital budgeting because, by centralizing, the firm is implicitly fore-casting home currency cash flows directly, and this provides a more accurate account of the value of the project to the parent.

EXAMPLE 3.1

A U.S. multinational corporation is considering a one-year project in Malta in which goods would be imported from the United States and sold in the local market. In local currency, the cash flow in one year is expected to be 200 thousand lira. Interest rates in the United States and Malta hap-pen to be identical, so the UIP equation suggests that the exchange rate in one year is expected to be the current spot rate of $2.5 per lira. However, the local currency cash flows and the ex-change rate are also expected to be interdependent. If the exchange rate is $2.0 per lira, the lira has depreciated and the firm will sell less, so the cash flow is expected to be 100 thousand lira. If the exchange rate is $3.00 per lira, the lira has appreciated and the firm will sell more, so the cash flow is expected to be 300 thousand lira. The company estimates that the probabilities attached to exchange rates of 2.0, 2.5, and 3.0 are equal (at 1/3). Hence, the expected dollar cash flow is ob-tained by calculating the average after computing the dollar cash flows under each scenario: $(1/3)(2 \times 100 + 2.5 \times 200 + 3 \times 300) = \$533.33$ thousand. In this case, covariance of the cash flows and exchange rates if $33.33 thousand and the expected dollar cash flow from the project can also be calculated as $E[CF_t S_t] = E[CF_t] \times E[S_t] + \text{cov}[CF_t, S_t] = 200 \times 2.53 + 3.33 = \$533.33$ thousand. Note that this is greater than $E[CF_t] \times E[S_t]$ due to the foreign exchange exposure, so the project will look more valuable from the viewpoint of centralized capital budgeting than from decentral-ized capital budgeting. If the cost of capital in both the dollar and the lira is 10 percent, the pres-ent value of the project based on centralization is $533.33/1.1 = \$484.85$ thousand and the present value of the project based on decentralization is $[200/1.1] \times 2.5 = \$454.55$ thousand. Because of the nature of the exposure, the project is more valuable to the parent than it looks on its own.

APPLICATION 3-5

INTERNATIONAL CAPITAL ASSET PRICING MODELS

Extensions of the Capital Asset Pricing Model (CAPM) to include not only covariance of project returns with world market returns but also covari-ance of project returns with exchange rate changes are currently being developed as International Capital Asset Pricing Models (ICAPM); for intro-ductions, see Adler and Dumas (1983) and Dumas (1994). Although there are several forms of the ICAPM, they all suggest that projects face both systematic market risk and foreign exchange risk, and that both risks are compensated by premia in an integrated international capital market. With these two factors, calculation of the cost of capital for a project requires knowledge of the project's beta with respect to a world market portfolio (β)

and its sensitivity to exchange rate changes, which we denote δ:

$$COC_{t,t+n} = R_{t,t+n} + \beta[R_{t,t+n}^M - R_{t,t+n}] + \delta\{E[\%\Delta S_{t,t+n}]\}$$

where $\delta\{E[\%\Delta S_{t,t+n}]\}$ is the exchange risk pre-mium. Some alternative formulations specify $\delta\{E[\%\Delta S_{t,t+n}] - R_{t,t+n}\}$ or $\delta\{R_{t,t+n}^* + E[\%\Delta S_{t,t+n}] - R_{t,t+n}\}$ as the exchange risk premium.

The discussion of the cost of capital in the chapter implicitly assumes that $\delta = 0$. If $\delta \neq 0$ and $E[\%\Delta S_{t,t+n}] \neq 0$, the cost of capital must be altered from the simpler CAPM calculation covered in the chapter to include the exchange risk premium. For

APPLICATION 3-5 (cont.)

example, O'Brien and Dolde (2000) estimate the cost of capital for Grand Metropolitan PLC, the British company often referred to as GrandMet. Using data for the period April 1991 through March 1997, they estimate that $\beta = 1.1017$ for GrandMet returns measured in U.S. dollars against a world market portfolio (also measured in U.S. dollars). They assume that $[R_{t,t+n}^M - R_{t,t+n}] = 5.40$ percent based on previous research. They also estimate, using data for the same period, that $\delta = -0.1182$ and $R_{t,t+n}^* + E[\%\Delta S_{t,t+n}] - R_{t,t+n} = -1.57$ percent. Note that O'Brien and Dolde (2000) use the expected deviation from uncovered interest parity as the relevant benchmark of the exchange risk. The implication of the negative δ is that the rate of return in U.S. dollars on currency deposits is expected to be lower than the U.S. dollar risk-free rate due to expected appreciation of the U.S. dollar and/or lower interest rates on the currency deposits. The deviation from UIP of -1.57 implies that the U.S. dollar is expected to appreciate (so foreign currencies are expected to depreciate) by 1.57 percent more than the interest differential suggests. The Eurodollar interest rate in April 1997 was 5.625 percent, which is taken to be the nominal risk-free interest rate, $R_{t,t+n}$. Hence,

the cost of capital denominated in U.S. dollars for GrandMet is:

$$
\begin{aligned}
COC_{t,t+n} &= R_{t,t+n} + \beta[R_{t,t+n}^M - R_{t,t+n}] \\
&\quad + \delta\{R_{t,t+n}^* + E[\%\Delta S_{t,t+n}] - R_{t,t+n}\} \\
&= 5.625 + 1.1017[5.40] \\
&\quad - 0.1182[-1.57] = 11.76\%.
\end{aligned}
$$

This cost of capital should therefore be used when taking the present value of a project in which the cash flows are denominated in U.S. dollars, such as when GrandMet is evaluating a new project in the United States that is substantially similar to its other projects worldwide.

Empirical studies of the ICAPM have estimated magnitudes of δ. One study by Jorion (1991) finds that, in a version of the simple ICAPM specified above, δ is not statistically significantly different from zero for a large sample of U.S. stock market data. The conclusion here is that exchange risk is diversifiable and thus not priced in aggregate in the stock market. However, another study by Dumas and Solnik (1995) rejects the hypothesis that δ is zero for a sample of data from the United States, United Kingdom, Germany, and Japan. Once again, then, managers must make judgments with respect to their specific projects.

3.6   DIVERSIFICATION OF PROJECTS

Occasionally, managers consider capital projects vis-à-vis the other projects a firm undertakes in an attempt to make the firm itself well diversified. The treatment of capital budgeting in this chapter has presented the modern finance approach in which the value of the project depends only on the returns from the project itself and how they covary with the returns on the market. The other projects undertaken by the firm are specifically not considered in the capital budgeting process.

In a broader context, in which diversification is beneficial because it reduces the costs of bankruptcy and preserves access to capital markets, the firm may want to consider a new project vis-à-vis the other projects it is undertaking. A portfolio of diverse projects is likely to be less risky than a portfolio of similar projects, as illustrated in Chapter 1. In this instance, diversification reinforces the benefits of centralized capital budgeting because of the desire to have projects in many currencies and many countries as long as the returns are not perfectly correlated. The capital budgeting decision would involve an analysis of cash flows for the company as a whole, and consideration of the returns and risks together would suggest that the firm will want to perform mean-variance optimization on its portfolio of projects. This is not a central topic in capital budgeting, however, and because the issue of diversification (and mean-variance optimization) is adequately considered elsewhere, we do not discuss the topic further in this chapter. We will return to some elements of this, however, when we consider risk management in Chapter 10.

3.7   ASSESSMENT OF INTERNATIONAL CAPITAL BUDGETING

In this chapter, we have presented an introduction to international capital budgeting and issues related to the cost of capital. In assuming familiarity with domestic capital budgeting, many technical issues related to forecasting cash flows have not been fully developed. In addition, many accounting issues have also been inadequately developed. By minimizing the treatment of these, however, we have been able to focus on issues pertaining to exchange rates and international costs of capital. For additional treatment of these and other issues, the reader may want to consult Eiteman (1991).

In many ways, international capital budgeting is more art than science. This is certainly true for estimating cash flows associated with a project. The centralization-versus-decentralization framework of capital budgeting presented here for analyzing the cash flows once they are estimated makes the rest of the analysis look easier. For an integrated global capital market, the analysis is straightforward and internally consistent. As a result, it is intuitively appealing. There are considerable doubts, however, that national equity markets are perfectly integrated. The framework is nonetheless useful as a benchmark, and is probably appropriate for most corporate capital budgeting decisions, at least as an approximation.

In the presence of nationally segmented capital markets, international capital budgeting becomes even more of an art than a science. With capital market segmentation, either because UIP does not hold *ex ante* or because the risk premium required for a project depends on who supplies the capital, there are several subtle revisions to the theory that mean only centralized capital budgeting makes sense. This is because the capital basically comes from the home country, and returns on projects must satisfy the home-country capital owners. The imperfections in equity capital markets represent an underdeveloped area of study in international finance at this point, although interest in international differences in the cost of capital is growing. At some future date, more definite conclusions on international capital budgeting may be available.

❖ SUMMARY OF CHAPTER OBJECTIVES

1. Value a foreign project using two methods of international capital budgeting.

There are two methods of evaluating a foreign project. The decentralized approach discounts local currency cash flows at the foreign cost of capital and then converts the net present value into home currency units at the prevailing spot rate. The centralized approach converts all local currency cash flows into the home currency, then discounts them at the home cost of capital.

2. Calculate the cost of capital for a foreign project and explain cost of capital parity.

The cost of capital for a foreign project is calculated from the Capital Asset Pricing Model. The domestic cost of capital uses domestic risk-free interest rates and a domestic market portfolio as benchmarks, while the foreign cost of capital uses foreign risk-free interest rates and a foreign market portfolio as benchmarks. With perfect integration of global capital markets, cost of capital parity implies that the difference between the domestic cost of capital and the foreign cost of capital exactly represents the expected percentage change in the exchange rate.

3. Value a foreign project in the presence of segmented capital markets.

When capital markets are segmented, cost of capital parity does not hold and centralized capital budgeting is preferred because it ensures that the foreign projects have returns which adequately compensate the domestic shareholders. Two types of capital market segmentation result in deviations from cost of capital parity: *ex ante* deviations from uncovered interest parity and differing project risk premia on foreign projects.

4. Explain the concept of foreign exchange exposure and how exposure affects international capital budgeting.

Foreign exchange exposure arises when local currency cash flows depend on the level of the exchange rate. When foreign exchange exposure is associated with a foreign project, the project should be evaluated using the centralized capital budgeting technique to properly account for the covariation between the local cash flows and the exchange rate in determining the home currency value of the cash flows.

5. Understand how projects relate to one another and affect the firm's overall risk.

To determine the value of a foreign project, it is not necessary to consider how the project interacts with other projects the firm undertakes. However, a firm may want to consider a new project vis-a-vis other projects when it is concerned with its degree of diversification, a topic which is taken up later in the book.

❖ QUESTIONS FOR REVIEW

1. [Class discussion] What is meant by the terms "centralized" and "decentralized" when applied to capital budgeting? Why might centralized and decentralized analyses of the same project lead to different net present values?
2. [Class discussion] What might lead companies in one country to have a lower cost of capital than similar companies in another?
3. GWU Associates is considering a one-year project in London. The project has an initial investment cost of $1 million and a net cash inflow of £800,000 in the next year. The cash inflow is an incremental cash flow net of income taxes at a 35 percent rate. The spot exchange rate is 1.5 $/£, and the interest rate on one-year government bonds is 10 percent in the United States and 8 percent in the United Kingdom. The required rate of return on the market portfolio is known to be 16 percent in the United States and 15 percent in the United Kingdom. An investment bank estimates that the project has a beta of 0.80 vis-à-vis the U.S. market portfolio and a beta of 0.70 vis-à-vis the U.K. market portfolio.

   a. If the project is analyzed using the decentralized capital budgeting technique, what is the net present value?

   b. If the project is analyzed using the centralized capital budgeting technique, what is the net present value?

4. A U.S. multinational corporation is considering a one-year project in Ruthenia. In local currency, the cash flow in one year is expected to be 1,000 pesos. The uncovered interest parity equation suggests that the exchange rate will be $2 per peso. However, the local currency cash flows and the exchange rate are also expected to be interdependent. If the exchange rate is $1.5 per peso, the cash flow is expected to be 1,500 pesos. If the exchange rate is $2.5 per peso, the cash flow is expected to be 500 pesos.

   a. If the probabilities of the exchange rates of $1.5, $2.0, and $2.5 per peso are 1/3 each, what is the expected dollar cash flow from the project?

   b. If the probabilities of the exchange rates of $1.5, $2.0, and $2.5 per peso are 1/3 each, what is the covariance between the cash flows and the exchange rates? (Be sure to include units in your answer.)

5. What is the present value (in U.S. dollars) of a project in Papua New Guinea which requires an initial investment of 100 million kina (the currency of Papua New Guinea, currently at US$1.2/kina) this year and is expected to have 75 million kina in cash flows next year and 150 million kina in cash flows in two years? Your bosses have told you to evaluate the project assuming that the risk-free interest rate in Papua New Guinea is 15 percent , that the required return on the market portfolio in Papua New Guinea is 22 percent, and that the beta of the project is 1.1.

6. What is the present value (in U.S. dollars) of a project in the Philippines which requires an initial investment of 500 million pesos (the currency of the Philippines, currently at US$0.04/peso) this year and is expected to have 250 million pesos in cash flows next year and 350 million pesos in cash flows in two years? Your bosses have told you to evaluate the project assuming that the risk-free interest rate in the United States is 5 percent, that the risk-free interest rate in the Philippines is 12 percent, that the required return on the market portfolio in the United States is 15 percent, and that the beta of the project is 1.1.

7. A U.S. multinational corporation is considering a new project in Poland which requires an initial investment of 700 million zloty. The project is expected to have profits of 400 million zloty in the first year of operations and 600 million zloty in the second year of operations. The current exchange rate is $0.35/zloty. The risk-free interest rate in the United States is 4 percent and the risk-free interest rate in Poland is 11 percent. The multinational thinks that the required rate of return on the market portfolio in the United States is 10 percent, and estimates that the project beta is about 0.90. There is no information on the required rate of return in Poland.

   a. What is the all-equity cost of capital you are able to calculate for this project? Does this require you to evaluate the project using the centralized or decentralized technique?

   b. What is the present value of the project?

8. A U.S. multinational company is considering a new project in Germany which requires an initial outlay of 3 million DM and generates 2 million DM in the first year of operations and 2 million DM in the second year of operations. The project would then be terminated without any salvage value. The current spot exchange rate is $0.60/DM. The risk-free interest rate in the United States is 7 percent and the risk-free interest rate in Germany is 4 percent. The managers of the multinational

consult German investment bankers who think that the required rate of return on the German market portfolio is 10 percent and that the project under consideration has a beta of about 1.1 with respect to the German market portfolio.

a. What is the all-equity cost of capital you are able to calculate for this project? Does this require you to evaluate the project using the centralized or decentralized technique?

b. What is the present value of the project?

9. A U.S. multinational corporation is considering a new project in Mexico. The project requires an initial investment of 800 million pesos. The project is expected to have profits of 400 million pesos in the first year of operations and 600 million pesos in the second year of operations. The current exchange rate is 8 pesos per U.S. dollar, or $0.125/peso. The risk-free interest rate in the United States is 4 percent and the risk-free interest rate in Mexico is 12 percent. The multinational thinks that the required rate of return on the market portfolio in the United States is 10 percent, and estimates that the project beta is about 0.90. The company has no information on the required rate of return in Mexico. The firm is able to borrow in the United States at an interest rate of 6 percent, and is able to borrow in Mexico at an interest rate of 15 percent.

a. What is the all-equity cost of capital you are able to calculate for this project? Does this require you to evaluate the project using the centralized or decentralized technique?

b. What is the present value of the project?

10. Coval Enterprises, a U.S. multinational corporation, is considering a new project in Germany. The project requires an initial investment of 2 million DM. The project is expected to have profits of 1.5 million DM in the first year of operations and 2.5 million DM in the second year of operations. The current exchange rate is $0.50/DM. The risk-free interest rate in the United States is 6 percent and the risk-free interest rate in Germany is 3 percent. The president of Coval Enterprises estimates that the required rate of return on the market portfolio in the United States is 12.36 percent, and that the required rate of return on the market portfolio in Germany is 9.18 percent. The president also estimates that the project beta is about 0.90, valued against either the U.S. or the German market.

a. What is the present value of the project if evaluated using the decentralized method of international capital budgeting?

b. What is the present value of the project if evaluated using the centralized method of international capital budgeting?

11. Extended exercise [Group project]: Polydemic-Canada's capital budgeting

You are the chief financial officer of Polydemic Enterprises, a U.S. multinational with operations spread throughout the world. You have the opportunity to undertake a five-year investment in Canada with the following projected cash flows:

REVENUE

1. Sales volume for the first year is estimated to be 200,000 units, and the selling price will be C$150.

2. Sales growth of 10 percent per year is expected for the following four years, and an annual price increase of 5 percent is expected.

COSTS

1. Local material and labor costs are expected to be C$40 per unit, with an annual rate of increase of 5 percent for the following four years.

2. Manufacturing overhead (excluding depreciation) is expected to be C$9 million for the first year of operation, and an annual rate of increase of 2 percent is expected for the following four years.

3. Selling and administrative costs are expected to be 10 percent of annual sales.

4. The parent company will levy a licensing fee of C$1 million the first year, and will raise the fee 10 percent per year.

5. Polydemic's effective marginal tax rate is 34 percent, which is the rate used in analyzing investment projects (assuming that the parent can take appropriate credits for taxes paid to the Canadian government).

Your assignment is to prepare a report to the board of directors that analyzes this project.

a. What are the net cash flows in each year?

b. The nominal risk-free interest rate in the United States is 10 percent. The nominal risk-free interest rate in Canada is 15.5 percent. Assume that the term structure of interest rates in both countries is flat. The Canadian dollar/U.S. dollar exchange rate is currently C$1 = US$0.75. There are well-developed financial markets for the Canadian dollar so a variety of forward contracts is readily available. Using the information given, what are the forward rates being quoted for the next five years?

c. The required return on the market portfolio of investment projects in the United States is 16 percent and in Canada is 21.8 percent. The capital budgeting department tells you that the beta for this project is probably 1.2. What is the all-equity cost of capital for this project in each country? How did the capital budgeting department arrive at the beta for this project?

d. You are now ready to assess the present value of the project in U.S. dollars. Start by assuming that all cash flows occur at the end of the year. Evaluate the project first using the decentralized method. Next evaluate the project using the centralized method, where the forward rates are considered unbiased predictors of future spot rates. How do your two answers compare? Should you undertake the project?

e. When you call your banker to arrange financing, he mentions that the forward rate is not an unbiased predictor of future spot rates. In his thirty years of banking, he has noticed that the uncovered interest parity hypothesis does not tend to hold between the United States and Canada. He thinks there is a premium of about two percentage points associated with the Canadian dollar. You now wish to reconsider the project. If the risk premium is taken to be two percentage points, what are the expected future spot exchange rates? Reevaluate the project using the centralized method and the new estimates of future spot rates. Compare the evaluations of the project using the decentralized method and the centralized method. Which method should you use?

❖ ENDNOTES

1. This chapter assumes that the reader is already familiar with domestic capital budgeting. The methodology of capital budgeting is covered in standard corporate finance textbooks, such as Grinblatt and Titman (1998), Chapters 9–12.

2. If this is not the case, then $(1 + COC^*)^t$ would be replaced with $\Pi_{i=0}^{t}(1 + COC_i^*)$.

3. Recall that $E[CF_t S_t] \neq E[CF_t] \times E[S_t]$ unless CF_t and S_t are independent. In this case, the firm will want to forecast home currency cash flows directly, and this is described later in the chapter.

4. One additional benefit of this is that, as there is no uncertainty about forward exchange rates,

any covariance between expected local currency cash flows and expected exchange rates is irrelevant and can properly be ignored.

5. For an introduction to the Capital Asset Pricing Model, see, for example, Grinblatt and Titman (1998), Chapter 5.

6. Converted into continuous time, the risk premia are identical:

$$1.4[\ln 1.15 - \ln 1.10] = 1.4[\ln 1.242 - \ln 1.188]$$
$$= .06223.$$

Furthermore, the costs of capital would be:

$$COC_{t,t+n} = \ln 1.10 + .06223 = .1575$$

and

$$COC_{t,t+n}^* = \ln 1.188 + .06223 = .2345.$$

❖ REFERENCES

Adler, Michael, and Bernard Dumas. "International Portfolio Choice and Corporation Finance: A Synthesis," *Journal of Finance,* 1983, pp. 925–984.

Agmon, Tamir, and Donald R. Lessard. "Investor Recognition of Corporate International Diversification," *Journal of Finance,* 1977, pp. 1049–1055.

Aliber, Robert Z. "A Theory of Direct Foreign Investment," in *The International Corporation: A Symposium,* ed. by C. P. Kindleberger, M.I.T. Press, 1970, pp. 17–34.

Bartov, Eli, Gordon M. Bodnar, and Aditya Kaul. "Exchange Rate Variability and the Riskiness of U.S. Multinational Firms: Evidence from the Breakdown of the Bretton Woods System," *Journal of Financial Economics,* 1996, pp. 105–132.

Buckley, Adrian. *International Capital Budgeting,* Prentice Hall, 1996.

Dumas, Bernard. "Partial Equilibrium versus General Equilibrium Models of the International Capital Market," Chapter 10 of *The Handbook of International Macroeconomics,* edited by Frederick van der Ploeg, Blackwell, 1994, pp. 301–347.

Dumas, Bernard, and Bruno Solnik. "The World Price of Foreign Exchange Risk," *Journal of Finance,* 1995, pp. 445–479.

Eiteman, David K. "Foreign Investment Analysis," *Handbook of International Accounting,* edited by Frederick D.S. Choi, John Wiley & Sons, 1991.

Fatemi, Ali M. "Shareholder Benefits from Corporate International Diversification," *Journal of Finance,* 1984, pp. 1325–1344.

Frankel, Jeffrey A. "The Japanese Cost of Finance: A Survey," *Financial Management,* Spring 1991, pp. 95–127.

Grinblatt, Mark, and Sheridan Titman. *Financial Markets and Corporate Strategy,* Irwin/McGraw-Hill, 1998.

Hekman, Christine R. "Capital Investment and Management in Global Businesses," Chapter 17 of *The Handbook of International Financial Management,* ed. by R. Z. Aliber, Dow Jones-Irwin, 1989, pp. 539–559.

Jorion, Philippe. "The Pricing of Exchange Rate Risk in the Stock Market," *Journal of Financial and Quantitative Analysis,* 1991, pp. 363–376.

Loderer, Claudio, and Andreas Jacobs. "The Nestlé Crash," *Journal of Financial Economics,* 1995, pp. 315–339.

McCauley, Robert N. and Steven A. Zimmer. "Explaining International Differences in the Cost of Capital," *Federal Reserve Bank of New York Quarterly Review,* Summer 1989, pp. 7–28.

O'Brien, Thomas J., and Walter Dolde. "A Currency Index Global Capital Asset Pricing Model," *European Financial Management,* forthcoming 2000.

Poterba, James M. "Comparing the Costs of Capital in the United States and Japan: A Survey of Methods," *Federal Reserve Bank of New York Quarterly Review,* Winter 1991, pp. 20–32.

Shapiro, Alan C. "Capital Budgeting for the Multinational Corporation," *Financial Management,* Spring 1978, pp. 7–16.

Shapiro, Alan C. "International Capital Budgeting," *Midland Corporate Finance Journal,* Spring 1983, pp. 26–45.

Stulz, Rene M. "Globalization of Capital Markets and the Cost of Capital: The Case of Nestlé," *Bank of America Journal of Applied Corporate Finance,* Fall 1995, pp. 30–38.

CHAPTER 4

FINANCING INTERNATIONAL PROJECTS

CHAPTER OBJECTIVES
AFTER READING THIS CHAPTER, YOU SHOULD BE ABLE TO:

❖ Revise the value of a foreign project to include the effects of financing part of the project with debt.

❖ Explain ways of financing the multinational corporation as a whole and why a subsidiary's capital structure is not independent of the parent's capital structure.

❖ Explain ways of financing the foreign subsidiary, including internal versus external financing, equity versus debt financing, and home currency versus foreign currency financing.

❖ Analyze the currency denomination of debt (home currency versus foreign currency) in terms of the uncovered interest parity theorem and the project's foreign exchange risk.

This chapter covers four main topics. The first section reconsiders international capital budgeting to include the effects of financing part of the project with debt. The second section considers ways of financing the multinational corporation as a whole with external capital, specifying that the capital structure of a subsidiary is not independent of the capital structure of the parent. Two main issues are thus parent versus subsidiary financing and equity versus debt financing. The third section turns more specifically to issues in financing the foreign subsidiary by surveying three main international financing decisions and the available methods of financing foreign projects. We discuss issues regarding internal versus external financing, equity versus debt financing, and home-currency-denominated versus foreign-currency-denominated financing. The fourth section focuses more closely on the currency denomination of debt financing by considering foreign exchange risk.

4.1   INTRODUCTION

Once a multinational corporation identifies a foreign project with positive net present value, it must consider different ways of financing the investment. This chapter therefore examines issues in international financing, usually focusing on a foreign subsidiary carrying out the project. In many respects, financing a foreign subsidiary is much like financing any domestic subsidiary. As discussed in Chapter 1, however, two new factors emerge when a firm enters foreign markets—multiple currencies and multiple governments—and these factors bear directly on a multinational's financing decision. In particular, changing currency values and different tax rates result in important distinctions between financing domestic and international subsidiaries.

4.2   INTERNATIONAL CAPITAL BUDGETING AND THE PRESENT VALUE OF DEBT

The evaluation of projects presented in Chapter 3 on international capital budgeting used an **all-equity cost of capital,** the required rate of return on corporate equity in the absence of corporate debt, as the discount rate applied to uncertain cash flows. Equity represents an ownership stake in the project, which will be rewarded with an unspecified stream of dividend payments. In reality, equity can be leveraged by financing a portion of the project with debt. Debt represents a contractual agreement to repay principal with interest on a specified schedule. The cost of debt is therefore typically lower than the cost of equity because debt represents a certain stream of cash flows. Firms thus have an incentive to use debt to leverage equity. However, the cost of debt and the cost of equity are both increasing functions of the amount of debt issued. Although debt may be cheaper than equity, the cost of equity rises as more debt is issued, and modern finance theory suggests that the weighted average cost of debt and equity is in fact constant because the return on assets is not altered by the composition of asset financing.

In an integrated world capital market without any tax or other incentives associated with borrowing, debt would carry a present value of zero. This is because the value of the interest and principal repayments discounted at the required market rate of return on the firm's contractual agreements simply produces the initial principal of the loan.

Consider, for example, a one-year loan of $1 million at an interest rate of 9 percent, The borrower receives $1 million now, and must pay $1,090,000 in one year. The present value of the $1,090,000 contractual obligation, at the market's required rate of return of 9 percent for the firm's contractual obligations, is $1,090,000/1.09 = $1,000,000. Hence, the net present value of the debt, the inflow of cash minus the present value of the obligation, is zero. Note that the firm uses its borrowing rate as the discount rate for the debt because this is a contractual flow at a known interest rate. The firm does not use the all-equity cost of capital because that represents the required rate of return on uncertain cash flows associated with equity in the project; the required rate of return on debt is simply the market interest rate for the firm.

The result that the present value of debt is zero also applies to foreign currency borrowing when the foreign interest rate on the firm's foreign debt is used to discount the foreign currency obligations; this is the typical decentralized procedure. The firm could also centralize the present value calculation by converting the foreign currency obligations into domestic currency at the expected future spot exchange rate implied by UIP and taking the present value using the domestic rate of return required on the firm's debt. However, this would still produce a present value of zero as long as UIP holds *ex ante*. (Furthermore, the firm could also decentralize the present value calculation for domestic debt by converting the domestic debt obligations into foreign currency and taking the present value using the foreign rate of return required on the firm's debt. This would still produce a present value of zero, as long as uncovered interest parity holds.)

If the world capital market is segmented into separate national capital markets such that *ex ante* deviations from UIP exist, the firm stands to profit from borrowing in a low-interest-rate currency, properly accounting for expected exchange rate changes, and similarly stands to lose from borrowing in a high-interest-rate currency, again properly accounting for expected exchange rate changes.

The method for calculating the present value of borrowing in a foreign currency is identical to the centralized capital budgeting technique, and is therefore only briefly considered here. Implementing centralized capital budgeting, the firm must first list all the foreign currency cash flows. Next, the firm converts the foreign currency cash flows into home currency units, being sure to take into account deviations from UIP in calculating the expected future spot rate. Finally, the firm discounts the cash flows at the firm's interest rate on domestic debt. The result will be positive if the firm is borrowing in a low-interest-rate foreign currency and is thereby taking advantage of expected deviations from uncovered interest parity. The result will be negative if the firm is borrowing in a high-interest-rate currency, perhaps paying to use debt to hedge the risk associated with the project (a concept which is developed in further detail later in this chapter). Note, however, that the result will be zero if the firm is borrowing domestically, by the same argument given above.

EXAMPLE 4.1

Teegen and Adoff, a U.S. multinational, is opening a new subsidiary in Brazil. It can borrow $9 million for one year in the United States at a market interest rate of 6 percent to help finance this subsidiary. The market interest rate on a similar loan in Brazil is 10 percent, but the Brazilian government is offering a low interest rate of 8 percent on a 10 million real loan as an incentive to open the subsidiary. The current exchange rate is $0.90/real, so the principal amounts are identical. The expected future exchange rate, based on market interest rates and UIP, is $0.90(1.06)/(1.10) = \$0.8673$/real. By borrowing in reals from the Brazilian government, the real payment in one year is $10,000,000(1.08) = 10,800,000$ reals. In U.S. dollars, this is expected to be $(10,800,000)(0.8673) = \$9,366,545$. The present value of the obligation, in dollars, is therefore $\$9,366,545/(1.06) = \$8,836,364$, and the net present value of this debt is $9,000,000 - 8,836,364 = \$163,636$. As UIP does not hold for interest rates at which Teegen and Adoff can borrow, the real loan from the Brazilian government adds $163,636 to the value of the project.

EXAMPLE 4.2

Beto and Associates, a U.S. MNC, is opening a new subsidiary in Mexico. It can borrow $10 million for one year in the United States at an interest rate of 8 percent, or it can borrow 50 million pesos for one year in Mexico at an interest rate of 15 percent. The current exchange rate is 5 pesos per dollar. A consensus seems to exist in the market suggesting that the peso will depreciate over the next year, but not by as much as the interest rate differential indicates. Beto and Associates expects the exchange rate to be 5.2 pesos per dollar in one year, whereas the interest differential suggests that the exchange rate will be $5(1.15)/(1.08) =$ 5.324 pesos per dollar. Note that the difference between 5.2 and 5.324 is approximately -2.4 percent, so the peso is expected to depreciate about 2.4 percent less than the interest differential indicates. Beto and Associates recognizes that it is able to match some of the peso assets purchased with peso liabilities from borrowing, thus "balancing" its position. By borrowing in pesos, and given the expectation that the peso exchange rate will be 5.2 pesos per dollar, Beto and Associates is expecting to pay more for the debt in pesos than it would pay in dollars, but is willing to pay the additional amount to match the assets purchased. The payment in one year is $50,000,000(1.15) = 57,500,000$ pesos. In dollars, this is expected to be $57,500,000/5.2 = \$11,057,692$. The present value of the obligation is therefore $11,057,692/(1.08) = \$10,238,604$, and the net present value of the loan is $\$10,000,000 - \$10,238,604 = -\$238,604$. As UIP is not expected to hold, the peso loan is more expensive, and Beto and Associates is effectively paying \$238,604 to match peso assets with peso liabilities. Note that this is approximately 2.4 percent of the value of the loan, which is exactly the expected percentage amount of the deviation from UIP.

ADJUSTED PRESENT VALUE

In nearly all countries, debt has an important advantage over equity because the interest paid on debt is nearly always deductible from income in calculating corporate taxes but dividends on equity are not. Hence, the after-tax cost of debt is less than the pretax cost of debt. Debt therefore creates additional value for a project by reducing taxes paid, so adjustments to the calculation of the project's present value must be made if it supports additional debt. The contribution to present value of issuing debt is thus calculated as the present value of tax savings. This present value can then be added to the present value of a project calculated using the all-equity cost of capital and the methods developed in Chapter 3. The method of adding the tax benefits of debt to the separately calculated present value of the project using the all-equity cost of capital is known as the **adjusted present value (APV)** approach.[1]

To illustrate the benefits of debt resulting from the tax-deductibility of interest payments, we continue the extended example used throughout Chapter 3. Recall that Victor Enterprises is undertaking a project in Switzerland. The U.S. risk-free interest rate is 10 percent and the Swiss risk-free interest rate is 18.8 percent (creating an 8 percent spread). Assume that Victor Enterprises' debt cost is 4 percent above the risk-free interest rate, regardless of whether it borrows U.S. dollars or Swiss francs. Hence, if UIP holds for risk-free interest rates, it will hold for Victor Enterprises' corporate interest rates. (In the third section of this chapter we consider the possibility that a firm's debt costs will be different in different markets, such that there will be deviations from UIP for interest rates applicable to the firm even if UIP holds for risk-free interest rates. For now, we consider the simpler case that UIP holds for the firm if UIP holds for risk-free interest rates.) Victor Enterprises' U.S. dollar borrowing rate is therefore 14.4 percent, using the formula for simple interest rates $[(1.04)(1.10) = 1.144]$. Similarly, Victor Enterprises' Swiss franc borrowing rate is 23.552 percent [because $(1.04)(1.188) = 1.23552$].

If Victor Enterprises has the opportunity to borrow U.S. dollar debt in the amount of \$12 million for three years, and the terms of the loan are to repay principal in three equal installments along with interest, the profile of cash flows will be as listed in Table 4-1. Interest is calculated on the previous year's outstanding principal. Interest payments are

TABLE 4-1 Cash Flows from Victor Enterprises' Dollar Loan

Year	Principal	Interest	Tax Shield	Total Cash Flow
0	12,000,000			12,000,000
1	−4,000,000	−1,728,000	604,800	−5,123,200
2	−4,000,000	−1,152,000	403,200	−4,748,800
3	−4,000,000	−576,000	201,600	−4,374,400

deductible from income in determining the amount of corporate taxes to be paid, so the **debt-related tax shield** is the pecuniary benefit to the company from the deductibility of interest because of a reduction in tax payments (previously included in the estimated cash flows). If Victor Enterprises faces a tax rate of 35 percent, then every dollar of interest paid reduces income taxes paid by thirty-five cents. This is labeled the tax shield in Table 4-1. The total cash flow in each year is presented in the last column. The present value of the cash flows, using the discount rate of 14.4 percent is:

$$PV = 12,000,000 - 5,123,200/1.144 - 4,748,800/1.144^2 - 4,374,400/1.144^3$$
$$= \$971,407.$$

This present value can also be calculated by directly figuring the present value of the tax shields:

$$PV = 604,800/1.144 + 403,200/1.144^2 + 201,600/1.144^3$$
$$= \$971,407.$$

so the adjustment due to financing is typically represented algebraically as:

$$\sum_{t=1}^{n} \frac{\tau R D_{t-1}}{(1 + R)^t}$$

where τ is the corporate tax rate, R is the interest rate on debt applicable to the firm, and D_{t-1} is the outstanding dollar-denominated debt on which interest is paid.

The value to Victor Enterprises of the debt financing presented in Table 4-1 is $971,407, and this amount should be added to the value of the investment project if the debt represents incremental borrowing associated with the specific project. Because the net present value of the project, as calculated in Chapter 3, is $2,291,320, the adjusted present value is:

$$APV = \$2,291,320 + \$971,407$$
$$= \$3,262,727.$$

For this centralized approach to project and financing evaluation, the adjusted present value can be more generally expressed algebraically as:

$$APV = \sum_{t=0}^{n} \frac{E_0[CF_t S_t]}{(1 + COC)^t} + \sum_{t=1}^{n} \frac{\tau R D_{t-1}}{(1 + R)^t}.$$

If Victor Enterprises has the alternative opportunity of borrowing in Swiss francs, the calculation changes a bit because there are expected gains or losses associated with borrowing in the foreign currency. The Swiss franc equivalent of a US$12 million loan is SFr15 million given that the spot exchange rate is $0.80/SFr. The cash flows associated with Victor Enterprises' Swiss franc borrowing are listed in Table 4-2, using the firm's interest rate on Swiss franc debt of 23.552 percent. In addition, the franc cash flows are converted to dollars at the expected future exchange rates implied by UIP. The present value of these cash flows is:

$$PV = 12,000,000 - 5,404,681/1.144 - 4,479,342/1.144^2 - 3,661,434/1.144^3$$
$$= \$1,407,450.$$

From the discussion in Chapter 3, we know that this is equivalent to taking the present value in Swiss francs and converting into dollars at the spot exchange rate:

$$PV = 15,000,000 - 7,296,320/1.23552 - 6,530,880/1.23552^2 - 5,765,440/1.23552^3$$
$$= 1,759,313 \text{ Swiss francs}$$
$$= \$1,407,450 \text{ at } \$.80/SFr.$$

And, as before, this is equivalent to taking the present value of the tax shields:

$$PV = 1,236,480/1.23552 + 824,320/1.23552^2 + 412,160/1.23552^3$$
$$= 1,759,313 \text{ Swiss francs}$$
$$= \$1,407,450 \text{ at } \$.80/SFr$$

so the present value of the tax shields can be represented algebraically as:

$$\left[\sum_{t=1}^{n} \frac{\tau R^* D^*_{t-1}}{(1 + R^*)^t} \right] S_0$$

where τ is again the corporate tax rate, R^* is the foreign interest rate on debt applicable to the firm, and D^*_{t-1} is the outstanding foreign-currency-denominated debt on which interest is paid. Under any of these calculations, this figure is larger than the debt shield from U.S. dollar borrowing because the interest payments in Swiss francs are higher, as the Swiss interest rate is higher. Because the interest differential reflects expectations of Swiss franc depreciation, we must adjust the principal for expected depreciation and calculate the value of taxes on the foreign exchange gains.

Under U.S. tax laws, gains (or losses) from currency transactions are treated as ordinary income (or loss) rather than as capital gains (or losses) because currency fluctuation is viewed as an interest substitute. Tax laws can be complex, though, so here we examine only the basic case; for more on foreign currency and taxation, see Chapter 10 of Doernberg (1993).

Over the course of the Victor Enterprises loan, the Swiss franc is expected to depreciate vis-à-vis the U.S. dollar, as indicated by the interest rate differential between the two countries. Victor Enterprises therefore expects to have foreign exchange gains associated with the erosion of its Swiss franc liability. The calculation of these expected exchange gains is also shown in Table 4-2, below the cash flows from the Swiss franc loan and repayment. The expected foreign exchange gains (or losses) are calculated as the difference between the U.S. dollar value of the principal repayments at the spot exchange rate of $0.80/SFr in effect when the loan originates and the U.S. dollar value of the expected principal repayments at the future exchange rates expected when the loan originates. These exchange gains are denominated in U.S. dollars, and are taxed at the firm's corporate tax rate of 35 percent. (Losses are deductible from income and

TABLE 4-2 Cash Flows from Victor Enterprises' Swiss Franc Loan

Swiss Franc Loan and Repayment

Year	Principal	Interest	Tax Shield	Total Cash Flow	Expected Exchange Rate	Conversion at Expected Rate
0	15,000,000			15,000,000	$0.80/SFr	$12,000,000
1	−5,000,000	−3,532,800	1,236,480	−7,296,320	$0.7407/SFr	−$5,404,681
2	−5,000,000	−2,355,200	824,320	−6,530,880	$0.6859/SFr	−$4,479,342
3	−5,000,000	−1,177,600	412,160	−5,765,440	$0.6351/SFr	−$3,661,434

Ex Ante Exchange Gains

Year	SFr Principal	Conversion at $0.80/SFr	Expected Exchange Rate	Conversion at Expected Rate	Expected Gain	Tax on Expected Gain
0	15,000,000	$12,000,000	$0.80/SFr	$12,000,000	0	0
1	−5,000,000	−$4,000,000	$0.7407/SFr	−$3,703,704	$296,296	$103,704
2	−5,000,000	−$4,000,000	$0.6859/SFr	−$3,429,355	$570,645	$199,726
3	−5,000,000	−$4,000,000	$0.6351/SFr	−$3,175,329	$824,671	$288,635

symmetrically reduce taxes paid at the rate of 35 percent.) The expected amount of the tax in each year, also denominated in U.S. dollars, is presented in the final column. These tax payments represent additional cash outflows in each year, and the present value of these cash flows is:

$$PV = -103,704/1.144 - 199,726/1.144^2 - 288,635/1.144^3$$
$$= -\$436,045$$

and this must be subtracted from the value of the debt shield calculated above. More generally, the tax payments on expected exchange gains can be expressed algebraically as:

$$\sum_{t=1}^{n} \frac{\tau(D_t^* - D_{t-1}^*)E_0[S_t - S_0]}{(1 + R)^t}$$

Hence, the value of borrowing in Swiss francs to finance part of this project is $1,407,450 - $436,045 = $971,405, which is the same as the value of borrowing in U.S. dollars to finance the project (with a little rounding error).

The APV of the Victor Enterprises project financed with Swiss francs is therefore:

$$APV = \$2,291,320 + \$971,405$$
$$= \$3,262,725$$

and this is identical to the present value of the project financed with dollar debt with a little rounding error. The APV using decentralized capital budgeting and borrowing in the foreign currency can more generally be expressed as:

$$APV = \left[\sum_{t=0}^{n} \frac{E_0(CF_t)}{(1 + COC^*)^t} \right] S_0 + \left[\sum_{t=1}^{n} \frac{\tau R^* D_{t-1}^*}{(1 + R^*)^t} \right] S_0$$
$$+ \sum_{t=1}^{n} \frac{\tau(D_t^* - D_{t-1}^*)E_0[S_t - S_0]}{(1 + R)^t}.$$

The result that borrowing in the domestic currency and borrowing in a foreign currency generate the same debt-related tax shield depends on the symmetric tax treatment of interest payments and foreign exchange gains and losses as well as uncovered interest parity. Recall from Chapter 2 that UIP asserts:

$$R_{t,t+n} - R_{t,t+n}^* = a\{E_t[\%\Delta S_{t,t+n}]\}.$$

Letting the notation for interest rates $R_{t,t+n}$ and $R_{t,t+n}^*$ now pertain to borrowing rates for the firm rather than to risk-free interest rates, symmetric tax treatment implies that tax benefits (or taxation of capital gains) are applied to all three elements in the equation such that:

$$(1 - \tau)R_{t,t+n} - (1 - \tau)R_{t,t+n}^* = a(1 - \tau)\{E_t[\%\Delta S_{t,t+n}]\}$$

where τ is the corporate tax rate. The term $(1 - \tau)R_{t,t+n}$ is the after-tax domestic interest rate applicable to the firm, $(1 - \tau)R_{t,t+n}^*$ is the after-tax foreign interest rate applicable to the firm, and $a(1 - \tau)\{E_t[\%\Delta S_{t,t+n}]\}$ is the after-tax foreign exchange gain or loss to the firm. If UIP holds before taxes, it subsequently holds after taxes. In reality, this is not always the case, and in such an environment domestic currency borrowing and foreign currency borrowing do not have the same present value because the tax implications are different.

APPLICATION 4-1

DEBT AND TAXES IN GREAT BRITAIN[2]

Tax laws in Great Britain create asymmetries between exchange gains and exchange losses associated with foreign currency borrowing. British firms, or subsidiaries doing business in Britain, can deduct interest payments from corporate income before figuring taxable profits. Exchange gains on foreign currency loans, however, are taxed as income. For example, if a U.K. firm borrows French francs and the franc subsequently depreciates, the foreign exchange gain resulting from the reduced value of the liability is taxed. This makes sense because any expected depreciation raises franc interest rates. As the higher interest payments are tax deductible, foreign exchange gains should be taxable to preserve UIP between French franc borrowing and U.K. pound borrowing.

Under U.K. tax law, however, foreign exchange losses on foreign currency loans are not tax deductible. If the U.K. firm borrows Swiss francs and subsequently has a foreign exchange loss because of franc appreciation, there is no tax relief. This does not make economic sense because expected appreciation lowers Swiss franc interest rates; the relatively lower interest payments are tax deductible, but the foreign exchange losses are not deductible, so UIP is not preserved when taxes are taken into account.

The firm is interested in the after-tax interest rates in the domestic and foreign currencies. If UIP holds before taxes, U.K. firms will not want to borrow in currencies expected to appreciate. Although the before-tax interest rate reflects expected appreciation, the fact that actual interest payments are tax deductible while foreign exchange losses are not means that UIP does not hold after taxes. Further, there are actually additional incentives to borrow in depreciating currencies because the exchange gains usually qualify for capital gains indexation; taxes are not paid on the nominal amount of the gain, but only on the real gain, which is the nominal gain adjusted downward for inflation. Hence, if UIP holds before taxes, the U.K. firm incurs lower after-tax borrowing costs if it borrows in a depreciating foreign currency rather than the U.K. pound, and incurs higher after-tax borrowing costs if it borrows in an appreciating foreign currency rather than the U.K. pound.

The adjusted present value method described earlier is clearly quite useful in capital budgeting analysis. The all-equity cost of capital is first used to evaluate the core of the project, excluding financing costs. Additional benefits of project-specific debt financing are then explicitly and simply added on. One main advantage of the APV method is that it makes calculating and using a weighted-average cost of capital unnecessary.

4.3   FINANCING THE MULTINATIONAL CORPORATION

A foreign project can be financed in many ways. Equity financing was presumed in the previous chapter, and the previous section of this chapter considered the benefits of debt financing. More subtly, the discussion up to this point has taken the view of the firm as a whole without any distinction between entities known as parent and subsidiary. The examination of Victor Enterprises' borrowing in U.S. dollars and in Swiss francs pertains to the firm as a whole. More specifically, the example pertains to the parent, because the parent's tax rate was used to calculate benefits of tax shields and additional taxes due by the parent in the presence of foreign exchange gains. There may be some differences in borrowing costs if the subsidiary borrows directly, such as differences in tax rates and the treatment of foreign exchange gains and losses. Nevertheless, the subsidiary is not independent of the parent, so the perspective of the firm as a whole is appropriate.

When examining the financing of a subsidiary, more factors come into play than when financing the firm as a whole. For example:

1. Financing may in general emanate from the parent's internal funds or may be raised externally. Internal funds, such as retained earnings, represent shareholder equity as the money could otherwise be paid out to the shareholders. Hence, existing internal funds are in fact external funds and may be treated as such. Nevertheless, these internal funds can be passed to the subsidiary as an internal transfer.
2. Financing may be obtained externally by the parent and then internally passed to a foreign subsidiary to finance a project. From the subsidiary's perspective, this is internal financing even though the funds originated externally.
3. Financing may be obtained externally directly by the foreign subsidiary, which we consider more explicitly in this section.

Figure 4-1 presents a schematic diagram of these three financing flows, further breaking each into equity and debt. Hence, external financing raised by the parent can take the form of equity or debt, internal financing transferred from the parent to the subsidiary can be structured as either equity or debt, and external financing raised directly by the subsidiary can take the form of equity or debt. Furthermore, all six of these elements can be denominated either in the home currency or in the foreign currency (the currency of the country in which the foreign subsidiary is located), so there appear to be twelve financing alternatives.

PARENT VERSUS SUBSIDIARY FINANCING

We begin looking at the twelve financing alternatives with an examination of external financing. In general, external financing for the project is external to the firm as a whole regardless of whether the parent or the subsidiary undertakes the financing. Hence, we treat external equity simply as external equity whether it is issued by the parent or the subsidiary. In reality, equity is rarely issued directly by a subsidiary because the returns on the foreign project are generally not separable from the returns on the firm as a whole

FIGURE 4-1   SCHEMATIC DIAGRAM OF FINANCING FLOWS

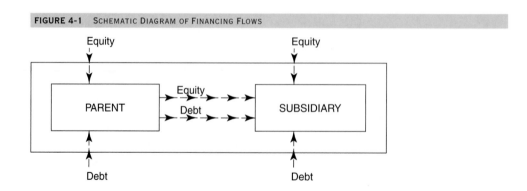

when paying dividends to external shareholders. In some instances, firms announce that obligations are to be tied to the fortunes of the subsidiary, such as when the parent issues equity as a **tracking stock,** a vehicle that tracks the returns of the subsidiary.

As there are extensive interactions with the parent, the plan is still best viewed from the standpoint of the entire firm.[3] Even if the returns on the foreign project are separable from the returns of the firm as a whole, it is irrelevant whether the equity is issued by the parent to track the returns of the subsidiary or by the subsidiary to track its own returns. In sum, external equity is external equity regardless of which entity undertakes the financing because it is external to the firm as a whole.

As with equity, external debt is generally external debt whether it is the liability of the parent or a subsidiary. The foundation for this analysis is the understanding that a subsidiary's liability is in fact the parent's liability, usually due to explicit loan guarantees by the parent, but also due to implicit loan guarantees by a parent concerned about its overall access to credit markets at favorable rates. Thus, because the financing is external to the whole firm, it does not matter who issues the debt—the parent or the subsidiary.

However, there are likely to be tax implications with debt that are not present with equity because the use of a foreign currency by a subsidiary located in the country that issues the currency (e.g., use of the Swiss franc by Victor Enterprises' subsidiary in Switzerland) results in deferral of foreign exchange gains and losses from the parent-country perspective. More importantly, this results in deferral of taxable income or tax-deductible loss in the parent country, because a firm's foreign exchange gains (losses) in the subsidiary are generally considered unrealized from the parent perspective until the subsidiary is sold, liquidated, or otherwise disposed of. Again, tax law can be complicated and we consider only the simplest case here; for further information see Chapter 10 of Doernberg (1993). The main point is that deferral of taxation on foreign exchange gains (or deferral of tax deductibility of losses) creates an asymmetry in borrowing decisions which depends on the unit (parent or subsidiary) arranging the borrowing.

BORROWING AT THE SUBSIDIARY

To see the asymmetry in borrowing decisions created by the deferral of taxation on foreign exchange gains (or deferral of tax deductibility of losses), reconsider Victor Enterprises' Swiss franc borrowing. In the previous section, we noted that the present value of debt shields on a Swiss franc loan must be combined with the tax payments on foreign exchange gains: $1,407,450 - $436,045 = $971,405. This is specifically the case when the parent borrows Swiss francs because taxes are due on foreign exchange gains as they occur. However, if a Swiss subsidiary of Victor Enterprises borrows Swiss francs, the subsidiary does not see the gains from its Swiss franc perspective; the U.S. taxes on the parent's foreign exchange gains are deferred, and are usually deferred indefinitely. The parent thus carries an unrealized foreign exchange gain on its consolidated books that is not taxed. (This aspect will become clearer in Chapter 6 when we examine accounting issues in more detail.) For tax purposes, the parent is usually not considered to realize the foreign exchange gain as income until the subsidiary is sold, liquidated, or otherwise disposed of. Hence, taxes on the foreign exchange gain on Victor Enterprises' Swiss franc loan (which have a present value of $436,045 when the parent borrows) can be indefinitely deferred if the Swiss subsidiary borrows the money (reducing the present value to zero). This effectively makes the present value of the loan the full amount of the debt shields, $1,407,450, when the Swiss subsidiary undertakes the borrowing.

The example of Victor Enterprises' Swiss franc loan demonstrates that when foreign interest rates are higher than home interest rates, $R^* > R$, there is a tax advantage to having the subsidiary borrow the foreign currency because taxes on foreign exchange gains are indefinitely deferred. Furthermore, there is also a tax advantage to having the subsidiary borrow the home currency because the subsidiary realizes both the benefits of the debt shields and of tax-deductible foreign exchange losses from the expected appreciation of the home currency. For example, reworking Victor Enterprises' dollar-denominated loan from the viewpoint of Victor Enterprises' subsidiary in Switzerland produces a present value of $971,407 associated with the debt shields plus a present value of $436,045 from the tax deductibility of foreign exchange losses in Switzerland due to dollar appreciation, for a total of $1,407,450. The offsetting gain to the parent from converting the Swiss franc losses back into U.S. dollars (basically undoing the losses from the parent's viewpoint) is again indefinitely deferred. Hence, we can conclude that, when foreign interest rates are higher than home interest rates, there is a tax advantage to having the subsidiary borrow regardless of the currency denomination of the debt. With both foreign currency and domestic currency borrowing, the present value of the loan is higher when the subsidiary borrows than when the parent borrows.

BORROWING AT THE PARENT

What if foreign interest rates are lower than home interest rates, $R^* < R$? In this case, there is a tax advantage to having the parent borrow. When foreign interest rates are lower than home interest rates, the foreign currency is expected to appreciate. Foreign-currency-denominated borrowing is thus associated with foreign exchange losses that can be deducted from income contemporaneously if the parent undertakes the borrowing. If, instead, the subsidiary borrows the foreign currency at the lower interest rate, the present value of the debt shields is less than the sum of the present value of the debt shields and the present value of the tax benefits from foreign exchange losses when the parent borrows the foreign currency.

Similarly, home-currency-denominated borrowing at the higher interest rate is more advantageous when done by the parent because there are no foreign exchange gains or losses. If, instead, the subsidiary borrows the home currency at the higher interest rate, the subsidiary realizes foreign exchange gains from the depreciation of the dollar, which are in turn taxed. Thus, the present value of the debt shields is reduced by the present value of the taxes on foreign exchange gains, resulting in a present value lower than when the parent undertakes the borrowing. Hence, the conclusion is that, when foreign interest rates are lower than home interest rates, there is a tax advantage to having the parent borrow regardless of the currency denomination of the debt. With both foreign currency and domestic currency borrowing, the present value of the loan is lower when the subsidiary borrows than when the parent borrows.

To briefly summarize, external financing is generally external financing of the firm as a whole whether it is a liability of the parent or a liability of the subsidiary. However, there are tax implications with external debt that make the value of the debt shields depend on which unit (parent or subsidiary) is doing the borrowing. When foreign interest rates are higher than home interest rates, $R^* > R$, there is a tax advantage to having the subsidiary borrow. Conversely, when foreign interest rates are lower than home interest rates, $R^* < R$, there is a tax advantage to having the parent borrow. Hence, borrowing should take place in the country where interest rates are highest. This is an extension of the notion from domestic finance that debt shields are more valuable when nominal interest rates are high because the tax break is greater; see, for example, Chapter 13 of Grinblatt and Titman (1998).

EQUITY VERSUS DEBT FINANCING

Next, consider the choice between equity and debt, again with respect to external financing. The choice is basically the same for the multinational as for the domestic corporation. If there are no tax implications or other market imperfections, the form of the obligations is of little importance: it doesn't matter whether the financing takes the form of equity or debt, or some combination of the two, because capital is capital and owners are owners. However, the deductibility of interest on debt before computing income taxes (compared to the nondeductibility of dividends on equity) causes firms to favor debt, at least up to some point. Increasing the amount of debt increases the probability of bankruptcy, and therefore increases both the cost of debt and the cost of equity. Firms that do not want to incur rising costs of debt and equity, and other costs of bankruptcy, will therefore limit their borrowing to an optimal level, which includes enough debt to take advantage of the tax shields but not so much debt that costs of capital are driven too high.

The typical situation is depicted in Figure 4-2, which shows **financial leverage,** the ratio of debt to the sum of debt and equity, on the horizontal axis and costs of financing on the vertical axes. The top line represents the cost of capital, increasing from an all-equity cost of capital as leverage increases. The lower line represents the after-tax cost of debt, which is constant at first but then increases as leverage increases because the probability of default increases. Note that the cost of debt is always below the cost of equity, due to the tax deductibility of interest. However, the firm cannot finance entirely with debt. The curved line in the middle represents the weighted average cost of equity and debt,

FIGURE 4-2 OPTIMUM LEVERAGE FOR A FIRM

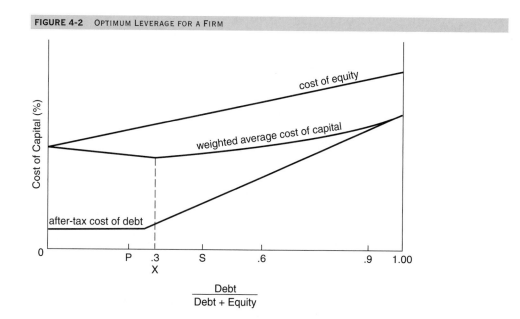

known as the **weighted average cost of capital (WACC),** at each level of leverage. The optimum leverage is that which minimizes the weighted average cost of capital, shown at point X in the diagram at around 30 percent debt. The diagram is based on the notion that firms which are more leveraged have higher probabilities of bankruptcy, and this drives up the costs of equity and debt. Hence, although firms want to take advantage of the tax-deductibility of interest, they have an incentive to limit their borrowing. In addition, firms which do not expect to fully benefit from tax deductibility of interest because their profits may not be consistently high enough will further limit their borrowing.[4]

The mix of equity and debt is also referred to as the firm's **capital structure.** The choice between equity and debt embodied in Figure 4-2 is important because the firm's external obligations are to outsiders who value these obligations according to a market equilibrium. Based on the earlier observation that external financing by any unit is external financing of the whole firm, it follows that the capital structure of the subsidiary is not independent of the capital structure of the parent. In fact, the capital structure of the whole firm is simply the weighted average of the external capital structures of all of its units. Figure 4-2 is therefore best understood as representing the capital structure of the firm as a whole. The optimal capital structure exists only for the firm as an integrated whole, and the firm can achieve this optimum through many different combinations of parent and subsidiary capital structures.[5]

With just one subsidiary, the firm's capital structure is a weighted average of the leverage of the parent and the leverage of the subsidiary (in which any internal financing between the two is netted out). Given that there is an optimum capital structure for the entire firm and that the capital structures of the parent and subsidiary are designed to produce this overall capital structure, the weighted average of the parent and the subsidiary's leverage should produce the minimum weighted-average cost of capital for the firm. For example, if the subsidiary is highly leveraged, perhaps at point S in Figure 4-2, then the parent must have less leverage, perhaps at point P, to make the overall leverage optimal (point X). Clearly, external financing of a subsidiary is simply a piece of the larger capital structure decision for the whole multinational.

The equity-versus-debt decision is more complex when there are international differences in tax rates. If tax rates at home and abroad are identical, the world could be regarded as one big tax jurisdiction and the choice between equity and debt would be exactly as developed. The discussion in this section has thus implicitly assumed that there is just one tax rate applicable to the firm as a whole. However, when tax rates are different in the home country and the foreign country, the issues become more complex. In fact, careful selection of the parent and subsidiary's capital structure may create additional value for the firm. These issues are taken up in the next section.

4.4   FINANCING THE FOREIGN SUBSIDIARY

Now that we have examined external financing, particularly comparing external financing by the parent to external financing by the subsidiary and comparing external equity to external debt, we are ready to consider remaining issues in financing direct foreign investment, or specific issues in financing the foreign subsidiary. From the viewpoint of financing the subsidiary, there are three binomial financing decisions facing the multinational:

1. whether to finance the investment using internal capital or external capital, or some combination of the two;
2. whether to finance the investment with equity or debt, or some combination;
3. whether to finance the investment using home or foreign-currency-denominated obligations.

These three binomial decisions produce eight financing alternatives (because $2 \times 2 \times 2 = 8$). Taking these issues as sequential decisions, we construct a tree of the eight alternatives in Figure 4-3. The first two of these decisions are conceptually no different from the financing decisions for a domestic project, but must be modified in the presence of international tax differences. The truly unique decision facing the multinational undertaking a foreign project is the last one. Although there appear to be eight financing alternatives, most of these alternatives are in reality not available. The following subsections examine financing alternatives, and point out what is and is not available.

INTERNAL VERSUS EXTERNAL FINANCING

First, consider the choice between internal and external financing. The firm is usually in a position to invest some of its internally-generated funds, such as retained earnings, in the new project. The alternative is to approach the external capital markets or financial intermediaries. The choice between internal and external financing is basically the same

FIGURE 4-3 METHODS OF FINANCING FOREIGN SUBSIDIARIES

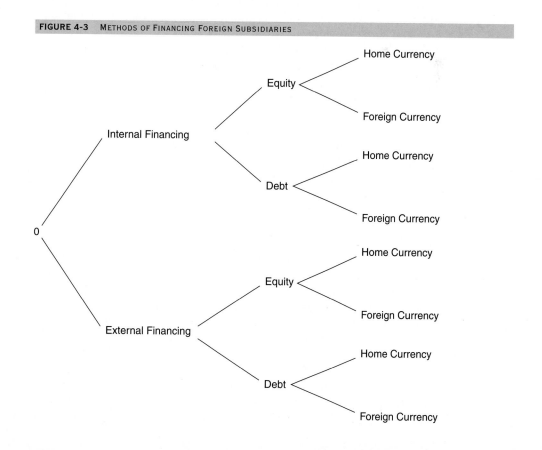

for the multinational as for the domestic corporation, and firms usually make the decision based on the amount of internal financing available and their degree of access to external financing. Hence, the issue of internal versus external financing does not matter too much.

However, there may be reasons for external finance to be used by one entity— parent or subsidiary—rather than the other. The previous section demonstrated that when foreign interest rates are higher than home interest rates there is a tax advantage to having the subsidiary borrow, and when foreign interest rates are lower than home interest rates there is a tax advantage to having the parent borrow. An important point is that no matter which entity undertakes the external finance, the funds can be passed to the other entity through internal financing flows. As we pointed out above, the parent may obtain external financing and then internally pass it to a foreign subsidiary to finance the project. However, it is also possible that the subsidiary may obtain external financing and internally pass it to the parent (representing something like negative internal financing for the subsidiary). We consider several implications of this possibility with respect to equity versus debt financing in the next subsection.

EQUITY VERSUS DEBT FINANCING

Like external financing, internal financing could be in the form of equity, in which the parent would hold an ownership stake in the project and collect dividends from the subsidiary, or in the form of debt, in which the parent would collect interest on its capital invested in the project. In a world without other distinctions between equity and debt, and because capital is capital, the firm would not care whether its claim on the project was called equity or debt. With tax implications, however, the choice between equity and debt is in fact an important one, and most subsidiaries are financed with a combination of internal debt and equity.

How do multinational firms decide between internal equity and internal debt in financing their subsidiaries? Chowdhry and Coval (1998) summarize the results of a model based on tax management. There are two keys to the analysis of the internal debt-equity financing decision. First, it is important to recognize that parent and subsidiary earnings are volatile and sometimes negative. Yet, regardless of the levels of earnings, debt financing requires contractually prespecified payments of interest from the subsidiary to the parent. Second, any dividend payments made from the subsidiary on parent-financed equity would be taken out of after-tax earnings, while most governments treat interest payments on debt as pretax costs. The tradeoff between the flexibility in timing repatriation equity financing offers and the potential tax benefits that debt offers is where the relative country tax rates play an important role.

Income to the parent from dividends on equity is taxed at the home-country tax rate with a full credit given for foreign taxes paid. As a benchmark, suppose that tax rates in the home country and the foreign country are identical at 35 percent, denoted $\tau = \tau^* = 0.35$. If the subsidiary is financed internally with equity, the subsidiary will pay a dividend to the parent from after-tax profits. If the dividend is $1, corresponding to $1.54 in pretax profits because $1.54[1 - .35] = 1.00$, then there are no further tax consequences at the subsidiary level (unless there are withholding taxes, which we ignore until Chapter 11 on international taxation). Although the $1 dividend is income to the parent, the parent has already paid taxes at the rate of $\tau^* = 0.35$ (for a total of $0.54) on the $1.54 before-tax profits and the parent gets a full credit against its domestic tax liability. Its domestic tax liability, since $\tau = 0.35$, is thus $0.35(\$1.54) = \$0.54$ minus the foreign tax credit of $0.54, for a net liability of zero. Hence, there are no tax consequences of paying a dividend.

In contrast to the treatment of dividends, interest income to the parent is taxed at the home-country rate without any further adjustment. If the subsidiary is financed internally with debt, the subsidiary will pay interest to the parent from pretax profits. To be consistent with the example of paying a dividend on equity, the interest payment would have to be $1.54 paid from pretax profits. With $\tau^* = 0.35$, an interest payment of $1.54 lowers foreign taxes paid by $.35(\$1.54) = \$0.54$. However, the $1.54 income to the parent is taxed in the home country at the rate of $\tau = 0.35$, so the parent pays $0.54 to the home government. Thus, the reduction in foreign income taxes by $0.54 is exactly offset by the increase in home income taxes of $0.54. Hence, there are no net tax consequences of paying interest. In this situation, the firm appears to be indifferent between internal financing structured as equity and structured as debt. However, debt requires payments according to a schedule regardless of the profits shown by the subsidiary, and the debt shield is only valuable if the firm has positive profits. Hence, the firm will not want to commit itself to a schedule of payments if there is a possibility of having profits be less than interest payments. The firm will thus prefer to structure the internal finance as equity because dividends do not have to be declared when profits are low or negative.

If the tax rate in the parent country is less than the tax rate in the subsidiary country, $\tau < \tau^*$, transferring funds in the form of interest payments to the parent is advantageous. This even suggests that the subsidiary should be financed entirely by internal debt. Suppose $\tau = 0.35$ and $\tau^* = 0.45$. If the subsidiary is financed by equity and the subsidiary pays a $1 dividend to the parent, $1.82 of pretax profits is repatriated because $\$1.00/(1 - .45) = \$1.82$. The parent's tax liability on the $1.00 dividend is $(.35)(\$1.82) = \$0.64$ minus the foreign tax credit of $(.45)(\$1.82) = \$0.82$, for a net value of $-\$0.18$. However, the home government does not refund $0.18, so the $0.18 is an **excess tax credit** which is forfeited, although there are some exceptions to this rule which are discussed in Chapter 11. (In this situation, the original project should be evaluated using the higher foreign tax payments, thus decreasing the present value.)

Consider, instead, internal financing in the form of debt. If the subsidiary pays $1.82 of interest to the parent, foreign taxes decline by $0.82 and home taxes rise by $0.64. As profits are already taxed at a higher rate abroad, there are no further implications of paying less tax abroad due to the interest deduction. Hence, the net effect is a decrease in total taxes paid of $\$0.82 - \$0.64 = \$0.18$, thus increasing the value of the firm as a whole. (In this situation, the original project should be evaluated using the higher foreign tax payments, then the present value of the internal loan—calculated using the tax differential—would be added to increase the adjusted present value of the project.) When $\tau < \tau^*$, internal financing should be structured as debt.

Although internal financing should be structured as debt when $\tau < \tau^*$, there is a limit to the amount of debt that a subsidiary can carry (and a mix between debt and equity is optimal). This is because the deductibility of interest payments requires the subsidiary to show profits against which to deduct the interest payments, and the volatility of earnings creates incentives for favoring the flexibility of repatriating the returns on equity. The benefit of debt—that it allows the firm to avoid the high subsidiary taxes—must be compared with the possibility that the firm is compelled to make interest payments from a subsidiary experiencing losses to a parent that has taxable earnings. This results in an increase in the multinational's total tax bill even though subsidiary earnings, and possibly overall earnings, are negative.

Now suppose the tax rate in the parent country exceeds the tax rate in the subsidiary country, $\tau > \tau^*$. In this case, transferring funds in the form of dividends is advantageous because this allows the firm to delay repatriation to periods in which the parent can use excess tax credits, and thereby creates the opportunity to avoid taxation at the parent level altogether. (Again, this will become clearer in Chapter 11.) Thus, the subsidiary should be financed entirely by internal equity. For example, suppose $\tau = 0.35$ and $\tau^* = 0.20$. If the subsidiary pays a \$1 dividend to the parent, this corresponds to \$1.25 of pretax profits because $\$1.00/(1 - 0.20) = \$1.25$. The tax liability of the parent company on the \$1.00 dividend is $(.35)(\$1.25) = \$0.44$ minus the foreign tax credit of \$0.25, for a net liability of $\$0.44 - \$0.25 = \$0.19$. Hence, declaring the dividend reduces the value of the firm by \$0.19. However, this liability is due only if a dividend is paid, so the firm can indefinitely defer the liability by retaining profits in the subsidiary, effectively parking profits in the low-tax jurisdiction.

Consider, instead, that the internal financing is in the form of debt. If the subsidiary pays \$1.25 of interest to the parent, foreign taxes decline by \$0.25 and home taxes rise by \$0.44. Hence, the net effect is an increase in total taxes paid of \$0.19, thus reducing the value of the firm as a whole. If the subsidiary is going to declare dividends at the same levels as would be specified by interest payments on debt, there is obviously no difference in the value of the firm under the two scenarios because each one lowers the firm's value by \$0.19. However, because interest would have to be paid but dividends do not have to be declared, the internal financing should be structured as equity.

An extension of the tax implications described above suggests that external debt should be obtained by the entity located in the high-tax country. If the tax rate in the parent country is less than the tax rate in the subsidiary country, $\tau < \tau^*$, the tax shields generated by subsidiary borrowing are generally more valuable than tax shields generated by parent borrowing, so the firm has an incentive to have the subsidiary borrow heavily. For example, Victor Enterprises will find a higher present value of its Swiss franc loan if it uses a higher Swiss tax rate to calculate the present value of debt shields. In the extreme, the subsidiary might even borrow heavily and subsequently internally provide equity to the parent (or other subsidiaries located in lower-tax jurisdictions).

Conversely, if the tax rate in the parent country exceeds the tax rate in the subsidiary country, $\tau > \tau^*$, the tax shields generated by parent borrowing are generally more valuable than tax shields generated by subsidiary borrowing. Victor Enterprises will find a lower present value of its Swiss franc loan if it uses a lower Swiss tax rate to calculate the present value of debt shields. The firm therefore has an incentive to have the parent borrow heavily, and subsequently provide equity to the subsidiary internally.

How do firms choose the capital structure of their foreign subsidiaries? Tax effects are obviously important, of the kind addressed earlier with regard to tax treatment and parent financing versus subsidiary financing, and of the kind just addressed with regard to differences in tax rates. In addition, the nominal interest rates on the debt are important, even when UIP holds, when taxes on foreign exchange gains can be indefinitely deferred at the parent level, as discussed above with respect to parent versus subsidiary financing. Putting these two arguments together basically produces a choice between parent company borrowing based on the parent's tax rate and the home-currency interest rate valued as:

$$\left[\sum_{t=1}^{n} \frac{\tau RD_{t-1}}{(1 + R)^t} \right] S_0$$

or subsidiary borrowing based on the subsidiary's tax rate and the foreign-currency interest rate valued as:

$$\sum_{t=1}^{n} \frac{\tau^* R^* D^*_{t-1}}{(1 + R^*)^t}.$$

When subsidiary borrowing produces a higher PV than parent borrowing, the subsidiary will be financed with a lot of debt; when subsidiary borrowing produces a lower PV than parent borrowing, the subsidiary will be financed with a lot of equity.

In addition to tax rates and interest rates, there are other factors determining how firms choose the capital structure of their foreign subsidiaries which are not considered here. For example, Chowdhry and Nanda (1994) point out that external debt supplements internal debt, and that the mix depends on international differences in tax rates: for any given level of total debt financing, higher (lower) corporate tax rates in the foreign country are associated with a larger (smaller) proportion of external debt, along with higher (lower) interest rates and a larger (smaller) probability of bankruptcy. In empirical studies, other factors which appear to influence the choice of subsidiary capital structure include size of the operation, degree of ownership and control by the parent, age of the subsidiary, the financial risk of the subsidiary, and political risk in the subsidiary country. A survey study of 156 subsidiaries of U.S. multinational corporations by Shao, Hasan, and Shao (1995) finds that the age of the subsidiary significantly increases the proportion of debt in the capital structure and confirms that the extent of financial risk significantly reduces the proportion of debt.[6]

HOME CURRENCY VERSUS FOREIGN CURRENCY FINANCING

The final decision with regard to financing the foreign subsidiary involves the choice of currency in which obligations are denominated. In principle, the four financing alternatives already discussed (internal equity, internal debt, external equity, and external debt) could be denominated either in the home or the foreign currency. However, this choice is irrelevant in many cases and unavailable in others.

With respect to internal financing, the denomination of the obligation is generally irrelevant. As the parent's asset is the subsidiary's liability, there is no valuation effect on the corporation as a whole. Similarly, the denomination of the asset/liability has no effect on the corporation as a whole. If the parent needs to convert foreign currency into the home currency, the subsidiary does not, and vice versa. This is a little like a father or mother giving a child an allowance when the parent carries only $20 bills and the child spends only $1 bills. If the parent must go to a bank to convert a $20 bill into twenty $1 bills before giving the child the allowance, the child does not need to worry about the conversion. However, if the parent gives the child a $20 bill, the child must

LEVERAGE OF MULTINATIONAL CORPORATIONS AND DOMESTIC CORPORATIONS

The discussion of capital structure has covered the multinational corporation as a whole and its entities. A related question is how the capital structure of multinational corporations compares to the capital structure of purely domestic corporations. As optimal leverage will be different for different firms, we do not know whether firms with foreign projects (MNCs) will be more or less leveraged than firms without foreign projects (DCs). If the foreign projects make the cost of equity higher for MNCs than for DCs (recall the box on "Betas of Foreign Projects Compared to Betas of Domestic Projects" in Chapter 3), or if access to foreign borrowing and tax benefits (of the type discussed in this section) makes the cost of debt lower for MNCs than for DCs, then multinationals should be more highly leveraged than domestics. On the other hand, if the foreign projects make the cost of equity lower for MNCs than for DCs, possibly because of diversification (again, see the box in Chapter 3), or if foreign projects make the cost of debt higher for MNCs than for DCs, perhaps because of the additional risk, multinationals should be less leveraged than domestics. Hence, we do not have a theoretical prediction for how leverage of MNCs will compare to leverage of DCs, so the issue is an empirical one.

Several articles, including Burgman (1996), Fatemi (1988), and Lee and Kwok (1988), have pointed out that the proportion of debt in the capital structure of multinational corporations is lower than that of domestic corporations. For example, over the period 1990–1994, the Standard and Poor's Compustat database suggests that the leverage of 973 multinationals (firms with positive sales from foreign operations) averaged 0.2745, meaning that 27.45 percent of total financing was in the form of debt. For 1,910 domestic corporations (firms without any sales from foreign operations), leverage averaged 0.2926, or 29.26 percent debt. Given the sample sizes and the dispersion, the difference is statistically significant.

With the fact firmly established that MNCs are less leveraged than DCs, the question in the literature right now is why this is the case. The current explanation is that agency costs of debt are higher for MNCs than DCs, meaning that it is harder for lenders and bondholders to monitor the activities of MNCs, perhaps because of the foreign projects. Hence, less debt is optimal. An alternative explanation, however, is that additional risks faced by MNCs, such as exchange risk and political risk, may make them riskier than DCs and less able to sustain debt even if they are internationally diversified. Although the reason for the result is still unclear, it appears certain that MNCs optimally have less debt in their capital structure than DCs.

---

go to a bank to convert the $20 bill into twenty $1 bills. The final outcome is the same: the parent has one less $20 bill and the child has twenty more $1 bills. At the same time, there is no overall effect on the combined wealth of the parent and the child. If there are no tax implications, and usually there are not, then a firm does not need to choose between home-currency-denominated financing and foreign-currency-denominated financing; internal capital is internal capital regardless of the currency in which it is denominated.

With external financing, the choice of currency denomination is more important because the obligation is due outsiders, and the subsidiary (and firm) must make cash payments in the appropriate currency. With respect to external equity, however, currency denomination is not really a choice for the firm. One predominantly institutional fact is that multinational corporations generally issue equity only in their home country denominated in home currency. An exception is Royal Dutch/Shell, which has two classes of shares denominated in two different currencies. One class is denominated in pounds and trades on the London stock exchange, and one is denominated in guilders and trades on the Amsterdam stock exchange. This arrangement is something of an institutional oddity, and results from the historical fact that Shell Transport and Trading originated in Britain and Royal Dutch Petroleum originated in Holland, before merging in 1905. The two classes of shares are treated symmetrically with respect to dividends: shareholders receive a fixed proportion of the pound and guilder dividends declared. Another example is Unilever N.V. and Unilever P.L.C., which are separately incorporated in the Netherlands and England, but have pooled cash flows since 1930. Hence, even in this example when two denominations of shares exist, the shares do not receive currency-specific dividends.[7]

It is thus rare for a multinational to issue a separate class of equity denominated in a foreign currency, although this sometimes occurs for a partially owned subsidiary. The Walt Disney Company, for example, issued new equity shares denominated in French francs at the request of the French government when it raised capital for Euro-Disneyland; Walt Disney Company kept a 49 percent ownership share and sold the remaining 51 percent to Europeans in an initial public offering. The Euro-Disneyland subsidiary thus has a genuine external equity obligation denominated in francs. Again, however, this situation is rare, and in practice is usually limited to cases in which a foreign government requires it. Additionally, there are situations in which a joint venture is formed between the MNC and a local partner, and the local partner puts up capital even though the MNC will maintain substantial control over the project.

Although firms basically issue equity only in their home country denominated in home currency, many do list the equity on foreign exchanges. For example, the Coca-Cola Company issues equity in the United States and lists it on the New York Stock Exchange, but in addition the equity is listed, or technically **cross-listed,** on the German exchange in Frankfort and the Swiss exchange in Zurich. Germans and Swiss can then buy shares of Coca-Cola in Germany or Switzerland using German marks or Swiss francs and receive dividends in marks or francs. However, the underlying obligation of Coca-Cola is in dollars and Coca-Cola pays dividends in dollars. A financial intermediary makes the conversion from dollars to marks or francs for the convenience of the German and Swiss investors and the shares all sell for the same price once converted into a common currency.

Multinational companies often cross-list their shares internationally in the belief that wider distribution of shares will lower the cost of capital, and that international distribution is less likely if shares are listed in only one country than if shares are listed in many countries. This may be one method of overcoming home bias in portfolios: if investors will not cross the border to get to the foreign shares, then the firm can take its shares across the border to the investors. A study by Miller (1999) empirically confirms that international cross-listing increases a firm's stock price and apparently lowers the firm's cost of capital.[8]

With external debt, the choice of currency denomination is once again important because the obligation is due outsiders, and the subsidiary (and firm) must make cash payments in the appropriate currency. In contrast to equity, however, the opportunities for a firm to issue debt in the capital markets or borrow from an intermediary in various currencies are numerous. This topic is so important that the next section examines it in more depth.

TABLE 4-3   Asset Financing of U.S. Foreign Affiliates

Type	Amount (billions)	Percent
Internal Equity from U.S. Parents	427	34.5
Internal Debt from U.S. Parents	25	2.0
External Equity from Other U.S. Sources	2	0.2
External Debt from Other U.S. Sources	22	1.8
External Equity from Foreign Sources	194	15.7
External Debt from Foreign Sources	567	45.8
TOTAL	1237	100

Source: Based on data reported in Martin Feldstein, "The Effects of Outbound Foreign Direct Investment on the Domestic Capital Stock," in *The Effects of Taxation on Multinational Corporations,* edited by Martin Feldstein, James R. Hines, Jr., and R. Glenn Hubbard, The University of Chicago Press, 1995, pp. 47–48.

SUMMARY OF FINANCING THE FOREIGN SUBSIDIARY

By way of summary, Table 4-3 presents the main financing alternatives available along with empirical estimates from Feldstein (1995) of the extent to which they are used. Due to the nature of the data, we need to make a few clarifications, and a few assumptions. The data represent how the value of assets of U.S. foreign affiliates are financed. A fair amount of this is retained earnings, so it does not necessarily represent how new foreign projects would be financed. Because the assets total $1,237 billion, the various forms of financing must total $1,237 billion, but this total includes all the assets of affiliates that are majority owned by U.S. firms as well as all affiliates that are wholly owned. A joint venture which is 51 percent owned by a U.S. multinational is thus considered to have assets which are wholly controlled by the U.S. multinational, even though the U.S. direct foreign investment is only 51 percent of the value of the assets. As a consequence, the external equity from foreign sources is probably higher than would really be representative of the way U.S. multinationals finance foreign projects. We also assume that capital from U.S. sources is denominated in U.S. dollars and that capital from foreign sources is denominated in the foreign currency, although this is not necessarily the case. With these assumptions, however, the figure suggests that the main sources of financing foreign assets are external foreign currency debt from foreign sources (46 percent), internal equity from U.S. parents (35 percent), and external equity from foreign sources (16 percent).

4.5   THE DEBT DENOMINATION DECISION

The major international debt financing decision the MNC faces is choosing the currency denomination of external debt. Namely, should the MNC borrow in the home country's currency or in the currencies of the countries in which subsidiaries are located? This is the last fork of Figure 4-3. The first section of this chapter examined the issue and demonstrated that, when UIP holds for interest rates pertaining to the MNC, the after-tax cost of the debt is identical between the two currencies. The second section demonstrated more specifically that the after-tax cost of debt is identical between the two currencies when the parent is doing the borrowing and the after-tax cost of debt is identical between the two currencies when the subsidiary is doing the borrowing, although the after-tax cost of debt may not be identical in a comparison between the parent and the subsidiary. Hence, we start with the observation that the currency denomination of debt does not affect the cost of the debt.

This section develops the analysis further by shifting the focus to both the project and the debt's risk characteristics that have not yet been considered. Debt financing is usually long term and is quite often associated with a specific project. Therefore, this section introduces the discussion of debt financing with respect to one project and one currency. We consider cases in which UIP holds, and cases in which UIP does not hold.

The currency denomination of external debt is important, and, as we shall see, in fact makes debt financing a useful management tool. We assume that the firm (without specifying parent or subsidiary) can either borrow at home in its home currency or in a subsidiary's country in the foreign currency.

By the 1990s, markets for international debt had been extensively developed. Issuing a **foreign bond,** one sold by a foreign issuer and denominated in the currency of the country of issue, became more common for MNCs. International banking has developed to a level at which most international banks will deal in many currencies and subsidiaries/branches of international banks or local banks will make loans to foreign borrowers. There are also possibilities to borrow at home in the foreign currency, but these are sufficiently rare that we rule them out. Occasionally, there are possibilities to borrow in the foreign market in the home currency. In the 1990s, the **offshore market,** in which a bond denominated in a currency other than that of the country in which the bond is issued, grew rapidly. However, we consider this offshore borrowing more like onshore borrowing (in the home country) than like foreign borrowing. In sum, the relevant characteristic of debt is the currency denomination rather than the actual location of borrowing.

The firm's debt denomination decision is sometimes cast as a choice between centralizing or decentralizing debt finance, referring primarily to the currency denomination, but also to the location of borrowing activity. If the firm borrows in the home country and thereby holds all debt denominated in the home currency, the firm is said to centralize debt financing. If the firm instead borrows in the countries where operations are located, or possibly to which it exports, and thereby holds debt denominated in the currencies of the various countries in which it operates, the firm is said to decentralize debt financing. There are advantages to each strategy, and the choice between the two usually depends on the characteristics of the firm. The rest of this chapter is designed to identify the advantages of each strategy and the characteristics of the firm that determine its debt denomination pattern.

Before continuing, it is worth noting that centralization of debt financing need not occur in the home country or in the home country currency, but may occur in another country and currency that the firm decides is appropriate. A Latin American firm, for example, may find centralizing its debt in the U.S. dollar appropriate.

FOREIGN CURRENCY DENOMINATED DEBT

The main advantage of having debt denominated in the foreign currency (or in the export market's currency) is that the debt service (interest payments and principal repayments) is denominated in the currency in which the subsidiary's revenues are received. In addition, the liability denominated in the foreign currency offsets the subsidiary's foreign currency assets. Thus foreign-currency debt can serve to offset the otherwise exposed net cash inflows and assets, reducing overall risk. When the foreign currency appreciates vis-à-vis the home currency, the value of the liability and the cost of the debt payments increase, but the values of the foreign assets and revenues typically increase as well. Using a decentralized debt denomination strategy, a multinational corporation can effectively hedge its balance sheet and income statement exposures and thereby reduce foreign exchange risk.

Consider the case of Victor Enterprises' Swiss subsidiary examined earlier in this chapter. The after-tax cost of borrowing in U.S. dollars is equal to the after-tax cost of borrowing in Swiss francs because UIP holds before taxes and taxes are applied symmetrically to interest rates and foreign exchange gains/losses. Thus, the firm will likely be indifferent between borrowing in dollars and francs.

However, consider the risk characteristics of both the project and the debt. When the Swiss franc appreciates, the project's assets and cash flows have higher values in terms of U.S. dollars. When the Swiss franc depreciates, the project's assets and cash flows have lower values in terms of U.S. dollars. If the firm borrows in U.S. dollars, there is no change in the value of the liability or debt service as the Swiss franc appreciates or depreciates. However, if the firm borrows in Swiss francs, the liability and the debt service change as the Swiss franc appreciates or depreciates. When the Swiss franc appreciates, the debt and debt service have higher values in terms of U.S. dollars, and when the Swiss franc depreciates the debt and debt service have lower values in terms of U.S. dollars. These fluctuations appear to be risky for the MNC, but the fluctuations in the value of the debt and debt service offset part of the fluctuations in the value of the assets and cash flows from the project. When the Swiss franc appreciates, the assets and cash flows have higher values, and the debt and debt service have higher values. When the Swiss franc depreciates, the assets and cash flows have lower values, and the debt and debt service have lower values. Hence, the project and the debt taken together are not as risky because the debt denomination matches the denomination of the assets and cash flows. As Victor Enterprises finds that the costs of borrowing in U.S. dollars and Swiss francs are identical, it should prefer the Swiss franc borrowing as a costless method of reducing the project's foreign exchange risk.

The advantage of centralizing debt in the home currency must therefore be on the cost side. For example, centralization may be less costly because of economies of scale in borrowing. Larger borrowings in one currency may carry a lower interest rate than many smaller borrowings in various currencies, and are probably associated with lower transaction and administration costs. More importantly, however, if effective interest rates are different across countries, representing deviations from UIP, then companies may reduce their borrowing costs by borrowing where interest rates are lowest. This is actually nothing more than the theme that capital flows from low-interest-rate countries to high-interest-rate countries, which was developed in Chapter 1.

A centralized debt denomination strategy therefore allows the multinational corporation to take advantage of interest rate disparities between countries, and this is what may induce a firm to centralize borrowings in a currency other than its home currency.

As taking advantage of borrowing in low-interest-rate countries and deploying the funds in high-interest-rate countries is the focus of centralized debt financing in international investment, it is useful to examine the reasons for interest differentials across countries. If one currency carries a higher effective interest rate than another, such that centralizing borrowing can reduce the firm's interest bill, there must be *ex ante* deviations from uncovered interest parity. These *ex ante* deviations may arise for any of the several reasons discussed in Chapter 2, such as capital market imperfections arising from government capital controls, transaction costs, information asymmetries, tax distortions, political risk, and exchange risk.

A more compelling reason explaining why firms face cross-country differences in interest rates is that they have differential access to markets. Put simply, a firm usually enjoys greater access to home-country debt markets with lower interest rates than foreign firms. This means that firms are usually at a disadvantage in foreign debt markets. The reasons for this disadvantageous position may depend on the availability of information in the host market and lack of familiarity with the firm, or on cultural and language differences. Sometimes, the reasons will be legal or political. The argument here is that countries have different borrowing rates for domestic and foreign borrowers, and not that borrowing rates across countries differ. Along similar lines, a firm may have access to subsidized financing in one country but not in another, as with export financing or other government programs. Borrowing rates the firm faces are therefore even less likely to conform to uncovered interest parity than treasury bill interest rates, because firms may face differential access to markets.

As Victor Enterprises is a U.S. MNC, differential access to markets most likely means that its access to credit markets is more favorable in the United States than in Switzerland. Suppose risk-free interest rates in the United States and Switzerland are still 10 percent and 18.8 percent, respectively, and that UIP still holds for these risk-free rates. Also, suppose that Victor Enterprises' debt cost is still 4 percent above the risk-free rate in the United States, as previously developed in Table 4-1 for a $12 million loan, resulting in a present value of $971,407. However, suppose that Victor Enterprises' debt cost is now 5 percent above the risk-free rate in Switzerland, making its Swiss franc borrowing rate 24.74 percent (because $(1.05)(1.188) = 1.2474$) rather than the earlier 23.552 percent. The borrowing rates applicable to Victor Enterprises no longer adhere to UIP, and Swiss franc borrowing will be costlier because of its comparative disadvantage. Table 4-4 modifies the calculation of the cash flows from Victor Enterprises' Swiss franc loan. The present value of the cash flows associated with the Swiss franc loan, using the centralized method, is thus:

$$PV = 12,000,000 - 5,490,481/1.144 - 4,532,305/1.144^2 - 3,685,954/1.144^3$$
$$= \$1,275,604$$

rather than $1,407,450 calculated earlier. Netting out the $436,045 present value of taxes on foreign exchange gains, the net present value of the Swiss franc loan is $1,275,604 − $436,045 = $839,559, which is less than the present value of $971,407 from borrowing in dollars.

THE RISK-RETURN TRADEOFF

Although *ex ante* deviations from uncovered interest parity are difficult to detect, managers' interpretations of *ex ante* deviations from uncovered interest parity affect their debt denomination decisions. If management believes that uncovered interest parity holds *ex ante* in the long run, but acknowledges that *ex post* deviations exist, the firm will decentralize finance. The costs of long-run financing decisions do not differ if uncovered

TABLE 4-4 Cash Flows from Victor Enterprises' Swiss Franc Loan with Unfavorable Interest Rate

Swiss Franc Loan and Repayment

Year	Principal	Interest	Tax Shield	Total Cash Flow	Expected Exchange Rate	Conversion at Expected Rate
0	15,000,000			15,000,000	$0.80/SFr	$12,000,000
1	−5,000,000	−3,711,000	1,298,850	−7,412,150	$0.7407/SFr	−$5,490,481
2	−5,000,000	−2,474,000	865,900	−6,608,100	$0.6859/SFr	−$4,532,305
3	−5,000,000	−1,237,000	432,950	−5,804,050	$0.6351/SFr	−$3,685,954

Ex Ante Exchange Gains

Year	SFr Principal	Conversion at $0.80/SFr	Expected Exchange Rate	Conversion at Expected Rate	Expected Gain	Tax on Expected Gain
0	15,000,000	$12,000,000	$0.80/SFr	$12,000,000	0	0
1	−5,000,000	−$4,000,000	$0.7407/SFr	−$3,703,704	$296,296	$103,704
2	−5,000,000	−$4,000,000	$0.6859/SFr	−$3,429,355	$570,645	$199,726
3	−5,000,000	−$4,000,000	$0.6351/SFr	−$3,175,329	$824,671	$288,635

interest parity holds in the long run, so there is no additional cost to denominating debt in the foreign currency and the firm will do so to hedge its exposure. If management believes that uncovered interest parity does not hold *ex ante,* for any of the reasons previously discussed, management must assess whether the deviation is large or small compared to the level of additional risk the firm would be acquiring by centralizing finance.

Some firms will be willing to pay the deviation in the form of higher foreign currency borrowing rates to hedge exposure. These are direct foreign investors who require a risk premium for holding claims denominated in a foreign currency. The larger interest payments are thus justified as payment of a premium to hedge exposure. Other firms will not be willing to pay the deviation, so will centralize borrowing in currencies with low real interest rates, thereby reducing their interest bill, and retain their exposure and the risk that goes with it. These are direct foreign investors who do not require a risk premium for holding claims denominated in a foreign currency.[9]

The intuition behind the debt denomination analysis given here is the same as any risk-return trade-off. The firm's decision will generally be influenced by two characteristics: the level of diversification of the firm and the risk aversion of managers and owners. If a firm is highly diversified with respect to exposure, that firm will be able to take on the additional exposure fairly easily and thus will lean toward centralizing finance. If a firm is not well diversified, however, it will lean toward decentralized finance to hedge the exchange risk. If managers or owners are highly risk averse, in that they want to avoid bankruptcy and the costs of financial distress, management will again lean toward decentralizing finance. If, on the other hand, managers or owners are not very risk averse, or are even risk neutral as implied by modern finance theory, management will lean toward centralizing debt finance.

To rigorously analyze the issues discussed in this section, consider a simple model of a U.S. MNC making a one-year investment in a foreign country that must decide whether to finance part of the investment by borrowing in U.S. dollars or the foreign currency. Let $I^*_{t,t+1}$ denote the foreign currency rate of return on assets, known with certainty (for convenience), and not affected by the financing decision. (The assumption that this rate of return is known with certainty is unrealistic, so the "Tools for Analysis" at the end of this chapter works through the case when there is uncertainty. This alternative model comes to the same conclusions presented here except in some unusual circumstances.) The expected dollar rate of return on assets $I_{t,t+1}$, is then the foreign currency return plus the expected exchange rate change:

$$I_{t,t+1} = I^*_{t,t+1} + E_t[\%\Delta S_{t,t+1}]$$

where there is no annualization factor because the horizon is one year. As the only uncertainty in the expected dollar rate of return is associated with exchange rate fluctuations, the standard deviation of the expected dollar return is equal to the standard deviation of exchange rate changes: $\sigma_I = \sigma_{\%\Delta S}$.

The rate of return on assets can be decomposed into a weighted average of the rate of return on debt, $I^d_{t,t+1}$, and the rate of return on equity, $I^e_{t,t+1}$:

$$I_{t,t+1} = \alpha I^d_{t,t+1} + (1 - \alpha)I^e_{t,t+1}$$

where α denotes the portion of the project financed with debt, $0 < \alpha < 1$. (We are ignoring the effect of taxes in this, although the model could be extended to account for taxes in a straightforward way.)

THE DENOMINATION OF DEBT
AT LAKER AIRWAYS

Laker Airways (International), Ltd., a U.K. firm, operated no-frills, cut-rate airline services between London and the United States from 1977 to 1982. The bankruptcy of Laker Airways in 1982 has been at least partially attributed to incorrectly choosing the currency denomination of debt. Laker received ticket revenues in both U.K. pounds and U.S. dollars, in roughly the same magnitude. Laker also had costs in both currencies because aviation fuel is priced in U.S. dollars and most other operating expenses, such as salaries, were incurred in U.K. pounds. Laker was a highly leveraged firm, however, and most of the debt was denominated in U.S. dollars; in 1981 it raised $131 million from a consortium of banks and had $147 million in loans

from the U.S. Export-Import bank. This configuration made total dollar outflows far higher than total dollar revenues, and total sterling inflows higher than total sterling expenses. As the pound depreciated to new lows in 1981 and 1982, Laker could not meet its dollar expenses with its sterling revenues. The currency mix of debt was too risky; less dollar debt and more sterling debt may have saved the company. Laker may have initially chosen the large dollar borrowings because management felt that its interest rate on dollar debt was more favorable than the interest rate on sterling debt. Hence, the risk-return trade-off is apparent. For Laker, though, the risk to the firm was too high and the ultimate return was far too low.

Sources: Srinivasulu, S.L., "Currency Denomination of Debt: Lessons from Rolls-Royce and Laker Airways," *Business Horizons,* September–October 1983, pp. 19–23; "A Falling Pound Takes the Air Out of Laker," *Business Week,* August 3, 1981, pp. 35–36; and "How Sir Freddie Shot Himself Down," *Business Week,* February 22, 1982, p. 38.

The cost of dollar debt would be quoted by lenders (knowing α) as $R_{t,t+1}$, such that $I_{t,t+1}^{d,h} = R_{t,t+1}$, where the superscript h denotes home currency financing. $I_{t,t+1}^{d,h}$ has a standard deviation of zero as there is no uncertainty about the nominal interest rate. The rate of return on equity is thus expected to be:

$$I_{t,t+1}^{e,h} = \{I_{t,t+1}^* + E_t[\%\Delta S_{t,t+1}] - \alpha R_{t,t+1}\}/\{1 - \alpha\}$$

with standard deviation $\sigma_{Ie,h} = \sigma_{\%\Delta S}/(1 - \alpha)$. Note that, like the return on equity, the standard deviation is leveraged by $(1 - \alpha)$. The standard deviation is also clearly an increasing function of α as well. (However, as $R_{t,t+1}$ is an increasing function of α, the return on equity $I_{t,t+1}^{e,h}$ is not necessarily an increasing function of α.)

The dollar-equivalent cost of foreign currency financing is expected to be $I_{t,t+1}^{d,f} = R_{t,t+1}^* + E_t[\%\Delta S_{t,t+1}]$, where the superscript f denotes foreign currency financing, which has a standard deviation of $\sigma_{\%\Delta S}$. The expected rate of return on equity is thus expected to be:

$$I_{t,t+1}^{e,f} = \{I_{t,t+1}^* + E_t[\%\Delta S_{t,t+1}] - \alpha\{R_{t,t+1}^* + E_t[\%\Delta S_{t,t+1}]\}\}/(1 - \alpha)$$
$$= \{I_{t,t+1}^* - \alpha R_{t,t+1}^* + (1 - \alpha)E_t[\%\Delta S_{t,t+1}]\}/(1 - \alpha)$$

with standard deviation $\sigma_{Ie,f} = \sigma_{\%\Delta S}$. In this case, the variation in dollar profits due to currency fluctuations is offset by equal variation in financing costs. Note that the standard deviation is $\sigma_{\%\Delta S}$ regardless of the amount of leverage (α) because of the offsetting effects.

Comparing the standard deviations of returns to equity, it is clear that $\sigma_{Ie,f}$ is less than $\sigma_{Ie,h}$. The firm will prefer foreign currency finance because $\sigma_{Ie,f} < \sigma_{Ie,h}$ if the profits are expected to be the same, $I^{e,f} = I^{e,h}$, or if the foreign currency borrowing makes expected profits higher, $I^{e,f} > I^{e,h}$. However, if home currency financing makes the return on equity higher, $I^{e,h} > I^{e,f}$, the firm will have to analyze the risk-return trade-off. Managers must ask whether they prefer higher profits, $I^{e,h}$, with higher risk, $\sigma_{Ie,h}$, or lower profits, $I^{e,f}$, with lower risk, $\sigma_{Ie,f}$.

EXAMPLE 4.3

Brauhaus, Inc., is an American firm based in Chicago that is testing a new beer brewing project in a section of Germany that used to be part of East Berlin. The test project requires a one-year investment for plant leasing and equipment rental, and Brauhaus intends to finance the project with 60 percent equity and 40 percent debt. The DM return on the brewing operations is known to be 15 percent for that year.

First consider the case where UIP holds. The expected exchange rate change is −2 percent, and the standard deviation of annual percentage changes in the exchange rate is 4 percentage points. The borrowing rate quoted for the firm in U.S. dollars is currently 11 percent. The borrowing rate quoted for the firm in German marks is 13 percent. The dollar return on equity if this investment is 40 percent financed in U.S. dollars is expected to be

$$I_{t,t+1}^{e,\$} = [15\% - 2\% - 0.4(11\%)]/0.60 = 14.33\%$$

with a standard deviation of $4/0.60 = 6.67$ percentage points. The dollar return on equity if this investment is 40 percent financed in DM is

$$I_{t,t+1}^{e,DM} = [15\% - 0.4(13\%) + 0.6(-2\%)]/0.60 = 14.33\%$$

with a standard deviation of 4 percentage points. The risk that the future exchange rate change is not −2 percent is fairly high, however, as the standard deviation of annual percentage changes in the exchange rate is 4 percentage points. The standard deviation of the project's returns is much higher if it is financed in dollars than if it is financed in marks, so the firm would prefer to finance in marks.

Now consider the case where UIP does not hold. If the firm does not expect the DM to depreciate by 2 percent, it must weigh the additional expected returns against the additional risk from borrowing in dollars. For example, the firm may know that the 11 percent interest rate quoted on dollars is a good rate because the U.S. lender does a lot of business with Brauhaus, and that the 13 percent rate on DM is fairly high because debt capital is currently scarce in Germany and the German lender does not have a relationship with Brauhaus. Suppose the firm does not expect any change in the exchange rate. When the project is financed 40 percent in dollars, the expected return on equity is

$$I_{t,t+1}^{e,\$} = [15\% - 0.4(11\%)]/0.60 = 17.67\%.$$

When the project is financed 40 percent in DM, the expected return on equity is

$$I_{t,t+n}^{e,DM} = [15\% - 0.4(13\%)]/0.60 = 16.33\%.$$

The firm would prefer to have a 17.67 percent return over a 16.33 percent return, but the higher return comes with a standard deviation of 6.67 percentage points and the lower return comes with a standard deviation of 4 percentage points. The firm clearly must decide which risk-return combination it prefers.

One thing we have omitted here is the opportunity to hedge the investment in the financial markets. As we have detailed an example for one year dealing with the German mark, a hedge should be fairly easy to obtain. This means that firms may be able to borrow in the United States at a favorable interest rate and then lock in an exchange rate in the forward market. (We consider this further in Chapter 9 on financial hedges.) The analysis would then include a forward premium (or discount) and involve substantially less exchange risk. The analysis in this chapter is more generally applicable, however, to longer-term borrowing and to investment projects in unusual currencies, where financial hedges are not readily available.

Up to this point, we have considered debt financing for a single foreign subsidiary or project. A multinational with several foreign subsidiaries or projects in different countries has the added flexibility of managing a portfolio of debt. As with any portfolio problem, debt management would benefit from diversification of currencies. In this instance, diversification reinforces the benefits of decentralization because of the desire to borrow in many currencies. It is important to remember, however, that diversification may come at a cost if centralization would reduce overall interest payments. If this is the case, managers may want to undertake risk-return analysis using the multinational corporation as a whole. Because this is of secondary importance, however, we do not take up the issue further in this chapter. The reader is referred to any financial investments textbook for a more thorough discussion. For the particular applications to debt financing, see Madura (1985). The analysis of debt management must be done as part of an overall assessment of exchange risk in the firm as the former is likely to be an important component of the latter.

❖ SUMMARY OF CHAPTER OBJECTIVES

1. Revise the value of a foreign project to include the effects of financing part of the project with debt.

A positive present value of debt arises due to deductibility of interest from income in calculating corporate taxes. The present value can be computed by discounting the cash flows from the debt and repayment at the rate of interest on the debt. The magnitude of the benefit from foreign borrowing is identical to the benefit from domestic borrowing under the following two conditions: (1) uncovered interest parity must hold before taxes; and (2) taxes must be applied to capital gains and losses symmetrically, and at the same rate at which the interest payments are deductible.

2. Explain ways of financing the multinational corporation as a whole and why a subsidiary's capital structure is not independent of the parent's capital structure.

The multinational corporation as a whole is financed with external capital, which may take the form of either equity or debt. The capital structure of the subsidiary is not independent of the capital structure of the parent because funds can be transferred internally between the subsidiary and the parent, and because the external financing is a liability of the corporation as a whole whether it is issued by the subsidiary or by the parent. There is an optimal capital structure for the firm as a whole, and the combination of the parent's capital structure and that of the subsidiary should together produce this optimal capital structure of the firm. When foreign interest rates are higher than home interest rates, there is a tax advantage to having the subsidiary borrow, and when foreign interest rates are lower than home interest rates there is a tax advantage to having the parent borrow, regardless of the currency denomination of the debt.

3. Explain ways of financing the foreign subsidiary, including internal versus external financing, equity versus debt financing, and home currency versus foreign currency financing.

The multinational firm must consider internal financing versus external financing and equity versus debt. However, these two decisions are fundamentally no different for the multinational corporation than they are for the domestic corporation. The unique decision facing the multinational is in choosing between obligations denominated in the home currency and those denominated in the foreign currency.

4. Analyze the currency denomination of debt (home currency versus foreign currency) in terms of the uncovered interest parity theorem and the project's foreign exchange risk.

The debt denomination decision is particularly important with respect to external debt financing. Most international debt financing is in fact project-specific, so the chapter largely concentrates on one foreign project and one foreign currency. In long-term debt markets, it is likely that there will be expected deviations from uncovered interest parity, particularly when the multinational has better access to its home country's capital markets (leading to favorable interest rates) than to foreign capital markets. This fact then gives rise to an important risk-return trade-off between centralizing and decentralizing debt finance: centralizing borrowing in a low-interest-rate currency will reduce the cost of financing, but decentralizing borrowing in many foreign currencies reduces the risks associated with the various projects.

❖ QUESTIONS FOR REVIEW

1. The Batt Corporation arranged a one-year, $1 million loan to fund a foreign project. The loan was denominated in French francs and carried a 10 percent nominal rate. The exchange rate at the time of the loan was 5.75 francs per dollar but dropped to 5.10 francs per dollar by the time the repayment came due. What effective interest rate did Batt end up paying on the foreign loan?

2. A U.S. multinational wants to evaluate the present value of a loan denominated in Australian dollars. It prefers to evaluate the Australian dollar debt using the typical decentralized technique, in which the Australian dollar cash flows are discounted and then converted to U.S. dollars at the prevailing spot rate. The spot exchange rate is currently $0.80/A$. The firm is considering three-year debt in the amount of A$12,500,000, at an interest rate of 26 percent. The loan structure provides for payment of interest and repayment of all principal in one lump sum three years from now. The corporation's tax rate is 34 percent, and the firm will be able to realize all benefits of the tax-related debt shield. As a point of reference, the firm's cost of borrowing in U.S. dollars is 14.4 percent.

   The risk-free interest rate in the United States is 10 percent and the risk-free interest rate in Australia is 18.8 percent. The firm decides to use uncovered interest parity to form expectations of future spot exchange rates, so the three-year-ahead forecast is $.8[1.10/1.188]^3 = 0.635065792$.

   One final tax consideration is that the United States will tax any foreign exchange gains associated with the repayment of principal or will allow deductions against other income for any foreign exchange losses. Hence, the present value of the tax payments on foreign exchange gains is expected to be:

   $$.34[.635065792 - .80][-12,500,000]/1.144^3 = \$468,189.$$

   a. What is the present value of the Australian dollar financing, using the typical decentralized technique?

   b. Instead of using the decentralized technique, the firm is considering a centralized technique, in which the Australian dollar cash flows are converted to U.S. dollars and subsequently discounted at the U.S. dollar cost of debt. If the firm uses uncovered interest parity in the risk-free deposit markets to forecast future exchange rates, what is the present value of the loan calculated to be? Carefully explain your reasoning.

3. A U.S. multinational wants to evaluate Australian dollar debt financing using a centralized technique, in which the Australian dollar cash flows are converted to U.S. dollars and subsequently discounted at the U.S. dollar cost of debt, which is currently 14.4 percent. The spot exchange rate is currently $0.80/A$. The firm is considering three-year debt in the amount of A$12,500,000, at an interest rate of 23.552 percent. The structure of the loan provides for payment of interest and repayment of all principal in one lump sum three years from now. The corporation's tax rate is 34 percent, and the firm will be able to realize all benefits of the tax-related debt shield. Hence, the repayment of debt net of tax shield amounts to:

$$(1.23552)^3(12,500,500) - .34[(1.23552)^3(12,500,000) - 12,500,000] =$$
$$\text{A\$ }19,809,774.$$

The risk-free interest rate in the United States is 10 percent and the risk-free interest rate in Australia is 18.8 percent. The firm decides to use uncovered interest parity to form expectations of future spot exchange rates, so the three-year ahead forecast is $.8[1.10/1.188]^3 = 0.635065792$.

One final tax consideration is that the United States will tax any foreign exchange gains associated with the repayment of principal or will allow deductions against other income for any foreign exchange losses. Hence, the present value of the tax on foreign exchange gains is expected to be:

$$.34[.635065792 - .80][-12,500,000]/1.144^3 = \$468,189.$$

a. If the firm uses a centralized technique to evaluate the debt, what is the present value in U.S. dollars?

b. Suppose that some of the firm's managers believe that the Australian dollar is not expected to depreciate as much as the interest differential indicates. In particular, their three-year forecast of the exchange rate is $0.6822/A$. What is the present value of the debt under this exchange rate forecast? Carefully explain your reasoning.

4. The main unique decision in international financing is the debt denomination decision. Suppose that Coval Enterprises, a U.S. multinational, is able to borrow $500,000 for one year in the United States at an interest rate of 10.24 percent, and is able to borrow DM 1 million for one year in Germany at an interest rate of 7.12 percent. The current exchange rate is $0.50/DM, the risk-free interest rate in the United States is 6.00 percent, and the risk-free interest rate in Germany is 3.00 percent. Coval Enterprises faces a tax rate of 35 percent and is able to deduct interest payments from corporate income before calculating tax liability, so debt creates a tax shield. In addition, the United States taxes foreign exchange gains on foreign-currency-denominated debt at 35 percent and allows deduction of foreign exchange losses on foreign-currency-denominated debt at 35 percent.

a. If Coval Enterprises borrows $500,000 for one year, what is the additional value that borrowing adds to the project in the form of debt-related tax shields?

b. If Coval Enterprises borrows DM 1 million for one year, what is the additional value that borrowing adds to the project in the form of debt-related tax shields (including tax effects from foreign exchange gains or losses)?

c. One theme in international financial management is that financial markets may be segmented or integrated. You may safely assume that the markets for risk-free securities in the United States and Germany are integrated in this question, so that uncovered interest parity holds. Even if the markets for risk-free securities in the United States and Germany are integrated, why might the markets for the equity and debt of Coval Enterprises be segmented?

5. [Class discussion] One stylized fact of multinational corporations is that foreign subsidiaries are capitalized with as little equity as possible and with as much intra-firm debt as possible.

   a. What are the advantages of internal debt over internal equity in financing a foreign subsidiary?

   b. How do the tax rates in the home and the host country affect the decision to use internal debt instead of internal equity?

   c. How would you choose the currency denomination of the internal debt?

   d. To what extent does the capital structure (debt versus equity) of the subsidiary really matter? Carefully explain your reasoning.

6. [Class discussion] One proposition regarding the capital structure of multinational corporations is that the capital structure of a foreign project or subsidiary is not separate from the capital structure of the parent.

   a. Carefully explain the main reasons why the proposition above is generally true.

   b. Now consider the implications of the proposition for financing a foreign subsidiary. How much does the capital structure of the subsidiary matter?

7. [Class discussion] What are the benefits and costs of decentralizing international finance such that corporate borrowings are denominated in the currencies of the countries in which the various subsidiaries operate?

8. [Group project] The internationalization of capital markets suggests that the world is moving toward an integrated, global capital market (and away from segmented domestic markets). Currently, multinational firms often list their stocks on foreign stock exchanges, an activity referred to as cross-listing. For example, Sony cross-lists its Japanese stock on the New York Stock Exchange. In many circumstances, the process of cross-listing can be expensive. What motivates companies to cross-list their stocks? What are the perceived benefits of cross-listing, and why do these benefits exist? Answer as fully and as carefully as you can.

9. A U.S. multinational is considering a new project in Portugal. The initial stage requires only one year of operations, during which the rate of return in Portuguese escudos is known to be 13 percent (without any uncertainty). The standard deviation of annual percentage changes in the Portuguese escudo vis-à-vis the U.S. dollar has historically been 6 percentage points. The firm is able to finance the entire operation by borrowing from a multinational bank. The borrowing rate quoted for the firm in the U.S. dollar is 7 percent and in the Portuguese escudo is 11 percent. The firm's managers believe that the Portuguese escudo will depreciate by 2 percent during the year of operations.

   a. What is the expected rate of return on this investment if it is financed in U.S. dollars? What is the standard deviation of this expected rate of return?

   b. What is the expected rate of return on this investment if it is financed in Portuguese escudos? What is the standard deviation of this expected rate of return?

   c. For this firm's expectations and its quoted interest rates, does uncovered interest parity hold? For this investment, what are the benefits and what are the costs of financing the project in Portuguese escudos?

10. A U.S. multinational is considering a new project in Denmark. The initial stage requires only one year of operations, during which the rate of return in Danish krone

is expected to be 12 percent. The firm is able to finance half of the operation by borrowing from a multinational bank; the other half of the investment will come from internal equity from the parent. The borrowing rate quoted for the firm in the Danish krone is 9 percent, and in the U.S. dollar is 8 percent. Managers of the firm believe that the Danish krone will depreciate by 2 percent during the year of operations.

a. What is the expected rate of return on this project before financing costs (i.e., if it is an all-equity-financed project)?

b. What is the expected rate of return on this project if it is financed half with equity and half with dollar-denominated debt?

c. What is the expected rate of return on this project if it is financed half with equity and half with krone-denominated debt?

11. The manager of a firm operating in the Sovereign Republic of Hacker is trying to decide whether to borrow, for one year, Hacker pschorrs at 8 percent or U.S. dollars at 12 percent. The current exchange rate is 4 Hacker pschorrs per U.S. dollar.

a. For what end-of-year exchange rate will the cost of these two choices be equal?

b. If the standard deviation of the exchange rate is 0.50 Hp/$, what is the standard deviation of the cost of dollar borrowing per dollar borrowed?

c. Suppose that the tax rate in Hacker is 40 percent. The firm is able to deduct interest payments from corporate income before calculating taxes, thereby lowering the after-tax cost of borrowing. The firm is also able to deduct exchange losses on foreign currency loans, but must also add exchange gains on foreign currency loans to taxable income. For what end-of-year exchange rate will the after-tax cost of these two choices be equal?

d. Again suppose that the tax rate in Hacker is 40 percent, and that the firm is able to deduct interest payments from corporate income before calculating taxes, but now suppose that exchange losses on foreign currency loans are not tax-deductible and exchange gains on foreign currency loans are not taxed as income. For what end-of-year exchange rate will the after-tax cost of the two choices be equal?

12. Vertigo, Inc., a U.S. corporation, is considering a foreign project. The project has an expected foreign currency rate of return of 20 percent with a standard deviation of 10 percentage points. The percentage change in the exchange rate between the U.S. dollar and the foreign currency is expected to be zero, with a standard deviation of 12 percentage points. The covariance between the foreign currency returns and the percentage changes in the exchange rate is 60 percentage points squared, such that the foreign currency returns are higher when the foreign currency appreciates. Vertigo is considering U.S. dollar debt and foreign currency debt to finance this project. The firm can borrow the entire amount in U.S. dollars at a fixed interest rate of 8 percent, or the entire amount in foreign currency at a fixed interest rate of 11 percent.

a. What is the simple correlation coefficient between foreign currency returns and exchange rate changes?

b. What is the standard deviation of the U.S. dollar returns if the project is financed with debt denominated in the foreign currency?

c. What is the standard deviation of the U.S. dollar returns if the project is financed with debt denominated in the U.S. dollar?

d. What is the additional U.S. dollar return (positive or negative) on the project expected from borrowing in the dollar over borrowing in the foreign currency?

TOOLS FOR ANALYSIS
Debt Financing with Project Risk

This section reconsiders the model of the debt de-nomination decision when there is uncertainty about the foreign currency rate of return on assets $I_{t,t+1}^*$ as well as uncertainty about exchange rate changes. Recall from the chapter that

$$I_{t,t+1}^{e,h} = \frac{I_{t,t+1}^* + E_t[\%\Delta S_{t,t+1}] - \alpha R_{t,t+1}}{1 - \alpha}$$

$$I_{t,t+1}^{e,f} = \frac{I_{t,t+1}^* - \alpha R_{t,t+1}^* + (1 - \alpha)E_t[\%\Delta S_{t,t+1}]}{1 - \alpha}$$

where $0 < \alpha < 1$. If $I_{t,t+1}^*$ is not known with certainty, then it adds an additional source of risk. If the standard deviation of $I_{t,t+1}^*$ is denoted σ_{I^*}, then the standard deviations of $I_{t,t+1}^{e,h}$ and $I_{t,t+1}^{e,f}$ are:

$$\sigma_{Ie,h} = \frac{\sqrt{\sigma_{I^*}^2 + \sigma_{\%\Delta S}^2 + 2\rho\sigma_{I^*}\sigma_{\%\Delta S}}}{1 - \alpha}$$

$$\sigma_{Ie,f} = \frac{\sqrt{\sigma_{I^*}^2 + (1 - \alpha)^2\sigma_{\%\Delta S}^2 + 2(1 - \alpha)\rho\sigma_{I^*}\sigma_{\%\Delta S}}}{1 - \alpha}$$

where ρ is the correlation coefficient between I^* and $\%\Delta S$. After some algebraic manipulation, we find that:

$$\sigma_{Ie,f} < \sigma_{Ie,h} \quad \text{when} \quad \alpha < 2(1 + \rho\sigma_{I^*}/\sigma_{\%\Delta S})$$

$$\text{and} \quad \sigma_{Ie,f} > \sigma_{Ie,h} \quad \text{when} \quad \alpha > 2(1 + \rho\sigma_{I^*}/\sigma_{\%\Delta S}).$$

In most circumstances, $\alpha < 2(1 + \rho\sigma_{I^*}/\sigma_{\%\Delta S})$. In particular, the condition is satisfied whenever $\rho \geq 0$. Hence, the firm will typically prefer foreign currency borrowing to reduce the risk of a foreign project. In some unusual cases involving $\rho < 0$ (but not all such cases), $\alpha > 2(1 + \rho\sigma_{I^*}/\sigma_{\%\Delta S})$, and the firm will actually prefer home currency borrowing to reduce the risk of a foreign project. The condition $\rho < 0$ implies that the foreign currency returns on a project decline when the foreign currency appreciates, as when the foreign project exports to the rest of the world and is hurt by foreign currency appreciation. If the effect is large enough, the firm will prefer home currency borrowing to reduce risk.

EXAMPLE 4.4
Suppose $\rho = -0.70$, $\sigma_{I^*} = 6$, $\sigma_{\%\Delta S} = 5$, and $\alpha = 0.35$. Since $2(1 + \rho\sigma_{I^*}/\sigma_{\%\Delta S}) = 2[1-0.7(6)/5] = 0.32$, we see that $\alpha > 2(1 + \rho\sigma_{I^*}/\sigma_{\%\Delta S})$. Hence, $\sigma_{Ie,f} > \sigma_{Ie,h}$, meaning that foreign currency borrowing is riskier than home currency borrowing.

Richer models of the debt denomination would allow combinations of home currency borrowing and foreign currency borrowing rather than just one or the other, and could allow α to be a choice variable.

❖ **ENDNOTES**

1. This is simply the international counterpart to the adjusted present value method undertaken in domestic finance; for example, see Grinblatt and Titman (1998), Chapter 12, or Luehrman (1997). Its appropriateness in international capital budgeting is highlighted by Lessard (1985).

2. Based on John F. Chown, "Tax Structures and Finance," Chapter 11 of *The Handbook of International Financial Management,* edited by Robert Z. Aliber, pp. 373–407.

3. In reality, parent companies rarely issue separate shares to track returns on a subsidiary, and subsidiaries rarely issue shares directly unless there is a compelling reason to do so. One example of a tracking stock, albeit domestic, is General Motors' class H shares, which are designed to track its Hughes Electronics subsidiary. This could also have been accomplished if the Hughes subsidiary had issued shares directly. In some instances, the subsidiary is not wholly owned by the parent and its capital structure is segmented from the parent's capital structure to interact with the other owners of capital in the project. In this case, the partially-owned subsidiary is probably best thought of as a separate company. One example of a subsidiary not wholly owned by the apparent parent is EuroDisney, which is less than half owned by the Walt Disney Company although it is solely operated by the Walt Disney Company. The rest of EuroDisney is owned by shareholders who purchase French-franc-denominated shares that directly track Euro-Disney rather than the Walt Disney Company as a whole.

4. There are also new theories of capital structure which suggest that the method of financing influences firm managers' investment decisions by providing incentives for the firm to undertake profitable investments and by allocating some control of the firm to people other than managers (such as bondholders or bankers). For a synthesis of the traditional and control-based theories, see Diamond (1994).

5. Hodder and Senbet (1990) develop this idea in a model of an equilibrium international capital structure based on international differences in taxes, the effects of inflation, and exchange rate changes. Their model implies that there is an optimum capital structure for the entire multinational corporation, and that the capital structures of the subsidiaries are designed to produce this overall optimal capital structure.

6. There are also studies of capital structure of firms across countries, such as Rutterford (1985) and Sekely and Collins (1988).

7. Dividend pooling implies that the value of the shares should be identical once converted to a common currency and adjusted for the proportions of shares. The fact that the separate shares have not been of equal value has been the topic of discussions, and suggests that international capital markets are segmented. For more, see Harvard Business School Case No. 9–296–077, "Global Equity Markets: The Case of Royal Dutch and Shell"; Froot and Dabora (1999); and Rosenthal and Young (1990).

8. For more on corporations listing their stock on foreign exchanges, see Saudagaran (1988) Mittoo (1994), and Howe and Madura (1990).

9. For more on the managerial implications, see Aliber (1989).

❖ REFERENCES

Aliber, Robert Z. "The Debt Denomination Decision," Chapter 13 of *The Handbook of International Financial Management,* ed. by R. Z. Aliber, Dow Jones-Irwin, 1989, pp. 435–451.

Burgman, Todd. "An Empirical Examination of Multinational Corporate Capital Structure," *Journal of International Business Studies,* 1996, pp. 553–570.

Chowdhry, Bhagwan, and Joshua D. Coval. "Internal Financing of Multinational Subsidiaries: Debt vs. Equity," *Journal of Corporate Finance,* 1998, pp. 87–106.

Chowdhry, Bhagwan, and Vikram Nanda. "Financing of Multinational Subsidiaries: Parent Debt vs. External Debt," *Journal of Corporate Finance,* 1994, pp. 259–281.

Chown, John F. "Tax Structures and Finance," *The Handbook of International Financial Management,* ed. by Robert Z. Aliber, pp. 373–407.

Diamond, Douglas W. "Corporate Capital Structure: The Control Roles of Bank and Public Debt with Taxes and Costly Bankruptcy," *Federal Reserve Bank of Richmond Quarterly Review,* Spring 1994, pp. 11–37.

Doernberg, Richard L. *International Taxation in a Nutshell,* West Publishing Co., 1993.

Fatemi, Ali M. "The Effect of International Diversification on Corporate Financing Policy," *Journal of Business Research,* 1988, pp. 17–30.

Feldstein, Martin. "The Effects of Outbound Foreign Direct Investment on the Domestic Capital Stock," in *The Effects of Taxation on Multinational Corporations,* edited by Martin Feldstein, James R. Hines, Jr., and R. Glenn Hubbard, The University of Chicago Press, 1995, pp. 43–63.

Froot, Kenneth A., and Emil M. Dabora. "How Are Stock Prices Affected by the Location of Trade?" *Journal of Financial Economics,* 1999, pp. 189–216.

Grinblatt, Mark, and Sheridan Titman. *Financial Markets and Corporate Strategy,* Irwin/McGraw-Hill, 1998.

Hodder, James E., and Lemma W. Senbet. "International Capital Structure Equilibrium," *Journal of Finance,* 1990, pp. 1495–1516.

Howe, John S., and Jeff Madura. "The Impact of International Listings on Risk: Implications for Capital Market Integration," *Journal of Banking and Finance,* December 1990, pp. 1133–1142.

Lee, Kwang Chul, and Chuck C.Y. Kwok. "Multinational Corporations vs. Domestic Corporations: International Environmental Factors and Determinants of Capital Structure," *Journal of International Business Studies,* 1988, pp. 195–217.

Lessard, Donald R. "Evaluating International Projects: An Adjusted Present Value Approach," Chapter 34 of *International Financial Management: Theory and Application,* ed. by Donald R. Lessard, John Wiley & Sons, Inc., 1985, pp. 570–584.

Luehrman, Timothy A. "Using APV: A Better Tool for Valuing Operations," *Harvard Business Review,* May-June 1997, pp. 145–154.

Madura, Jeff. "Development and Evaluation of International Financing Models," *Management International Review,* 1985, no. 4, pp. 17–27.

Miller, Darius. "The Market Reaction to International Cross-Listings: Evidence from Depository Receipts," *Journal of Financial Economics,* 1999, pp. 103–123.

Mittoo, Usha R. "Evaluating the Foreign Listing Decision in a Capital Budgeting Framework," *Managerial Finance,* 1994, pp. 22–35.

Rosenthal, Leonard, and Colin Young. "The Seemingly Anomalous Price Behavior of Royal Dutch Shell and Unilever NV/PLC," *Journal of Financial Economics,* 1990, pp. 123–141.

Rutterford, Janette. "An International Perspective on the Capital Structure Puzzle," *Midland Corporate Finance Journal,* Fall 1985, pp. 60–72.

Saudagaran, Shahrokh M. "An Empirical Study of Selected Factors Influencing the Decision to List on Foreign Stock Exchanges," *Journal of International Business Studies,* Spring 1988, pp. 101–127.

Sekely, William S., and J. Markham Collins. "Cultural Influences on International Capital Structure," *Journal of International Business Studies,* Spring 1988, pp. 87–100.

Shao, Lawrence Peter, Iftekhar Hasan, and Alan T. Shao. "Determinants of International Capital Structure for U.S. Foreign Subsidiaries," *Multinational Business Review,* Fall 1995, pp. 67–77.

Srinivasulu, S.L. "A Falling Pound Takes the Air Out of Laker," *Business Week,* August 3, 1981, pp. 33–36.

Srinivasulu, S.L. "How Sir Freddie Shot Himself Down," *Business Week,* February 22, 1982, p. 380.

Srinivasulu, S.L. "Currency Denomination of Debt: Lessons from Rolls-Royce and Laker Airways," *Business Horizons,* September–October 1983, pp. 19–23.

FOREIGN INVESTMENT STRATEGY

5.1   Introduction
5.2   Positive Present Value and Economic Rent
5.3   Modes of International Business
5.4   Theories of Direct Foreign Investment
5.5   Real Options in International Capital Budgeting

CHAPTER OBJECTIVES

AFTER READING THIS CHAPTER, YOU SHOULD BE ABLE TO:

❖ Explain the source of positive present value in investment projects.

❖ Compare different modes of international business by analyzing their present values.

❖ Understand wholly-owned foreign investment projects in terms of theories of direct foreign investment.

❖ Value projects in terms of the future opportunities to change the investment.

This chapter covers four main topics. The first section explores the sources of positive present value projects. We discuss both cost-based and revenue-based sources. The second section then considers different international business modes and makes a comparison of their present values. We then discuss and evaluate the major theories of DFI. We conclude with an analysis of the impact of managerial flexibility on international capital budgeting decisions.

5.1   INTRODUCTION

This chapter is the last in the trilogy of chapters analyzing the evaluation and financing of foreign projects. Chapter 3 examined foreign project evaluation in terms of present value calculations and the cost of capital, and Chapter 4 examined foreign project financing and its integration with MNC financing for the firm as a whole. This chapter serves as an overview of foreign project evaluation and financing by explicitly considering underlying sources of positive present value. As such, this chapter is much less technical than the preceding two chapters and much more conceptual. It begins with the premise that the source of positive present value for any project is a comparative advantage in the use of resources that produces an excess return on the project. We are particularly interested in the excess return on capital, which represents a return to capital in excess of the return the shareholders, the owners of capital, require. How a firm pursues this excess return on behalf of the shareholders is the firm's **corporate strategy,** a plan to identify, develop, and exploit a comparative advantage in the use of resources.

In international business, an excess return can be captured through many different modes of operation, including simple import/export businesses, license and franchise agreements with foreign entities, joint ventures with foreign firms, and the wholly-owned direct foreign investments we considered in Chapters 3 and 4. Each one of these modes has advantages and disadvantages, and they must be compared to select the mode which maximizes present value. However, there are particularly rich theories of wholly-owned DFI, which typically seek to explain the existence of DFI in terms of comparative advantages in the use of resources that MNCs have over their host-country counterparts. These theories are often based on corporate strategies for seeking excess returns that are particularly international when compared to more general theories of excess returns. Although there are some microeconomic elements here, theories of DFI are predominantly examined in a macroeconomic context vis-à-vis models of international capital flows and international investment. This perspective focuses attention on financial aspects of DFI to subsequently examine financial management in multinational corporations.

Foreign investment strategy often involves project analysis, which goes beyond valuation using present value techniques. In general, a firm may be able to alter the nature of a project depending on the state of the operating environment—such as by expanding the project when circumstances are favorable and contracting the project when circumstances are unfavorable. This approach presents a difficulty for present value analysis because the methodology is designed to evaluate projects which are fixed over time, although there is uncertainty over cash flows generated by the fixed project. In the extreme, the firm might be able to delay a project and subsequently undertake it fully if circumstances become more favorable. Alternatively, the firm might be able to abandon a project already started if circumstances become unfavorable. Present value calculations in these situations are inadequate because they do not accurately value the flexibility of a project, which is alterable over time. The alterations possible in capital investment projects have become known as **real options,** representing such opportunities as the option to start a project or the option to abandon a project, and attention to the value created by these real options is an important part of investment strategy.

This chapter brings together many issues in international capital budgeting, international financing, and foreign investment strategy. The balance of theory from domestic finance relating to the sources of firm profitability and theory from international finance relating to capital flows represents the crossroads at which international financial management exists. This is a blend of micro- and macro-economics: domestic microeconomics provides foundations for corporate finance while international macro-economics provides most of the concepts distinguishing international corporate finance from domestic corporate finance. We continue discussion of these issues in the next part of the book on foreign exchange exposure, risk, and hedging.

5.2 POSITIVE PRESENT VALUE AND ECONOMIC RENT

Corporations are in business to capture profit for the shareholders. Projects with positive present value generate profits in excess of the return required by the owners of capital—the shareholders—and therefore create additional value for them. Economists call this excess return **economic rent,** broadly defined as the return to a factor of production in excess of the return in its next-best use. This concept is the foundation of corporate strategies which seek to maximize the value of the firm because economic rent results from a firm's comparative advantage in the use of resources, either on the production or on the sales side.[1]

Chapters 3 and 4 calculated the present value of cash flows and tax-related debt shields for hypothetical foreign projects. The adjusted present value (APV), the present value of a project adjusted for the effects of financing, was shown as:

$$APV = \sum_{t=0}^{n} \frac{E_0[CF_t S_t]}{(1 + COC)^t} + \sum_{t=1}^{n} \frac{\tau RD_{t-1}}{(1 + R)^t}$$

using the centralized capital budgeting technique, where all notation is as defined earlier. Firms maximize value by undertaking all projects with $APV > 0$, or picking the highest APVs among mutually exclusive projects.

With all firms undertaking all projects with $APV > 0$, an equilibrium would emerge where all profitable projects are being done. At the margin, in fact, $APV=0$ and only projects with $APV < 0$ remain. Hence, a firm expecting a positive APV on a project should wonder why a positive APV exists. After all, if there is really a positive APV, wouldn't some other firm already be doing the project?

This is a direct analogy to the efficient markets hypothesis for portfolio investments, which suggests that prices of financial assets reflect all available information. If a stock analyst, for example, expects an excess return on a particular stock, he must wonder why other stock analysts have not also discovered the expected excess return on that stock and already bid up the price of the stock to eliminate the excess return. By analogy, if a project has an expected positive APV, there must be a reason for the excess return that explains why another firm has not already undertaken the project. The reason usually depends on real (physical) market imperfections in the markets for the inputs to make the products or in the markets for the sale of the final product output as opposed to imperfections in financial markets. These real imperfections explain the sources of a firm's comparative advantage in the use of resources, or economic rent.

We present economic rent in terms of microeconomic diagrams of revenues and costs because the topic has been extensively developed using such methodology. After using estimates of cash flows in capital budgeting and financing, diagrams also represent an efficient way to convey a lot of information concisely in the form of revenue schedules and cost schedules in which cash flows are a function of the quantity of output. We also introduce the diagrams here in anticipation of using them again in Chapter 7 to examine the effects of exchange rate changes on economic rents.

The traditional example of economic rent is the return to a fixed supply of land. The land is assumed to be idle if not put to use, so there is no opportunity cost in using the land. Figure 5-1 contains a diagram of the quantity of land on the horizontal axis and the price of land on the vertical axis. As shown in Figure 5-1, a fixed supply of land produces pure rent for the land's owners because the market-clearing price of the land depends on the demand for the land. Any positive price received for the land exceeds the owner's cost of producing the land, and furthermore exceeds the price of the next-best alternative use of the land, which would be zero if the land is idle, so the entire price received is economic rent. The principle can be extended to include any natural resources on the land; for example, a natural water source (perhaps Evian or Perrier) would provide economic rent to the firm bottling and selling the water or an oil reserve would provide economic rent to the firm extracting it.[2]

In finance, economic rent on capital is profit in excess of the profit in its next-best use, or a return in excess of the return required. This return in excess of the required return is often referred to as **economic profit** to distinguish it from accounting profit, which includes the required return in addition to any excess return. When the firm purchases assets and inputs at market prices that subsequently yield output that is worth more than the cost of the inputs, the firm's owners capture economic rents. In this situation, the rent results from the firm's comparative advantage in the use of resources. It is thus natural to ask why the firm is able to improve on the market values of the assets and inputs. Two sources of rent or profit often considered by economists are: (1) profits from being a low-cost producer, and (2) profits from monopoly or oligopoly power. A firm will have positive economic rent only if it has a comparative advantage in operating assets and using inputs due to one or both of these sources. Without the advantage, competition determines the return to capital from operating the assets using inputs as simply the required return on capital.

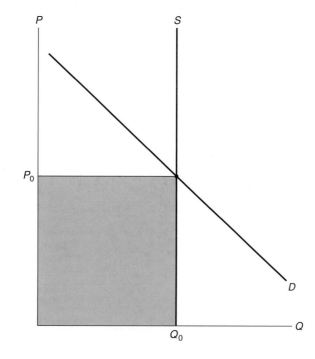

FIGURE 5-1 ECONOMIC RENT WITH FIXED RESOURCE SUPPLY

A fixed resource supply is represented by the vertical line labeled S at Q_0, and the demand for the resource is represented by the downward-sloping line labeled D. The market-clearing price is P_0, and when the opportunity cost of the use of the resource is zero, the entire amount of the price represents economic rent. With price P_0 and quantity Q_0, total economic rent is the shaded area.

COST-BASED STRATEGY

When the firm has a cost advantage, it is able to add economic value to the market value of assets and inputs used in production. These advantages might be due to cutting-edge technology, proprietary production processes, or managerial techniques that competitors do not have. In the "Tools for Analysis" at the end of this chapter, we provide mathematical details about profit maximization for a firm and the calculation of economic rent. Here, we summarize the results graphically, as is typical in courses on managerial economics. Figure 5-2 illustrates the situation for a price-taking firm with a cost advantage. The average cost of production is represented by the U-shaped curve labeled AC, and the marginal cost of production is represented by the upward-sloping curve labeled MC. Even if the firm is a price taker in a perfectly competitive market—such that the marginal revenue curve, MR, is flat at the equilibrium price of the product—the firm will enjoy economic profits as long as the marginal revenue exceeds the firm's minimum average cost. In Figure 5-2, the cost structure reflected in MC and AC is sufficiently low to produce economic rent. The optimum quantity of output is Q_0, which is determined by the intersection of MR and MC. Hence, the profit margin, or economic rent per unit, is measured by the difference between the price of the goods sold and the average cost of goods sold at that quantity, $(P_0 - C_0)$. The shaded area thus represents the total amount of economic rent. Firms that enjoy economic rent due to comparative advantages in production are often said to follow a **cost-based strategy.**

REVENUE-BASED STRATEGY

When a firm has market power to set prices, it enjoys monopoly rents from marketing its products. The monopolistic advantages may be natural, or may be bestowed on a firm through patents, trademarks, copyrights, exclusive franchises, brand recognition, product differentiation, or any other unique aspect capable of producing market power for the firm. In all of these situations, the firm will face a downward-sloping demand curve for

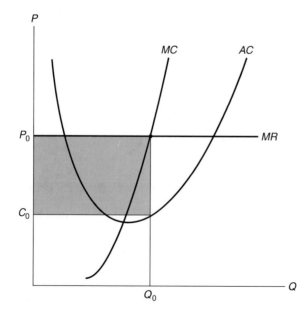

FIGURE 5-2   ECONOMIC RENT FOR A PRICE-TAKING FIRM

A price-taking firm is able to sell at a constant price, which is represented by the flat marginal revenue curve labeled MR at P_0. The cost structure is represented by the average cost curve, AC, and the marginal cost curve, MC. The optimum quantity of output is at Q_0, determined by the intersection of MR and MC. At Q_0, the average cost of output is C_0, which is determined by the position of Q_0 along the AC curve. Economic rent per unit of output is thus $(P_0 - C_0)$ and the total amount of rent is the shaded area.

its product, and consequently experience a downward-sloping marginal revenue curve as well. These downward slopes imply that the firm is a price maker, although the price the firm chooses must correspond to the quantity of output the firm wishes to sell as well. Once again, at the end of this chapter, we provide mathematical details about profit maximization and economic rent in this scenario, and here we summarize the results graphically. Figure 5-3 depicts a simple linear demand curve, D, and the marginal revenue curve derived from it, MR. The cost structure of the firm is once again reflected in the marginal cost and average cost curves, MC and AC. The optimum quantity of output is Q_0, again determined by the intersection of MC and MR. The selling price is P_0, determined by the position of Q_0 on the demand curve. The monopoly rent per unit is therefore $(P_0 - C_0)$, and the shaded area represents the total rent. Firms that enjoy economic rent due to comparative advantages in sales and marketing are often said to follow a **revenue-based strategy.**

The depictions of economic rent in these microeconomic diagrams represent the returns to capital in excess of the return required by the owners of capital for a particular period (such as a year). If there is no economic rent, the expected cash flows from the investment exactly compensate the owners of capital for the use of the capital. In Chapter 3, we used the capital asset pricing model (CAPM) to determine the required rate of return on capital invested in a project. For example, the CAPM may indicate that the required rate of return is 15 percent. In this situation, every hundred dollars of capital put into a project this year is expected to receive $115 next year (in a one-year project). Thus, there is no economic rent and the present value of the project is zero:

$$PV = -100 + 115/1.15 = 0.$$

If there is economic rent, then the cash flows in one year must be expected to exceed $115 by exactly the dollar amount of economic rent, represented by shaded areas in

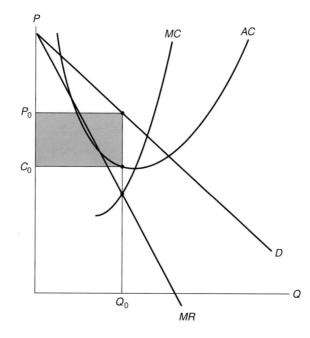

FIGURE 5-3 ECONOMIC RENT FOR A PRICE-MAKING FIRM

A price-making firm faces a downward-sloping demand curve for its product, D, and derives a downward-sloping marginal revenue curve from it, MR. The cost structure is represented by the average cost curve, AC, and the marginal cost curve, MC. The optimum quantity of output is at Q_0, determined by the intersection of MR and MC. The optimum price is P_0, determined by the position of Q_0 along the demand curve. The average cost of output is C_0, determined by the position of Q_0 along the AC curve. Economic rent per unit of output is thus $(P_0 - C_0)$, and the total amount of rent is the shaded area.

Figures 5-2 and 5-3, and the present value of the project will be positive. (For further explanation, see the numerical example at the end of this chapter.)

If a project will yield economic rent over several periods, the shaded areas for every year must be added up over time. As economic rent one year into the future is worth less than economic rent this year, the adding up involves a present value calculation where the cost of capital is again the relevant discount rate:

$$PV = \sum_{t=0}^{n} \frac{E_0[\text{rent}_t]}{(1 + COC)^t}$$

and the similarity of this calculation to the present value calculation in capital budgeting is obvious. In fact, the present value of the economic rent is exactly the same as the present value calculation from the capital budgeting problem examined in Chapter 3 (with an adjustment for the effects of financing calculated in Chapter 4).

If there is economic rent associated with a project, there will be a positive present value. If there is no economic rent associated with a project, but the revenues completely cover all costs including the required rate of return on capital, the present value will be zero. Just as there might be positive economic rent representing economic profit, there might be negative economic rent associated with economic losses, in which case the present value of the project will be negative.

The above analysis requires some slight modification when debt creates value through the tax-deductibility of interest, but the main conclusions remain intact. The debt shields essentially allow some projects with negative present values in cash flows to have positive adjusted present values, but this number of projects is really quite small. The reason such instances will be rare is that deductibility of interest is valuable only when there are profits from which the interest can be deducted. Hence, projects need to have positive cash flows even to warrant an adjustment for the value created by debt. Positive APV therefore does not result from financing the project. Instead, economic rent produces a positive present value in cash flows

$$PV = \sum_{t=0}^{n} \frac{E_0[CF_tS_t]}{(1 + COC)^t} > 0$$

rather than a positive present value of debt shields. Financing creates value, but should not be the only reason APV > 0 because financing does not represent a source of economic rent. If a project is only profitable because of debt-related tax shields, it is generally not worth doing because the firm does not have a demonstrated comparative advantage in the use of resources in production and marketing. Firms with an ability and willingness to profit from financial market imperfections of the kind examined in Chapter 4, such as by borrowing where the cost of debt is low, may not even need the project. For example, a firm wanting to borrow where the cost of debt is low may be able to borrow there without ever establishing a project.

Taking this discussion to its logical conclusion, corporate investment strategy should be based on seeking economic rents by identifying, evaluating, and developing comparative advantages in the use of resources. In the literature on business strategy, the comparative advantages in the use of resources are also referred to as **competitive advantages and core competencies.** Effective corporate planning should be grounded in a thorough understanding of the firm's specific advantages, regardless of what they are called. In addition, it should be grounded in understanding the barriers to entry that would prevent competitors from eroding these advantages over time. Before undertaking a project, the firm should verify its comparative advantage in the use of resources employed in the project.

This section on present value and economic rent has been about general business strategy, and there is nothing uniquely international about the concepts. However, the concept of economic rent is an important foundation of many theories of international business. To a certain extent, such theories simply seek to explain why international business is profitable. Some focus on the production or cost side, suggesting that some international business is production-oriented or input-seeking. An example of an international business that is input seeking might be Exxon drilling for oil in foreign countries. On the other hand, some theories focus on the demand or revenue side, suggesting that some international business is market-seeking. This might be the case when Coca-Cola sells its beverages in foreign markets.

In both situations, the theories seek to identify the firm's main source of comparative advantage in the use of resources which gives rise to economic rent. In some instances, the reasons for profits on foreign projects are no different than the reasons for profits on domestic projects. In others, an effort is made to explain why it is more profitable to undertake a foreign project than a domestic one. Furthermore, some theories consider why it is more profitable for a multinational corporation to undertake the foreign project than for a host-country firm to do so. With these concepts in mind, the next section introduces and analyzes the main modes of international business. The subsequent section then examines theories of DFI more thoroughly. In addition, we return to the concept of economic rent in Chapter 7 when we investigate the effects of exchange rate changes on the amount of economic rent received by a firm.

5.3   MODES OF INTERNATIONAL BUSINESS

A firm can choose among several modes of operation to extract economic rent from its comparative advantages in the use of resources associated with a foreign project. The preceding two chapters chiefly considered a wholly-owned DFI, typically represented by a subsidiary. In reality, there are many forms of business associated with less commitment of capital, less operating control, and less risk than DFI that nonetheless allow a firm to capture economic rent.

INTERNATIONAL TRADE, LICENSE/FRANCHISE AGREEMENTS, JOINT VENTURES, AND WHOLLY-OWNED DFI

The hierarchy of modes typically examined in international business, from the least amount of risk to the greatest, is:

1. an export or import operation based at home
2. a license or franchise agreement with a foreign firm or individual
3. a joint venture with a foreign firm
4. a wholly-owned direct foreign investment

The international trade operation—an export or import business—represents the least risky mode because it requires no capital investment abroad, although it would generally require capital investment at home. Such an operation is designed to exploit the firm's comparative advantage in the use of resources either on the input side through imports or on the output side through exports. The main disadvantage of an international trade operation is that it typically involves higher transportation costs, international tariffs, and other expensive barriers associated with crossing an international border.

License and franchise agreements represent low-risk alternatives because they generally require no capital investment either abroad or at home. **Licensing** is an arrangement in which a firm with a comparative advantage in the use of resources (the licensor) grants legal permission to another firm or individual (the licensee) to use specified components of its production or marketing process, typically for a limited amount of time. The licensed components may include patents, copyrights, trademarks, technology, managerial skills, and the like. The licensee then typically produces and markets a product in the foreign country similar to one the licensor produces and markets at home.

Franchising is an arrangement in which a firm with a comparative advantage in the use of resources (the franchisor) grants a package of support services to another firm or individual (the franchisee) to undertake production and/or marketing in a specified location. Franchise contracts generally cover more aspects of the foreign operation and have a longer duration than licensing contracts. The package might include product input supplies, production equipment, ongoing management assistance, advertising and promotional materials, strategic planning, and so on. Franchising may also involve some financing, particularly in the early stages of developing the foreign business.

With both licensing and franchising agreements, the licensee/franchisee typically compensates the licensor/franchisor with royalties and fees. This income is the main incentive for the firm to enter into a licensing or franchising agreement, and is particularly attractive as there is no capital commitment. However, the firm must recognize that licensing or franchising is a substitute for import/export operations and DFI. A main reason for a corporation to enter into a license or franchise agreement with a foreign entity is that the foreign entity has some advantages of its own operating in the foreign country. For example, the licensee/franchisee may be more familiar with the local business environment or may have better access to local distribution channels. In addition, the licensee or franchisee may be able to avoid some costs associated with distance that import/export operations or DFI would incur. The transportation and tariff costs associated with import/export operations are obviously avoided. Similarly, costs of international travel and international communication (phones, faxes), which MNCs would incur to manage and monitor the foreign project, are reduced. With licensing and franchising, however, there are some costs that would not be associated with import/export operations or DFI. These include the costs of monitoring the licensee or franchisee to ensure quality, and the opportunity cost of sharing the economic rents to preserve performance incentives for the licensee or franchisee. There is an additional risk inherent in sharing corporate secrets with an outside party; the outside party could become a full-fledged competitor.

In comparison to international trade and licensing/franchising operations, an international joint venture with one or more foreign firms represents a riskier form of international business for most MNCs because it typically requires the commitment of capital abroad and substantial responsibility for running the foreign project. In comparison to wholly-owned DFI, though, an international joint venture is usually not as risky because it requires less commitment of capital abroad and somewhat less responsibility for running the foreign project. The capital committed by the firm going abroad to enter into a joint venture is nevertheless considered DFI because the firm maintains operating control over its share of the investment.

Typically, the perception of the advantage of a joint venture is that the firm does not have to contribute the entire amount of capital required for a foreign project. In addition, the firm may be able to exploit its own comparative advantages in the use of resources without sustaining a comparative disadvantage from undertaking a foreign project if it selects partner corporations with knowledge of the foreign environment, or some other advantage that the home country firm does not have. However, the benefits of a joint venture may be partially reduced if extra costs result from having to negotiate with, continuously monitor, and provide performance incentives to the partner(s). In extreme circumstances, the benefits of a joint venture may be more than completely offset if the marriage does not work out, if the partner turns out to be incompetent or corrupt, or if the partner turns into a full-fledged competitor. Hence, not all joint ventures create value.

The riskiest form of international business is typically thought to be the form generally considered throughout this book: the wholly-owned direct foreign investment, such as a foreign subsidiary. In this operation, the parent company maintains 100 percent operating control, takes responsibility for all of the financing, and accordingly takes on all the risk involved in the foreign project.

The four modes of international business—ranging from import/export operations through license/franchise agreements and joint ventures to wholly-owned DFI—can be thought of as competing ways to extract economic rents. In this sense, they are mutually exclusive projects. That is, a firm can typically undertake a foreign project through only one of the four modes, and selection of one mode precludes the others. If a company makes a license or franchise agreement with a foreign firm, for example, import/export operations, joint ventures with other firms, and a wholly-owned subsidiary in that location are usually not possible. Hence, in selecting the mode of international business, the firm with the competitive advantage in the use of resources should determine which mode produces the highest present value.

PRESENT VALUE COMPARISONS OF MODES

Although this book examines wholly-owned DFI in great detail, the other modes of international business are sometimes just as important and may be more profitable. The methodology of Chapter 3 for international capital budgeting can be applied to all modes of international business in straightforward ways. The topics of Chapter 4 on financing international projects are, however, typically limited to the cases of joint ventures and wholly-owned DFI in which the firm must provide capital for the foreign project. The international trade and licensing/franchising alternatives typically do not require the commitment of capital abroad and are therefore much simpler than the cases of DFI considered. Hence, although the focus of the book is on DFI, the principles explained throughout are applicable to the entire range of international business operations.

As an example, reconsider Victor Enterprises' project in Switzerland, which was the extended example used in Chapters 3 and 4 to discuss project evaluation and financing. In the base case, using the cash flows in Table 3-2 and the debt financing in Table 4-1, the establishment of a wholly-owed subsidiary representing 100 percent DFI produces an adjusted present value of:

$$APV = \$2,291,320 + \$971,407 = \$3,262,727$$

which we now use as a benchmark for comparison with other modes of international business in Switzerland.

Suppose, as an alternative to wholly-owned DFI, Victor Enterprises has the opportunity to undertake the project as a joint venture with a Swiss firm. If the project itself is not altered by the joint ownership, the required rate of return on the equity investment will continue to be 17 percent in dollars or 26.36 percent in francs. If the joint venture is 50 percent owned by Victor Enterprises and 50 percent owned by the Swiss firm, each partner will contribute half of the initial SFr 20 million capital investment. Furthermore, if the project is not altered by joint ownership, each partner will receive half of the subsequent cash flows. In addition, if the project is partially funded with $12 million, or SFr 15 million in external debt, reducing the equity contribution required of each partner to SFr 2,500,000, each partner will receive half of the debt-related tax shields associated with the debt. In short, each joint venture partner will receive half of the APV of the project, or $1,631,364.

Viewed from the standpoint of Victor Enterprises, the APV of $1,631,364 from a joint venture is clearly less desirable than the APV of $3,262,727 from a wholly-owned DFI, so Victor Enterprises should not undertake the joint venture in lieu of the wholly-owned DFI because it will be splitting its rents with its partner. This conclusion is based on the explicit assumption that the project and its cash flows are not altered by the joint ownership structure. If, on the other hand, the joint venture changes the cash flows, the valuation would be different. For the joint venture to create value, the project revenues must be higher or the project cost must be lower, or both. For example, the Swiss partner may have some competitive advantages in the use of resources in production or marketing that Victor Enterprises does not have, thus increasing the APV of the joint venture. In addition, there might be capital market advantages associated with the joint venture (producing a cost of equity lower than 17 percent in dollars or 26.36 percent in SFr or a cost of debt lower than 14.4 percent in dollars or 23.552 percent in SFr). For Victor Enterprises to prefer the joint venture over the wholly-owned project, however, the advantages in higher revenue, lower production costs, and lower financing costs must be large enough to produce an APV greater than $3,262,727 on Victor Enterprises' half of the project.

Now suppose that Victor Enterprises has the opportunity to undertake a license or franchise agreement with a Swiss firm. In this scenario, the Swiss firm will be responsible for all of the initial investment, as well as all of the ongoing expenses. In exchange for allowing the Swiss firm to produce and market its product in Switzerland, Victor Enterprises will receive a royalty payment. As Victor Enterprises has already eliminated the joint venture alternative in favor of wholly-owned DFI, it is interested in comparing the present value of the royalties from the license/franchise agreement to the present value of the DFI. Suppose the license/franchise agreement stipulates that the Swiss firm will remit 7.5 percent of the gross revenues to Victor Enterprises. If the revenues are once again not altered by the ownership change, then Victor Enterprises will receive royalty payments of:

Year	SFr Cash Flows
1	$50,000,000 \times .075 = 3,750,000$
2	$55,000,000 \times .075 = 4,125,000$
3	$60,000,000 \times .075 = 4,500,000$

and will have to pay corporate income taxes on the royalties at the rate of 35 percent. Hence, Victor Enterprises will receive after-tax cash flows of:

Year	SFr Cash Flows
1	$3,750,000 \times (1 - .35) = 2,437,500$
2	$4,125,000 \times (1 - .35) = 2,681,250$
3	$4,500,000 \times (1 - .35) = 2,925,000$

and will calculate the present value as:

$$PV = 2,437,500/1.2636 + 2,681,250/1.2636^2 + 2,925,000/1.2636^3$$
$$= \text{SFr } 5,058,036$$
$$= \$4,046,429 \text{ at } \$0.80/\text{SFr.}$$

This amount is also the adjusted present value, APV, for Victor Enterprises because the license or franchise agreement does not increase Victor Enterprises' debt capacity.

Because the APV of $4,046,429 from the license/franchise royalties exceeds the APV of $3,262,727 from the wholly-owned subsidiary by $783,702, Victor Enterprises clearly prefers the licensing/franchising agreement.

However, the licensee/franchisee must recognize that the royalty payment to Victor Enterprises is a rather large expense. In fact, if the structure of the project and the amount of the other cash flows are not altered, the APV of the project to the licensee is negative by the exact amount of the increase in APV to Victor Enterprises, −$783,702, and Victor Enterprises will not be able to find a licensee/franchisee willing to undertake the project. Hence, the APV of the project itself is not changed, and the distribution of the APV between the licensor and licensee is a zero-sum game. As with the joint venture, the total APV is simply split between Victor Enterprises and its licensee/franchisee. Further, to make Victor Enterprises better off, the licensee/franchisee must be worse off. However, as with the joint venture, the license or franchise agreement will create value when the revenues from the project are higher, the production costs are lower, or both. In addition, there might again be capital market advantages associated with the license/franchise agreement if the licensee/franchisee has a lower cost of equity or debt.

As a final alternative, suppose Victor Enterprises considers undertaking the project by setting up a production operation in the United States and exporting the final output to Switzerland for sale to consumers. If the nature of the project is substantially similar to the project establishing production in Switzerland, the cost of capital for the project will remain at 17 percent in dollars. As a benchmark, suppose that the revenues and costs are generally the same except for transportation and tariff costs associated with the export operation. For simplicity, assume that the transportation and tariff costs are expected to amount to $1 million per year for each of the three years the project is in operation. Hence, the dollar cash flows adjusted for transportation and tariff costs are:

Year	U.S.$ Cash Flows
0	−16,000,000
1	7,407,407 − 1,000,000 = 6,407,407
2	8,230,453 − 1,000,000 = 7,230,453
3	9,525,987 − 1,000,000 = 8,525,987

and the present value is:

$$PV = -16,000,000 + 6,407,407/1.17 + 7,230,453/1.17^2 + 8,525,987/1.17^3$$
$$= U.S.\$ 81,735$$

so that, adjusting for the benefits of debt financing, the APV is:

$$APV = \$81,735 + \$971,407 = \$1,053,142.$$

Due to the transportation and tariff costs, the APV of this project is substantially lower than the APV of the project involving both production and sales in Switzerland. For exporting to produce a higher APV, the revenues must be higher or, more likely, the costs of production in the United States must be lower. One way to have lower costs would be when the exports can be produced from existing production facilities or by expanding existing production facilities rather than by creating new ones. The additional output, for example, may serve to reduce the firm's average costs, allowing it to capture economies of scale.

The example of the mutually exclusive approaches to Victor Enterprises' Swiss project suggests that choosing among the modes of international business requires an extensive analysis of the changes in cash flows that each alternative entails (which has not been illustrated here). If the project's cash flows are completely unaltered by changes in ownership and operation, the wholly-owned DFI will always dominate. This is because, with DFI, Victor Enterprises will not have to share its rents with a foreign firm, as it would under a joint venture or a licensing/franchising agreement, and will not have to incur the transportation and tariff costs involved with an export operation. The feasibility of the alternative modes of international business therefore depends on changes in cash flows, which either raise the revenues or lower the costs substantially when a foreign firm gets involved or when production is located in the home country.

5.4   THEORIES OF DIRECT FOREIGN INVESTMENT

DFI can be examined in a macroeconomic perspective in addition to the microeconomic perspective presented in the previous section. When the firm chooses import/export operations or licensing/franchising, there is no capital flow from one country to another, so the macroeconomic questions must be addressed separately. For a joint venture and wholly-owned subsidiary, however, an international capital flow exists in the form of DFI, so the macroeconomic questions can be addressed more directly.

Chapter 1 noted that DFI is different from portfolio investment and intermediated investment because the asset's owner maintains operating control over the asset. Recall that models of international investment were presented in Chapter 1 to provide a basic reason for international capital flows, but that those models do not explain what form the international investment will take. In other words, they do not distinguish DFI from portfolio investment and intermediated investment. Our discussions of economic rent and modes of international business may therefore suggest why certain international capital flows take place as DFI rather than as portfolio or intermediated investment. There is a macroeconomic need for a theory of DFI that explains why the owner maintains operating control of the asset, and this section presents some of the prominent theories. Often, theories of DFI explain comparative advantages in the use of resources that MNCs have over their host-country counterparts, which means that DFI includes not only the transfer of capital, but other inputs as well, such as managerial talent or technology.

WHAT SHOULD A THEORY OF DFI SEEK TO EXPLAIN?

The first challenge for a theory of DFI is to determine which countries will be source countries (or home countries) and which will be host countries, an issue often referred to as the **locational indication.** In other words, a theory of DFI should explain data on country patterns of investment, or why certain countries (such as Japan) tend to be home countries and certain countries (such as Mexico) tend to be host countries. The main models of international capital flows considered in Chapter 1 simply require an interest rate differential such that $r^* > r$; that is, returns abroad are higher than domestic returns. With respect to DFI, however, there is in reality not a lot of evidence that investments are related to relative, economy-wide rates of return. Theories of DFI should therefore indicate something in addition to or instead of the interest rate argument for locational indication in an effort to explain why project rates of return are higher abroad than they are domestically.

Considering that profits and rents for the firm arise from the difference between revenues and costs, certain locational advantages might be derived from lower production costs (as in the theory of comparative advantage typically applied to international trade), and certain advantages might be derived from higher revenues. Hence, although the locational question is predominantly a macroeconomic question related to international capital flows, some of the answers must include an examination of microeconomic phenomena in the theory of the firm. There are several possible reasons for a locational advantage.

Firms often cite lower labor costs abroad as a locational advantage. These lower labor costs will generally translate into higher returns. IBM, for example, may discover that rather than export American-made computers to Mexico, it can achieve a higher return by both producing and selling in Mexico where labor costs are substantially lower. Many firms will produce abroad and even re-export to the home country to take advantage of lower labor costs. In the late 1980s, for example, many Japanese electronics companies moved their production operations from Japan to Thailand. They produced in Thailand with substantially lower labor costs; they then re-exported their products back to Japan, allowing them to achieve a higher profit margin than before.

Plentiful, accessible resources provide another reason for locational advantage. If deposits of natural resources (such as minerals) or other kinds of raw materials are inexpensive to develop in the host country, project returns are likely to be higher. Availability of other inputs, such as technology, will also translate into higher returns.

Government policies that create market imperfections can also play a part in creating locational advantage. For example, trade barriers can create a market that is free of competition from imports, so domestic production may yield a high profit margin. DFI is then a particularly attractive prospect if exports from the home country are limited; this is often called tariff-jumping DFI. For example, as the possibility of a protected European common market grows, many foreign companies with high export volumes to Europe—particularly Japanese auto makers—are constructing production facilities in Europe itself. More generally, any government policies that create market imperfections make DFI an economically rational corporate strategy (see Brewer, 1993).

Large, expanding markets may offer high rates of return too. A company may wish to set up production in such a country, rather than simply export, to lower transportation costs and to take full advantage of the opportunities such markets present. This may be another explanation for the manufacturing rush into Europe. It is certainly an explanation for investment in Germany to gain access to Eastern Europe.

One financial reason for a locational advantage is based on currency values. Products produced in countries with undervalued currencies are much more competitive in a global marketplace than those produced in countries with overvalued currencies. This implies that countries with undervalued currencies have lower manufacturing costs, and therefore increased returns. The currency value is especially important for exporters and re-exporters. For example, Japanese auto makers, in particular Honda and Toyota, have taken advantage of the fall of the U.S. dollar by exporting cars from their U.S. assembly lines back to Japan.

A tax argument is also associated with locational advantage. Firms may have an incentive to locate where taxes are low to boost profits. Countries with low taxes might therefore offer higher after-tax returns.

Finally, countries with safe investment climates—that is, stable political and social environments—pose little risk to investments, allowing for higher expected returns. Some economists believe that this is a reason for the proliferation of direct foreign investment in the United States during the first part of the 1980s. The United States was simply one of the safest places in the world to invest. This, in fact, is just one aspect of political behavior by multinationals; for more see Boddewyn (1988).

We discuss many of the financial arguments for locational advantage again in greater detail later in this book. For example, the effects of an undervalued currency are thoroughly developed in Chapter 7 on economic exposure. The effect of taxation on international investment and DFI is analyzed in Chapter 11, and the role of the political environment is examined in Chapter 12. The other arguments for locational advantage (labor cost, resources and technology, trade barriers, market availability, and so on) are generally discussed in international production and marketing books, and are therefore not further developed here.

The locational advantage indicates where investment will take place and what countries will provide the investment, but does not explain why firms will use DFI instead of portfolio or intermediated investment. Therefore, the second item a theory of DFI should explain is precisely why DFI exists instead of portfolio or intermediated investment. Models of international capital flows are generally unable to explain what

APPLICATION 5-2

THE PRODUCT CYCLE THEORY AND PRODUCTION OF ELECTRONICS

The electronics sector has been important to the growth of high-technology fields in the United States , especially in the Silicon Valley and Boston. Recent downturns in these industries and areas have caused some observers to argue that businesses are leaving the early technology centers for lower-cost locations. A study by Sherwood-Call (1992) examines this issue and demonstrates that the pattern is consistent with the product cycle theory, which suggests early innovations are concentrated geographically, but proximity to the innovating region becomes less important than other costs as the product's market grows and standardized production technologies are developed.

Table 5-1 presents various measures of production, costs, and technological sophistication for electronics industries in several important electronics-producing countries. In 1988, the United States dominated the world electronics industry with a 38 percent market share. The United States also outranks other producing countries by most measures of technological sophistication, such as telephones per capita. However, the cost of doing business in the United States is relatively high, as per capita GDP is high (although second to Japan). There are signs that U.S. domination of the industry is declining; the growth rate in U.S. production between 1984 and 1988 was only 1 percent, by far the

TABLE 5-1 Electronics Sectors in Selected Countries

	U.S.	Japan	EC*	S. Korea	Taiwan	Singapore	Brazil	India	World
Value of Electronics Production ($M, 1988)	186,232	127,208	115,136	9,103	7,890	7,651	3,876	2,314	486,718
% of World Total (1988)	38.3	26.1	23.7	1.9	1.6	1.6	0.8	0.5	100
% of World Total (1984)	43.0	22.5	21.9	0.9	1.1	0.8	0.6	0.2	100
Real Annual Growth Rate (%, 1984–88)	1	8	6	24	15	23	11	23	4
Production/GDP (%, 1987)	3.9	4.6	2.6	6.0	10.0	28.6	1.0	1.7	N/A
Production ($000)/ Employment	104.9	105.9	79.2	35.8	40.7	107.8	15.1	11.6	N/A
Total Electronics Employment (000, 1986)	1776	1201	1454	254	194	71	257	200	N/A
Annual Growth Rate (%, 1980–86)	1.3	9.6	1.5	9.8	2.6	−0.2	N/A	N/A	N/A
General Technology Characteristics									
Telephones/1000 Pop. (1986)	791	558	520	186	228	417	84	4	N/A
Scientists & Engineers (000, 1986)	787	575	468	47	42	2	33	100	N/A
Scientists & Engineers/ Million Pop.	3,230	4,712	1,443	1,116	2,149	923	230	128	N/A
GDP per Capita ($, 1987)	18,393	19,448	13,137	2,881	3,794	7,654	2,304	326	N/A

Note: "Electronics" is defined here to include materials and components, software, computers, telecommunications equipment, business equipment (copiers, facsimile machines, and so on), and instruments.
*EC data exclude Portugal and Greece.

Source: Carolyn Sherwood-Call, "Changing Geographical Patterns of Electronic Components Activity," Federal Reserve Bank of San Francisco *Economic Review,* 1992, no. 2, Table 1, p. 27.

APPLICATION 5-2 (cont.)

slowest among the countries included in the table. Electronics industry growth rates in countries that offer much lower costs were all in double digits, demonstrating stronger growth than the countries that dominated world production in 1988.

Other evidence is also available. According to the Semiconductor Industry Association, the share of U.S. company production in total world semiconductors fell fairly steadily, from 65 percent in 1977, to 60 percent in 1982, 45 percent in 1987, and 38 percent in 1988, before slightly rebounding to 40 percent in 1990. Furthermore, these numbers understate the movement of the semiconductor outside the United States, as U.S.-based companies have moved to offshore production even as foreign companies have increased their production.

The conclusion here is that the United States' share of the total worldwide electronics industry has fallen dramatically, while nations with lower costs and less developed technological infrastructures are gaining market share. This result is consistent with expectations based on the product life cycle theory. The United States does continue to play an important role in the industry, however, suggesting that complete standardization of the industry either has not yet occurred or will never occur in the fast-changing world of high-tech production.

the market, they will be internalized and undertaken by the firm itself. Buckley and Casson (1976) apply the Coase argument internationally to explain the existence of DFI by multinational firms.[5]

OPEC investments in the United States provide an example of internalization. Many OPEC oil companies have built or purchased refineries to be used in the process of bringing their oil to the American market. Some OPEC oil companies have even established or acquired the actual retail gas stations as well. Apparently, these companies have discovered that refining their oil in their own refineries in the United States and selling their gas in their own gas stations is cost-effective vertical integration. In other words, internalizing all of these transactions reduces the number of market transactions required and raises profits by lowering transactions costs.

The main emphasis in the internalization theory is usually on knowledge, because knowledge is not easily traded in markets. Knowledge is difficult to price, difficult to sell if it is proprietary, and generally has the properties of a public good. This theory is therefore similar to the technological advantages theory applied to firm-specific knowledge.

The internalization theory differs, however, in that the possession of unique information is not what gives the firm an advantage. Rather, the process of internalizing that information provides the advantage. After all, some firms with information advantages choose to export to foreign markets, license or franchise the information to foreign producers, or even sell the information to foreigners. The theory of internalization, in fact, has been developed principally to explain why DFI takes place when a firm has an ownership advantage rather than license/franchise agreements or joint ventures. All firms have firm-specific knowledge, but not all firms can internalize all aspects of that knowledge. Costs of internalization may be prohibitive for some firms. Specifically, accounting and control costs may be high, communications and transportation costs may be high, and so on. Conversely, some firms can internalize transactions without having much firm-specific knowledge if they have exceptional managerial capabilities.

An example of effective internalization capacity may be the successful Japanese management style that has become the subject of much recent study. Many people argue that the reason the Japanese auto companies can operate assembly lines in the United States and produce superior cars, even while using the same labor, the same materials, and even, in some cases, the same assembly lines as their American counterparts, is that they have a superior style of management. Toyota essentially took over a GM plant in California, and Mazda took over a Ford plant in Michigan, and both Japanese firms succeeded in making profitable ventures out of unprofitable ones predominantly due to managerial talent. Their ability to internalize aspects of automotive production to the extent that it prevails in their various subsidiaries gives them a significant advantage over their domestic competition.

IMPERFECTIONS IN SECURITIES MARKETS

The first macroeconomic theory of DFI examines imperfections in securities markets. In countries with no organized markets for equities or debt or with financial markets that are thin or illiquid, such as developing countries, DFI may be a good substitute for portfolio investment. This theory is developed by Ragazzi (1973). The basic argument also holds for other countries with impediments to investing in their markets, such as legal restrictions, capital controls, currency controls, prohibitive tax regulations, or even information processing difficulties. DFI therefore reaps the benefits of higher returns that simply cannot be achieved through portfolio investment.

An example of securities markets imperfections is Heinz's operations in Zimbabwe. While Zimbabwe has no real securities market for portfolio investment, it has potential for high returns because it offers advantages in its arable land and its well-developed road and rail system. In 1982, the H. J. Heinz Company acquired a family-owned vegetable oil and soap manufacturer in Zimbabwe. Subsequently, the operation was able to produce Heinz tomato soup and baked beans by helping local farmers grow the necessary tomatoes and beans. Now, Heinz and its investors are reaping Zimbabwe's high returns, which were not available via any Zimbabwe securities market, through direct investment.

Further development of the securities markets imperfections theory adds the benefits of diversification. DFI in countries where portfolio and intermediated investment are difficult or unavailable serves to diversify the investors' portfolios to an extent that may not have been possible without DFI. Even if real returns are equal, there will be benefits of diversifying risk internationally. For example, the Heinz project in Zimbabwe might diversify its other projects, making Heinz a more stable firm. Rather than holding a lot of shares of smaller foreign corporations to achieve diversification, investors can alternatively hold shares in a multinational corporation. The development of diversification motives for DFI is associated with Rugman (1976, 1977), although some empirical evidence in Jacquillat and Solnik (1978) suggests that "multinationals are poor tools for diversification."

EXCHANGE RISK THEORY

Another macroeconomic theory of DFI is Aliber's (1970) exchange risk theory, in which the risk that exchange rate changes will severely alter the home-currency value of a foreign investment provides a barrier to portfolio investment and intermediated investment by risk-averse investors. Portfolio investors and financial intermediaries who manage capital thus require a premium on interest rates and returns in countries with certain weak or volatile currencies to compensate them for the exchange risk when they invest in those countries. The result is that real interest parity does not hold when left to portfolio investors and financial intermediaries. In this situation, flows of portfolio and intermediated investment are inadequate, and further investment opportunities exist exclusively for DFI. In other words, the door to the country is left open for direct investment as a substitute for portfolio and intermediated investment.

With DFI, the investor maintains management control of the enterprise and can structure operations to reduce the risks from currency fluctuations. Portfolio and intermediary investors cannot structure operations to reduce these risks because they do not have operating control over the investment, so the investment is exposed to more exchange risk. This means that direct foreign investments do not require as great a premium for holding exchange risk as intermediated or portfolio investments.

Recent development of the exchange risk theory (Aliber, 1993) extends the argument to include not only bilateral comparisons of interest rates, but the role of exchange rates as well. The main idea is that undervaluation of a currency creates a locational advantage as a host country because that country is then a relatively low-cost center of production globally. Foreign capital will be eager to take advantage of these low production costs. Simultaneously, acquisition of assets in the country by foreigners is relatively inexpensive due to the weakness of the currency. Conversely, overvaluation of a currency creates a locational advantage as a source country because that country is a relatively high-cost center of production globally while the acquisition of foreign assets is relatively inexpensive due to the strength of the currency.[6] Capital will be eager to pursue relatively attractive overseas production opportunities.

EVALUATION OF THEORIES OF DFI

This section briefly assesses how each theory of DFI meets the following three criteria: (1) locational advantages, (2) why DFI is chosen over portfolio investment and intermediated investment—or the existence of an overcompensating ownership advantage, and (3) the prevalence of cross-hauling in DFI. As this treatment is fairly brief, and because evaluation of the theories is necessarily subjective, the reader may want to think about more than the simplest elements presented here.

The technological advantages theory proves to be fairly successful when evaluated vis-à-vis the three established criteria. Generally, it is one of the most accepted theories of DFI, as well as one of the first. It accounts for locational advantage by viewing source countries as those countries with technological advantages and host countries as those without. While that works well for source country designation, the theory is somewhat weak in viewing host countries as simply countries without technological advantages. In other words, it doesn't really indicate where DFI will be located or what the locational advantages are.

Furthermore, this theory contradicts the data presented in Chapter 1, which suggested that most host countries are technologically advanced rather than technologically deficient. It explains an overcompensating advantage quite well in that firm-specific technologies and skills would clearly provide DFI with an advantage over domestic competitors. Finally, it succeeds in explaining cross-hauling, as it is quite possible for firm-specific technologies to exist in different countries, causing these countries to invest reciprocally in each other.

The product cycle theory, which is probably the most famous theory of DFI, does not fare as well when judged against the criteria. While the theory does provide a locational indication (source countries are those with new products and skilled labor, and host countries are those with low-cost unskilled labor), its implication contradicts the data presented in Chapter 1, which suggests that most host countries are high- rather than low-wage countries. Furthermore, the theory does not give an indication of an over-compensating advantage that DFI has over domestic competition, which is particularly important because the product is standardized. In other words, it does not indicate why foreign rather than domestic investors must control production when domestic investors ought to be able to exploit low-cost unskilled labor as well as or better than foreigners. Finally, the product cycle theory explains only a one-way flow of investment—from high wage countries to low-wage countries—so it does not provide a viable explanation for the cross-hauling patterns observed in the world.[7]

The oligopoly models do not directly meet many of our established criteria. While source countries are viewed as those with oligopolistic firms, the theory gives no indication of what the host countries would be. Oligopolistic firms can simply locate anywhere. Because the growth incentive supersedes any evaluation of returns, no overcompensating advantage is identified that these firms have over the domestic competition. Perhaps simply being an oligopoly is enough of an overcompensating advantage in that oligopolistic (quasi-monopolistic) rents are available. The oligopoly theory is, however, able to account for cross-hauling patterns, as oligopolies can originate in many different countries and locate anywhere.

The internalization theory of DFI fares quite well when evaluated according to our criteria. Because it is similar to the technological advantages theory, it shares the same advantages and disadvantages. Source countries are defined as those with the capacity to internalize market transactions or firm-specific technologies and skills, and host countries are those without this capacity. As discussed on page 190, this is a rather weak host country indication because there is no specific locational advantage. An overcompensating advantage exists in the firm-specific advantages attained from management's ability to internalize proprietary information. Finally, the theory explains cross-hauling patterns in that firms in many different countries have the capacity to internalize, and therefore internalize into many other countries.

The securities market imperfections theory, if broadly interpreted, is also quite effective. The source countries are those with capital, and the host countries are those with securities market imperfections and little capital. The theory explains why DFI is chosen over portfolio investment as portfolio investment is unavailable or has some additional costs associated with it. The theory also includes an overcompensating advantage relative to domestic investment as the availability of capital, a home-country-specific advantage. This theory was specifically designed to explain the one-way flow of DFI from developed countries into developing countries during the 1960s and 1970s, so it cannot easily explain the two-way flows involved in cross-hauling. However, it may be able to explain cross-hauling if every country has securities market imperfections when viewed from abroad, and if the quest for diversification is strong enough to make over-compensating advantage unnecessary.

Finally, the exchange risk theory stands up well with respect to the three criteria outlined above. It views source countries as those with small currency premiums (low real interest rates), and host countries as those with high currency premiums (high real interest rates). It identifies a country-specific overcompensating advantage in DFI's ability to exploit the interest rate disparity associated with the risk premium on the host country currency. Unfortunately, the exchange risk theory provides no explanation of the cross-hauling patterns: a country's currency has either a high or a low risk premium, so there cannot be two-way investment.

Clearly, no single theory can explain all DFI, so an eclectic approach to the theories may be the best method of analysis. Dunning (1977, 1979, 1981) has contributed the most to development of an eclectic approach through an organizing framework known as OLI: Ownership, Location, and Internalization. That is, the firm must have an ownership advantage, a foreign site must offer a locational advantage, and the firm must be able to internalize foreign production itself rather than through licensing agreements or other contract markets.

Many eclectic theories are possible. One may draw on the microeconomic technological advantages theory to establish firm-specific overcompensating advantages and cross-hauling, as well as on the macroeconomic exchange risk theory to establish country patterns and locational advantages. Many other combinations are possible, of course, but are not discussed here; the foundations of the basic theories discussed above should enable readers to formulate their own eclectic theory.

5.5   REAL OPTIONS IN INTERNATIONAL CAPITAL BUDGETING

One final area in the realm of foreign investment strategy is setting up opportunities for future investments, as opposed to setting up the investments themselves. As we explained in the introduction to this chapter, such opportunities have become known as *real options*, because prior planning gives the firm an option to make a real (physical) investment. Symmetrically, there may be an option to discontinue a current real project. As discussed in Chapter 3 on pages 106–112, capital budgeting is typically approached using present value analysis, which essentially involves forecasting future cash flows and then boiling down future prospects until they are sterilized of their timing and their riskiness. This is done by determining an appropriate discount rate that reflects both the time value of money and the riskiness of the cash flows.

However, capital budgeting projects will often have built-in options, and the present value will systematically misvalue such projects. For example, a firm could have an option to delay a capital project. In this case, the firm would own the option to purchase and develop land or other resources if output prices turn out to justify development costs. On the other hand, a firm could also hold an abandonment option, where the firm retains the right to abandon the project and partially recover its investment costs if market conditions or operating costs change in a sufficiently adverse way. A firm could also retain the option to alter a project's operating scale. For example, it could expand the scale if market conditions turned out to be more favorable than expected. A final example would be an option to switch the input or output mix. In this case, a firm would have the opportunity to alter the sources of its inputs or the types of and markets for its output if the prices of each adjusted sufficiently. (For more on the basics of real options, see Amran and Kulatilaka (1999a and 1999b) or Luehrman (1998a and 1998b).)

In the international setting, real options are likely to be present in a wide range of capital budgeting cases because input and output prices fluctuate with exchange rate changes. Opportunities to alter input sourcing, change output mix, or redirect exports to new markets are omnipresent in a setting of multiple markets with fluctuating currency values. Indeed, with the devaluation of Southeast Asian currencies in 1997, Japanese automakers shifted the output mix of their subsidiaries in Thailand and Indonesia from production of autos for the local markets to production of parts for developed country markets.[8] This flexibility is often given as a major reason for corporate multinationality and for value creation through multinationals; for example, see de Meza and van der Ploeg (1987) and Kogut and Kulatilaka (1994).

Present value analysis cannot appropriately deal with capital budgeting situations with built-in options for a couple of reasons. First, PV requires forecasts of expected future cash flows, which take the firm investment decisions as given. By explicitly ignoring path-contingent decisions, which give the firm the opportunity to exploit good states and avoid bad ones, PV is likely to underestimate future cash flows. Second, when cash flows depend not only on financial price risk, but also on firm decisions, which are often contingent on the realization of these prices, PV analysis offers no guidance about what the necessary adjustments to the discount rate ought to be.

Although it is the subject of considerable current research in finance, capital budgeting with options is unfortunately still an inexact science mainly because valuing managerial flexibility is highly complicated. When firms face projects with a degree of managerial flexibility, the problem of quantifying the impact this flexibility has on the timing and riskiness of cash flows, which is necessary from a capital budgeting standpoint, rapidly becomes intractible. In what follows, we will use an extended capital budgeting example to provide insights into the types of considerations that are important to bear in mind when valuing projects with built-in options.

Consider the Shalini Motor company which is considering a project to produce and sell automobiles in the country of Shumway. The subsidiary will be entirely self-contained, with costs and revenues determined in the currency of Shumway, the tyle. Currently, the dollar risk-free interest rate is 8 percent, the tyle risk-free interest rate is 4 percent, and the exchange rate is $1.8/tyle. Shalini Motors has the option of undertaking the project this year or delaying the project until next year. We focus on the case where all set-up costs are in dollars, so the company makes the initial investment in dollars, and this investment is not affected by exchange rate changes. If the project is undertaken today, year 0, the initial required investment is $18.6 million. If delayed one year, the required investment will increase to $20 million, but there is no uncertainty about this, so the present value of the future investment is calculated using the risk-free interest rate: $20 million/1.08 = $18.519 million. Hence, this present value reflects only the one year delay of the investment.

Once up and running, the Shumway subsidiary expects to produce and sell 24,000 cars per year for three years at a profit of 200 tyle per car, for annual cash flows of 4.8 million tyles for three years. The project is expected to take some time before it becomes operational. In particular, cash flows will begin in year 2 if the project is committed to today and in year 3 if the firm delays commitment by one year. During the year in between the initial investment and the initial cash inflows, the project is not operational and therefore does not face operating risk—only (potentially) exchange rate risk. Once up and running, however, the project faces operating risk, and the estimated dollar cost of capital is 20 percent.

There is considerable uncertainty about the future exchange rate. In particular, Shalini Motors estimates that with 50 percent probability next year's exchange rate will appreciate to $2.3/tyle, and with 50 percent probability the exchange rate will depreciate to $1.6/tyle. The expected value of next year's exchange rate is thus $(0.5)(2.3) + (0.5)(1.6) = \$1.95/tyle$.

Although our analysis is completely generalizable, for simplicity suppose that during subsequent years the exchange rate has an expected appreciation of 4 percent per year, with a 50 percent probability of appreciating 24 percent and a 50 percent probability of depreciating 16 percent. Note that we are assuming that exchange rate fluctuations are completely diversifiable beyond year 1. Uncovered interest parity is expected to hold: the tyle is expected to appreciate by 4 percent per year, which exactly offsets the 4 percent interest differential. However, note that between year 0 and year 1, uncovered interest parity is not expected to hold. The tyle is expected to appreciate by 8.33 percent to $1.95/tyle, and this exceeds the 4 percent interest differential. As discussed in Chapter 2, the failure is likely due to an exchange rate risk premium which is causing a failure of real interest parity, and therefore of uncovered interest parity as well. A measure of the risk premium can be obtained from the following adjusted version of UIP:

$$E[(\$/tyle)_1](1 + R^{tyle})/(1 + R^\$ + RP) = (\$/tyle)_0$$
$$(\$1.95/tyle)(1.04)/(1.08 + RP) = \$1.8/tyle$$

where RP is the unknown risk premium. Solving the equation, we find $(1.08 + RP) = 1.1267$, so $RP = 4.67\%$. As the risk premium is not zero, it is clear that either our exchange rate projections do not match those of the rest of the market or the market is attaching an additional 4.67 percent risk premium to fluctuations in the dollar value of the tyle between year 0 and year 1. From year 1 onward, this risk premium is zero because UIP is expected to hold.

PRESENT VALUE ANALYSIS

Based on the information above, expected exchange rates are projected as follows:

Year 1	Year 2	Year 3	Year 4	Year 5
$1.95/tyle	$2.03/tyle	$2.11/tyle	$2.19/tyle	$2.28/tyle

If the project is undertaken this year and because it earns 4.8 million tyles in years 2, 3, and 4, expected dollar cash flows (in millions) will be:

Year 1	Year 2	Year 3	Year 4	Year 5
0	$9.73	$10.12	$10.53	$0

and likewise, if the project is undertaken next year, expected dollar cash flows will be as follows:

Year 1	Year 2	Year 3	Year 4	Year 5
0	0	$10.12	$10.53	$10.95

As the operating risk of the project's dollar cash flows requires a cost of capital of 20 percent, cash flows must be discounted at this rate for the time the project is in operation. If the project is undertaken this year, the present value in year 1 (in millions) is:

$$PV_1 = \$9.73/1.2 + \$10.12/1.2^2 + \$10.53/1.2^3$$
$$= \$21.24 \text{ million.}$$

If undertaken next year, or year 1, the present value of future cash flows in year 2 (in millions) is:

$$PV_2 = \$10.12/1.2 + \$10.53/1.2^2 + \$10.95/1.2^3$$
$$= \$22.08 \text{ million}$$

and the present value in year 1 requires discounting this $22.08 million one more period. As when we discounted the initial investment of $20 million at the risk-free rate to reflect the delay of the investment, we discount $22.08 from year 2 to year 1 at the risk-free rate. This is because exchange rate risk from year 1 onward is assumed to be diversifiable (i.e., no exchange rate risk premium exists), so the future cash flows need only be discounted for being delayed an additional year. Hence, the present value of the cash flows in year 1, if the project is undertaken in year 1, is:

$$PV_1 = \$22.08/1.08$$
$$= \$20.45 \text{ million.}$$

Now we must consider the year 0 present values based on these year 1 present values. At what rate should we discount these figures to obtain present values for year 0? From year 0 to year 1, the only risk facing the project is that of exchange rate fluctuations during the first year, which, during this period, are not diversifiable. As a result, to discount cash flows for time and risk, we use a cost of capital of 8 percent + 4.67 percent = 12.67 percent, which adds the exchange rate risk premium calculated above to the risk-free rate.

Hence, net of investment costs, the year 0 present value of the project if committed to today is:

$$PV_0 = \$21.24/1.1267 \text{ million} - \$18.6 \text{ million}$$
$$= \$248,000.$$

The project delayed one year looks worse:

$$PV_0 = \$20.45/1.1267 \text{ million} - \$18.52 \text{ million}$$
$$= -\$386,590.$$

Thus, it appears the firm should undertake the project immediately and obtain the positive net present value of $248,000 instead of delaying the project (and receiving −$386,590). However, this analysis ignores the value of the option to delay. If Shalini Motors delays the investment by one year, it will undertake the project only if the exchange rate appreciates and it can therefore avoid the exchange rate risk. The option to delay can be included in the valuation by using alternative decision techniques, such as decision tree analysis or contingent claim analysis.

DECISION TREE ANALYSIS

Decision tree analysis recognizes that a delay in the project enables management to make a decision in the future about whether or not to undertake the project. A decision tree is constructed based on current and future choices, and the project is evaluated by starting from the last decision node and working toward the present. At each decision node, we assume that optimal decisions will be made in the future. In the example of the investment in Shumway, the decision in year 0 is whether to invest immediately or to delay, and if the year 0 decision is to delay, the decision in year 1 is whether to under-take the project. Figure 5-4 presents this decision tree. The final decision node is in year 1, at which time the exchange rate has either appreciated to $2.3/tyle or depreciated to $1.6/tyle. If it has depreciated, the present value at year 1 is negative:

$$PV_1 = (4.8 \times 1.73/1.2 + 4.8 \times 1.80/1.2^2 + 4.8 \times 1.87/1.2^3)/(1.08) - 20$$
$$= -\$3.22 \text{ million.}$$

Note that we are using the expected exchange rates in years 3, 4, and 5 conditional on the exchange rate having dropped to $1.6/tyle in year 1 (knowing the exchange rate is expected to appreciate by 4 percent per year from $1.6/tyle in year 1 to $1.73/tyle in year 3, and so on). On the other hand, if the tyle appreciates to $2.3/tyle in year 1, the present value is positive:

$$PV_1 = (4.8 \times 2.49/1.2 + 4.8 \times 2.59/1.2^2 + 4.8 \times 2.69/1.2^3)/(1.08) - 20$$
$$= \$4.12 \text{ million.}$$

Clearly, the optimal decision in year 1 is to undertake the project only if the exchange rate has appreciated.

Next, we move to the year 0 decision node. The present value of the project if the decision to invest is delayed to year 1 is the expected future cash flows (the present value from the optimal year 1 decision) discounted at an appropriate rate. Given the optimal decision in year 1, Shalini will undertake the project only if the exchange rate has appreciated (50 percent probability), resulting in a present value in year 1 of

FIGURE 5-4   DECISION TREE FOR SHUMWAY PROJECT

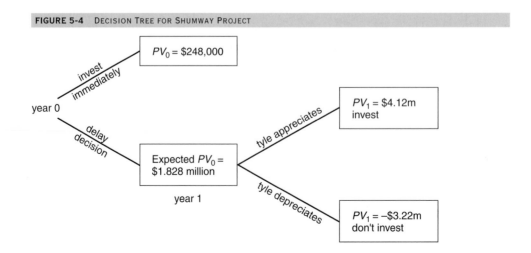

$4.12 million. If the exchange rate depreciates, Shalini will abandon the project and the present value is zero. The expected cash flow, therefore, is $(0.5)(\$4.12) = \$2.06$ million.

What discount rate should be used to calculate the present value in year 0? If time 0 exchange rate risk were diversifiable, we would simply discount by the risk-free rate. On the other hand, if the exchange risk is not diversifiable, the discount rate calculated above of 12.67 percent is inappropriate because it applies only if we plan to implement the project irrespective of the exchange rate fluctuations. As we are planning to implement the project only when the exchange rate appreciates, the project's risk has actually increased and a higher discount rate is warranted. This is because, in planning to implement the project only when the exchange rate has appreciated, we have effectively levered up on exchange rate risk.

Unfortunately, there is no easy way to identify an appropriate discount rate. For now, we will calculate the present value assuming the 12.67 percent rate is appropriate. In this case, the present value of the project in year 0 will be $\$2.06/1.1267 = \$1.828$ million. Compared to the present value if the project is undertaken immediately, $248,000, it is clear the project should be delayed. According to the decision tree analysis, the value of the option to delay is $\$1.828 - \$0.248 = \$1.580$ million.

CONTINGENT CLAIM ANALYSIS

Another method of analysis, contingent claim analysis, explicitly recognizes that Shalini owns an option to undertake the project next year, which is known as a *call option* on the investment (and "call" is a general term for an option to buy). Contingent claim analysis properly values an option on a project exposed to nondiversifiable risk using option valuation techniques developed for financial options markets. We will use the binomial pricing method to value Shalini's call option. To use the binomial method, we find risk-neutral valuation probabilities—that is, probabilities that investors are using to value assets sensitive to dollar/tyle exchange rate risk. In risk-neutral valuation, the probabilities are adjusted to reflect the risk of the project and discounting is done at the risk-free rate.

This approach contrasts with the usual method of leaving the probabilities alone and adjusting the discount rate to reflect risk. The reason the discount rate must be adjusted is that doing so is the only way to properly address the fact that an option does not expose its investor to a constant degree of risk across all possible outcomes. In the present case, the investment is only exposed to exchange rate fluctuations if the tyle appreciates and not if it depreciates. The only way to accommodate this fact is to embed the risk premium in the probabilities directly, so that a given state's probability jointly takes into account the likelihood of the state occurring as well as the risk associated with its occurrence.

In the Shumway example, the current exchange rate is $1.8/tyle and is anticipated to be either $2.3/tyle or $1.6/tyle next year with equal probability. To derive risk neutral probabilities, we simply adjust these probabilities until we have a risk-neutral exchange rate forecast under which uncovered interest parity holds. In this way, we embed the risk premium which was causing a violation of uncovered interest parity into the probabilities used to assess expectations:

$$[(p)(2.3) + (1 - p)(1.6)][(1.04)/(1.08)] = 1.8,$$

where p is the probability of an appreciated exchange rate under the risk-neutral valuation. Remember that this is not the true probability of appreciation, but is a hypothetical probability that also incorporates risk. This is the probability that would prevail if investors did not care about the risks associated with the dollar/tyle exchange rate, and therefore uncovered interest parity would be expected to hold. Solving, we get $p = 0.385$. Note that this is lower than the true probability of 0.5 because risk-averse investors, if not allowed to adjust the discount rate of returns exposed to a particular risk, must move probability from good states to bad states to lower the value of these returns and incorporate the risk into their valuation.

Using the new risk-neutralized probabilities, we are now positioned to value the project. If the exchange rate depreciates, the year 1 value of future cash flows will be:

$$PV_1 = (4.8 \times 1.73/1.2 + 4.8 \times 1.80/1.2^2 + 4.8 \times 1.87/1.2^3)/(1.08)$$
$$= \$16.78 \text{ million.}$$

Correspondingly, if the exchange rate appreciates, the value of future cash flows will be:

$$PV_1 = (4.8 \times 2.49/1.2 + 4.8 \times 2.59/1.2^2 + 4.8 \times 2.69/1.2^3)/(1.08)$$
$$= \$24.12 \text{ million.}$$

Hence, from a contingent claims standpoint, Shalini owns an option to invest in the project at an exercise price of $20 million, the investment required in year 1. This option will be exercised only if the exchange rate appreciates, for a net present value of $24.12 - \$20 = \$4.12$ million. Now all that remains is to take the expected value of the option in year 1 and discount it by the risk-free rate into year 0. We discount at the risk-free rate because, when using the risk-neutral probabilities to determine the year 1 expected value, we only need to still adjust the cash flows for timing. Hence, the value of the project in year 0 (in millions) is:

$$PV_0 = (0.385)(\$4.12)/(1.08)$$
$$= \$1.47 \text{ million.}$$

The value of the option to delay, therefore, is $1.47 million $- \$248,000 = \$1,220,431$. Note that both of these values are considerably lower than those derived in the decision tree analysis. This is because here we have properly taken into account the higher risk of a project conditionally exposed to the dollar/tyle exchange rate.

The analysis above can be generalized to allow for a greater number of future states. For example, to make this scenario more realistic, we can allow for two states in six months, branching to four in one year. This scenario effectively gives us four possible outcomes at the end of the year. We can make the interval between nodes shorter and shorter to accommodate a large number of possible outcomes at the end of the year.

❖ SUMMARY OF CHAPTER OBJECTIVES

1. Explain the source of positive present value in investment projects.

The source of positive present value for any project is a comparative advantage in the use of resources that produces a return on capital in excess of the return the shareholders require.

2. Compare different modes of international business by analyzing their present values.

An excess return can be captured through many different modes of operation, including simple import/export businesses, license and franchise agreements with foreign entities, joint ventures with foreign firms, and wholly-owned direct foreign investments. These methods should be compared using present value analysis to select the most valuable opportunity.

3. Understand wholly-owned foreign investment projects in terms of theories of direct foreign investment.

Theories of DFI typically seek to explain the existence of DFI in terms of comparative advantages in the use of resources that MNCs have over their host-country counterparts. They are based on corporate strategies for seeking excess returns, which are particularly international when compared to more general theories of excess returns.

4. Value projects in terms of the future opportunities to change the investment.

The alternations possible in capital investment projects, such as the option to start or expand a project, or the option to abandon or scale back a project, are valuable to a firm. However, the value is not included in traditional present value analysis, and needs to be calculated separately using real option valuation.

❖ QUESTIONS FOR REVIEW

1. Weinress and Donegan, a U.S. consulting company based in Arlington, Virginia, is considering opportunities for business in Holland. The company has examined the amount of Dutch business available and the costs associated with this business, and it has considered different modes of business. One way to do business would be to essentially export their services by working for Dutch consulting contracts in the United States and simply visiting Holland as necessary, although this would require some expansion of the Virginia office. A second way to do business would be to open a small subsidiary in Amsterdam and hire staff to do the work there with supervision from the United States. A final alternative would be to engage in a 50/50 joint venture with a Dutch firm, Knoppers, with which Weinress and Donegan has worked before. One advantage of the joint venture is that additional business would be available and costs would be less than the costs incurred from either of the other two ways of doing business, but the profits would of course be split in half. For a two-year horizon, the U.S. dollar cash flows associated with the three possible modes of doing business are shown below.

	Year 0	Year 1	Year 2
Exporting	−100,000	300,000	300,000
Direct Foreign Investment	−1,000,000	700,000	900,000
Joint Venture	−700,000	800,000	1,000,000

The cash flows for the joint venture are for the whole project, before splitting with Knoppers. As the project is essentially the same regardless of the mode adopted, the cost of capital for the project is 15 percent for each mode under consideration. What is the present value of exporting? What is the present value of direct foreign investment? What is the present value of the joint venture? Based on present value analysis, which way of serving the Dutch market should Weinress and Donegan choose?

2. [Class discussion] Theories of Direct Foreign Investment (DFI) need to identify the reason why DFI occurs instead of portfolio investment or intermediated investment. In this regard, they usually identify an overcompensating advantage that a

multinational firm has over its host-country competitors. What are the overcompensating advantages identified by the major theories of DFI? What theories are particularly successful in this regard and what theories are relatively unsuccessful?

3. True or False: Indicate whether the statement is true or false and clearly explain why.

   a. The product cycle theory of direct foreign investment postulates that direct foreign investment results when firms react to the threat of losing markets as the product matures by expanding overseas and capturing the remaining rents from development of the product.

   b. Because local firms have an inherent cost advantage over foreign investors, multinationals can succeed abroad only if their advantages cannot be purchased or duplicated by local competitors.

   c. According to the internalization theory of direct foreign investment, multinational corporations will grow larger and larger without limit as they replace market transactions with internal transactions.

4. [Class discussion] What does Aliber's "currency area" theory of direct foreign investment (DFI) suggest is the main determinant of DFI, and how credible is this argument in the context of modern finance theory?

5. [Class discussion] The phenomenon of cross-hauling occurs in all of the international investment accounts. What is cross-hauling and why is it of theoretical concern? What theories of DFI can explain this phenomenon, and how do they explain it? What theories cannot explain cross-hauling and why not?

6. [Class discussion] Foreign investments are conventionally assumed to involve additional costs of distance and costs due to unfamiliarity with foreign governments, languages, legal systems, and distribution channels. In a domestic context, positive net present value (NPV) typically originates from economic rents on a firm's competitive advantages, including technological information, marketing expertise, and managerial talent. How do these advantages explain why direct foreign investment occurs? Explain why the NPV might be higher on the foreign project than on a competing domestic project, and explain why the NPV might be higher when undertaken by the foreign (multinational) firm than a competing local firm.

7. [Group project] Several theories of direct foreign investment highlight firm-specific and/or home-country-specific advantages that enable a multinational corporation (MNC) to compete against host-country firms that typically are more familiar with the local business environment and do not have high costs associated with operating a project or subsidiary at a distance from the parent. Consider a perfectly competitive market, in which both MNCs and local firms are price takers.

   a. Draw a diagram showing the cost structure of a price taker and a market price well above minimum average cost. Given that any firm is a price taker, how can a firm capture any economic rent (profits in excess of the opportunity cost of capital)? Show the requirements in the diagram, and indicate what the amount of economic rent would be.

   b. With specific reference to a perfectly competitive market, what are some examples of firm-specific or country-specific advantages that MNCs may have which overcompensate for their lack of familiarity with local markets and the additional costs of distance they must incur? In other words, what explains the ability of multinationals to capture economic rent even if the MNC is a price taker?

8. [Group project] Several theories of direct foreign investment highlight firm-specific and/or home-country-specific advantages which enable a multinational corporation (MNC) to compete against host-country firms which typically are more

familiar with the local business environment and do not have the high costs associated with operating a project or subsidiary at a distance from the parent. Consider an imperfectly competitive market, in which an MNC is price-maker because it experiences a downward-sloping demand curve for its products.

    a. Draw a diagram depicting the downward-sloping demand curve the firm faces and its cost structure (in terms of average cost and marginal cost). Given this information, what price would the firm select for its output, and how much would it sell? Is the firm collecting any "economic rent" (or profit in excess of the opportunity cost of capital)? If so, show the rent in the diagram.

    b. What are some examples of firm-specific or country-specific advantages which a MNC might possess which enables it to experience a downward-sloping demand curve? In other words, what explains the origin of economic rent for MNCs which are price-makers, and why are they price-makers in the first place?

9. [Class discussion] With regard to direct foreign investment strategy, modern finance suggests that an equilibrium would occur in which all projects with positive net present value are already undertaken. Relaxing this efficient markets hypothesis, how can foreign projects have positive net present values?

10. In the example of real options in international capital budgeting for the automobile project in Shumway, suppose the current exchange rate is $1.878/tyle instead of $1.80/tyle but all other data are unchanged. How does this affect the problem?

TOOLS FOR ANALYSIS
Mathematics of Profit and Rent Maximization

This section develops the mathematical specifications of the firm's profit-maximizing behavior. The firm is assumed to know the production function for its output, which specifies the quantity of output as a function of the quantities of inputs such as labor, capital, natural resources, and so on. The firm must pay the market equilibrium cost for all of these inputs. The cost function for the firm's product expresses the cost of production as a function of the quantity produced, and is derived from the production function and the market costs of the inputs. The cost function additionally includes any fixed cost associated with production, which is not a function of the quantity of output produced.

    The cost function, which we now denote C, summarizes the firm's production costs and may take any form. Suppose, for example,

$$C = Q^3 - 14Q^2 + 69Q + 128$$

where Q is the quantity of output produced (e.g., in thousands) and C is measured in dollars. (Because C is measured in dollars, there is nothing uniquely international about production. In Chapter 7, however, we reconsider the cost function to be expressed in foreign currency in certain circumstances and translate it into dollars using the exchange rate. As a result, C will be a function of the exchange rate.) The average cost function, AC, summarizes costs per unit of output and can be represented as:

$$AC = [Q^3 - 14Q^2 + 69Q + 128]/Q$$
$$= Q^2 - 14Q + 69 + 128/Q$$

and the marginal cost curve, MC, summarizes the increase in total cost required to produce an additional unit of output:

$$MC = dC/dQ = 3Q^2 - 28Q + 69$$

and these are the AC and MC curves plotted in Figures 5-2 and 5-3.

    If the firm is a price taker, it is able to sell any amount of output without affecting the price, P, measured in dollars. (Again, Chapter 7 reconsiders the price to be quoted in foreign currency in certain circumstances and translates it into dollars using the exchange rate.) Revenues are thus the price times the quantity of output, $P \times Q$. Suppose, for example, $P = 89$. The firm's profits, Π, are expressed as revenues minus costs:

$$\Pi = 89Q - [Q^3 - 14Q^2 + 69Q + 128].$$

The firm's objective is to pick the quantity of output, Q, to maximize profits, so:

$$d\Pi/dQ = 89 - 3Q^2 + 28Q - 69 = 0$$

and, solving, $Q = 10$. This amounts to setting MC equal to P, which was done graphically in Figure 5-2. When $Q = 10$, $\Pi = 472$, and this represents economic rent, the shaded area in Figure 5-2.

If the firm is a price maker, it faces a downward-sloping demand curve and must take into account the effect of producing and selling additional units on the price received. Suppose, for example, the demand curve is:

$$P = 132 - 8Q$$

where P is again measured in dollars (although again Chapter 7 reconsiders this). The revenue for the firm is thus:

$$P \times Q = 132Q - 8Q^2$$

and the marginal revenue, MR, represents the additional amount of revenue from selling a unit of output, recognizing that the additional unit sold reduces the price on every unit sold:

$$MR = d(PQ)/dQ = 132 - 16Q.$$

Once again, the firm's goal is to pick Q to maximize profits,

$$\Pi = 132Q - 8Q^2 - [Q^3 - 14Q^2 + 69Q + 128]$$

so:

$$d\Pi/dQ = 132 - 16Q - 3Q^2 + 28Q - 69 = 0$$

and $Q = 7$. This amounts to setting MC equal to MR, which was done graphically in Figure 5-3. When $Q = 7$, $\Pi = 264$, and this represents economic rent, the shaded area in Figure 5-3.

As the cost functions already include payment for the use of capital at the rate the owners of capital

require, the economic rent deriving from the profit maximization objective is a specific period's expected cash flows in excess of the required return on the capital used in the project. Suppose the production project represented by the cost function C above requires an initial investment of 500, and the output will be sold one period later. If the required rate of return is 15 percent, then the cash flow one period later must be $500(1.15) = 575$ to compensate the capital's owners for the use of their capital. In this situation, there is no economic rent and the present value of the project is zero:

$$PV = -500 + 575/1.15 = 0$$

In the example above for the price-taking firm, economic rents amounted to 472. This represents a return above the required return for capital, which is still 575, so the present value of the project will be positive:

$$PV = -500 + (575 + 472)/1.15 = 410,$$

and this is simply the present value of 472 discounted at 15 percent, $472/1.15 = 410$.

The mathematics developed here can be easily extended to projects that span multiple periods by considering the amount of economic rent rendered in each period. Furthermore, the profit maximization problem for the firm is often expressed as the choice of a sequence of quantities in future periods, Q_t for $t = 0,1,2,3, \ldots$, to maximize the discounted present value of the stream of profits:

$$\max \sum_{t=0}^{n} \frac{E_0[P_t Q_t - C_t]}{(1 + COC)^t}$$

where C_t is again a function of Q_t, and P_t may also be a function of Q_t. As with the one-period example above, the rents received over multiple periods can also be discounted at the required rate of return on capital to find the present value of the stream of rents:

$$PV = \sum_{t=0}^{n} \frac{E_0[\text{rent}_t]}{(1 + COC)^t}$$

and the similarity of this to the present value calculation in capital budgeting is obvious.

❖ **ENDNOTES**

1. For further development of issues relating economic rent to corporate strategy, see "Primer: Economic Concepts for Strategy" in Besanko, Dranove, and Shanley, 1996, pp. 1–37.

2. Individuals with rare talent also capture economic rent. For example, a high-level manager may be paid $1 million a year for her unusual leadership ability. If the manager's next best al-

ternative is to be an accountant at $50,000 per year, she captures $950,000 in economic rent. An entertainer whose next best alternative is to be a waiter captures economic rent, as does a surgeon whose next best alternative would be in family medicine. As an individual, you should develop talents that enable you to capture economic rent for yourself.

3. Hood and Young (1979) and Markusen (1995) present predominantly microeconomic approaches to the theories of DFI, asking why firms undertake DFI rather than export from home or establish license/franchise agreements with foreign firms. Because the answers focus on firm operations, they do not shed much light on the macroeconomic questions concerning capital flows. In fact, both articles begin by taking the overcompensating ownership advantage of the firm as given and subsequently examining the locational decisions.

4. For additional support, see the discussion by Rugman (1980, 1981, 1985, 1986). Ethier (1986)

presents a formal mathematical treatment of internalization, in which the internalization decision is endogenous within a simple general equilibrium model of international trade.

5. A related theory of direct foreign investment, associated with Magee (1977), is known as the *appropriability theory.* In this theory, a firm with technological advantages exploits the advantage itself for the purpose of keeping the technology away from its rivals in foreign countries. By developing its technology in foreign markets, the firm deters competitors from entering.

6. A similar argument is presented in Froot and Stein (1991) in terms of an increase in domestic wealth as the domestic currency strengthens. Wealthier countries then acquire more assets abroad.

7. For a reconsideration of the product cycle theory, see Vernon (1979).

8. See Lisa Shuchman, "Japanese Auto Makers Shift Strategies to Keep Plants Viable in Southeast Asia," *Wall Street Journal,* January 28, 1998, p. A1.

❖ REFERENCES

Aliber, Robert Z. "A Theory of Direct Foreign Investment," in *The International Corporation: A Symposium,* ed. by C. P. Kindleberger, M.I.T. Press, 1970, pp. 17–34.

Aliber, Robert Z. "The Theory of Direct Foreign Investment and the Multinational Paradigm," Chapter 5 of *The Multinational Paradigm,* M.I.T. Press, 1993, pp. 169–207.

Amran, Martha, and Nalin Kulatilaka. *Real Options: Managing Strategic Investment in an Uncertain World,* Harvard Business School Press, 1999a.

Amran, Martha, and Nalin Kulatilaka. "Disciplined Decisions: Aligning Strategy with the Financial Markets," *Harvard Business Review,* January–February 1999b, pp. 95–104.

Besanko, David, David Dranove, and Mark Shanley. *The Economics of Strategy,* John Wiley & Sons, Inc., 1996.

Boddewyn, Jean J. "Political Aspects of MNE Theory," *Journal of International Business Studies,* Fall 1988, pp. 341–363.

Brewer, Thomas L. "Government Policies, Market Imperfections, and Foreign Direct Investment," *Journal of International Business Studies,* First Quarter 1993, pp. 101–120.

Buckley, Peter J., and Mark Casson. *The Future of the Multinational Enterprise,* Holmes & Meier Publishers, Inc., 1976.

Caves, Richard E. "International Corporations: The Industrial Economics of Foreign Investments," *Economica,* February 1971, pp. 1–27.

Coase, Ronald. "The Nature of the Firm," *Economica,* November 1937, pp. 386–405.

de Meza, David, and Frederick van der Ploeg. "Production Flexibility as a Motive for Multinationality," *Journal of Industrial Economics,* March 1987, pp. 343–351.

Dunning, John H. "Trade, Location of Economic Activity, and the Multinational Enterprise: A Search for an Eclectic Approach," in *The International Allocation of Economic Activity,* edited by B. Ohlin, P. Hesselborn, and P. Wiskman, MacMillan, 1977.

Dunning, John H. "Explaining Changing Patterns of International Production: In Defence of the Eclectic Theory," *Oxford Bulletin of Economics and Statistics,* November 1979, p. 269–295.

Dunning, John H. *International Production and the Multinational Enterprise,* George Allen and Unwin, 1981.

Ethier, Wilfred J. "The Multinational Firm," *Quarterly Journal of Economics,* November 1986, pp. 805–833.

Froot, Kenneth A., and Jeremy C. Stein. "Exchange Rates and Foreign Direct Investment: An Imperfect Capital Markets Approach," *Quarterly Journal of Economics,* November 1991, pp. 1191–1271.

Helpman, Elhanan. "A Simple Theory of Trade with Multinational Corporations," *Journal of Political Economy,* June 1984, pp. 451–471.

Helpman, Elhanan. "Multinational Corporations and Trade Structure," *Review of Economic Studies,* July 1985, pp. 443–457.

Hood, Neil, and Stephen Young. "The Determinants of Foreign Direct Investment," Chapter 2 of *The Economics of Multinational Enterprise,* Longman Group, 1979, pp. 44–86.

Hymer, Stephen. *The International Operations of National Firms: A Study of Direct Foreign Investment,* Ph.D. Dissertation, Massachusetts Institute of Technology, 1960; M.I.T. Press, 1976.

Hymer, Stephen, and Robert Rowthorn. "Multinational Corporations and International Oligopoly: The Non-American Challenge," in *The International Corporation: A Symposium,* ed. by C. P. Kindleberger, M.I.T. Press, 1970, pp. 57–91.

Jacquillat, Bertrand, and Bruno Solnik. "Multinationals are Poor Tools for Diversification," *Journal of Portfolio Management,* Winter 1978, pp. 8–12.

Kindleberger, Charles P. *American Business Abroad: Six Lectures on Direct Investment,* Yale University Press, 1969.

Knickerbocker, Frederick T. *Oligopolistic Reaction and Multinational Enterprise,* Harvard University, 1973.

Kogut, Bruce, and Nalin Kulatilaka. "Operating Flexibility, Global Manufacturing, and the Option Value of a Multinational Network," *Management Science,* January 1994, pp. 123–139.

Lizondo, J. Saúl. "Foreign Direct Investment," in *Determinants and Systemic Consequences of International Capital Flows,* Washington: International Monetary Fund, 1991.

Luehrman, Timothy A. "Investment Opportunities as Real Options: Getting Started with the Numbers," *Harvard Business Review,* July-August 1998a, pp. 51–67.

Luehrman, Timothy A. "Strategy as a Portfolio of Real Options," *Harvard Business Review,* September-October 1998b, pp. 89–99.

Magee, Stephen. "Information and the MNC: An Appropriability Theory of Direct Foreign Investment," in *The New International Economic Order,* edited by Jagdish Bhagwati, Cambridge: M.I.T. Press, 1977, pp. 317–340.

Markusen, James R. "Multinationals, Multi-Plant Economics, and the Gains from Trade," *Journal of International Economics,* May 1984, pp. 205–226.

Markusen, James R. "The Boundaries of Multinational Enterprises and the Theory of International Trade," *Journal of Economic Perspectives,* Spring 1995, pp. 169–189.

Ragazzi, Giorgio. "Theories of the Determinants of Direct Foreign Investment," *IMF Staff Papers,* July 1973, pp. 471–498.

Rugman, Alan M. "Risk Reduction by International Diversification," *Journal of International Business Studies,* Fall/Winter 1976, pp. 75–80.

Rugman, Alan M. "Risk, Direct Investment, and International Diversification," *Weltwirtschaftliches Archiv,* 1977, part 3, pp. 487–500.

Rugman, Alan M. "Internalization as a General Theory of Foreign Direct Investment: A Re-Appraisal of the Literature," *Weltwirtschaftliches Archiv,* 1980, pp. 365–379.

Rugman, Alan M. *Inside the Multinationals: The Economics of Internal Markets,* New York: Columbia University Press, 1981.

Rugman, Alan M. "Internalization is Still a General Theory of Foreign Direct Investment," *Weltwirtschaftliches Archiv,* 1985, pp. 570–575.

Rugman, Alan M. "New Theories of the Multinational Enterprise: An Assessment of Internalization Theory," *Bulletin of Economic Research,* 1986, pp. 101–118.

Sherwood-Call, Carolyn. "Changing Geographical Patterns of Electronic Components Activity," Federal Reserve Bank of San Francisco *Economic Review,* no. 2, 1992, pp. 25–35.

Shuchman, Lisa. "Jamanese Auto Makers Shift Strategies to Keep Plants Viable in Southeast Asia," *Wall Street Journal,* January 28, 1998, p. A1.

Vernon, Raymond. "International Investment and International Trade in The Product Cycle," *Quarterly Journal of Economics,* May 1966, pp. 190–207.

Vernon, Raymond. "The Product Cycle Hypothesis in a New International Environment," *Oxford Bulletin of Economics and Statistics,* November 1979, pp. 255–267.

PART

III

MANAGING FOREIGN EXCHANGE RISK

Having considered the major issues that make evaluating, financing, and understanding an overseas project different from a domestic project in Part II, a focus basically on getting a project started, this part of the book considers financial issues pertaining to the project once it is operating. The main financial challenge a firm faces upon becoming multinational is what to do about exchange rate changes, and the five chapters in this part introduce the concepts of foreign exchange exposure, risk, and risk management. Properties of exchange rates and various international parity theorems, which were introduced in Chapter 2, are once again important tools in analyzing exposure, risk, and hedging. In addition, the management decisions are again treated within the centralization-versus-decentralization framework used in Chapters 3 and 4. The chapters in this part therefore build on the foundations begun in Parts I and II.

Issues in risk assessment and management have been studied in many different situations. Macroeconomic risks—which are usually considered to be exogenous when viewed from the level of the firm—include interest rate risk, inflation risk, and commodity price risk (such as oil price risk), as well as exchange rate risk. Familiarity with these other types of risk and methods of managing these risks will be advantageous in our study of foreign exchange risk. After all, the concepts of exposure, risk, and hedging are quite general.

Although some attention will be paid to interest rate, inflation, and commodity price risk, the truly unique risk confronted by direct foreign investment—which is rarely an issue in domestic investment—is foreign exchange risk. This is not to imply that the other risks are minor, but that they are simply not the center of attention in this book. For readers wishing to study these other macroeconomic risks, and readers needing an introduction or review of risk assessment and management, the articles by Rawls and Smithson (1990) and Smith, Smithson, and Wilford (1989) should be helpful. In addition, Chapter 25 of Brealey and Myers (1992) focuses on "Hedging Financial Risk," and Part IV of Grinblatt and Titman (1998) is about "Risk Management" with a particular focus on interest rate risk.

Chapter 6, "Translation and Transaction Exposure," addresses the simplest numerical approaches to measuring what the firm has at stake. Accountants have examined foreign exchange exposure for a relatively long time because they are faced with the task of consolidating the financial statements of foreign branches and subsidiaries, which are kept in various local currencies, into the parent company's financial statements, which are kept in home currency units. Under the Bretton-Woods system of fixed exchange rates, accountants had a relatively easy life as long as a devaluation or revaluation did not occur. Once any type of realignment occurred, however, accountants had to decide which exchange rates were to be used for various accounting purposes. They were also faced with posting the inevitable foreign exchange gains and losses associated with the impact exchange rate changes had on the firm's accounts. With the break-down of the Bretton-Woods system and the shift to a floating exchange rate system in the 1970s, the task became even more complicated. Chapter 6 examines the accountant's concept of translation exposure as currently prescribed by the Financial Accounting Standards Board. Limitations of the translation exposure concept will also be addressed in the latter part of the chapter, and an alternative focus on the treasury concept of transactions exposure will be suggested. Although this is an improvement, transactions exposure also suffers from a few deficiencies, and these are presented at the end of the chapter.

Chapter 7, "Economic Exposure," addresses all-encompassing measures of what the firm has at stake. Because translation and transaction exposure measurements both suffer from deficiencies, economists and financial analysts have developed the concept of economic exposure, which suggests that managers are to be concerned with the impact of exchange rate changes on the entire value of the firm. A complete analysis therefore evaluates the effect of exchange rate changes on the ongoing revenues and costs of the firm, as well as on the assets and liabilities in the balance sheet. Furthermore, managers are to be concerned only with the effects of real exchange rate changes—which are the observed nominal exchange rate changes adjusted for inflation. Because quantifying economic exposure is obviously much more difficult than quantifying translation and transaction exposure, the basic thrust of the chapter is conceptual. At the conclusion of the chapter, however, the concept of economic exposure as an econometric regression coefficient is presented for those readers with a basic knowledge of regression analysis.

Chapter 8, "The Risk of Foreign Exchange Exposure," examines the foreign exchange risk associated with exposures covered in Chapters 6 and 7. The risk associated with an individual exposure is measured by the standard deviation of the currency in which the exposure is denominated. The chapter subsequently contains an examination of modern portfolio theory applied to exchange risk management with multiple currencies. The centralization-versus-decentralization framework is reintroduced as a way of thinking about overall risk. The principle of foreign currency diversification is established, and the general benefits of centralized financial management are illustrated through a few examples. The principle is then extended to include interest rates in an application of the theory, and of the centralization-versus-decentralization paradigm, to international cash management.

Chapter 9, "Hedging with Financial Instruments," examines financial tools for hedging foreign exchange risk. The chapter begins by looking at the simplest hedges, using forward markets and money markets, which relies on an interest parity theorem introduced in Chapter 2, known as covered interest parity, linking forward exchange rates to spot exchange rates through interest rates on the currencies involved. Although the analysis is conducted in nominal terms rather than in real terms, covered interest parity captures intuition about why future spot exchange rates are not expected to be the same as the current spot exchange rate. Subsequently, the principles of hedging are extended to more advanced financial hedges. In particular, the uses of foreign currency futures and options are analyzed. The presentation considers hedges which reduce but don't eliminate the risk of a position and account for positions that are contingent on some other event. The use of futures contracts to hedge exposure builds on the covered interest parity theorem, but recognizes that a perfect hedge is generally not available. The use of options contracts to hedge exposure is most appropriate when the exposure is contingent on something else, such as a bid being accepted, because the option gives the right to buy or sell currencies without the obligation to do so. Although options appear to give the purchaser the right to keep the upside gains at the same time he or she is getting rid of the downside losses, the option premium accounts for this asymmetry. As long as the option is priced fairly in efficient markets, however, an option may be used to hedge a variety of transactions without being expensive.

Chapter 10, "Risk Management Strategy," concludes the discussion of foreign exchange exposure, risk, and hedging by looking at motivations for hedging and management strategies to reduce exchange risk. This chapter is an overview of the nature of hedging, and is fairly conceptual. It reviews the types of exposure introduced in Chapters 6 and 7 and carefully examines whether transactions are associated with economic exposure. It also examines why firms might have a preference for a known home-currency transaction amount rather than a gamble with the same expected value involving potential gains or losses. The chapter also focuses on distinctions among economic exposure in the short run, intermediate run, and long run, and considers additional reasons why firms hedge. With these distinctions, we reconsider the value of hedging with financial instruments, and address why options hedges seem to be so important in practice. As additional methods of managing foreign exchange risk, the chapter introduces short-term transactions management (other than financial hedges) and intermediate-term operating management. The latter draws on the growing literature in international business strategy, international marketing, and international production. In the long run, the firm should be in equilibrium vis-à-vis its competitors and the level of the exchange rate.

The five chapters in this part focus on another major theme of the book: that analysis of the impact of exchange rate changes and methods to mitigate these effects should be based on inflation-adjusted exchange rate changes, rather than on purely nominal changes. This is predominantly an application of the purchasing power parity proposition, and therefore shows up primarily in Chapter 7 on economic exposure and Chapter 10 on risk management strategies for multinational corporations. However, we acknowledge that analysis of nominal exchange rate exposure is important in the context of real exchange rate exposure for two reasons. First, as developed in Chapter 6, nominal measurement is easy when the limitations of the analysis are taken into account. Second, as developed in Chapter 9, nominal hedging is easy for short-term exposures as long as nominal exposures also represent real economic exposures. The analysis of risk in Chapter 8 draws the two perspectives together by suggesting that, as an empirical proposition, nominal and real exchange rate changes are almost identical anyway.

❖ REFERENCES

Brealey, Richard A., and Stewart C. Myers. *Principles of Corporate Finance,* McGraw-Hill, 1992.

Grinblatt, Mark, and Sheridan Titman. *Financial Markets and Corporate Strategy,* Irwin/McGraw-Hill, 1998.

Rawls, S. Waite, III, and Charles W. Smithson. "Strategic Risk Management," *Continental Bank Journal of Applied Corporate Finance,* Winter 1990, pp. 6–18.

Smith, Clifford W., Jr., Charles W. Smithson, and D. Sykes Wilford. "Managing Financial Risk," *Continental Bank Journal of Applied Corporate Finance,* Winter 1989, pp. 27–48.

TRANSLATION AND TRANSACTION EXPOSURE

CHAPTER OBJECTIVES
AFTER READING THIS CHAPTER, YOU SHOULD BE ABLE TO:

❖ Define the concepts of foreign exchange exposure, translation exposure, and transaction exposure.

❖ Calculate the accounting measures of exposure.

❖ Calculate exposure based on upcoming, known cash flows that a corporate treasurer might prefer over the traditional accounting measurement.

This chapter begins by defining various concepts of exposure. It then details the application of translation exposure, the traditional, accounting measure of exposure. We pay a fair amount of attention to exceptions to translation accounting rules and the reasoning behind these exceptions. The chapter then shifts the focus to transaction exposure, an exposure measure which focuses on known cash flows rather than balance sheet items.

6.1   INTRODUCTION

Once the multinational corporation establishes direct foreign investment abroad, it is immediately confronted with foreign exchange risk. If the exchange rate changes, the home currency value of assets and liabilities denominated in the foreign currency changes. Furthermore, the home currency value of the income stream the foreign investment generates changes. This is the first of a pair of chapters that examines the extent to which foreign operations of multinational corporations are exposed to changes in exchange rates. The main focus here is on the accounting approach, although we make some modifications to allow for a transactions-based approach. By understanding these two approaches, with or without the details presented throughout this chapter, the foundation is set for an all-encompassing examination in Chapter 7.

6.2   FOREIGN EXCHANGE EXPOSURE

Several concepts of foreign exchange exposure have been developed throughout the past few decades, but they all share a common underlying definition. **Foreign exchange exposure** is the degree to which a company is affected by exchange rate changes. It is a measure of what the company has at stake. Exposure is of concern because it indicates the magnitude of any foreign exchange gain or loss corresponding to a particular exchange rate change. This relationship is reflected in the simple formula:

$$\text{FX Gain (Loss)}_{t,t+n} = [S_{t+n} - S_t][\text{Exposure}_t]$$

where FX Gain (Loss)$_{t,t+n}$ is the foreign exchange gain or loss and $[S_{t+n} - S_t]$ is the change in the spot exchange rate over the period. The exposure is denominated in the underlying local currency, the exchange rates are quoted as home currency units per local currency, and the foreign exchange gain or loss is denominated in home currency units.

EXAMPLE 6.1

A U.S. multinational corporation is holding a 10,000 Swiss franc account receivable. If the exchange rate when it was obtained was SwF 1 = $0.75 and the exchange rate at maturity is SwF 1 = $0.90, there is an exchange gain or loss equal to:

$$[\$0.90/\text{SwF} - \$0.75/\text{SwF}][\text{SwF } 10,000] = \$1,500$$

or a gain of $ 1,500.

Of the many concepts of exposure that have been developed, three are important. Figure 6-1 diagrams these concepts and profiles the contemporary treatment of them. Accountants developed the earliest concepts of exposure, because they faced the task of translating foreign currency amounts into the home currency for financial reporting. Any time the exchange rate changes, accountants face different exchange rates to be applied to different things at different points in time. These translation problems are dealt with first in the concept of translation exposure. Because translation exposure focuses only on the accountant's need to translate financial statements, the concept has several deficiencies when used as a tool for management decisions. We therefore present a more refined focus on translation exposure, transactions exposure, as an alternative foundation for analysis. We treat both translation and transaction exposure in this chapter.

The final branch of the diagram in Figure 6-1 applies to the subject of Chapter 7, economic exposure. Economic exposure is defined separately because even the concept of transaction exposure is too narrow to allow us to analyze the impact of exchange rate changes on the entire firm's ongoing operations.

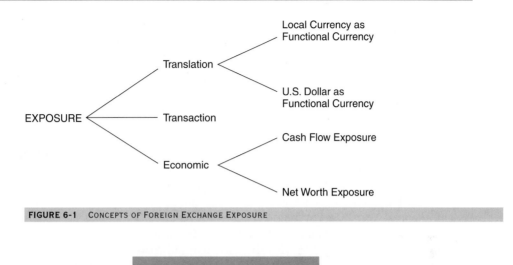

FIGURE 6-1   CONCEPTS OF FOREIGN EXCHANGE EXPOSURE

6.3   TRANSLATION EXPOSURE

Accounting rules vary across countries, so no single presentation of accounting for foreign investments is truly adequate. However, understanding the rules for a particular country illuminates the issues involved and makes subsequent study of other countries' rules more straightforward. As this book is aimed primarily at a U.S. audience, we consider the main accounting features pertaining to U.S. firms with investments abroad. Many other countries follow these same rules, or make slight modifications to them, so the principles are in fact more general than they might appear.

Under generally accepted U. S. accounting principles, the nature of financial reporting for a firm with foreign investments depends on the type and extent of the overseas operations. It is important to distinguish large, significant ownership and control from moderate or small stakes in foreign operations. If a company owns very little—usually less than 10 percent—of the voting shares in a foreign corporation, the investment is not considered a direct foreign investment and is accounted for using the cost method. With the **cost method,** the corporation carries the foreign investment on the balance sheet at cost, calculated at the exchange rate prevailing at the time of the investment, and dividends are recognized as they are received, calculated at the exchange rate in effect when they are received.

If a company owns a moderate share but not a majority—usually between 10 and 50 percent—of the voting stock in a foreign corporation, the investment is considered direct foreign investment and is recorded using the equity method. In the **equity method,** the initial investment is recorded at cost, but periodic adjustments for changes in the value of the investment are made based on the owned share of profits and losses.

If a company owns a controlling interest in a foreign operation, usually defined to be more than 50 percent of the voting stock of a foreign operation, consolidation of the owned share of the balance sheet and income statement into the owner's balance sheet and income statement is required. When the parent company acquires a majority stake in a foreign enterprise, it records the investment as an asset on its balance sheet, and the foreign company shows the parent's investment as an equity stake. Subsequently, the parent's share of the foreign enterprise is periodically consolidated into the parent's balance sheet in a process that nets the parent's investment asset against the foreign enterprise's equity. Because the foreign enterprise's balance sheet is denominated in the foreign currency, changes in the exchange rate affect the consolidation because they affect the U.S. dollar value of the foreign currency.

From the standpoint of foreign exchange exposure, this is the situation in which we are most interested. In particular, this chapter develops examples of wholly-owned subsidiaries in which a parent company owns 100 percent of the voting shares of the foreign enterprise. The same principles apply to foreign branches, which are not the legally separate entities that subsidiaries are, if separate records are kept at all. **Translation exposure,** or **accounting exposure,** is the degree to which the value of a firm's foreign-currency-denominated accounts on the balance sheet are affected by exchange rate changes. In the United States, accounting standards are set by a private foundation called the Financial Accounting Standards Board (FASB). Translation exposure is currently defined for U.S. firms by Financial Accounting Standards Board Statement No. 52, which has been in effect since 1982 (FASB-52). A parent is also required to consolidate its share of the income statement of a majority-owned foreign enterprise, and we will examine the exposure of the income statement as warranted.

PRINCIPAL FEATURES OF FASB-52

There are many ways to translate a foreign subsidiary's balance sheet for consolidation into the parent company's balance sheet. The method usually prescribed by FASB-52 is known as the **current rate method,** in which all assets and liabilities on the balance sheet are translated at the exchange rate prevailing on the date of the balance sheet statement. All items in the equity account, such as the value of capital stock and retained earnings, are translated at their historical rates, which were the rates in effect when they were originally posted to the subsidiary's balance sheet. This method therefore allows for isolation of the exchange rate effects on the capital account, which implies that only the capital investment is at stake. We give examples of the current rate method shortly to clarify the translation procedure.

As the current rate method translates all assets and liabilities at the current exchange rate, FASB-52 therefore quantifies translation or accounting exposure as the difference between total assets and total liabilities on the balance sheet. This, by accounting definition, equals the capital account. As a long-term investment, again, only the equity in the subsidiary is at risk. In terms of the foreign exchange gain or loss equation presented earlier, the net asset position (assets minus liabilities) or book value of capital is used as the measurement of exposure.

The final prescription of FASB-52 is that translation gains or losses bypass the income statement and are accumulated in a separate equity account in the balance sheet. This separate account is usually called "cumulative translation adjustment" or something similar. The logic for this procedure is that the translation gains and losses are unrealized until the foreign operations are sold or discontinued. As such, the unrealized gains and losses should not be shown on the income statement because doing so will unnecessarily change the reported profit. Indeed, with highly volatile exchange rates, the reported profits could be wildly fluctuating from quarter to quarter because of short-term exchange gains and losses. By accumulating them on the balance sheet until the activity is sold or discontinued, only the to-date aggregate gain or loss is important at any given period.

TRANSLATION USING THE CURRENT RATE METHOD

By way of illustration, this section presents two examples of translation using the usual features of FASB-52. The first example translates a balance sheet that has not changed over the course of the year. This simplification allows us to focus on the balance sheet to the exclusion of the income statement. The second example introduces income earned during the year that is posted to retained earnings, and therefore requires examination of the end-of-period balance sheet and the period's income statement.

EXAMPLE 6.2
Continental Labs, a U.S. firm based in Seattle, operates a new wholly-owned subsidiary in France that produces and sells industrial chemicals. The subsidiary was started with FF 10,000 in capital when the exchange rate was FF 5 = $1. Profits of FF 2,000 were retained in the first year of operation, when the exchange rate remained at FF 5 = $1. The balance sheet for the subsidiary at the beginning of the second year is shown in Column 1 of Table 6-1. At the end of the second year, the balance sheet is completely unchanged, implying that there are no additional retained profits. If the exchange rate remains at FF 5 = $1, the translation of the balance sheet is the simple case shown in Column 2, where the total assets are valued at $24,000 and the total equity is valued at $2,400. There are no foreign exchange gains or losses because the exchange rate does not change. If the franc depreciates to FF 6 = $1, however, there will be exchange losses because the net assets or equity will be worth less in U.S. dollar terms. Assets and liabilities are translated at the current rate of FF 6 = $1, while the equity accounts are translated at their historic rates of FF 5 = $1. Table 6-2 presents a translation exposure report for Continental Labs of France based on the balance sheet in Table 6-1. This report demonstrates that exposure is FF 12,000, which is simply the total French franc assets minus the total liabilities, or the parent company's equity position in

TABLE 6-1   Balance Sheet for Continental Labs of France Translated Using the Current Rate Method

	1 *French* *Francs*	2 *5 FF* *= $1*	3 *6 FF* *= $1*	4 *4 FF* *= $1*
ASSETS				
Cash	10000	2000	1667	2500
Accounts Receivable	6000	1200	1000	1500
Inventory	14000	2800	2333	3500
Plant and Equipment (net)	90000	18000	15000	22500
TOTAL ASSETS	120000	24000	20000	30000
LIABILITIES AND EQUITY				
Accounts Payable	16000	3200	2667	4000
Current Debt	4000	800	667	100
Long-Term Debt	88000	17600	14666	22000
TOTAL LIABILITIES	108000	21600	18000	27000
Capital Stock	10000	2000	2000	2000
Retained Earnings	2000	400	400	400
Cumulative Translation Adjustment			(400)	600
TOTAL EQUITY	12000	2400	2000	3000
TOTAL LIAB. AND EQUITY	120000	24000	20000	30000

TABLE 6-2   Translation Exposure Report for Continental Labs of France Based on the Current Rate Method

Cash	FF	10000
Accounts Receivable		6000
Inventory		14000
Plant and Equipment (net)		90000
TOTAL ASSETS EXPOSED	FF	120000
Accounts Payable	FF	16000
Current Debt		4000
Long-Term Debt		88000
TOTAL LIABILITIES EXPOSED	FF	108000
NET ASSETS EXPOSED	FF	12000

the subsidiary. Using the formula from the first section of this chapter, the loss due to franc depreciation is therefore:

$$\text{FX Gain (Loss)} = (\$1/6 \text{ FF} - \$1/5 \text{ FF})(\text{FF } 12,000) = -\$400$$

and this loss is shown as the cumulative translation adjustment in Column 3 of Table 6-1. If the franc appreciates to FF $4 = \$1$, however, there will be gains because the French net assets or equity are worth more in U.S. dollar terms. The gain is:

$$\text{FX Gain (Loss)} = (\$1/4 \text{ FF} - \$1/5 \text{ FF})(\text{FF } 12,000) = \$600$$

and this is shown with the translation of the balance sheet in Column 4 of Table 6-1.

When a foreign subsidiary is profitable in a given period, the income from the operation is partially exposed to exchange rate changes. Under the current rate method, all items in the income statement are translated at an appropriately-weighted average exchange rate to reflect conditions over the period. As a result, income is translated at the period average exchange rate and is therefore exposed to the extent that the end-of-period exchange rate is different than the period average exchange rate.

As a simple case, the period's average exchange rate may be the average of the beginning and ending exchange rates: $(1/2)(S_{t+n} + S_t)$. Income is exposed to the extent that the ending exchange rate, S_{t+n}, is different than the period average, $(1/2)(S_{t+n} + S_t)$, so:

$$\text{FX Gain (Loss)}_{t,t+n} = [S_{t+n} - (1/2)(S_{t+n} + S_t)][\text{Income}_t]$$
$$= [S_{t+n} - S_t][1/2][\text{Income}_t],$$

suggesting that half of the period's income is exposed, or alternatively that income is exposed to half of the exchange rate change. The period average exchange rate may be some weighting of exchange rates throughout the period, so the notion that the exposure of income is 50 percent is only an approximation. The next example demonstrates income statement exposure when the average exchange rate is not the average of beginning and ending exchange rates.

EXAMPLE 6.3

Polydemic Enterprises is a U.S. multinational corporation with operations all over the world. It recently opened a new subsidiary in Greece. The beginning exchange rate was 135 drachmas per dollar. Over the first quarter of operations, the drachma fell to 150 drachmas per dollar, and the period average exchange rate was 140 drachmas per dollar. The ending balance sheet is shown in Table 6-3 and the period's income statement is shown in Table 6-4. This translation

TABLE 6-3   Polydemic-Greece's Balance Sheet in Drachmas and Translated into Dollars (figures in millions)

	1 *Drachmas*	*2* *Rate*	*3* *Dollars*
ASSETS			
Cash	300.0	150	2.00
Receivables	112.5	150	0.75
Inventory	67.5	150	0.45
Plant & Equipment (net)	405.0	150	2.70
TOTAL ASSETS	885.0		5.90
LIABILITIES AND CAPITAL			
Current Payables	140.0	150	0.93
Long-Term Debt	400.0	150	2.67
Common Stock	135.0	135	1.00
Retained Earnings	210.0	140	1.50
Cumulative Translation Adjustment			(0.20)
TOTAL LIABILITIES AND CAPITAL	885.0		5.90

at 140 drachmas per dollar is shown in the second column of Table 6-4. The translation of the balance sheet is shown in the third column of Table 6-3. All assets and liabilities are translated at the period-end exchange rate of 150 drachmas per dollar. The common stock is translated at the historical rate of 135 drachmas per dollar. The retained earnings are translated at the average exchange rate for the period in which they are earned, or 140 drachmas per dollar, and this rate will be the historical exchange rate for 210 drachmas of retained earnings into the future. The cumulative translation adjustment arises from two components. The first is the effect of drachma depreciation on the value of the capital stock:

$$(\$1/150 \text{ drachmas} - \$1/135 \text{ drachmas})(135 \text{ drachmas}) = -\$0.1$$

and the second is the effect of drachma depreciation on retained earnings between the period average exchange rate and the end of the period exchange rate:

$$(\$1/150 \text{ drachmas} - \$1/140 \text{ drachmas})(210 \text{ drachmas}) = -\$0.1,$$

so the total cumulative translation adjustment is a loss of $ 0.2.

The translation adjustment described here is a simple version of the translation adjustment that shows up in the annual reports of every corporation with foreign affiliates. These translation adjustments are accumulated over time, until an activity is sold

TABLE 6-4   Polydemic-Greece's Income Statement in Drachmas and Translated into Dollars (figures in millions)

	1 *Drachmas*	*2* *Dollars*
Revenue	3500	25.0
Cost of Goods Sold	2000	14.3
Depreciation of Plant & Equipment	1000	7.1
Office Expenses	80	0.6
PRE-TAX INCOME	420	3.0
Income Taxes	210	1.5
NET INCOME	210	1.5

or disposed of. Accountants therefore need to keep records on all the historical exchange rates at which the items in the capital account are translated. It should be clear from our example, though, that to construct a balance sheet in home currency units, the only information you need is the beginning-of-period balance sheet in home currency units and the exchange rate, the period's retained earnings and average exchange rate, and the end-of-period exchange rate.

A brief look at the recent history of nominal exchange rates will explain the temporal patterns of translation gains and losses. In Chapter 2 we saw that there was a decade-long dollar cycle during the 1980s. Between the beginning of 1980 and the end of 1984, the U.S. dollar appreciated with respect to nearly every other industrial country's currency. During this period, U.S. corporations with operations abroad consistently recorded translation losses because the U.S. dollar value of the equity at stake declined. Between the beginning of 1985 and the end of 1987 the dollar depreciated against these same industrialized currencies. Corporations with operations abroad recorded foreign exchange gains during this period as the U.S. dollar value of foreign-currency-denominated equity increased. By the end of 1987, the U.S. dollar had approximately returned to its 1980 level, completing what some authors refer to as a dollar cycle.

If the exposure of an overseas affiliate was constant over this eight-year period, the accumulated translation adjustment at the end of the dollar cycle would be approximately what the accumulated translation adjustment was at the beginning of 1980. This eight-year dollar cycle should emphasize why short-term translation gains and losses are not very important in evaluating periodic income statements. Short-term gains and losses are simply not integral parts of the business' profitability. It is clear why corporations should treat foreign exchange gains and losses as unrealized until an activity is sold or discontinued.

EXCEPTIONS TO THE PRINCIPAL FEATURES OF FASB-52

There are some circumstances in which the principles outlined above are considered inappropriate for translating foreign affiliates' balance sheets for consolidation. The exceptions to the principal features of FASB-52 center around the determination of the unit's **functional currency,** or the currency of the primary economic environment in which the affiliate operates. The functional currency is usually considered the currency of the country in which the operation is based. In examples 6.2 and 6.3, the functional currency is the French franc (in example 6.2) or Greek drachma (in example 6.3). These branches or subsidiaries collect revenue in francs or drachmas and incur expenses in francs or drachmas, and have all the accounts in their balance sheets actually denominated in francs or drachmas.

FASB-52 sometimes defines the functional currency of a foreign operation as the parent company's home currency, the U.S. dollar, rather than the local currency. These cases fall into two basic categories. First, the reporting requirements change if the foreign operation is considered an integral part of the parent's operations. Second, the reporting requirements change if the foreign affiliate is located in a highly inflationary country.

EXCEPTION 1: THE FOREIGN OPERATION IS AN INTEGRAL PART OF THE PARENT'S OPERATIONS

Certain foreign operations are not self-contained units. At a simple level, a foreign operation that functions as just a sales office for the parent simply imports goods and sells them in the foreign market. In this instance, the operation is clearly an integral part of

TRANSLATION EXPOSURE
AT WENDY'S INTERNATIONAL, INC.

Wendy's International, Inc., operates approximately 90 Wendy's fast-food restaurants in Canada. Prior to 1995, these were the company's only foreign operations; all other Wendy's restaurants in foreign countries were operated by franchise owners. In 1995, Wendy's International acquired Tim Hortons, a Canadian restaurant chain. The Consolidated Balance Sheets for the whole company contain translation adjustments that result from exchange rate changes. The Consolidated Balance Sheet for 1994, Table 6-5, which is prior to the acquisition of Tim Hortons, shows

TABLE 6-5 Balance Sheet of Wendy's International, Inc.

January 1, 1995, and January 2, 1994 *(Dollars in thousands)*	*1994*	*1993*
Assets		
Current assets		
Cash and cash equivalents	$ 119,639	$ 71,698
Short-term investments, at market	15,292	40,647
Accounts receivable, net	28,015	27,381
Notes receivable, net	7,446	5,259
Deferred income taxes	13,067	12,244
Inventories and other	19,702	21,478
	203,161	178,707
Property and equipment, at cost		
Land	222,671	203,651
Buildings	359,503	329,023
Leasehold improvements	189,243	182,519
Restaurant equipment	335,474	289,242
Other equipment	53,265	65,197
Capital leases	63,531	64,148
	1,223,687	$1,133,780
Accumulated depreciation and amortization	(457,368)	(426,496)
	766,319	707,284
Cost in excess of net assets acquired, net	30,780	24,314
Deferred income taxes	16,142	15,250
Other assets	69,690	70,931
	$1,086,092	$ 996,486
Liabilities and Shareholders' Equity		
Current liabilities		
Accounts and drafts payable	$ 69,845	$ 68,735
Accrued expenses		
Salaries and wages	22,173	16,288
Taxes	15,248	14,935
Insurance	26,037	21,345
Other	11,409	11,160
Income taxes	1,683	2,896
Deferred income taxes	3,108	2,299
Current portion of long-term obligations	57,674	5,611
	207,177	143,269

APPLICATION 6-1 (cont.)

TABLE 6-5 (cont.)

January 1, 1995, and January 2, 1994
(Dollars in thousands)	*1994*	*1993*
Long-term obligations		
Term debt	104,842	156,741
Capital leases	40,018	43,892
	144,860	200,633
Deferred income taxes	39,799	40,859
Other long-term liabilities	12,758	10,930
Commitments and contingencies		
Shareholders' equity		
Preferred stock, authorized: 250,000 shares		
Common stock, $.10 stated value, authorized: 200,000,000 shares		
Issued: 101,787,000 and 100,823,000 shares, respectively	10,179	10,082
Capital in excess of stated value	171,004	161,238
Retained earnings	503,712	430,866
Translation adjustments	(19)	1,347
Pension liability adjustment	(3,212)	(2,572)
	681,664	600,961
Treasury stock at cost: 29,000 shares	(166)	(166)
	681,498	600,795
	$1,086,092	$ 996,486

a cumulative translation adjustment balance of −$19,000 at the end of 1994, indicating that the Canadian operations had experienced net translation losses since they were established. As Wendy's International operated in only one foreign country, several observations about the foreign operations can be made.

By comparing the translation adjustments on the balance sheets for 1993 and 1994, the foreign exchange gain (or loss) for 1994 can be calculated: −$19 − $1,347 = −$1,366 thousand. This translation gain (loss) consists of several components. First, it represents the foreign exchange gains (losses) from the beginning-of-year equity position in the Canadian restaurants. Second, it reflects gains (losses) from the income statement due to any difference between the period average exchange rate and the end of period exchange rate. Finally, it also reflects reversals of prior gains (losses) for restaurants which have been franchised (sold) or closed, because the cumulative translation gains or losses have to be realized when the operations are discontinued by removing them

from the cumulative translation adjustment account and taking them to the income statement.

As Wendy's does not report the Canadian affiliates' balance sheet, the magnitude of translation exposure is unclear. An estimate is possible, however. The 1994 beginning-of-period exchange rate between the U.S. dollar and the Canadian dollar is known to have been $0.7553/C$. The end-of-period exchange rate is known to have been $0.7129/C$. From this information and the known foreign exchange loss in 1994, a rough estimate of the exposure can be made. We can plug the known data into the formula for exchange gains (losses) and solve for the unknown translation exposure:

$$-1{,}366 \text{ thousand} = (\$0.7129/\text{C\$} - \$0.7553/\text{C\$}) \times \text{C\$ exposure.}$$

Solving, Wendy's C$ exposure is revealed to be C$32,317 thousand.

The first part of Table 6-6 reports estimates of Wendy's International's Canadian dollar translation exposure for 1992 to 1994. All the figures are in excess of 20 million Canadian dollars, or more

APPLICATION 6-1 (cont.)

TABLE 6-6   Wendy's International, Inc., Translation Exposure

Year	Number of Canadian Restaurants	Cumulative Translation Adjustment (thousands)	Translation Gain (Loss) (thousands)	Exchange Rate ($/C$)	Estimated Translation Exposure (thousands)
1991	82	$4,412	—	0.8654	—
1992	91	$2,072	−$2,340	0.7867	C$29,733
1993	92	$1,347	−$725	0.7553	C$23,089
1994	96	−$19	−$1,366	0.7129	C$32,317
1995	—	−$4,511	—	0.7331	—
1996	—	−$5,712	−$1,201	0.7298	C$363,939
1997	—	−$18,191	−$12,479	0.6987	C$401,254

than C$250,000 per restaurant. After the acquisition of Tim Hortons in 1995, the accounting for translation gains and losses became more complicated. Nearly all foreign operations are in Canada, but a few company-owned restaurants now exist outside of North America. In addition, the firm combines the cumulative translation adjustment with other unspecified adjustments to the equity section of the consolidated balance sheet. Assuming that the effect of non-Canadian foreign restaurants is small, and that the other adjustments to shareholder equity are small, we can estimate the Canadian dollar exposure when Tim Hortons is included with Wendy's. The last rows of Table 6-6 indicate that exposure jumped to C$363,939 thousand in 1996 and C$401,254 in 1997.

the parent's operations. A similar situation arises with respect to re-export facilities abroad. If the nature of the operation is to import inputs from the parent, perform some light manufacturing or assembling, and re-export finished products to the United States, the operation is again an integral part of the parent's operations. In these situations, the fact that the foreign operation is an integral part of the parent's operation implies that accounting for the foreign operation should result in statements quite similar to those that would be produced if foreign operations were posted directly to the parent's books. The functional currency is therefore the U.S. dollar rather than the local currency, because a dollar perspective more accurately describes the situation. The main implication is that foreign exchange gains or losses associated with monetary assets and liabilities are considered to have an important impact on the parent company's value, and are thus recorded in the income statement as they occur.

EXCEPTION 2: THE FOREIGN OPERATION IS IN A HIGH-INFLATION COUNTRY

Operations of any type that are located in highly inflationary countries suffer from related problems. In these economies, the local currency is not a very effective functional currency. Revenues and costs measured in an inflationary local currency and converted into dollars at an exchange rate reflecting relative depreciation may produce dollar-equivalent amounts that don't represent the true situation. Furthermore, any foreign exchange losses that result from the inevitable depreciation of the currency should be considered an integral part of doing business in that country and should be realized as the currency depreciates rather than accumulated *ad infinitum.* After all, such foreign exchange losses are not at all likely to be reversed and therefore represent real costs to the firm that should be reflected in the parent's financial statements. For highly inflationary countries, defined by FASB-52 as countries in which 100 percent inflation is achieved in a 3-year period, the functional currency of foreign operations located in the country must be the U.S. dollar.

CHANGES IN TRANSLATION METHODOLOGY

For the cases in which the functional currency of a foreign operation is the U.S. dollar, FASB-52 provides for translation of the financial statements using the **temporal method,** in which all monetary assets and liabilities are translated at the current exchange rate and non-monetary assets and liabilities are translated at historical exchange rates. The term "temporal" refers to timing, or the distinction between items translated at current exchange rates versus items translated at historical rates. In the temporal method, inventory is considered a monetary asset if it is valued on the balance sheet at market value but is considered a non-monetary asset if it is valued at historical cost.

The logic behind using the monetary/non-monetary distinction for balance sheet items is that any translation gains and losses on monetary accounts are presumed to reflect meaningful components of expenses or revenue because the monetary accounts are denominated in nominal units of foreign currencies that closely approximate market values. On the other hand, translation gains and losses associated with non-monetary accounts are understood to be less meaningful because the accounts reflect historic book values rather than actual market values. As FASB-52 makes this distinction between monetary and non-monetary accounts, and translates monetary accounts at the current exchange rate, translation exposure is therefore quantified as the difference between monetary assets and monetary liabilities, where inventory may or may not be a monetary asset.

For the exceptional cases when the U.S. dollar is the functional currency, FASB-52 also stipulates that translation gains/losses be taken to the income statement rather than directly to the balance sheet. Such gains and losses are considered important components of doing business in a given time period, and are therefore to be realized as they occur. Because this income or expense affects the period's profits, it affects the amount posted to retained earnings, and the balance sheet will balance without the need for a cumulative translation adjustment.

TRANSLATION USING THE TEMPORAL METHOD

To illustrate translation requirements when the U.S. dollar is the functional currency, example 6.4 returns to the simple case in which the balance sheet does not change over the course of the year.

EXAMPLE 6.4

Suppose Continental Labs of France no longer produces industrial chemicals but is set up to import chemicals produced in the United States for sale to French companies. Because these operations are an integral part of the company's activities, the functional currency is the U.S. dollar and translation is undertaken using the temporal method. Table 6-7 presents the translation exposure report and Table 6-8 presents the balance sheet and translation. Inventory is shown on Continental's balance sheet at historic cost so it is considered a non-monetary asset. Translation exposure is measured as total monetary assets, FF 16,000, minus

TABLE 6-7   Translation Exposure Report for Continental Labs of France Based on the Temporal Method

Cash	FF	10000
Accounts Receivable		6000
TOTAL ASSETS EXPOSED	FF	16000
Accounts Payable	FF	16000
Current Debt		4000
Long-Term Debt		88000
TOTAL LIABILITIES EXPOSED	FF	108000
NET ASSETS EXPOSED	FF	−92000

the monetary liabilities, FF 108,000, or FF −92,000, as shown in Table 6-7. The negative sign here represents a net liability position, so exchange depreciation will make the firm better off because the liabilities are worth less in U.S. dollar terms. Note that there is no cumulative translation adjustment line in the equity section of the balance sheet in Table 6-8. Instead, foreign exchange gains and losses have been shown in the income statement and are reflected in the retained earnings amount. If the franc depreciates to FF 6 = $1, the foreign exchange gain or loss is:

$$(\$1/6 \text{ FF} - \$1/5 \text{ FF})(\text{FF} -92{,}000) = \$3067.$$

Adding the existing retained earnings translated at the historic rate brings the total retained earnings to $3467, which is shown in Column 3 of Table 6-8. If the franc appreciates to FF 4 = $1, the firm will be worse off because the liabilities have a higher value in U.S. dollar terms. The exchange gain or loss is:

$$(\$1/4 \text{ FF} - \$1/5 \text{ FF})(\text{FF} -92{,}000) = \$-4600$$

and adding the original retained earnings of $400 brings this to $−4200, which is shown in Column 4.

TABLE 6-8   Balance Sheet for Continental Labs of France Translated Using the Temporal Method

	1 *French Francs*	2 *5 FF = $1*	3 *6 FF = $1*	4 *4 FF = $1*
ASSETS				
Cash	10000	2000	1667	2500
Accounts Receivable	6000	1200	1000	1500
Inventory	14000	2800	2800	2800
Plant and Equipment (net)	90000	18000	18000	18000
TOTAL ASSETS	120000	24000	23467	24800
LIABILITIES AND EQUITY				
Accounts Payable	16000	3200	2667	4000
Current Debt	4000	800	667	100
Long-Term Debt	88000	17600	14667	22000
TOTAL LIABILITIES	108000	21600	18000	27000
Capital Stock	10000	2000	2000	2000
Retained Earnings	2000	400	3467	(4200)
TOTAL EQUITY	12000	2400	5467	(2200)
TOTAL LIAB. AND EQUITY	120000	24000	23467	24800

Example 6.4 demonstrates that subsidiaries which are simply not self-contained should include foreign exchange gains and losses in the income statement to accurately reflect the effect on the parent's operations. Similarly, operations of any kind that are conducted in highly inflationary currencies should include foreign exchange gains and losses in the income statement because they are not likely to be reversed in the future. Highly inflationary currencies do not go through an exchange rate cycle. In this scenario, classifying exchange losses (there are rarely any gains) as unrealized in the balance sheet would misrepresent the nature of the losses, so they are realized in the income statement as they are incurred.

OVERVIEW OF TRANSLATION EXPOSURE

Figure 6-2 summarizes the required methodology for translating financial reports of overseas subsidiaries. We begin with financial statements recorded in the host country currency. Step 1 is to determine the functional currency given the characteristics of the foreign operations. If the host country currency is used, step 2 involves the translation of the financial statements into the home country currency using the current rate method. The resulting foreign exchange gains or losses are accumulated in the balance sheet as unrealized translation adjustments. If, on the other hand, the home country currency is used as the functional currency, step 2 requires the translation to the functional currency using the temporal method. Furthermore, the foreign exchange gains or losses are realized on the income statement in the period in which they occur. The third and final step, regardless of the functional currency used, requires the consolidation of the overseas affiliate's financial statements into the parent company's financial statements.[1]

A foreign operation's functional currency can also change over time. For example, Brazil has traditionally been considered a highly inflationary country, requiring the U.S. dollar to be the functional currency of U.S. multinationals' operations there, but the 1994 Real Plan has successfully reduced inflation and most U.S. multinationals now use the Brazilian real as the functional currency of operations in that country. General

FIGURE 6-2 FINANCIAL REPORTING UNDER FASB-52

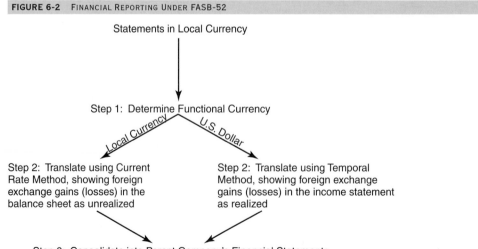

Statements in Local Currency

Step 1: Determine Functional Currency

Local Currency   U.S. Dollar

Step 2: Translate using Current Rate Method, showing foreign exchange gains (losses) in the balance sheet as unrealized

Step 2: Translate using Temporal Method, showing foreign exchange gains (losses) in the income statement as realized

Step 3: Consolidate into Parent Company's Financial Statements

Motors has a Brazilian subsidiary, GM do Brasil, and this is part of GM's consolidated financial statements. The GM 1997 Annual Report discloses the change in translation methodology:

> During the years ended December 31, 1997, 1996, and 1995, GM recorded the financial performance of operations in Brazil using the U.S. dollar as the functional currency due to GM's classification of the Brazilian economy as highly inflationary. Accordingly, translation gains and losses were recognized as incurred in the consolidated income statement. Statement of Financial Accounting Standards No. 52, Foreign Currency Translation, defines a highly inflationary economy as one that has cumulative inflation of approximately 100 percent or more over a three-year period. In mid-1997, the Brazilian three-year cumulative inflation rate fell below the 100 percent level. As a result, GM evaluated historical inflation rate trends and certain other factors and determined that it should no longer classify the Brazilian economy as highly inflationary. As a result, beginning January 1, 1998, GM will record the financial performance for operations in Brazil using the local currency as the functional currency with translation gains and losses recorded in the stockholders' equity section of the consolidated balance sheet.[2]

The concept of translation exposure is based on the necessary translation of financial statements into the parent company's currency. It is quite easy to measure, and that is its chief advantage. On a general level, however, it suffers from several major deficiencies. In one sense, it is too narrow because it concentrates on the balance sheet to the exclusion of the income statement and the firm's ongoing operations. Even known future transactions are not included unless they are already posted to the balance sheet. It is also based on book values of assets acquired and liabilities incurred in the past, rather than market values of assets and liabilities. In addition, it measures gains and losses using nominal exchange rate changes and does not adjust changes in values for inflation.

6.4 TRANSACTION EXPOSURE

One improvement over measuring translation exposure is to examine **transaction exposure,** or **contractual exposure,** which is the degree to which cash and known transactions denominated in a foreign currency and already entered into for settlement at a future date are affected by exchange rate changes. The reason for this improvement is twofold. First, translation exposure not associated with actual cash flows is excluded, so fixed assets such as land, plant and equipment, and physical inventory are thrown out of the exposure measurement. This approach is similar to the monetary/nonmonetary distinction of translation exposure in the temporal method. Second, all contractual commitments that do not show up on the balance sheet (called **off-balance-sheet items**) are included in the measurement, such as signed contracts for future sales. Corporate treasurers often prefer a transactions approach to exposure because it gives an indication of how exchange rate changes will affect cash flows; gains and losses associated with known transactions are likely to be realized relatively soon.

EXAMPLE 6.5

Table 6-9 presents a transaction exposure report for Continental Labs of France, which is the hypothetical firm examined in Tables 6-1, 6-2, 6-7 and 6-8. The transaction exposure of cash and accounts receivable is the same as the translation exposure, because any exchange rate changes directly affect their home currency value. Note, however, that the inventory and net plant and equipment are not considered exposed under definitions of transaction exposure because there is no known cash flow associated with inventory or plant and equipment. Continental Labs of France has off-balance-sheet items in signed sales contracts, however, that represent known cash inflows of FF 25,000. The exposure of accounts payable, current debt, and long-term debt is the same for transaction exposure as it is for translation exposure. Off-balance-sheet liabilities include a foreign exchange contract to sell FF 7000 for U.S. dollars and purchase commitments for raw materials in the amount of FF 4000. The transaction exposure is therefore FF −78,000, a liability or net cash outflow position. This means that the firm will be better off with a depreciation of the French franc because the U.S. dollar equivalent of the cash outflows will be smaller.

The transaction exposure report is a managerial report, typically prepared for the corporate treasury office, and is not for public release. Treasurers use the report to get an indication of what elements of exposure will lead to realized foreign exchange gains and losses in the near future. As such, it is often more useful to organize the transactions data by the month, quarter, or year in which the cash flow will occur. The report would thus contain a column for each month, quarter, or year into the future, as far out as is relevant. The example in Table 6-9 is basically the total of the monthly or quarterly columns. In essence, the transaction exposure report becomes more of a foreign currency cash flow budget, and the activity is occasionally referred to as "funds flow mapping." The gains and losses associated with the transactions are not posted to the firm's financial reports, as they are subsequently handled in the consolidation and translation process. The transactions exposure report thus provides managers with information on the exposure which will affect the value of the firm, but the accounting issues are separate.

There are also transaction exposure reports for domestic firms which engage in foreign-currency-denominated transactions but do not maintain financial records in foreign currencies. In this case, the gains and losses are posted to the firm's financial statements as they occur, although firms have some discretion about exactly how and when the accounting is done, often depending on the type of transaction.[3] The most common approach to recording these transactions is to record the complete transaction at the spot exchange rate prevailing on the date the transaction occurs. At subsequent balance sheet dates, nonmonetary accounts remain at historical cost, while monetary ac-

TABLE 6-9 Transaction Exposure Report for Continental Labs of France		
Cash	FF	10000
Accounts Receivable		6000
Signed Sales Contracts		25000
TOTAL EXPOSED ASSETS AND CASH INFLOWS	FF	41000
Accounts Payable	FF	16000
Current Debt		4000
Long-Term Debt		88000
Foreign Exchange Sales Contract		7000
Purchase Commitments		4000
TOTAL EXPOSED LIABILITIES AND CASH OUTFLOWS	FF	119000
NET TRANSACTION EXPOSURE	FF	−78000

counts are adjusted to reflect exchange rate changes. Hence, the transaction exposure report provides direct information on the gains and losses which must be realized.

The transaction exposure report is an improvement over the translation exposure report because it considers the elements of exposure that most directly affect the firm's value. By focusing on cash and known transactions, transaction exposure is also very easy to measure. However, it also suffers from several deficiencies. First, it ignores all of the firm's ongoing operations, implicitly assuming that noncontractual cash flows are not exposed. There is no explicit consideration of the revenues and costs that are denominated in the foreign currency on a regular basis and how these revenues and costs may change as exchange rates change. Second, transaction exposure ignores the economic valuation of fixed assets and inventory in its focus on known cash flows. This may be myopic if market values of assets and liabilities change as exchange rates change. Third, like translation exposure, transaction exposure concentrates on nominal exchange rate changes without any analysis of inflation. Hence, an appreciation of the local currency in the nominal exchange rate would result in a foreign exchange gain even if the exchange rate change were simply the result of higher inflation in the home country. As we will see in Chapter 7, economic exposure effectively solves these three problems.

APPLICATION 6-2

TRANSACTION EXPOSURE AT BOSTON BEER COMPANY[4]

The Boston Beer Company, the maker of Samuel Adams beers, brews and sells beer, ale, and cider products in the United States. Although the company does market its products in selected foreign countries, substantially all of its $200 million in sales and $100 million in assets are in America. However, the company faces transaction exposure because it has entered into foreign-currency-denominated contracts for the supply of a portion of its hops requirements. As disclosed in their annual report for 1998, "these contracts, which extend through crop 2004, specify both the quantities and prices to which the company is committed. The prices are denominated in German marks and English pound sterling. Hop purchase commitments outstanding at December 26, 1998 totaled $34.9 million." (p. 38).

Boston Beer does recognize that the dollar price of the hops therefore changes as exchange rates fluctuate. During 1997 and 1998, the company used forward contracts to hedge against the impact of exchange rate fluctuations, but as of December 26, 1998, the company had no forward contracts outstanding. Hence, the total transaction exposure was the $34.9 million off-balance-sheet cash outflow associated with the hops purchase commitments.

In its quantitative and qualitative disclosures about market risk, the company applied a sensitivity analysis to reflect the impact of a hypothetical 10 percent depreciation of the dollar. The estimated potential loss in pretax earnings from such an exchange rate change is reported as $3.5 million, simply 10 percent of the transaction exposure. With pretax earnings of approximately $14 million, a $3.5 million foreign exchange loss would wipe out 25 percent of the earnings. However, the company adds, "It should be noted that the potential earnings impact from fluctuations in foreign currency exchange rates relates to contracts that extend six years (p. 26)," so $3.5 million represents the maximum potential impact over a six year period.

❖ **SUMMARY OF CHAPTER OBJECTIVES**

1. Define the concepts of foreign exchange exposure, translation exposure, and transaction exposure.

Foreign exchange exposure is the degree to which a company is affected by exchange rate changes. Translation exposure, or accounting exposure, is the degree to which the value of a firm's foreign-currency-denominated accounts on the balance sheet are affected by exchange rate changes. Transaction exposure, or contractual exposure, is the degree to which cash and known transactions denominated in a foreign currency and already entered into for settlement at a future date are affected by exchange rate changes.

2. Calculate the accounting measures of exposure.

Translation exposure of a foreign subsidiary is normally measured as the difference between total assets and total liabilities on the balance sheet, although some adjustment for the current period's income is also possible. When the foreign subsidiary is an integral part of the parent's operations or operates in a highly inflationary country, translation exposure is measured as the difference between monetary assets and monetary liabilities, and adjustment for current income becomes quite difficult.

3. Calculate exposure based on upcoming, known cash flows which a corporate treasurer might prefer over the traditional accounting measurement.

Transaction exposure measures the net cash and known cash inflows against known cash outflows.

❖ **QUESTIONS FOR REVIEW**

1. The balance sheet below pertains to a U.S. multinational corporation's subsidiary in Erehwon. The subsidiary was formed on December 31, 1994, to operate only in the Erehwon market.

AMALGAMATED INDUSTRIES: EREHWON SUBSIDIARY
December 31, 1994
thousands of Erehwon peronis

Assets		*Liabilities*	
Cash and Receivables	3000	Current Liabilities	4000
Inventory	4500	Long-Term Debt	5000
Fixed Assets (net)	7000	*Capital*	
		Capital Stock	5500
TOTAL ASSETS	14500	TOTAL LIAB + CAP	14500

a. If the Erehwon peroni is the functional currency, what is the amount of foreign exchange exposure the company faced on December 31, 1994?

b. On December 31, 1994, the exchange rate was $0.40/peroni. On December 31, 1995, the exchange rate was $0.50/peroni. There was no income for 1995 and none of the balance sheet accounts changed during 1995. What foreign exchange gain or loss did the parent company show, and where did the firm show it?

c. Suppose that during 1995 the subsidiary had net income of 1,500 thousand peronis, and all income was retained as cash. On December 31, 1995, all other asset and liability accounts were unchanged from their December 31, 1994, amounts. The exchange rates were as specified in (b), and the average exchange rate for 1995 was $0.46/peroni. What foreign exchange gain or loss would the parent company have shown, and where would the firm have shown it?

d. If the U.S. dollar was the functional currency, rather than the Erehwon peroni as stated in (a), what was the amount of foreign exchange exposure the company faced on December 31, 1994? If there was no income during 1995 and all balance sheet accounts were unchanged, as in (b), what foreign exchange gain or loss would the parent company have shown, and where would the firm have shown it?

2. If a U.S. company starts a new subsidiary in Papua New Guinea on January 1 with an equity stake of 700 million kina (the currency of Papua New Guinea), and earns 300 million kina of income during the year which is posted to the retained earnings account, what will the equity section of the December 31 balance sheet converted into U.S. dollars look like? The exchange rate on January 1 was $1.25/kina, the exchange rate on December 31 was $1.05/kina, and the company uses the average of the beginning and ending exchange rates as the period average exchange rate. (You may assume that the translation follows FASB-52's current rate method.)

3. The balance sheet below represents the end-of-year balance sheet for a new wholly-owned subsidiary of a U.S. multinational corporation operating in Poland. All amounts are shown in millions of zloty, the local currency. The subsidiary was incorporated on January 1, 1994, when the exchange rate was $0.50/zloty. Since the subsidiary has been in operation for only one year, the Retained Earnings represent only the current year's profits.

CLICK ENTERPRISES OF POLAND
Balance Sheet
December 31, 1994
millions of zloty

Assets		Liabilities	
Cash	100	Accounts Payable	100
Accounts Receivable	100	Long-Term Debt	600
Inventory	100	Common Stock	300
Plant & Equip. (net)	800	Retained Earnings	100
TOTAL	1100	TOTAL	1100

You are faced with the task of converting this balance sheet into U.S. dollars for consolidation into the parent company's balance sheet. The exchange rate on December 31, 1994, is $0.45/zloty. Inventory is carried at historical cost, and the associated historical exchange rate is $0.50/zloty. The historical rate for plant and equipment and for the initial equity (common stock) in the subsidiary is also $0.50/zloty. The average exchange rate for 1994 was $0.48/zloty.

a. Assuming that the subsidiary in Poland is self-contained and that Poland is not a highly inflationary country, show the conversion to U.S. dollars.

b. Over the past decade, Poland has occasionally experienced high inflation, and there is some concern that inflation will again be a big problem in the near future. If, on December 31, 1994, Poland had experienced more than 100 percent inflation over the previous three years, translation of the balance sheet would have to follow slightly different rules. Show the conversion to U.S. dollars if Poland must be considered a highly inflationary country.

4. If a U.S. company starts a new subsidiary in Poland on January 1 with an equity stake of 400 million zlotys, and earns 200 million zlotys of income during the year which is posted to the retained earnings account, what will the equity section of the December 31 balance sheet converted into U.S. dollars look like? The exchange rate on January 1 was $0.45/zloty, the exchange rate on December 31 was $0.55/zloty, and the company uses the average of the beginning and ending exchange rates as the period average exchange rate. (You may assume that the translation follows FASB-52's current rate method.)

5. [Class discussion] Consider the balance sheet below.

CONRAD INDUSTRIES CONSOLIDATED
December 31, 1992
thousands of dollars

Assets		*Liabilities and Capital*	
Cash	6000	Debt	100000
Inventory	1850		
Plant and Equipment	95000	Common Stock	2000
		Retained Earnings	500
		Translation Adjustments	350
TOTAL ASSETS	102850	TOTAL LIAB. AND CAPITAL	102850

This is the December 31, 1992, consolidated balance sheet for Conrad Industries, a holding company with three subsidiaries. The subsidiary in the United States, more than 25 years old, was formed with $100,000 in equity. It showed retained earnings of $350,000 on December 31, 1991. Conveniently, no profit or loss was shown for 1992.

A subsidiary in Alpha was created on January 1, 1992. This subsidiary is self-contained, so uses the current rate method of translating its financial statements from Alphan pounds into U.S. dollars. On January 1, 1992, the exchange rate was $4/Alphan pound. On December 31, 1992, the exchange rate was $6/Alphan pound. The average exchange rate for 1992 was $5/Alphan pound. Profits of 50 thousand Alphan pounds for 1992 were retained as cash.

A subsidiary in Beta was also created on January 1, 1992. This subsidiary is a sales unit for the parent, so it does not have any nonmonetary assets or inventory. As it is not self-contained, it uses the temporal method of translating its financial statements from Betan pesos to U.S. dollars. On January 1, 1992, the exchange rate was $0.20/Betan peso. On December 31, 1992, the exchange rate was $0.15/Betan peso. The average exchange rate for 1992 was $0.17/Betan peso. There were no profits or losses from this subsidiary in 1992 when expressed in Betan pesos.

Conveniently, none of the assets or liabilities on the balance sheets of the three subsidiaries changed over the year, except for the profits retained as cash in the Alpha subsidiary.

a. How much equity did Conrad Industries put into its subsidiary in Alpha on January 1, 1992? (Give the answer denominated in Alphan pounds.)

b. What was the foreign exchange exposure of the subsidiary in Alpha on December 31, 1992? (Again, give the answer denominated in Alphan pounds.)

c. How much equity did Conrad Industries put into its subsidiary in Beta on January 1, 1992? (Give the answer denominated in Betan pesos.)

d. What was the foreign exchange exposure of the subsidiary in Beta on December 31, 1992? (Again, give the answer denominated in Betan pesos.)

6. Consider the balance sheet below.

ATLAS INDUSTRIES: ASMARA SUBSIDIARY
December 31, 1988
thousands of Asmaran aegeans

Assets		Liabilities	
Cash and Receivables	4500	Current Liabilities	4000
Inventory	4500	Long-Term Debt	6000
Fixed Assets (net)	7000	*Capital*	
		Capital Stock	6000
TOTAL ASSETS	16000	TOTAL LIAB. + CAPITAL	16000

This balance sheet is for a multinational corporation's subsidiary in the Republic of Asmara. The subsidiary was formed on December 31, 1988, to operate only in the Asmaran market. Inventory is carried on the balance sheet at historic cost, rather than at market value. On December 31, 1988, the exchange rate was $1.25/aegean.

a. What was Atlas Industries of Asmara's translation or accounting exposure on December 31, 1988, as measured by FASB-52, assuming that the Asmaran aegean is the functional currency?

b. At the end of 1989, the subsidiary's balance sheet had to be translated into U.S. dollars in preparation for consolidation into the parent company's balance sheet. If the exchange rate was $1.00/aegean on December 31, 1989, what was the translation gain or loss? Assume that the balance sheet did not change over the course of the year and that there was no profit or loss from operations during 1989.

c. The only off-balance-sheet transaction known on December 31, 1988, was a forward contract to purchase 1000 thousand aegeans with U.S. dollars. What was Atlas Industries of Asmara's transaction exposure on December 31, 1988?

d. What would Atlas Industries of Asmara's translation exposure have been on December 31, 1988, if Asmara had been generally experiencing inflation of 100 percent per year?

e. If the exchange rate was $0.75/aegean on December 31, 1989, what would the translation gain or loss have been if Asmara had been experiencing inflation of 100 percent per year? Assume that the balance sheet did not change over the course of the year and that there was no profit or loss from operations during 1989.

7. Shown below is the balance sheet for Proctor & Gamble's subsidiary in Papua New Guinea (P&G in PNG) on December 31, 1996, denominated in thousands of Papua New Guinea kina.

P&G in PNG
December 31, 1996
thousands of PNG kina

Assets		Liabilities	
Cash	300	Accounts Payable	300
Accounts Receivable	300	Short-Term Debt	300
Inventory	300	Long-Term Debt	800
Plant & Equipment (net)	900	*Equity*	
		Common Stock	300
		Retained Earnings (1996)	100
TOTAL	1800	TOTAL	1800

This subsidiary was created on January 1, 1996, so it has been in operation for only the 1996 year. The exchange rate on January 1, 1996, was $1.25/kina. The exchange rate on December 31, 1996, was $1.35/kina. The average exchange rate for the period was $1.30/kina. All earnings for 1996 have been retained as cash. The inventory is shown at its historical cost (on January 1, 1996). The firm has determined that the functional currency is the PNG kina.

a. Show the translation of the P&G in PNG balance sheet for December 31, 1996.

b. Show the calculation of the translation gain or loss.

8. Shown below is the balance sheet of MMM Corporation's subsidiary in Poznan, Poland, on December 31, 1996, denominated in thousands of Polish zloty.

MMM Corporation of Poznan, Poland
December 31, 1996
thousands of Polish zloty

Assets		*Liabilities*	
Cash	250	Accounts Payable	250
Accounts Receivable	100	Short-Term Debt	350
Inventory	300	Long-Term Debt	550
Real Estate	450	Prepaid Deliverables	150
Plant	400	*Equity*	
Equipment	400	Common Stock	500
		Retained Earnings	100
TOTAL	1900	TOTAL	1900

The subsidiary was created on January 1, 1996, so it had been in operation for only one year, and all earnings from 1996 were retained as cash. The exchange rate on January 1, 1996, was $0.35/zloty. The exchange rate on December 31, 1996, was $0.40/zloty. The average exchange rate for the period was $0.36/zloty. The inventory is shown at historical cost. The firm also had one unusual nonmonetary liability: MMM had already collected 150 thousand zloty from a Polish firm that ordered a large amount of supplies, and MMM promised to deliver the supplies within the next year.

a. What was the translation exposure of MMM Corporation of Poznan, Poland, on December 31, 1996, if the zloty was the functional currency? If there were no changes in the balance sheet over 1997, what was the translation gain (loss) if the exchange rate was $0.35/zloty on December 31, 1997, based on this exposure? Where does this gain (loss) appear on the financial statements?

b. What was the translation exposure of MMM Corporation of Poznan, Poland, on December 31, 1996, if the dollar was the functional currency? If there were no changes in the balance sheet over 1997, what was the translation gain (loss) if the exchange rate was $0.35/zloty on December 31, 1997, based on this exposure? Where does this gain (loss) appear on the financial statements?

9. Shown below is the balance sheet for Black Bear Enterprises's subsidiary in Mexico on December 31, 1996, denominated in millions of Mexican pesos.

Black Bear Enterprises
December 31, 1996
millions of Mexican pesos

Assets		Liabilities	
Cash	400	Accounts Payable	400
Accounts Receivable	400	Short-Term Debt	400
Inventory	400	Long-Term Debt	800
Plant & Equipment (net)	800	*Equity*	
		Common Stock	200
		Retained Earnings (1996)	200
TOTAL	2000	TOTAL	2000

The subsidiary was created on January 1, 1996, so it had been in operation for only the 1996 year. The exchange rate on January 1, 1996, was $0.13/peso. The exchange rate on December 31, 1996 was $0.15/peso. The average exchange rate for the period was $0.14/peso. All earnings for 1996 have been retained as cash, but there are no other changes in the balance sheet. The inventory is shown at its historical cost (on January 1, 1996).

a. Suppose that the firm has determined that the functional currency is the Mexican peso. What was the accounting exposure on January 1, 1996? Given the exchange rate change (from $0.13/peso to $0.15/peso), what are the foreign exchange gains or losses associated with this exposure? Given that the 1996 earnings are retained as cash, and are therefore exposed, what are the foreign exchange gains or losses associated with this exposure? Where are these gains or losses reported in the U.S. parent's financial statements?

b. Now suppose that the firm has determined that the functional currency is the U.S. dollar. What was the accounting exposure on January 1, 1996? Given the exchange rate change (from $0.13/peso to $0.15/peso), what are the foreign exchange gains or losses associated with this exposure? Where are these gains or losses reported in the U.S. parent's financial statements? (Given that the 1996 earnings are retained as cash, they are also exposed, but you do not need to worry about them.)

c. Compared to transaction exposure and economic exposure, what are the advantages and limitations of translation (accounting) exposure?

10. [Group project] Extended exercise: Polydemic-Greece's translation and transaction exposure

   You are the head accountant of Polydemic Enterprises, a U.S. multinational corporation with operations spread throughout the world. In evaluating Polydemic's new Greek subsidiary a few weeks ago, the chief executive officer became nervous about the volatility of the Greek drachma/U.S. dollar exchange rate and the effect a drachma depreciation would have on the subsidiary. He has asked you to look into the consequences.

   Polydemic-Greece is a self-contained subsidiary that produces textile manufacturing equipment and markets to manufacturers in Greece. The beginning-of-quarter exchange rate was 135 drachmas per dollar. You think the drachma may depreciate about 11 percent by the end of the quarter, to 150 per dollar.

The current balance sheet for Polydemic-Greece is given below.

Polydemic-Greece
Balance Sheet
Beginning of Quarter
millions of drachmas

Assets		*Liabilities and Capital*	
Cash	90.0	Current Debt	140.0
Receivables	112.5	Long-Term Debt	400.0
Inventory (historical cost)	67.5	Common Stock	135.0
Plant and Equipment (net)	405.0		
TOTAL	675.0	TOTAL	675.0

Additional off-balance-sheet information is provided below.

1. Signed sales agreements total 372.5 million drachmas.
2. Purchase commitments total 25 million drachmas.
3. An interest payment on long-term debt of 10 million drachmas is due at the end of the quarter.
4. Outstanding sales bids total 200 million drachmas.

a. Prepare a report for the CEO concerning Polydemic-Greece's translation and transaction exposure. After you present the exposure report, answer the following specific questions.

1. What will happen if the drachma depreciates to 150 drachmas per dollar?
2. Where would any exchange losses or gains be reported in the financial statements?
3. If Polydemic-Greece were not engaged in manufacturing the textile equipment but were only a sales office for U.S.-manufactured equipment, what analyses would have to be revised? (This means you should work through the analysis again.)
4. Do you think the exposure reports you have prepared accurately measure Polydemic-Greece's exposure to exchange rate changes?
5. What are your attitudes toward hedging translation and transaction exposure?

b. By the end of the quarter, the exchange rate actually appreciated to 100 drachmas per dollar, after having been 135 drachmas per dollar since the subsidiary was created. The average exchange rate for the quarter was 120 drachmas per dollar. The subsidiary had net income of 240 million drachmas for the quarter, and all income has been retained as cash. Coincidentally, all other asset and liability accounts remain unchanged. Construct Polydemic-Greece's balance sheet in U.S. dollars in preparation for consolidation into the parent's financial statements.

❖ **ENDNOTES**

1. The material in this chapter is principally an overview of translation; for greater detail see, for example, "Translation of Foreign Currency Financial Statements," Chapter 13 of Radebaugh and Gray (1993), pp. 338–374, or "Foreign Currency Translation," Chapter 4 of Choi and Mueller (1992), pp. 137–205.

2. Based on General Motors 1997 Annual Report, p. 52.

3. For more details, see, for example, "Accounting for Foreign Currency Transactions and Foreign Currency Derivatives," Chapter 12 of Radebaugh and Gray (1993), pp. 310–337,

or the section on Foreign Currency Transactions in "Foreign Currency Translation," Chapter 4 of Choi and Mueller (1992), pp. 175–185.

4. Based on the Boston Beer Company 1998 Annual Report.

❖ REFERENCES

AlHashim, Dhia D., and Jeffrey S. Arpan. *International Dimensions of Accounting,* PWS-Kent Publishing Co., 1988.

Choi, Frederick D.S., and Gerhard G. Mueller. *International Accounting,* second edition, Prentice-Hall, 1992.

Mueller, Gerhard G., Helen Gernon, and Gary Meek. *Accounting: An International Perspective,* Irwin, 1987.

Radebaugh, Lee H., and Sidney J. Gray. *International Accounting and Multinational Enterprises,* third edition, John Wiley and Sons, 1993.

Schweikart, James A., Sidney J. Gray, and Clare B. Roberts. *International Accounting: A Case Approach,* McGraw-Hill, 1994.

Stickney, Clyde P. "Accounting Considerations in International Finance," Chapter 11 of *The Handbook of International Financial Management,* edited by Robert Z. Aliber, Dow Jones-Irwin, 1989.

CHAPTER 7

ECONOMIC EXPOSURE

CHAPTER OBJECTIVES

AFTER READING THIS CHAPTER, YOU SHOULD BE ABLE TO:

❖ Explain the concept of economic exposure.

❖ Analyze a firm's cash flow exposure.

❖ Evaluate a firm's net worth exposure.

❖ Interpret a quantitative measurement of economic exposure from a coefficient in a simple regression.

In this chapter, we examine the economic exposure of a firm. We look at cash flow exposure in the first section, and net worth exposure in the second section. In the final section of this chapter, however, we present the quantitative measurement of economic exposure as a coefficient in a simple regression.

7.1   INTRODUCTION

The concepts of translation and transaction exposure, which we covered in the previous chapter, are useful for accountants faced with consolidating financial statements or treasurers who must make short-term decisions about how to deal with known contractual obligations denominated in foreign currencies. They each have deficiencies, however, when a longer-run analysis is required. Translation exposure, for example, ignores all off-balance-sheet commitments and includes exposure for fixed assets that are not associated with cash flows. Transaction exposure ignores the ongoing operations of the firm and changes in the value of assets and inventory. Furthermore, both methods concentrate on nominal exchange rate changes without any analysis of inflation. In this chapter, therefore, we develop a more comprehensive evaluation of exposure.

Figure 7-1 reproduces the diagram of different types of exposure introduced in Figure 6-1. The final concept to be covered here is **economic exposure,** which is the extent to which the market value of a firm or subsidiary changes when exchange rates change. This concept has two components: cash flow exposure and net worth exposure. Exposure is an improvement over the other concepts not only because it integrates the firm's ongoing operations and the valuation of fixed assets and inventory, but also because it accounts for exchange rate changes that result from differences in national inflation rates. This last point highlights the fact that the foundations of economic exposure rest in the proportionality propositions of international finance. We presented the key proposition of importance, purchasing power parity (PPP), which directly relates an exchange rate to the behavior of prices in two countries, in Chapter 2. We now consider how real exchange rate changes affect the firm, rather than the purely nominal exchange rate changes that we examined in Chapter 6. The primary focus of this chapter will be on developing a framework for thinking about the economic risks a firm operating internationally faces. Most of the analysis in this chapter is conceptual, relying on economic intuition to explain the issues, although in the final section we present the quantitative measurement of economic exposure as a coefficient in a simple regression.

The concepts of translation and transaction exposure examined in Chapter 6 are not obsolete, but are applicable only to specific functions in statement consolidation or to short-term gains and losses associated with known contractual cash flows. For longer-term competitive strategy, managers must have a thorough understanding of economic exposure, which incorporates cash flow or income statement exposure, as well as net worth exposure or an economic interpretation of the balance sheet. The three upcoming chapters discuss methods of assessing the risk of foreign exchange exposure and managing foreign exchange exposure.

FIGURE 7-1 CONCEPTS OF FOREIGN EXCHANGE EXPOSURE

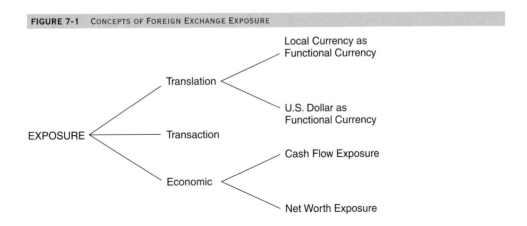

7.2   ANALYZING CASH FLOW EXPOSURE

The most important part of economic exposure evaluates the firm's ongoing cash flows or its income statement. Economic exposure is meaningful only from a real standpoint, or abstracting from inflation. **Cash flow exposure,** or **income statement exposure,** sometimes also referred to as **real operating exposure,** is the extent to which a company's real revenues and expenses are affected by exchange rate changes. The expenses we analyze, however, do not include depreciation of real assets, debt repayment, or interest payments. We deal with these issues later in the section on net worth exposure. It should be clear that depreciation should be excluded because it does not represent a cash flow. Debt repayment should be excluded because it does not constitute an expense even though it is a cash flow. Interest expense could be included, but because it is directly related to debt, we do not analyze it as cash flows. We examined the topics of debt and interest in detail in Chapter 4, so we do not consider them further here.

To examine the role of cash flow exposure, we take as an example a U.S. corporation's British subsidiary. We will analyze the effects of a British pound devaluation on the subsidiary's revenues, costs, profits, and production volume. There are five basic cases, which are discussed in turn. We develop mathematical specifications of these cases in the "Tools for Analysis" at the end of this chapter, so the development here is strictly conceptual.

CASE 1: NO DEVIATIONS FROM PPP

As the first scenario, we look at the subsidiary in the situation where purchasing power parity holds. When PPP holds, nominal exchange rate changes correspond to differences in national inflation rates and there are no real exchange rate changes. Hence, a depreciation of the British pound is the result of higher inflation in the United Kingdom than in the United States. Here, the pound price of the product will rise in accordance with British inflation. Obviously, nominal depreciation of the pound means that the price will not rise as much when converted into U.S. dollars. Because PPP holds, the rise in the U.S. dollar equivalent of the pound price will correspond to U.S. inflation. This means that the real U.S. dollar price will remain unchanged.

If PPP holds, then, there is no real effect on the subsidiary's revenues. The same analysis will hold for production costs. The nominal rise in costs due to British inflation will be partially offset by the depreciation of the pound. This depreciation yields cost rises that correspond only to U.S. inflation, thereby leaving real production costs unchanged in constant U.S. dollars. As real revenues and real costs are not affected, the real profit margin does not change. Furthermore, nominal changes do not have any effect on the physical volume of production, so real profits clearly remain unchanged too.

CASE 2: REAL EXCHANGE RATE CHANGES AND THE SELF-CONTAINED SUBSIDIARY

The second scenario examines the effect of real exchange rate depreciation on an entirely self-contained subsidiary. In this case, the British operation services a local market and undertakes all production in that market. Figure 7-2 illustrates the usual case of

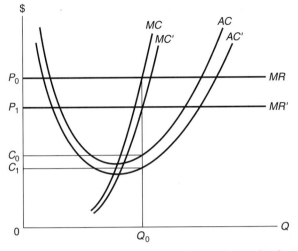

A price-taking subsidiary is able to sell at a constant foreign currency price which is converted into dollars at the prevailing exchange rate, shown as the MR curve at P_0. The cost structure is denominated in the foreign currency and also converted into dollars, shown as AC and MC. The optimum quantity of output is at Q_0, at which C_0 is the average cost per unit and the margin is $(P_0 - C_0)$. A depreciation of the foreign currency reduces the dollar-equivalent MR proportionately, shifting the MR curve downward to MR' at P_1. In addition, the depreciation reduces the cost structure, shifting the AC and MC curves downward to AC' and MC' in the same proportions as the shift in the MR curve. The optimum quantity of output remains at Q_0, although the margin declines in proportion to the exchange rate change to $(P_1 - C_1)$.

FIGURE 7-2   REAL EXCHANGE RATE CHANGES AND A SELF-CONTAINED PRICE-TAKING SUBSIDIARY

a firm functioning as a price taker in a perfectly competitive local environment. The marginal revenue curve is horizontal at the market-determined price of the output. The company's marginal cost curve is upward-sloping. The intersection of these two schedules determines the firm's output. The distance between marginal revenue and average cost at the quantity of output produced represents the profit margin—or profit per unit sold—to the firm. Note, however, that the vertical axis is denominated in U.S. dollars because that is what the parent company is concerned with.

If the British pound depreciates in real terms, the pound price of the output does not change—because the firm is a price taker in the British market—so the U.S. dollar value of the price must change. Hence, the marginal revenue curve in U.S. dollars shifts downward with the depreciation by the proportionate amount of the depreciation. As all costs are incurred in pounds, the cost structure shifts down as well—and by the same proportion. The end result is that the volume of output is unchanged. The U.S. dollar value of the revenue has decreased, however, because each unit is sold at the same pound price, but the pound is worth less. Similarly, the U.S. dollar costs have decreased, and in the same proportion. However, this means that the firm's profit margin is lower in U.S. dollar terms as long as revenues are greater than costs. The firm's profits are therefore lower.

A real appreciation of the local currency would similarly make the multinational corporation's subsidiaries more profitable. Again, the local currency price and cost structures do not change, so output remains the same. The profit margin and total profits

of the subsidiary therefore remain unchanged in local currency units, but an appreciation of the currency makes them worth more in home currency units. Gillette Co., a U.S.
multinational in the health and beauty products industry, benefited from the appreciation of European currencies between 1986 and 1990. In fact, over 60 percent of Gillette's
earnings come from outside the United States, primarily from Europe. According to the
assistant treasurer of Gillette, Gian Camuzzi, "We basically manufacture everything we
need for European markets in Europe," so the benefit of local currency appreciation
"comes in the profit exchange."[1]

The reason for the result above appears to be the fact that the firm is a price taker
in the local market. Indeed, the company cannot raise the price of its product because
it is in a perfectly competitive industry and there is no pricing flexibility. However, the
result is the same when the firm is a price-making monopolist, because, after a devaluation of the pound, the firm will still not find changing the pound price optimal. The key
is that the demand curve facing the firm is denominated in pounds. The situation is depicted in Figure 7-3. The downward-sloping demand curve is the dollar equivalent of
the downward-sloping pound-denominated demand curve. When a depreciation of the
pound occurs, the pound-denominated demand curve does not change, so the dollar-
equivalent demand curve shifts down in proportion to the depreciation. As with the case
of a price taker, the cost curves shift down in proportion to the depreciation. Hence, the
marginal revenue and marginal cost curves intersect at the same volume regardless of
the level of the real exchange rate. The depreciation makes the U.S. dollar equivalent
profits worth less, but does not change the pricing policy or production volume.[2]

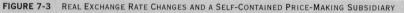

FIGURE 7-3   Real Exchange Rate Changes and a Self-Contained Price-Making Subsidiary

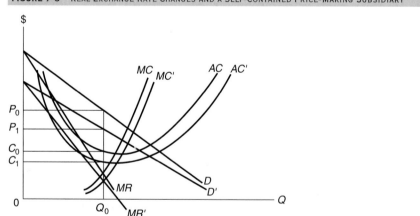

A price-making subsidiary faces a downward-sloping demand curve in the foreign country, which is
converted from foreign currency into dollars at the prevailing exchange rate and shown as D. The
marginal revenue curve derived from the demand curve is MR. The cost structure is also denominated in the foreign currency and converted into dollars, shown as AC and MC. The optimum quantity of output is at Q_0, at which the margin is $(P_0 - C_0)$. A depreciation of the foreign currency
reduces the dollar-equivalent demand curve proportionately, shifting D downward to D'. In addition,
the MR curve shifts downward to MR'. Depreciation also reduces the cost structure, shifting the AC
and MC curves downward to AC' and MC' in the same proportions as the shifts in D and MR. The
optimum quantity of output remains at Q_0, although the margin declines in proportion to the exchange rate change to $(P_1 - C_1)$.

The scenario outlined here, in which the corporation is in worse condition after depreciation and better condition after appreciation, is generally the most common outcome for multinational firms operating abroad. The next two scenarios examine divergences from the assumption that the subsidiary is self-contained.

CASE 3: REAL EXCHANGE RATE CHANGES AND A WORLD OUTPUT MARKET

Now, let us examine a subsidiary operating in Britain but functioning in a world market for output. This would be true of any product facing competition from imports or being priced according to world supply and demand. For simplicity, we assume here that the world price is determined in U.S. dollars and is invariant to changes in the value of the U.S. dollar. Clearly, this is not a perfect description of reality, but the basic principles do not change with small changes in world market prices. We will return to the issue of determining the world market price later in this section. In terms of Figure 7-4, our assumption means that the marginal revenue schedule is fixed in terms of the U.S. dollar price. Depreciations of the pound therefore do not affect this marginal revenue schedule. The depreciations, however, affect the cost schedules because all inputs are from the British factor markets. In particular, depreciation shifts the marginal cost schedule downward, just as before. In this case, however, the firm will increase production because Britain has become a low-cost producer of the product. Any output not consumed in the United Kingdom is simply sold to the world market, so the subsidiary is used as an export platform. The profit margin for the firm also increases as the average cost

FIGURE 7-4   REAL EXCHANGE RATE CHANGES AND A PRICE TAKER IN A WORLD OUTPUT MARKET

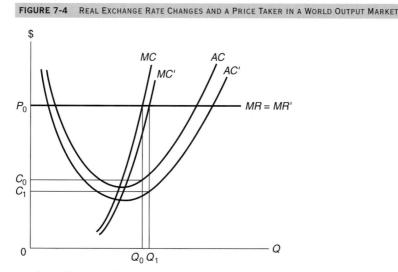

A price-taking subsidiary competing in a world output market is able to sell at a constant dollar price, shown as the MR curve at P_0. The cost structure is denominated in the foreign currency and converted into dollars, shown as AC and MC. The optimum quantity of output is at Q_0, at which the margin is $(P_0 - C_0)$. A depreciation of the foreign currency has no effect on the world market price in dollars. However, depreciation reduces the cost structure, shifting the AC and MC curves downward to AC' and MC' in the same proportions as the change in the exchange rate. The optimum quantity of output increases to Q_1, and the margin increases to $(P_0 - C_1)$.

curve shifts down. Hence, the firm's total profits increase because of both the increase in the profit margin and the increase in the volume of output. In this scenario, the firm is unambiguously better off because of the depreciation.

The result that a firm competing in a world output market is better off after a local currency depreciation holds for a price-making monopolist, as long as the relevant demand curve is denominated in U.S. dollars. Figure 7-5 illustrates the situation. In a world output market denominated in dollars, the demand curve and its marginal revenue curve are not affected by British pound depreciation. However, the cost curves shift downward because all inputs are from British factor markets. In fact, the cost curves move down in proportion to the exchange rate change. Note that the lower cost structure allows the company to lower the dollar price of the good and increase the number of units sold. Hence, the firm benefits from higher profits per unit because price decreases less than average cost decreases and it benefits from higher volume.

There are many examples of firms that do better after depreciation, or worse after appreciation. Oil companies operating in Latin America are clearly better off when the local currencies depreciate in real terms because the world price of the oil is not affected but the firm's production costs are lower. Although the U.S. dollar has been assumed to be the world's currency, this is not always the case. The world price for Japanese automobiles logically depends on the Japanese yen, for example. In fact, the depreciation of the U.S. dollar vis-à-vis the Japanese yen in the latter half of the 1980s made Honda's Ohio plant such a low-cost producer of Japanese automobiles that the United States became an exporter of Japanese cars!

FIGURE 7-5   REAL EXCHANGE RATE CHANGES AND A PRICE MAKER IN A WORLD OUTPUT MARKET

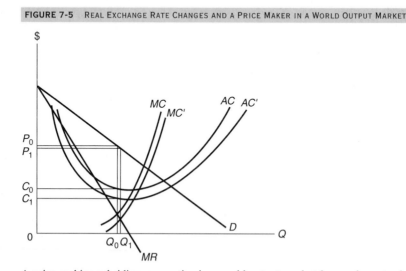

A price-making subsidiary competing in a world output market faces a downward-sloping demand curve denominated in dollars, shown as D, associated with marginal revenue curve MR. The cost structure is denominated in the foreign currency and converted into dollars, shown as AC and MC. The optimum quantity of output is at Q_0, at which the margin is $(P_0 - C_0)$. A depreciation of the foreign currency has no effect on D or MR, but reduces the cost structure and shifts the AC and MC curves downward to AC' and MC' in proportion to the exchange rate change. The optimum quantity of output increases to Q_1, the dollar price declines to P_1, and the margin increases to $(P_1 - C_1)$.

EXPOSURE AT HONDA MOTOR COMPANY

In 1979, Honda Motor Company decided to build an automobile production plant in Marysville, Ohio, where the firm already had a motorcycle plant. Honda Accords began coming off the assembly line in December, 1982. This made Honda the first Japanese automaker to manufacture in the United States. Other cars were produced over the subsequent years as capacity expanded at the Marysville facility.

Most Hondas produced in the United States are sold in the United States, but exchange rates have given Honda North America an advantage in foreign markets as well. By 1987, Honda began exporting Ohio-produced Japanese cars to other countries, such as Taiwan. In 1988, Honda even began exporting Ohio-made Japanese cars to Japan.

Honda wanted to increase its market share in the high-margin luxury car market in Japan, but the market wasn't large enough to produce luxury cars in Japan. It began to service the Japanese market for these models from the United States because the yen was very strong vis-à-vis the U.S. dollar, at approximately 155 yen to the dollar. "The comparative costs of producing a car in the United States have become very competitive under the current yen-dollar exchange rate," according to Koji Hirao of the Long-Term Credit Bank of Japan. At the low yen/dollar exchange rate, the costs of raw materials such as steel were cheaper in the United States. By mid-1988, the exchange rate fell to 125 yen/dollar, further favoring U.S. production. Honda planned to sell 5,000 of its Ohio-made cars in Japan in 1988, more than the total amount of U.S. cars sold in Japan in 1987.

The stock price of Honda Motor Company rose 44 percent during the first quarter of 1988 with news of these surging car sales in Japan. By 1992, with the yen still around 125 per dollar, Honda sold about 20,000 of these reverse import cars in Japan. By 1994, with the yen averaging an even lower 100 per dollar, Honda exported more than 100,000 vehicles. Other car makers are following Honda; Mazda planned to take advantage of the low dollar by exporting 2,500 Ford Probes made in its Michigan plant. The general conclusion is that exchange rate changes clearly affect international production and trade patterns, and Honda was particularly successful in reacting to the changing yen/dollar exchange rate.

Sources: "A Hot American Car May Hit Japan: The Honda," *Business Week,* January 26, 1987, p. 50; "Honda's Coupe Is a Coup," *Fortune,* May 9, 1988, p. 6; "The Americanization of Honda," *Business Week,* April 25, 1988, p. 90–93; "Honda Motor Sees Strength in Yen Hurting Its Sales," *The Wall Street Journal,* March 8, 1993, p. B7D; and "The Outlook: Midwest Exports Blunt Some Effects of Strike," *Wall Street Journal,* March 25, 1996, p. 1.

CASE 4: REAL EXCHANGE RATE CHANGES AND A WORLD INPUT MARKET

The fourth scenario for consideration is what happens when the output market is priced in pounds but the inputs are all priced in dollars. While this is an extreme case, it is not unusual for some firms to have a large proportion of the final product composed of imported inputs. For instance, a British auto parts company will have its costs depend heavily on the price of steel, an input which is largely priced in dollars. This situation is shown in Figure 7-6. Here, the depreciation of the pound shifts the U.S. dollar marginal revenue curve downward because sales in the United Kingdom are worth less. If all inputs are priced in U.S. dollars, however, the cost function does not shift down. The unfortunate result is that the affiliate must cut production to reduce costs. The affiliate's profit margin declines also. Profits have therefore declined greatly because of the combined fall in the profit margin and in volume.

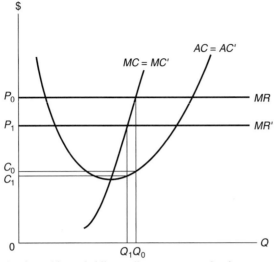

A price-taking subsidiary sells at a constant foreign currency price which is converted into dollars at the prevailing exchange rate, shown as the MR curve at P_0. For the case of a world input market, the cost structure is denominated in dollars, shown as AC and MC. The optimum quantity of output is at Q_0, at which the margin is $(P_0 - C_0)$. A depreciation of the foreign currency reduces the dollar-equivalent MR proportionately, shifting the MR curve downward to MR' at P_1. However, the depreciation has no effect on the cost structure. The optimum quantity of output falls to Q_1, and the margin declines to $(P_1 - C_1)$.

FIGURE 7-6   REAL EXCHANGE RATE CHANGES AND A PRICE TAKER IN A WORLD INPUT MARKET

The result in which the firm competing in a local output market from a world input market is in worse condition after a depreciation of the local currency similarly holds for a price maker. Figure 7-7 analyzes this scenario. The cost structure is stable in U.S. dollars, so pound depreciation does not alter their positions. However, the demand and marginal revenue curves shift down in proportion to the pound depreciation. The optimum pricing strategy is to lower the U.S. dollar price of the good and to cut the volume. Note that this implies that the pound price of the good is higher, inducing a decline in volume. By examining the relative positions of the two demand curves, the decline in dollar price is shown to be less than the depreciation of the pound reflected in the downward shift of the demand curve, further confirming that the pound price of the good increases.

CASE 5: REAL EXCHANGE RATE CHANGES AND WORLD OUTPUT AND INPUT MARKETS

The final scenario is a combination of Cases 3 and 4 in which the subsidiary is competing in a world output market but is simultaneously producing the output with factors supplied in a world input market. In this scenario, there are no shifts in the marginal revenue curve denominated in dollars as the pound depreciates. Similarly, there are no shifts in the cost curves as the pound depreciates either. Affiliates in this environment therefore face no economic exposure viewed from the perspective of the U.S. parent company.

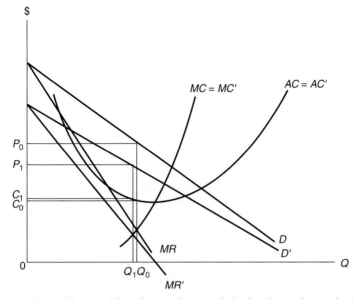

A price-making subsidiary faces a downward-sloping demand curve in the foreign country, which is converted from foreign currency into dollars at the prevailing exchange rate and shown as D. The marginal revenue curve is MR. For the case of a world input market, the cost structure is denominated in dollars, shown as AC and MC. The optimum quantity of output is at Q_0, at which the margin is $(P_0 - C_0)$. A depreciation of the foreign currency reduces the dollar-equivalent demand curve proportionately, shifting D downward to D' and MR downward to MR'. Depreciation has no effect on the cost structure. The optimum quantity of output declines to Q_1, and the margin declines to $(P_1 - C_1)$.

FIGURE 7-7   REAL EXCHANGE RATE CHANGES AND A PRICE MAKER IN A WORLD INPUT MARKET

THE CURRENCY HABITAT OF PRICE

In our discussion of Cases 3, 4, and 5, we raised the question of how the world price of a good or service, or of an input, is determined. In our examples, the world price was assumed to be determined in the U.S. dollar. As the example of Honda illustrated, however, the U.S. dollar is not always the currency pricing the product. In the world marketplace for automobiles, the value of the yen is obviously important. Similarly, the Unisys Corporation finds that personal computers and random access memory chips are two products whose price is mostly determined in yen and Pacific Rim currencies. World market prices determined by foreign currencies complicate the analysis of shifts in the marginal revenue and cost curves, but do not alter the fundamental conclusions. The key to analysis is simply to ask how the curves move with movements in other currencies.

Flood and Lessard (1986) have called the currency in which the price of a good tends to be the most stable the **currency habitat of price;** other authors have referred to **a currency of determination.** For many goods that are traded in truly worldwide markets, such as coffee, sugar, or cocoa, the U.S. dollar might be the currency habitat of price essentially because the U.S. dollar is the world's currency. For goods produced only within the United States or only by American investment, the currency habitat of price is likely to be the U.S. dollar. For other goods, such as automobiles, personal computers, or random access memory chips, Asian currencies may be the currency habitats. For still other goods, such as wine, European currencies may be the currency habitats.

If the currency habitat of price is the home currency, or even the local currency, the analysis follows the cases outlined above. Simply ask what happens to the marginal revenue and cost curves when the bilateral home currency/local currency exchange rate changes. If the currency habitat is a third currency, the firm will have to monitor this third currency and analyze changes in the marginal revenue or marginal cost curves resulting from these third currency movements, the impact on operations denominated in the local currency, and their value in home currency units. Clearly, more analysis is necessary when the currency habitat of price is a third currency, and the firm may face more exchange risk.

The issue of the currency habitat of price is also important for firms that operate only domestically, but compete against foreign imports. In the United States, California wine producers are aware that the U.S. dollar price of wine is greatly affected by foreign competition. When the U.S. dollar is low, the world price of wine is high by dollar standards and domestic vintners are able to increase production. The French franc and the Italian lira are of particular influence in pricing wine for the obvious reason that France and Italy are the world's primary wine exporters. Hence, the domestic wine industry must analyze foreign currency exposure in much the same way as a firm with a foreign subsidiary operating in a world input market (Case 4). For the California vintners, the cost curves do not change with changes in the value of the U.S. dollar vis-à-vis the franc or the lira, but the marginal revenue curve does. When the U.S. dollar appreciates with respect to European currencies, the marginal revenue curve shifts downward because the currency habitat of the price of wine is the European currency.

Another way to think about this exercise is to put the currency habitat of price (rather than the U.S. dollar) on the vertical axis of the marginal revenue and marginal cost schedule graph. Changes in the value of the currency will then not alter the marginal revenue curve, but the cost curves of the California vintners will shift upward when the dollar appreciates. The Americans will then have to cut production and their profits will decrease. This analysis is the same as in Case 3, with the adjustment that the foreign currency that is the currency habitat of price is plotted on the vertical axis rather than the home currency.

It is also interesting to note that some service industries that are not often thought of as exporters are in fact affected by exchange rate changes. The tourism industry is one such example. The economy of the Bahamas is highly dependent on tourism. By some estimates, one-third of the Bahamian GNP is derived from tourism and one-half of its employment is in the tourism sector. The currency of the Bahamas is the Bahamian dollar, which is pegged to the U.S. dollar at a one-to-one rate. There are no currency controls, so Bahamian monetary policy maintains the peg as a truly market exchange rate. When the Bahamian dollar depreciates relative to the Canadian dollar and European currencies because the U.S. dollar depreciates, the Bahamas becomes a low-cost producer of worldwide tourist services and the volume of tourists going to the Bahamas increases. This is the same analysis as in Case 3.

Most visitors to the Bahamas, however, are American. It may appear that there is little exposure because the Bahamian dollar/U.S. dollar exchange rate cannot change. Unfortunately, the U.S. dollar and its equivalent, the Bahamian dollar, are not necessarily the currency habitats for tourism. When the dollar is high, Americans are encouraged to visit other resorts where the dollar is worth more. This logic follows the analysis in Case 4. Hence, by pegging the Bahamian dollar to the U.S. dollar, the Bahamian government may actually increase the exposure of the tourism sector; when the dollar is high, Europeans, Canadians, and Americans go where the local currency is not pegged to the U.S. dollar.

One final way to think about price determination in the presence of many different currency influences is to visualize the currency habitat in terms of a currency basket. This currency basket is likely to be more stable than any of the underlying currencies. For random access memory chips, currencies in the basket are likely to be the yen, the dollar, and a variety of other Pacific Rim currencies. For wine, the currencies are likely to be the franc, the lira, the dollar, and a few other European currencies. For tourism, the currencies of nearly every country could be included—especially those with warm climates and lots of sun. When analyzing the exposure of operations facing a currency basket as the habitat of price, the movement of the home currency vis-à-vis the currency basket becomes the key variable.

SUMMARY OF CASH FLOW EXPOSURE

As we have seen, ongoing cash flows and the income statement are only truly exposed to the extent that there are deviations from PPP. In the first case—where PPP holds—there is no shift in either the revenues or the costs, so there is no exposure. In the second case, where the foreign operation is self-contained, the profit margin between revenues and costs is directly affected by real exchange rate changes, so there is moderate exposure. In the third and fourth cases, the margin effect is combined with changes in the firm's volume of sales and production to increase the firm's exposure to real exchange rate changes. In the fifth case, there is again no change in the revenues or costs, so there is no exposure. Table 7-1 summarizes the findings of these five cases.

To correctly analyze the effects of exchange rate changes on revenues and costs, three aspects must be examined. First, analysts must look at the effect of a deviation from PPP on the marginal revenue denominated in the home country's currency. This effect necessarily depends on whether the firm is a price taker or a price maker in the marketplace. Second, they must look at the effect on the marginal and average costs denominated in

TABLE 7-1 Summary of Results from Local Currency Depreciation (All values refer to real U.S. dollar values)

Case	U.S. Dollar Price	U.S. Dollar Average Cost	U.S. Dollar Margin	Volume	U.S. Dollar Profits
1. PPP Holds	No Change	No Change	No Change	No Change	No Change
2. Real Depreciation, Self-Contained Subsidiary	Decrease	Decrease	Decrease	No Change	Decrease
3. Real Depreciation, World Output Market	Price Taker: No Change Price Maker: Decrease	Decrease	Increase	Increase	Increase
4. Real Depreciation, World Input Market	Decrease	No Change	Decrease	Decrease	Decrease
5. Real Depreciation, World Output and Input Market	No Change	No Change	No Change	No Change	No Change

the home country's currency. Together, these explain what happens to the profit margin as exchange rates change; Lessard and Lightstone (1986) logically refer to the combined effects of price and cost changes on the profit margin as the **margin effect.** Finally, however, it is important to examine the quantity of output produced and sold; will the exchange rate change cause a cut in volume or will it allow for an expansion? Lessard and Lightstone (1986) logically refer to this effect as the **volume effect.** Together, the margin effect and the volume effect determine what happens to the firm's total profits.

Obviously, the firm's ongoing cash flow exposure is quite difficult to quantitatively measure, and as a result is not measured very accurately or too frequently. As a concept, however, it is important to understand.[3] Cash flow exposure exists only to the extent that there are deviations from PPP exchange rates. As we will discuss further in Chapter 10, if there are never any real exchange rate changes, then foreign operations are never exposed!

7.3   ANALYZING NET WORTH EXPOSURE

The second component of economic exposure, **net worth exposure,** or **economic balance sheet exposure,** is the extent to which a company's real net asset position is affected by exchange rate changes. By real net asset position, we mean the market value of the total assets net of the market value of the liabilities. In other words, we are interested in the economic value of the balance sheet rather than the book or accounting value. Recall that the items in the balance sheet, such as plant and equipment and debt, have been separated from the cash flow items; this separation ensures that items are not counted twice. The separation is designed so that we may examine balance sheet items on their own. We will proceed by examining nonmonetary assets in the balance sheet first, and then focus on monetary assets and liabilities.

NONMONETARY ASSETS

Consider first the market value of nonmonetary assets, such as real estate, plant and equipment, and even inventory. The value of these assets most likely rises with local inflation. We are, of course, interested in the real U.S. dollar value of the assets. Hence, they are exposed to exchange rate changes only to the extent that there are deviations from PPP. To continue with our British subsidiary example, real estate, plant and equipment, and even inventory are typically valued less in U.S. dollars if there is a real devaluation of the pound.

When analyzing nonmonetary assets, a distinction between expected and unexpected deviations from PPP becomes important. For example, any expected real depreciations are generally reflected in the assets' U.S. dollar price, assuming there are integrated liquid markets for these assets. Otherwise, potential buyers would simply wait for the expected real depreciation before purchasing the assets. Hence, nonmonetary assets are exposed only to the extent that there are unanticipated deviations from PPP. This means that the economic exposure should not be measured by the deviation of the exchange rate from PPP, but rather as the deviation of the actual exchange rate from the expected exchange rate.

It is not unusual to expect real deviations from PPP. For example, real exchange rate changes may be anticipated if there is a tendency toward PPP or if there is mean reversion in the exchange rate series. The exchange rate does not follow a smooth function of the currency values; instead, it fluctuates around the true relationships, resulting in overvalued and undervalued currencies that experience subsequent movements back toward PPP equilibrium. Unfortunately, these expected real exchange rates can be hard to measure and therefore are often neglected. In such cases, the focus is on the whole real exchange rate, regardless of whether any deviations are expected or unexpected.

MONETARY ASSETS AND LIABILITIES

Monetary assets and liabilities are exposed to deviations from PPP as well. One difference between nonmonetary and monetary assets and liabilities is that monetary assets and liabilities carry nominal returns determined by the interest rates on the instruments. This means that any real depreciation of a currency reduces the value of the net asset position in home currency units, as long as the depreciation is not compensated by a higher interest rate than would otherwise prevail. Technically, then, monetary assets and liabilities are exposed only to the extent that there are deviations from uncovered interest parity (UIP). For example, a bond denominated in pounds is worth less in dollars if there is a real devaluation that is not compensated by a higher real interest rate. This means that any expected real devaluations will raise local currency interest rates. Hence, these monetary assets are exposed only to the extent that there are unanticipated deviations from UIP. This is almost exactly what we said about nonmonetary assets and PPP, but with a different line of reasoning.

Often, there will be changes in the value of a monetary asset or liability for reasons other than exchange rate changes. As an example, consider the real value of a pound bond again. If the relevant interest rates are fixed *ex ante* and the currency subsequently experiences unexpected inflation, the real value of the bond decreases. This decrease, however, should be considered inflation exposure rather than foreign exchange exposure. In other words, the erosion of the value of the bond is due to British inflation and is independent of any currency argument.

The exposures associated with monetary and nonmonetary positions can clearly be aggregated because all that matters in each is the magnitude of any unanticipated deviations from PPP or UIP. As we saw in Chapter 2, deviations from PPP (pertinent to nonmonetary assets) and deviations from UIP (pertinent to monetary assets and liabilities) are nearly identical to one another. The important point to remember is that the relevant information pertains to market rather than book values.

7.4   MEASURING EXPOSURE USING REGRESSION ANALYSIS

A statistical measure of economic exposure can be provided using historical data of cash flows or net worth and linear regression analysis. Using cash flows in each period as a dependent variable and the relevant exchange rate as an independent variable, the output from estimating the following equation can be examined:

$$CF_t = \alpha + \beta S_t + u_t$$

where CF_t denotes the cash flows in home currency units in period t, and S_t is the spot exchange rate in terms of home currency units per foreign currency unit. The estimated beta coefficient, $\beta = \text{Cov}(CF_t, S_t)/\text{Var}(S_t)$, therefore measures the sensitivity of cash flows to the level of the exchange rate, which is precisely a quantitative measurement of the exposure denominated in foreign currency units. As an example, if the beta estimate is one million pounds, the statement "we have historically had an annual cash flow exposure of one million pounds" can be made. The R^2 statistic from the equation measures the fraction of cash flow variability explained by the variation in the exchange rate. If the R^2 is low, exchange rates do not explain cash flows very well.[4]

Given the extensive discussion in this chapter about purchasing power parity, it is clear that the regression above should be run in real values. The cash flows should therefore be deflated by a price index to make comparisons more meaningful. More importantly, however, the exchange rate should be the real exchange rate defined earlier rather than simply the nominal exchange rate. If the regression is run using nominal values, the exposure estimate will be biased.

As an example, consider a case in which PPP holds between the United States and the United Kingdom. In such a situation, there is no exposure under economic definitions. If inflation in America is running at 10 percent per year and there is no inflation in England, the U.S. dollar must be depreciating at a rate of 10 percent per year to maintain purchasing power parity. If the nominal regression is run, however, the cash flows will be increasing at 10 percent per year due to dollar inflation and the spot exchange rate will be rising at 10 percent per year reflecting the nominal depreciation. The beta coefficient will pick up this proportional increase on each side over time and most analysts would incorrectly attribute this effect to exposure. Using real cash flows and real exchange rates removes the proportional changes due to nominal differences, so the beta coefficient comes out to be zero when PPP holds. This is unambiguously the correct estimate of exposure.

The technique can be applied in many different ways. For example, the firm's net asset value can be regressed onto the exchange rate to see what the net worth exposure is. Another regression may use the firm's total market value. Jorion (1990) uses stock returns to determine the exchange-rate exposure of U.S. multinationals. Lagged values of the exchange rate can be used if some adjustment lag in cash flows is postulated. Finally, all of these regressions can be run in differences, if the firm is interested in finding out how exchange rate changes account for changes in the relevant dependent variables:

$$CF_{t+n} - CF_t = \alpha + \beta[S_{t+n} - S_t] + u_t.$$

This is essentially what is implied in the formula shown in Chapter 6:

$$\text{FX Gain (Loss)}_{t,t+n} = [S_{t+n} - S_t][\text{Exposure}_t],$$

which is now used to econometrically estimate exposure given changes in cash flows, profits, or values [here referred to as FX Gain (Loss)$_{t,t+n}$] and changes in exchange rates $[S_{t+n} - S_t]$. The beta estimate captures the unknown exposure. Econometricians often prefer differencing because the differenced series are usually more stationary, or stable, than the undifferenced series. The equation can also be run in differences of logs of variables. Using the real exchange rate, this is precisely the deviation from the relative version of purchasing power parity discussed at the beginning of this chapter. Finally, as discussed in the next chapter, it can be run in percentage changes.

ECONOMIC EXPOSURE OF AMERICAN AIRLINES

American Airlines (AMR) is a leader in the global air transportation industry, and foreign exchange exposure is an important concern for the company. Net foreign currency cash flows have increased from $119 million in 1986 to $393 million in 1990. International revenue has grown from 19.3 percent of the system total in 1986 to approximately 26.7 percent in 1990. Consequently, managers and analysts need to know how the profitability of the airline will be affected by exchange rate changes.

To assess the exposure of American Airlines, Bilson (1994) examined the price of AMR stock. Although the main interest is in the effect of exchange rates on the stock price, other factors that affect the stock price include the overall performance of the stock market and the price of oil (which directly affects airline fuel costs). A regression equation of the price of AMR stock using monthly data over the period January 1985 to December 1991 revealed (with standard errors in parentheses):

$$\ln P_{AMR} = -3.5396 + 0.9829 \ln P_{S\&P}$$
$$(.9471) \quad (.1107)$$
$$- 0.1793 \ln P_{OIL} - 0.7753 \ln S_{\$/DM}$$
$$(.0716) \quad\quad (.1617)$$
$$R^2 = 0.53 \quad AR(1) = 0.72 \quad D\text{-}W = 1.81$$

where $\ln P_{AMR}$ is the (natural) logarithm of the stock price, $\ln P_{S\&P}$ is the logarithm of the Standard and Poor's 500 stock index, $\ln P_{OIL}$ is the logarithm of the contract price of crude oil futures, and $\ln S_{\$/DM}$ is the logarithm of the $/DM exchange rate. (The equation has been estimated using a correction for serial correlation.) The coefficients on $\ln P_{S\&P}$ and $\ln P_{OIL}$ are as expected; when the stock market does well, the price of AMR stock increases, and when oil prices rise, the price of AMR stock falls. For exchange risk, the focus is on the $/DM exchange rate because over 75 percent of revenues outside of North America are from Europe. The negative coefficient on $\ln S_{\$/DM}$ implies that American Airlines is hurt by dollar depreciation. Because the equation is estimated in logarithms, the coefficients can be interpreted as elasticities; with respect to the exchange rate, a 1 percent appreciation of the DM is associated with a 0.77 percent drop in the stock price.

Why is American Airlines hurt by dollar depreciation? Given that the airline has foreign currency revenues, an analyst might expect American Airlines to benefit from the depreciation of the dollar as foreign currency revenues become more valuable when converted into dollars. One explanation for the reverse outcome is that the load factor (or number of passengers) could drop as the dollar depreciates. Bilson points out that for Americans using international air travel services, depreciation of the dollar increases the total costs of international travel by raising the prices of foreign hotels, restaurants, other travel services, and shopping. American overseas travel is therefore likely to be adversely affected by the dollar depreciation, and American Airlines will experience lower load factors and may reduce its ticket prices. Depreciation of the dollar will certainly make travel to the United States by foreigners less expensive, but if foreign travelers have a preference for their national airlines, then U.S. carriers will be adversely affected.

Sources: Bilson, John F.O., "Managing Economic Exposure to Foreign Exchange Risk: A Case Study of American Airlines," Chapter 10 of *Exchange Rates and Corporate Performance,* edited by Yakov Amihud and Richard M. Levich, Irwin Professional Publishing, 1994, pp. 221–246.

EXPOSURE OF AMERICAN AND JAPANESE AUTOMAKERS IN THE U.S. MARKET

One concern often expressed in the financial press is that competition among firms within an industry is directly affected by exchange rates. For example, the dollar/yen exchange rate is often assumed to influence the relative position of American and Japanese auto producers. In August, 1994, as the yen/dollar exchange rate hovered around 100, the *Wall Street Journal* reported that Toyota was increasing prices on vehicles sold in North America "to reflect the yen's sharp rise against the dollar." The article concluded that "[t]hough the Big Three American auto makers have also raised prices on some vehicles in advance of the 1995 model year, a significant jump in Toyota's prices would likely hurt its standing in the U.S. market."

In an investigation of competition in the automobile industry, Barber, Click, and Darrough (1999) empirically estimate the effects of changes in the dollar/yen exchange rate on sales quantities of American and Japanese firms in the U.S. market. The full analysis controls for changes in the price of oil and changes in U.S. domestic income, which are often thought to affect sales quantities of American and Japanese firms differently. In addition, exchange rate changes are adjusted to remove any effects due to oil price changes or income changes. Hence, one advantage of the analysis is that foreign exchange exposure is clearly separated from oil price exposure and income (or business cycle) exposure. The investigation also examines the timing of effects by considering both an immediate short-run effect that takes place in the same month as the exchange rate change and subsequent convergence to a long-run equilibrium which is empirically completed after approximately eighteen months.

The macroeconomic system estimated with exchange rates, oil prices, and income suggests that the standard deviation of monthly exchange rate changes is 0.017 cents per yen, or about 2.69 percent of the series average of 0.631 cents per yen. An exchange rate change of this magnitude is revealed to have a long-run effect of 0.027 cents per yen, or about 4.28 percent of the series average, after working its way through the macroeconomy over the course of a year. The short-run effects of an exchange rate change on the quantity of automobiles sold are small, but the long-run effects are qualitatively more important.

The main result is that the 4.28 percent appreciation of the yen vis-à-vis the dollar increases the total quantity of automobiles sold by American producers by about 1.53 percent and decreases the total quantity of automobiles sold by Japanese producers by about 1.57 percent. (As the quantity of American automobiles sold is greater than the quantity of Japanese cars sold, this translates into an increase in the overall market of about 1 percent.) This is fairly convincing evidence that yen appreciation vis-à-vis the dollar does benefit the American producers and hurt the Japanese producers.

Results for individual firms using the three major American and three major Japanese firms suggest some variation in the effects. The 4.28 percent appreciation of the yen vis-à-vis the dollar increases the quantity of automobiles sold by each of the American producers and decreases the quantity of automobiles sold by each of the Japanese producers as follows:

Chrysler	+1.92%	Honda	−0.29%
General Motors	+1.52%	Toyota	−1.57%
Ford	+1.35%	Nissan	−1.96%

Hence, Chrysler and Nissan are the most severely affected by exchange rate changes, and Honda is hardly affected at all. The overall conclusion is clear: yen appreciation vis-à-vis the dollar benefits each of the three American automobile producers and hurts each of the three Japanese producers selling in the U.S. market.

Source: Barber, Brad M., Reid W. Click, and Masako N. Darrough, "The Impact of Shocks to Exchange Rates and Oil Prices on U.S. Sales of American and Japanese Automakers," *Japan and the World Economy,* January 1999, pp. 57–93. The quotes from the *Wall Street Journal* are from August 26, 1994, p. A3.

❖ SUMMARY OF CHAPTER OBJECTIVES

1. Explain the concept of economic exposure.

Economic exposure is the extent to which the market value of a firm or subsidiary changes when exchange rates change.

2. Analyze a firm's cash flow exposure.

Cash flow exposure is the extent to which a company's real revenues and expenses are affected by exchange rate changes. To analyze a firm's cash flow exposure, you need to consider three things: (1) the type of deviation from PPP (appreciation or depreciation); (2) the nature of the foreign operation (whether it is a self-contained subsidiary, operates in a world output market, operates in a world input market, or operates in both world output and input markets), and (3) the structure of competition (whether the firm is a price-taker or a price-maker in the market).

3. Evaluate a firm's net worth exposure.

A firm's net worth exposure is the extent to which a company's real net asset position is affected by exchange rate changes. To evaluate the net worth exposure, consider how the market value of both assets and liabilities changes as exchange rates change.

4. Interpret a quantitative measurement of economic exposure from a coefficient in a simple regression.

The coefficient in a regression of historical cash flows onto historical exchange rates is a quantitative measure of economic exposure. In the simplest regression, the coefficient—for example, 1 million pounds—allows one to make a statement like "we have historically had an annual cash flow exposure of one million pounds." There are many variations of the simple regression, such as using logarithms of or changes in the data.

❖ QUESTIONS FOR REVIEW

1. [Class discussion] There are three measures of exposure traditionally studied: translation, transaction, and economic. Discuss the advantages and limitations of using each measure of exposure. Which of these should managers focus on? Carefully explain your answer.

2. [Class discussion] True or False: Indicate whether the statement is true or false and clearly explain why.
   a. A U.S. corporation operating in the Puerto Rican tourism sector does not face foreign exchange exposure because Puerto Rico uses the U.S. dollar.
   b. If the law of one price holds for the commodity a firm sells, the firm will not face foreign exchange exposure on sales revenues.
   c. The currency habitat of the price of a homogeneous commodity (e.g., tin) is the U.S. dollar.

3. Acme, Inc., a U.S. multinational corporation, has a subsidiary in Mexico which sells goods in the Mexican market which are produced entirely using U.S. dollar inputs. Because of local competition, the subsidiary is a price taker in Mexican pesos.
   a. Draw a diagram of the firm's cost structure and the marginal revenue line. In the diagram, show the initial level of profit from the Mexican operations. Briefly describe the amount of profit.

b. Now consider what happens if the Mexican peso depreciates by 15 percent. Show the effects of depreciation in the diagram. Specify the new level of profit from the Mexican operations. Describe the profit change in terms of the margin effect and the volume effect.

4. Mitchell Enterprises, a U.S. multinational corporation, sells cocoa beans it produces in Ghana. The cocoa beans are sold in a perfectly competitive world output market priced in U.S. dollars. Production in Ghana consists entirely of Ghanaian cedi costs: local land rents, Ghanaian labor costs, and local transport costs.

   a. Draw a diagram of the firm's cost structure and the marginal revenue line denominated in dollars. In the diagram, show the initial level of economic profit (economic rent) from the Ghanaian operations. Briefly describe the amount of profit.

   b. Now consider what happens if the Ghanaian cedi appreciates 10 percent against the U.S. dollar. Show the effects of the appreciation in the diagram. Specify the new level of profit (rent) from Ghanaian operations, and briefly describe the amount of profit. Describe the change in terms of the margin effect and the volume effect.

5. Consider a firm competing in a market in which it is a price taker.

   a. Draw the cost structure of the firm and the marginal revenue line. As a manager, you are required to decide how much to produce given the situation. Indicate in the diagram the quantity of production and sales that you choose. Next, indicate the amount of economic profit or economic rent the firm receives. Where does the profit/rent come from?

   b. Now suppose the firm is a self-contained subsidiary of a U.S. multinational corporation operating in Portugal. What happens to the value of the profit/rent if the Portuguese escudo appreciates by 5 percent? Show the effects of the appreciation in the diagram and indicate the new quantity and the new rent.

6. Your boss has asked you to analyze the foreign exchange exposure of a subsidiary in Erehwon. The subsidiary sells exclusively in Erehwon, taking in revenues denominated in Erehwon grolsch. The market is strictly local, and the subsidiary does not compete in a world output market. However, the market is not perfectly competitive so the demand for the product is downward-sloping. The costs of production are also strictly local, denominated in Erehwon grolsch, and marginal costs rise with the quantity produced. Prepare a diagram of marginal cost, demand, and marginal revenue curves with the U.S. dollar price on the vertical axis and quantity on the horizontal axis.

   a. Show what the optimum quantity of output/sales is for the subsidiary, and what the optimum (U.S. dollar equivalent) price is.

   b. Your boss is worried that the Erehwon grolsch will depreciate by 10 percent. Assuming that this is a self-contained subsidiary (as just explained), show what happens when there is a 10 percent depreciation of the grolsch in the diagram. What happens to the optimum quantity of output/sales for the subsidiary? What happens to the optimum (U.S. dollar equivalent) price following the 10 percent depreciation? What happens to the Erehwon grolsch price following the 10 percent depreciation?

7. Pluto Enterprises has a subsidiary in New Zealand which produces a unique product for export to the rest of the world. All costs are denominated in New Zealand dollars. Because the product is unique and is produced for a world market, the firm sees a downward-sloping demand curve denominated in U.S. dollars.

   a. Draw the subsidiary's marginal cost curve and the demand curve for the product, along with the marginal revenue curve derived from the demand curve. Show the optimal quantity of output and the optimal U.S. dollar price.

   b. Consider what happens if the New Zealand dollar appreciates by 10 percent. Show the effects of the NZ$ appreciation in the diagram. Be sure to show the effects on the optimal quantity produced and the effects on the optimal U.S. dollar price of the product. Briefly explain the effects.

   c. What happens to the subsidiary's U.S. dollar profits after the New Zealand dollar appreciated by 10 percent? Answer as completely as possible.

   d. What happens to the price of the product denominated in New Zealand dollars?

8. Ace, Inc., a U.S. multinational corporation, has a subsidiary in Mexico that sells goods in the Mexican market that are produced entirely using U.S. dollar inputs.

   a. Because of local competition, the subsidiary may be a price taker in Mexican pesos. Draw a diagram of the firm's cost structure and the marginal revenue line. In the diagram, show the optimum quantity of sales and the profit margin (price minus average cost). Now consider what happens if the Mexican peso depreciates (in real terms) by 5 percent. Show the effects of depreciation in the diagram, and show the new optimum quantity of sales and the new profit margin.

   b. In the absence of extensive competition, the subsidiary may face a downward-sloping demand curve and therefore be a price-maker in Mexican pesos. Draw a diagram of the firm's cost structure and the demand curve and marginal revenue line. In the diagram, show the optimum quantity of sales, the optimum price, and the profit margin. Now consider what happens if the Mexican peso depreciates (in real terms) by 5 percent. Show the effects of depreciation in the diagram, and show the new optimum quantity of sales, the new price, and the new profit margin.

   c. Compare the situations in a and b, explaining what happens to the optimum quantity of sales and the profit margins in response to the 5 percent depreciation of the peso. Which of these situations has a larger exposure to exchange rate changes?

9. Draw a diagram of cost curves and a constant marginal revenue curve with the U.S. dollar price on the vertical axis and quantity on the horizontal axis. Suppose this represents a U.S. beef firm's export platform in Argentina. (In other words, the firm's subsidiary in Argentina exports its beef to the rest of the world.) Assume that the U.S. dollar is the currency habitat of the price of the beef. Also suppose that there is a fixed exchange rate between the U.S. dollar and the Argentine peso, but that inflation in Argentina is less than inflation in the United States over the course of a year. How are the subsidiary's operations affected by this situation? (Consider what happens to the real exchange rate, and consider the margin effects and the volume effects separately before explaining the total effect.)

10. [Group project] The economy of the Bahamas is highly dependent on tourism. By some estimates, one-third of GNP is derived from tourism and one-half of Bahamian employment is in the tourism sector. The currency of the Bahamas is the Bahamian dollar, which is pegged to the U.S. dollar at a one-to-one rate. There are no currency controls, so Bahamian monetary policy maintains the peg as a truly market exchange rate.

   a. The Royal Bahamian Hotel, just outside of Nassau, is owned by a French hotel corporation, Le Meridien. Assume that the property caters entirely to European and Canadian visitors, who stay longer than Americans. Does the Royal Bahamian face cash flow exposure viewed from the French parent's standpoint?

b. The British Colonial Hotel, in Nassau, is owned by an American hotel corporation, Best Western. This property caters almost exclusively to American visitors, who typically come for short visits. Does the British Colonial face cash flow exposure viewed from the American parent's standpoint?

11. [Group project] Tokyo Disneyland, a large amusement theme park, opened to the public in 1983. It is owned and operated by Oriental Land Company under a license agreement with the Walt Disney Company of Burbank, California, which owns and operates Disneyland in Anaheim, California, and Walt Disney World in Orlando, Florida. The Walt Disney Company's involvement in Tokyo Disneyland is minimal. However, the Walt Disney Company receives a 10 percent royalty payment from admissions and a 5 percent royalty payment from merchandise and food sales, all naturally paid in Japanese yen. For fiscal year 1984, royalty receipts amounted to approximately $35 million. For the Walt Disney Company as a whole, total revenue was $1.7 billion and net income was $98 million in fiscal 1984. The yen royalty receipts from Tokyo Disneyland were expected to grow at 10 to 20 percent per year as the new theme park attracted the interest of Japanese vacationers and foreign tourists traveling to Tokyo. The Walt Disney Company became concerned about the exposure and risk of the yen royalty receipts to fluctuations in the yen/dollar exchange rate. The company therefore began an analysis of the foreign exchange exposure and risk, as well as appropriate ways to manage it.

Analyze the Walt Disney Company's foreign exchange exposure from the yen royalty receipts. How will fluctuations in the value of the yen affect Disney's profits from Tokyo Disneyland? Use a diagram to help you form your judgments. How large is the exposure? How large is the foreign exchange risk? Is it appropriate for Disney to examine the yen royalty receipts separate from the cash flows of the other Disney amusement parks worldwide?

12. [Class discussion] When examining the economic exposure of assets (or liabilities), what determines the degree of exposure for nonmonetary assets (or liabilities) and what determines the degree of exposure for monetary assets (or liabilities), and does this mean that nonmonetary assets (or liabilities) and monetary assets (or liabilities) should not be added together in this examination?

13. As the chief financial officer of a U.S.-based company, you have been analyzing the foreign exchange exposure of a subsidiary your company has in an emerging market known as Erehwon. You are worried because the value of the Erehwon fromage has been extremely volatile with respect to the U.S. dollar. You are thinking of estimating some regressions of real dollar revenues, costs, profits, and prices onto the real dollar/fromage exchange rate. In particular, you are thinking of estimating the regressions in logarithmic form so that the coefficients may be interpreted as elasticities.

a. Assume that the coefficient on the exchange rate from the regression of revenues is 1, meaning that a 1 percent increase in the dollar/fromage exchange rate increases dollar revenues by 1 percent. Also assume that the coefficient on the exchange rate from the regression of costs is 1, meaning that a 1 percent increase in the dollar/fromage exchange rate increases dollar costs by 1 percent. What do you think the coefficient on the exchange rate from the regression of profits will be? What do you think the nature of the subsidiary's operations is?

b. You run a regression of profits onto the exchange rate in logarithmic form and produce the following equation:

$$\ln[\text{profits}] = 5 - 1.75 \ln[\text{dollars/fromage}]$$

where both coefficients are statistically significant. What does this imply about the nature of the subsidiary's operation?

c. If the coefficient on the exchange rate from the regression of the dollar price of the good is 1, what is the currency habitat of the price of the good?

d. If the coefficient on the exchange rate from the regression of the dollar price of the good is 1, what would you expect the coefficient on the exchange rate to be in a regression of the fromage price of the good?

TOOLS FOR ANALYSIS
Mathematics of Cash Flow Exposure

This section builds on the "Tools for Analysis" in Chapter 5 to examine the mathematics of cash flow exposure. As before, the cost function for the firm's product expresses the cost of production as a function of the quantity produced, and is derived from the production function and the market costs of the inputs. The cost function additionally includes any fixed cost associated with production, which is not a function of the quantity of output produced. For production in the United States or for foreign production with inputs priced in a dollar-denominated world input market, the cost function may again be:

$$C = Q^3 - 14Q^2 + 69Q + 128$$

where Q is the quantity of output produced (e.g., in thousands) and C is measured in dollars. When foreign production uses inputs whose prices are denominated in the foreign currency, the cost function may be measured in foreign currency, denoted C^*, and converted into dollars at the real exchange rate, e:

$$C = eC^* = e[Q^3 - 14Q^2 + 69Q + 128].$$

When inputs are priced in dollars, the average cost and marginal cost functions are as before:

$$AC = [Q^3 - 14Q^2 + 69Q + 128]/Q$$
$$= Q^2 - 14Q + 69 + 128/Q$$
$$MC = dC/dQ = 3Q^2 - 28Q + 69$$

and these are the AC and MC curves plotted in Figures 7-6 and 7-7. When inputs are priced in foreign currency and converted into dollars at the real exchange rate, the average cost and marginal cost curves are:

$$AC = e[Q^3 - 14Q^2 + 69Q + 128]/Q$$
$$= e[Q^2 - 14Q + 69 + 128/Q]$$
$$MC = dC/dQ = deC^*/dQ$$
$$= e[3Q^2 - 28Q + 69]$$

and these are the AC and MC curves plotted in Figures 7-2 through 7-5.

If the firm is a price taker, it is able to sell any amount of output without affecting the price. If the firm is a price taker in a dollar-denominated world output market, it is able to sell at price P, measured in dollars. Suppose $P = 89$ again. If the firm is a price taker in the foreign market, it is able to sell at price P^*, measured in foreign currency, which is equivalent to eP^* in dollars. For simplicity, suppose $P^* = 89$ also. Considering that there are two price-taking scenarios and two input-price scenarios, four situations are possible.

If the subsidiary is self-contained, such that it is a price taker in the local currency and the production uses inputs priced in the foreign currency, the firm's profits are:

$$\Pi = e[89Q] - e[Q^3 - 14Q^2 + 69Q + 128]$$
$$= e\{89Q - [Q^3 - 14Q^2 + 69Q + 128]\}$$

Profit maximization reveals:

$$d\Pi/dQ = e[89 - 3Q^2 + 28Q - 69] = 0$$

and $Q = 10$ regardless of the exchange rate. Thus, there is no change in quantity when the exchange rate changes. When $Q = 10$, $\Pi = [e][472]$, so profit depends directly on the real exchange rate. Thus, a 1 percent depreciation of the foreign currency causes profits to decrease by exactly 1 percent, and a 1 percent appreciation of the foreign currency causes profits to increase by exactly 1 percent. This is the situation depicted in Figure 7-2.

When the subsidiary is competing in a dollar-denominated world output market, but production uses inputs priced in the foreign currency, the firm's profits are:

$$\Pi = [89Q] - e[Q^3 - 14Q^2 + 69Q + 128].$$

Profit maximization reveals:

$$d\Pi/dQ = 89 - 3eQ^2 + 28eQ - 69e = 0.$$

Solving, Q is a decreasing function of the exchange rate:

$$Q = \frac{28 + \sqrt{-44 + 1068/e}}{6}$$

and profit is similarly a decreasing function of the exchange rate. For example, if $e = 1$, then $Q = 10$ and $\Pi = 472$. If $e = 1.1$, $Q = 9.74$ and $\Pi = 431.34$. If $e = 0.9$, $Q = 10.3$ and $\Pi = 515.15$. This is the situation depicted in Figure 7-4.

When the subsidiary is producing with inputs priced in a dollar-denominated world input market, but selling as a price-taker in the foreign currency, the firm's profits are:

$$\Pi = e[89Q] - [Q^3 - 14Q^2 + 69Q + 128].$$

Profit maximization reveals:

$$d\Pi/dQ = 89e - 3Q^2 + 28Q - 69 = 0.$$

Solving, Q is an increasing function of the exchange rate:

$$Q = \frac{28 + \sqrt{-44 + 1068e}}{6}$$

and profit is similarly an increasing function of the exchange rate. For example, if $e = 1$, then $Q = 10$ and $\Pi = 472$. If $e = 1.1$, $Q = 10.27$ and $\Pi = 562.22$. If $e = 0.9$, $Q = 9.71$ and $\Pi = 384.26$. This is the situation depicted in Figure 7-6.

The final scenario, when the subsidiary is competing in a dollar-denominated world output market and producing with inputs priced in a dollar-denominated world input market, is basically the domestic scenario covered in Chapter 5. The situation is therefore depicted in Figure 5-2.

If the firm is a price maker, it faces a downward-sloping demand curve and must take into account the effect of producing and selling additional units on the price received. In a dollar-denominated world output market, for example, the demand curve might be:

$$P = 132 - 8Q$$

where P is again measured in dollars. The revenue for the firm is thus:

$$P \times Q = 132Q - 8Q^2$$

and the marginal revenue is:

$$MR = d(PQ)/dQ = 132 - 16Q.$$

In a segmented foreign market, the demand curve might be expressed in foreign currency and converted into dollars at the real exchange rate:

$$eP* = e[132 - 8Q]$$

where $P*$ is measured in the foreign currency. The dollar-equivalent revenue for the firm is thus:

$$e[P* \times Q] = e[132Q - 8Q^2]$$

and the marginal revenue is:

$$MR = d(eP*Q)/dQ = e[132 - 16Q].$$

Once again, the firm's goal is to pick Q to maximize profits. As with the case of the price-taking firm, there are four scenarios.

When the subsidiary is self-contained, such that it is a price taker in the local currency and the production uses inputs priced in the foreign currency, the firm's profits are:

$$\Pi = e[132Q - 8Q^2] - e[Q^3 - 14Q^2 + 69Q + 128]$$

so:

$$d\Pi/dQ = e[132 - 16Q - 3Q^2 + 28Q - 69] = 0$$

and $Q = 7$ regardless of the exchange rate. Thus, $P* = 76$ regardless of the exchange rate. Profits are therefore $\Pi = [e][264]$, and once again respond directly to exchange rate changes. This is the situation depicted in Figure 7-3.

When the subsidiary is competing in a dollar-denominated world output market, but production uses inputs priced in the foreign currency, the firm's profits are:

$$\Pi = [132Q - 8Q^2] - e[Q^3 - 14Q^2 + 69Q + 128]$$

so:

$$d\Pi/dQ = 132 - 16Q - e[3Q^2 - 28Q + 69] = 0.$$

Solving, Q is a complicated function of the exchange rate:

$$Q = \frac{-16 + 28e + \sqrt{256 + 688e - 44e^2}}{6e}$$

and profit is similarly complicated. As an example, if $e = 1$, then $Q = 7$ and $P = 76$, so $\Pi = 264$. If $e = 1.1$, then $Q = 6.936$ and $P = 76.51$, so $\Pi = 237.26$. If $e = 0.9$, $Q = 7.07$ and $P = 75.44$, so $\Pi = 290.87$. This is the situation depicted in Figure 7-5.

When the subsidiary is producing with inputs priced in a dollar-denominated world input market, but selling as a price taker in the foreign currency, the firm's profits are:

$$\Pi = e[132Q - 8Q^2] - [Q^3 - 14Q^2 + 69Q + 128]$$

so:

$$d\Pi/dQ = e[132 - 16Q] - [3Q^2 - 28Q + 69] = 0.$$

Solving, Q is a complicated function of the exchange rate:

$$Q = \frac{28 - 16e + \sqrt{-44 + 688 + 256e^2}}{6}$$

and profit is similarly complicated. As an example, if $e = 1$, then $Q = 7$ and $P = 76$, so $\Pi = 264$. If $e = 1.1$, then $Q = 7.06$ and $P = eP^* = 1.1 \times 75.5 = 83.0$, so $\Pi = 317.26$. If $e = 0.9$, $Q = 6.93$ and $P = eP^* = 0.9 \times 76.57 = 68.91$, so $\Pi = 210.87$. This is the situation depicted in Figure 7-7.

The final scenario, in which the subsidiary is competing in a dollar-denominated world output market and producing with inputs priced in a dollar-denominated world input market, is basically the domestic scenario covered in Chapter 5. The situation is therefore depicted in Figure 5-3.

❖ ENDNOTES

1. "How Dollar's Plunge Aids Some Companies, Does Little for Others," *The Wall Street Journal,* October 22, 1990, p. 1.
2. For an in-depth analysis of exchange rate exposure for firms with market power, see Luehrman (1990).
3. See Pringle (1990) for a presentation on how to conduct an exposure audit, a method that a firm can use to qualitatively measure cash flow exposure internally.
4. For further development of regression analysis as applied to economic exposure, see Adler and Dumas (1984) and Garner and Shapiro (1984).

❖ REFERENCES

Adler, Michael, and Bernard Dumas. "Exposure to Currency Risk: Definition and Measurement," *Financial Management,* Summer 1984, pp. 41–50.

Barber, Brad M., Reid W. Click, and Masako N. Darrough. "The Impact of Shocks to Exchange Rates and Oil Prices on U.S. Sales of American and Japanese Automakers," *Japan and the World Economy,* January 1999, pp. 57–93.

Bilson, John F.O. "Managing Economic Exposure to Exchange Risk: A Case Study of American Airlines," Chapter 10 of *Exchange Rates and Corporate Performance,* edited by Yakov Amihud and Richard M. Levich, Irwin Professional Publishing, 1994, pp. 221–246.

Coughlin, Cletus C., and Kees Koedijk. "What Do We Know About the Long-Run Real Exchange Rate?" *Federal Reserve Bank of St. Louis Review,* January-February 1990, pp. 36–48.

Flood, Eugene, Jr., and Donald R. Lessard. "On the Measurement of Operating Exposure to Exchange Rates: A Conceptual Approach," *Financial Management,* Spring 1986, pp. 25–36.

Garner, Kent, and Alan Shapiro. "A Practical Method of Assessing Foreign Exchange Risk," *Midland Corporate Finance Journal,* Fall 1984, pp. 6–17.

Hekman, Christine. "A Financial Model of Foreign Exchange Exposure," *Journal of International Business Studies,* Summer 1985, pp. 83–99.

Hekman, Christine. "Measuring Foreign Exchange Exposure: A Practical Theory and its Applications," *Financial Analysts Journal,* September-October 1983, pp. 59–65.

Jorion, Philippe. "The Exchange-Rate Exposure of U.S. Multinationals," *Journal of Business,* no. 3, 1990, pp. 331–345.

Lessard, Donald R., and John B. Lightstone. "Volatile Exchange Rates Can Put Operations at Risk," *Harvard Business Review,* July-August 1986, pp. 107–114.

Luehrman, Timothy A. "The Exchange Rate Exposure of a Global Competitor," *Journal of International Business Studies,* Second Quarter 1990, pp. 225–242.

Pringle, John J. "Managing Foreign Exchange Exposure," *Continental Bank Journal of Applied Corporate Finance,* Winter 1990, pp. 73–82.

Pringle, John J., and Robert A. Connolly. "The Nature and Causes of Foreign Currency Exposure," *Continental Bank Journal of Applied Corporate Finance,* Fall 1993, pp. 61–72.

THE RISK OF FOREIGN EXCHANGE EXPOSURE

8.1   Introduction
8.2   Exchange Risk with One Currency
8.3   Exchange Risk with Multiple Currencies
8.4   Exchange Risk in International Cash Management

CHAPTER OBJECTIVES
AFTER READING THIS CHAPTER, YOU SHOULD BE ABLE TO:

❖ Calculate foreign exchange risk with respect to a single currency exposure and the standard deviation of its value.

❖ Calculate foreign exchange risk with multiple currencies by applying portfolio techniques.

❖ Analyze foreign exchange risk in international cash management by considering interest rates on deposits as well as the currency movements.

This chapter is dedicated to foreign exchange risk. In the first section, we analyze the concept of foreign exchange risk with respect to a single currency exposure and the standard deviation of its value. In the second section, we examine exchange risk with multiple currencies by building on the concepts from the first section. In the third section, we apply the analysis of multiple currencies to exchange risk in international cash management by considering interest rates on deposits as well as the currency movements.

8.1   INTRODUCTION

Chapters 6 and 7 looked at different measures of foreign exchange exposure. It is clear from those chapters that changes in exchange rates have an impact on the home currency value of foreign operations. This chapter shifts the focus from measuring exposure to examining the *risk* associated with the exposure. This chapter also applies the portfolio theory of currency movements to exchange risk management and international cash management with multiple currencies.

Foreign exchange risk provides the rationale for hedging foreign currency exposure, or activities that can prevent or reduce foreign exchange losses. Exposure alone is not enough to justify hedging, but the risk associated with it is. If individuals or companies are risk-averse—that is, have a preference for a sure amount of wealth over a gamble involving the same expected value but also the possibility of gains or losses—they will be better off when they hedge exposure. We examine financial hedges involving forward contracts and/or money market contracts, as well as futures and options contracts, in the next chapter.

8.2 EXCHANGE RISK WITH ONE CURRENCY

The last two chapters addressed a firm's foreign exchange exposure, but did not actually explain the risk associated with an exposure. **Foreign exchange risk** is the variability in the value of an exposure—a firm, subsidiary, project, or investment position—that is caused by uncertainty about exchange rate changes. As usual in finance, this risk is measured as a variance or standard deviation. In this case, we will examine the variance or standard deviation of exchange rates and their effect on changes in the value of the investment position.

Foreign exchange risk is a function of two underlying variables: the volatility of exchange rates and the degree of exposure. If the exchange rate is fixed and is expected to remain at the same rate, there is very little foreign exchange risk and managers should not be too concerned even if they are heavily exposed. This is because the degree to which cash flows can be affected by exchange rate changes is limited. If the firm is exposed but the variance of the exchange rate is very low, foreign exchange risk is small and managers should be only moderately concerned. This is because, even with heavy exposure, the value of the firm will not change much when exchange rates change. If the firm is exposed and the variance of the exchange rate is very high, managers should be quite concerned. In fact, managers should be more concerned the higher the exposure. It therefore follows that the magnitude of foreign exchange risk depends on a combination of the volatility of the exchange rate and the amount of foreign exchange exposure. However, the analysis is more complicated than is apparent because we are again often concerned with the volatility of real exchange rates rather than nominal exchange rates.

When the exchange rate is fixed in nominal terms, there is still foreign exchange risk because the real exchange rate changes when there are inflation differentials. Hence, the magnitude of foreign exchange risk more specifically depends on a combination of the volatility of real exchange rates and the amount of the foreign exchange exposure. As demonstrated later in this chapter, though, volatilities of nominal and real exchange rates are empirically very similar for most currencies, so a distinction is not always necessary in practical terms.

This chapter considers a simple formula for calculating foreign exchange risk: the product of the degree of exposure (converted to the home currency) and the standard deviation of percentage changes in the exchange rate for the relevant currency. In other words, we figure the standard deviation of a position based on information on the size of the position and the standard deviation of returns on the position:

$$\sigma(XS_{t+n}) = XS_t \times \sigma_{\%\Delta S}$$

where X is the exposure denominated in local currency. The exchange rates S_t and S_{t+n} are quoted as dollars per foreign currency, and $\sigma_{\%\Delta S}$ is the standard deviation of percentage changes in the exchange rate. Note that this formula does not directly figure the standard deviation of a position's future value. Using this formula is similar to figuring the standard deviation of a stock market position using the current value of the position and the standard deviation of returns on the stock rather than directly figuring the standard deviation of the future value of the stock. To account for an expected future value, the formula can be modified to:

$$\sigma(XS_{t+n}) = X \times E[S_{t+n}] \times \sigma_{\%\Delta S}.$$

EXAMPLE 8.1

Doug's Delights, a Chicago gourmet store, has a £1 million receivable due in one year. The standard deviation of the percentage changes in the $/£ exchange rate is 15 percentage points for a one-year horizon, and the distribution of percentage changes is assumed to be normal. Based on the published forward rate, Doug's Delights expects the exchange rate to be $2/£ in one year. The distribution of the future $/£ exchange rate is therefore centered at $2/£ with values for one, two, and three standard deviations as shown in the upper panel of Figure 8-1. The exchange rate will be within 15 percent of $2/£ with a probability of 68 percent, within 30 percent of $2/£ with a probability of 95 percent, and within 45 percent of $2/£ with a probability of 99.7 percent.

Based on the expected future spot rate of $2/£, Doug's Delights' £1 million receivable is expected to be worth $2 million. Furthermore, the foreign exchange risk of this position is $2 million × 15 percentage points = $300,000, resulting in the distribution shown in the lower panel of Figure 8-1. Doug's Delights can expect the value of the receivable to range from $1.7 million to $2.3 dollars with 68 percent probability, from $1.4 million to $2.6 million with 95 percent probability, and from $1.1 million to $2.9 million with 99.7 percent probability.

PERCENTAGE CHANGES IN EXCHANGE RATES

The assumption that the risk of an exposure is the product of the home currency value of the exposure and the standard deviation of percentage changes in the relevant exchange rate allows us to use formulas developed in portfolio investment theory to figure standard deviations of portfolios of exposures.[1] It also directly uses an empirical characteristic of exchange rate data: that percentage changes in exchange rates more closely follow the normal distribution than either levels of exchange rates or simple changes in exchange rates. There is disagreement about whether percentage changes in exchange rates are actually normally distributed, so we use the normal distribution as a convenient simplification. (Empirically, the tails in exchange rate distributions are often found to be fatter than suggested by the normal distribution.)

The standard deviation of the percentage changes in the exchange rate is also more useful than analyzing the standard deviation of the exchange rate itself (or the simple change in the exchange rate) because percentage changes can be directly compared across currencies. The standard deviation of percentage changes in the exchange rate also summarizes the risk that the change in the exchange rate will be different from what is anticipated, without requiring an explicit formulation of anticipated exchange rate changes.

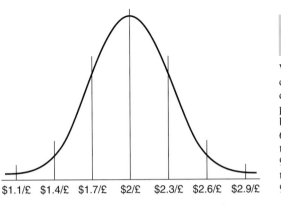

FIGURE 8-1   DISTRIBUTION OF $/£ EXCHANGE RATE AND VALUES OF A £1 MILLION RECEIVABLE

With an expected future spot exchange rate of $2/£ and a standard deviation of 15 percentage points, the exchange rate will be between $1.7/£ and $2.3/£ with 68% probability, will be between $1.4/£ and $2.6/£ with 95% probability, and will be between $1.1/£ and $2.9/£ with 99.7% probability.

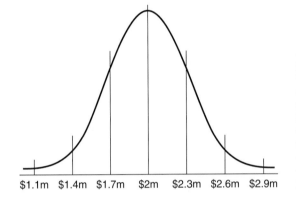

A £1 million receivable is expected to be worth $2 million when the expected future spot exchange rate is $2/£. The receivable is expected to be between $1.7 million and $2.3 million with 68% probability, between $1.4 million and $2.6 million with 95% probability, and between $1.1 million and $2.9 million with 99.7% probability.

For transactions that are contractually set in nominal amounts, the risk of nominal exchange rate changes is important. Hedging instruments, which are examined in the next chapter, are also defined in nominal terms. Hence, it is entirely appropriate to focus on nominal exchange rate changes and nominal exchange risk. In light of the purchasing power parity proposition that formed the basis of our analysis of economic exposure in Chapter 7, however, the exchange rate that is important for evaluating economic exchange risk is the real exchange rate. Due to problems with measuring inflation in short intervals, real exchange rate changes are somewhat hard to measure, so empirical work usually concentrates on nominal exchange rate changes in the short run. In practice, movements in nominal exchange rates generally reflect the real risk involved anyway, particularly for the currencies of developed countries. This is because, as discussed in Chapter 2, most nominal exchange rate changes reflect real exchange rate changes as well. Nevertheless, this chapter considers both nominal and real exchange rate changes to the extent possible, to demonstrate this point.

Table 8-1 presents the standard deviations of monthly, quarterly, and annual percentage changes for several exchange rates during the period 1977–1998. The DM/$ exchange rate, for example, is shown to have an unannualized standard deviation of 2.74 percentage points for a one-month holding period. The Italian lira/$ exchange rate is shown to have a standard deviation of 2.58 percentage points, making it less risky than the mark. The Canadian dollar is even less risky vis-à-vis the U.S. dollar, with a standard

TABLE 8-1 Standard Deviations of Percentage Changes in Exchange Rates (unannualized and annualized, 1977–1998)

| Currency | Monthly | | Quarterly | | Annual |
	Unannualized	Annualized	Unannualized	Annualized	
Euro	3.38	40.59	5.79	23.15	12.84
UK Pound	2.66	31.97	5.31	21.23	12.65
French Franc	2.66	31.95	5.49	21.95	12.84
German Mark	2.74	32.89	5.68	22.73	12.34
Italian Lira	2.58	30.93	5.58	22.32	12.64
Swiss Franc	3.18	38.16	6.66	26.66	13.52
Canadian Dollar	1.06	12.68	1.91	7.65	4.78
Japanese Yen	3.10	37.15	6.15	24.59	13.06
Australian Dollar	2.21	26.49	4.57	18.29	9.84
Mexican Peso	5.58	66.96	12.26	49.05	34.33
Argentine Peso	15.42	185.05	37.38	149.53	108.49
Chilean Peso	2.48	29.75	5.96	23.86	16.49
Brazilian Real	11.49	137.94	31.06	124.24	104.21

Source: Authors' calculations based on data in International Monetary Fund, International Financial Statistics.

deviation of 1.06. The riskiest currency listed is the Argentine peso, with a standard deviation of 15.42 percentage points.

EXAMPLE 8.2

Doug's Delights, the Chicago gourmet store, has just booked a £1 million receivable due in one month. The standard deviation of the percentage changes in the $/£ exchange rate is 3.4 percentage points for a one-month horizon, and the distribution of percentage changes is assumed to be normal. Based on the published 30-day forward rate, Doug's Delights expects the exchange rate to be $2/£ in one month, so Doug's Delights' £1 million receivable is expected to be worth $2 million. Furthermore, the foreign exchange risk of this position is $2 million × 3.4 percentage points = $68,000. Doug's Delights can expect the value of the receivable to range from $1,932,000 to $2,068,000 dollars with 68 percent probability, from $1,864,000 to $2,136,000 with 95 percent probability, and from $1,796,000 to $2,204,000 with 99.7 percent probability, in one month.

The standard deviations in Table 8-1 clearly depend on the length of the holding period, so the magnitude of foreign exchange risk also depends on the length of the holding period. Note that the unannualized standard deviations increase as the holding period lengthens from one month to one quarter to one year. Hence, exposures held for a short period are not as risky as exposures held for a longer period simply because there isn't as much time to experience exchange rate changes. However, note that the quarterly standard deviations are clearly less than three times the monthly standard deviations and that the annual standard deviations are less than twelve times the monthly standard deviations or four times the quarterly standard deviations.

This means that an exposure held for one quarter is not three times as risky as an exposure held for one month, or that an exposure held for one year is not twelve times as risky as an exposure held for one month or four times as risky as an exposure held for one quarter. In fact, note that the annualized standard deviations decline as the holding period increases from one month to one quarter, and from one quarter to one year.

Hence, a position held for a longer period of time is less risky than a position held for a short period of time on an annualized basis.

There is really nothing magical about this, because a quarter consists of three draws from the monthly distribution and a year consists of twelve draws from the monthly distribution or four draws from the quarterly distribution. Specifically, consider the quarterly distribution. If the variance of monthly percentage changes in the exchange rate is constant and the exchange rate changes are independent across three months in a quarter, the variance of annualized percentage changes for a quarter is simply one-third of the variance of annualized percentage changes for a month.[2] The quarterly annualized standard deviation is therefore $\sqrt{1/3}$ times the monthly annualized standard deviation. Similarly, the annual standard deviation is $\sqrt{1/12}$ times the monthly annualized standard deviation or $\sqrt{1/4}$ times the quarterly annualized standard deviation.

8.3   EXCHANGE RISK WITH MULTIPLE CURRENCIES

Exchange risk management is not easy when just one foreign currency is of concern, so it should be obvious that exchange risk management is even harder when two or more foreign currencies are involved. The central problem in assessing foreign exchange exposure and risk with multiple currencies is that exposures and risks in different currencies cannot simply be added together. When exposures in two foreign currencies are being analyzed, the correlation of the currency movements vis-à-vis the home currency becomes extremely important. If the two foreign currencies are highly positively correlated, meaning that they tend to move together with respect to the home currency, then they can be treated as effectively the same currency. The total exposure, then, is approximately the sum of the two separate exposures. If the two currencies are not perfectly correlated, however, the total exposure should not be considered the sum of the two separate positions, but, rather, something less. This is because gains in one position may be expected to offset losses on another position, at least to some degree. Clearly, the magnitude of exchange risk depends on how currencies fluctuate with respect to each other.

When exchange rates are not highly positively correlated, **currency diversification** reduces the overall foreign exchange risk. Currency diversification is the activity of holding a portfolio of many currency exposures to avoid excessive exposure to any one source of currency risk. Well-diversified firms face less foreign exchange risk than poorly-diversified firms for a given aggregate level of exposure. This section rigorously examines foreign exchange risk with multiple currencies and how firms can reduce risk.

NOMINAL EXCHANGE RATE CHANGES

To examine exchange risk management with multiple currencies, we must begin by examining correlations and covariances of the currencies. Table 8-2 presents the correlation matrix and the covariance matrix for annualized quarterly percentage changes of several currencies vis-à-vis the U.S. dollar for the period 1977 to 1998. The correlation table indicates, for example, that the correlation between the French franc and the German mark is very high (.956), which would lead us to treat exposures in the two currencies as being practically in the same currency. In fact, now that the German mark and French franc are irrevocably fixed to each other as part of European monetary

TABLE 8-2   Covariances and Correlations of Percentage Changes in Exchange Rates

Covariance Matrix

	UK	France	Germany	Italy	Switzerland	Canada	Japan	Australia	Mexico
UK	446.0								
France	325.4	479.8							
Germany	342.5	475.4	515.1						
Italy	350.4	435.9	435.7	495.2					
Switzerland	392.2	499.6	542.9	465.6	707.2				
Canada	29.7	15.6	10.4	26.8	8.2	61.7			
Japan	251.1	324.5	346.5	274.5	441.2	6.7	599.1		
Australia	110.2	80.5	58.8	81.6	73.8	54.3	114.6	334.9	
Mexico	−48.3	−123.3	−232.6	−84.9	−238.9	−18.8	−86.3	212.4	2391.9

Correlation Matrix

	UK	France	Germany	Italy	Switzerland	Canada	Japan	Australia	Mexico
UK	1								
France	0.703	1							
Germany	0.715	0.956	1						
Italy	0.746	0.894	0.863	1					
Switzerland	0.698	0.858	0.899	0.787	1				
Canada	0.179	0.090	0.058	0.153	0.039	1			
Japan	0.486	0.605	0.624	0.504	0.678	0.035	1		
Australia	0.285	0.201	0.142	0.200	0.152	0.377	0.256	1	
Mexico	−0.047	−0.115	−0.210	−0.078	−0.184	−0.049	−0.072	0.237	1

Source: Authors' calculations based on data in International Monetary Fund, International Financial Statistics.

unification, the correlation is expected to be unity in the future. This means that the risk of a portfolio of exposures in these two currencies is the simple sum of the standard deviations of the separate positions.

The correlation between the Canadian dollar and the German mark, however, is close to zero, suggesting that we could treat the exposures as being statistically independent. There are therefore substantial advantages of currency diversification in this case, so the risk of a portfolio of exposures in these two currencies is considerably less than the sum of the standard deviations of the separate positions.

Formally, the variance of the value of a portfolio of n assets is:

$$\sum_{i=1}^{n} Q_i^2 \, \text{Var}(R_i) + \sum_{i=1}^{n} \sum_{j=1}^{n} Q_i Q_j \, \text{Cov}(R_i, R_j)$$
$$\text{for } i \neq j$$

where Q_i is the aggregate value of each asset i held, and R_i is the return on the asset. As the covariance between two currencies equals their correlation coefficient multiplied by their standard deviations, this equation is equal to:

$$\sum_{i=1}^{n} Q_i^2 \, \text{Var}(R_i) + \sum_{i=1}^{n} \sum_{j=1}^{n} Q_i Q_j \, \text{Corr}(R_i, R_j) \sqrt{\text{Var}(R_i) \, \text{Var}(R_j)}$$

for $i \neq j$. These formulas can be used to determine the variances of various portfolios to choose the least risky alternative.[3]

EXAMPLE 8.3

Suppose the variance of annualized quarterly percentage changes in the lira/\$ exchange rate is 525 percentage points squared and the variance of percentage changes in the DM/\$ exchange rate is 560 percentage points squared. Also suppose that the correlation coefficient between these two currencies is 0.96, so that the covariance is 520 percentage points squared. The exchange risk associated with exposure consisting of \$100 worth of Italian lira and \$100 worth of DM is almost the simple sum of the standard deviations of the lira and the DM because the correlation is very high. Letting R_{IL} denote the percentage changes in the Italian lira and R_{DM} denote the percentage changes in the DM,

$$100^2 \, \mathrm{Var}(R_{IL}) + 100^2 \, \mathrm{Var}(R_{DM}) + 2(100^2) \, \mathrm{Cov}(R_{IL}, R_{DM})$$
$$= 100^2 [\mathrm{Var}(R_{IL}) + \mathrm{Var}(R_{DM}) + 2 \, \mathrm{Cov}(R_{IL}, R_{DM})]$$
$$= 100^2 [525 + 562 + 2(520)]$$
$$= 100^2 [2127]$$

so the standard deviation is 4612 cents or \$46.12 on the \$200 portfolio. This is somewhat less than the simple sum of the standard deviations of the lira and the DM, which is \$46.58, but is close because the correlation is very high.

EXAMPLE 8.4

Suppose the variance of annualized quarterly percentage changes in the British pound is 540 and the variance of the Mexican peso is 1900. The correlation between these two currencies is zero, so the covariance is zero.

The exchange risk associated with exposure consisting of \$100 worth of British pounds and \$100 worth of Mexican pesos is therefore substantially less than the sum of the separate standard deviations because the currency movements are independent. Using the same formula used in the previous example, the variance is $100^2 [540 + 1900] = 100^2 [2440]$ so the standard deviation is \$49.40 on the \$200 portfolio. Note that this is considerably less than the simple sum of the separate standard deviations, which is \$66.83, because of the lack of correlation.

REAL EXCHANGE RATE CHANGES

We focused on nominal exchange rate changes. When inflation differentials affect nominal exchange rates, however, we know that exposure should be measured with respect to deviations from purchasing power parity (PPP). The analysis of correlations and covariances is therefore more meaningful when carried out using real exchange rates. Consider the Mexican peso, for example. This currency has historically moved in just one direction—down—so we should be interested in the volatility of the real exchange rate rather than the volatility of the nominal exchange rate. Purely nominal changes in exchange rates therefore should not be attributed to exchange risk.

Table 8-3 presents correlation and covariance matrixes of annualized percentage changes in real exchange rates. As before, the real exchange rate is calculated using the transformation:

$$e_t = S_t P_t^* / P_t$$

where the spot exchange rate is quoted in U.S. dollars per local currency and e_t denotes the real spot exchange rate. From Table 8-3 it is clear that the variance of the Mexican

TABLE 8-3   Covariances and Correlations of Percentage Changes in Real Exchange Rates

Covariance Matrix

	UK	France	Germany	Italy	Switzerland	Canada	Japan	Australia	Mexico
UK	491.1								
France	319.8	462.2							
Germany	339.7	465.0	518.8						
Italy	357.9	418.7	427.8	490.7					
Switzerland	391.1	495.4	541.4	461.6	707.4				
Canada	25.9	18.3	19.2	33.7	23.9	64.5			
Japan	257.4	322.1	350.2	284.0	452.0	22.1	616.6		
Australia	126.3	109.3	97.6	111.0	116.1	59.9	133.9	349.7	
Mexico	6.4	−46.7	−101.7	13.7	−148.3	−4.3	39.9	121.7	1561.3

Correlation Matrix

	UK	France	Germany	Italy	Switzerland	Canada	Japan	Australia	Mexico
UK	1								
France	0.671	1							
Germany	0.673	0.950	1						
Italy	0.729	0.879	0.848	1					
Switzerland	0.664	0.866	0.894	0.784	1				
Canada	0.145	0.106	0.105	0.189	0.112	1			
Japan	0.468	0.603	0.619	0.516	0.684	0.111	1		
Australia	0.305	0.272	0.229	0.268	0.233	0.399	0.288	1	
Mexico	−0.007	−0.055	−0.113	−0.016	−0.141	−0.014	−0.041	0.165	1

Source: Authors' calculations based on data in International Monetary Fund, International Financial Statistics.

peso is much smaller when analyzed in real terms: 1561 versus 2392. The peso is simply not as risky to hold in real terms as it appears in nominal terms. The variances of the other currencies do not change as much, demonstrating that nominal exchange rate changes primarily reflect real exchange rate changes for these countries.

By calculating the percentage changes of the real exchange rate, we are calculating precisely the deviations from purchasing power parity examined in Chapters 2 and 7. The "Tools for Analysis" at the end of this chapter provides a mathematical exposition of this. The point, once again, is that when inflation differentials affect nominal exchange rate changes, foreign exchange exposure and risk should be measured with respect to deviations from PPP. Analyzing exchange risk with multiple currencies using real exchange rates takes this into account.

EXAMPLE 8.5

Suppose the variance of percentage changes in the real British pound is 578, and the variance of the real Mexican peso is 795. Also, suppose that the correlation between these two currencies is zero, so the covariance is zero. The real exchange risk associated with exposure consisting of $100 worth of British pounds and $100 worth of Mexican pesos is less than the nominal exchange risk leads us to believe. The variance is $100^2 [578 + 795] = 100^2 [1373]$, so the standard deviation is $37.05 on the $200 portfolio. Note that this is less than the standard deviation of the nominal exchange rates, which was $49.40, because holding the peso is not as risky in real terms as it appears in nominal terms.

MANAGING EXCHANGE RISK WITH MULTIPLE CURRENCIES

Centralized exchange risk management can reduce the overall foreign exchange risk at a low cost by taking advantage of the portfolio diversification effect, and this is the major advantage of centralized foreign exchange risk management compared to the alternative of decentralizing management to the foreign affiliates. The centralized exchange risk manager is able to net the exposure positions of several subsidiaries against one another and identify what the main sources of currency risk are. For example, French automaker Renault considers the geographic diversification in risk analysis. According to Thierry Moulonguet, deputy director of Renault's finance department, "We deal in the Deutschemark, the British pound, the Italian lira, the Spanish peseta, and other [European currencies]. . . . We feel that so many currencies gives us a natural hedge, that the balance of countries is a hedge in itself. Clearly, there are times when currency movements are going to hurt you, but overall, we think our policy is sound."[4]

EXAMPLE 8.6

The following matrix presents the variances and covariances of the monthly changes in real exchange rates for the French franc, Swiss franc, and Mexican peso. Above the diagonal, the correlation coefficients are provided.

	French franc	*Swiss franc*	*Mexican peso*
French franc	12.6	.87	−.19
Swiss franc	12.4	16.1	−.21
Mexican peso	−5.5	−6.9	64.3

R.J. Enterprises has three divisions, each with an exposure of $100,000 worth of foreign currency; one is long in French francs, one is short in Swiss francs, and one is long in Mexican pesos. As exchange risk manager, Dan Sang is concerned with the risk of the aggregate exposure and ways to reduce it. Letting R_{FF} represent the percentage changes in the French franc, R_{SF} represent the percentage changes in the Swiss franc, and R_{MP} represent the percentage changes in the Mexican peso, the variance of the portfolio is:

$$100000^2[\text{Var}(R_{FF}) + \text{Var}(R_{SF}) + \text{Var}(R_{MP}) - 2\,\text{Cov}(R_{FF}, R_{SF})$$
$$+ 2\,\text{Cov}(R_{FF}, R_{MP}) - 2\,\text{Cov}(R_{SF}, R_{MP})]$$
$$= 100000^2[12.6 + 16.1 + 64.3 - 2(12.4) + 2(-5.5) - 2(-6.9)]$$
$$= 100000^2[71]$$

so the standard deviation is 842,610 cents or $8,426 out of a $100,000 portfolio. Mr. Sang knows that centralized exposure management can reduce the amount of hedging necessary. He recognizes that the French franc and the Swiss franc are highly correlated. This means that the long position in French francs is offset almost entirely by the short position in Swiss francs, so he does not need to hedge these two exposures. The standard deviation of the aggregate exposure is due almost entirely to the risk from the Mexican peso position. A single exposure of $100,000 worth of pesos would be associated with a standard deviation of about $8,000, and this is the bulk of the $8,426 total exposure, so the most important hedge would simply be on the Mexican peso position. This would leave a portfolio with a variance of $100000^2[12.6 + 16.1 - 2(12.4)] = 100000^2[3.9]$ or a standard deviation of $1,975.

The centralized exposure manager can be aided in his task of reducing exchange risk by using an optimization program that is capable of figuring the minimum variance portfolio of exposures. These programs generally solve for optimal shares, or weights, given a variance-covariance matrix. Formally, the program minimizes:

$$\sum_{i=1}^{n} Q_i^2 \, \text{Var}(R_i) + \sum_{i=1}^{n} \sum_{j=1}^{n} Q_i Q_j \, \text{Cov}(R_i, R_j)$$
$$\text{for } i \neq j$$

subject to:

$$\sum_{i=1}^{n} Q_i = 1$$

and given the variance-covariance matrix, where the Q_i are now interpreted as weights, or proportions of total exposure. Although the exposure manager can be aided in his task of reducing exposure by referring to the minimum-variance portfolio, this does not mean that the goal of the manager should be to minimize variance, because there are indeed costs to achieving such a portfolio. Such costs include both transactions costs and managerial costs.

By solving the optimization problem, though, the manger is able to see what the best pattern of moving out of different currencies or into other currencies would be. The solution to the optimization problem should give the manager a good idea of what the minimum attainable risk level for the portfolio of exposures is, given the currencies and exposure positions used. Sensitivity analysis can be conducted by consecutively dropping (or even adding) currencies which the manager is not willing (or is willing) to hold. By excluding certain currencies, such as the Mexican peso in the example above, the manager would be indicating a preference for completely hedging these currencies. To completely eliminate risk, of course, the manager would exclude all foreign currencies and end up holding only the U.S. dollar, the home currency. The program can also be amended to account for transactions costs, such as the bank fee for converting a foreign currency into dollars or the costs of acquiring a hedge for a position. The manager can thus use the program to evaluate the trade-off between risk reduction and the costs of hedging.

APPLICATION 8-1

VALUE AT RISK

Risk management has become a major endeavor by academics, practitioners, and regulators, and a cornerstone of recent interest is a class of models called "Value at Risk" (VAR) models. In short, VAR summarizes the greatest possible loss over a specified horizon within a given confidence interval. For example, a $20 million portfolio might have a value at risk of $3.94 million for one month at the 95 percent confidence interval, which means that the value of the portfolio will decline no more than $3.92 million during the next month 95 times out of 100.

The most common VAR models estimate variance-covariance matrixes of asset returns using historical time series, and assume that the distributions of asset returns are normal. Portfolio risk is a function of the risk of each asset and the correlations among the returns on the assets, as described in this chapter. The value at risk is calculated from the standard deviation of the portfolio, given the appropriate horizon, and the critical values of the normal distribution. Suppose the standard deviation of a portfolio of currency exposures is 10 percentage

APPLICATION 8-1 (cont.)

points for a one-year horizon. Since 95 percent of all returns fall within 1.96 standard deviations of the mean return, the value at risk of a $20 million portfolio is:

$$VAR = 0.10 \times 1.96 \times \$20 \text{ million}$$
$$= \$3.92 \text{ million.}$$

Management may convey this information in non-technical language by saying something like, "The most we can lose over a year, under normal market conditions, is $3.92 million."

Several commercial VAR models are available, including J.P. Morgan's RiskMetrics and Banker's Trust's RAROC. The models have been developed primarily for assessing the risk of banks and other financial firms, and U.S. bank regulatory agencies now require commercial banks to use VAR assessment to determine the amount of capital required to cover the market risk exposure of trading activities. However, VAR models are increasingly being applied to nonfinancial firms—particularly to multinational corporations—and the U.S. Securities and Exchange Commission now requires companies to disclose information about their market risks and derivatives activities which may be reported as value at risk.

The Ford Motor Company provides an example of value at risk analysis applied to a multinational corporation. It reports in its 1998 Annual Report that it uses a VAR analysis to evaluate foreign exchange exposure:

"The primary assumptions used in the VAR analysis are as follows:

- A historical time series analysis (variance/covariance) is used to calculate changes in the value of currency derivative instruments (forwards and options) and all significant underlying exposures. The VAR includes an 18-month exposure horizon and a one-month holding period.

- The VAR analysis calculates the potential risk, within a 99% confidence level, on firm commitment exposures (cash flows), including the effects of foreign currency derivatives. (Translation exposures are not included in the VAR analysis.) The model generally assumes currency prices are normally distributed and draws volatility data from the currency markets.

- Estimates of correlations of market factors primarily are drawn from the JP Morgan RiskMetrics datasets.

Based on our overall currency exposure (including derivative positions) during 1998, the risk during 1998 to our pre-tax cash flow from currency movements was on average less than $300 million, with a high of $350 million and a low of $200 million. At December 31, 1998, currency movements are projected to affect our pre-tax cash flow over the next 18 months by less than $325 million, within a 99% confidence level. Compared with our projection at December 31, 1997, the 1998 VAR amount is approximately $75 million higher, primarily because of increased currency exchange rate volatility and increased exposure. (Ford Motor Company 1998 Annual Report, p. 42.)"

For more on VAR, see Simons (1996) for an introduction or Jorion (1997) for a comprehensive treatment.

EXCHANGE RISK AND THE VARIABILITY OF CASH FLOWS

The previous analysis gives an idea of the risk involved with a portfolio of exposures, but does not relate the risk to an overall volatility for the firm. The portfolio standard deviation we have determined could be large or small when compared to the standard deviation of total cash flows or the value of the firm. Hence, some comparison of the two is ultimately necessary. One way would be to construct a simple ratio of the exposure portfolio's standard deviation to the standard deviation of the value of the firm's cash flows, or to the standard deviation of the firm's market value, both of which would indicate the level of foreign exchange risk as a percent of total risk.

There is also a way of evaluating foreign exchange risk when ongoing cash flows or the value of the firm are being evaluated based on regression analysis. Chapter 7 presented a regression of foreign exchange exposure which produced an empirical measurement of the level of exposure. This regression is analogous to exchange risk. Statistically, a useful measure of exchange risk is the R^2 value representing the percent of variation in the dependent variable explained by the independent variables. If the R^2 statistic is low, not much of the variability of the dependent variable (the left-hand variable, such as cash flow or market value of the firm) can be explained by variation in the exchange rate, so there is not a great deal of exchange risk.

This observation is separate from the value of the beta coefficient, the estimate of the exposure. A regression could have a statistically significant beta coefficient and still have a low R^2, indicating that there is indeed foreign exchange exposure but that it does not affect the dependent variable (cash flows or the market value) very much. If the R^2 is high, however, the exchange rate variability explains a large amount of cash flow (or market value) variability, so there is a significant level of exchange risk. The numerical values of low and high R^2s are hard to define. As exchange rate movements are usually not the major forces driving cash flows or market values, the R^2 statistics in these equa-

---

APPLICATION 8-2

FOREIGN EXCHANGE RISK MANAGEMENT AT 3M

Minnesota Mining and Manufacturing, the 3M Company, depends on non-U.S. markets for slightly more than half of its corporate sales. The company is thus concerned about exchange rates and foreign exchange risk associated with these sales. In 1998, for example, foreign sales volume increased about 4 percent and foreign selling prices were up about 2 percent, but this 6 percent total increase in foreign sales revenue was completely undone by a 6 percent depreciation of the foreign currencies against the dollar.

Foreign sales are also typically associated with foreign-currency-denominated costs, reducing net exposure. For example, about 75 percent of 3M sales in Brazil (representing 6 percent of total sales) are from locally produced products, helping to protect Brazilian sales and profits from a weakening Brazilian real. Nevertheless, flat foreign sales in 1998 were also associated with a small (2 percent) decline in foreign operating income, so costs clearly did not decline enough. "A financial

risk management committee, composed of senior management, provides oversight for risk management and derivative activities. This committee determines the company's financial risk policies and objectives, and provides guidelines for derivative instrument utilization (3M Company 1998 Annual Report, p. 26)." 3M's foreign sales occur throughout Europe, the Middle East, Asia, the Pacific, Latin America, Africa, and Canada, and are therefore well diversified. Costs are similarly well diversified. The risk management committee recognizes this diversification: "Our wide geographic presence and extensive local manufacturing capability help minimize the company's overall currency risk (p. 26)."

With relatively little overall currency risk, relatively little hedging is necessary. In fact, based on derivative instruments outstanding at December 31, 1998, the company estimates that probable near-term changes in exchange rates would not materially affect its financial statements or operations.

Source: The 3M Company 1998 Annual Report.

tions are never very high. In practice, an R^2 of just a few percent is usually enough to be concerned about.

Foreign exchange risk with multiple currencies can also be compared to the total variability of the cash flows by using the regression analysis method. The only difference is that real cash flows at time t, RCF_t, are regressed onto several different real exchange rates, e_{1t}, e_{2t}, and so on. The equation would be:

$$RCF_t = \alpha + \beta_1 e_{1t} + \beta_2 e_{2t} + \cdots + u_t$$

where the coefficients β_1, β_2, etc., measure the exposure of cash flows with respect to different foreign currencies. The R^2 statistic from this regression again gives an indication of the total foreign exchange risk vis-à-vis the overall variability of cash flows. Once again, the methodology is generally applicable in that the market value of the firm or similar data can be used as the dependent variable. With multiple currencies, some care should be exercised to use distinctly different currencies as independent variables.

As we have seen, the empirical characteristics of some currencies are practically indistinguishable from others, as is the case for currencies in the European monetary union. For such currencies, including more than one currency from the group would lead to multicollinearity in the regression, and might produce dubious results. Hence, it may be appropriate to use just one European currency as a proxy for all European currencies.

8.4 EXCHANGE RISK IN INTERNATIONAL CASH MANAGEMENT

This section considers a specialized application of the principles addressed in the section on foreign exchange risk with multiple currencies to the study of international cash management. In this section, **cash management** refers to the manipulation of short-term financial assets which serve as a store of wealth for the firm. Cash can be held in national treasury bills, money markets, and offshore deposits, among other short-term financial assets. When a portfolio of cash is examined, as opposed to a portfolio of exposures, managers will be inclined to pay attention to the nominal rates of return on the various currencies.

For all short-term financial assets or deposits, there is a nominal interest rate that varies by currency. It is therefore natural to think about a trade-off between the return on the deposit and the riskiness of the currency. Cash managers may be willing to hold more risk if it is compensated by higher returns. The portfolio problem therefore becomes more complex because it no longer relates to variances and covariances alone. In the presence of expected returns, the problem becomes a standard mean-variance optimization problem. The analysis including expected returns also alters the variance-covariance matrix, because it incorporates interest rate volatility and the covariances of interest rates with exchange rate changes into the covariance matrix.

The analysis contained in the rest of this section introduces the returns associated with short-term deposits, and acknowledges the importance of mean-variance optimization, but proceeds to dispel the importance of nominal returns in international cash management. The thesis of this section is that currency co-movements should be the major focus of international cash management. Currency diversification reduces the overall risk of the cash portfolio, and in exactly the same way that diversification reduces the exchange risk associated with a portfolio of exposures. Incorporating expected returns into a mean-variance optimization problem is a natural activity. Cleary, however, if the uncovered interest parity proposition holds, the dollar-denominated returns in all currencies are expected to be the same:

$$R^*_{t,t+n} + a\{E_t[\%\Delta S_{t,t+n}]\} = R_{t,t+n}$$

from the uncovered interest parity equation. Consider what happens if uncovered interest parity holds especially well in the short-term offshore deposit markets where investors can quickly and easily move in and out of different currencies with just a phone call.[5] Because the expected dollar returns are the same in all currencies, there is no risk/return trade-off and the analysis of risk alone is sufficient for the cash management decisions. Mean-variance optimization simply produces the minimum variance portfolio.

The previous discussion suggests there are two possible approaches to international cash management: an analysis of nominal returns and an analysis of deviations from uncovered interest parity. Table 8-4 presents the variance-covariance and correlation ma-

TABLE 8-4   Covariances and Correlations of Returns on Deposits

Covariance Matrix

	US	UK	France	Germany	Italy	Switzerland	Canada	Japan	Australia	Mexico
US	8.6									
UK	−2.4	480.5								
France	−8.6	322.1	465.6							
Germany	−6.5	344.9	464.9	508.7						
Italy	−3.6	340.9	410.0	414.4	466.9					
Switzerland	−7.5	393.7	493.6	538.2	449.7	712.9				
Canada	12.4	35.2	24.2	20.5	38.3	21.8	83.2			
Japan	−6.5	253.7	326.0	342.6	266.0	439.7	15.6	603.0		
Australia	0.3	129.4	100.3	81.6	104.0	95.7	65.7	122.5	356.1	
Mexico	−8.8	−8.1	−90.3	−191.9	−1.2	−199.5	53.8	−14.0	206.0	2236.8

Correlation Matrix

	US	UK	France	Germany	Italy	Switzerland	Canada	Japan	Australia	Mexico
US	1									
UK	−0.037	1								
France	−0.135	0.681	1							
Germany	−0.098	0.698	0.955	1						
Italy	−0.056	0.720	0.879	0.850	1					
Switzerland	−0.096	0.673	0.857	0.894	0.780	1				
Canada	0.465	0.176	0.123	0.100	0.195	0.089	1			
Japan	−0.090	0.471	0.615	0.619	0.501	0.671	0.069	1		
Australia	0.006	0.313	0.246	0.192	0.255	0.190	0.382	0.264	1	
Mexico	−0.064	−0.008	−0.089	−0.180	−0.001	−0.158	0.125	−0.012	0.231	1

Source: Authors' calculations based on data in International Monetary Fund, International Financial Statistics.

trixes for the dollar-equivalent nominal returns on foreign currency deposits. The volatility of the deposit consists of the volatility of the nominal foreign interest rate, the volatility of the percentage changes in the exchange rate, and (twice) the covariance between these two items.

DEVIATIONS FROM UNCOVERED INTEREST PARITY

The second approach to international cash management involves an analysis of deviations from uncovered interest parity. This method is preferable because, just as exposure of physical assets was best measured theoretically by deviations from PPP, the exposure of monetary assets and liabilities is best measured theoretically by deviations from UIP.

Chapter 2 established that most *ex post* deviations from uncovered interest parity are due to deviations from PPP, suggesting that the volatility of *ex post* deviations from uncovered interest parity is likely to be approximated by deviations from PPP. In fact, this is confirmed by looking at Table 8-5, the covariance and correlation matrixes for *ex post* deviations from uncovered interest parity. For most currencies, Table 8-5 is not very different from Table 8-3. By looking at the volatility of deviations from PPP only, we would ignore the volatility of the other three components and all the covariance terms. For international cash management, however, a firm may want to diversify inflation risk, so may want to do a full analysis of the volatility of deviations from uncovered

TABLE 8-5 Covariances and Correlations of Excess Returns on Deposits

Covariance Matrix

	UK	France	Germany	Italy	Switzerland	Canada	Japan	Australia	Mexico
UK	493.8								
France	341.6	491.3							
Germany	362.4	488.5	530.2						
Italy	355.4	430.7	433.0	482.6					
Switzerland	412.1	518.3	560.8	469.3	736.4				
Canada	33.8	29.0	23.2	38.1	25.4	67.0			
Japan	271.1	349.6	364.2	284.7	462.2	18.2	624.6		
Australia	140.1	117.1	96.4	115.8	111.5	61.6	137.2	364.0	
Mexico	11.6	−64.4	−168.0	19.7	−174.7	58.8	9.9	223.0	2262.9

Correlation Matrix

	UK	France	Germany	Italy	Switzerland	Canada	Japan	Australia	Mexico
UK	1								
France	0.694	1							
Germany	0.708	0.957	1						
Italy	0.728	0.885	0.856	1					
Switzerland	0.683	0.862	0.897	0.787	1				
Canada	0.186	0.160	0.123	0.212	0.114	1			
Japan	0.488	0.631	0.633	0.519	0.681	0.089	1		
Australia	0.330	0.277	0.219	0.276	0.215	0.395	0.288	1	
Mexico	0.011	−0.061	−0.153	0.019	−0.135	0.151	0.008	0.246	1

Source: Authors' calculations based on data in International Monetary Fund, International Financial Statistics.

interest parity using information like that contained in Table 8-5. A simple focus on volatility of deviations from PPP is likely to be useful under most circumstances because it is similar to the full analysis. Ignoring interest rate volatility implicitly assumes that the real currency changes are the most significant elements of risk when dealing with international cash management.

The conclusion from the previous analysis is that international cash management is largely the same activity as exchange risk management with multiple currencies, whether the focus is on deviations from PPP or deviations from UIP. Currency diversification again reduces the overall risk of the cash portfolio, and central management of the portfolio can reduce risk further. This diversification is a major advantage of centralizing cash management rather than decentralizing it to the subsidiary level.

EXAMPLE 8.7

Lemberg, Inc., is a holding company in Boston that operates manufacturing subsidiaries throughout the world. Lemberg's subsidiaries in Germany, Italy, Canada, and Brazil are each holding $100,000 worth of local currency as precautionary cash balances. The variances and covariances of the monthly returns in excess of U.S. dollar returns are given below.

	mark	lira	C $	real
German mark	9.6	.96	.32	.12
Italian lira	8.3	7.8	.33	.19
Canadian dollar	1.0	0.9	1.1	.16
Brazilian real	3.3	4.6	1.5	75.1

The variance of Lemberg's portfolio viewed from its Boston headquarters is

$$100{,}000^2[9.6 + 7.8 + 1.1 + 75.1 + 2(8.3) + 2(1.0) + 2(3.3) + 2(0.9) + 2(4.6) + 2(1.5)]$$
$$= 100{,}000^2[132.8]$$

so the standard deviation is $11,524 on the $400,000 portfolio. To reduce the standard deviation, a centralized money manager would reduce holdings in the DM and lira as they are practically the same currency. She could move money into the Canadian dollar because its volatility is very low. For example, converting $100,000 from the German mark into the Canadian dollar reduces the standard deviation to $100{,}000^2[7.8 + 4(1.1) + 75.1 + 4(0.9) + 2(4.6) + 4(1.5)] = \$10{,}300$. The manager could also adopt hedges to reduce risk further, such as eliminating exposure in the Brazilian real as it is the most volatile. Holding a portfolio of $200,000 worth of lira and $200,000 worth of Canadian dollars, for example, produces a standard deviation of $6,542.

Being able to optimally rearrange the portfolio composition of cash balances is the major advantage of centralized cash management. Beyond simply rearranging the portfolio, the centralized cash manager can decide which hedges she should apply to reduce the standard deviation of the portfolio further. Similarly, the manager can decide what currencies to move out of altogether by converting positions into dollars. If entirely eliminating risk is the objective, the cash balances should all be centralized and held in U.S. dollars. The firm's objective largely depends on the magnitude of foreign exchange risk resulting from holding cash balances in comparison to overall foreign exchange risk. For most nonfinancial firms, risk in cash management is likely to be a small component of overall risk. However, because it is more manageable than other forms of risk, it usually receives a lot of attention.

TREASURY MANAGEMENT
AT PROCTER & GAMBLE

Over the past decade, Procter & Gamble has centralized a wide variety of treasury functions in its Cincinnati headquarters. According to Roger C. Stewart, assistant treasurer for global treasury, "We've spent a large sum to build a global treasury database that will help us manage foreign-exchange exposures, outstanding debt and our investment portfolio."

Procter & Gamble, a global consumer products company, sells in 140 countries and has full production and sales operations in 55 countries. In 1994, global sales totaled $30 billion, approximately half of which were foreign, and profits were $2.2 billion. The firm holds approximately $2.3 billion in global cash and short-term investments. Its foreign exchange exposures are in the billions of dollars as well, because it ships raw materials and finished products from one country to another and because it earns a significant portion of its profits in foreign currencies. (In fact, more than one-third of its exposure is cross-currency, between Deutsche marks and French francs or Deutsche marks and British pounds, rather than simply vis-à-vis the dollar.) Procter & Gamble also has $1 billion of foreign-currency debt in its portfolio of $6.3 billion of external debt.

Centralization of the treasury operations has taken place over the past ten years. Before 1985, Procter & Gamble was very decentralized, with each subsidiary doing virtually all of its own foreign exchange, cash management, and borrowing. Regional consolidation took place between 1985 and 1993, as the company established supranational treasury operations in offices in Europe, Asia, Latin America, Eastern Europe, the Far East, and a few other areas. In 1994, the company began to look at treasury operations on a global basis to capture greater economies of scale.

The system currently in place has regional treasurers in charge of Europe, Latin America, and the Far East. In fact, Procter & Gamble opened a financial services company, Dublin Docks, in Ireland in 1994 to house its global cash pool and debt. In Cincinnati, however, Mr. Stewart has a global cash/investment manager, a foreign exchange risk manager, and a global debt manager. These officers work with the regional treasurers to develop strategies, policies, and procedures, and then report to the vice president and treasurer.

Although centralization requires "a lot of paperwork and phone calls," and there are a lot of nuances from a tax standpoint (on investment returns, pricing on debt and foreign exchange, and so on), Procter & Gamble expects to have increased returns on its cash, better risk management of foreign exchange, and savings on borrowing costs by pooling the companies' positions. In addition, centralization is providing increased knowledge of subsidiaries' activities around the world. According to Stewart, "I'm much more at ease now that I can tell senior management what our income statement's going to look like at 1.7 Deutsche marks to the dollar. Two years ago, I couldn't answer that question."

Source: Roger C. Stewart, "Balancing on the Global High Wire," *Financial Executive,* September/October 1995, pp. 35–39.

There will occasionally be circumstances in which a manager believes that uncovered interest parity does not hold *ex ante* in the offshore or other money markets. Chapter 2 contains a much broader discussion on *ex ante* deviations from uncovered interest parity; such deviations would arise when investors are not indifferent between holding assets with the same expected rate of return but denominated in different currencies, or if there are barriers to capital mobility. If *ex ante* deviations are expected, a full mean-variance optimization analysis would be appropriate. Any financial investment textbook will explain how to perform such an analysis. In such circumstances, the manager will want to place more cash where the risk-adjusted return is high. For a more complete analysis of rates of return on currency deposits along with the variance of the deposits (mean-variance optimization in cash management), see Madura and Nosari (1984b) and Swanson and How (1986).

❖ **SUMMARY OF CHAPTER OBJECTIVES**

1. Calculate foreign exchange risk with respect to a single currency exposure and the standard deviation of its value.

For a single exposure, the foreign exchange risk is simply the product of two components: the magnitude of the exposure stated in home currency units (rather than foreign currency units) and the standard deviation of percentage changes in the exchange rate.

2. Calculate foreign exchange risk with multiple currencies by applying portfolio techniques.

Exchange risk with multiple currencies examines the portfolio effect of dealing with several currencies, so an analysis of the covariation of currency movements is important. A portfolio's risk is calculated from an equation taken from investment theory. There are two primary conclusions. First, currency diversification reduces the overall risk of exposure positions. Second, centralized financial management can reduce risk further at a low cost by taking account of the diversification effect.

3. Analyze foreign exchange risk in international cash management by considering interest rates on deposits as well as the currency movements.

The introduction of nominal interest rates raises a potential trade-off between foreign exchange risk and the returns on cash balances. However, if uncovered interest parity holds, dollar-equivalent returns in all currencies are expected to be the same. Thus, the cash management decisions become substantially the same as the exchange risk management decisions. With respect to the standard deviation, the components of volatility other than deviations from PPP tend to be very small, so currency movements are shown to be the major focus of decision-making, with little role for interest rates.

❖ **QUESTIONS FOR REVIEW**

1. One simple way of analyzing the foreign exchange risk associated with an exposed position is to examine the product of the exposure and the standard deviation of percentage changes in exchange rates:

$$\sigma(XS_{t+n}) = XS_t \times \sigma_{\%\Delta S}$$

This is particularly useful when the expected future spot rate is equal to the current spot rate. Consider a U.S. company that has an account receivable denominated in French francs for FF 50,000 which will be collected in one quarter. The current spot exchange rate is US$0.20/FF, and the firm believes the random walk hypothesis of exchange rate forecasting for the quarterly horizon, such that the spot exchange rate expected for next quarter is the same as the current spot rate. However, the standard deviation of quarterly percentage changes in the $/FF exchange rate has historically been 6 percentage points. Assuming that the exchange rate changes follow a normal distribution, show a diagram of the distribution of the U.S. dollar value of the receivable.

2. Suppose an American firm has US$100 worth of accounts payable in Canadian dollars and US$100 worth of accounts payable in Australian dollars, and needs to know the standard deviation of the portfolio of payables. The firm knows that, for a 90-day horizon:

> standard deviation of percentage changes in the US$/C$ = 8 percentage points
> standard deviation of percentage changes in the US$/A$ = 20 percentage points
> correlation between percentage changes in US$/C$ and US$/A$ = .35

What is the standard deviation of the portfolio?

3. Suppose the annualized variance of quarterly percentage changes in the real French franc is 300 and the variance of the real Swiss franc is 600. Also, suppose that the correlation coefficient between these two currencies is 0.90.

   a. What is the covariance between the French franc and the Swiss franc?

   b. What is the standard deviation of a portfolio of $100 worth of French francs and $100 worth of Swiss francs?

4. An American firm has $100 worth of accounts payable in German marks and $100 worth of accounts payable in Japanese yen. The firm knows that, for a one-year horizon:

> standard deviation of percentage changes in the $/DM = 15 percentage points
> standard deviation of percentage changes in the $/¥ = 11 percentage points
> correlation between percentage changes in $/DM and $/¥ = .30

   a. Consider the exposures separately. What is the standard deviation of the $100 worth of accounts payable in German marks? What is the standard deviation of the $100 worth of accounts payable in Japanese yen? (Be sure to specify units in both answers.) Comparing these two, which one is riskier?

   b. Consider the exposures together. What is the standard deviation of the portfolio of the $100 worth of accounts payable in German marks and $100 worth of accounts payable in Japanese yen? (Again, specify units.) In this example, is there very much diversification?

5. Bukovac and Simon, a Washington, D.C. trading company, is assessing the risk of a portfolio of two exposures: US$ 100 worth of Irish pounds and US$ 100 worth of Belgian francs. The treasurer's office reports that, on an annual basis, the variance of percentage changes in the US$/I£ exchange rate has been 225, the variance of percentage changes in the US$/BFr has been 144, and the covariance between percentage changes in the US$/I£ and percentage changes in the US$/BFr has been 126.

   a. What is the correlation coefficient between percentage changes in the US$/I£ and percentage changes in the US$/BFr? Interpret this correlation coefficient as best as you can: are these two currencies uncorrelated, highly correlated, mildly correlated, or something different?

   b. What is the standard deviation of the portfolio of US$ 100 worth of Irish pounds and US$ 100 worth of Belgian francs?

c. Draw the distribution of potential U.S. dollar values of the portfolio, assuming that the percentage changes in portfolio value are normally distributed, and show the intervals of the value of the portfolio which would be expected 68 percent of the time and 95 percent of the time.

6. The following matrix displays the variances and covariances of monthly percentage changes in three fictitious currencies versus the U.S. dollar. The units are monthly percentage points squared. Assume that percentage changes in exchange rates are normally distributed.

	Almazas	*Pripps*	*Sagres*
ALMAZAS	14		
PRIPPS	15	20	
SAGRES	00	08	10

a. You have $100 worth of pripps, and the expected exchange rate change is zero for the following month. What is the range of the expected portfolio value one month from now with 95 percent probability?

b. Are movements in the almaza and the pripp (vis-à-vis the dollar) highly correlated? What is the correlation coefficient?

c. What is the standard deviation of a portfolio of $100 worth of almazas and $100 worth of sagres?

d. What is the standard deviation of a portfolio of $100 worth of pripps and $100 worth of sagres?

7. [Class discussion] In international cash management, managers have a choice between managing only foreign exchange risk or managing foreign exchange and interest rate risk together. Considering only nominal changes in exchange rates and nominal interest rates, do you expect the inclusion of interest rate risk in the analysis to suggest that the cash portfolio is more or less risky than an examination of foreign exchange risk alone? Would you advise cash managers to manage only foreign exchange risk or foreign exchange and interest rate risk together? Answer as completely as possible.

8. [Group project] You are analyzing the foreign exchange exposure of a U.S. corporation's subsidiary in the United Kingdom. One aspect of your analysis involves empirical estimation of regressions based on data from the subsidiary. You have data on the quarterly U.S. dollar cash flows from the subsidiary, calculated from pound cash flows and the exchange rate in effect each quarter. You regress these series onto a constant, the $/pound exchange rate, a lagged value of the $/pound exchange rate, the $/yen exchange rate, and a lagged value of the $/yen exchange rate. Of course, you converted everything to real values before you ran the regressions. The results of the regressions are listed, where the coefficients are all statistically significant at conventional levels. The adjusted R^2 statistic is 0.10.

$$CF_{\$,t} = 1000 + 45\,S_{\$/\pounds,t} + 20\,S_{\$/\pounds,t-1} + 5500\,S_{\$/\yen,t} + 2500\,S_{\$/\yen,t-1} + \varepsilon_t$$

a. As the pound appreciates against the dollar, what happens to the dollar cash flows from the subsidiary in the United Kingdom?

b. Although the subsidiary is in the United Kingdom, why might you include an exchange rate other than the $/pound exchange rate in the regression analysis? What is your interpretation of the fact that the coefficients on the $/yen exchange rates are larger than the coefficients on the $/pound exchange rates?

   c. In the previous equation, what happens to the cash flows from the U.K. subsidiary as the yen appreciates? Why might this be the case?

   d. Why might you include lagged values of relevant exchange rates in your regression analysis? Explain your reasons using the regression equation given, such as by interpreting the coefficients on $S_{\$/£,t-1}$ and $S_{\$/¥,t-1}$.

   e. What is your interpretation of the adjusted R^2 statistic?

9. Erehwon Imports has subsidiaries in Chile, Italy, and Switzerland. The currencies have the following annual variance-covariance structure (in percentages squared):

	peso	lira	franc
peso	900		
lira	−400	500	
franc	−350	450	550

   a. The exposures of next year's cash flows to exchange rate changes, converted into millions of dollars, are $50 for the Chilean operation, $25 for the Italian subsidiary, and $30 for the Swiss subsidiary. If there are no expected changes in the exchange rates over the next year, what is the range of next year's total dollar cash flows with 95 percent probability?

   b. Hedging which of these three exposures reduces risk the most?

10. [Class discussion] A U.S. investor has a portfolio of French, German, Italian, and Dutch bonds. Is this portfolio less risky in U.S. dollar terms now that the euro is the common currency of Europe, since the portfolio is now only exposed to a single exchange rate rather than to four exchange rates for the franc, mark, lira, and guilder?

TOOLS FOR ANALYSIS
Percentage Changes in the Real Exchange Rate Represent Deviations from Purchasing Power Parity

By calculating the percentage changes of the real exchange rate, we are calculating precisely the deviations from purchasing power parity examined in Chapters 2 and 7. To find the percentage changes of the real exchange rate, we use the formula:

$$\ln[e_{t+n}] - \ln[e_t] = \ln[S_{t+n}P^*_{t+n}/P_{t+n}] - \ln[S_tP^*_t/P_t]$$

that is, the natural log of the real exchange rate at time $t+n$ minus the natural log of the real exchange rate at time t gives the percentage change of the real exchange rate between t and $t+n$. Through simple transformation, this is the same as:

$$[\ln(S_{t+n}) - \ln(S_t)] - [\ln(P_{t+n}) - \ln(P_t)]$$
$$+ [\ln(P^*_{t+n}) - \ln(P^*_t)]$$

where the first term is the percentage change in the nominal exchange rate, the second term is the percentage change in the domestic price level, and the third term is the percentage change in the foreign price level. Using the notation introduced in Chapter 2, this is simplified to be:

$$[\%\Delta S_{t,t+n}] - \pi_{t,t+n} + \pi^*_{t,t+n}$$

where $\pi_{t,t+n}$ represents an inflation rate over the period t to $t+n$. This final expression is exactly what we defined as the deviation from relative PPP, denoted in Chapter 2 as $\phi_{t,t+n}$.

❖ Endnotes

1. Note that we also assume that the position is precisely known and does not covary with the exchange rate.

2. $\text{Var}[(1/3)(\text{month1} + \text{month2} + \text{month3})] = (1/9)\text{Var}(\text{month1} + \text{month2} + \text{month3}) = (1/9)(3)[\text{Var}(\text{month})] = (1/3)\text{Var}(\text{month})$, assuming independence across the three months.

3. For further empirical analysis, see Madura and Nosari (1984a).

4. Quoted in Christopher Farrell, "A Garden Full of Hedges," *Business Week,* April 19, 1993, pp. 96–97.

5. Actually, as discussed in Chapter 2, economists do not agree that this is the case. This chapter assumes that uncovered interest parity holds *ex ante* for offshore deposits to focus attention on other aspects of international cash management. We reconsider *ex ante* deviations from uncovered interest parity at the end of our discussion.

❖ References

Jorion, Philippe. *Value at Risk: The New Benchmark for Controlling Market Risk,* Irwin Professional Publishing, 1997.

Levy, Haim. "Optimal Portfolio of Foreign Currencies with Borrowing and Lending," *Journal of Money, Credit, and Banking,* August 1981, pp. 326–341.

Madura, Jeff, and E. Joe Nosari. "Utilizing Currency Portfolios to Mitigate Exchange Rate Risk," *Columbia Journal of World Business,* Spring 1984a, pp. 96–99.

Madura, Jeff, and E. Joe Nosari. "Global Money Management," *Financial Executive,* June 1984b, pp. 42–47.

Simons, Katerina. "Value at Risk—New Approaches to Risk Management," *New England Economic Review,* September/October 1996, pp. 3–13.

Soenen, L. A., and Raj Aggarwal. "Corporate Foreign Exchange and Cash Management Practices," *Journal of Cash Management,* March/April 1987, pp. 62–64.

Swanson, Peggy E., and William S. Y. How. "Portfolio Diversification by Currency Denomination: An Approach to International Cash Management with Implications for Foreign Exchange Markets," *Quarterly Review of Economics and Business,* Spring 1986, pp. 95–103.

HEDGING WITH FINANCIAL INSTRUMENTS

CHAPTER OBJECTIVES

AFTER READING THIS CHAPTER, YOU SHOULD BE ABLE TO:

❖ Hedge a transaction using a forward contract on foreign exchange.

❖ Hedge a transaction using international money markets.

❖ Compare forward and money market hedges, specifically in the context of equilibrium in the financial markets.

❖ Analyze foreign currency swaps.

❖ Hedge an exposure using foreign currency futures contracts.

❖ Compare forward and futures hedges, specifically in the context of equilibrium in the financial markets.

❖ Hedge an exposure using foreign currency options contracts.

❖ Compare forward and options hedges, specifically in the context of equilibrium in the financial markets.

This chapter is an in-depth look at hedging using financial instruments. In the first section, we look at forward market hedges, which use the forward contracts introduced in Chapter 1 to offset an exposure. In the second section, we examine money market hedges, which use borrowing and lending in the money markets—such as the offshore markets introduced in Chapter 1—to hedge an exposure. In the third section, we compare forward and money market hedges, specifically in the context of equilibrium in the financial markets. With the main principles of hedging established in these first sections, the rest of the chapter considers some more sophisticated financial hedges. In the fourth section, we consider a combination of forward and money market instruments known as a "swap," and in the fifth section, we consider hedging with foreign currency futures, financial contracts similar to forward contracts that are traded on an organized exchange. In Section six, we compare forward and futures hedges, again with a focus on market equilibrium. In the seventh section, we look at hedging with foreign currency options, financial contracts that give the purchaser the right but not the obligation to exchange currency, and in the eighth section, we compare forward and option hedges, with particular attention to an equilibrium in these markets.

9.1 INTRODUCTION

This chapter examines techniques for eliminating or reducing foreign exchange risk by hedging foreign exchange exposure using a variety of financial instruments. The financial hedges we examine in this chapter—foreign currency forward contracts, money market contracts, swap agreements, futures contracts, and options—can be very useful for firms that desire to reduce foreign exchange exposure and risk. Although the analysis is generally more technical than other chapters in this book, we develop several simple rules of thumb to make hedging strategy more understandable.

Hedging with financial instruments is an increasingly important area of international financial management. When corporations hold derivatives, either for hedging or for speculation, they are increasingly responsible for reporting their derivative positions to their shareholders. The U.S. Securities and Exchange Commission requires some disclosure of the risk involved with derivatives positions. The Financial Accounting Standards Board (FASB) also recently issued Statement No. 133 specifying accounting methods for derivative instruments and hedging activities, which will take effect for fiscal years beginning after June 15, 1999.

FASB-133 requires that every derivative instrument be recorded in the balance sheet as either an asset or a liability based on its fair value, and that changes in value be recognized in current earnings unless specific hedge accounting criteria are met. The hedge accounting allows a derivative's gains and losses to be offset by related results on the hedged item on the income statement. The company must also formally document, designate, and assess the effectiveness of transactions that receive hedge accounting. As a result, considerably more information about corporate use of financial instruments to hedge foreign exchange exposure positions will be available in the near future.

9.2 FORWARD MARKET HEDGES

The forward contracts introduced in Chapter 1 can be used to perfectly protect known future contractual cash flows, such as exposed transactions. If the firm is expecting a foreign currency cash inflow on a specific date, it should sell the currency forward in the

FIGURE 9-1 HEDGING AN EXPOSURE WITH A FORWARD CONTRACT

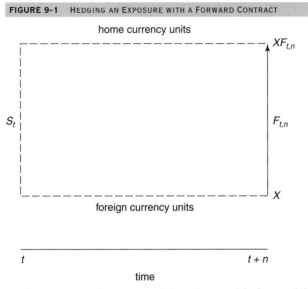

The home currency is represented along the top of the box, and the foreign currency is represented along the bottom of the box. The time horizon from t to $t + n$ is represented by the length of the box. The current spot exchange rate is S_t and the current forward rate for settlement n periods into the future is $F_{t,n}$, both quoted in terms of home currency units per foreign currency. A foreign currency exposure of X is hedged using a forward contract, locking in a home currency value of $X F_{t,n}$. A receivable is hedged by selling foreign currency forward and a payable is hedged by buying foreign currency forward.

same magnitude for the same date. If the firm is expecting a foreign currency cash out-flow on a specific date, it should buy the currency forward in the same magnitude for the same date. Figure 9-1 summarizes this principle.

When hedging using forward contracts, the spot exchange rate (denoted S_t, and quoted in home currency units per foreign currency unit) essentially becomes irrel-evant. Instead, the n-period-ahead forward rate quoted for the time the actual trans-action is to take place (denoted $F_{t,n}$, and again quoted in home currency units per foreign currency unit) becomes relevant.

If the firm has a foreign currency inflow of X, it can lock in a home currency value of $X[F_{t,n}]$, and this is what the firm should record in its financial statements. If the firm has a foreign currency outflow of X, it can also lock in a home currency value of $X[F_{t,n}]$. In both cases, the firm should use the forward rate to convert the foreign currency cash flow into dollars rather than the current spot rate because the transaction and currency conversion will occur in the future at the currently-known forward exchange rate. The future value is thus clearly based on the forward rate. This fact also implies that the unknown future spot exchange rate, S_{t+n}, is irrelevant because conversion will occur at the forward rate. The hedge therefore protects a transaction from losses due to adverse movements in the ex-change rate, but also removes the gains due to beneficial movements in the exchange rate.

EXAMPLE 9.1

Wattenmaker, Inc., is a large buyer and seller of cotton based in Pittsburgh. On June 1, Wattenmaker agreed to sell DM 1,000,000 of cotton to a textile firm in Frankfort, to be paid for on June 1 of the following year. As all of Wattenmaker's costs are incurred in

U.S. dollars, the DM account receivable is associated with economic exposure. The $/DM exchange rate is $0.65/DM and the one-year-ahead forward rate is $0.62/DM. To protect itself against DM depreciation, Wattenmaker decides to sell one million DM forward. Hence, Wattenmaker locks in a dollar value of the account receivable of:

$$DM\ 1,000,000(\$0.62/DM) = \$620,000.$$

One year later, the spot exchange rate is $0.58/DM. Wattenmaker benefits from the forward contract because it is able to sell marks at $0.62. The value of the DM receivable on the spot market is DM 1,000,000 ($0.58/DM) = $580,000. The gain on the forward contract is DM 1,000,000 ($0.62/DM − $0.58/DM) = $40,000. Hence, the total dollar cash inflow to the firm is $580,000 + $40,000 = $620,000. However, the total dollar cash inflow is always $620,000, regardless of what the spot exchange rate is, because gains (or losses) on the forward contract always offset losses (or gains) on the spot position. If the spot rate had instead been $0.65/DM, the value of the DM receivable on the spot market would have been $650,000. The gain on the forward contract would have been 1,000,000 ($0.62/DM − $0.65/DM) = −$30,000, a loss. Thus, the total dollar cash inflow to the firm is still $650,000 − $30,000 = $620,000. The nature of hedging with forward contracts is to lock in the future home currency value of a foreign-currency-denominated transaction, which will be obtained regardless of the future spot exchange rate.

EXAMPLE 9.2

Shepard Cellular of Providence, Rhode Island, manufactures car phones for sale in the United States. Shepard purchases its transistors from Lin Electronics Corporation, a Japanese firm. On January 1, Shepard purchased ¥15,000,000 worth of transistors to be paid for on July 1—180 days later. Although the spot yen/dollar exchange rate was holding steady at ¥150/$, Shepard was concerned about a possible yen appreciation between January and the payment date. The manager realized that any yen appreciation would mean that the cost of the transistors would increase. However, he knew that the revenues from selling cellular phones in the United States would not increase with yen appreciation. Hence, the transaction exposure is associated with economic exposure.

Shepard decided to avoid taking any unnecessary risks and signed a forward contract to purchase ¥15,000,000 on July 1. He locked in a six-month forward rate of ¥145/$. Hence, his account payable, or the cost of the transistors, was locked in at:

$$(¥15,000,000)(\$1/¥145) = \$103,448.$$

Six months later, the spot exchange rate had dropped to ¥135/$. Had Shepard not purchased the forward contract, it would have had to pay $111,111 for the ¥15,000,000 worth of transistors. The gain on the forward contract is the difference between the spot rate and the forward rate on the day the contract matures, multiplied by the size of the contract, which is here (¥15,000,000)($1/¥135 − $1/¥145) = $7,663. Hence, the total cash flow is $111,111 − $7,663 = $103,448.

Because forward contracts can be used to perfectly hedge known future contractual cash flows when the date of the transaction and the maturity of the forward contract are exactly matched, the overall gain or loss on the transaction and the forward contract is zero. This is because any gains (losses) on the transaction are perfectly offset by losses (gains) on the forward contract. This can be expressed in the equation:

$$\text{Gain(Loss)} = X(S_{t+n} - F_{t,n}) + (F_{t,n} - S_{t+n}) = X[0] = 0$$

where X is the amount of the exposure measured in the local currency. The term $(S_{t+n} - F_{t,n})$ represents the gain (loss) on the original transaction, which is the difference between the spot rate on the date the transaction is settled and the forward rate entered into on the date the transaction was established. The term $(F_{t,n} - S_{t+n})$ represents the gain (loss) on the forward contract itself, the difference between the forward rate at which currency conversion takes place and the spot rate at which conversion can take place outside the forward contract.

Note that the gain (loss) on the forward contract completely offsets the loss (gain) from the underlying transaction. The relevant benchmark for the gain (loss) on the transaction is the forward rate rather than the spot rate on the date the transaction was established because the forward rate establishes the future value of the transaction. Although this is the economically meaningful approach, accounting for the transaction and the hedge is usually separated into different components. By expanding the previous equation we get:

$$\text{Gain(Loss)} = X[(S_{t+n} - S_t) + (S_t - F_{t,n}) + (F_{t,n} - S_{t+n})]$$

where $(S_{t+n} - S_t)$ represents the gain (loss) on the transaction due to the spot exchange rate change and $(S_t - F_{t,n})$ represents the gain (loss) on the forward contract due to the forward premium or discount, which is obviously known at the time the transaction is entered into. Accounting for the transaction and the hedge often requires the transaction to be posted at the current spot rate (rather than the forward rate) and the difference between the spot rate and the forward rate to be reported as a foreign exchange gain (loss). Once the transaction is settled and the future spot exchange rate is known, there are gains and losses on the original transaction and the forward contract. Together, the three gains (losses) sum to zero.[1]

9.3   MONEY MARKET HEDGES

Firms that have access to money markets for different currencies are able to borrow and lend in such a way that a hedge can be constructed. Of primary importance are offshore currency deposits, or Eurocurrency deposits, introduced in Chapter 1. These are bank deposits denominated in a currency other than the currency of the country in which the deposit is located. There are also offshore currency loans, or Eurocurrency and Eurodollar loans.

A money market hedge using Eurocurrency deposits or loans can be used to perfectly protect known future cash flows as long as maturity dates match the specific date on which a transaction will take place. If the firm is expecting a foreign currency inflow, it can borrow the present value of the foreign currency at a fixed interest rate now and convert it into the home currency. The firm would then put the home currency amount on deposit, at a fixed interest rate, until it received the foreign currency inflow as something of collateral on the foreign currency loan. When the firm receives the foreign currency inflow, it uses it to pay off the foreign currency loan and the home currency deposit becomes the cash inflow. By using the money market hedge, the firm therefore locks in the value of the cash inflow in terms of home currency units.

If the firm is expecting a foreign currency outflow, it will want to put the present value of the cash outflow on deposit in foreign currency using the equivalent amount of borrowed home currency. When the foreign currency outflow is due, it is paid out of the foreign currency deposit previously arranged. Home currency is then used to repay the home currency loan. By undertaking the money market hedge, the firm locks in the home currency value of the cash outflow.

Figure 9-2 summarizes money market hedging. If the firm is expecting a foreign currency inflow of X, it should borrow $X/[1 + i^*_{t,t+n}]^{1/a}$ in foreign currency, where $i^*_{t,t+n}$ is the simple annual interest rate on the foreign currency (in discrete time) and a is the annualization factor. This amount should be converted into the home currency at the prevailing spot exchange rate, resulting in $S_t[X]/1[1 + i^*_{t,t+n}]^{1/a}$ home currency units. In turn, this amount should be put on deposit at interest rate $i_{t,t+n}$, so the home currency equivalent of the foreign currency cash inflow is ensured to be $S_t[X][1 + i_{t,t+n}]^{1/a}/[1 + i^*_{t,t+n}]^{1/a}$.

Similarly, if the firm will have a foreign currency outflow of X, it should put $X/[1 + i^*_{t,t+n}]^{1/a}$ in foreign currency on deposit at interest rate $i^*_{t,t+n}$. This amount would come from a home currency loan of $S_t[X]/[1 + i^*_{t,t+n}]^{1/a}$. When the cash outflow occurs, the firm will pay off the home currency loan, with interest, for a total of $S_t[X][1 + i_{t,t+n}]^{1/a}/[1 + i^*_{t,t+n}]^{1/a}$. For both the inflow and the outflow, the firm should record $S_t[X][1 + i_{t,t+n}]^{1/a}/[1 + i^*_{t,t+n}]^{1/a}$ in its financial statements rather than use only the spot exchange rate S_t because the relative interest differential indicates what the opportunity cost is of holding one currency vis-à-vis the home currency.

EXAMPLE 9.3

Shuckers Restaurants is a successful American seafood chain. In the winter, when domestic salmon harvests slow, they purchase most of their salmon from Araujo-Northwestern Fishing Company, a Canadian fishing outfit. On June 1, the owner of Shuckers bought C$250,000 of chinook salmon to be paid for on December 1. The spot exchange rate was $0.8/C$, but the owner was worried about possible Canadian dollar appreciation. She knew that any Canadian

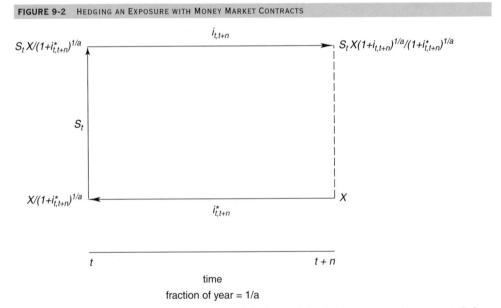

FIGURE 9-2 HEDGING AN EXPOSURE WITH MONEY MARKET CONTRACTS

The home currency is represented along the top of the box and the foreign currency is represented along the bottom of the box. The time horizon from t to $t + n$ is represented by the length of the box, and spans the fraction of a year $1/a$. The home interest rate from t to $t + n$ is $i_{t,t+n}$, the foreign interest rate from t to $t + n$ is $i^*_{t,t+n}$ and the current spot exchange rate is S_t. A foreign currency exposure—receivable (or payable)—of X is hedged by borrowing (or lending) its present value at the foreign interest rate, $X/(1 + i^*_{t,t+n})^{1/a}$, exchanging in the spot market using home currency in the amount of $S_t X/(1 + i^*_{t,t+n})^{1/a}$, and lending (or borrowing) at the home interest rate to yield a future value of $S_t X (1 + i_{t,t+n})^{1/a}/(1 + i^*_{t,t+n})^{1/a}$.

dollar appreciation would raise the cost of the salmon, but she also knew that she could not raise the price of a salmon dinner to her customers because she would lose business to her competitors.

She called her bank and was quoted a Canadian dollar interest rate of 14 percent and a U.S. dollar interest rate of 10 percent. She therefore needed to put C$250,000/1.14$^{1/2}$ = C$234,146 on deposit to cover her liability. She took out a loan of $187,317 which was converted into C$234,146 in the spot market at $0.80/C$. Six months later, Shuckers' owner withdrew the money from the Canadian dollar deposit, which after six months at 14 percent annually had grown to C$250,000, and paid for the fish. Then she paid back the U.S. loan of $187,317 with interest, for a total of $187,317(1.10$^{1/2}$) = $196,460. The amount paid for the fish was thus $196,460, and is entirely independent of the spot exchange rate on December 1.

9.4 COMPARING FORWARD AND MONEY MARKET HEDGES

With both forward and money market hedges available, a firm may be interested in comparing the two hedges to determine which is more advantageous, either locking in a higher value of a receivable or a lower value of a payable. Firms thus choose the hedge which is the most profitable, but as firms (or other traders) do this, an equilibrium emerges in which any difference in the two hedges disappears. The rates of return on Eurocurrency deposits thereby precisely determine the relationship between spot exchange rates and forward exchange rates.

Assume, for the sake of example, that U.S. dollars on deposit in London carry a 12 percent annual rate of return. Also assume that German marks on deposit in London carry an 8 percent annual rate of return. As both deposits are exactly the same in all respects except for the currency of denomination, the interest rate spread must indicate the percentage difference between the spot rate and the forward rate. In this particular example, the U.S. dollar must be selling at approximately a 4 percent forward discount and the German mark must be selling at a 4 percent forward premium. This means that the one-year-ahead dollar/mark forward rate is approximately 4 percent above the spot rate.

We examined the relationship between interest rate differentials and the forward premium or discount in Chapter 2. It is known as *interest rate parity* or *covered interest parity*. The home currency equivalent of a foreign-currency-denominated cash flow using a forward hedge is $XF_{t,n}$. The home currency equivalent of a foreign-currency-denominated cash flow using a money market equivalent is $XS_t[1 + i_{t,t+n}]^{1/a}/[1 + i^*_{t,t+n}]^{1/a}$. Setting these equal, and canceling the exposed position, interest rate parity is precisely the interest parity equation:

$$S_t[1 + i_{t,t+n}]^{1/a}/[1 + i^*_{t,t+n}]^{1/a} = F_{t,n}$$

using the simple interest rates we have been studying. As discussed in Chapter 2, the covered interest parity theorem holds because arbitrage activity eliminates any deviation.

EXAMPLE 9.4

Sardy Enterprises is an American import-export firm. On May 1, Sardy signed a deal to sell merchandise to a company in the United Kingdom for £1,000,000. Unfortunately, there was a one-year delay before the shipment would arrive and payment would be received. The owner, Marc Sardy, was thus quite concerned about the possibility of pound depreciation during the next year.

With the present spot exchange rate at $2.037/£, the one-year interest rate on the Eurodollar at 8 percent, the one-year interest rate on the Europound at 10 percent, and a one-year forward rate of $2.000/£, Sardy was quite confused about whether he should engage in a forward market hedge or a money market hedge. After some research, he concluded that the hedges would work equally well. Sardy constructed the following comparison:

Forward Hedge	*Money Market Hedge*
(£1,000,000)($2/£) = $2,000,000	[(£1,000,000)/(1.10)][$2.037/£][1.08] = $1,999,964

which indicates that the two hedges were equivalent because the $36 difference is due to rounding the forward rate to three decimal places. Using interest rates on Eurocurrency deposits, the interest rate parity theorem or covered interest parity was demonstrated to hold.

The fact that covered interest parity holds means that a firm cannot be better off using a money market hedge than a forward contract if one exists. In fact, a firm will always find it more profitable to use the forward markets than the money markets because the firm most likely must borrow at a rate above the interbank offshore lending rate or put funds on deposit at a rate below the interbank offshore deposit rate. This situation creates disadvantageous deviations from covered interest parity for the firm. Exceptions occur only when the firm can borrow at a concessional rate (a rate below the interbank rate) or lend at a premium rate (a rate above the interbank rate), both of which create advantageous deviations from covered interest parity for the firm. Unfortunately, however, these exceptions are rare.

9.5   SWAPS

Forward and money market agreements are often combined in relatively sophisticated ways to form another derivative known as a **swap,** an agreement in which two parties repay each other's loans. Currency swaps, in their simplest form, involve exchanging repayment of two fixed-interest-rate loans denominated in different currencies. This is easier to explain through an example. Consider Kaul Computers, located in Ann Arbor, MI, which is interested in obtaining financing in Swiss francs to hedge exposure generated by its exports to Switzerland. Likewise, Seyhun Confectioners, a Swiss chocolate maker based in Lausanne, Switzerland, is interested in obtaining a dollar liability to hedge its sales in the United States.

Each company takes out a 10-year fixed-rate loan for $100 million in its local currency. Kaul obtains a dollar loan with an interest rate of 10 percent while Seyhun obtains a Swiss franc loan at 9.6 percent. At a current exchange rate of $0.80/SFr, the payment schedules look as follows:

Year	*Kaul Computers*	*Seyhun Confectioners*
0	$100 million	SFr 125 million
1	($10 million)	(SFr 12 million)
2	($10 million)	(SFr 12 million)
3	($10 million)	(SFr 12 million)
⋮	⋮	⋮
10	($110 million)	(SFr 137 million)

Then, through an intermediary such as an investment bank, Kaul and Seyhun agree to exchange repayment of each other's loans. This means that Kaul will receive $10 million from Seyhun each year to cover repayment of its dollar loan (and $110 million in Year 10) in return for making payments of SFr 12 million each period (and SFr 137 million in the final period) to cover Seyhun's Swiss franc loan. Cash flows, net of swap payments, now look as follows:

Year	Kaul Computers	Seyhun Confectioners
0	$100 million	SFr 125 million
1	(SFr 12 million)	($10 million)
2	(SFr 12 million)	($10 million)
3	(SFr 12 million)	($10 million)
⋮	⋮	⋮
10	(SFr 137 million)	($110 million)

In this way, Kaul and Seyhun have both achieved liabilities in their desired currencies without having to access overseas capital markets.

THE ALL-IN COST OF A CURRENCY SWAP

When calculating the overall cost of raising funds through a swap transaction, firms typically appeal to an "all-in" cost calculation. The all-in cost is the effective foreign-currency interest rate, net of transaction costs, that the firm pays on the proceeds from the swap transaction. The formula calculates the discount rate, i, that equates swap payments with net swap proceeds:

$$(\text{Swap Principal} - \text{Swap Fees})/S_0 = \text{Payment}_1/(1 + i) + \text{Payment}_2/(1 + i)^2 \\ + \text{Payment}_3/(1 + i)^3 + \cdots + \text{Payment}_n/(1 + i)^n$$

where S_0 is the current exchange rate (in home currency per foreign currency) and n is the total number of years in the swap. In our example, suppose that Kaul Computers has to pay a fee of $1 million to the intermediary to execute the swap transaction. The all-in cost would then be the value which equates both sides of the following equation:

$$(\$100 \text{ million} - \$1 \text{ million})/(\$0.80/\text{SFr}) = (\text{SFr 12 million})/(1 + i) \\ + (\text{SFr 12 million})/(1 + i)^2 + (\text{SFr 12 million})/(1 + i)^3 \\ + \ldots + (\text{SFr 137 million})/(1 + i)^{10}$$

Solving for i, using either a financial calculator or a spreadsheet, Kaul's all-in cost is determined to be 9.76 percent. Hence, if Kaul cannot borrow in Swiss francs directly at 9.76 percent, then the swap is advantageous.

SWAPS AS SEQUENCES OF FORWARD CONTRACTS

Because swaps are exchanges of fixed amounts of currency at specific future dates, they can be thought of as sequences of currency forward contracts. In the simplest case, the swap of one-year obligations is exactly a one-year forward contract. In our example, if we assume the loans are to be repaid (interest plus principal) at the end of Year 1, then the swap is no different than Kaul agreeing today to pay Seyhun SFr 137 million in one year in return for $100 million. Hence, the implied forward rate is calculated from:

$$(\text{SFr 137 million})(F_{0,1}) = \$110 \text{ million}$$

such that $F_{0,1} = 0.8029$. In the swap of 10-year loans, we can calculate the forward exchange rates implied by the swap flows based on the cash flows exchanged:

Year	Kaul Computers	Seyhun Confectioners	Implied Forward Rate
0	$100 million	SFr 125 million	$F_{0,0} = S_0 = \$0.80/\text{SFr}$
1	(SFr 12 million)	($10 million)	$F_{0,1} = \$0.8333/\text{SFr}$
2	(SFr 12 million)	($10 million)	$F_{0,2} = \$0.8333/\text{SFr}$
3	(SFr 12 million)	($10 million)	$F_{0,3} = \$0.8333/\text{SFr}$
⋮	⋮	⋮	⋮
10	(SFr 137 million)	($110 million)	$F_{0,10} = \$0.8029/\text{SFr}$

Note that the sequence of implied forward rates need not equal actual market forward rates, but as a whole the two should resemble each other.

THE MARKET FOR FOREIGN EXCHANGE SWAPS

A natural question is why swaps have become so popular when they can be replicated by simply borrowing in the desired currency in the first place, as with the money market hedges discussed earlier, or by borrowing at home and purchasing a sequence of long-dated forward contracts. The answer involves a variety of factors, including the segmentation of international debt markets, the liquidity of long-dated futures contracts, and exploitation of relative borrowing advantages or differential access to markets.

At the source of the demand for swap transactions is the apparent segmentation of international borrowing markets. The point is simply that capital markets, in spite of their trend toward increased globalization, continue to price the obligations of firms differently, and hence demand different interest rates from the same firm. Whether these divergences arise from different assessments of the riskiness of an obligation or differential demands for a given obligation is open to debate. However, differences in a given firm's cost of debt across markets are frequent and can be significant.

Although firms can easily convert short-dated obligations into desired currencies by using currency forward and futures contracts, the costs in doing so with long-dated obligations are generally prohibitive. Few banks are interested in taking the opposite side of a series of long-dated forward contracts, and hence bid-ask spreads tend to represent a significant portion of the total price. As a result, firms rarely convert obligations into different currencies by purchasing long-dated forward contracts. Swaps, on the other hand, because they match parties interested in converting long-dated obligations into each other's currency, enjoy a liquidity that makes their transaction costs attractively low.

A final reason that swaps have enjoyed high popularity is because they do not require that firms be matched according to their credit quality. However, before explaining why, it is important to point out that swap transactions are not risk free. Firms using swaps to hedge are exposed to "counter-party risk," the risk that the other firm engaged in the swap might default. In this case, the first firm retains the right-of-offset and will cancel its side of the swap payments. The firm now must find a replacement counter-party with which it can resume swap payments. However, doing so at the pre-specified swap terms may no longer be possible if the exchange rate has moved sufficiently against the firm (nor may it be prudent if the exchange rate has moved in the firm's favor). If this happens, the firm will face a gain or loss, depending on the movement of the exchange rate and the corresponding terms of the replacement swap. The point is that swaps carry a special kind of default risk—the risk, in the event of counter-party default, of facing market risk due to exchange rate changes. However, as long as firms are appropriately compensated for bearing this risk, swap transactions are still possible.

The reason that swaps of differing credit qualities benefit from the exchange of obligations, even in the presence of counter-party risk, is that firms' relative advantage in borrowing in their home currencies may generate sufficient gains from trade. To see this phenomenon, we return to the previous example. Suppose that the Swiss franc borrowing costs for Kaul are 15 percent, whereas the US$ borrowing costs for Seyhun are 9 percent. Combining these with our earlier assumptions about domestic borrowing costs, we have:

	Borrowing costs	
	$	*SFr*
Kaul Computers	10%	15%
Seyhun Confectioners	9%	9.6%

Note that Seyhun Confectioners enjoys an absolute advantage borrowing in both the US$ and the Swiss franc. However, Seyhun's advantage is relatively stronger in the Swiss franc. Hence, together the firms are better off if they borrow at home and swap rather than borrowing in their desired currencies. To see why this is advantageous, note that annual U.S. dollar interest payments if each firm borrows in its desired (foreign) currency are $24 million (at the current exchange rate):

$$(\$100 \text{ million})(0.09) + (\text{SFr } 125 \text{ million})(0.15)(\$0.80/\text{SFr}) = \$24 \text{ million.}$$

On the other hand, annual U.S. dollar interest payments under the swap are $19.6 million (at the current exchange rate):

$$(100 \text{ million})(0.10) + (\text{SFr } 125 \text{ million})(0.096)(\$0.80/\text{SFr}) = \$19.6 \text{ million.}$$

Hence, the combined savings from the swap transaction are $4.4 million per year. Kaul simply needs to offer terms which make the swap (as opposed to direct US dollar borrowing) worthwhile for Seyhun. Kaul must offer Seyhun at least $1 million per year over the 10 year period or $6.1 million (the present value of $1 million per year for 10 years) up front.

9.6   HEDGING WITH FOREIGN CURRENCY FUTURES

Other financial contracts are available that are similar to forward contracts. **Futures contracts** are contracts which specify delivery of fixed quantities of foreign currencies on a set delivery date in the future that are traded on an organized exchange. This means that the contracts are standardized by size and delivery date to make trading easier. The futures exchange rates are the prices of the futures contracts, and are subject to specified price increments.

While futures contracts are similar to forward contracts, the following important differences are worth emphasizing:

1. Forward contracts are written by banks and traded only in an inter-bank market with the prices set in the contract, while futures contracts are traded on an organized exchange with the prices determined through market trading.
2. The size of a forward contract is individually tailored to the customer's needs and is generally very large, typically in excess of $1 million, while the size of a futures contract is standardized yet is comparatively small, around $100,000.
3. The date of maturity for a forward contract is individually tailored to the customer's needs and can be on any business day, while with a futures contract, the date of maturity cannot be individually tailored and delivery can only occur on the specific dates determined by the organized exchange.
4. The settlement of a forward contract occurs on the date determined in the contract and rarely requires that any cash be paid before that date, while futures contracts require daily settlement of gains and losses within the exchange that necessitates establishing a margin account with some capital (ranging from about 1 percent up to 10 percent of the position) paid in advance.

The largest foreign currency futures exchange is the International Monetary Market (IMM) of the Chicago Mercantile Exchange. Futures contracts on major currencies have been trading on the IMM since 1972. Currently, futures contracts are available in nine currencies: 12.5 million Japanese yen; 125,000 German marks; 100,000 Canadian dollars; 62,500 British pounds; 125,000 Swiss francs; 100,000 Australian dollars; 500,000 Mexican pesos; 100,000 Brazilian reals; 100,000 euros; 500,000 French francs; 100,000 New Zealand dollars; 500,000 Russian rubles; and 500,000 South African rand.

The IMM has determined only four delivery dates per year, coinciding with the end of each calendar quarter. Table 9-1 presents an example of the daily listing of futures prices on the IMM. It lists the opening price of the contract, the high, the low, the closing price, and the change, as well as the contract's lifetime high and low. The column at the right labeled *open interest* indicates the number of contracts in effect, representing both a buyer of the contract and a seller. Buying a futures contract obligates the buyer to take delivery of the foreign currency, and selling the futures contract obligates the seller to deliver the foreign currency.

The standardization of futures contracts appears to make these contracts much less useful than forward contracts in hedging. Similarly, maintaining the required margin account appears to make futures contracts more cumbersome than forward contracts. These features, however, are actually the futures contract's major advantages over forward contracts in hedging. As futures are traded on organized exchanges, they can be liquidated prior to maturity at any time at relatively little cost. Because of this ease of liquidity, firms can use futures to hedge whenever a transaction date is not definite. Nearly all forward contracts are settled by actual delivery of the foreign currency on the maturity date, while almost no futures contracts are settled by actual delivery of the foreign currency on the maturity date because positions are closed out before the maturity date arrives. Although the size of futures contracts is standardized, their smaller size

TABLE 9-1	Currency Futures Prices Chicago Mercantile Exchange, Thursday, June 24, 1999

CURRENCY

	Open	*High*	*Low*	*Settle*	*Change*	Lifetime *High*	Lifetime *Low*	*Open Interest*
JAPAN YEN (CME)—12.5 million yen; $ per yen (.00)								
Sept	.8299	.8314	.8270	.8303	+ .0002	.9500	.7680	90,715
Dec	.8390	.8414	.8384	.8413	+ .0002	.9600	.8257	11,104
Mr00	....	....	....	.8531	+ .0002	.8931	.8369	113
Est vol 11,703; vol Wed 9,345; 101,932, −2.								
DEUTSCHEMARK (CME)—125,000 marks; $ per mark								
Sept	.5314	.5357	.5299	.5352	+ .0041	.6300	.5282	23,688
Dec	....	....	....	.5389	+ .0041	.6120	.5316	192
Est vol 3,706; vol Wed 3,687; open int 23,880, +435.								
CANADIAN DOLLAR (CME)—100,000 dlrs.; $ per Can $								
Sept	.6800	.6820	.6793	.6800	− .0001	.7080	.6310	58,572
Dec	.6812	.6816	.6810	.6807	− .0001	.6930	.6320	2,550
Mr00	.6825	.6825	.6820	.6815	− .0001	.6940	.6425	526
June	.6829	.6829	.6829	.6824	− .0001	.6950	.6547	177
Est vol 4,084; vol Wed 7,881; open int 61,838, −402.								
BRITISH POUND (CME)—62,500 pds.; $ per pound								
Sept	1.5818	1.5906	1.5744	1.5894	+ .0082	1.6980	1.5744	61,867
Est vol 7,936; vol Wed 25, 510; open int 61,973, +13.								
SWISS FRANC (CME)—125,000 francs; $ per franc								
Sept	.6530	.6579	.6508	.6570	+ .0045	.7831	.6491	63,233
Est. vol 11,097; vol Wed 13,831; open int 63,379, +1.								
AUSTRALIAN DOLLAR (CME)—100,000 dlrs.; $ per A.$								
Sept	.6586	.6608	.6574	.6590	+ .0004	.6745	.5825	27,252
Est vol 550; vol Wed 1,555; open int 27,281, −94.								
MEXICAN PESO (CME)—500,000 new Mex. peso, $ per MP								
Sept	.10265	.10280	.10120	.10173	− .00067	.10350	.06350	13,413
Dec	.09770	.09770	.09730	.09748	− .00072	.84345	.06700	3,166
Mr00	.09335	.09335	.09315	.09350	− .00067	.09500	.08135	3,093
Est vol 5,356; vol Wed 4,669; open int 19,682, −151.								
BRAZILIAN REAL (CME)—100,000 Braz. reals; $ per reals								
July	.55250	.55250	.55250	.55350	− .00050	.76050	.48500	294
Est vol 10; vol Wed 25; open int 315, +20.								
EURO FX (CME)—Euro 125,000; $ per Euro								
Sept	1.0393	1.0474	1.0366	1.0467	+ .0079	1.2374	1.0332	39,065
Dec	1.0452	1.0530	1.0446	1.0539	+ .0079	1.2409	1.0420	257
Est vol 9,497; vol Wed 8,850; open int 39,322, −27.								

Source: The Wall Street Journal, June 25, 1999, p. C16. Reprinted by permission.

makes them more appropriate than forward contracts for hedging smaller transactions. Hence, futures contracts can be quite useful for hedging exposure, particularly accounts receivable.

Futures contracts do, however, have limitations. For example, they are available in only few currencies and are therefore often unavailable in a currency a firm wants to hedge. Sometimes, a firm will be forced to use a **cross-hedge,** which is hedging an exposed position in one currency with a futures contract in another currency. An example would be hedging a French franc exposure with Deutsche mark futures. Also, because the contractual amounts of futures contracts are set at standardized levels, firms are forced to round off the hedge to the nearest whole number of contracts. Thus, a perfect hedge is not generally available in the futures market.

BASIC PRINCIPLES OF HEDGING WITH FOREIGN CURRENCY FUTURES

The simplest use of hedging with futures contracts is to establish a futures position that offsets an existing exposure one-for-one, such as hedging SFr 500,000 with four SFr 125,000 contracts. In this case, the firm will buy or sell futures contracts at date t for intended liquidation at date $t + n$. The price of the futures contract at t is denoted $Z_{t,T}$, where T represents the maturity date of the contract. The price of the futures contract at $t + n$, which is unknown at t, is $Z_{t+n,T}$. The gain or loss on the hedged position is:

$$\text{Gain(Loss)} = X[(S_{t+n} - bS_t) - (Z_{t+n,T} - Z_{t,T})]$$

where X is the amount of exposure measured in the local currency, and also represents the aggregate futures position. The term b is defined to be the interest rate ratio:

$$b = [1 + i_{t,t+n}]^{1/\hat{a}}/[1 + i^*_{t,t+n}]^{1/\hat{a}}$$

where $\hat{a}$ is the annualization factor for the interval from t to $t + n$. The term bS_t is identical to the forward rate and, as before, represents the future home currency value of the future foreign currency cash flow that takes place at time $t + n$. Recall that the value of a foreign currency receivable or payable should be calculated using the forward rate rather than the spot rate because the relative interest rate differential indicates the opportunity cost of holding one currency vis-à-vis another currency. The term $(S_{t+n} - bS_t)$ is therefore the deviation of the future spot exchange rate from this interest-rate-adjusted spot exchange rate (or the forward rate) at inception of the position. The term $(Z_{t+n,T} - Z_{t,T})$ is the change in the price of a futures contract maturing at time T over the time period from t, inception of the position, to $t + n$, liquidation of the position. Note that, for simplicity, in calculating gains and losses, we are ignoring any adjustment for the timing of gains received or losses paid through daily settlement in the margin account, as well as any opportunity cost associated with holding balances in the margin account. Hence, there are three dates to keep in mind:

$$t\text{-----------------------}t + n\text{-----------------------}T$$
$$\quad\text{inception}\qquad\qquad\text{liquidation}\qquad\qquad\text{contract maturity}$$

because futures contracts are not usually held until maturity.

As an empirical approximation, the futures price $Z_{t,T}$ is determined according to the interest rate parity theorem or covered interest parity in the same way the forward rate was determined:

$$Z_{t,T} = S_t[1 + i_{t,T}]^{1/a}/[1 + i^*_{t,T}]^{1/a}$$

where a is the annualization factor for the interval from t to T. Otherwise, riskless arbitrage profits would be possible between forward contracts and futures contracts or between money market contracts and futures contracts. In reality, arbitrage with futures contracts is a little harder than arbitrage with forward and money market contracts, because of the margin requirement and transactions costs. Nevertheless, the interest rate parity theorem has been found to hold for futures contracts, as demonstrated in Cox, Ingersoll, and Ross (1981).

FUTURES CONTRACTS HELD TO MATURITY

From the previous formulas, it soon becomes evident that a futures contract held to maturity enables a perfect hedge to be created. If a futures contract is held to maturity, $t + n = T$, so $i_{t+n,T} = 0$ and $i^*_{t+n,T} = 0$. This means that $Z_{t+n,T} = S_{t+n}$, implying that the futures price on the contract's maturity date is identical to the spot exchange rate. In addition, $Z_{t,T} = bS_t$ so the futures price at t is identical to the forward rate for a contract maturing at T. The equation for a foreign exchange gain or loss simplifies to:

$$\text{Gain(Loss)} = X[(S_{t+n} - bS_t) - (S_{t+n} - bS_t)] = X[0] = 0$$

and a perfect hedge is created. This is the same result that prevails with the forward contract because a futures contract held to maturity is equivalent to a forward contract with the same maturity date; after all, both forwards and futures are priced according to covered interest parity.

EXAMPLE 9.5

Durrell Enterprises is a major international design firm with headquarters in Cincinnati. On January 15, the owner, Amy Durrell, signs a contract to supply SFr 500,000 worth of consulting services to a Swiss firm, with payment to occur on March 30, two and one-half months later. Durrell then hedges the cash inflow by selling four March futures contracts to Foster & Co. in Washington, D.C. The spot exchange rate on January 15 is $0.75/SFr and the futures price for March contracts is $0.7643/SFr. The Eurocurrency interest rate on dollars is 15 percent and on Swiss francs is 5 percent.

Durrell opened a margin account to settle gains and losses on the position daily. On March 30, the spot exchange rate and the futures exchange rate are $0.72/SFr. This means that the cumulative gain on the short futures position is:

$$\text{SFr } -500{,}000(0.72 - 0.7643) = \$22{,}150.$$

This is offset by a loss on the original receivable of:

$$\text{SFr } 500{,}000(0.72 - b(0.75)) = \$-22{,}175$$

where $b = (1 + .15)^{1/4.8}/(1 + .05)^{1/4.8} = 1.0191332$ and the annualization factor is determined to be 12 months/2.5 months = 4.8. Because the contract was held to maturity, the hedge was essentially perfect:

$$\text{Gain(Loss)} = \text{SFr } 500{,}000[(0.72 - (1.0191332)(0.75)) - (0.72 - 0.7643)] = \$-25$$

which is close to zero. The nonzero result is due to the fact that the futures price of 0.7655 must be rounded to four decimal places, whereas bS_t contains more decimal places.

FUTURES CONTRACTS NOT HELD TO MATURITY

When futures contracts are not held to maturity, futures hedges are not perfect because the remaining time to maturity on the futures contract is priced using covered interest parity, so the futures price has not yet converged to the spot price. Furthermore, the relative interest rates at the time the position is liquidated are not known in advance and most likely change over the interval through liquidation anyway.

The problem can be clarified with reference to the basic property of the **term structure of interest rates,** the configuration of interest rates with different maturities. The relationship between an interest rate over an interval from t to T and corresponding interest rates over an interval from t to $t+n$ and another over an interval $t+n$ to T is:

$$[1 + i_{t,T}]^{1/a} = [1 + i_{t,t+n}]^{1/\hat{a}}[1 + i_{t+n,T}]^{1/\tilde{a}}$$

where $\tilde{a}$ is the annualization factor over the interval from $t+n$ to T. There are now three annualization factors—a, $\hat{a}$, and $\tilde{a}$—such that $1/a = 1/\hat{a} + 1/\tilde{a}$. Using this data, the equation for the gain or loss on the futures hedge is simplified to:

$$\text{Gain(Loss)} = X[(S_{t+n} - bS_t) - c(S_{t+n} - bS_t)]$$

where c is defined as:

$$c = [1 + i_{t+n,T}]^{1/\tilde{a}}/[1 + i^*_{t+n,T}]^{1/\tilde{a}}.$$

Hence, whenever c is not equal to one, the hedge will not be perfect.

The problem can be fixed, however, by altering the amount of the hedge, as opposed to using an equal offsetting position in the futures market. In particular, the optimal hedge would involve $1/c$ foreign currency units of foreign currency futures. This makes the gain or loss equal to zero because $(c)(1/c) = 1$. When $c > 1$, the hedge should involve a smaller amount of currency futures than the original currency exposure being hedged, and the optimal amount would be $1/c$. Similarly, when $c < 1$, the hedge should involve a larger amount of currency futures than the original amount being hedged, and the optimal amount is again $1/c$.

This strategy has two big problems. First, c is based on interest rates for a period in the future and is therefore not known at time t. It can be inferred, however, by looking at the term structure of interest rates and extracting the implied future interest rate. Second, even if the interest rates can be inferred from the term structure of interest rates, they are likely to change a lot as news about the economy becomes available over the period from t to $t+n$. Hence, c is stochastic and using a hedge ratio of $1/c$ sets the expected gain (loss) equal to zero, but does not produce a perfect hedge.

This technique of hedging is usually referred to as **delta hedging** because it attempts to offset the change (often denoted by the Greek letter delta) in the value of the exposure with an opposite change in the value of the hedge position. To do this, the size of the hedge must be frequently adjusted as c changes, which is cumbersome. Therefore, to concentrate on the basic principles of hedging with futures, for the rest of this section we will continue assuming that we hedge an open position with an equal short position in the futures market.

EXAMPLE 9.6

On January 15, Durrell Enterprises signs another consulting contract with a Swiss firm for SFr 250,000 with payment to occur April 30. The owner, Amy Durrell, decides to hedge the exposure using futures contracts again. On January 15, she sells two June Swiss franc futures contracts. The spot rate is \$0.75/SFr, the futures rate is \$0.7819/SFr, and interest rates on Eurocurrency deposits are 5 percent on the Swiss franc and 15 percent on the U.S. dollar. On April 30, when she liquidates the position, the spot rate is \$0.71/SFr, the futures rate is \$0.7260/SFr, and interest rates are 5 percent on the Swiss franc and 20 percent on the U.S. dollar. The gain or loss on the position is:

$$\text{Gain(Loss)} = \text{SFr } 250,000[(0.71 - (1.026886)(0.75)) - (0.7260 - 0.7819)] = \$-1,067$$

where $b = [1 + .15]^{3.5/12}/[1 + .05]^{3.5/12} = 1.0268886$. Since the futures contracts are not held to maturity, the hedge cannot be perfect because the spot and futures prices do not converge.

Why use futures contracts if they generally cannot construct perfect hedges? The most important reason is that there may be uncertainty about the transaction date, above denoted $t + n$, anyway. Consider, for example, an account receivable. A firm knows that the account will be paid sometime, but may not know whether it will be paid next month or the month after. Similarly, consider an asset that might be held for a long time before being sold, but which the owner wants to hedge. In this case, the owner could easily create an offsetting position in the futures market and roll over the contracts until he sells the asset.

Another situation in which an imperfect futures hedge might be used is when the amount of the transaction is not precise or is subject to some uncertainty, and rounding the hedge is required anyway. The futures market also allows the hedge to be altered in the future as new information on the transaction amount becomes available, an activity that is not readily available in the forward market. A final instance in which an imperfect futures hedge might be used is when the transaction is simply too small to be hedged in the forward market.

Although futures contracts do not eliminate risk, they definitely reduce risk. We can measure the effectiveness of hedging as the percentage of the unhedged risk eliminated by the purchase of futures contracts. Let the unhedged risk be measured as the variance of $(S_{t+n} - bS_t)$. Let the hedged risk be measured by the variance of $(Z_{t+n,T} - Z_{t,T})$. The following formula calculates the hedging effectiveness mathematically:

$$\left[1 - \frac{\text{Var}[(S_{t+n} - bS_t) - (Z_{t+n,T} - Z_{t,T})]}{\text{Var}(S_{t+n} - bS_t)}\right] \times 100$$

We know that $\text{Var}[(S_{t+n} - bS_t) - (Z_{t+n,T} - Z_{t,T})]$ is less than $\text{Var}(S_{t+n} - bS_t)$ because we have seen that the long position in the foreign currency is offset by the short position in the futures market and vice versa.

We can also measure the hedged risk as a percent of the open risk using the concept of standard deviations. The following formula figures the standard deviation of the hedged position relative to the standard deviation of the unhedged position and expresses it as a percent:

$$\sqrt{\frac{\text{Var}[(S_{t+n} - bS_t) - (Z_{t+n,T} - Z_{t,T})]}{\text{Var}(S_{t+n} - bS_t)}} \times 100$$

where the variables are as defined before.

EXAMPLE 9.7

Durrell Enterprises begins to do more and more business with firms in Switzerland as time goes on. The owner, Amy Durrell, decides to provide up to 90 days for clients to pay an invoice. However, she discovers that the average length of time for payment is 60 days. She continues to hedge in the futures market, buying and selling contracts as accounts receivable fluctuate, but wants to know how the hedged risk compares to the unhedged risk. Using historical data for 60-day intervals, she determines that the $\mathrm{Var}(S_{t+n} - bS_t)$ is approximately 0.0016, the $\mathrm{Var}(Z_{t+n, T} - Z_{t,T})$ is approximately 0.0020, and the $\mathrm{Cov}[(S_{t+n} - bS_t),$ $(Z_{t+n, T} - Z_{t,T})]$ is approximately 0.0017. This means that the $\mathrm{Var}[(S_{t+n} - bS_t) - (Z_{t+n, T} - Z_{t,T})]$ is:

$$\mathrm{Var}(S_{t+n} - bS_t) + \mathrm{Var}(Z_{t+n,T} - Z_{t,T}) - 2\,\mathrm{Cov}[(S_{t+n} - bS_t),(Z_{t+n,T} - Z_{t,T})]$$
$$= 0.0016 + 0.0020 - 2(0.0017) = 0.0002.$$

Hence, the measure of hedging effectiveness is:

$$[1 - (0.0002/0.0016)] \times 100 = 87.5\%$$

meaning that hedging has removed 87.5 percent of the variance, implying that 12.5 percent of the variance remains. The hedged risk as a percent of open risk is:

$$\sqrt{0.0002/0.0016} \times 100 = 35.4\%.$$

or simply the square root of 0.125.

As there is clearly at least some risk in futures hedges whenever futures contracts are not held to maturity, it makes sense for a manager to choose a futures hedge with the minimum level of risk possible. The firm is able to exert control not over the standard deviations of exchange rates and futures rates, but over the quantity of futures used to hedge the exposure. It is possible to calculate the hedge with the minimum variance by specifying the optimum **hedge ratio,** the quantity of futures purchased or sold for each unit of exposure. Because this is somewhat difficult, however, we omit the calculation here but provide complete detail and an example in the "Tools for Analysis" at the end of this chapter. Here, we merely point out that it is possible to have less risk by using a hedge that does not match up the futures position with the exposed position on a one-for-one basis.

SUMMARY OF HEDGING WITH FUTURES

Futures contracts, as compared to forward contracts, nearly always fail to completely remove risk, so are most likely to be used as hedging tools in three particular instances. First, futures contracts would be used when the transaction date is not definite. This was the case discussed in the preceding material with respect to accounts receivable and assets for which no transaction is scheduled. Second, futures contracts would be used when the transaction amount is not precise. In this case, estimating and rounding the hedge is required anyway, and the futures market allows the hedge to be altered in the future if the need arises. Third, the futures market would be a useful hedge if the transaction was too small for the forward market.

The actual maturity date of the futures contract selected is of little importance in all three of these hedges. The only thing built into the differences in prices on contracts of different maturities is the relationship in the term structure of interest rates. Just as a hedge can be liquidated before maturity, the hedge can always be rolled over into new futures contracts as necessary by liquidating near-maturity contracts and acquiring long-maturity contracts.

The analysis of futures hedges developed here addresses the role of liquidation before maturity. In this regard, the analysis can apply directly to forward contracts not held to maturity. For example, a firm may have a six-month forward contract it wants to close out after four months. It can do this either by negotiating to settle early, or simply by taking an offsetting two-month forward contract. In either case, however, there is the risk that interest rates and exchange rates have changed, so the hedge of the original exposure will not be perfect. This is identical to the problems with futures hedging, so the firm anticipating closing out a forward contract before maturity should investigate the minimum variance hedge ratio.

9.7   COMPARING FORWARD AND FUTURES HEDGES

With both forward and futures contracts available, a firm may be interested in explicitly comparing the two hedges to determine which is more advantageous. Firms thus choose the hedge which is the most profitable, but as firms (or other traders) make this choice, an equilibrium emerges in which any difference in the two hedges disappears. Differences may manifest themselves in transactions costs, such as a firm having a large transaction that might entail high broker fees in the futures market but not in the forward market. A comparison of forwards and futures must also consider the risks involved, as futures hedges generally do not eliminate risk.

EXAMPLE 9.8

Recall Sardy Enterprises, the American import-export firm that signed a deal to sell merchandise to a company in the United Kingdom for £1,000,000 payable on May 1. Sardy is concerned about the possibility of pound depreciation during the next year. Sardy had earlier compared forward and money market hedges, from which it had concluded that there was no difference between the two because covered interest parity held.

Sardy is now interested in comparing forward and futures hedges. The present spot exchange rate is $2.037/£, the interest rate on the Eurodollar is 8 percent, the interest rate on the Europound is 10 percent, and the one-year forward rate is $2.00/£.

Sardy now also checks the price of a futures contract with his broker. The broker explains that a June contract and a September contract are currently being traded, but certainly no contract for next May 1. Sardy would therefore have to sell either of the available contracts and roll them over until selling a contract maturing in June of the following year, which he would liquidate on May 1.

In response to a question from Sardy regarding the price of the futures contract next May, the broker explains that the price would be $2.000/£ given current interest rates and based on covered interest parity, but that that would change as interest rates change. Hence, the future futures price of $2/£ is an expected value, and there is uncertainty about the actual future futures price of the contract on the May 1 liquidation date. Sardy constructed the following comparison of the hedges:

Forward Hedge	Futures Hedge (based on expected value)
(£1,000,000)($2/£) = $2,000,000	(£1,000,000)($2/£) = $2,000,000

Sardy concludes that the two hedges have the same expected value, but recognizes that there is no uncertainty about the forward hedge and there is uncertainty about the futures hedge.

Sardy decides to investigate the risk associated with the futures contracts to compare the risk of the unhedged position to the risk of the position hedged with a forward contract and the risk of the position hedged with futures contracts. Sardy discovers that the unhedged position has a variance of $\text{Var}(S_{t+n} - bS_t) = 0.0900$ for a one-year horizon. Hence, the standard deviation is 0.300, which has units of dollars per pound. (Note that although this is a different measure than the one developed in Chapter 8, the two measures are similar. In particular, the standard deviation of \$0.300/£ around the forward rate of \$2.000/£ is 15 percent.) The distribution of the unhedged position is shown in the first panel of Figure 9-3. Note that the position could have gains or losses of (£1 million × \$0.300/£) = \$300,000 within one standard deviation, gains or losses of \$600,000 within two standard deviations, and gains or losses of \$900,000 within three standard deviations. The forward hedge of the transaction locks in a value of \$2,000,000 without any uncertainty. The probability distribution is thus simply a spike at \$2,000,000 with 100 percent probability, as shown in the second panel of Figure 9-3. Sardy also determines that a position hedged with futures contracts has a variance of $\text{Var}[(S_{t+n} - bS_t) - (Z_{t+n,T} - Z_{t,T})] = 0.010$ based on data for the one-year horizon. The standard deviation of the hedged positon is therefore \$0.100/£. The distribution of the position hedged with futures contracts is shown in the third panel of Figure 9-3. Note that the position could have gains or losses of (£1 million × \$0.100/£) = \$100,000 within one standard deviation, gains or losses of \$200,000 within two standard deviations, and gains or losses of \$300,000 within three standard deviations.

In comparing the unhedged position to the hedged position using futures, the first and third panels of Figure 9-3 suggest that the gains and losses of the hedged position are clearly one-third the size of the gains or losses corresponding to the unhedged position. Hence, the hedged risk as a percent of open risk is intuitively 33%, which can also be calculated mathematically:

$$\sqrt{0.0010/0.0090} \times 100 = 33.33\%.$$

9.8   HEDGING WITH FOREIGN CURRENCY OPTIONS

Foreign currency options provide another financial instrument that can be used to hedge foreign exchange exposure. A **foreign currency option** contract is a financial instrument that gives the holder the right but not the obligation to sell or buy currencies at a set price (called the **strike price** or **exercise price**) either on a specific date or before some expiration date. If the option contains the right to sell a currency, it is called a **put** on the currency. If the option contains the right to buy a currency, it is called a **call** on the currency. If the option can be exercised only on the maturity date, it is called a **European option.** If the option can be exercised at any time prior to the maturity date, it is called an **American option.** The price or value of the option is called the **premium.**

The Philadelphia Exchange is the largest trading center in the United States for foreign currency options on spot exchange rates. Figure 9-4 on page 302 illustrates that options on six currencies are typically available: the Australian dollar, British pound, Canadian dollar, Japanese yen, Swiss franc, and the euro. In addition, options are also available on the German mark and the French franc, but trading in these has been thin since the introduction of the euro; the value of the euro is fixed at 1.95583 marks and 6.55957 francs. Note in Figure 9-4 that the size of each option is standardized in amounts equal to half the size of the corresponding futures contract on the IMM. There are also standardized maturity dates corresponding to a month, usually one, two, and three months into the future. Additionally, there are standardized strike price intervals for the options.

The Philadelphia Exchange trades both American (not labeled) and European (labeled) options. Most of the options expire mid-month (third Wednesday of the month), but the ones labeled EOM expire at the end of the month (last Friday of the month). There are also cross-currency options between the British pound and German mark and between the Japanese yen and German mark, although quotes are not reported in Figure 9-4 because of thin trading. Options are also available from banks and some over-the-counter exchanges, but these are not reported in the financial pages of newspapers.

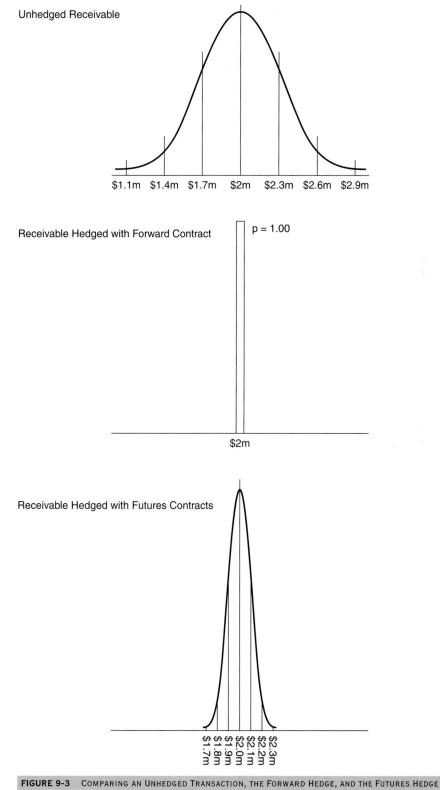

FIGURE 9-3 COMPARING AN UNHEDGED TRANSACTION, THE FORWARD HEDGE, AND THE FUTURES HEDGE

FIGURE 9-4   CURRENCY OPTIONS PRICES PHILADELPHIA EXCHANGE, THURSDAY, JUNE 24, 1999

OPTIONS
PHILADELPHIA EXCHANGE

	Calls		Puts	
	Vol.	Last	Vol.	Last
CDollr				67.93
50,000 Canadian Dollar EOM-European style.				
68 Jun	8	0.11	16	0.16
68 Jul	...	...	16	0.48
Euro				103.22
100 Sep	...	...	100	0.48
102 Aug	...	0.01	2	0.79
104 Sep	243	2.01	...	0.01
SFranc				64.64
62,500 Swiss Franc EOM-European style.				
67 Jun	...	...	320	2.30
Australian Dollar				65.88
50,000 Australian Dollars-European style.				
65 Sep	...	0.01	30	0.72
50,000 Australian Dollars-cents per unit.				
66½ Jul	10	0.34	...	0.01
British Pound				157.93
31,250 Brit. Pound EOM-European				
158 Jul	...	...	3	1.45

	Calls		Puts	
	Vol.	Last	Vol.	Last
31,250 Brit. Pounds-cents per unit.				
152 Sep	...	0.01	100	0.36
157 Sep	...	0.01	2	1.76
158 Aug	50	1.72	...	0.01
159 Jul	100	0.67	...	0.01
161 Aug	50	0.67	...	...
162 Jul	100	0.10	...	0.01
Euro				103.22
62,500 Euro-European style				
104 Jul	...	...	10	1.38
Japanese Yen				82.00
6,250,000 J. Yen-100ths of a cent per unit.				
80½ Sep	...	0.01	42	0.85
82 Sep	...	0.01	5	0.85
83 Sep	...	0.01	8	1.76
85 Sep	...	...	1	3.28

	Calls		Puts	
	Vol.	Last	Vol.	Last
6,250,000 J. Yen-European Style.				
80 Aug	...	0.01	16	0.46
82 Jul	15	1.00	...	0.01
84 Sep	1	1.20	...	0.01
Swiss Franc				64.64
62,500 Swiss Francs-European Style.				
64 Jul	...	...	82	0.27
64 Aug	...	...	16	0.47
64 Sep	16	1.82	16	0.62
65 Jul	...	...	48	0.67
65 Sep	16	1.30	64	0.93
66 Jul	...	...	64	1.31
66 Aug	...	...	64	1.41
66 Sep	...	0.01	48	1.53
67 Jul	...	...	32	2.16
Call Vol 814			Open Int.... 39,242	
Put Vol 1,105			Open Int.... 31,285	

Source: The Wall Street Journal, June 25, 1999, p. C17. Reprinted by permission.

BASIC PRINCIPLES OF HEDGING WITH FOREIGN CURRENCY OPTIONS

The major benefit of using options in hedging is that, because they give the holder the right but not the obligation to trade currencies, they can be used to hedge potential transactions, or transactions that are contingent on something else. For example, they can be used to hedge bids that have not yet been accepted, or to hedge an unknown quantity of inventory sales at a pre-specified price before it is sold. [For further development, see Giddy (1983) and Giddy and Dufey (1995).] The firm does not want to hedge with forward or futures contracts because that would entail an obligation that would lead to gains or losses if the bids are not accepted or the quantities vary too much.

EXAMPLE 9.9

On June 1, Shepard Cellular of Providence, Rhode Island, submitted a yen-denominated bid to provide Atsumi Electronics of Tokyo with an order of cellular phones. Shepard will not know whether the bid is accepted until the announcement of the winning bid is made on December 1. The president, Adam Shepard, may still want to protect the firm from possible yen depreciation in case it wins the bid and is awarded a contract. Mr. Shepard would not want to use a forward contract or futures contract hedge, however, because that would entail an obligation to sell dollars in the future. If Shepard Cellular loses the bid, it will not have yen revenues but will still have to honor any yen forward or futures contracts. Hence, the appropriate financial instrument is an option. In particular, Shepard wants a put on yen.

If the bid is for a total cost of ¥300,000,000, and the current spot exchange rate is ¥150/$, Mr. Shepard may want to ensure that he receives approximately $2,000,000 for the sale. If he purchases put options to sell ¥300,000,000 for dollars at a strike price of ¥150/$, he effectively locks in minimum revenues of $2,000,000, less the total cost of the put options. If the yen depreciates such that the dollar appreciates to more than 150 ¥/$, Shepard can simply exercise the ¥300,000,000 option if he wins the bid and receive $2,000,000 for the cell phones, again less the cost of the options. This is the worst the firm can do. If the dollar depreciates to less than 150 ¥/$, Shepard will not exercise the options if he receives the bid. In this case, he can receive even more than $2,000,000 for the cell phones if he exchanges the ¥300,000,000 at the spot rate. If Atsumi does not award the contract to Shepard, Shepard can let the options expire and there will be no further consequences. If the options have value, however, Shepard can sell them or exercise them and enjoy cash inflows despite the fact that the company lost the cell phone sale.

Options may also be useful whenever a firm wants to protect itself from the downside risk of exposure but reap some of the benefits on the upside. As options are priced in efficient markets, however, the firm pays for the privilege of keeping the upside. The expected return on the option is therefore generally not positive. Nevertheless, if options are priced in efficient markets, they are not unusually expensive; the expected return on an option may therefore not be negative either. Firms recognizing this may use options to hedge transactions when they are willing to pay to eliminate a large part of the downside risk—everything in excess of the amount paid in the premium—but keep most of the upside gains—everything in excess of the amount paid in the premium. We note this now, but discuss it further in the next section when comparing the option hedge to the forward hedge. For convenience, we more narrowly define the usefulness of options in this section to be limited to contingent cash flows, as in Giddy (1983) and reaffirmed in Giddy and Dufey (1995).

When options are used to hedge contingent cash flows, the choice of a strike price is largely irrelevant. If the strike price makes the option far into the money, though, it is tantamount to a forward position because exercise of the option is nearly certain. Similarly, if the strike price makes the option far out of the money, it is useless because exercise of the option is almost completely unlikely.

The strike price and the premium together also determine the floor or ceiling established for the potential transaction, so they must be examined carefully. The more favorable the floor or ceiling, the higher the premium. The relationship between the strike price and the premium is discussed in depth in the next subsection. For now, we provide a brief look at how the strike price and the premium determine the floor or ceiling on a transaction.

Figure 9-5 presents the profit profile for a put option, which can be used to hedge foreign currency inflows. The put establishes a floor price for the exchange rate. The horizontal axis in Figure 9-5 plots a range of potential exchange rates, in dollars per foreign currency. The vertical axis plots the profit or loss on the option. Point X denotes the strike price of the option. Anytime the spot exchange rate is higher than X, the put will not be exercised because the option's owner will be better off selling the foreign currency in the spot market.

Because the option costs something in advance, however, the profit on the option is negative in the amount of the option premium, P. Any time the spot price is below X, the value of the put increases one-for-one with depreciation of the foreign currency. Hence, the owner of the option breaks even when the spot rate is $(X - P)$, which is the floor price established by the hedge. As the option premium is paid before the option is exercised, there should be a slight adjustment reflecting the opportunity cost of holding the option rather than some other investment. Because this adjustment is small, however, it is ignored here.

Figure 9-6 presents the profit profile for a call option, which can be used to hedge foreign currency outflows. The call establishes a ceiling price for the exchange rate. Anytime the spot rate is below the strike price X, the call will not be exercised. The profit in this case is negative, reflecting the cost of the option, P. Anytime the spot price rises above X, the profits increase one-for-one with appreciation of the foreign currency.

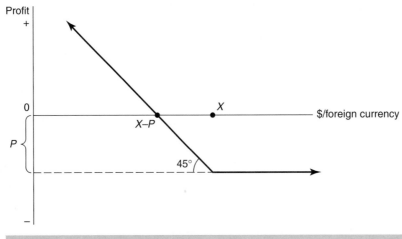

FIGURE 9-5   PROFIT PROFILE FOR PUT OPTION

A put option on a foreign currency gives the holder the right to sell the foreign currency at a strike price X, quoted in terms of dollars per foreign currency. The horizontal axis plots a range of potential exchange rates and the vertical axis plots the profit or loss on the option. The put premium is denoted by P. When the spot exchange rate S is above the strike price X, the option is not exercised and the profit on the option is $-P$, a loss. Whenever the spot exchange rate is below X, the option is exercised and the profit is the difference between the strike price and the spot price, less the premium, $X - S - P$. The break-even point is when the difference between the strike price and the spot price is identical to the premium, or when $S = X - P$. When a put is used to hedge a receivable, a floor on the value of each unit of foreign currency is established at $X - P$.

When the spot price reaches $(X + P)$, the owner of the option breaks even, and this point is the ceiling price established by the hedge. Again, there should be a slight adjustment reflecting the opportunity cost associated with paying the option premium in advance, but for simplicity, we ignore this adjustment here.

EXAMPLE 9.10

Tiki Enterprises of Chicago imports a lot of foreign beer and wine for sale by the bottle. Some of the alcohol is rare, so Tiki must bid for it in mail auctions. On September 15, Tiki bid DM 500,000 for a rare German beer, but will not know whether the bid was successful until December 15. To protect against mark appreciation, the owner of Tiki Enterprises, Mr. Ciral, purchased a DM 500,000 call option from his bank. The strike price is $0.65/mark, and the option premium is one cent per mark. Tiki has therefore locked in a ceiling price of approximately $0.66/mark, for a maximum total payment of $330,000. If the spot price of the mark appreciates to $0.70/mark, Tiki will exercise the option and purchase marks at $0.65/mark, so will pay $325,000 plus the $5000 option premium for the alcohol. If the mark depreciates to $0.60/mark, however, the firm will be better off buying marks on the spot market and letting the option expire unused; it therefore pays $300,000 plus the $5000 option premium for the alcohol.

Other characteristics of the appropriate option are relatively easy to select. The term to maturity should extend out as far as the contingent cash flow, but any additional time is not useful to the firm and therefore isn't worth the extra cost. (We examine the relationship between price and time to maturity again in the next section on options pricing.) Similarly, the choice between a European option and an American option is generally not too difficult. Most hedgers prefer the flexibility of the American option,

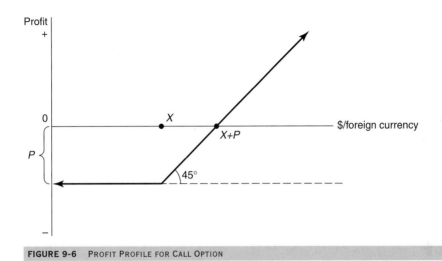

FIGURE 9-6 PROFILE PROFILE FOR CALL OPTION

A call option on a foreign currency gives the holder the right to buy the foreign currency at a strike price X, quoted in terms of dollars per foreign currency. The horizontal axis plots a range of potential exchange rates and the vertical axis plots the profit or loss on the option. The call premium is denoted by P. When the spot exchange rate S is below the strike price X, the option is not exercised and the profit on the option is $-P$, a loss. Whenever the spot exchange rate is above X, the option is exercised and the profit is the difference between the spot price and the strike price, less the premium, $S - X - P$. The break-even point is when the difference between the spot price and the strike price is identical to the premium, or when $S = X + P$. When a call is used to hedge a payable, a ceiling on the value of each unit of foreign currency is established at $X + P$.

but they end up paying more for the American option than the corresponding European option. (Again, we explain this assertion in the next section, but it can be taken as a fact for now.) If the uncertain transaction is only to occur on an option's maturity date, the firm would likely purchase the European option to save money. In this case, the added flexibility of the American option doesn't mean anything to the firm.

If the firm purchases an option from an organized exchange, it always has an opportunity to re-sell the option before maturity. This is particularly valuable if the firm does not have the potential cash flow being hedged, because some of the costs may be recovered or a profit might be possible. It is also valuable if the option would be exercised before maturity, because the option may be more valuable to someone outside the firm than what its immediate exercise value is to the firm. (We will further examine this, too, in the next section on the pricing of options.) Figure 9-7 diagrams the decision analysis when selling an option can occur.

EXAMPLE 9.11
Medici Management Moguls, a U.S. multinational, bids to provide catering and food service contracts all over the world. On July 20, it bid A$200,000,000 for a job in Australia. The winning bid will not be announced until October 1, however, and Medici Management Moguls is interested in protecting itself from possible Australian dollar depreciation. It buys 4,000 October put options on the Australian dollar on the Philadelphia Exchange, so that it can resell the options on the exchange if it does not use them. The strike price is $0.80/A$ and the premium is one cent per Australian dollar. This means that the firm has locked in a floor price of approximately $0.80/A$ − $0.01/A$ = $0.79/A$, for a total cash inflow of $158,000,000. There is also a brokerage fee associated with the purchase of options on the Philadelphia Exchange,

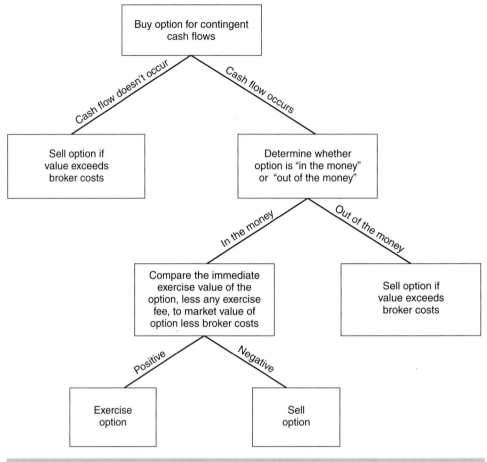

FIGURE 9-7 Strategy for Hedging with Options when Resale is Possible

which would have the effect of further reducing the floor, but this is small and is ignored here for simplicity.

When the winning bid is announced on October 1, the options still have approximately one month to maturity. If Medici Management Moguls does not receive the contract on which it bid in Australia, it will simply sell the options on the Philadelphia Exchange if the value of the options is still high enough to cover additional brokerage costs. If the contract is accepted, however, Medici will receive cash payment on October 1.

Its decision about what to do with the options depends on the spot price of the Australian dollar on October 1 and the value of the options on the Philadelphia Exchange. If the spot exchange rate is above $0.80/A\$, the firm will be better off converting the Australian dollar payment into U.S. dollars in the spot market. With about a month to maturity, however, the option previously purchased will have a positive value on the organized exchange. If the value of the option is high enough to cover additional brokerage costs, Medici Management Moguls should sell the options; after all, the internal value to the firm is zero. If the spot exchange rate on October 1 is below $0.80/A\$, the firm will be benefitting from having purchased options to hedge the cash inflow.

Before it simply exercises the options to take delivery of U.S. dollars in exchange for Australian dollars, however, the firm should compare the immediate exercise value to the value of the options in the market. If the spot exchange rate is $0.76/$A, for example, the immediate exercise value is $0.04/A$. With about a month to maturity, however, the value of the options will be higher than this, and if it is sufficiently above $0.04/A$ to cover additional brokerage costs, the firm should sell the options on the organized exchange and then sell the Australian dollars on the spot market.

BASIC PRINCIPLES OF PRICING OPTIONS ON SPOT FOREIGN EXCHANGE

This section outlines some basic principles of pricing foreign exchange options. The purpose is not to present precise pricing formulas, but rather to explain the patterns observed in Figure 9-4 by appealing to economic intuition. The principles are useful in selecting a floor price or ceiling price for a hedge, picking the duration of the option, and choosing American versus European options. For a fully developed model of foreign currency options pricing, see Garman and Kohlhagen (1983). For more discussion on pricing, see Abuaf and Schoess (1990), Hopper (1995), and Chapter 7 of Grabbe (1996). Here, we present seven main principles of options pricing.

1. *The value of an option on its expiration date is either its immediate exercise value or zero, whichever is higher.* Obviously, the price cannot be higher than the immediate exercise value, sometimes known as the **intrinsic value,** because the alternative is to simply purchase foreign exchange in the spot market. The value of an option can clearly never become negative because the owner has the right to throw it away.

2. *If two options are identical in all respects with the exception of the exercise price, a call option with a higher exercise price will always have a lower value and a put option with a higher exercise price will always have a greater value than the corresponding options with lower exercise prices.* Clearly, a call option with a higher

---

HEDGING AT WESTINGHOUSE

In 1989, Westinghouse put together a $50 million bid to upgrade a Swiss power plant. If the bid were accepted, Westinghouse would pay subcontractors and suppliers in five currencies. The Swiss utility would pay for the project in Swiss francs, though. According to Frank Maier, Westinghouse's banking director, "We had to come up with a Swiss franc price based on a five-year payment schedule that was worked up in dollars." Any depreciation of the Swiss franc would clearly throw off cost projections and reduce profits on the project.

After analyzing the movements of foreign currencies with respect to the U.S. dollar, Maier concluded that the exposure was about $28 million. Since the exposure was contingent on receiving the contract, Maier purchased an option from a bank to hedge the potential exposure. Westinghouse lost the bid, but the currencies moved in Westinghouse's favor while the Swiss utility was making its decision, so the value of Westinghouse's options increased. In the end, Westinghouse made $1.2 million on the hedge. According to Maier, "It was more profit than they had in the job originally."

Source: "Why Multinationals Are Rushing Into Economic Hedging," *Corporate Finance,* February 1990, pp. 51–53.

exercise price introduces a higher ceiling, and is therefore worth less. Similarly, a put option with a higher exercise price introduces a higher floor, and is therefore worth more. In terms of Figure 9-4, it's clear that if you read down a column for call options the prices get smaller, and if you read down a column of put options the prices get higher.

3. *At all times prior to expiration, an American option will have a value larger than its immediate exercise value.* Because an American option can be exercised at any time, it will always have a value at least as large as its immediate exercise value. As the probability that the option will become more in the money is always greater than zero, an American option will be worth more than its immediate exercise price. As a European option can be exercised only at maturity, it may have a value lower than its immediate exercise value.

4. *If two American options are identical in all respects with the exception of the length of the contract, the longer contract will have a greater value at all times.* This is clear because the option with the longer term to maturity is more flexible than the option with the shorter term to maturity; the latter is always inferior to the former. As European options can be exercised only on the maturity date, the one with the longer term to maturity is not more flexible than the one with a shorter term to maturity, so will not necessarily be worth more.

5. *Prior to expiration, an American option has a value at least as large as the corresponding European option.* This is clearly because the American option can be exercised anytime before maturity, so is unambiguously more flexible than a similar European option.

6. *A larger (positive) differential between the domestic interest rate and the foreign interest rate, $(i - i^*)$, increases the price of a call and decreases the price of a put.* This asserts that option values are affected by interest rate differentials in much the same way that forward and futures contracts are.

7. *The value of the option increases as the volatility of the underlying currency increases.* This occurs because high volatility increases the amount and the probability the option could potentially be in the money sometime before maturity.

The seven principles of option pricing presented here are based on complicated option pricing models. At the heart of these models is the efficient-markets hypothesis that the premium reflects all available information on the current exchange rate, domestic and foreign interest rates, and estimates of the volatility of the currency, as well as characteristics of the option itself such as the strike price and time to maturity. The implication here is that the premium is the expected value of the option, in that the distribution of possible future values of the exchange rate make the option profitable for the purchaser and unprofitable for the writer (if the premium is not taken into account).

A writer would certainly not charge less than the expected value of the option because he does not want to lose money. When options are priced in efficient markets, the writer would also not charge more than the expected value of the option because a competitor would be able to undercut his price. Hence, an equilibrium in an efficient market occurs when the premium represents the expected value of the option. As the premium is paid/collected in advance, it more specifically represents the present value of the expected future value of the option.

SUMMARY OF HEDGING WITH OPTIONS

Options contracts are appropriately chosen for hedging transactions that are uncertain. In other words, options are useful if there is uncertainty over whether a transaction will take place, such as when the transaction is contingent on another event, or uncertainty over the size of the transaction. This uncertainty is often thought of as "quantity risk" because the firm doesn't know the quantity of the foreign currency involved, and in particular might have a quantity as low as zero. In most other situations explored in this chapter, the firm knows the foreign currency amount but is worried about the "price risk" because it does not know the exchange rate.

Options may be used if the firm is uncertain about the amount of the transaction yet desires a perfect hedge of the transaction. The firm can use an approximate futures hedge if the amount of the transaction is uncertain, but the hedge would not be perfect. To construct a better hedge for an uncertain amount, the firm must purchase ample options to cover the highest cash flows possible. Once the magnitude of the transaction is known, the firm can resell any excess options or leave them to expire.

Options are also appropriate whenever a firm wants to protect itself from most of the downside risk but reap most of the profits on the upside on a known transaction (appropriately accounting for the option premium paid). We consider this scenario in the next section by comparing an option hedge to a forward hedge.

9.9   COMPARING FORWARD AND OPTION HEDGES

In the previous section, we considered the use of options broadly, and particularly the use of options to hedge contingent cash flows. In this section, we consider the use of options to hedge known transactions to explain the nature and costs of protecting the transaction from most of the downside risk but being able to reap some, but not all, of the upside potential. We do this by comparing the option hedge to the forward hedge.

For a receivable, a floor is established below the strike price as a result of the premium paid for the options, and there is upside potential when the foreign currency appreciates. For a payable, a ceiling is established above the strike price as a result of the premium, and there is upside potential when the foreign currency depreciates. Recall the proposition that when options are priced in efficient markets the premium reflects the present value of the expected future value of the option. This proposition implies that an equilibrium price of the option is one which does not alter the expected value of the hedged transaction. The option does, however, alter the distribution of potential outcomes. For a hedged receivable, the floor is below the expected value and some outcomes are above the expected value. For a hedged payable, the ceiling is above the expected value and some outcomes are below the expected value.

EXAMPLE 9.12

Recall Sardy Enterprises, the American import-export firm that signed a deal to sell merchandise to a company in the United Kingdom for £1,000,000 for which it will receive payment in one year. Sardy is thus concerned about the possibility of pound depreciation during the next year. The present spot exchange rate is $2.037/£, the interest rate on the Eurodollar is 8 percent, the interest rate on the Europound is 10 percent, and the one-year forward rate is $2.00/£.

LUFTHANSA'S AIRCRAFT PURCHASE

In 1986 the financial press reported that Lufthansa, the German airline, purchased $500 million of new U.S. aircraft in early 1985 with payment due in early 1986, one year later. The transaction hit the news because Lufthansa reportedly paid approximately DM 1,364 million, which was more than the $500 million liability converted at the prevailing spot exchange rate, $.447/DM, or DM 1,118 million. This happened because Lufthansa decided to hedge half of the purchase price using forward contracts at a time when the dollar subsequently depreciated against the DM. However, it is not clear whether Lufthansa and the financial press should be disappointed with this outcome.

Lufthansa's cash flows are predominantly in DM. The purchase of dollar-denominated aircraft meant that Lufthansa would have to convert DM into dollars to pay off the liability. Lufthansa purchased a forward contract for half of the liability, or $250 million, and decided to leave the other half of the transaction exposed. The forward contract obligated Lufthansa to purchase dollars in early 1986 at a rate of approximately $0.31/DM. From March 1985 to March 1986, however, the dollar depreciated (and the DM appreciated) from $0.30/DM to $0.45/DM. Hence, Lufthansa would have benefited from not having taken out the forward contract in 1985, but the dollar depreciation was uncertain at the time the forward contract was entered into. In the end, Lufthansa paid about DM 1,364 million under the transactions set up. Had the airplane purchase been fully hedged, Lufthansa would have paid about DM 1,610 million. However, attention focused on the fact that Lufthansa would have paid about DM 1,118 million if it had done nothing at all.

Lufthansa's aircraft purchase raises some difficult questions about hedging. One question is whether Lufthansa should be disappointed about the *ex post* outcome of the decision to hedge half of the dollar cash outflow. The answer is probably no, as long as the hedge was appropriate in the first place. In early 1985, Lufthansa was concerned that dollar appreciation would cause it to pay more DM for the aircraft, and accordingly decided to hedge part of the dollar cash outflow. If the dollar had indeed appreciated, Lufthansa would have been in a position of paying less for the aircraft than the spot rate in 1986 would suggest. (In this case, however, Lufthansa may have been attacked for incompletely hedging the transaction.)

Ex ante, Lufthansa simply wanted to reduce the risk associated with having to buy $500 million with DM, and hedging half of the cash outflow accomplished that. With DM volatility at approximately 16 percent per annum at the time, the unhedged position would have had a standard deviation of approximately $(0.16 \times 500/0.30 =)$ DM 267 million. By locking in the DM cost of $250 million, Lufthansa reduced the standard deviation of the aircraft purchase to half that, or DM 133 million. This *ex ante* reduction in risk is the main purpose of hedging, so Lufthansa should not be disappointed with the results *ex post.*

Another question is whether options would have been more appropriate than forward contracts, because they give the purchaser the right but not the obligation to transact at a specified exchange rate. It seems obvious that Lufthansa would have then benefitted from depreciation of the dollar without having to pay the consequences resulting from appreciation of the dollar. In other words, it would have been hedged if the dollar appreciated, thus locking in a maximum price for the aircraft, but it would have been able to keep the upside gains if the dollar depreciated. This strategy is more in the realm of speculation, as risk reduction does not require the asymmetric characteristics of the options hedge. Furthermore, the strategy is expensive. An at-the-money option would have cost Lufthansa about 6 percent of the transaction, or $30 million dollars for a $500 million hedge.

If the objective of hedging is to avoid paying more for the aircraft than you have to, then options appear to be an expensive way to reap the upside gains without ever experiencing the downside losses. Boards of directors are typically reluctant to pay out premiums (currency insurance) over and above the cost of the goods themselves. *Ex ante,* it was not obvious that a $30 million option would be worth the cost to Lufthansa. Only with hindsight does the strategy appear so profitable.

Source: Neil McGeown, "Lufthansa: A Case Study in Options," *Market Perspectives: Topics on Options and Financial Futures,* September 1986.

Mr. Sardy talks to a broker who quotes the premium on a European-style put option with a strike price of $2/£ and maturity one year from now at 11.07 cents per pound.[2] Hence, for the £1 million pound exposure, the total cost of options would be (£1,000,000)($0.1107/£) = $110,700, or about 5.5 percent of the transaction value ($2,000,000 based on the forward rate). Sardy is thus interested in comparing the forward hedge to an option hedge, recognizing that the latter would be a way of protecting the transaction from serious downside risk without completely giving up all of the upside gains.

Given the information available, Sardy believes that the expected future spot exchange rate is $2/£ because he knows that the forward rate is an unbiased predictor. The possible future spot exchange rates are furthermore assumed to be normally distributed around $2/£. The first panel of Figure 9-8 therefore repeats the distribution of possible transaction values for the un-hedged exposure based on the forward rate as a predictor of the future spot rate and the standard deviation of the open position considered earlier, $0.30/£ (or approximately fifteen percentage points in the teminology of Chapter 8). The second panel repeats the distribution of the transaction hedged with the forward contract, which is simply a spike with probability of 100 percent at $2,000,000.

Sardy is now ready to analyze the distribution of the transaction hedged with options. Because the distribution of possible future spot exchange rates is symmetric around $2/£, Sardy recognizes that a put option with a strike price equal to the forward rate is likely to be exercised with 50 percent probability and likely to be allowed to expire with 50 percent probability because half of the distribution of possible exchange rates falls below the strike price and half is above the strike price, respectively. When the spot exchange rate is below $2/£, the value of the £1 million pound receivable is equal to the product of the strike price and the magnitude of the exposure less the amount of the premium paid for the options:

$$(\$2.00/£)(£1,000,000) - (\$0.1107/£)(£1,000,000) = \$1,889,300.$$

This is the floor that the option hedge establishes, in that the hedged receivable will never be worth less than $1,889,300 (although an adjustment should be made to reflect the fact that the premium is paid one year before the option is exercised). It is possible, however, that the exchange rate will appreciate above $2.00/£, in which case the option will be allowed to expire because the receivable can be sold on the spot market for more than it can through the option. In fact, half of the distribution of future spot exchange rates is above $2/£, so Sardy can expect to have more than $1,889,300 with a probability of 50 percent. With a standard deviation of $0.30/£, the exchange rate will be between $2.00/£ and $2.300/£ with a probability of 34 percent, half of 68 percent, because we are interested in one standard deviation only in one direction. If the exchange rate is $2.3/£, the value of Sardy's receivable is:

$$(\$2.30/£)(£1,000,000) - (\$0.1107/£)(£1,000,000) = \$2,189,300.$$

Hence, Sardy's receivable will be between $1,889,300 and $2,189,300 with 34 percent probability.

Continuing with the distribution of possible exchange rates, the standard deviation of $0.30/£ implies that the exchange rate will be between $2/£ and $2.60/£ with probability 47.5 percent, or half of 95 percent. This implies that the exchange rate will be between $2.30/£ and $2.60/£ with a probability of 13.5 percent, or 47.5 − 34 percent. If the exchange rate is $2.6/£, the value of Sardy's receivable is:

$$(\$2.60/£)(£1,000,000) - (\$0.1107/£)(£1,000,000) = \$2,489,300.$$

Hence, Sardy's receivable will be between $2,189,300 and $2,489,300 with 13.5 percent probability. Finally, the standard deviation of $0.30/£ implies that the exchange rate will be between $2/£ and $2.90/£ with a probability of 49.85 percent (half of 99.7 percent), so the exchange rate will be between $2.60/£ and $2.90/£ with a probability of 2.35 percent (or 49.85 percent— 13.5 − 34 percent). If the exchange rate is $2.9/£, the value of Sardy's receivable is:

$$(\$2.90/£)(£1,000,000) - (\$0.1107/£)(£1,000,000) = \$2,789,300.$$

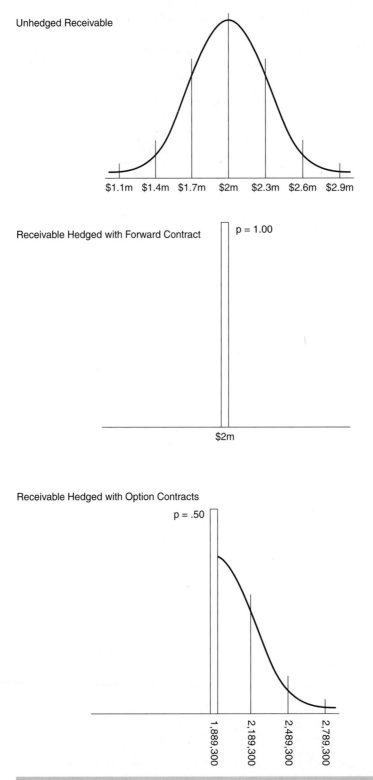

FIGURE 9-8 COMPARING AN UNHEDGED TRANSACTION, THE FORWARD HEDGE, AND THE OPTION HEDGE

An approximate distribution of the value of the receivable hedged using options is shown in the third panel of Figure 9-8. With 50 percent probability, the hedged receivable will be worth $1,889,300, and with 50 percent probability, the hedged receivable will be worth more than $1,889,300 based on the upper half of the normal distribution with a standard deviation of $0.30/£. (Once again, it would be appropriate to alter all values discussed here to account for the fact that the option premium is paid one year before the exposed cash flow takes place. This action would have the effect of reducing all future values shown in the third panel of Figure 9-8. We omit it for the sake of simplicity.)

By looking at Figure 9-8, it is not immediately clear whether Sardy is better off with the forward hedge or the option hedge. However, an equilibrium between forward and option markets is one where the transaction hedged with the forward contract represents the expected value of the transaction hedged with the option contracts. The third panel of Figure 9-8 indeed suggests that the expected value could be $2,000,000 based on the pictured distribution. Hence, Sardy should conclude that, on average, the option hedge does not put him in better or worse condition than the forward hedge. The choice thus boils down to comparing the distribution of possible outcomes, or comparing $2,000,000 known with certainty to the distribution ranging from 1,889,300 to slightly more than $2,789,300 shown in the third panel.

Because option hedges do not alter the expected value of an exposed position when option premiums are determined in efficient markets, such hedges simply rearrange the distribution of possible outcomes by establishing a floor or ceiling and a continuum of opportunities to reap gains in excess of the premium paid. Some observers have therefore considered option hedges of little use, except when the cash flow being hedged is associated with some uncertainty of actually occurring (as addressed in the previous section). However, if the option sets a floor or ceiling at a level sufficient to prevent the firm from facing financial difficulties which it might face in the absence of the hedge, then the objective of hedging has been achieved. We reconsider this in a broader view of hedging strategy presented in Chapter 10. However, this does not imply that an option hedge is superior to a forward hedge, just that it is superior to no hedge at all.

❖ SUMMARY OF CHAPTER OBJECTIVES

1. Hedge a transaction using a forward contract on foreign exchange.

Forward contracts are designed to hedge large foreign currency transactions for which the amount and date are known. A receipt of foreign currency is hedged by selling the foreign currency forward and a payment of foreign currency is hedged by buying the foreign currency forward.

2. Hedge a transaction using international money markets.

Money market hedges require borrowing and lending in the international money markets. A receipt of foreign currency is hedged by borrowing the foreign currency and holding the home currency, and a payment of foreign currency is hedged by holding the foreign currency and borrowing the home currency.

3. Compare forward and money market hedges, specifically in the context of equilibrium in the financial markets.

In equilibrium, forward and money market hedges are identical. However, because private borrowers must usually borrow at an interest rate above the inter-bank rate, and as depositors put money on deposit at an interest rate slightly below the inter-bank rate, forward contracts are usually cheaper than money market hedges. Money market

HEDGING WITH FINANCIAL INSTRUMENTS AT COCA-COLA

The Coca-Cola Company derived approximately 74 percent of its $5 billion of 1998 operating income outside the United States, so the company is definitely concerned about foreign exchange risk. The company manages most of its foreign currency exposures on a consolidated basis, which allows it to "net certain exposures and take advantage of any natural offsets" (1998 Annual Report, p. 30) of the types discussed in Chapter 8. The company uses derivative financial instruments to further reduce net exposure to currency fluctuations, primarily by hedging specific transactions. As discussed in its 1998 Annual Report (p. 30):

> We do not enter into derivative financial instruments for trading purposes. As a matter of policy, all our derivative positions are used to reduce risk by hedging an underlying economic exposure. Because of the high correlation between the hedging instrument and the underlying exposure, fluctuations in the value of the instruments are generally offset by reciprocal

changes in the value of the underlying exposure. The derivatives we use are straightforward instruments with liquid markets.

In disclosing the magnitude of derivative financial instruments held, the report states that "We enter into forward exchange contracts and purchase currency options . . . to hedge firm sale commitments denominated in foreign currencies. We also purchase currency options . . . to hedge certain anticipated sales" (p. 51). The company also uses swaps to hedge foreign exchange exposure. Table 9-2 summarizes the financial instruments held for foreign currency management. Although the magnitude of Coca-Cola's foreign currency derivative portfolio is large at $3 billion to $4 billion, the net amount of assets minus liabilities is much smaller, at ±1 billion. In turn, this is a small portion of the company's $19 billion in assets and $19 billion in annual sales revenue.

Source: The Coca-Cola Company 1998 Annual Report.

TABLE 9-2   Derivative Financial Management Instruments for Foreign Currency Management at Coca-Cola (millions of dollars)

	December 31, 1998		December 31, 1997	
Derivative Insturment	*Notional Principal*	*Maturity*	*Notional Principal*	*Maturity*
Forward Contracts				
Assets	809	1999–2000	1,286	1998–1999
Liabilities	1,325	1999–2000	465	1998–1999
Swap Agreements				
Assets	344	1999–2000	178	1998
Liabilities	704	1999–2002	1,026	1998–2002
Purchased Options				
Assets	232	1999	1,051	1998
Total Derivatives	3,414		4,006	
Net Assets less Liabilities	−644		1,024	

Source: The Coca-Cola Company 1998 Annual Report, pp. 51–52.

hedges are more advantageous than forward contracts only if the firm can borrow at a below-market interest rate or lend at an above-market interest rate. However, money market hedges are also useful when forward contracts are not readily available.

4. Analyze foreign currency swaps.

Swap agreements are essentially forward and money market contracts combined, and are useful when a somewhat longer time horizon—such as a decade—is involved in the hedge.

5. Hedge an exposure using foreign currency futures contracts.

Futures contracts are like forward contracts, but are traded on an organized exchange. A receipt of foreign currency is hedged by selling futures contracts and a payment of foreign currency is hedged by buying futures contracts. Futures contracts are important hedging tools when a cash flow transaction date is not certain, when the transaction amount is not precise, and when a transaction is too small to be hedged in the forward market.

6. Compare forward and futures hedges, specifically in the context of equilibrium in the financial markets.

In equilibrium, forward and futures contracts are identical. However, some institutional characteristics, such as the required deposit into a margin account for futures contracts, provide reasons for forward and futures prices to diverge.

7. Hedge an exposure using foreign currency options contracts.

Options contracts give the purchaser of the contract the right to exchange currencies in the future without the obligation to do so. They are most appropriately chosen to hedge a transaction that is not certain to occur, but may also be used if a firm wants to protect itself from most of the downside on a known transaction but reap some of the profits on the upside. A receipt of foreign currency is hedged using a put option and a payment of foreign currency is hedged using a call option.

8. Compare forward and options hedges, specifically in the context of equilibrium in the financial markets.

As an option has an asymmetric distribution of pay-offs, comparing forward and options hedges is difficult. However, in equilibrium, the expected value of a transaction hedged with an option is identical to the known value of the transaction hedged with a forward contract.

❖ **QUESTIONS FOR REVIEW**

1. A U.S. corporation will receive 2.5 million Portuguese escudos in 1 year and wishes to hedge this in the forward market. Assume that the forward rate quoted between the U.S. dollar and the Portuguese escudo is $0.006633/escudo. What action is taken in the forward market? How much is this firm's receivable in U.S. dollars?

2. Suppose a U.S. company, Johnson Enterprises, buys manufacturing equipment from a French company for FF 1 million. Payment will occur in one year, and Johnson wants to protect the dollar value of this payable. After calling its lead bank,

Johnson decided to use a money market hedge. The spot exchange rate is $0.20/FF. The bank provided the following borrowing and lending rates:

	Deposit Rate (in percent)	Lending Rate (in percent)
1-year U.S. dollar	8	10
1-year French francs	12	14

Explain the money market hedge which protects the dollar value of Johnson's payable, and calculate the U.S. dollar value which is locked in by the money market hedge.

3. The spot exchange rate between the French franc and the U.S. dollar on a certain date is FF 6 = $1 and the 1-year forward exchange rate is FF 6.25 = $1.

   a. A U.S. multinational corporation will receive 6 million French francs in one year. If it wishes to lock in the dollar value of the receipts now, what action should it take in the forward market and what is the future dollar value of the receivable?

   b. What is the forward premium or discount on the French franc?

   c. If the one-year French franc simple-interest Eurocurrency rate is 8 percent, what is the U.S. dollar simple-interest Eurocurrency rate?

   d. What money market hedge is equivalent to the forward hedge used in question a? Be sure to give amounts of currencies.

4. [Class discussion] In general, are money market hedges preferred to forward market hedges, or vice versa? When would the preference be reversed?

5. GWU Associates has an account receivable of 300,000 Belgian francs which will be collected in one year. The current spot exchange rate is $0.0300/Belgian franc. The firm wishes to hedge this transaction to protect itself from foreign exchange risk. A bank provides the following interest rate quotes for deposits and loans:

	Deposit Rate (in percent)	Loan Rate (in percent)
1-year U.S. dollar	10	14
1-year Belgian francs	12	15

and simultaneously quotes a forward rate of $0.0295/Belgian franc. Compare a money market hedge to a forward market hedge using this information. Which hedge should GWU Associates choose? Is this a typical outcome when comparing forward and money market hedges?

6. Suppose the French company LeBlanc sold $1 million of wine glasses to Lemberg Enterprises, an American company. The sale, denominated in U.S. dollars, occurred in January and payment is to occur in July, six months later. The company decided to hedge this transaction in the forward market to avoid foreign exchange exposure. At the time of the transaction, the spot exchange rate was 5.000 FF/$, and the six-month forward rate was 5.115 FF/$. A six-month Euro-franc deposit carried an interest rate of 15.12 percent. The company records the account receivable converted at the spot rate, for a value of FF 5 million.

   a. What is the forward premium (discount) on the U.S. dollar vis-à-vis the French franc?

   b. Assuming that covered interest parity holds, what is the Euro-dollar interest rate?

   c. If the spot rate on the date of payment is 5.100 FF/$, what will the company record as the foreign exchange gain (loss) on the receivable?

   d. If the spot rate on the date of payment is 5.100 FF/$, as in c, what will the company record as the foreign exchange gain (loss) on the forward contract?

7. Currency futures contracts are traded on organized exchanges. Suppose you sell a contract on Australian dollars in the amount of A$100,000 on the Chicago Mercantile Exchange at $0.7900/A$. Upon maturity of the contract, the futures price is $0.7500/A$.

   a. Have you made money or lost money? How much have you made or lost?

   b. If you hold your position to maturity, what do you do to settle the contract? How are the gains or losses paid?

8. [Class discussion] What are the main disadvantages of hedging with futures contracts compared to hedging with forward contracts?

9. A Boston consulting firm signed a contract to sell consulting services to an Australian firm for A$1,000,000 on April 15. Payment is to occur on July 15. To protect itself from Australian dollar depreciation, the firm decides to hedge the transaction in the futures market. It therefore sells September Australian dollar futures contracts, which are traded in units of A$100,000. Additional information:

   i. The spot exchange rate on April 15, S_t, is $0.82/A$.

   ii. The September futures rate on April 15, $Z_{t,T}$, is $0.7992/A$.

   iii. The interest rate on U.S. dollar Eurocurrency deposits is 12 percent on April 15.

   iv. The interest rate on Australian dollar Eurocurrency deposits is 18 percent on April 15.

   v. The spot exchange rate on July 15, S_{t+n}, is $0.75/A$.

   vi. The September futures rate on July 15, $Z_{t+n,T}$, is $0.7410/A$

   a. What is the U.S. dollar equivalent of the A$1,000,000 account receivable? (HINT: Both of these are future values.)

   b. If the firm sells ten futures contracts to hedge the A$1,000,000 account receivable, what is the total gain or loss of the account receivable and the futures hedge?

10. [Class discussion] In what kinds of situations would you advise someone to hedge a foreign currency exposure using foreign currency options?

11. A firm has decided to purchase a call option on British pounds. The strike price written into the option is $1.55/£ and the premium is 3 cents per pound.

   a. Using a diagram, show the profit profile for the option. Label the diagram carefully, showing the strike price, premium, and break-even point.

   b. The company is also considering a call option with a strike price of $1.57/£. Will the premium on this be higher or lower than the premium on the call with the strike price of $1.55/£? Show the profit profile for this option in the same space used in part a, carefully considering what happens to the strike price, the premium, and the break-even point.

12. A U.S. company may have a cash inflow of 125,000 DM within the next quarter and decides to hedge this potential inflow using American-style options. The current spot rate is $0.60/DM and the company purchases options with a strike price of $0.56/DM for 0.5 cents per DM.

   a. How much does the company pay for the options to hedge the total cash flow?

   b. What approximate boundary price of the exchange rate has the company locked in? (Specify ceiling or floor.)

c. If interest rates on DM increase, but interest rates on the U.S. dollar remain the same and the spot rate remains at $0.60/DM, what happens to the value of the option?

d. If the company receives payment six weeks later and the spot rate on that date is $0.63/DM, what should the firm do with the foreign currency and with the option?

13. Your U.S.-based company might have an inflow of 125,000 DM in May from a bid you recently submitted to supply services to a German company. You are thinking of hedging this contingent cash flow using options. Shown below is the options trading report from the Philadelphia Exchange. The spot rate is 72.68 cents per DM, or $0.7268/DM. You are considering the use of American style options.

62,500 German marks-cents per unit

Strike	Expiration	Calls Vol.	Calls Last	Puts Vol.	Puts Last
70½	May	. . .	. . .	700	0.26
71	May	. . .	. . .	1000	0.35
72½	May	. . .	. . .	4	0.83
72½	Jun	. . .	. . .	3	1.50
74	May	2	0.60	. . .	. . .
74	Jun	2	1.16	. . .	. . .
74½	May	. . .	. . .	10	2.11
75	May	4	0.37	. . .	. . .

a. When you call your broker to purchase the options that will hedge the potential cash flow, what do you order? Be sure to indicate the quantity of options desired and whether you need puts or calls.

b. If you decide to purchase options with a strike price of 72.5 cents per DM, what is the total options premium paid?

c. If the options are exercised, what is the dollar cash flow from selling services to the German company? (Don't forget to account for the options premium.)

d. What is the options premium as a percent of the value of the currency exchanged?

14. A U.S. multinational corporation is considering a one-year investment in the Durango stock market.

   i. The standard deviation of annual returns on the Durango market index in tuskers (the local currency) is 20 percentage points.

   ii. The standard deviation of annual percentage changes in the Durango tusker/U.S. dollar exchange rate is 14 percentage points.

   iii. Empirical studies have shown that the Durango market index is not exposed to exchange rate changes; in other words, the tusker returns in the Durango market as a whole are not affected by currency appreciation or depreciation.

The corporation is considering an imperfect hedge for this investment using futures contracts with a hedge ratio of unity.

   i. The standard deviation of annual percentage changes in the value of the futures contracts is 16 percentage points.

   ii. The covariance between annual percentage changes in the exchange rate and annual percentage changes in the value of futures contracts is 210 percentage points squared. (Hence, the correlation coefficient is 0.9375.)

    a. What is the standard deviation of unhedged dollar returns on the Durango stock market?

    b. What is the standard deviation of the percentage changes in the hedged exchange rate?

    c. What is the hedged foreign exchange risk as a percent of open risk?

    d. If the multinational corporation undertakes the imperfect currency hedge, what is the standard deviation of the hedged dollar returns on the Durango stock market?

TOOLS FOR ANALYSIS

The Minimum Variance Futures Hedge

This section calculates the minimum variance futures hedge by specifying the optimum hedge ratio, the quantity of futures purchased or sold for each unit of exposure. We specifically deal with the case in which the cash flow denominated in foreign currency is known with certainty. The method can also be used when the cash flow denominated in foreign currency is uncertain; for this, see Kerkvliet and Moffett (1991).

    Let $H = (N)(Q)/X$ be the hedge ratio, where N is the number of futures contracts, Q is the size of each contract, and X is the amount of exposure denominated in local currency units. The gain or loss on the position hedged with futures using a hedge ratio H is:

$$\text{Gain(Loss)} = X[(S_{t+n} - bS_t) - (H)(Z_{t+n,T} - Z_{t,T})]$$

The variance of the gain or loss is therefore:

$$\text{Var} = X^2\{\text{Var}(S_{t+n} - bS_t) + H^2\,\text{Var}(Z_{t+n,T} - Z_{t,T}) - 2(H)\text{Cov}[(S_{t+n} - bS_t),(Z_{t+n,T} - Z_{t,T})]\}$$

where S_t is again the spot exchange rate and $Z_{t,T}$ is the futures price of a contract maturing at time T.

    The hedge ratio H is selected to minimize the variance by applying principles of calculus. Setting:

$$\frac{d\text{Var}}{dH} = \frac{X^2(2(H)\text{Var}(Z_{t+n,T} - Z_{t,T}) - 2\text{Cov}[(S_{t+n} - bS_t),(Z_{t+n,T} - Z_{t,T})])}{} = 0$$

and, solving for H, we find that:

$$H = \frac{\text{Cov}[(S_{t+n} - bS_t),(Z_{t+n,T} - Z_{t,T})]}{\text{Var}(Z_{t+n,T} - Z_{t,T})}$$

is the optimal hedge ratio. This hedge ratio produces the lowest level of risk possible. Of course, the actual hedge based on hedge ratio H must be rounded to the nearest whole number of contracts. Once H is found, the number of contracts to purchase is $N = (H)(X)/Q$.

One way to find the minimum variance hedge ratio H is by using regression analysis and historical data. When $(S_{t+n} - bS_t)$ is regressed onto $(Z_{t+n,T} - Z_{t,T})$, the beta coefficient is the covariance between the dependent variable and the independent variable divided by the variance of the independent variable. Hence, the beta coefficient is precisely the minimum variance hedge ratio. This technique is particularly useful in choosing cross-hedges, such as when a French franc exposure is hedged using DM futures.

    When a hedge ratio is used, hedging effectiveness is:

$$\left[1 - \frac{\text{Var}[(S_{t+n} - bS_t) - (H)(Z_{t+n,T} - Z_{t,T})]}{\text{Var}(S_{t+n} - bS_t)}\right] \times 100$$

and after substituting in the defintion of the minimum-variance hedge ratio, H, and performing algebraic manipulations, this expression is simplified to:

$$(\text{Corr}[(S_{t+n} - bS_t),(Z_{t+n,T} - Z_{t,T})])^2 \times 100$$

where $\text{Corr}[(S_{t+n} - bS_t),(Z_{t+n,T} - Z_{t,T})]$ denotes the simple correlation coefficient between $(S_{t+n} - bS_t)$ and $(Z_{t+n,T} - Z_{t,T})$. Clearly, the hedge is more effective the higher the correlation. (Recall from statistics that the correlation between two variables is the covariance between the two variables divided by the standard deviation of each variable.)

    In the presence of a hedge ratio, the hedged risk as a percent of open risk becomes:

$$\sqrt{\frac{\text{Var}[(S_{t+n} - bS_t) - (H)(Z_{t+n,T} - Z_{t,T})]}{\text{Var}(S_{t+n} - bS_t)}} \times 100$$

and substituting in for the optimal hedge ratio H, this expression is simplified to:

$$\sqrt{1 - (\text{Corr}[(S_{t+n} - bS_t),(Z_{t+n,T} - Z_{t,T})])^2} \times 100$$

where again it is clear that the hedge is more effective the higher the correlation.

EXAMPLE 9.13

Recall the case of Durrell Enterprises from the examples in the chapter. For Durrell's hedge involving the Swiss franc, $\text{Var}(S_{t+n} - bS_t) = 0.0016$, $\text{Var}(Z_{t+n,T} - Z_{t,T}) = 0.0020$, and $\text{Var}[(S_{t+n} - bS_t) - (Z_{t+n,T} - Z_{t,T})] = 0.0002$, and $\text{Cov}[(S_{t+n} - bS_t), (Z_{t+n,T} - Z_{t,T})] = 0.0017$. The optimal hedge ratio for Durrell Enterprises' ongoing business with Swiss firms, based on the historical data given, is $H = [0.0017/0.0020] = 0.85$. As the correlation coefficient is:

$$\text{Corr}[(S_{t+n} - bS_t), (Z_{t+n,T} - Z_{t,T})]$$
$$= \frac{0.0017}{\sqrt{0.0016}\,\sqrt{0.0020}} = .95$$

the hedge ratio of 0.85 removes $.95^2 = .9025$ or 90.25 percent of the variance, so hedging is 90.25 percent effective. The hedge ratio of 0.85 is therefore more effective than a hedge ratio of 1 (which produced hedging effectiveness of 87.5 percent). Alternatively, the hedge ratio reduces the hedged risk as a percent of open risk to:

$$\sqrt{1 - (.95)^2} \times 100 = 31.22\%$$

This is slightly less risk than the 35.4 percent based on a hedge ratio of 1. The total of Swiss franc accounts receivable for Durrell Enterprises is SFr 6.47 million, so the appropriate number of futures contracts to buy is $N = (H)(X)/Q = (.85)(6,470,000)/(125,000) = 44$ contracts.

❖ ENDNOTES

1. For more details, see, for example, "Accounting for Foreign Currency Transactions and Foreign Currency Derivatives," Chapter 12 of Radebaugh and Gray (1993), pp. 310–337, or the section on Foreign Currency Transactions in "Foreign Currency Translation," Chapter 4 of Choi and Mueller (1992), pp. 175–185.

2. This is the price of a European option when the annual standard deviation of exchange rate changes is 15 percentage points, given the spot rate, the dollar interest rate, the pound interest rate, the strike price, and the time to maturity given in the example.

❖ REFERENCES

Abuaf, Niso, and Stephan Schoess. "Foreign-Currency Options," Chapter 16 of *The Handbook of International Financial Management,* ed. by R. Z. Aliber, Dow Jones-Irwin, 1990, pp. 499–538.

Choi, Frederick D. S., and Gerhard G. Mueller. *International Accounting,* second edition, Prentice-Hall, 1992.

Cox, John, Robert Ingersoll, and Steven Ross. "The Relationship Between Forward and Futures Prices," *Journal of Financial Economics,* 1981, number 9, pp. 321–346.

Garman, Mark B., and Steven W. Kohlhagen. "Foreign Currency Option Values," *Journal of International Money and Finance,* 1983, volume 2, pp. 231–237.

Giddy, Ian. "The Foreign Exchange Option as a Hedging Tool," *Midland Corporate Finance Journal,* Fall 1983, pp. 32–42.

Giddy, Ian, and Gunter Dufey. "Uses and Abuses of Currency Options," *Bank of America Journal of Applied Corporate Finance,* Fall 1995, pp. 49–57.

Grabbe, J. Orlin. *International Financial Markets,* Prentice-Hall, 1996.

Handjinicolaou, George. "The Forward Foreign Exchange Market: An Alternative for Hedging Currency Risks," Chapter 13 of *The Handbook of Currency and Interest Rate Risk Management,* edited by Robert J. Schwartz and Clifford W. Smith, Jr., New York Institute of Finance, 1990, pp. 13-1–13-38.

Hodrick, Robert J. *The Empirical Evidence on the Efficiency of Forward and Futures Foreign Exchange Markets,* Harwood Academic Publishers, 1987.

Hopper, Gregory P. "A Primer on Currency Derivatives," Federal Reserve Bank of Philadelphia *Business Review,* May/June 1995, pp. 3–14.

Kerkvliet, Joe, and Michael H. Moffett. "The Hedging of an Uncertain Future Foreign Currency Cash Flow," *Journal of Financial and Quantitative Analysis,* December 1991, pp. 565–578.

Radebaugh, Lee H., and Sidney J. Gray. *International Accounting and Multinational Enterprises,* third edition, John Wiley & Sons, 1993.

CHAPTER 10

RISK MANAGEMENT STRATEGY

CHAPTER OBJECTIVES
AFTER READING THIS CHAPTER, YOU SHOULD BE ABLE TO:

❖ Assess foreign exchange risk and design risk management strategy for the short run, the intermediate run, and the long run.

❖ Describe some short-run techniques to manage transactions that are exposed to foreign exchange risk.

❖ Formulate intermediate-run operating strategies to manage foreign exchange risk.

❖ Analyze risk management strategy from a broad perspective.

This chapter provides a broad perspective on issues in international risk management. In the first section, we examine the nature of foreign exchange risk and risk management in a temporal context using a "short" run, an "intermediate" run, and a "long" run. The second section then discusses short-run transactions management, and the third section discusses intermediate-run operations management. By way of synthesis, the final section considers the nature of risk management from a general perspective.

10.1   INTRODUCTION

Part III, on Managing Foreign Exchange Risk, has thus far contained chapters on translation and transaction exposure, economic exposure, the risk of foreign exchange exposure, and the mechanics of hedging with financial instruments. These provide the foundations for formulating an overall risk management strategy, a topic which has received major managerial interest during the past decade; for example, see the Cummins, Phillips, and Smith (1998) survey. At this point in Part III, many questions regarding an overall risk management strategy remain unanswered, so this chapter seeks to turn attention away from the more technical issues addressed in Chapters 6 to 9 to develop a broader perspective on risk management. In particular, this chapter moves the focus of managing foreign exchange exposure away from hedging with financial instruments to more general issues concerning risk management strategy. As such, it draws together several ideas presented in the previous four chapters and expands the outlook.

10.2   FOREIGN EXCHANGE RISK AND RISK MANAGEMENT IN THE SHORT RUN, INTERMEDIATE RUN, AND LONG RUN

Chapters 6 to 9 provide the tools for analyzing foreign exchange risk, but have not yet been tied together to provide guidance for managers within a firm. Although Chapters 6 and 7 examine definitions and measurements of exposure, one question left hanging is, "How much should managers worry about each measure of exposure?" Similarly, Chapter 8 examines the volatility of exchange rates, but another question left unanswered is, "How much should managers worry about exchange rate changes?" And finally, although Chapter 8 introduces active management of diversification and Chapter 9 considers hedging with financial instruments to reduce foreign exchange risk, the big question that remains unanswered is, "How much should managers worry about managing foreign exchange risk?" To a certain extent, these questions are difficult to answer because the answers are not precise. Furthermore, academics or practitioners within finance and international economics are not in agreement about what the answers are. As a result, this chapter cannot give definitive answers to the questions, but will provide sketches of answers based on the current status of knowledge in risk management.

To help answer the three questions, consider a stylized time line containing a short run, an intermediate run, and a long run. At this point, the duration of the short run is unspecified, and the point at which a long run begins is unspecified, but a discussion of the answers to the questions will help develop the time line framework further.

HOW MUCH SHOULD MANAGERS WORRY ABOUT EACH MEASURE OF EXPOSURE?

As there are several different exposure concepts, a manager needs to decide how much to worry about each one. Translation or accounting exposure essentially considers the difference between the book value of assets and liabilities denominated in a foreign currency, and therefore has the limitations discussed in Chapter 6. It focuses on the balance sheet to the exclusion of the income statement, and on book values rather than economic values and actual cash flows. In practice, changes in the balance sheet may have little effect on the ongoing operations of the firm. The concept is thus too narrow, and managers should therefore not worry about translation exposure very much, if at all. As translation exposure is essentially superseded by the concept of net worth exposure, introduced in Chapter 7 as the economic interpretation of balance sheet exposure, the economic value of assets and liabilities on the balance sheet will still be important. This issue is taken up again later. Consequently, we can now dismiss translation exposure from further discussion.

The second concept of exposure, transaction exposure, is similarly limited, but in a more rational way. The focus on known, contractual cash flows overlooks all the ongoing revenues and expenses not contractually specified. However, the focus on known, contractual cash flows has the advantage of isolating transactions that have a definite, and generally immediate, impact on a company's profits. As exchange rates change, there will be gains and losses carried directly to the income statement as transactions are consummated. As a result, managers should worry about transaction exposure in a short run context—focusing on transactions that will take place within a year or two and not quite as much on transactions that are scheduled after that. Transaction contracts nearly always specify nominal currency amounts, so hedging specific transactions using the financial instruments described in Chapter 9 will protect the firm from any unanticipated exchange rate changes—whether nominal or real. This means that transactions are easy to hedge precisely because they are known, contractual amounts, and the financial instruments used in hedging are quoted in nominal terms. Because forward, money market, futures, and options contracts are generally available for a horizon of a year or two, hedging transactions exposure makes sense in the short run.

Economic exposure, both cash flow exposure and net worth exposure, is what managers should ultimately worry about because it defines the firm's competitive position by focusing mainly on its ongoing operations and cash flows. The chief disadvantage of focusing on economic exposure is that it is very difficult to quantitatively measure, partially because there are no contracts or pieces of paper specifying amounts that are exposed, but also because the focus is on real exchange rate changes rather than on nominal exchange rate changes. In addition, measurement is difficult because analysis must stretch beyond a horizon of a year or two, into an intermediate run. Hence, managers should worry about economic exposure as part of strategic analysis that extends beyond the short run. Another problem with economic exposure is that, even when managers figure out the nature of the firm's economic exposure, managing the exposure in the intermediate run is difficult. Hedging cash flow exposure is difficult due to the ongoing and non-contractual nature of the concept. Furthermore, financial instruments are simply not very useful in this case because they are specified in nominal amounts and do not extend very far into the future. Net worth exposure is a little easier to measure and hedge if assets and liabilities are stated in market values. Unfortunately, a net worth hedge in the absence of a cash flow hedge is so incomplete as to become useless. Managing economic exposure is thus more art than science.

Up to now, we have addressed hedging concerns with respect to transactions exposure. However, the firm is ultimately concerned with economic exposure. It is therefore important to examine transaction exposure by carefully evaluating whether there is underlying economic exposure. Thus, a manager must determine what happens to both the revenues and the costs as exchange rates change to verify that a specific transaction is associated with economic exposure. Making his determination requires that he evaluate transactions for cash inflows with respect to what will happen to cash outflows as exchange rates change, and that he evaluate transactions for cash outflows with respect to what will happen to cash inflows as exchange rates change. Will a depreciation of a foreign currency that reduces the value of a known, contractual receivable also reduce costs even if these costs are not contractually specified? Will an appreciation that raises the value of a known, contractual payable allow the firm to raise prices to offset the higher cost? In other words, a complete picture needs to be reviewed by putting the transaction into perspective vis-à-vis the firm's overall cash flows.

Whenever a currency movement affects revenues and costs equally, the transaction is not associated with much economic exposure—only the profit margin is exposed. In some cases, the relevant comparison is between the (market) value of assets and liabilities on the balance sheet. If a change in the home currency market value of an asset is equal to the change in the home currency market value of a liability, the transaction is not associated with economic exposure. When transactions are not associated with economic exposure they should obviously not be hedged.

The chief distinction between transactions exposure and economic exposure is the degree of certainty associated with the cash flows. The former involves uncertainty only about the home currency value of the cash flow, but not about the foreign currency value. Economic exposure, on the other hand, nearly always involves uncertainty about both the home and the foreign currency value of the cash flow. Hence, by its very nature, economic exposure is much harder to quantify and therefore much more difficult to hedge. The financial hedges we examined earlier—forwards, money markets, futures, and options—are clearly useful only over a short run, precisely because their duration is limited to a few years or less. However, these financial instruments are as effective in hedging economic exposure as they are in hedging transactions exposure within this time period. As the quantity and timing of cash flows is not known precisely, the hedging activity is a little more difficult. Nevertheless, there are indeed examples of firms using financial instruments to hedge economic exposure in the short run, although they must recognize that financial hedges are imperfect and temporary.

HOW MUCH SHOULD MANAGERS WORRY ABOUT EXCHANGE RATE CHANGES?

Properties of exchange rates give indications of how much managers should worry about exchange rate volatility. Chapter 8 provides quantitative data on the standard deviations of percentage changes in exchange rates. One result presented there is that the standard deviation of annualized percentage changes declines as the horizon lengthens from one month to one quarter to one year. This result can be extended to show that the standard deviation of average annual exchange rate changes declines as the length of the holding period increases from one year to two years, then to five years and ten years, and so on. Thus, as an empirical proposition, exchange risk declines as the short run gives way to the intermediate run because the volatility of exchange rates declines. In addition, however, there are theoretical propositions which reinforce this result, mainly purchasing power parity and uncovered interest parity that were introduced in Chapter 2 and applied to the discussion of exposure and risk in both Chapters 7 and 8.

LUFTHANSA'S AIRCRAFT PURCHASE (REVISITED)

Chapter 9 presents the basic facts about Lufthansa's purchase of U.S. aircraft in early 1985, with payment due in early 1986. Various financial hedges were applied to the $500 million liability. From a broader perspective, however, Lufthansa's aircraft purchase raises some more subtle questions about hedging.

One question is whether economic exposure was really associated with transaction exposure when Lufthansa purchased the aircraft. To the extent that Lufthansa was acquiring an asset with this liability, an important consideration is what happens to the value of the asset as the value of the exchange rate changes. A loss on the cash outflow might be offset by a gain in the value of the assets and vice versa; the firm pays more (less) DM for the aircraft but the aircraft are worth more (less) when denominated in DM. This would be the case if the market value of the aircraft was stable in dollars. It is highly likely that the market value of the U.S. aircraft, which is literally a mobile asset, is determined in dollar-denominated worldwide markets, which means that the DM value of the aircraft probably declined as the dollar fell. In this case, Lufthansa not only paid more than it would have in the absence of the hedge, but, more importantly, it paid more than the market value of the aircraft. It either showed the loss from the forward contract on the income statement or recorded the value of the aircraft at an improperly high amount on the balance sheet. In either case, the bottom line is that Lufthansa most likely introduced economic exposure where none previously existed.

A related question is how the firm's ongoing cash flows are affected by dollar/DM exchange rate changes. Considering that the aircraft are being purchased to generate revenues in the form of future passenger receipts, Lufthansa (and Lufthansa's shareholders) should value the assets as the present value of the profits generated from putting the assets into service.

If passenger revenues are tied to the U.S. dollar such that a depreciation of the dollar reduces Lufthansa's DM receipts, then the profitability of operating the aircraft is lower. This would be the case if Lufthansa faced competition from U.S. airlines. Lufthansa might also enjoy lower fuel costs with the depreciation of the dollar, because jet fuel is basically priced in dollars, but these lower costs might not be enough to offset the reduction in revenue. Hence, Lufthansa may face operating exposure on the purchase of the aircraft after all.

The dollar depreciation causes the present value of profits to be lower, so Lufthansa would have best preserved the positive net present value of the capital projects by paying less for the aircraft. In this scenario, Lufthansa most likely exacerbated its economic exposure by hedging the purchase of the aircraft, because this introduced additional economic exposure where a natural hedge of underlying operating exposure already existed. In fact, Lufthansa could have constructed an operating hedge by financing the aircraft over their useful lives using debt denominated in dollars. As the dollar depreciates and profits fall, the value of the liability (along with the interest and principal payments) will also fall.

It is also possible, however, that passenger revenues are tied to the U.S. dollar such that a depreciation of the dollar increases Lufthansa's DM receipts. This would be the case if the dollar depreciation stimulates more visits to the United States and other parts of the world by Germans who use Lufthansa. Accompanied by a reduction in fuel costs, profitability would increase. Hence, dollar depreciation causes the present value of profits to be higher, so dollar appreciation causes the present value of profits to be lower.

Lufthansa should therefore protect itself from having to pay more for the aircraft when the dollar appreciates, so it should hedge the $500 million cash outflow. This strategy will best preserve the positive net present value of the capital project. Furthermore, if Lufthansa decides to finance the purchase of the aircraft over their useful lives, it should not denominate the debt in dollars.

The length of the holding period is important in assessing how much managers should worry about exchange rate changes. Chapter 8 considers the short-run focus on monthly, quarterly, and annual standard deviations, and reveals that annual standard deviations tend to range from 10 to 15 percentage points for different industrial currencies. Figure 10-1 uses this information as the starting point for developing the relationship between risk and time. Note that there are two lines in Figure 10-1, one starting at 10 and one starting at 15 for the first year. Moving to the right, the standard deviation of average annual percentage changes in exchange rates declines as the length of the holding period increases. This decline is based on having multiple draws from the annual distributions of exchange rate changes, with standard deviations of 10 and 15, that are assumed to be independent. For example, with a holding period of two years there are two draws from the annual distributions.

Using the standard deviation of 10 percentage points, the standard deviation of the average annual exchange rate change for two years is:

$$[\mathrm{Var}(1/2\,X + 1/2\,Y)]^{1/2} = [1/4\,\mathrm{Var}(X + Y)]^{1/2} = [1/4(\mathrm{Var}\,X + \mathrm{Var}\,Y)]^{1/2}$$
$$= [1/4(2\,\mathrm{Var}\,X)]^{1/2} = [1/2\,\mathrm{Var}\,X]^{1/2} = [1/2]^{1/2}[\mathrm{Var}\,X]^{1/2}$$
$$= [1/2]^{1/2}[\sigma_X] = [.7071][10] = 7.071$$

where X is the exchange rate change in the first year and Y is the exchange rate change in the second year, and X and Y are both drawn from the same distribution with a standard deviation of 10.

FIGURE 10-1   STANDARD DEVIATION OF AVERAGE ANNUAL EXCHANGE RATE CHANGES AS A FUNCTION OF HOLDING PERIOD

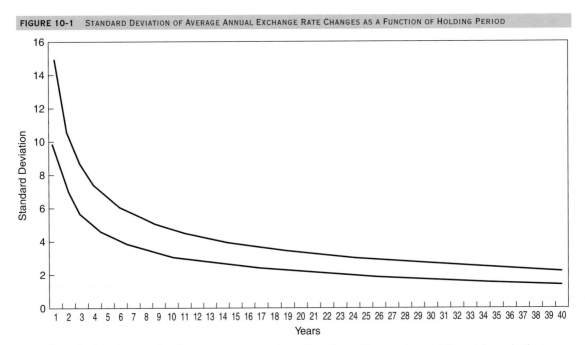

Annual standard deviations of exchange rate changes of $\sigma = 10$ and $\sigma = 15$ percentage points are shown in the two lines: note that the lower line begins at 10 and the upper line begins at 15 for the 1-year holding period. As the length of the holding period increases, the standard deviation of average annual percentage changes declines in accordance with the formula $[1/n]^{1/2}[\sigma]$, where n is the number of years.

Similarly, using the standard deviation of 15 percentage points, the standard deviation of the average annual exchange rate change for a two-year holding period is $[.7071][15] = 10.6066$. In general, the standard deviation of the average annual exchange rate change for n years is $[1/n]^{1/2}[\sigma]$, where σ is either 10 or 15 in our examples. Thus, the standard deviation drops to half at the four-year holding period, and to one-third at the nine-year period.

EXAMPLE 10.1

Barak Enterprises is considering an investment in Japanese yen which would take the form of a yen-denominated bond. For simplicity, the term structure of interest rates is assumed to be flat at 3 percent. The annual standard deviation of percentage changes in the $/¥ exchange rate has historically been about 13 percentage points. This means that a one-year investment in yen at 3 percent is expected to have a dollar-equivalent return in the range from −23 to 29 percent with 95 percent probability (representing two standard deviations). The average annual standard deviation of percentage changes in the exchange rate for a five-year horizon is $[1/5]^{1/2}[13] = 5.2$ and that for a ten-year horizon is $[1/10]^{1/2}[13] = 4.1$. A five-year investment at a yen rate of 3 percent is thus expected to have a dollar-equivalent average annual return in the range of −7.4 to 13.4 percent with 95 percent probability. A ten-year investment at 3 percent is expected to have a dollar-equivalent average annual return in the range of −5.2 to 11.2 percent with 95 percent probability. As the holding period of the investment increases from one year to five years to ten years, the position is associated with less foreign exchange risk.

Based on empirical characteristics, it is clear that a short run extending to a year or two is characterized by relatively high risk because the volatility of exchange rates is highest, and that an intermediate run from about two years to approximately ten years is characterized by moderate risk because the volatility of exchange rates is much less. This is similar to the analysis of domestic stock market investments, in which the short run is characterized by high risk because the annual volatility is high but the intermediate run is characterized by moderate risk because annual changes even out for longer holding periods. Beyond ten years, which might be called a "long run," exchange risk (or stock market risk, for that matter) is fairly low. In fact, the standard deviation of average annual exchange rate changes asymptotically approaches zero.

The implication here is that managers should in fact worry about exchange rate changes in the short run more than in the intermediate run, and should not worry about exchange rate changes in the long run very much at all. One caveat is that managers who are concerned about the value of a position on a particular date, known as the **terminal value,** should be aware that the standard deviation of the terminal value is larger as the horizon lengthens, even though the average annual standard deviation decreases, because there is more time for exchange rate changes to occur. The main point, however, is that the standard deviation of the terminal value ten years into the future is much less than ten times the standard deviation of a terminal value one year in the future.

In addition to empirical characteristics, theoretical propositions reinforce a focus on short-run and intermediate-run exchange rate changes. Specifically, purchasing power parity (PPP) and uncovered interest parity (UIP) are generally expected to hold in the long run as equilibrium conditions. In fact, the empirical examination of PPP and UIP in Chapter 2 demonstrates that the propositions tend to hold in a long-run sense. From the standpoint of foreign exchange risk, then, PPP suggests that there is no real exchange risk associated with cash flows and nonmonetary assets and liabilities in the long run, and UIP suggests that there is no real exchange risk of monetary assets and liabilities in the long run.

However, even if PPP and UIP hold in the long run, Chapter 2 demonstrates that there are clearly deviations from the propositions before then, in the short run and the intermediate run. As a result, there is exchange risk in the short and intermediate runs because there are deviations from PPP and UIP. Furthermore, the discussions in Chapters 2 and 8 demonstrate that in a short run of a year or two, nominal and real exchange rate changes are nearly identical because prices are relatively stable. In an intermediate run, perhaps from two to ten years, prices can be adjusted with more flexibility, and a distinction between nominal and real exchange rates is more meaningful. As a result, the short run deviations from PPP and UIP can be characterized by the changes in nominal exchange rates and the intermediate run deviations can be characterized by changes in real exchange rates.

This perspective has managerial implications because it suggests that managers should worry more about nominal exchange rate changes in the short run and subsequently focus on real exchange rate changes in the intermediate run. However, PPP and UIP also suggest that managers should not worry about either nominal or real exchange rate changes in the long run.

HOW MUCH SHOULD MANAGERS WORRY ABOUT MANAGING FOREIGN EXCHANGE RISK?

The discussion of exposure and exchange rate changes can now be used to begin a discussion about managing foreign exchange risk. So far, we have suggested that managers should worry about transactions exposure in the short run, because transaction exposure is easily measured and foreign exchange gains and losses directly and immediately affect the firm's income. The short run is also characterized by relatively volatile exchange rates, as deviations from PPP and UIP are common. Finally, the nature of the exchange risk can be represented by nominal exchange rate changes because they closely track real exchange rate changes. Hence, hedging transactions exposure is particularly appropriate in the short run because financial instruments, denominated in nominal currency amounts, are available for a horizon of one or two years. More generally, managing transactions in the short run is appropriate, where hedging is just one form of managing.

Another form is actively managing the benefits from diversification, as we discuss in Chapter 8 both with respect to exposure and with respect to international cash management. The next section in this chapter considers a few other techniques of short-run transactions management. The main point here is that an initial building block of risk management strategy appropriately focuses on transactions in the short run.

After the short run, risk management strategy must be different. We have suggested that managers should worry about economic exposure in the intermediate run, because economic exposure captures the firm's competitive position with respect to real exchange rate changes. The intermediate run is characterized by moderate exchange rate volatility, and deviations from PPP and UIP are still present. However, the nature of exchange risk can be represented by real exchange rate changes rather than nominal exchange rate changes because prices are more easily adjusted. Hedging is thus not a very viable approach to managing exchange risk in the intermediate run because the duration of most financial instruments is not long enough to be of use and such contracts are specified in nominal rather than real terms. As a result, the firm must consider operating techniques to manage economic exposure in the intermediate run.

Operating techniques to manage economic exposure in the intermediate run center on marketing and production decisions, but there is a financial technique embodied in long-term debt management as well. In this regard, the usefulness of hedging economic exposure with financial instruments is, in fact, limited to the time required to restructure operations through marketing and production plans. From the operating perspective, the short run is thus characterized by relatively fixed marketing and production plans, such as fixed marketing budgets and fixed input commitments. The intermediate run is characterized by an ability to alter marketing and production plans to respond to changes in real exchange rates, thereby managing exchange risk. These operating responses should be mixed, but should generally follow a simple principle: firms should react to deviations from PPP by curtailing activities where currency movements are disadvantageous and by expanding activities where currency movements are advantageous. As a result, the firm as a whole probably displays less variation in income as exchange rates change. In addition, however, the firm as a whole also tends to have lower foreign exchange losses and higher foreign exchange gains; thus, managing foreign exchange risk in the intermediate run creates value for the firm.

To exploit deviations from PPP to create firm value, the firm must have pre-planned flexibility in the intermediate run to alter marketing and production operations. According to some authors, this flexibility is the key to designing a global business strategy; for elaboration, see Kogut (1985a and 1985b) and Aaker and Mascarenhas (1984). This flexibility can be viewed as a portfolio of real options on foreign exchange of the kind covered in Chapter 5, and in fact suggests that foreign exchange risk is good because it adds value. We examine these marketing, production, and financial components of global business strategies thoroughly in a later section, after the section on short-term transactions management, so we do not discuss them further here. The main point we want to convey now is that a major building block of risk management strategy appropriately focuses on operations management in the intermediate run.

After an intermediate run, risk management strategy must yet again be different. We have already suggested that managers should not worry about exchange rate changes in the long run, because the long run is characterized by relatively stable exchange rates and a return to PPP and UIP. Hence, there is no exchange risk and management of exchange risk is not necessary. Hedging and other techniques of managing transactions are useless in the long run. In addition, marketing and production adjustments which prove to be so useful in the intermediate run are not effective in the long run. Market entry and exit will in fact enforce this. In the long run, the firm should itself be back to equilibrium with respect to marketing and production operations.

To ensure that the present value of long run profits is maximized in this equilibrium, the firm needs to make all long-run operating decisions based on the long-run PPP real exchange rate, with relatively little regard for the exact exchange rate in effect when the decision is made. This means that projections of future cash flows required in the capital budgeting decision must take into account long run equilibrium exchange rates. Hence, a firm selecting a production site should base the decision on the long-run comparative advantage of the location rather than on what might be a short-run deviation from the PPP exchange rate. For a firm that does not make long-run decisions based on the long-run PPP exchange rate, the result is a sub-optimal operating structure for the long run.

At an extreme, firms that are set up solely to profit from short-run deviations from PPP cannot survive in the long run. We developed these issues more technically in Chapter 3 on international capital budgeting and Chapter 5 on foreign investment strategy, so we only summarize here in the context of long run equilibrium. The main point of this discussion is that a final building block of risk management strategy appropriately recognizes that there is no foreign exchange risk in the long run.

SUMMARY OF FOREIGN EXCHANGE RISK IN THE SHORT RUN, INTERMEDIATE RUN, AND LONG RUN

To provide an overview of the discussion in this section, Table 10-1 considers the time line developed and the three questions discussed previously: (1) "How much should managers worry about each measure of exposure?" (2) "How much should managers worry about exchange rate changes?" (3) "How much should managers worry about managing foreign exchange risk?" The main point of the discussion of the short run is that an initial building block of risk management strategy appropriately focuses on transactions in the one- to two-year horizon. The main point of the discussion of the intermediate term is that a major building block of risk management strategy appropriately focuses on operations management in the two- to (perhaps) ten-year horizon. The main point of the discussion of the long run is that a final building block of risk management strategy appropriately recognizes that there is no foreign exchange risk in the long run.

The discussion of the short run, intermediate run, and long run suggests that risk management strategy should be based on managing the firm's economic value. The short-run transactions management strategy is thus based on ensuring the firm's sur-

TABLE 10-1 Foreign Exchange Risk and Risk Management Strategy in the Short Run, Intermediate Run, and Long Run ($t = 0$ represents the current time period)		
short run	*intermediate run*	*long run*
$t = 0$ - - - - - - - - - - - - - - - - - - - | - | ->		
focus on transactions exposure	focus on economic exposure	
hedging is easy	hedging is more difficult	
exchange rate volatility is high	exchange rate volatility is moderate	exchange rate volatility is low and approaches zero
deviations from PPP and UIP are common	deviations from PPP and UIP exist	PPP and UIP hold
exchange risk is predominantly nominal	exchange risk is predominantly real	no exchange risk
transactions management important (hedging, active diversification, and other techniques)	operations management important (marketing and production changes, appropriate long-term debt policy)	no risk management necessary
marketing and production plans are fixed	marketing and production plans are flexible	marketing and production plans are in long-run equilibrium

vival into the intermediate run. It is characterized by deviations from PPP and fairly high volatility of exchange rates, but also by relatively fixed marketing and production operations. As a result, financial hedges and short-run transactions management are useful in dealing with foreign exchange risk to ensure the firm's survival.

In turn, the intermediate-run strategy is based on maintaining—and perhaps increasing—the firm's economic value and on ensuring the firm's survival into the long run. While the intermediate run is characterized by deviations from PPP, it is also characterized by lower volatility of exchange rates and more flexibility in marketing and production

---

APPLICATION 10-2

EXCHANGE RISK MANAGEMENT AT WATERFORD CRYSTAL

Waterford Crystal, of Kilbarry, Ireland, exports specialty glassware to the United States. It faced a potentially disastrous situation in 1985 as the U.S. dollar began to sink against the Irish pound. A wine decanter that sold in the United States for $150 translated into 148 pounds in 1985, but by 1986 translated into just 106 pounds.

Waterford, however, locked in an exchange rate for a significant part of its anticipated U.S. receivables by buying forward contracts on the Irish pound in 1985. The forward position stretched out for two years, or until 1987. In 1986, Waterford was able to translate $50 million in U.S. sales into 48 million pounds instead of the 37 million it would have reported at the current exchange rate. Financial hedges clearly cannot be sustained beyond the short run, however.

After 1987, Waterford was forced to make operating changes to cope with the fall of the dollar. The short-run financial hedging strategy was useful to Waterford, however, because budgets, staff, markets, and production processes were relatively fixed over the two-year period. By hedging, the company was buying the time necessary to make substantive changes in operating procedures.

Waterford changed its strategy for dealing with foreign currencies by purchasing British china-

maker Wedgwood Plc. in 1986, primarily to diversify operations. Waterford was originally heavily exposed to fluctuations in the U.S. dollar/Irish pound exchange rate because most of its revenue was in dollars while nearly all of its costs were in Irish pounds. Wedgwood has more limited exposure to the U.S. market because it sells worldwide. The diversification worked well for two reasons. First, sales revenues were less dependent on the dollar and more dependent on the Japanese yen, which are not highly correlated currencies vis-à-vis the Irish pound. Waterford-Wedgwood now has just 30 percent of sales in the U.S. dollar, and an expanded presence in Japan. Second, the costs incurred in British pounds diversified the cost structure because the British pound and the Irish pound are not highly correlated vis-à-vis any of the currencies in which revenues are received. The acquisition of Wedgwood therefore reduced the foreign exchange risk of Waterford.

In 1991, Waterford Crystal launched a cheaper "Marquis" line of crystal that is made not in Ireland, but in Germany, Portugal, and Yugoslavia. This served to further diversify the corporation's cost structure. Diversification can clearly be an important intermediate-term strategy to help ensure that the firm survives in the long run.

Source: Stern, Richard L., "(Dangerous) fun and games in the foreign exchange market," *Forbes,* August 22, 1988, pp. 69–72, and Timberlake, Cotton, "Waterford Crystal Appears on the Way to Recovery After Major Cost-Cutting," *Wall Street Journal,* January 24, 1992, p. A7A.

operations, so marketing and production strategies can be used to respond to the deviations from PPP. This strategic response is important because the usefulness of financial hedges and transactions management has declined; these purely tactical responses reach limits due to the relatively short duration of the instruments and management techniques.

Finally, the long run is based on the firm's competitive equilibrium. It is characterized by a return to PPP, and low volatility of exchange rates, so the firm must be in its long-run comparative advantage to survive.

10.3   SHORT-RUN TRANSACTIONS MANAGEMENT

Chapter 9 considers financial instruments that are useful in hedging, and this chapter has heretofore considered this type of hedging as the main risk management issue in the short run. Chapter 8 additionally considers some types of risk management in the context of managing the portfolio of risks and a portfolio of international cash balances. We therefore need to reconsider these types of risk management in addition to financial hedging in the short run.

One point we made in Chapter 8 (see pp. 267–268) was that firms face a choice of whether to centralize or decentralize the management of foreign exchange risk and international cash balances. Centralization means that the management of foreign exchange risk will be done from the corporation's headquarters office or some specialized location. Decentralization, on the other hand, means that the management of foreign exchange risk will be delegated to the various subsidiaries. Centralization allows subsidiaries to transfer foreign exchange transactions to the headquarters, but decentralization allows subsidiaries to retain more control of the transactions and remain accountable. The advantages of centralization are usually greater than the advantages of decentralization, though, and companies are increasingly centralizing short-run transactions management.

At Tate and Lyle, a British food multinational, a "central treasury group adds value by freeing the subsidiaries from hedging concerns, thus allowing the divisions to concentrate on core businesses," according to Tate and Lyle treasurer David Creed.[1] We now consider the centralization-versus-decentralization paradigm for hedging along with other methods of short-term transactions management.

DIVERSIFICATION

When deciding whether to centralize or decentralize exchange risk management, the portfolio diversification effect should be taken into account. For example, the overall foreign exchange risk viewed from the headquarters may not be as great as segmented foreign exchange risks viewed from each subsidiary. A central exposure manager can reduce the overall foreign exchange risk at a low cost by taking advantage of the portfolio effect, and this is a major advantage of centralizing exposure management rather than decentralizing it to the subsidiary level. The problem with decentralizing exposure management is that, by seeing a tree rather than the forest, the firm will have a myopic tendency to hedge everything to protect the subsidiary's operation.

Centralized exposure management more correctly analyzes the subsidiary's contribution to the firm's overall exchange risk and reduces the amount of hedge transactions required to achieve a given level of safety for the firm. A firm will also want to examine the costs of centralization, which may include more communications and personnel expenses to extract information from the subsidiaries, but these are likely to be small in any benefit-cost analysis. Although it seems that setting up an additional administrative office would be costly, there are likely to be economies of scale in exposure management and savings in transactions costs that can be captured through centralization.

As with exchange risk management, central management of the cash portfolio can reduce risk efficiently through diversification, and this is a major advantage of centralizing cash management rather than decentralizing it to the subsidiary level. Central management of the cash portfolio would be cumbersome and costly for the day-to-day transactions balances of foreign operations, but it is appropriate for any excess cash and the precautionary cash balances firms usually hold to cover unexpected transactions that may occur. The development of international cash management in Chapter 8 therefore pertains only to the cash balances that foreign branches and subsidiaries are able to usefully pool among themselves. This creates a central cash depository, either globally or on a region-by-region basis.

This is something of an international counterpart to concentration banking, in which payments are collected at several banks located throughout a country and subsequently transferred to a concentration account at the firm's main bank.[2] Pooling surplus cash balances in a central cash depository has the additional advantage of enabling firms to reduce the total precautionary balances that are required to meet a certain level of safety if several affiliates pool. However, this is no different from pooling precautionary balances in domestic operations, so this section concentrates on the currency diversification effect. Pooling internationally may lead to a greater reduction in the total precautionary balances required because the cash flows are likely to be less interdependent than for a purely domestic corporation, but this issue is secondary.

This section shifts the focus away from managing the stock of foreign exchange exposure and the stock of precautionary cash balances held by moving toward an analysis of the flow of transactions denominated in different currencies. Transactions management can be analyzed in the same centralization-versus-decentralization framework used before. Centralization means that the management of certain transactions will be done from the corporation's headquarters office or some specialized location, such as a central cash depository. Decentralization means that the management of certain transactions will be delegated to the various subsidiaries. In transactions management, the firm will want to compare the costs of centralization to the costs of decentralization. Centralization, for example, is likely to entail higher administrative and communications costs, but decentralization may entail higher processing and transactions costs. If central management of the day-to-day transactions of foreign operations would be cumbersome and costly, these transactions are efficiently decentralized to the level of the subsidiary. However, there are many intracorporate transactions and non-local-currency transactions than can be efficiently centralized.

In this section, four particular activities in transactions management are addressed: (1) the routing of cash balances, (2) payments netting in intracorporate transactions, (3) leading and lagging in intracorporate transactions, and (4) reinvoicing imports and exports.

ROUTING OF CASH BALANCES

The central cash depository created for international cash management must route cash balances among subsidiaries and act as a pooling center for precautionary cash balances. For example, the central cash depository can route surplus cash from the subsidiary in France to cover a shortfall in cash at the subsidiary in Sweden. With subsidiaries in many different countries, multilateral routing can become quite complex, so the central cash depository provides essential coordination. The benefit of this, which in fact is the main reason for a central cash pool, is that one unit is not borrowing short-term funds at a relatively high interest rate as another unit maintains idle cash balances on deposit at a relatively low interest rate.

By acting as an intermediary, the central cash pool also facilitates the conversion from one currency to another whenever necessary. The central cash depository does not need to make as many foreign exchange conversions because it keeps inventories of various currencies at its disposal. Furthermore, the central cash facility can probably execute conversions at lower transactions costs than the various operating units because the transaction size is likely to be larger and the central cash facility is apt to experience economies of scale in foreign exchange conversions. Hence, efficient routing of cash balances adds to firm value.

PAYMENTS NETTING

Another important function of centralized transactions management is in reducing the number of intracompany payments that take place. In any multinational corporation, payments between affiliates for inputs and services are numerous. To reduce the amount of cash transmitted, payments can be netted against one another in a process known as **payments netting.** Bilateral payments netting can be used, for example, to net a $1 million payment from subsidiary A to subsidiary B against a $2 million payment from subsidiary B to subsidiary A; in this case, only a payment of $1 million from subsidiary B to subsidiary A needs to be made.

Multilateral payments netting extends the concept to any number of subsidiaries. For example, subsidiary A may owe subsidiary B a $1 million payment, subsidiary B may owe subsidiary A a $2 million payment, and subsidiary C may owe subsidiary B a $1 million payment. In this case, only a payment of $1 million dollars from subsidiary C to subsidiary A needs to be made, despite the fact that no other transactions between subsidiaries A and C have taken place. Although payments can be made directly between affiliates under multilateral netting, the central cash depository may act as an intermediary or clearing house to (generally) reduce the number of transactions to at most one per subsidiary.[3]

Multilateral payments netting is really no different in a multinational corporation than it is in a purely domestic conglomerate; the only significant difference is that multiple currencies are involved. Once again, then, the central cash depository can facilitate the conversion from one currency to another as necessary. One other difference between multinational and domestic corporations is that by dealing in multiple currencies the multinational also encounters restrictions imposed by various governments. In addition to currency controls, many governments in fact explicitly restrict payments netting. The multinational must therefore pay attention to a myriad of complex laws for multilateral payments netting to work. Once again, however, efficient payments netting adds to firm value.

LEADING AND LAGGING

One particular method of routing cash balances by using the payments netting system is to accelerate payments to an affiliate that needs cash and delay payments from the same affiliate that are due all the other affiliates, an activity known as **leading and lagging.** This practice is useful to get additional liquidity into a particular subsidiary, but it comes at the cost of reducing liquidity in the other subsidiaries. Leading and lagging has aroused the suspicion of governments that view this activity as an undocumented intracorporate loan, so there are legal constraints to the extent to which it can be used. In this regard, however, it may still face less governmental interference than an intracorporate loan. Under U.S. tax law, subsidiaries do not have to pay or receive interest on intracompany accounts for up to six months, but they do have to pay or receive interest on intracorporate loans. Hence, leading and lagging is another way to inject liquidity into the subsidiary needing it, and it creates value for the firm.

REINVOICING

Centralized transactions management can also be used to concentrate foreign exchange exposure in one location via a practice in which a centralized transaction manager uses **reinvoicing** of import and export transactions in each subsidiary's local currency. For example, the German subsidiary may be importing one million Swiss francs of component parts. The central cash facility can purchase the inputs for the German subsidiary in Swiss francs, and subsequently sell the inputs to the German subsidiary in Deutsche marks. Although the reinvoicing center transfers the title to the goods, the goods move directly to the German subsidiary. By reinvoicing the acquisition, the central cash manager takes on the transactions exposure and relieves the German subsidiary of any foreign exchange risk. If reinvoicing is used consistently, each subsidiary can be left to operate exclusively in its own local currency, and foreign exchange risk management can be centralized in one location. Reinvoicing is thus an important function in a multinational corporation. There are government limits to reinvoicing, however, to prevent the multinational corporation from using reinvoicing simply to shift profits to low-tax jurisdictions. Nevertheless, efficient reinvoicing creates value.

10.4   INTERMEDIATE-RUN OPERATIONS MANAGEMENT

This section shifts the focus from the short run to the intermediate run by examining the basic components of global business strategies that can be implemented to manage economic exposure. Such strategies should focus on marketing operations, production operations, and financial structure. The first two of these are addressed as ways to manage cash flow or income statement exposure, and the final one is addressed under management of net worth or balance sheet exposure. Throughout this section, the discussion concentrates on the level of the real exchange rates and appropriate managerial reactions to observed real exchange rate changes.

In this regard, the analysis is a follow-up to Chapter 7 on economic exposure. To a lesser degree, managers should adjust the operating strategies to reflect both observed and anticipated exchange rate changes.[4]

MANAGING CASH FLOW EXPOSURE

In the generally long list of things a firm can do to manage cash flow exposure, there are really just two objectives. One is to manage the demand or revenue side of the business through marketing, and the other is to manage the supply or cost side through the production process. The key to successful implementation requires pre-planned flexibility and a fast, active response to exchange rate signals. Two caveats are in order. First, the marketing strategies developed in the following sections make sense only when the firm is not functioning completely in a world output market. If the firm is functioning in a world output market, the location of marketing activity would be generally independent of the exchange rate. Second, the production strategies developed below make sense only when the firm is not functioning completely in a world input market (in the sense developed in Chapter 7), and when the firm can export output to other countries. If this were not the case, the location of production activity would be generally independent of the exchange rate. The meaning of these comments will become clearer as we develop the strategies in the next few paragraphs.

MARKETING MANAGEMENT

Under marketing management, the major focus should be on increasing sales in countries where the currency is overvalued with respect to a PPP benchmark, and reducing sales in countries where the currency is undervalued. Although increased marketing activity where the currency has depreciated may restore the profit margin, the company as a whole should seek revenues where the currency has appreciated because these revenues are more valuable when converted into home currency units. To achieve increased sales in overvalued currencies, the firm may want to reduce marketing activity where the currency is undervalued. The promotional strategy should reflect this focus by increasing advertising, merchandising, and the sales force where currencies are the strongest at the expense of promotions elsewhere.

Hence, pre-arranged flexibility in the marketing budget is important. Marketing dollars should be free to flow where the marginal benefits from marketing activities are the highest. Of course, this strategy implies that the marginal costs of marketing efforts need to be constant or at least not rise as much as the benefits in response to appreciation. This is generally the case because marketing activity usually has a bigger impact on marginal revenue than on marginal cost.

Product design and development is also an important component of the marketing strategy. Although new products should be introduced based on their long-run competitive merits vis-à-vis the long-run PPP real exchange rate, the optimal place to introduce new products may be where the currency is overvalued. This is the case both because the revenues are relatively valuable and because it is easier to justify high market-entry costs. In countries where the currency is undervalued, introduction of new products may increase interest in the firm's wares, but this strategy is likely to be expensive. A focus on high-volume or high-margin products is probably more prudent under such circumstances.

The reasoning behind product development choices can be applied to market development decisions as well. Although new markets should be selected based on long-run sales forecasts and long-run PPP real exchange rates, a location where the exchange rate is currently overvalued will be favored if all other things are equal. Again, for both product introduction and market entry, prearranged flexibility is important.

Marketing management also involves pricing strategy, and firms with some market power will want to reevaluate their price structures to maximize profits. In particular, firms will want to lower the local currency price of their products wherever the currency is overvalued to capture a larger market, as long as there is some stability in the home currency cost structure. Conversely, the firm could raise the local currency price where the currency is undervalued to increase the profit margin, again as long as there is some stability in the home currency cost structure. This activity requires some degree of pre-arranged flexibility in the pricing arrangement and a quick response to exchange rate signals. Note that firms in competitive industries that are price takers in local markets by definition do not have the necessary pricing flexibility. All of these conclusions emerge from the analysis in Chapter 7, so the reader may want to review the diagrams presented there.

Pricing strategy, as is evident from the discussion here, is simply an application of the cash flow or income statement exposure detailed in Chapter 7. By way of example, Figure 7-7 analyzes a foreign currency depreciation for a firm with market power and price flexibility. The cost structure is stable in U.S. dollars, so foreign currency depreciation depresses the demand and marginal revenue curves proportionately. The optimum pricing strategy is to lower the U.S. dollar price of the good, but not by as much as the depreciation (represented by the vertical distance between the demand curves), so the foreign currency price increases. Quantity therefore declines.

This is also shown in Figure 10-2, in which the demand and marginal revenue curves are drawn as stable functions of the local currency. Foreign currency depreciation corresponds to dollar appreciation so the marginal cost curve shifts up. Clearly, the local currency price increases and the firm sells less output. Hence, the dollar margin has decreased and the volume has decreased, so profits have decreased.

With the fall in the value of the U.S. dollar in the early 1990s, many foreign companies were forced to adjust dollar prices. For example, Paris-based Charles Jourdan "was under pressure to pass through to U.S. customers double-digit price rises on its $95 to $395 shoes."[5] The company realized that, according to the chief executive of the

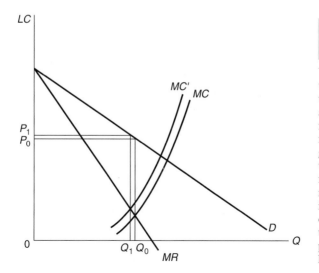

FIGURE 10-2 LOCAL CURRENCY PRICE CHANGES AS REAL EXCHANGE RATES CHANGE

With the local currency price on the vertical axis, a depreciation of the local currency is reflected as an appreciation of the dollar. For a firm with market power and price flexibility, the demand and marginal revenue curves are stable in the local currency. With inputs from a world market denominated in dollars, the cost structure is stable in dollars, so appreciation of the dollar shifts the cost structure upward. The local currency price increases and the firm sells less output, so profits decline.

U.S. subsidiary, "The American consumer is not willing to swallow those price increases." The solution? Charles Jourdan should "[h]ang on to his U.S. customers by squeezing his profit margins—and pray for a stronger dollar by spring." Although Charles Jourdan viewed the decision as a short-run solution, the company planned to reevaluate pricing strategy again several months later.

PRODUCTION MANAGEMENT

Production management is on the opposite side of the marketing management coin. Just as marketing activity should focus on countries where the currency is overvalued, production activity should focus on countries where the currency is undervalued. Production should therefore be shifted from countries where the currency is high, which means that the plant is a relatively high-cost producer, to countries where the currency is low, which means that the plant is a relatively low-cost producer. This means that, to the extent possible, expatriate labor in the production line should be moved from countries with overvalued currencies to countries with undervalued currencies. In addition, input components can be sourced from countries where the exchange rate is low rather than from countries where the exchange rate is high.

Both of these strategies require some built-in flexibility in the production processes. Long-run production design therefore needs to reflect the desire for a high degree of flexibility from the outset, and the cost of such flexibility needs to be weighed against the benefits. Although the firm needs to be profitable in long-run equilibrium, it may not choose the minimum long-run average cost capacity because excess capacity adds value when firms can profit from flexibility.

Changes in the production process are also important in the global production management strategy. Although investment in new technology and other efforts to improve productivity should be based on long-run comparative advantage and PPP exchange rates, the optimal place to introduce such changes may be where the currency is low because the location is already in a relatively favorable position. The investment can be more easily justified because production volume is high while the location is realizing a comparative advantage, and because the plant's higher profits can absorb the costs of the new investment.

In locations where appreciation of the currency makes production costs higher, some effort to improve productivity may restore the profit margin, but the multinational should develop the advantaged centers first. The multinational corporation is thus a portfolio of real options on foreign exchange, as discussed in Chapter 5, and the foreign exchange risk increases the value of the options to expand investments. Similar reasoning pertains to the location of new production facilities. Although the plant location decision should be based on long-run comparative advantage and PPP real exchange rates, a location where the currency is currently undervalued will be favored if all other things are equal.

MANAGING NET WORTH EXPOSURE

Although managing cash flow or income statement exposure is probably the most important aspect of a global business strategy to manage economic exposure (because it directly affects the ongoing profitability of the firm), attention needs to be given to the market value of the stock of assets and liabilities in the firm. Attending to this area

EXCHANGE RATES AND CORPORATE PRICING STRATEGY

The effect of exchange rate changes on prices of imports and exports has been a fertile area of empirical investigation. Knetter (1994) studies the pricing of exports from Germany to various destinations, reporting many different versions of regressions of export prices onto exchange rates. One is a time-series regression of the log of the DM price of a German export shipped to the United States onto the log of the dollar/DM exchange rate and the log of income in the United States :

$$\ln P_{DM} = \alpha + \beta \ln S_{\$/DM} + \gamma \ln Y_{US}.$$

Because logarithms are used, coefficients are interpreted as elasticities, so that β represents the percentage change in the DM price of the exported good for a 1 percent change in the $/DM exchange rate. In this set-up, the β coefficients are expected to be between −1 and 0. Although Knetter reports results for many different commodities (using annual data for 1975–1987), shown here are the β coefficients for automobiles (by engine size) and a few adult beverages, with standard errors in parentheses:

Commodity	β (s.e.)	Commodity	β (s.e.)
Autos under 1 L.	−1.00 (0.18)	Beer	−0.57 (0.17)
Autos 1.5–2 L.	−0.65 (0.22)	White wine	−0.22 (0.02)
Autos 2–3 L.	0.03 (0.11)	Sparkling wine	−0.18 (0.32)
Autos over 3 L.	0.03 (0.13)		

From these results, it seems that smaller automobiles face price exposure to exchange rate changes, but larger automobiles do not face price exposure at all. The coefficient of −1 on autos under 1 liter means that a 1 percent appreciation of the DM reduces the DM export price by 1 percent such that the dollar import price would remain unchanged. The coefficient of −.65 on autos 1.5–2

liters means that a 1 percent appreciation of the DM reduces the DM export price by 0.65 percent, passing through the remaining 0.35 percent of the exchange rate change to the dollar price. The coefficients on autos 2–3 liters and over 3 liters are not statistically different from zero, implying that DM appreciation does not alter the DM export price so there is full pass-through of exchange rate changes to the dollar import price. Overall, there appears to be more price competition in the small car market than in the large, luxury car market.

Similar conclusions follow from the analysis of coefficients on the beverages listed. Exports of German beer seem to face more price exposure in the U.S. market than exports of white wine. A 1 percent appreciation of the DM reduces the DM export price of beer 0.57 percent (increasing the dollar price by the remaining 0.43 percent) and the price of white wine by 0.22 percent (increasing the dollar price by 0.78 percent). However, the coefficient on sparkling wine is not statistically different from zero, suggesting that the DM price does not respond to exchange rate changes so there is full pass-through to the dollar price. Overall, there appears to be more price competition in the beer market than in the white wine market, and no price competition in the sparkling wine market.

What determines the β coefficients and the degree of exchange rate pass-through to import prices? The answer is: Primarily the nature of competition and the degree to which the firm is able to set the product price in various markets. In certain national markets, firms must be price-takers, as in the small car market in the United States. In other national markets, firms have a sufficiently differentiated product and can set the price with relatively little concern, as in the large car market or the sparkling wine market in the United States. In this case, there may simply be one home currency price for the product in the home country or in the world, such that foreigners must pay the price regardless of what happens to the exchange rate.

APPLICATION 10-3 (cont.)

Many products fall between these two extremes, giving the firm some market power to alter the price to the consumer in response to exchange rate changes while simultaneously not setting just one home currency price. This is most important when the exporting firm faces segmented national markets and can set a different price in each country to which it exports, as in the mid-size auto market or the beer and white wine markets in the United States.

Source: Knetter, Michael M., "Exchange Rates and Corporate Pricing Strategies," Chapter 9 of *Exchange Rates and Corporate Performance,* edited by Yakov Amihud and Richard M. Levich, Irwin Professional Publishing, 1994, pp. 181–219.

requires managing the firm's net worth or economic balance sheet exposure, specifically by managing the underlying currency denominations of the assets and liabilities.

The most common way to offset the local currency exposure of nonmonetary assets, such as plant and equipment, is to undertake long-term borrowing in the same local currency. In this manner, a devaluation that reduces the value of the physical assets also reduces the value of the liability. If a firm wants to hold a completely unexposed balance sheet position, where again the exposures are measured in market values, the firm needs to denominate the net asset position in the home country currency. As the net asset position is equal to the market value of the equity in the subsidiary, the parent firm thereby achieves a complete hedge on its investment.

An important way to manage overall economic exposure, however, requires engineering the net worth or balance sheet exposure to offset cash flow or income statement exposure. The net worth position that offsets a firm's cash flow exposure is called a **balance sheet hedge,** and is the financial component of the global business. If a firm's cash flow is adversely affected by a local currency depreciation, a net local currency liability position in the balance sheet will offset the income statement exposure because the home currency value of the liability will decline. Such a position can be arranged by denominating even more assets in the home currency and debt or other liabilities in the local currency. If necessary, local currency borrowings can be converted into home currency securities and simply retained as assets.

EXAMPLE 10.2

A subsidiary of Lane, Inc., operating in Australia, has an annual cash flow exposure of 10 million (real) Australian dollars, possibly determined using regression analysis. This means that a one cent depreciation of the Australian dollar in terms of the U.S. dollar generates $100,000 in foreign exchange losses. If the real discount rate is 5 percent, the present value of the annual exposure in perpetuity is (A$ 10 million/.05 =) 200 million dollars, in the absence of any growth in exposure. Hence, the present value of the foreign exchange losses resulting from a 1 cent depreciation is 2 million dollars. This means that the net local currency liability position in Lane's balance sheet should be 200 million Australian dollars, such that a 1 cent depreciation of the Australian dollar in terms of the U.S. dollar causes a $2 million foreign exchange gain. The easiest way to achieve this is to borrow in Australian dollars whatever quantity will leave a net liability position of 200 million Australian dollars in the balance sheet.

The principle of a balance sheet hedge is similar for other types of firms. If an export platform is adversely affected by local currency appreciation, a net asset position in the relevant currency in the balance sheet offsets the income statement exposure because appreciation makes the local currency assets more valuable. If the firm is exporting to certain developed markets, and is therefore exposed to changes in the export market's currency, the net asset position in the balance sheet should be achieved by borrowing in the currencies of the export markets. For example, if an Australian subsidiary is exporting to Japan, some debt should be denominated in yen. When the yen is high, the Australian dollar value of the debt payments is high, but the Australian dollar value of the sales to Japan is also high. When the yen is low, the Australian dollar value of the sales to Japan is low, but the Australian dollar value of the debt is also low. Similarly, if the Australian subsidiary is exporting to the United States, some debt should be denominated in dollars.

In a similar analysis, purely domestic firms that face foreign competition can also benefit from balance sheet hedging strategy. For example, domestic wine producers that operate only within the United States face European competition such that when the dollar is high vis-à-vis European currencies their cash flows decrease. When the dollar is high, consumers switch to foreign imports and cut back on consumption of domestic varieties. The balance sheet hedge for domestic vintners would be to denominate some of their borrowing in European currencies so that when their cash flows decrease the value of their debt also decreases.

10.5   THE NATURE OF RISK MANAGEMENT

As discussed in the section on "Foreign Exchange Risk and Risk Management in the Short Run, Intermediate Run, and Long Run" at the beginning of this chapter, risk management strategy should be based on managing the firm's economic value. There are two ways this objective can be interpreted. One is that managing the economic value reduces the volatility of the firm's value by reducing the volatility of income and return on assets without altering the firm's expected value. A second interpretation is that managing the firm's economic value creates value in that the firm's expected value is higher in the presence of a risk management strategy.

RISK AVERSION

If risk management reduces the volatility of firm value without altering the expected value, we immediately need to ask why this might be desirable. Up to now, we have essentially justified risk management by reference to **risk aversion,** the preference for a known home currency amount over a gamble with the same expected value involving potential gains or losses. However, even the reason for risk aversion is less clear. The firm may be risk averse because it would then be assured of using all tax credits and tax deductions to which it is entitled. More often, the explanation is that managers or stockholders are risk-averse. Even if firms are risk-neutral in profit maximization, the shareholders are likely to be risk-averse so value may be added when the firm manages risk. If shareholders are risk-averse, however, they are perfectly able to construct a diversified portfolio or to hedge a firm's foreign exchange exposure whenever a firm does not hedge itself.

One argument for corporate hedging activity, though, is that firms are likely to be more efficient than shareholders in this endeavor. For example, the hedging costs to the firm are likely to be much lower due to the higher transaction volume, and information on exposure and risk is much better within the firm than outside.

However, it may be that managers are risk averse and therefore choose risk management policies that maximize their own welfare. If managers are in danger of losing their jobs when an exchange rate change makes a project unprofitable (and they don't have comparable positions readily available elsewhere), they have strong personal incentives to hedge the exchange rate change. Shareholders in turn let managers hedge because doing so provides incentives for managers to maximize the firm's value as they maximize their own welfare. (For a formal model, see Stulz, 1984.) In any case, hedging may be a response to somebody's risk aversion. (For more, see Dufey and Srinivasulu, 1983.)

If corporations prefer a known home currency transaction amount over a gamble with the same expected value involving potential gains or losses, the nature of risk aversion requires that corporations give up the chance for upside foreign exchange gains to protect themselves from possible downside foreign exchange losses. With forward, money market, and futures hedges, the symmetry of the hedge makes it practically costless.

Using options for hedging appears to be different, because firms protect themselves from most of the potential foreign exchange losses without giving up much of the potential upside gains. However, the cost of the option reflects the market's evaluation of the potential for upside gains, so the firm pays for the privilege of keeping the upside gain when it pays the option premium. As options are priced in an efficient market, the expected value of the option cannot be positive. However, the expected value of the option may not be negative either, so no harm is done when managers hedge transactions with options—the payoff distribution is simply a little different than with forwards, money markets, and futures hedges.[6]

Ultimately, risk aversion is a fairly weak reason for a firm to undertake a risk management program. After all, managers should simply focus on maximizing the firm's value. Furthermore, as there is no exchange risk in the long run when PPP and UIP hold, short-run gains and losses will even out by averaging to zero over the long run. This is, in fact, true—as long as there is a long run. However, the true value of risk management may be in ensuring that the firm gets to the long run.

LOSS AVERSION

An alternative to risk aversion is **loss aversion,** which recognizes that risk is a concern because of the downside losses rather than because of the upside gains. As discussed in the first part of this chapter, short-run transactions management strategy should be based on ensuring survival of the firm into the intermediate run. In turn, intermediate-run strategy is based on ensuring survival of the firm into the long run. Provided that long-run operating strategies are based on the long-run PPP real exchange rate, the firm will be maximizing the present value of profits. It is the deviations from PPP in the short run and intermediate run that can have an impact on the firm and prevent it from surviving into the long run.

If foreign exchange gains occur, the firm reports higher profits and pays additional taxes, and may be able to put the after-tax profits to good use, but that is pretty much the end of the story. In contrast, if foreign exchange losses occur, the firm will report lower profits, and possibly even negative profits. Lower profits reduce taxes paid, but may also have repercussions elsewhere. The firm may have more difficulty raising capital if profits are lower, or may be required to pay higher costs of capital. Similarly, customers may recognize a precarious financial situation and decide to make purchases from financially stronger competitors, particularly in durable goods sectors.

Negative profits due to foreign exchange losses may also cause firms to lose the current benefits of tax credits and tax deductions. Furthermore, negative profits may even cause the firm to seek bankruptcy protection, the costs of which increase losses even more, or may even cause the firm to cease operations. Bankruptcy is not necessarily bad if the firm's resources are more productively employed by another firm elsewhere in the economy. If this is not the case, managers and shareholders are justified in wanting to avoid bankruptcy. Under such circumstances, managers and shareholders are obviously not so much worried about the impacts of foreign exchange gains as they are about the impacts of foreign exchange losses.

The firm is therefore justifiably concerned about the short- and intermediate-run variability of its cash flow because of the need to avoid financial distress and bankruptcy. If the firm encounters capital constraints in the short run, it may be forced to go out of business, and the long run never arrives. An active risk management program that reduces the variability of cash flows will thus lower the probability of bankruptcy, and this may make the firm's cost of borrowing lower, or at least increase the firm's access to debt markets.

As the probability of bankruptcy is also affected by the firm's ratio of debt to equity, risk management activities may also increase the firm's debt capacity; see Dolde (1995) for empirical evidence. An extension of this argument, made in Froot, Scharfstein, and Stein (1993), is that if external sources of finance are more costly than internally generated funds, risk management adds value because it helps ensure that a corporation has sufficient internal funds available to take advantage of profitable investment opportunities. Once again, then, risk management helps the firm avoid short-run and intermediate-run capital constraints to survive into the long run.

FINANCIAL DISTRESS

Because the value of hedging rests in preventing financial distress in the short and intermediate runs, it follows that the only risk worth managing is that which may have a material impact on the value of the firm's periodic cash flows. A large quantity of exposure, with a corresponding possibility for a large foreign exchange gain or loss in relation to the total cash flows, is therefore worth hedging, whereas a small quantity of exposure probably is not. Similarly, an exposure associated with a currency that has a high standard deviation of percentage changes, and a corresponding possibility for a large gain or loss in relation to the total cash flow, is of more concern than exposure in a currency with a low standard deviation.

The exact point at which foreign exchange exposure and risk are worth worrying about is a function of the firm's or market's tolerance for the risk associated with the variability of the cash flow. Large, highly diversified firms may not be at much risk from foreign exchange exposure at all, because few transactions are large enough to threaten the firm and standard deviations of currencies do not translate into high standard deviations of cash flows. Conversely, small, poorly diversified firms are at greater risk from foreign exchange exposure, because more transactions are large enough to threaten the firm and standard deviations of currencies result in higher standard deviations of cash flows.

With the observation that the only risk worth managing is that which may have a material impact on the firm's cash flows, the approach to hedging discussed in Chapter 9 can be put into context. Most of the hedging literature is developed to deal with a mythical corporation facing an occasional, large foreign exchange transaction. In certain cases, the relevant question is what happens to the market value of an asset or liability as exchange rates change. Although these isolated transactions or individual assets or liabilities hardly represent the normal operations of multinational corporations, they provide a useful benchmark for analysis.

We are ultimately interested, of course, in the net exposed position at a particular time; the hedging concepts easily generalize. However, the transactions which pose the most risk for a multinational corporation are usually the rare, large foreign exchange transactions anyway. This fact suggests that the earlier transaction-by-transaction approach to hedging is indeed appropriate.

ELIMINATION OF DOWNSIDE LOSSES

One corollary to the observation that the value of hedging is in preventing short-run and intermediate-run financial distress is that the hedge is valued only for its elimination of downside losses. After all, managers and shareholders are not as worried about the impacts of foreign exchange gains as they are about the impacts of foreign exchange losses. This suggests that a more complicated, asymmetric approach to foreign exchange risk may be necessary—which is not captured by the simple standard deviation in Chapter 8.

If such considerations are important, they suggest that options are more justifiable as hedging tools than previously asserted because of the asymmetric pay-off structure. Giddy and Dufey (1995) even suggest that there are costs to symmetric hedges (such as forwards, money markets, and futures) when losses on the hedge are reported separately from (typically implicitly reported) gains on the underlying exposure. Corporate officers often have to explain these legitimate derivatives losses to managers, directors, bondholders, and shareholders, any of whom may not understand the legitimacy of the losses. In turn, the careers of the corporate officers may be affected by this misunderstanding. Hence, options provide a solution to this problem because there is no possibility for loss (beyond the amount of the premium paid).

Managers thus also have an incentive to undertake profitable projects when they are simultaneously allowed to hedge profits using options. As Froot, Scharfstein, and Stein (1993) point out, the asymmetric hedge also allows managers to maintain a minimum amount of investment for the firm through tough times, while providing flexibility to increase investment in good times when the profitability of the investment is even higher.

Note that none of the reasons for risk management or hedging has yet suggested that the firm finds the activities profitable. In hedging, managers are not betting against the market. They therefore cannot protect transactions from exchange rate changes expected in the marketplace, because the prices of all the financial instruments are determined in efficient markets and therefore already incorporate market expectations of exchange rate changes. It follows that hedging activity protects the firm from

HEDGING PRACTICES AT GENERAL ELECTRIC AND AT&T

GENERAL ELECTRIC

For the most part, General Electric uses a portfolio approach to hedging. The portfolio is 50 percent forward contracts, 25 percent currency options, and 25 percent spot market orders based on exchange rate movements (e.g., orders to stop loss or take profit at certain exchange rates). Yet, GE often finds that the standard practice for hedging yen contracts turns out to be inappropriate. As the assistant treasurer, David Rusate, puts it, "Conventional theory tells us to avoid all risk by transacting in U.S. dollars—bill in dollars and take payment in dollars. Period. The fall back is to bill customers in their local currency and hedge 100 percent of it with a forward contract. But isn't that speculation?"

His reasoning is as follows. GE conducts significant business in the Japanese market and competes directly against U.S. and Japanese companies for market share. Say GE chose to hedge its yen receivables, but a major U.S. competitor went unhedged. On January 1, 1993, the spot rate was 125 yen/$. Locking in the receivables, they use forward rates averaging 124.85, giving them a slight benefit because the yen is the premium currency. As it turns out, the average exchange rate ends up being 111.05 yen per dollar. The problem? As Rusate puts it, "If your competitor went unhedged, used stop/loss orders or used put options to hedge its yen exposure, it now has additional margin to come after your market share."

The point is that under some conditions, firms will have incentives to construct their hedging strategies in terms of what their competition is doing. Although this doesn't mean that a company should follow its competition in placing bets at a roulette wheel in Las Vegas, there is some extent to which firms should consider their risks in the context of their competition's strategy.

General Electric also tries to keep its individual business units well-educated about risk management. For instance, business units are encouraged to bill in premium currencies and receive invoices in discount currencies. In early 1995, the Japanese yen was a premium currency, while the Italian lira was trading at a discount. GE was bidding $4.3 million for a Japanese turbine order with three-year delivery. A Japanese competitor had submitted a yen bid. Rusate then instructed the GE unit to bill in yen, converting the bid into 431 million yen at the spot rate of 98.75. As soon as they received the purchase order, they purchased forward contracts to guarantee the unit $4.6 million—an additional $300,000 at no risk. Of course, as Rusate has pointed out, if the yen appreciates significantly beyond the forward rates, GE may experience an opportunity cost—one that may be gained by unhedged competitors.

On the other side, purchasing managers are encouraged to bill in discount currencies. For example, when GE located an Italian supplier for laundry pumps, it first negotiated the price in dollars. At that point, Rusate urged the manager to, " . . . disarm the supplier by offering to take the billing in lira if we get this bell or whistle—in return for the risk we're taking, of course." Then, the manager suggested that they simply convert the dollars to lira using the exchange rate in the day's newspaper—this was, of course, the spot price. According to Rusate, "Because the Italian supplier's representatives are sales managers, not currency experts, they're ready to sign the purchase order."

AT&T

AT&T has about $3 billion in gross foreign exchange exposures and an annual trade-in of $15 to $20 billion in the foreign-exchange marketplace. The company directs all of its units and divisions to report any exposure above $1 million to the treasury organization, as they leave all hedging decisions with the treasury rather than the operational managers. AT&T only hedges transactions exposures, viewing translation exposures as long-term. As assistant treasurer, Errol Harris puts it, "When we invest in another country, those investments are

APPLICATION 10-4 (cont.)

long-term, so we're not as concerned about fluctuations in foreign currencies. And if we realize a loss or a gain, it's reflected in the equity account, not the income statement."

AT&T does not hedge the bottom-line profit/ loss number. It does, however, cover any exposures incurred along the way. For instance, if they incur expenses that are obviously components of the income-statement number, they hedge the various components—but they do not hedge the bottom line as a total. As Harris puts it, "We strongly believe in avoiding speculation, and we must have an underlying reason to engage in the marketplace."

AT&T focuses on three forms of internal controls as part of its risk-management program. First, they carefully distinguish between individuals who execute transactions in the marketplace and those who confirm and settle the transactions. Second, they employ frequent internal audits and rely on external auditors to ensure that their foreign-exchange group is following the policies and procedures that they have established. Finally, they have judicious approval levels: The foreign exchange manager can approve transactions up to $50 million, the assistant treasurer can approve those up to $100 million, and the treasurer must approve those greater than $100 million.

Source: "The Reins on Risk," *Financial Executive,* July/August 1995, pp. 18–23.

unexpected exchange rate changes only. If a firm lets its expectations differ from the market expectations reflected in interest rate differentials or option premiums, the firm is speculating rather than hedging. And, in fact, a firm need not have transactions exposure to speculate in the foreign exchange markets.

APPLICATION 10-5

HEDGING PRACTICES
AT BAXTER INTERNATIONAL

At Baxter International, independent oversight of risk-management operations is a high priority. They follow three simple guidelines. First, they try to educate a wide range of people within the company in the proper use of risk management tools. They send members of their internal-audit, accounting, tax, and legal departments to derivatives training. According to Paul Collier, capital markets director, "If you have only one or two people in your firm who truly understand your derivatives transactions, you may have a case where the same person originates a trade and effectively manages the back office." Second, Baxter finds it worthwhile to make many of its risk-management decisions by

consensus. This means Baxter sometimes misses an opportunity when the market moves because its decision-making process takes longer. But ultimately, it works as an effective check-and-balance system, as Baxter's treasury department only makes transactions with which people in other departments are comfortable. Finally, Baxter tries to interact and share information with several investment banks concurrently—all of which understand their business and goals. In developing these long-term relationships with the banks, they obtain an additional source of checks and balances. As Collier puts it, "You can be sure if one bank has a great idea for you, the other banks will try to poke holes in it."

Source: "The Reins on Risk," *Financial Executive,* July/August 1995, pp. 18–23.

A slightly different issue is whether risk management more generally creates value. This was the second interpretation of managing the economic value of the firm considered at the beginning of this section. The issue of whether risk management creates value is largely unresolved, but the intuition for creating value has been presented earlier in this chapter in the discussion of marketing and production management. If marketing resources are allocated where currencies are overvalued and are taken away from locations where currencies are undervalued, the firm as a whole is more profitable than it would have been if nothing had been done in response to exchange rate changes. Similarly, if production is increased where currencies are undervalued and is decreased where currencies are overvalued, the firm as a whole is more profitable than it would have been if nothing had been done. In this sense, risk management may indeed create value as well as reduce the variability of firm value.

❖ SUMMARY OF CHAPTER OBJECTIVES

1. Assess foreign exchange risk and design risk management strategy for the short run, the intermediate run, and the long run.

In the short run, foreign exchange risk focuses on transactions that occur within one to two years, which are easily hedged using the techniques developed in Chapter 9. In the intermediate run, foreign exchange risk requires operating responses because short-term solutions expire. In the long run, there is no foreign exchange risk because purchasing power parity holds.

2. Describe some short-run techniques to manage transactions that are exposed to foreign exchange risk.

Short-run transactions management is useful in managing foreign exchange risk. Cash balances can be routed from subsidiaries with surpluses to subsidiaries with shortfalls, and the central office facilitates the conversion from one currency to another. Payments netting among subsidiaries also reduces the number of intracompany payments that take place and facilitates the conversion from one currency to another. "Leading and lagging" is when the payments netting system is used to accelerate payments to and delay payments from an affiliate that needs cash. Reinvoicing can be used to concentrate foreign exchange risk in one location by restating import or export prices in each subsidiary's local currency.

3. Formulate intermediate-run operating strategies to manage foreign exchange risk.

Operating strategies in marketing, production, and finance directly build on the analysis of the firm presented in Chapter 7. With respect to marketing management, the main goal is to increase sales in countries where the currency is overvalued by using price, product, and promotion strategies. With respect to production management, the goal is to increase production in countries where the currency is undervalued by changing production and technology strategies. Financial management recognizes the goal of offsetting cash flow exposures by constructing an offsetting balance sheet hedge.

4. Analyze risk management strategy from a broad perspective.

Risk aversion and loss aversion are the main motivations for risk management. The value of risk management is derived from preventing financial distress and bankruptcy in the short and intermediate runs to ensure survivability into the long run. Thus, the only risk worth managing is that which may have a material impact on the value of the firm's cash flows.

❖ QUESTIONS FOR REVIEW

1. Traditionally, the analysis of foreign exchange exposure, risk, and hedging has been the most important topic in international business finance.
   a. What are the three measures of exposure traditionally studied, and what are the advantages and disadvantages of using each one?
   b. What measure or measures of exposure should managers focus on? Should managers hedge exposures?

2. Weiner Amalgamated is considering an investment in DM-denominated bonds. For simplicity, the term structure of German interest rates can be assumed to be flat at 6 percent. The annual standard deviation of percentage changes in $/DM exchange rates has historically been about 12 percentage points.
   a. What is the range of dollar-equivalent returns on DM bonds for the 95 percent probability level if the investment is held for one year?
   b. What is the range of dollar-equivalent average annual returns on DM bonds for the 95 percent probability level if the investment is held for ten years?
   c. What is the range of dollar-equivalent average annual returns on DM bonds for the 95 percent probability level if the investment is held for twenty years?

3. [Class discussion] In designing a hedging strategy, firms might do well to consider a short-term strategy, an intermediate-term strategy, and a long-term strategy. What characterizes each horizon? What would be an appropriate hedging strategy for each horizon? Carefully explain your answer.

4. [Class discussion] A multinational corporation headquartered in Boston with operations in forty different countries is revising its production schedule and its marketing efforts for the current year. What adjustments should it make if there has been an unanticipated, large currency appreciation in Alpha and an unanticipated, large currency depreciation in Beta?

5. Daimler-Benz, a German multinational, exports cars to the U.S. market. The firm has some market power because of its upscale product line, and therefore faces a downward-sloping demand for its cars in the United States.
   a. Draw two diagrams showing the demand curves for the firm's product line, one denominated in US$ and one denominated in DM; as the cars are being sold in the United States, the demand curve is stable with respect to the US$. Also show in both diagrams the marginal cost curve for the firm; as the cars are produced in Germany, the marginal cost curve is stable with respect to the DM. In both diagrams, find the optimal quantity of cars sold in the United States. In both diagrams, show the price charged for the cars (in $ and in DM). Briefly explain your answer.
   b. Now consider what happens if the US$ appreciates by 10 percent against the DM. Show the effects of dollar appreciation in both diagrams. What happens to the optimal quantity of cars sold in the United States? What happens to the price charged for the car (in $ and in DM)? Briefly explain your answer.

6. Your company is thinking of entering a new market in Germany. Your assistant has presented you with the following regression of the log of a competitor's product price in Germany onto the $/DM exchange rate:

$$\ln P_{DM} = 5 - 0.33 \ln S_{\$/DM}$$

where the average exchange rate over the period of estimation has been 0.65 dollars per DM. What can you tell about the price of the product in Germany and the effect of exchange rate changes?

7. The subsidiary of Oliver Enterprises operating in the United Kingdom has an annual cash flow exposure of £10 million (in real terms), which is expected to remain at this level in perpetuity. Oliver Enterprises assumes that the real discount rate is 4 percent. How would Oliver Enterprises construct a hedge of this cash flow exposure in its U.K. subsidiary's net worth position?

8. [Class discussion] One debate in international business finance is whether hedging foreign exchange exposure creates value for a firm.

   a. Why does theoretical finance suggest that hedging does not create value?

   b. Why does applied finance suggest that hedging does create value?

9. True or False: Indicate whether the statement is true or false and clearly explain why.

   a. In response to a local currency depreciation, a multinational should increase marketing efforts to sell more output and recover profit.

   b. Multinational corporations hedge because their stockholders cannot.

   c. Management of financial risk creates value.

10. [Group project] According to an article in the *Financial Times* ("Centralization Lessens the Risk," April 18, 1997, Survey of Foreign Exchange, p. 3):

    . . . [I]n the 1980s Jaguar, the carmaker, hedged its potential US dollar proceeds and set its U.S. car prices at a level competitive to those of its U.S. counterparts. However, Jaguar had not considered competition from Germany. When the Germans started to sell their cars at a lower price mainly due to the rise in the U.S. dollar, Jaguar found that it was locked into its price levels due to the foreign exchange hedge.

    Suppose a Jaguar car sells for $50,000 in the United States and the exchange rate is £0.60/$. The one-year forward rate quoted by a U.K. bank is £0.60/$. Jaguar plans to sell 100,000 cars at $50,000 each during the next year, and decides to hedge by using forward contracts to ensure the pound equivalent of the sales. One year later, the spot exchange rate is £0.75/$.

    a. Under what circumstances would the one-year forward rate be equal to the current spot rate?

    b. If Jaguar is able to sell all 100,000 cars at $50,000, how much is the pound revenue if converted at the spot rate? What is the gain or loss on the forward contract? What are the net pound proceeds to Jaguar?

    c. Now consider the problem with the German competition: the price of luxury cars is lower. Jaguar might have to cut price to $45,000 to sell all 100,000 cars. What are the net pound proceeds to Jaguar, in view of the forward hedge it must honor?

    d. Jaguar feels that it cannot cut price because of its forward position. Does Jaguar face any risk if it does not cut price?

    e. Given the problem created by the hedge, consider whether Jaguar is doing the right thing. Would you recommend that Jaguar stop hedging? Can you suggest a better hedging plan?

❖ ENDNOTES

1. Based on "Centralization Lessens the Risk," *Financial Times,* April 18, 1997, Survey on Foreign Exchange, p. 3.
2. For more on the advantages of concentration banking, see Brealey and Myers, 1991, Chapter 31.
3. For more on netting, see Anvari (1986), Bokos and Clinkard (1983), Srinivasan and Kim (1986), and Glass (1994).
4. For more on this, see Aggarwal and Soenen (1989). In addition, Srinivasulu (1981) presents

case analyses of Volkswagen and Rolls Royce in the context of business strategy.

5. Quoted in Joan E. Rigdon and Valerie Reitman, "Pricing Paradox: Consumers Still Find Imported Bargains Despite the Weak Dollar," *Wall Street Journal,* October 7, 1992, p. 1.
6. Not everyone agrees with this. In fact, many economists suggest that corporations end up paying for more than they need in a hedge—see Giddy and Dufey (1995)—which is why options are typically regarded as expensive.

❖ REFERENCES

Aaker, David A., and Briance Mascarenhas. "The Need for Strategic Flexibility," *Journal of Business Strategy,* Fall 1984, pp. 74–82.

Aggarwal, Raj, and Luc A. Soenen. "Managing Persistent Real Changes in Currency Values: The Role of Multinational Operating Strategies," *Columbia Journal of World Business,* Fall 1989, pp. 60–67.

Anvari, M. "Efficient Scheduling of Cross-Border Cash Transfers," *Financial Management,* Summer 1986, pp. 40–49.

Bokos, William J., and Anne P. Clinkard. "Multilateral Netting," *Journal of Cash Management,* June/July 1983, pp. 24–34.

Brealey, Richard A., and Stewart C. Myers. "Cash Management," Chapter 31 of *Principles of Corporate Finance,* McGraw-Hill, Inc., 1991.

Coughlin, Cletus C., and Kees Koedijk. "What Do We Know About the Long-Run Real Exchange Rate?" *Federal Reserve Bank of St. Louis Review,* January/February 1990, pp. 36–48.

Cummins, J. David, Richard D. Phillips, and Stephen D. Smith. "The Rise of Risk Management," *Federal Reserve Bank of Atlanta Economic Review,* First Quarter 1998, pp. 30–40.

Dolde, Walter. "Hedging, Leverage, and Primitive Risk," *The Journal of Financial Engineering,* volume 4, number 2, 1995, pp. 187–216.

Dufey, Gunter, and S. L. Srinivasulu. "The Case for Corporate Management of Foreign Exchange Risk," *Financial Management,* Winter 1983, pp. 54–62.

Froot, Kenneth A., David S. Scharfstein, and Jeremy C. Stein. "Risk Management: Coordinating Corporate Investment and Financing Policies," *Journal of Finance,* December 1993, pp. 1629–1658.

Giddy, Ian H., and Gunter Dufey. "Uses and Abuses of Currency Options," *Bank of America Journal of Applied Corporate Finance,* Fall 1995, pp. 49–57.

Glass, Garrett R. "A Primer on Netting," *Journal of Commercial Lending,* October 1994, pp. 18–25.

Knetter, Michael M. "Exchange Rates and Corporate Pricing Strategies," Chapter 9 of *Exchange Rates and Corporate Performance,* edited by Yakov Amihud and Richard M. Levich, Irwin Professional Publishing, 1994, pp. 181–219.

Kogut, Bruce. "Designing Global Strategies: Comparative and Competitive Value-Added Chains," *Sloan Management Review,* Summer 1985a, pp. 15–28.

Kogut, Bruce. "Designing Global Strategies: Profiting from Operational Flexibility," *Sloan Management Review,* Fall 1985b, pp. 27–38.

Srinivasan, VenKat, and Yong H. Kim. "Payments Netting in International Cash Management: A Network Optimization Approach," *Journal of International Business Studies,* Summer 1986, pp. 1–20.

Srinivasulu, S. L. "Strategic Response to Foreign Exchange Risks," *Columbia Journal of World Business,* Spring 1981, pp. 13–23.

Stulz, Rene. "Optimal Hedging Policies," *Journal of Financial and Quantitative Analysis,* June 1984, pp. 127–140.

MANAGING INTERNATIONAL TAXATION AND POLITICAL RISK

This final part of the book examines two public policy issues involving direct foreign investment, along with the ways a firm manages these interventions by the various governments involved. These are often thought of as special topics within the field of international financial management, and both have generated sizable practitioner and academic literatures. Although they are special topics, and might therefore be considered optional, they are clearly linked to the first ten chapters of the book.

The first area in which governments and multinationals must interact is corporate income taxation. Chapter 11, "International Taxation," looks at both the public policy issue, providing the conceptual foundation for analyzing capital taxation, and tax management within a firm. Of course, an exclusively domestic firm must interact with its domestic government regarding taxation, but the issue becomes more complicated when a firm is a multinational because the firm must interact with multiple governments. This interaction means more than simply dealing with foreign taxation of foreign income in various foreign countries, because foreign income is potentially taxed in both the foreign country and the home country. Hence, the multinational must interact with different governments over the same income and navigate potentially contradictory public policies.

Corporate tax planning is now regarded as an important element of business strategy, even in the purely domestic context; see, for example, Scholes and Wolfson (1992). Recently, international taxation has been a fertile area of academic research, both in international finance and in public finance, and the chapter on international taxation conveys a sense of the results of that research.

The second area in which governments and multinational corporations must interact is political interventions. Chapter 12, "Political Risk," looks at motivations for government intervention in direct foreign investments, and at how multinationals can assess and manage the intervention. In some sense, an exclusively domestic firm must consider political risk emanating from its domestic government, but the concern necessarily increases when a firm becomes a multinational because it must interact with multiple governments and navigate potentially contradictory public policies. Once again, multinationals must do more than simply deal with political risk in foreign operations emanating from foreign governments, because foreign operations are potentially affected by interventions from both the host and the home country. This topic has a fairly long history of research interest, by both academics and practitioners.

Topics taken up here are dependent on the analyses in Parts I to III because they build on the tools and foundations provided earlier. The issues inherent in international taxation and political risk are viewed within the context of international capital flows introduced in Chapter 1 and extended in Chapter 2. Both areas provide additional reasons for real interest parity to fail, and consequently for uncovered interest parity to fail. The managerial aspects build on the capital budgeting and financing issues taken up in Chapters 3 and 4. Tax management is additionally related to the accounting concepts introduced in Chapter 6, and political risk is analyzed in much the same way that foreign exchange risk is analyzed throughout Part III. Hence, no new themes are introduced in this part of the book, although the two topics are applications of the earlier themes to specific issues.

❖ REFERENCE

Scholes, Myron, and Mark Wolfson. *Taxes and Business Strategy: A Planning Approach,* Prentice Hall, 1992.

INTERNATIONAL TAXATION

CHAPTER OBJECTIVES
AFTER READING THIS CHAPTER YOU SHOULD BE ABLE TO:

❖ Compare the effects of taxation on debt financing to the effects of taxation on equity financing.

❖ Describe various types of host government and home government tax policies.

❖ Make decisions regarding the allocation of profit among a firm's foreign branches by allocating costs, setting transfer prices, and reducing tariffs paid.

❖ Decide whether to establish foreign operations as branches or as subsidiaries when there is no profit repatriation; design a dividend policy for optimal profit repatriation in the context of the branch versus subsidiary decision.

This chapter examines the international tax policies of host and home countries and the management strategies of firms to reduce total taxes paid. In the first section, we review the tax implications for debt financing that we discussed in Chapter 4 as a transition to studying the tax implications for equity. In the second section, we examine international tax policies of both host and home governments. We then proceed to define and examine various tax management decisions. In the third section, we introduce an example that we will revisit throughout the subsequent sections. The first decisions pertain to the allocation of profit among a firm's foreign operations with respect to the firm's ability to allocate costs, manipulate transfer prices, and reduce tariff payments, and we cover these in the fourth section. In the fifth section of the chapter, we focus on the tax implications of establishing foreign operations as branches and as subsidiaries. We analyze these implications in terms of profit allocation without repatriation, and then with respect to establishing a dividend policy for profit repatriation. In the final two sections, we discuss some intertemporal considerations and broadly assess tax policy and tax management.

11.1 INTRODUCTION

This chapter introduces foundations of international taxation. Specifically, we are concerned with corporate income taxes, which are generally conceived as taxes on the returns to equity capital. In the discussion of international capital budgeting in Chapter 3, we alluded several times to tax payments but did not present much discussion on the calculation of taxes due. This chapter completes the picture by analyzing the structure of tax payments and techniques of tax management. We also considered taxes in Chapter 4 with respect to their effects on debt financing and the capital structure of a subsidiary. In this chapter, we review the basic concepts as they are comparatively straightforward and represent a natural springboard into what follows. Any implications which were not fully developed in Chapter 4 will become much clearer as we present the details here.

This chapter begins with an essential framework for thinking about both host and home country policies. However, the main objective of this chapter is to describe tax management within a firm. The chapter develops an extended example to illustrate the techniques of international tax management, and itemizes eleven international tax management principles. The goal of international tax management is to increase corporation-wide profits by reducing the total amount of taxes paid. Firms are able to use several techniques to accomplish this goal, including cost allocation among subsidiaries, setting transfer prices on goods and services traded among subsidiaries, and determining whether to set up foreign operations as branches or as subsidiaries. An understanding of these techniques—and legal implementation of them—will help managers increase the value of their firms.

11.2 TAXATION AND DEBT FINANCING

We introduced taxes in previous chapters predominantly with respect to the treatment of debt financing. Chapter 4 examined the management implications of the deductibility of interest payments when figuring corporate income for tax purposes. Because interest on debt is a deductible expense when figuring corporate income, there is clearly a distinction between the pre-tax and the after-tax interest rate applicable to the firm. We noted that the deductibility of interest payments on debt (regardless of denomination) and the treatment of capital losses (or gains) on principal increase the present value of an investment over what it would be if financed entirely with equity capital. To calculate the additional benefit, we introduced the Adjusted Present Value (APV) method to figure the value of the debt-related tax shield to the corporation. Most countries also allow realized foreign exchange losses associated with debt principal denominated in appreciating currencies to be deducted from income, and also tax foreign exchange gains associated with debt principal denominated in depreciating currencies, so that uncovered interest parity is preserved.

The implications of the tax-deductibility of interest payments and the treatment of foreign exchange gains and losses on principal reflect a general principle in international taxation: the returns to debt are distinct from the returns to equity in any investment project. Interest payments are therefore separated from the rest of corporate income when figuring the corporate income tax liability, which means that the corporate income tax is designed as a tax on the returns to equity only. Chapter 4 discussed the implications of this tax system for the firm's capital structure. A loan from the parent to the foreign subsidiary provides an opportunity to return funds to the parent in the form of interest, which is advantageous when the parent's country has a lower tax rate than the subsidiary's country. Conversely, equity financing of foreign subsidiaries allows for reinvestment of profits and postponement of home country taxes until profits are repatriated as dividends, which is advantageous when the parent's country has a higher tax rate than the subsidiary's country. Hence, debt financing is desirable in high-tax environments and equity financing is desirable in low-tax environments. One final point is that equity financing offers added flexibility in timing repatriation.

Separation of the returns to debt from the returns to equity raises questions concerning the taxation of returns to debt. By convention, the lender is taxed on the returns to debt when he receives interest. Furthermore, the lender is usually taxed by the home government only. International debt flows, then, are really no different from domestic debt flows because the lender pays the same tax rate to the same government no matter where the capital is loaned. Hence, our analysis of international taxation will not focus on the returns to debt, but will focus instead only on the returns to equity.

11.3   INTERNATIONAL TAX POLICY

Analyzing taxation of equity returns is conceptually more difficult than analyzing the taxation of debt returns because there is an imbroglio of tax laws pertaining to the former. In contrast to the taxation of debt returns, equity returns are taxed in the host country, and may be taxed in the home country—possibly even at a different time. International tax policy is thus determined through often-complex interactions between host and home governments. By convention, the host government acts first and the home government determines policies vis-à-vis the host government. This section is therefore divided into two subsections, one on host government policies and one on home government policies. In reality, there is more interaction and conflict between governments than this simple outline would suggest, and some of the prime concerns are taken up in the next section.

HOST GOVERNMENT TAX POLICIES

The general international arrangement prevailing with respect to taxation of corporate profits is that the host country gets the first opportunity—or the "first crack"—to tax income produced within its borders. Specifically, the host country gets to decide its tax rates on corporate profits first. The after-local-tax rate of return to the home country investor on direct foreign investment is therefore $r^*(1 - \tau^*)$ where r^* is the foreign rate of return and τ^* is the foreign tax rate.

In addition, however, the host country is able to set other **withholding taxes,** which are taxes imposed on capital paid to the parent as they are taken out of the country. The withholding taxes may be imposed on dividends or repatriation of profits, license and royalty fees, and other revenues paid, whereas these funds would escape taxation if they remained in the host country. For example, the after-tax rate of return if profits are not repatriated is $r^*(1 - \tau^*)$, but the after-tax rate of return if all profits are repatriated is $r^*(1 - \tau^*)(1 - \tau_w^*)$ where τ_w^* is the additional withholding tax on repatriated profits. Clearly, the withholding tax acts as an incentive to reinvest earnings in the host country.

HOME GOVERNMENT TAX POLICIES

The home government's tax policies are much more complicated than those of the host government because the home country must establish tax policies relative to the previously-determined host country's policies. In particular, the home country must establish tax policy with respect to two factors: (1) treatment of foreign income and foreign taxes paid and (2) the timing of taxation. We treat these two factors separately.

In what follows, we assume that the home government's tax rate on foreign income is the same as the tax rate on domestic income. This is not necessarily the case, but generally prevails in practice. Some governments may be interested in taxing foreign profits at a different rate than the domestic rate. This practice would obviously introduce more complexities and create more distortions, but the analysis of different tax rates is just a direct extension of the kinds of analysis given elsewhere in this book. We do not take up the analysis here, however, so that we may concentrate more closely on the benchmark cases.

TREATMENT OF FOREIGN INCOME AND FOREIGN TAXES PAID

Given that there is a domestic tax rate on corporate income, there are four basic ways in which a home country government can treat foreign income and foreign taxes paid. The next four paragraphs outline these possibilities.

The easiest way to treat foreign income is to *exempt* it from domestic taxation. The firm will simply not be taxed on any income that it has earned abroad, and thus the foreign tax rate governs taxes paid by the firm. The after-tax rate of return is therefore $r^*(1 - \tau^*)$, as presented previously, abstracting from withholding taxes.

A second possibility is to tax profits earned overseas at the same rate as profits earned at home, and then give a full tax *credit* for the foreign taxes paid (generally both income taxes and withholding taxes, although this need not be the case). Hence, the home tax rate generally governs taxes paid by the firm. In practice, home countries limit tax credits to the company's domestic tax liability on total foreign income, which means that the multinational enterprise pays the foreign or domestic tax rate—whichever is higher. The after-tax rate of return is therefore:

$$\min[r^*(1 - \tau^*), r^*(1 - \tau)]$$

once again abstracting from withholding taxes.

A third possibility is to tax foreign profits at the domestic tax rate but then give a *deduction* for foreign taxes paid, rather than a full credit. Foreign taxes paid therefore only reduce total taxable income. The after-tax rate of return is $r^*(1 - \tau^*)(1 - \tau)$, again ignoring the role of withholding taxes. Here, there is some double taxation of foreign income occurring. This system is therefore not often used.

The fourth possibility would be to tax foreign profits, but then give no recognition for foreign taxes paid. In other words, complete *double taxation* of foreign income occurs. The after-tax rate of return is $r^*(1 - \tau^* - \tau)$, again ignoring any withholding taxes. This is not used as a method of taxation anywhere, but is presented merely to complete the list. Hence, no matter how much multinational corporations complain about taxation, things could be worse.

EXAMPLE 11.1

Peripatetic Enterprises, a multinational corporation headquartered in Nide, has foreign income of $1000 from its affiliate operating in Serendip. The government of Serendip imposes a corporate income tax of 35 percent. The government of Nide taxes domestic income at 45 percent, but has not decided what the treatment of foreign income and foreign taxes paid will be. Peripatetic therefore figures its income under all four schemes outlined previously while awaiting Nide's tax decision.

	Exemption	*Credit*	*Deduction*	*Double Tax*
Foreign Income	$1000	$1000	$1000	$1000
Foreign Taxes Paid	350	350	350	350
Home Taxes Paid	0	100	293	450
Net Income	$ 650	$ 550	$ 357	$ 200

If foreign income is exempted from further taxation in Nide, Peripatetic will simply pay Serendip 35 percent, so it will end up with after-tax income of $650. If Nide taxes foreign income at 45 percent but gives a complete credit for foreign taxes paid, Peripatetic's home tax bill is $[(.45)(1000) - 350] = \$100$; after-tax income is $550. If Nide taxes foreign income at 45 percent and gives a deduction for foreign taxes paid, Peripatetic's home tax bill is $(.45)(1000 - 350) = \$293$; after-tax income is $357. If Nide chooses to tax foreign income and completely ignore foreign taxes paid, Peripatetic's home tax bill is $(.45)(1000) = 450$; after-tax income is just $200. As expected, Peripatetic prefers the tax exemption. Beyond that, Peripatetic prefers the tax credit over the tax deduction, and prefers either of these over double taxation.

TIMING OF TAXATION

The timing of home government taxation also plays an important role in the establishment of the home country's tax policy towards foreign income. There are two major policies possible.

First, a country may choose to tax foreign equity returns during the fiscal year in which they are earned, a situation sometimes called **contemporaneous taxation.** This set-up exists in the United States (and most other countries) for foreign branches of multinationals. A **branch** is not incorporated separately from the parent and is therefore considered an extension of the parent rather than a separate entity. The profits from these branches are therefore consolidated into the parent's income statement and taxes are consequently paid when the foreign profits are earned.

Alternatively, taxation may occur at the time profits are repatriated as dividends, a situation known as **tax deferral.** In the United States (as well as most other countries that tax the foreign income of their multinational corporations), this set-up exists for foreign subsidiaries of multinationals. A **subsidiary** is an affiliate of a multinational corporation that is incorporated in the country in which it operates, and is therefore considered a separate legal entity. Thus, subsidiary profits are taxed by the home government only when they come home. The basic implication of this policy is that tax deferral encourages profits to be reinvested abroad rather than repatriated.

SUMMARY OF INTERNATIONAL TAX POLICY

The first-crack principle means that the host country government sets the corporate income tax rate on returns to equity earned within its borders, as well as any withholding taxes on financial outflows. The home country government is left to react to the host country's policies by deciding the treatment of foreign income and foreign taxes paid in domestic taxation, as well as the timing of taxes. In practice, some countries exempt foreign income from taxation but most countries tax foreign income and give a full credit for foreign taxes paid. Countries could alternatively give a deduction for foreign taxes paid, or even fail to recognize foreign taxes paid altogether. Taxation can be either contemporaneous, as is the case for branches of U.S. corporations abroad, or deferred until repatriation of profits occurs, as is the case for foreign subsidiaries of U.S. corporations.

Clearly, relative tax rates affect the investment decisions of multinationals. All other things equal, the multinational prefers to invest where taxes are lower. This explanation is often given as one reason for the inflow of direct foreign investment into the United States after the first round of tax cuts in the early 1980s. The Tax Reform Act of 1986 further lowered the marginal corporate income tax rate, from 46 percent to 34 percent, and this may help explain why inflows were speeding up in 1986 and 1987. Because the United States was a low-tax country, foreign corporations had an incentive to invest there.

Economists often study the effects of taxes on the investment decisions of multinationals and on international capital flows in general. As taxes typically create distortions to the equilibrium that would otherwise prevail, they are associated with losses to global output and welfare. "Tools for Analysis I" considers several aspects of tax distortions on the allocation of capital and resulting changes in output and welfare. The results of the analysis are important with respect to the public policy aspects of international taxation, but are somewhat beyond the managerial scope of this chapter.

Tax laws are in reality not as simple as the framework presented here. As an overview, however, the theoretical material in this part of the chapter serves to set up the analysis of international tax management presented in the rest of the chapter. With any rule of thumb regarding tax laws, there are always exceptions. For example, in the United States some subsidiary income is taxed regardless of when it is repatriated; this is known as "Subpart F" income. Roughly speaking, Subpart F pertains to passive income (interest, royalties, etc.) earned in the foreign subsidiaries that could have easily or properly been attributed to the U.S. parent company. We do not discuss Subpart F income further in this book, but it is important to recognize that this exception—and others—can be researched more fully in sources dedicated strictly to international taxation. In general, we will keep our tax analysis simple, so that we can coherently draw up strategies and conclusions toward tax laws that may be used in some modified fashion as the analysis becomes more complicated. For more details on the U.S. tax system, see McDaniel (1989), Ault and Bradford (1990), Billings (1990) or Bodner (1991).

INTERNATIONAL TAX POLICY AND REINVESTMENT

One stylized fact presented in Chapter 1 was that over half of U.S. DFI flows are actually reinvested earnings. The following table summarizes some of the recent evidence on the reinvestment of foreign earnings abroad. The reinvestment ratio represents the fraction of earnings reinvested, so for 1993 53 percent of total earnings were reinvested, and reinvested earnings accounted for 51 percent of total flows of direct foreign investment.

U.S. REINVESTMENT ABROAD

		1992	1993
A	Total Earnings	$48.7 b	$56.1 b
B	Reinvested Earnings	$14.5 b	$29.6 b
C	Reinvestment Ratio	.30	.53
D	Outflows of DFI	$39.9 b	$59.2 b
E	B as percent of D	36%	50%

However, Hines and Hubbard (1990) point out that this aggregate conceals a dichotomy among firms: the vast majority of multinationals' subsidiaries do not pay dividends to the parent and a small number of multinationals' subsidiaries pay significant dividends because they are in advantageous tax situations.

Some observers assert that high rates of reinvestment represent over-investment abroad. Given the nature of the tax system, this may be correct. Any earnings from foreign subsidiaries that are repatriated must usually pay a withholding tax in the foreign country, and must pay an additional tax to the U.S. government if the U.S. corporate income tax rate is higher than the foreign tax rate (combined with the withholding tax). Hence, a corporation may prefer to reinvest abroad even if the real returns are lower because it escapes these additional tax burdens. However, this may not represent overinvestment if firms plan for the reinvestment in advance, such as by underinvesting initially to preserve profitable opportunities for reinvestment of profits. In addition, firms may initially undercapitalize their foreign investments, transferring less equity and financing using more debt, in anticipation of future retained earnings.

Chapter 1 also pointed out that relatively little foreign investment inflows into the United States consists of reinvested earnings. Recent evidence on the reinvestment of foreign earnings in the United States is presented in the table below.

FOREIGN REINVESTMENT IN THE UNITED STATES

		1992	1993
A	Total Earnings	$ −4.8 b	$−1.0 b
B	Reinvested Earnings	$−11.7 b	$−9.4 b
C	Inflows of DFI	$ 9.9 b	$ 21.4 b

These figures suggest that repatriation of earnings to the home country has been common recently, despite losses on operations in the United States. Because of the negative numbers, reinvestment ratios and percentages of inflows of DFI attributable to reinvested earnings are not calculated.

Source: From "Foreign Direct Investment in the U.S.: Detail for Historical-Cost Position and Related Capital and Income Flows, 1993" and "U.S. Direct Investment Abroad: Detail for Historical Costs Position and Related Capital and Income Flows, 1993" *Survey of Current Business,* August 1994, pp. 98–161.

11.4   INTERNATIONAL TAX MANAGEMENT

The rest of this chapter develops analyses of tax management through an extended example, which is used as the framework for defining, explaining, and drawing conclusions concerning the various tax management decisions. We consider the operations of C&C Enterprises, a multinational corporation headquartered in Chicago which manufactures ski paraphernalia and sporting goods. C&C Enterprises operates a self-contained branch in Japan, and branches in Canada and Ireland that manufacture exclusively for export to branches in Great Britain and Germany, respectively. To make the exposition as streamlined as possible, we assume that there are no U.S. operations other than the home office in Chicago; the costs of this office are fully charged to the foreign branches, so there is no domestic profit or loss. The relevant information on each affiliate is found in Table 11-1. The income statements of the foreign operations are presented in the upper portion of the figure. Goods shipped from one country to another are currently transferred at $16 per unit; this figure determines the revenue in the exporting branch and the cost of goods sold in the importing branch. Other revenues and costs of goods sold are shown in the figure. Import duties—currently zero—and other expenses are shown on separate lines. There are no physical assets in these operations, so there is no depreciation shown in the income statements. The difference between revenues and costs is pre-tax income in the foreign country. Foreign income taxes are then paid at the following rates: 28 percent in Canada, 35 percent in Britain, 30 percent in Ireland, 56 percent in Germany, and 42 percent in Japan.

The tax structure used in the United States, C&C's home country, is based on the worldwide tax principle: gross foreign branch income is taxed and a full credit is given for foreign taxes paid up to the amount of the U.S. tax liability. The U.S. tax rate is 34 percent. The U.S. tax liability on branch income is calculated in the middle section of Table 11-1, determined as 34 percent of $260,000, or $88,400, less foreign taxes paid amounting to $88,100, for a net tax liability of $300 for the particular example. The net branch income is therefore $171,600. This is the benchmark result for analyzing all of C&C's forthcoming tax management decisions.

To focus attention on the major implications of our analysis, discussion is built around eleven general International Tax Management Principles derived from our analysis of C&C Enterprises. Table 11-1 will be extensively revised throughout this chapter. First, relevant decisions for branches will be considered. Second, relative considerations in establishing branches versus subsidiaries will be considered. Note that the bottom portion of Table 11-1 is set up for analyzing subsidiaries, as opposed to branches, and will be used later in the chapter.

As a final caveat, note that Table 11-1 is stated entirely in dollars, implying that the income statements from foreign branches (or, later, subsidiaries) have already been translated from the local currencies. All the issues of foreign exchange translation discussed in Chapter 6 are still present, but we strip away exchange rates in order to focus on taxation. For completeness, however, we note that branch remittances are translated at the exchange rate prevailing when the remittance is sent to the parent, and that remaining branch earnings are translated using the average exchange rate for the year. Similarly, dividends from subsidiaries are translated into dollars at the exchange rate prevailing on the date that the dividend is paid, and the elements in the calculation of the tax credit are also translated at that exchange rate.

TABLE 11-1 Income Statements for C&C Enterprises: Initial Situation as Branch Structure

Foreign operations are set up as branches. Goods shipped from Canada to Britain and from Ireland to Germany are transferred at $16 per unit, and there are no import duties in Britain or Germany. Foreign income tax rates are: 28 percent in Canada, 35 percent in Britain, 30 percent in Ireland, 56 percent in Germany, and 42 percent in Japan. The U.S. tax rate is 34 percent, and the tax liability on branch income is calculated in the middle section of the table. Total foreign branch income is $260,000, so the gross U.S. tax liability is $88,400. Foreign tax credits total $88,100 so net U.S. tax liability is $300. Income from foreign operations is $171,600.

	Canada	Britain	Ireland	Germany	Japan	Total
INCOME STATEMENT						
Revenue	16 160000	260000	16 160000	250000	120000	260000
Cost of Goods Sold	50000	160000	40000	160000	100000	88400
Import Duty		0		0		88100
Other Expenses	15000	50000	20000	65000	30000	300
Pre-Tax Income	95000	50000	100000	25000	−10000	171600
Foreign Income Taxes	0.28 26600	0.35 17500	0.3 30000	0.56 14000	0.42 0	0
NET FOREIGN INCOME	68400	32500	70000	11000	−10000	
BRANCH INCOME*						
Taxable Branch Income	0 95000	0 50000	0 100000	0 25000	0 −10000	260000
Gross U.S. Income Tax						0.34 88400
U.S. Foreign Tax Credit	26600	17500	30000	14000	0	88100
Net U.S. Branch Taxes Due						300
NET BRANCH INCOME						171600
Excess Tax Credits						0
SUBSIDIARY INCOME						
Gross Dividend Paid	0	0	0	0	0	0
Gross-Up for Foreign Taxes	0	0	0	0	0	0
U.S. Taxable Income	0	0	0	0	0	0
Gross U.S. Income Tax	0	0	0	0	0	0.34 0
U.S. Foreign Tax Credit	0	0	0	0	0	0
U.S. Withholding Tax Credit	0.25 0	0 0	0.25 0	0.25 0	0.2 0	0
Net U.S. Taxes on Dividends	0	0	0	0	0	0
NET DIVIDENDS						0
REINVESTED EARNINGS	0	0	0	0	0	0
Excess Tax Credits						0
INCOME FROM FOREIGN OPERATIONS						171600
Excess Tax Credits						0

*NOTE: 0 = BRANCH, 1 = SUBSIDIARY

11.5   ALLOCATION OF PROFITS AMONG FOREIGN BRANCHES

C&C Enterprises is presently concerned with allocating pre-tax profits among foreign branches to maximize after-tax profits. The first step is to review cost allocation. The general accounting rule for allocating expenses is that a dollar spent on generating income in a particular foreign country should be allocated to, and deducted from revenue in, that country. Certain expenses, however, such as home office overhead, research and development expenses, and even the interest payments on parent company debt, are not directly attributable to specific operations. These are examined in the first subsection below.

The second step is to review the pricing of goods transferred from one subsidiary to another, known as **transfer prices,** both in the absence and the presence of import duties charged on the transfer price in the foreign country. We discuss these issues in the second and third subsections, respectively. Although we explicitly consider transfer prices on goods traded within the corporation, the theory of transfer pricing also applies to fees levied by the parent on the foreign operation for managerial and technical services and to royalty payments for the use of technology, patents, copyrights, and other compensation to the parent.[1]

COST ALLOCATION

The expenses incurred at C&C Enterprises' headquarters in Chicago total $50,000. Each of the five foreign branches of C&C Enterprises is currently charged $10,000 for these overhead expenses. This is included as part of "other expenses" in the financial statement of Table 11-1.

The vice-president of finance, Wayne Lin, suggests allocating the headquarters costs to the high-tax countries, reasoning that the biggest tax deductions are available there. He produces Table 11-2, which allocates all overhead costs to Germany, the highest tax country. Total taxes paid abroad decline from $88,100 to $83,400. When this is done, however, the tax liability to the U.S. government increases from $300 to $5000 and net branch income remains unchanged at $171,600. Hence, the taxes are shifted from foreign countries to the United States, but total taxes paid remain the same. Mr. Lin is puzzled.

The puzzle is explained by another manager, Toby Leavitt. She points out that the United States taxes total branch income and gives a credit for total foreign taxes paid, regardless of where the income is earned and the taxes are paid. In other words, U.S. tax liability is not figured on a branch-by-branch basis. As cost allocation does not affect total branch income before taxes, the gross U.S. tax liability (before credits) is not affected by changes in cost allocation. As long as the U.S. tax liability on foreign income (before credits) exceeds total foreign taxes paid, allocation of costs does not affect net branch income. It clearly affects what government receives the tax revenue, but it does not affect the total taxes the corporation pays.

On the other hand, the firm does not want the U.S. tax liability on foreign income (before credits) to fall short of total foreign taxes paid because it cannot use all the tax credits generated by foreign taxes paid. When the credits from foreign taxes exceed the U.S. tax liability, the firm is said to have **excess tax credits.** If the firm cannot use all the tax credits generated abroad, however, reallocating costs to high-tax countries will reduce total taxes paid and increase after-tax profits. This rule naturally applies only up

TABLE 11-2 Income Statements for C&C Enterprises: Branch Structure with Costs Allocated to High-Tax Country

Headquarters costs spread across the five branches, included in "Other Expenses," are aggregated and allocated to the high-tax country, Germany. This does not change total foreign branch income, however, so gross U.S. income tax remains at $88,400 and income from foreign operations remains at $171,600. This illustrates International Tax Management Principle I.

	Canada	Britain	Ireland	Germany	Japan	Total
INCOME STATEMENT						
Revenue	16 160000	260000	16 160000	250000	120000	
Cost of Goods Sold	50000	160000	40000	160000	100000	
Import Duty		0		0	0	
Other Expenses	5000	40000	10000	105000	20000	
Pre-Tax Income	105000	60000	110000	−15000	0	
Foreign Income Taxes	0.28 29400	0.35 21000	0.3 33000	0.56 0	0.42 0	
NET FOREIGN INCOME	75600	39000	77000	−15000	0	
BRANCH INCOME*						
Taxable Branch Income	0 105000	0 60000	0 110000	0 −15000	0 0	260000
Gross U.S. Income Tax						0.34 88400
U.S. Foreign Tax Credit	29400	21000	33000	0	0	83400
Net U.S. Branch Taxes Due						5000
NET BRANCH INCOME						171600
Excess Tax Credits						0
SUBSIDIARY INCOME						
Gross Dividend Paid	0	0	0	0	0	0
Gross-Up for Foreign Taxes	0	0	0	0	0	0
U.S. Taxable Income	0	0	0	0	0	0
Gross U.S. Income Tax	0	0	0	0	0	0
U.S. Foreign Tax Credit	0	0	0	0	0	0
U.S. Withholding Tax Credit	0.25 0	0 0	0.25 0	0.25 0	0.2 0	0.34 0
Net U.S. Taxes on Dividends	0	0	0	0	0	0
NET DIVIDENDS						0
REINVESTED EARNINGS	0	0	0	0	0	0
Excess Tax Credits						0
INCOME FROM FOREIGN OPERATIONS		0	0	0	0	171600
Excess Tax Credits	0	0	0	0	0	0

*NOTE: 0 = BRANCH, 1 = SUBSIDIARY

to the point at which the firm breaks even; if additional cost allocations will cause losses at subsidiaries in high-tax countries, the expenses are essentially wasted because losses do not generate negative taxes. The main ideas of cost allocation involving branches are summarized in International Tax Management Principle I.

INTERNATIONAL TAX MANAGEMENT PRINCIPLE I

If there are no excess tax credits, cost allocation decisions do not matter for branches. If there are excess tax credits, show branch profits in the lowest-tax jurisdictions by allocating costs to the highest-tax jurisdictions, without making profits negative.

Primarily because of government rules governing cost allocation, there are limits to the extent to which a firm is able to reduce its tax burden by managing cost allocation. Expenses not directly allocable—such as the home office expenses considered above, or research and development costs—are generally to be allocated based on proportions of assets, proportions of sales revenues, proportions of gross income, or some combination of these. The firm must usually choose a method of allocation and then use it until material circumstances change. Apportionment according to the asset base is the most stable of the three methods, and seems to be preferred by accountants and governments alike. However, it turns out that the restriction on cost allocation implied by asset proportions is not as limiting as presumed because firms have come to manage the location of assets, such that more mobile assets are now shown in the high-tax countries. There are limits to cost allocation, however, because firms must formulate internal guidelines to make the best use of information conveyed by cost allocation. Decision-making may be hampered by distorted information resulting from accounting manipulation designed to reduce taxes. As Caves (1982) puts it, "the MNE hoping to confuse the tax collector runs some danger of confusing itself (pp. 246–247)."

TRANSFER PRICING

The vice president of marketing, Dan Sang, advocates altering the company's transfer pricing structure to show profits in the low-tax jurisdictions. He produces Table 11-3, which raises the transfer price from $16 to $18 on goods shipped from Canada to Britain and from Ireland to Germany. This increase reduces total foreign taxes paid to $81,500 from the benchmark $88,100. Once again, however, the net branch income remains unchanged at $171,600 because the U.S. tax liability increases to $6,900 from $300. Ms. Leavitt again explains that transfer pricing does not matter when the firm does not have excess tax credits. If the firm were generating excess tax credits, however, the strategy of allocating profits to low-tax countries would make sense. Once again, this rule holds only up to the point at which profits become zero because losses do not generate negative tax liabilities. The main ideas of transfer pricing are summarized in International Tax Management Principle II.

INTERNATIONAL TAX MANAGEMENT PRINCIPLE II

If there are no excess tax credits, transfer pricing decisions do not matter for branches. If there are excess tax credits, show branch profits in the lowest-tax jurisdictions by following a simple rule:

> If one branch is selling to a foreign branch, set the transfer price as high as possible when $\tau^* > \tau$ without making profits negative, and as low as

TABLE 11-3 Income Statements for C&C Enterprises: Branch Structure with Transfer Price Increased

The transfer price on goods shipped from Canada to Britain and from Ireland to Germany is raised to $18 per unit to show profits in low-tax countries. Once again, this increase does not change total foreign branch income or gross U.S. income tax liability so income from foreign operations remains at $171,600. This illustrates International Tax Management Principle II.

	Canada	Britain	Ireland	Germany	Japan	Total
INCOME STATEMENT						
Revenue	18 180000	260000	18 180000	250000	120000	260000
Cost of Goods Sold	50000	180000	40000	180000	100000	88400
Import Duty		0		0		81500
Other Expenses	15000	50000	20000	65000	30000	6900
Pre-Tax Income	115000	30000	120000	5000	−10000	171600
Foreign Income Taxes	0.28 32200	0.35 10500	0.3 36000	0.56 2800	0.42 0	0
NET FOREIGN INCOME	82800	19500	84000	2200	−10000	
BRANCH INCOME*						
Taxable Branch Income	115000	30000	120000	5000	−10000	260000
Gross U.S. Income Tax						0.34 88400
U.S. Foreign Tax Credit	32200	10500	36000	2800	0	81500
Net U.S. Branch Taxes Due						6900
NET BRANCH INCOME						171600
Excess Tax Credits						0
SUBSIDIARY INCOME						
Gross Dividend Paid	0	0	0	0	0	0
Gross-Up for Foreign Taxes	0	0	0	0	0	0
U.S. Taxable Income	0	0	0	0	0	0
Gross U.S. Income Tax	0	0	0	0	0	0.34 0
U.S. Foreign Tax Credit	0	0	0	0	0	0
U.S. Withholding Tax Credit	0.25 0	0	0.25 0	0.25 0	0.2 0	0
Net U.S. Taxes on Dividends						0
NET DIVIDENDS						0
REINVESTED EARNINGS	0	0	0	0	0	0
Excess Tax Credits						0
INCOME FROM FOREIGN OPERATIONS						171600
Excess Tax Credits						0

*NOTE: 0 = BRANCH, 1 = SUBSIDIARY

365

possible when $\tau^* < \tau$ without making profits negative, where τ is the tax rate on profits earned by the first branch and τ^* is the tax rate on profits earned by the foreign branch.

Again primarily because of government rules, the extent to which the firm can manage transfer pricing to show profits in the low-tax jurisdictions is limited. Governments strive for transfer prices that reflect arms-length transactions. This is easy if there is a competitive market for the identical good outside the firm. The practical implication here is that firms in competitive industries are highly constrained. This is not usually the case for most multinational corporations, however, so the firm has some leeway in determining arms-length prices. The firm may establish a reasonable discount from the final resale price, which is called the **resale price method,** but it is difficult to determine this price for any intermediate product. The firm may also establish a reasonable mark-up over the cost of producing the good, which is called the **cost-plus method,** but defining and calculating the cost of a product is not easy. For further details, see Kim and Kim (1999).

Overall, the problems associated with methods of determining transfer prices give a firm an interval of acceptable transfer prices, from which managers are free to pick the most favorable. Once again, there are limits to this freedom because firms must make decisions based on the transfer prices used; the transfer price selected should therefore be set to have economic meaning as well as to reduce taxes. In addition, the transfer prices are subject to government scrutiny by tax-collection authorities. One objective of the U.S. government has been to crack down on transfer price manipulation by foreign firms operating in the United States. An Internal Revenue Service (IRS) study of tax returns for 1992 estimated that foreign companies understated their U.S. income by more than $1 billion. On a country-by-country basis, Japanese corporations allegedly understated income by $508 million, British corporations by $463 million, Canadian corporations by $134 million, and German corporations by $120 million.[2] Most of the understatement was attributed to inappropriate transfer prices. The Internal Revenue Service has subsequently pursued stricter enforcement of transfer pricing laws to collect more tax revenue.

TARIFFS AND TRANSFER PRICING

Just as things are going smoothly for Ms. Leavitt, Britain and Germany introduce 20 percent import tariffs. The tariffs are levied on the transfer prices selected by C&C Enterprises, and are deductible expenses in figuring the branches' income taxes. Ms. Leavitt, holding fast to her earlier convictions, advocates maintaining the $16 transfer price, arguing that transfer prices do not matter if there are no excess tax credits. The result is shown in Table 11-4; note that net branch income declines to $129,360 because of the import tariffs paid.

The Presidents of C&C Enterprises assume that this is the best they can do until the new vice president of marketing, Marc Sardy, suggests that, despite Ms. Leavitt's convictions, the firm should adjust the transfer pricing policy. Mr. Sardy argues that the firm can minimize the import duty paid by setting transfer prices as low as possible. C&C's accountants determine that they can justify transfer prices as low as $14, so in Table 11-5 Mr. Sardy tries pricing the transfers at $14. Total import duties paid fall from $64,000 (shown in Table 11-4) to $56,000, or by $8,000. Total foreign income taxes rise from $62,900 to $69,220, or by $6,320. The U.S. tax liability, however, falls from $3,740

TABLE 11-4 Income Statements for C&C Enterprises: Branch Structure with Import Tariffs Introduced
Britain and Germany introduce 20 percent import tariffs, thus reducing total foreign branch income to $196,000 and income from foreign operations to $129,360.

	Canada		Britain		Ireland		Germany		Japan		Total
INCOME STATEMENT											
Revenue	16	160000		260000	16	160000		250000		120000	196000
Cost of Goods Sold		50000		160000		40000		160000		100000	66640
Import Duty			0.2	32000			0.2	32000			
Other Expenses		15000		50000		20000		65000		30000	
Pre-Tax Income		95000		18000		100000		−7000		−10000	
Foreign Income Taxes	0.28	26600	0.35	6300	0.3	30000	0.56	0	0.42	0	
NET FOREIGN INCOME		68400		11700		70000		−7000		−10000	
BRANCH INCOME*	0		0		0		0		0		
Taxable Branch Income		95000		18000		100000		−7000		−10000	196000
Gross U.S. Income Tax											0.34 66640
U.S. Foreign Tax Credit		26600		6300		30000		0		0	62900
Net U.S. Branch Taxes Due											3740
NET BRANCH INCOME											129360
Excess Tax Credits											0
SUBSIDIARY INCOME											
Gross Dividend Paid		0		0		0		0		0	0
Gross-Up for Foreign Taxes		0		0		0		0		0	0
U.S. Taxable Income		0		0		0		0		0	0
Gross U.S. Income Tax		0		0		0		0		0	0.34 0
U.S. Foreign Tax Credit		0		0		0		0		0	0
U.S. Withholding Tax Credit	0.25	0	0	0	0.25	0	0.25	0	0.2	0	0
Net U.S. Taxes on Dividends		0		0		0		0		0	0
NET DIVIDENDS		0		0		0		0		0	0
REINVESTED EARNINGS		0		0		0		0		0	0
Excess Tax Credits		0		0		0		0		0	0
INCOME FROM FOREIGN OPERATIONS											129360
Excess Tax Credits		0									0

*NOTE: 0 = BRANCH, 1 = SUBSIDIARY

TABLE 11-5 Income Statements for C&C Enterprises: Branch Structure with Import Tariffs Introduced and Transfer Price Decreased

Britain and Germany have 20 percent import duties. Because import duties paid generate deductible expenses rather than tax credits, the firm favors a lower transfer price to lower the import duties paid, as long as it can use the tax credits generated by higher income tax payments. The transfer price on goods shipped is lowered to $14 per unit. Foreign branch income increases from $196,000 to $204,000. Gross U.S. income tax liability increases from $66,640 to $69,360, but foreign tax credits increase from $62,900 to $69,220. Income from foreign operations increases from $129,360 to $134,640. This illustrates International Tax Management Principle III.

	Canada	Britain	Ireland	Germany	Japan	Total
INCOME STATEMENT						
Revenue	14 140000	260000	14 140000	250000	120000	
Cost of Goods Sold	50000	140000	40000	140000	100000	
Import Duty		0.2 28000		0.2 28000		
Other Expenses	15000	50000	20000	65000	30000	
Pre-Tax Income	75000	42000	80000	17000	-10000	
Foreign Income Taxes	0.28 21000	0.35 14700	0.3 24000	0.56 9520	0.42 -10000	
NET FOREIGN INCOME	54000	27300	56000	7480	-10000	
BRANCH INCOME*						
Taxable Branch Income	75000	42000	80000	17000	-10000	204000
Gross U.S. Income Tax	0	0	0	0	0	0.34 69360
U.S. Foreign Tax Credit	21000	14700	24000	9520	0	69220
Net U.S. Branch Taxes Due						140
NET BRANCH INCOME						134640
Excess Tax Credits						0
SUBSIDIARY INCOME						
Gross Dividend Paid	0	0	0	0	0	0
Gross-Up for Foreign Taxes	0	0	0	0	0	0
U.S. Taxable Income	0	0	0	0	0	0
Gross U.S. Income Tax	0	0	0	0	0.34 0	0
U.S. Foreign Tax Credit	0	0	0	0	0	0
U.S. Withholding Tax Credit	0.25 0	0 0	0.25 0	0.25 0	0.2 0	0
Net U.S. Taxes on Dividends	0	0	0	0	0	0
NET DIVIDENDS	0	0	0	0	0	0
REINVESTED EARNINGS	0	0	0	0	0	0
Excess Tax Credits	0	0	0	0	0	0
INCOME FROM FOREIGN OPERATIONS						134640
Excess Tax Credits						0

*NOTE: 0 = BRANCH, 1 = SUBSIDIARY

to $140, or by $3,600. To Ms. Leavitt's surprise, Mr. Sardy's suggestion increases net branch income by $(8,000 - 6,320 + 3,660 =)$ $5,280 to $134,640. How does this happen? The fact is that an import tariff—in generating a deductible expense—does not generate a U.S. tax credit. This makes the firm favor a low transfer price as long as it can use the tax credits generated by higher income tax payments because credits are more valuable than deductions.

If there are excess tax credits, the decision is a little more complicated because a trade-off must be made between higher tariff payments and higher income tax payments. As there are excess tax credits, there is no need to worry about residual tax liabilities to the home government. "Tools for Analysis II" contains the mathematics of this trade-off. The change in a firm's profits can be expressed as a function of the tax rates and the change in the transfer price as follows:

$$\text{change in profits} = [\tau^* - \tau - \tau_d^*(1 - \tau^*)] \times \text{change in transfer price}$$

where τ is the income tax rate in the exporting country, τ_d^* is the import duty in the importing country, and τ^* is the income tax rate in the importing country. The intuition behind this is that managers must compare τ^*, which is the foreign tax paid on marginal profits booked in the importing country, to $[\tau + \tau_d^*(1 - \tau^*)]$, which is the total tax bill associated with marginal profits booked in the exporting country. The latter naturally includes the exporting country's income tax rate, but also includes the additional (after-tax) import duty charged by the importing country when the high transfer price is implemented.

EXAMPLE 11.2

Loki Technologies, a U.S. multinational, manufactures computer equipment in Ruthenia for export to Xenon. Accountants have decided they can justify a transfer price anywhere between $1,000 and $1,200, and they are aware they have excess tax credits from operations in other countries so residual tax liabilities to the U.S. government are always zero. The corporate income tax rate in Ruthenia is 30 percent, and the corporate income tax rate in Xenon is 45 percent. There is also an import duty of 10 percent for all computer equipment imported into Xenon. This means that:

$$\text{change in profits} = [.45 - .30 - .10(.55)] \times \text{change in transfer price}$$
$$= [.095] \times \text{change in transfer price}$$

so increasing the transfer price increases the firm's global profits. The high transfer price of $1200 should be used to show profits in Ruthenia, despite the higher import duty paid to Xenon.

Setting transfer prices in the presence of tariffs is clearly more difficult than setting them in the absence of tariffs. However, the intuition behind the transfer pricing decision is straightforward. The results of this section are summarized in International Tax Management Principle III.

INTERNATIONAL TAX MANAGEMENT PRINCIPLE III

If there are no excess tax credits, use the lowest possible transfer price between branches in the presence of import tariffs. If there are excess tax credits, minimize branch taxes paid in the presence of import tariffs by comparing τ^* to $[\tau + \tau_d^*(1 - \tau^*)]$:

Use the high transfer price if $\tau^* > [\tau + \tau_d^*(1 - \tau^*)]$ without making profits negative, and use the low transfer price if $\tau^* < [\tau + \tau_d^*(1 - \tau^*)]$ without making profits negative.

TABLE 11-6 Summary of Branch Tax Management Principles

Decision	Firm Does Not Have Excess Tax Credits	Firm Has Excess Tax Credits
Cost Allocation	Does not matter	Allocate costs to high-tax countries
Transfer Pricing	Does not matter	Show profits in low-tax countries
Transfer Pricing with Tariff	Low transfer price	Minimize total taxes by comparing τ^* to $\tau + \tau_d^*(1 - \tau^*)$

SUMMARY

The implications of tax management for branches are summarized in Table 11-6. With respect to all three decisions discussed—cost allocation, transfer pricing, and transfer pricing in the presence of tariffs—there is an important distinction between whether the firm can use all tax credits generated abroad or whether some tax credits cannot be used. Cost allocation and simple transfer pricing decisions do not matter if the firm does not have excess tax credits, and the firm unambiguously prefers the low transfer price in the presence of an import duty. If the firm has excess tax credits, it wants to allocate profits to low-tax jurisdictions, to the extent permissible by law, through cost allocation and simple transfer pricing decisions. For transfer pricing in the presence of an import duty, a comparison between the marginal tax on profits booked in one country and the marginal tax on profits booked in the other country is necessary. For more specific recommendations for the case of a firm with excess tax credits, see the International Tax Management Principles in the text.

11.6 BRANCH VERSUS SUBSIDIARY STATUS

In this section, we consider the tax implications of the distinction between establishing foreign operations as branches and as subsidiaries. The difference is in the timing of taxation. Multinational corporations establishing foreign branches effectively centralize finances, meaning that taxes on profits are paid when earned. Multinational corporations establishing foreign subsidiaries effectively decentralize finances, causing taxes to be paid only when profits are repatriated.

There are many considerations in choosing between a branch and a subsidiary other than tax treatment. For example, a multinational may separately incorporate the components of its business to limit legal liability. Sometimes, host countries require multinationals to set up subsidiaries. In what follows, there is therefore something of an overemphasis on the tax aspects. With that warning, however, we will proceed given that tax management is the focus of this chapter.

BRANCH VERSUS SUBSIDIARY STATUS
WITHOUT REPATRIATION

The vice president of finance, Mr. Sardy, recently promoted from the position in marketing, announces that he wants to convert all foreign branches into subsidiaries to defer U.S. tax payments. In Table 11-7, he converts all operations to subsidiaries with

TABLE 11-7 Income Statements for C&C Enterprises: Branch Structure Converted to Subsidiary Structure

Income statements correspond to the initial situation in Table 11-1 but foreign operations are set up as subsidiaries. The U.S. tax liability on subsidiary income would be calculated in the bottom section of the table, but without repatriation of profits there is no U.S. tax liability. Income from foreign operations rises from $171,600 to $171,900 without the U.S. tax liability. This illustrates International Tax Management Principle IV.

	Canada	Britain	Ireland	Germany	Japan	Total
INCOME STATEMENT						
Revenue	16 160000	260000	16 160000	250000	120000	
Cost of Goods Sold	50000	160000	40000	160000	100000	
Import Duty		0		0		
Other Expenses	15000	50000	20000	65000	30000	
Pre-Tax Income	95000	50000	100000	25000	−10000	
Foreign Income Taxes	0.28 26600	0.35 17500	0.3 30000	0.56 14000	0.42 0	
NET FOREIGN INCOME	68400	32500	70000	11000	−10000	
BRANCH INCOME*						
Taxable Branch Income	1	1	1	1	1	0
Gross U.S. Income Tax	0	0	0	0	0	0.34 0
U.S. Foreign Tax Credit	0	0	0	0	0	0
Net U.S. Branch Taxes Due						0
NET BRANCH INCOME						0
Excess Tax Credits						0
SUBSIDIARY INCOME						
Gross Dividend Paid	0	0	0	0	0	0
Gross-Up for Foreign Taxes	0	0	0	0	0	0
U.S. Taxable Income	0	0	0	0	0	0
Gross U.S. Income Tax						0.34 0
U.S. Foreign Tax Credit	0	0	0	0	0	0
U.S. Withholding Tax Credit	0.25 0	0 0	0.25 0	0.25 0	0.2 0	0
Net U.S. Taxes on Dividends						0
NET DIVIDENDS						0
REINVESTED EARNINGS	68400	32500	70000	11000	−10000	171900
Excess Tax Credits						0
INCOME FROM FOREIGN OPERATIONS						171900
Excess Tax Credits						0

*NOTE: 0 = BRANCH, 1 = SUBSIDIARY

no repatriation of their profits. Mr. Sardy's idea has merit, as income from foreign operations increases to $171,900 from the benchmark of $171,600. Clearly, this is because C&C Enterprises can now defer the $300 tax liability to the United States until repatriation occurs. If taxes are lower abroad, the firm defers the residual tax liability to the United States until profits are repatriated. The increase in income from foreign operations therefore comes specifically because the operations in Canada and Ireland (low-tax countries relative to the United States) are able to defer the U.S. tax liability.

There is another force at work in Table 11-7, however. Although there is no increase in income from converting the operations in Britain and Germany because taxes are higher in those countries than in the United States, the firm is able to retain the excess foreign tax credits until profits are repatriated if the operations are established as subsidiaries. Otherwise, the excess foreign tax credits would expire. Under current U.S. tax law, tax credits can be carried back two years or forward five years. The firm anticipating the ability to use excess tax credits further into the future is therefore advised to establish subsidiaries in the high-tax countries to accumulate the tax credits.

If operations show losses, different considerations apply. It is advantageous to establish unprofitable operations as branches rather than as subsidiaries if the losses can be used to offset other firm profits. This is one implication of consolidating foreign branch operations into the parent company. However, the profits to be offset by foreign branch losses must generally be other foreign profits, which limits the usefulness of foreign branch losses. The parent company can recognize subsidiary losses, on the other hand, only upon liquidation of the operation. While this rule sounds like a disadvantage, it means the losses can be accumulated rather than simply lost.

The details are more complicated because foreign branch losses in excess of foreign profits generate excess tax credits which can be carried back two years or forward five years. In general, firms establish unprofitable operations as branches on the premise that the tax credits are more valuable in the near term than upon liquidation of the operation. For example, if a foreign operation is expected to lose money for a period of time before becoming profitable, the firm will benefit from establishing the operation as a branch in the early stages and subsequently converting it to a subsidiary once profits can be maintained. (However, the United States now imposes a *conversion tax* making the conversion from branch to subsidiary less advantageous.) In the example we have been analyzing, C&C Enterprises would consider keeping the Japanese operations set up as a branch if it could use the losses to offset some profits elsewhere. As in Table 11-7, however, because C&C cannot use the Japanese losses to offset other foreign income, the operation could be established as a subsidiary to accumulate the losses.

The rules developed in this section are summarized in International Tax Management Principle IV.

INTERNATIONAL TAX MANAGEMENT PRINCIPLE IV
If there is no repatriation of profits, establish profitable operations as subsidiaries. If a foreign operation posts losses rather than profits, it is advisable to set it up as a branch if the losses can be used to offset profits elsewhere, but to set it up as a subsidiary if this is not the case.

ALLOCATION OF SUBSIDIARY PROFITS
WITHOUT REPATRIATION

Mr. Sardy, the vice president of finance, proceeds to advocate allocating the home-office overhead costs to high tax countries as a way of increasing subsidiary profits. This means increasing overhead allocation to Germany until profits are eliminated, and allocating the rest to Britain. Allocations to Canada and Ireland are reduced because tax rates are lower, and allocations to Japan are reduced because losses do not generate negative tax liabilities. Table 11-8 demonstrates the results: income from foreign operations rises $9,950 to $181,850 because expenses have been allocated where the value of the tax deduction is the highest, minimizing the overall foreign tax liability. This is summarized in International Tax Management Principle V.

> **INTERNATIONAL TAX MANAGEMENT PRINCIPLE V**
> If there is no repatriation, show subsidiary profits in the lowest-tax jurisdictions by allocating costs to the highest-tax jurisdictions, without making profits negative.

Note that Principle V is quite similar to Principle III, which applies to branches in the presence of excess tax credits. As discussed before, there are limits—both government-imposed and practical—to allocations of cost across subsidiaries, but firms practice tax-minimizing cost allocation to the extent they can.

Mr. Sardy also advocates altering transfer prices to show profits in low-tax jurisdictions as another method of increasing subsidiary income. His recommendations are shown in Table 11-9, where the high transfer price of $18 is used. In this figure, the original cost allocations have been restored for ease of comparison. The strategy increases income from foreign operations to $178,500 from the benchmark (in Table 11-7) of $171,900, for a gain of $6,600. The proposal illustrates International Tax Management Principle VI.

> **INTERNATIONAL TAX MANAGEMENT PRINCIPLE VI**
> If there is no repatriation, show subsidiary profits in the lowest-tax jurisdictions by following a simple rule:
> > If one subsidiary is selling to a foreign subsidiary, set the transfer price as high as possible when $\tau^* > \tau$, and as low as possible when $\tau^* < \tau$, without making profits negative.

Once again, note that this result derives from the same principle developed for branches in the presence of excess tax credits. In addition, there are limits to transfer pricing. Nevertheless, firms practice tax-minimizing transfer pricing to the extent they can. Cross-section studies indicate that profit rates of U.S. multinationals are higher in low-tax countries than in high-tax countries; see Grubert and Mutti (1991) and Hines and Rice (1994). In addition, U.S. firms with tax haven affiliates have lower U.S. tax liabilities than similar firms without affiliates in tax havens; see Harris, Morck, Slemrod, and Yeung (1993). Both of these findings are indicative of income-shifting activities.

Of course, Principles V and VI can be combined to increase income even more. For the C&C Enterprises example, achieving this increase is left as an exercise for the reader.

TABLE 11-8 Income Statements for C&C Enterprises: Subsidiary Structure with Costs Allocated to High-Tax Countries

Headquarters costs spread across the five subsidiaries, included in "Other Expenses," are aggregated and allocated to the high-tax countries, Germany and Britain. Without repatriation of profits, there is no U.S. tax liability. As a result, income from foreign operations rises from $171,900 to $181,850. This illustrates International Tax Management Principle V.

	Canada	Britain	Ireland	Germany	Japan	Total
INCOME STATEMENT						
Revenue	16 160000	260000	16 160000	250000	120000	0
Cost of Goods Sold	50000	160000	40000	160000	100000	0
Import Duty		0		0		0
Other Expenses	5000	55000	10000	90000	20000	0
Pre-Tax Income	105000	45000	110000			0
Foreign Income Taxes	0.28 29400	0.35 15750	0.3 33000	0.56	0.42	0
NET FOREIGN INCOME	75600	29250	77000			0
BRANCH INCOME*						
Taxable Branch Income	1	1	1	1	1	0
Gross U.S. Income Tax	0	0	0	0	0	0.34
U.S. Foreign Tax Credit	0	0	0	0	0	0
Net U.S. Branch Taxes Due						0
NET BRANCH INCOME						0
Excess Tax Credits						0
SUBSIDIARY INCOME						
Gross Dividend Paid	0	0	0	0	0	0
Gross-Up for Foreign Taxes	0	0	0	0	0	0
U.S. Taxable Income	0	0	0	0	0	0
Gross U.S. Income Tax						0.34
U.S. Foreign Tax Credit						0
U.S. Withholding Tax Credit	0.25 0	0 0	0.25 0	0.25 0	0.2 0	0
Net U.S. Taxes on Dividends						0
NET DIVIDENDS						0
REINVESTED EARNINGS	75600	29250	77000	0	0	181850
Excess Tax Credits						0
INCOME FROM FOREIGN OPERATIONS						181850
Excess Tax Credits						0

*NOTE: 0 = BRANCH, 1 = SUBSIDIARY

TABLE 11-9 Income Statements for C&C Enterprises: Subsidiary Structure with Transfer Price Increased

The transfer price on goods shipped from Canada to Britain and from Ireland to Germany is raised to $18 per unit to show profits in low-tax countries. Without repatriation of profits, there is no U.S. tax liability. As a result, income from foreign operations rises from $171,900 to $178,500. This increase illustrates International Tax Management Principle VI.

	Canada	Britain	Ireland	Germany	Japan	Total
INCOME STATEMENT						
Revenue	18 180000	260000	18 180000	250000	120000	
Cost of Goods Sold	50000	180000	40000	180000	100000	
Import Duty		0		0		
Other Expenses	15000	50000	20000	65000	30000	
Pre-Tax Income	115000	30000	120000	5000	−10000	
Foreign Income Taxes	0.28 32200	0.35 10500	0.3 36000	0.56 2800	0.42 0	
NET FOREIGN INCOME	82800	19500	84000	2200	−10000	
BRANCH INCOME*						
Taxable Branch Income	1 0	1 0	1 0	1 0	1 0	0
Gross U.S. Income Tax	0	0	0	0	0	0.34
U.S. Foreign Tax Credit	0	0	0	0	0	0
Net U.S. Branch Taxes Due						0
NET BRANCH INCOME						0
Excess Tax Credits						0
SUBSIDIARY INCOME						
Gross Dividend Paid	0	0	0	0	0	0
Gross-Up for Foreign Taxes	0	0	0	0	0	0
U.S. Taxable Income	0	0	0	0	0	0
Gross U.S. Income Tax						0.34
U.S. Foreign Tax Credit	0	0	0	0	0	0
U.S. Withholding Tax Credit	0.25 0	0 0	0.25 0	0.25 0	0.2 0	0
Net U.S. Taxes on Dividends						0
NET DIVIDENDS						0
REINVESTED EARNINGS	82800	19500	84000	2200	−10000	178500
Excess Tax Credits						0
INCOME FROM FOREIGN OPERATIONS						178500
Excess Tax Credits						0

*NOTE: 0 = BRANCH, 1 = SUBSIDIARY

APPLICATION 11-2

EXCESSES IN INTERNATIONAL TRANSFER PRICING

The incentives to set transfer prices at tax-reducing levels occasionally lead firms into fraudulent excesses. A study of invoice prices by professors John S. Zdanowicz and Simon J. Pak reported in major financial periodicals suggested that "phony" prices enable importers and exporters to launder dirty money, cheat the tax authorities, and make the U.S. balance of trade look worse than it is. They report finding that razor blades from Israel were priced at 3 cents, while identical blades from Panama were priced at $29.35. The price of a telephone imported from Hong Kong ranged between $3.18 and $2,400. The reason for these huge disparities is that underpriced exports and overpriced imports shift corporate profits out of the United States, presumably to lower-tax countries. Among the other excessive transfer prices they found for 1994 data:

Instant Print Cameras	France	3.05
Pianos	France	38.00
Missile/Rocket Launchers	Egypt	38.20
Refrigerators	Australia	20.39

Examples of Abnormally High U.S. Import Price

Truck Tires	Sweden	$2,266.00
Toilet Paper	Japan	6.00
Brassieres	Italy	131.33
Spark Plugs	Canada	70.00
Instant-Print Cameras	Japan	2,538.00
FAX Machines	Canada	16,283.00

Zdanowicz and Pak estimate that the total amount of lost U.S. taxes due to these abnormal trade prices was $39.54 billion, and that the $166 billion merchandise trade deficit may have been overstated by more than $100 billion.

Specific companies have not been revealed by Zdanowicz and Pak, but public records show that the Treasury Department is prosecuting transfer pricing excesses at some companies.

Examples of Abnormally Low U.S. Export Prices

Radial Tires	Colombia	$ 3.03
Snow Plows	Jamaica	267.70
Spark Plugs	Taiwan	0.01

Source: Damon Darlin, "Salad Oil, $720," *Forbes,* August 14, 1995, p. 56 and Mickie Valente, "U.S. Losing More than the Trade War," *The Tampa Tribune,* April 22, 1995, Business & Finance p. 1.

Now consider the management decisions again if Britain and Germany introduce a 20 percent import duty on the transfer price. Without making any adjustments to the benchmark case in Table 11-7, income falls—as shown in Table 11-10—to $133,100. Mr. Sardy, who now has immense familiarity with international transfer pricing, analyzes the marginal tax rates paid on profits shown in Canada versus profits shown in Britain, and on profits shown in Ireland versus profits shown in Germany. The decision rule is (once again) based on the calculation developed for profits in the section on branches operating in the presence of excess tax credits. This rule is presented as International Tax Management Principle VII.

INTERNATIONAL TAX MANAGEMENT PRINCIPLE VII

If there is no repatriation of profits, minimize total subsidiary taxes paid in the presence of import tariffs by comparing τ^* to $\tau + \tau_d^*(1 - \tau^*)$:

Use the high transfer price if $\tau^* > \tau + \tau_d^*(1 - \tau^*)$, and use the low transfer price if $\tau^* < \tau + \tau_d^*(1 - \tau^*)$, without making profits negative.

TABLE 11-10 Income Statements for C&C Enterprises: Subsidiary Structure with Import Tariffs Introduced. Britain and Germany introduce 20 percent import tariffs, thus reducing income from foreign operations from $171,900 to $133,100.

	Canada	Britain	Ireland	Germany	Japan	Total
INCOME STATEMENT						
Revenue	16 160000	260000	16 160000	250000	120000	
Cost of Goods Sold	50000	160000	40000	160000	100000	
Import Duty		0.2 32000		0.2 32000		
Other Expenses	15000	50000	20000	65000	30000	
Pre-Tax Income	95000	18000	100000	−7000	−10000	
Foreign Income Taxes	0.28 26600	0.35 6300	0.3 30000	0.56 0	0.42 0	
NET FOREIGN INCOME	68400	11700	70000	−7000	−10000	
BRANCH INCOME*						
Taxable Branch Income	1 0	1 0	1 0	1 0	1 0	0
Gross U.S. Income Tax	0	0	0	0	0	0.34 0
U.S. Foreign Tax Credit	0	0	0	0	0	0
Net U.S. Branch Taxes Due						0
NET BRANCH INCOME						0
Excess Tax Credits						0
SUBSIDIARY INCOME						
Gross Dividend Paid	0	0	0	0	0	0
Gross-Up for Foreign Taxes	0	0	0	0	0	0
U.S. Taxable Income	0	0	0	0	0	0
Gross U.S. Income Tax	0	0	0	0	0	0.34 0
U.S. Foreign Tax Credit	0	0	0	0	0	0
U.S. Withholding Tax Credit	0.25 0	0 0	0.25 0	0.25 0	0.2 0	0
Net U.S. Taxes on Dividends						0
NET DIVIDENDS						0
REINVESTED EARNINGS	68400	11700	70000	−7000	−10000	133100
Excess Tax Credits						0
INCOME FROM FOREIGN OPERATIONS						133100
Excess Tax Credits						0

*NOTE: 0 = BRANCH, 1 = SUBSIDIARY

The intuition for this principle is the trade-off between higher tariff payments and higher income tax payments. For subsidiaries not repatriating profits, the multinational corporation should seek to minimize tax payments. If profits are booked in the importing country using a low transfer price, the marginal tax is just τ^*. If profits are booked in the exporting country by using a high transfer price, the marginal tax is $\tau + \tau_d^*(1 - \tau^*)$, where $\tau_d^*(1 - \tau^*)$ is the marginal effective import duty when a deduction on income taxes is permitted.

Using International Tax Management Principle VII for the goods C&C Enterprises ships from Canada to Britain, $\tau^* = .35$ and $\tau + \tau_d^*(1 - \tau^*) = .28 + .20(1 - .35) = .41$, Mr. Sardy should choose the low transfer price. Similarly, for goods shipped from Ireland to Germany, $\tau^* = .56$ and $\tau + \tau_d^*(1 - \tau^*) = .30 + .20(1 - .56) = .388$, Therefore, Mr. Sardy should choose the high transfer price. When the appropriate transfer prices are implemented, the results indicate that a loss occurs in Germany, so the transfer price must be scaled back some. Mr. Sardy calculates the transfer price at which the German subsidiary breaks even to be $15.41, rounded to two decimal places. The total income from foreign operations associated with the optimal transfer prices is shown to be $137,205 in Table 11-11, which represents an increase of $4,105 over $133,100.

PROFIT REPATRIATION THROUGH DIVIDENDS

C&C Enterprises now finds that it needs to repatriate profits from its foreign affiliates. The vice president of finance, Mr. Sardy, is constructing recommendations for repatriation policy. He knows that profits repatriated from subsidiaries located in countries in which the income tax rate is below the U.S. income tax rate will be required to pay the differential to the U.S. government. Furthermore, Sardy finds that some countries have withholding taxes on these dividends paid by subsidiaries to the parent. These withholding taxes generate tax credits against the U.S. tax liability, but Sardy isn't sure that C&C Enterprises will be able to use all the tax credits. He notes that profits repatriated from branches in most foreign countries escape the withholding tax, however, because the operation is already considered part of the parent company anyway. There is similarly no additional tax liability to the U.S. government because the profits were taxed at the time they were earned. Hence, his first conclusion is International Tax Management Principle VIII.

> **INTERNATIONAL TAX MANAGEMENT PRINCIPLE VIII**
> Repatriate profits from branches first because this action is without tax consequences.

As Mr. Sardy advocated establishing everything abroad as subsidiaries, he does not have branch profits to repatriate. He therefore goes to the other extreme and determines what happens if all profits are repatriated from the subsidiaries. Table 11-12 demonstrates that the overall income from foreign operations declines to $134,550. Compared to the benchmark in which all operations are branches, this is a decline of $37,050 from $171,600. The biggest difference is due to the additional withholding taxes paid that result in $33,650 of excess tax credits that C&C Enterprises cannot use. If the firm could use all the tax credits generated by the withholding tax, the distinction between branches and subsidiaries would matter less. The remaining $3,400 is associated with the tax benefit of the $10,000 in losses from the Japanese branch, which is not a benefit if it is established

TABLE 11-11 Income Statements for C&C Enterprises: Subsidiary Structure with Import Tariffs Introduced and Optimal Transfer Prices Determined

Britain and Germany have 20 percent import tariffs. Comparing the tax rate in Britain to the sum of the tax rate in Canada plus the after-tax import tariff in Britain reveals that a low transfer price is preferred. The transfer price is thus set at $14 for goods shipped from Canada to Britain. Comparing the tax rate in Germany to the sum of the tax rate in Ireland plus the after-tax import tariff in Germany reveals that a high transfer price is preferred. However, the high transfer price must not result in losses at the German subsidiary, so the transfer price is set to eliminate profits there. The optimal transfer price is thus set at $15.41 for goods shipped from Ireland to Germany. Income from foreign operations rises from $133,100 to $137,205. This illustrates International Tax Management Principle VII.

	Canada	Britain	Ireland	Germany	Japan	Total
INCOME STATEMENT						
Revenue	14 140000	260000	15.41 154100	250000	120000	
Cost of Goods Sold	50000	140000	40000	154100	100000	
Import Duty		0.2 28000		0.2 30820		
Other Expenses	15000	50000	20000	65000	30000	
Pre-Tax Income	75000	42000	94100	80	−10000	
Foreign Income Taxes	0.28 21000	0.35 14700	0.3 28230	0.56 44.8	0.42 0	
NET FOREIGN INCOME	54000	27300	65870	35.2	−10000	
BRANCH INCOME*	1	1	1	1	1	
Taxable Branch Income	0	0	0	0	0	0
Gross U.S. Income Tax	0	0	0	0	0	0.34
U.S. Foreign Tax Credit	0	0	0	0	0	0
Net U.S. Branch Taxes Due						0
NET BRANCH INCOME						0
Excess Tax Credits						0
SUBSIDIARY INCOME						
Gross Dividend Paid	0	0	0	0	0	0
Gross-Up for Foreign Taxes	0	0	0	0	0	0
U.S. Taxable Income	0	0	0	0	0	0
Gross U.S. Income Tax	0	0	0	0	0	0.34
U.S. Foreign Tax Credit	0	0	0	0	0	0
U.S. Withholding Tax Credit	0.25 0	0 0	0.25	0.25 0	0.2 0	0
Net U.S. Taxes on Dividends	0	0	0	0	0	0
NET DIVIDENDS	0	0	0	0	0	0
REINVESTED EARNINGS	54000	27300	65870	35.2	−10000	137205
Excess Tax Credits	0	0	0	0	0	0
INCOME FROM FOREIGN OPERATIONS	54000	27300	65870	35.2	−10000	137205
Excess Tax Credits	0	0	0	0	0	0

*NOTE: 0 = BRANCH, 1 = SUBSIDIARY

TABLE 11-12 Income Statements for C&C Enterprises: Subsidiary Structure with Total Repatriation of Profits

Repatriation of profits from subsidiaries results in additional foreign tax liabilities due to withholding taxes imposed on dividend payments and in an additional U.S. tax liability. Withholding taxes are 25 percent on dividends paid from Canada, Ireland, and Germany. With total repatriation of profits from Canada, Britain, Ireland, and Germany, the U.S. taxable income is equivalent to foreign pre-tax income, $270,000. There is no income from Japan to be repatriated, and losses cannot offset profits repatriated from elsewhere. The U.S. tax liability is calculated in the bottom section of the table. The gross U.S. income tax liability is 34 percent of $270,000, or $91,800. Credits for foreign taxes paid, including withholding taxes, offset the gross U.S. income tax liability. Foreign income taxes amount to $88,100 and withholding taxes amount to $37,350, for total tax credits of $125,450, more than offsetting the U.S. tax liability, and resulting in excess tax credits of $33,650. Income from foreign operations in Canada, Britain, Ireland, and Germany is the total amount of dividends, $181,900, minus the withholding taxes paid, $37,350, or $144,550. Compared to Table 11-1, income from foreign operations with a subsidiary structure ($134,550) is less than income from foreign operations with a branch structure ($171,600) due to the withholding taxes and the treatment of losses at the Japanese operation. With total repatriation, C&C Enterprises would be better off with a branch structure. This illustrates International Tax Management Principles VIII and IX.

	Canada	Britain	Ireland	Germany	Japan	Total
INCOME STATEMENT						
Revenue	16 160000	260000	16 160000	250000	120000	
Cost of Goods Sold	50000	160000	40000	160000	100000	
Import Duty		0		0	0	
Other Expenses	15000	50000	20000	65000	30000	
Pre-Tax Income	95000	50000	100000	25000	-10000	
Foreign Income Taxes	0.28 26600	0.35 17500	0.3 30000	0.56 14000	0.42 0	
NET FOREIGN INCOME	68400	32500	70000	11000	-10000	
BRANCH INCOME*						
Taxable Branch Income	1	1	1	1	1	0
Gross U.S. Income Tax	0	0	0	0	0	0.34 0
U.S. Foreign Tax Credit	0	0	0	0	0	0
Net U.S. Branch Taxes Due						0
NET BRANCH INCOME						0
Excess Tax Credits						0

SUBSIDIARY INCOME

Gross Dividend Paid	68400	32500	70000	11000	0	181900
Gross-Up for Foreign Taxes	26600	17500	30000	14000	0	
U.S. Taxable Income	95000	50000	100000	25000	0	270000
Gross U.S. Income Tax	0.25	0	0.25	0.2	0	0.34 / 91800
U.S. Foreign Tax Credit	26600	17500	30000	14000	0	88100
U.S. Withholding Tax Credit	17100	0	17500	2750	0	37350
Net U.S. Taxes on Dividends	0.25	0	0	0.2	0	0
NET DIVIDENDS						144550
REINVESTED EARNINGS	0	0	0	−10000	0	−10000
Excess Tax Credits	0	0	0	0	0	33650

INCOME FROM FOREIGN OPERATIONS

INCOME FROM FOREIGN OPERATIONS	134550
Excess Tax Credits	33650

*NOTE: 0 = BRANCH, 1 = SUBSIDIARY

APPLICATION 11-3

TAX EVASION AT SUNRIDER

Manipulations to reduce tax liabilities are sometimes so tempting that they lead to tax evasion. One of the biggest U.S. tax evasion cases in recent history centered around Tei-Fu and Oi-Lin Chen and their family business, Sunrider Corporation, which makes and sells herbal products—teas, cosmetics, and food supplements—in 25 countries. In 1997, the Chens and Sunrider were "accused of using foreign companies they controlled to overcharge Sunrider by from 50 to 900 percent for ingredients, thus drastically understating its profits and their U.S. tax liability (Emshwiller, 1997, p. A1)" in a complex transfer pricing scheme. The money parked abroad would allegedly then be used to purchase assets. The Chens and Sunrider were indicted in Los Angeles federal court, accused of underreporting their income by $125 million during the period 1987 to 1990. The U.S. government asserted that there was deliberate mispricing of goods in foreign trade as a means of tax fraud. The Chens asserted that the U.S. government simply didn't understand Sunrider's complex but legal way of pricing raw materials.

The heart of the suit involved both import duties and income taxes. The indictment said that Mr. Chen helped create companies in Taiwan and Hong Kong to buy herbal raw materials overseas for Sunrider's production facility in the United States. There were apparently two sets of invoices: one for the Customs Service showing low prices paid and one for the IRS showing high prices paid. When Mr. Chen became concerned about being caught, he told the Customs Service that the prices listed on customs declarations were too low and paid $2.3 million in extra import duties. In the end, the firm paid more import duty, but the additional payment was small compared to the savings in corporate taxes. "Chen admitted to a Sunrider employee that he was willing to pay U.S. Customs money he did not owe in order to avoid paying his true income tax liability to the IRS (Emshwiller, 1997, p. A6)." Essentially, it was cheaper to pay the higher import tax on a high transfer price for the raw materials than to pay a higher income tax on higher profits that would result from a low transfer price on the raw materials. By disguising profits as import costs, Sunrider effectively shifted earnings to its Taiwan and Hong Kong subsidiaries.

Sunrider did not get away with this scheme. The Chens paid $93 million to the U.S. government to settle part of the dispute in July 1997. Then the Chens pleaded guilty to felony charges of tax evasion in September 1997.

Sources: John R. Emshwiller, "Tea Totaler: Overpricing of Herbs Was Key to Tax Scam, L.A. Prosecutors Say: Sunrider Made Profits Seem to Vanish, It's Alleged, In Export-Import Abuse," *The Wall Street Journal,* January 7, 1997, p. A1; "Sunrider's Chens to Pay $93 Million in Tax Dispute," *The Wall Street Journal,* July 3, 1997, p. C16; "Couple Plead Guilty to Felony Charges In Tax-Evasion Case," *The Wall Street Journal,* September 5, 1997, p. C16.

as a subsidiary because the firm cannot repatriate losses until liquidation. The lesson from this is summarized in International Tax Management Principle IX.

INTERNATIONAL TAX MANAGEMENT PRINCIPLE IX
If there is full repatriation of profits, and there are no excess tax credits, the decision between establishing a branch or a subsidiary generally does not matter. If there is full repatriation of profits, and there are excess tax credits, establish branches to generally avoid the withholding taxes on profit repatriation. As before, establish unprofitable operations as branches to receive immediate tax benefits.

Consider now the situation in which C&C Enterprises does not need to repatriate everything. What subsidiaries should C&C tap first for dividends? The answer depends on the withholding tax rate and the additional tax liability to the U.S. government. For example, Mr. Sardy notices that there is no withholding tax on dividends paid from Britain, and as the tax rate in Britain is higher than the tax rate in the United States, there will be no tax liability to the United States. Table 11-13 demonstrates that repatriation of the $32,500 in after-tax income (which corresponds to the $50,000 in pre-tax income) from Britain does not alter the overall $171,900 in income from foreign operations compared to the case of no repatriation shown in Table 11-7 because the firm has no additional cash outflows. C&C Enterprises therefore receives a net dividend of $32,500. The U.S. firm receives a foreign tax credit in the amount of the $17,500 United Kingdom tax payment. However, because the tax rate in Britain is higher than the tax rate in the United States, $500 in excess tax credits is effectively wasted.

What happens if C&C Enterprises repatriates $32,500 in profits from one of its other subsidiaries? As this would be partial repatriation of the profits from any individual subsidiary, the foreign tax payment needs to be adjusted to reflect the portion of profits repatriated. The formula for pro-rating tax payments is:

$$\frac{\text{Gross Dividend Paid}}{\text{Net Foreign Income}} \times \text{Foreign Income Taxes.}$$

Hence, repatriation of $32,500 in after-tax income from Canada is increased, or **grossed up,** by (32,500/68,400)(26,600) = $12,639 to become $45,139 in pre-tax income. This is shown in Table 11-14. The gross U.S. income tax is then 34 percent of $45,139, or $15,347. The firm receives exactly $12,639 in foreign income tax credits. Because there is a 25 percent withholding tax on dividends repatriated from Canada, the government of Canada collects $8,125 and the net cash dividend drops to $24,375 before any U.S. income taxes are paid. This withholding tax generates an additional tax credit of $8,125, so the U.S. tax liability is reduced to zero and excess tax credits total (12,639 + 8,125 − 15,347=) $5,417. The net dividend (gross dividend minus withholding taxes and additional U.S. tax liability) is therefore exactly $24,375.

For comparison, consider what happens if C&C Enterprises repatriates $32,500 in after-tax income from its subsidiary in Ireland. This is shown in Table 11-15. The dividend is grossed up by (32,500/70,000)(30,000) = $13,929 to be $46,429 in pre-tax income. The 25 percent withholding tax once again eliminates any U.S. tax liability on the repatriation and reduces the net dividend to $24,375. This case is not exactly the same, however, because the excess tax credits total $6,268. To the extent that C&C Enterprises does not want to unnecessarily waste tax credits, repatriation from Canada would be preferred over repatriation from Ireland.

The analyses of the preceding three paragraphs can be summarized in International Tax Management Principle X.

INTERNATIONAL TAX MANAGEMENT PRINCIPLE X
If there is partial repatriation from subsidiaries, pay dividends from subsidiaries where the sum of the withholding tax and the additional tax liability to the U.S. government is the lowest. If there are several opportunities with the same marginal cash outflows, repatriate from countries which would result in the least excess tax credits.

TABLE 11-13 Income Statements for C&C Enterprises: Subsidiary Structure with Repatriation from Britain

Partial repatriation of foreign profits is sufficient, so C&C decides to repatriate from Britain as there is no withholding tax and no additional U.S. tax liability. A dividend of $32,500 repatriates $50,000 in British income. Income from foreign operations remains at $171,900. There is a $500 excess tax credit because British income taxes paid ($17,500) exceed the gross U.S. tax liability ($17,000). This illustrates International Tax Management Principle X.

	Canada	Britain	Ireland	Germany	Japan	Total
INCOME STATEMENT						
Revenue	16 160000	260000	16 160000	250000	120000	
Cost of Goods Sold	50000	160000	40000	160000	100000	
Import Duty		0 0	0 0	0 0		
Other Expenses	15000	50000	20000	65000	30000	
Pre-Tax Income	95000	50000	100000	25000	-10000	
Foreign Income Taxes	0.28 26600	0.35 17500	0.3 30000	0.56 14000	0.42 0	
NET FOREIGN INCOME	68400	32500	70000	11000	-10000	
BRANCH INCOME*						
Taxable Branch Income	1 0	1 0	1 0	1 0	1 0	0
Gross U.S. Income Tax	0	0	0	0	0	0.34 0
U.S. Foreign Tax Credit	0	0	0	0	0	0
Net U.S. Branch Taxes Due						0
NET BRANCH INCOME						0
Excess Tax Credits						0
SUBSIDIARY INCOME						
Gross Dividend Paid	0	32500	0	0	0	32500
Gross-Up for Foreign Taxes	0	17500	0	0	0	
U.S. Taxable Income	0	50000	0	0	0	50000
Gross U.S. Income Tax	0	0	0	0	0	0.34 17000
U.S. Foreign Tax Credit	0	17500	0	0	0	17500
U.S. Withholding Tax Credit	0.25 0	0 0	0.25 0	0.25 0	0.2 0	0
Net U.S. Taxes on Dividends	0	0	0	0	0	0
NET DIVIDENDS						32500
REINVESTED EARNINGS	68400	0	70000	11000	-10000	139400
Excess Tax Credits						500
INCOME FROM FOREIGN OPERATIONS						171900
Excess Tax Credits						500

*NOTE: 0 = BRANCH, 1 = SUBSIDIARY

TABLE 11-14 Income Statements for C&C Enterprises: Subsidiary Structure with Partial Repatriation from Canada

If partial repatriation from Canada is chosen, the withholding tax reduces the amount of the dividend. With a 25 percent withholding tax, a dividend of $32,500 (identical to the dividend from Britain in Table 11-13) is reduced by $8,125 to $24,375. Income from foreign operations is thus reduced $8,125 to $163,775. There is an excess tax credit of $5,417 because Canadian taxes paid ($20,764) exceed the gross U.S. tax liability ($15,347). This further illustrates International Tax Management Principle X.

	Canada	Britain	Ireland	Germany	Japan	Total
INCOME STATEMENT						
Revenue	16 160000	260000	16 160000	250000	120000	
Cost of Goods Sold	50000	160000	40000	160000	100000	
Import Duty		0		0		
Other Expenses	15000	50000	20000	65000	30000	
Pre-Tax Income	95000	50000	100000	25000	-10000	
Foreign Income Taxes	0.28 26600	0.35 17500	0.3 30000	0.56 14000	0.42 0	
NET FOREIGN INCOME	68400	32500	70000	11000	-10000	
BRANCH INCOME*						
Taxable Branch Income	1 0	1 0	1 0	1 0	1 0	0
Gross U.S. Income Tax	0	0	0	0	0	0.34 0
U.S. Foreign Tax Credit	0	0	0	0	0	0
Net U.S. Branch Taxes Due						0
NET BRANCH INCOME						0
Excess Tax Credits						0
SUBSIDIARY INCOME						
Gross Dividend Paid	32500	0	0	0	0	32500
Gross-Up for Foreign Taxes	12639	0	0	0	0	
U.S. Taxable Income	45139	0	0	0	0	45139
Gross U.S. Income Tax						0.34 15347
U.S. Foreign Tax Credit	12639	0	0	0	0	12639
U.S. Withholding Tax Credit	0.25 8125	0 0	0.25 0	0.25 0	0.2 0	8125
Net U.S. Taxes on Dividends						0
NET DIVIDENDS						24375
REINVESTED EARNINGS	35900	32500	70000	11000	-10000	139400
Excess Tax Credits						5417
INCOME FROM FOREIGN OPERATIONS						163775
Excess Tax Credits						5417

*NOTE: 0 = BRANCH, 1 = SUBSIDIARY

TABLE 11-15 Income Statements for C&C Enterprises: Subsidiary Structure with Partial Repatriation from Ireland

If partial repatriation from Ireland is chosen, the 25 percent withholding tax reduces the amount of the dividend by $8,125 so income from foreign operations is reduced $8,125 to $163,775. There is an excess tax credit of $6,268 because Irish taxes paid ($22,054) exceed the gross U.S. tax liability ($15,786). This further illustrates International Tax Management Principle X.

	Canada	Britain	Ireland	Germany	Japan	Total
INCOME STATEMENT						
Revenue	16 160000	260000	16 160000	250000	120000	
Cost of Goods Sold	50000	160000	40000	160000	100000	
Import Duty		0	0	0	0	
Other Expenses	15000	50000	20000	65000	30000	
Pre-Tax Income	95000	50000	100000	25000	−10000	
Foreign Income Taxes	0.28 26600	0.35 17500	0.3 30000	0.56 14000	0.42 0	
NET FOREIGN INCOME	68400	32500	70000	11000	−10000	
BRANCH INCOME*						
Taxable Branch Income	1	1	1	1	1	0
Gross U.S. Income Tax	0	0	0	0	0	0.34 0
U.S. Foreign Tax Credit	0	0	0	0	0	0
Net U.S. Branch Taxes Due						0
NET BRANCH INCOME						0
Excess Tax Credits						0
SUBSIDIARY INCOME						
Gross Dividend Paid	0	0	32500	0	0	32500
Gross-Up for Foreign Taxes	0	0	13929	0	0	
U.S. Taxable Income	0	0	46429	0	0	46429
Gross U.S. Income Tax						0.34 15786
U.S. Foreign Tax Credit	0	0	13929	0	0	13929
U.S. Withholding Tax Credit	0.25 0	0 0	0.25 8125	0.25 0	0.2 0	8125
Net U.S. Taxes on Dividends			0			0
NET DIVIDENDS						24375
REINVESTED EARNINGS	68400	32500	37500	11000	−10000	139400
Excess Tax Credits						6268
INCOME FROM FOREIGN OPERATIONS						163775
Excess Tax Credits						6268

*NOTE: 0 = BRANCH, 1 = SUBSIDIARY

The subject of partial repatriation of income raises a final issue in the branch versus subsidiary debate. International Tax Management Principle IV implies that the firm should have a clear preference for subsidiaries if no repatriation is to occur, to defer U.S. tax payments and accumulate excess tax credits. International Tax Management Principles VIII and IX imply that the firm should have a preference for branch status if substantial repatriation is to occur, to avoid withholding taxes on dividend payments. A trade-off between establishing branches and subsidiaries is therefore involved if partial repatriation is to occur, and this is summarized as International Tax Management Principle XI.

> **INTERNATIONAL TAX MANAGEMENT PRINCIPLE XI**
> If there is partial repatriation from foreign operations, compare the advantage of tax deferral associated with a subsidiary against the withholding taxes incurred upon repatriation from the subsidiary in deciding whether to establish a subsidiary or a branch.

SUMMARY

The choice between establishing a branch or a subsidiary is dependent on the firm's intention to repatriate profits through dividends. If no repatriation takes place, profitable operations should be set up as subsidiaries to defer U.S. taxes on foreign earnings or to accumulate tax credits. Unprofitable operations should usually be established as branches to offset other firm income. For the profitable subsidiaries, the cost allocation and transfer pricing decisions correspond to the case of branch profits with excess tax credits. As summarized in Table 11-6, costs should be allocated to high-tax countries, transfer prices in the absence of tariffs should be set so as to allocate profits in the low-tax countries, and transfer prices in the presence of import tariffs should be determined through a comparison between the marginal tax on profits booked in one country and the marginal tax on profits booked in the other country.

If repatriation of profits occurs, international tax management is more difficult. Profits should be repatriated from branches first because this action is without tax consequences. If full repatriation occurs, establishing branches generally avoids withholding taxes on repatriated profits. This option is clearly useful if the firm has excess tax credits, but does not matter if the firm is able to use all the tax credits generated. As before, unprofitable operations should be set up as branches to offset other income immediately. With partial repatriation from subsidiaries, dividends should be paid from subsidiaries where the sum of the withholding tax and the additional tax liability to the U.S. government is the lowest. If several operations result in the same marginal cash outflow, the firm should minimize excess tax credits. With partial repatriation, the firm should compare the advantage of tax deferral associated with a subsidiary against the withholding taxes incurred upon repatriation from a branch in deciding which to establish. Although these statements may seem complex and inconclusive, they represent only a simple introduction to dividend repatriation. For further analysis, see Hines and Hubbard (1990) and Altschuler, Newlon, and Randolph (1995).

11.7   INTERTEMPORAL CONSIDERATIONS

The extended example analyzed in this chapter involves only one time period, and only barely alludes to other periods by reference to benefits from deferring tax payments and using excess tax credits before they expire. In reality, tax management decisions involve many periods. Benefits from deferring tax payments can be shown as the difference between the tax liability if paid today versus the present value of the tax liability paid sometime in the future. From an accounting standpoint, the existence of multiple periods means that firms need to keep information on profits and tax payments until the subsidiary is sold or liquidated. Furthermore, firms need to follow some inventory method when deciding which profits they will repatriate. Although the analysis becomes considerably more complicated when the framework is extended to multiple periods, most of the intuition developed above will carry forward to the multi-period setting.[3] Before proceeding, however, a couple of important intertemporal considerations merit discussion.

The main aspect in a multi-period setting that deserves attention in tax planning is a firm's investment horizon. For multinational firms facing high home-country tax rates and subject to taxation on worldwide income at home, the investment horizon will determine the rate of return relevant to various investment projects. A firm faced with only a one-year investment horizon can focus on the before-tax rates of returns of different investments. This is because total taxation will ultimately take place at the parent tax rate when it is repatriated at the end of the year. On the other hand, when the investment horizon is sufficiently long, the after-local-tax rates of return become relevant. The reason for this is that when after-tax earnings are reinvested in the project, rather than repatriated to the parent, the portion of returns available for reinvestment becomes the key concern. For further discussion of intertemporal tax considerations facing a multinational, along with general discussions of tax planning as an element of business strategy, see Chapters 13 and 14 of Scholes and Wolfson (1992).

11.8   ASSESSMENT OF INTERNATIONAL TAX POLICY AND MANAGEMENT

Returns to equity are fundamentally taxed at the corporate income tax rate in the country in which they are earned, while returns to debt are taxed in the country to which the interest is remitted. The public policy implication of this convention is that if a foreigner is willing to put capital in your country, as a host you prefer equity over debt because the equity returns are taxed and the debt returns are not. Conversely, if domestic capital is being invested abroad, as a source country you prefer to have the outflows in the form of debt rather than equity because debt returns are taxed at the full value of the interest received back in the home country, whereas equity returns are primarily taxed abroad. Clearly, this dichotomy of interests between the host and home countries can create a struggle to control the equity and debt flows between the countries.

It should be clear that the imbroglio of possible tax laws pertaining to equity returns makes international financial management much more difficult. The returns to the parent from undertaking a foreign investment depend quite clearly on the tax rates abroad and at home, as well as on the home country's treatment of foreign income and foreign taxes paid. In most cases, this means that the parent's cash flows depend critically on the company's policy regarding the repatriation of foreign profits.

With respect to international tax management, the basic strategy is to increase corporate profits by reducing the amount of taxes paid. This chapter therefore examines several basic tax management decisions. Although the development is extensive, the framework is actually oversimplified. The example analyzed takes one decision at a time and looks at extreme cases; no attempt is made to put everything together. Managers have several tools at their disposal to incorporate multiple time periods and examine several decisions at once—chief among them are linear programming packages, calculus, and computer simulations. However, these extensions are beyond the scope of this book; see the references at the end of the chapter for more information. This chapter has the relatively modest goal of providing the intuition behind tax management decisions through a series of spreadsheets—and this intuition generalizes to the other cases.

The discussion of tax payments in this chapter serves to emphasize the difference between project cash flows and parent cash flows. In the capital budgeting analysis, the multinational corporation should be concerned about parent cash flows on the assumption that only funds repatriated to the parent can be used to finance new investments and pay shareholder dividends. This means that the projected cash flows must make adequate allowance for foreign income taxes, withholding taxes, and residual tax liabilities to the home country. Returns on the foreign investment may be higher to the extent that profits from subsidiaries can be suitably reinvested abroad, thus delaying repatriation and home-country taxation. If no dividends are ever paid, though, the value of the project to the home company is nil, and the project would not have been undertaken in the first place. Hence, the firm must make some projection of the dividend stream, and the tax payments associated with it, in the capital budgeting problem, and then proceed to value the parent's cash flows.

❖ SUMMARY OF CHAPTER OBJECTIVES

1. Compare the effects of taxation on debt financing to the effects of taxation on equity financing.

By convention, the lender is taxed in the home country on returns to debt when he receives the interest, and the borrower deducts the cost of interest from taxes in the host country. In contrast, the lender is not taxed in the home country on the total returns to equity, but the borrower is taxed on the returns to equity in the host country.

2. Describe various types of host government and home government tax policies.

Host governments get the first crack at taxing equity income, and thus set the corporate profits tax rate and any withholding taxes. The home government then determines the treatment of foreign income and foreign taxes paid. If foreign income is taxed, foreign taxes paid may generate domestic tax credits, tax deductions, or neither, and domestic taxes may be imposed either contemporaneously or when repatriation of profits occurs.

3. Make decisions regarding the allocation of profit among a firm's foreign branches by allocating costs, setting transfer prices, and reducing tariffs paid.

Decisions depend on whether the firm can use all the tax credits generated abroad or not. If not, simple cost allocation and transfer pricing decisions do not matter, and a firm always prefers a low transfer price in the presence of an import duty. If all tax credits can be used, the firm wants to allocate profits to low-tax jurisdictions, and will compare marginal taxes on profits booked in either of two countries in the presence of an import tariff.

4. Decide whether to establish foreign operations as branches or as subsidiaries when there is no profit repatriation; design a dividend policy for profit repatriation and revisit the question of establishing branches versus subsidiaries.

The choice between a branch and a subsidiary is dependent on the firm's intention to repatriate profits. If no repatriation takes place, profitable operations should be set up as subsidiaries to defer U.S. taxes on foreign earnings or to accumulate tax credits. If full repatriation occurs, establishing branches generally avoids withholding taxes on repatriated profits. With partial repatriation from subsidiaries, dividends should be paid from subsidiaries where the sum of the withholding tax and the additional tax liability to the U.S. government is the lowest. With partial repatriation, the firm should also compare the advantage of tax deferral associated with a subsidiary against the withholding taxes incurred upon repatriation from a branch in deciding which to establish.

❖ QUESTIONS FOR REVIEW

1. Diego, Chica, & Cleo, Inc., is a multinational headquartered in Tecate, a newly independent country. Diego, Chica, & Cleo has foreign income of $10,000 from its subsidiary in the United States, where the corporate income tax rate is 35 percent. The government of Tecate imposes a corporate income tax of 40 percent on domestic income, but has not determined what the treatment of foreign income and foreign taxes paid will be. Calculate Diego, Chica, and Cleo's Tecate tax bill and net foreign income under each of the following possible tax situations.
   a. Tecate decides not to tax foreign income.
   b. Tecate decides to tax foreign income at 40 percent, and to give a full credit for foreign income taxes paid up to the amount of the Tecate tax liability.
   c. Tecate decides to tax foreign income at 40 percent and give a tax deduction for foreign taxes paid.
   d. Tecate decides to tax foreign income at 40 percent but does not recognize foreign taxes paid, assuming corporations could file for a refund of foreign taxes paid.

2. The situation of Diego, Chica, & Cleo, Inc., in question 1 is now complicated by a 10 percent withholding tax imposed by the United States on repatriation of profits (in the form of dividends).
   a. What is the total tax paid to the U.S. government on Diego, Chica, & Cleo's $10,000 of income, considering both the corporate profits tax and the withholding tax on repatriated profits?
   b. What is Diego, Chica, & Cleo's Tecate tax bill and net foreign income under each of the four possible tax situations listed in question 1, assuming that the withholding tax paid is treated the same as the U.S. income tax paid?

3. Fat Fred Amalgamated, headquartered in Chicago, has an operation in Yamow, where the tax rate is 28 percent, and an operation in Zenon, where the tax rate is

41 percent. Neither country has a withholding tax on repatriated income. There are profits in both operations, as shown by the following income statements.

	Yamow	Zenon
Revenue	$100,000	$100,000
Cost of Goods Sold	40,000	50,000
Administrative Expenses	20,000	20,000
Pre-Tax Income	$40,000	$30,000
Foreign Income Tax	11,200	12,300
Net Foreign Income	$28,800	$17,700

Administrative Expenses consist solely of home office overhead allocated evenly between the two operations. The U.S. corporate tax on foreign income is 35 percent with a tax credit given for foreign taxes paid. If the foreign operations are set up as branches, U.S. tax on foreign income is due as earned. If the foreign operations are set up as subsidiaries, U.S. tax on foreign income is due upon repatriation of foreign profits.

a. If both operations are set up as branches, what is the tax liability to the United States and what are the total taxes paid?

b. Suppose the operations are set up as branches. How should the $40,000 home office overhead be allocated to reduce total taxes paid?

c. If the operations in Yamow and Zenon are instead set up as subsidiaries but there is no repatriation of profits, what is the tax liability to the United States and what are the total taxes paid?

d. Suppose the operations in Yamow and Zenon are set up as subsidiaries and there is no repatriation of profits. How should the $40,000 home office overhead be allocated to reduce total taxes paid?

e. If the operations in Yamow and Zenon are set up as subsidiaries and there is full repatriation of profits, what is the tax liability to the United States and what are the total taxes paid?

f. Suppose the operations in Yamow and Zenon are set up as subsidiaries and there is full repatriation of profits. How should the $40,000 home office overhead be allocated to reduce total taxes paid?

4. Refer to the situation of Fat Fred Amalgamated described in question 3.

a. If no repatriation of profits is planned, should the foreign operations be set up as branches or subsidiaries?

b. If total repatriation of profits is planned, should the foreign operations be set up as branches or subsidiaries?

c. Suppose the operation in Yamow is set up as a subsidiary and Fat Fred Amalgamated decides to pay a dividend of $15,000 to the parent. What is the U.S. tax liability and what is the net dividend after taxes? (Also assume that the home office overhead is divided evenly between the two subsidiaries, as shown in the original income statements.)

d. Suppose the operation in Zenon is set up as a subsidiary and Fat Fred Amalgamated decides to pay a dividend of $15,000 to the parent. What is the U.S. tax liability and what is the net dividend after taxes? (Also assume that the home office overhead is divided evenly between the two subsidiaries, as shown in the original income statements.)

e. Suppose the operations in Yamow and Zenon are set up as subsidiaries and Fat Fred Amalgamated decides to pay a dividend of $15,000 from one of the two. Which subsidiary should pay the dividend?

5. Etemadi and Co., a U.S. firm with subsidiaries in Chile and Brazil, can justify a transfer price anywhere between $600 and $800 per unit for cookware sets shipped from Chile to Brazil while simultaneously preserving positive profits in both locations. The corporate income tax rate in Chile is 30 percent and the corporate income tax rate in Brazil is 40 percent. There is no repatriation of profits currently planned, and Etemadi has no excess tax credits elsewhere.

   a. Should Etemadi use the high transfer price or the low transfer price for goods shipped from Chile to Brazil?

   b. Suppose Brazil introduces an import tariff of 20 percent. With the import tariff, should Etemadi use the high transfer price or the low transfer price for goods shipped from Chile to Brazil?

6. [Group project] If C&C Enterprises combines International Tax Management Principles V and VI, which are illustrated separately in Tables 11-8 and 11-9, what is the income from foreign operations?

7. Gizmo International is a U.S.-based multinational corporation that ships gizmos to its subsidiaries in Canada, Mexico, and Australia. The marginal profits tax rate in the United States is 40 percent. The marginal profits tax rate is 30 percent in Canada, 50 percent in Mexico, and 40 percent in Australia. The subsidiaries in all three countries are profitable and able to remit dividends. The United States taxes foreign income only when repatriated, and allows a credit for taxes paid.

   a. Gizmo can justify setting a transfer price anywhere between $20 and $25 per gizmo and can determine this price separately for gizmos shipped to Canada, Mexico, and Australia. What should the transfer price for gizmos shipped to each location be, and why? If each country introduces an import tariff of 20 percent on gizmos, what should the transfer prices for gizmos be?

   b. Gizmo decides to repatriate $1 million in profits from one of its subsidiaries. Which subsidiary should pay the dividend and why? (Ignore the import tariffs introduced in a.)

8. Shown are income statements for two foreign operations in which the first operation exports all of its output to the second operation for sale. The transfer price is currently set at $20 per unit, and there is a 10 percent import duty for goods imported into the second country. The income tax rate in the first country is 26 percent and the income tax rate in the second country is 39 percent.

	1	2
Revenue	200000	300000
Cost of Goods Sold	50000	200000
Import Duty		20000
Other Expenses	70000	69000
Pre-tax Income	80000	11000
Foreign Income Tax	20800	4290
NET FOREIGN INCOME	59200	6710

The parent company is headquartered in the United States, which has a 35 percent income tax rate and follows the worldwide taxation system giving a full tax credit for foreign income taxes paid. Income from branches is taxed contemporaneously and income from subsidiaries is taxed at the time dividend repatriation occurs. Both of the foreign countries impose a 5 percent withholding tax on cash dividends paid out from subsidiaries, but repatriation from branches does not face tax consequences.

    a. If the two foreign operations are set up as branches, what is the tax liability to the United States from foreign operations, and what is the excess tax credit position of the company?

    b. If the two foreign operations are set up as subsidiaries and no repatriation of profits occurs, what is the tax liability to the United States from foreign operations, and what is the excess tax credit position of the company?

    c. If the two foreign operations are set up as subsidiaries and no repatriation of profits occurs, what should the transfer price be if managers can justify setting the transfer price anywhere in the interval from $18 to $22?

    d. If the parent corporation decides to repatriate $40,000 of pre-tax income from the operation in the first foreign country, and that operation is set up as a subsidiary, what is the cash dividend net of all applicable taxes? (Note that the $40,000 is half of the operation's total pre-tax income.)

9. Harpoon, Inc., is a U.S. multinational corporation that ships small appliances to its subsidiary in Austria. The marginal profits tax rate in the United States is 34 percent, and the marginal profits tax rate in Austria is 55 percent. The U.S. taxes foreign subsidiary income only when repatriated, and allows a credit for foreign taxes paid. Austria has a 20 percent withholding tax on dividend payments, for which the United States gives a complete tax credit. Harpoon's accountant has just informed you that she can justify setting a transfer price anywhere between $100 and $150 on microwave ovens shipped to Austria.

    a. What should the transfer price be?

    b. If Austria introduces an import tariff of 25 percent on microwave ovens, and permits this to be a deductible expense in figuring the subsidiary's income tax, what should the transfer price be?

    c. If $100 in pretax profits is repatriated from Austria, how much cash does the parent receive? (Ignore the import tariff introduced in question b.)

    d. If $100 in pretax profits is repatriated from Austria, what is Harpoon's additional tax burden or excess tax credit in the United States? (Again, ignore the import tariff introduced in question b.)

10. [Class discussion] If a foreign operation is incurring losses, what is the most appropriate structure (branch or subsidiary) to reduce after-tax losses?

TOOLS FOR ANALYSIS I
Global Welfare, Tax Neutrality, and National Welfare

Returns on equity are taxed in the host country, and may be taxed in the home country—possibly even at a different time. This situation may lead to distortions in equity capital allocation. This section applies the MacDougall model of optimum international investment presented in "Tools for Analysis I" of Chapter 1 to the market for equity capital in the presence of tax-

ation. From the analysis, we are able to develop ways of analyzing general principles of taxation as well as the welfare effects of international tax policies.

In the Chapter 1 "Tools for Analysis," we used the MacDougall diagram to analyze all types of capital flows: direct foreign investment (DFI), portfolio investment, and intermediated investment. Here, however, we will focus on the MacDougall diagram as it pertains to the equity capital form of direct foreign investment, because international corporate taxation applies only to the returns on this equity capital. As we saw in the first section of the chapter, different tax conventions apply to debt financing, so we want to separate the returns on debt. Similarly, we want to separate the flows of capital categorized as portfolio investment and intermediated investment, because different tax conventions apply to these categories too.

From the MacDougall model, we know that global welfare is maximized if capital is free to flow toward countries in which the marginal product of capital is highest. If taxes do not alter the optimum allocation of capital, taxation is said to be *neutral*. The next two subsections examine two types of tax neutrality: capital export neutrality and capital import neutrality.

Capital Export Neutrality

Capital export neutrality, sometimes referred to as domestic neutrality, means that taxes do not distort a

capital owner's choice between domestic and foreign investments. In other words, taxation is export neutral if domestic and overseas investments that earn the same pre-tax rates of return also yield the same after-tax rates of return. If capital export neutrality is violated, the capital owner will have an incentive to invest more where the tax rate is lower, thereby realizing a higher after-tax rate of return.

Figure 11-1 illustrates a typical violation of capital export neutrality. The home country is shown on the left-hand axis, and the host country is shown on the right-hand axis. The marginal products of capital are shown by MPK and MPK*, respectively, and the initial allocation of capital is at k. From the previous presentation of the MacDougall model, we know that the optimum allocation of capital is at k'. In Figure 11-1, however, the home country imposes a corporate profits tax of τ while the foreign country does not impose any tax. This action introduces a distinction between the actual pre-tax marginal product of capital and the after-tax marginal product of capital, $MPK(1-\tau)$.

FIGURE 11-1   THE MACDOUGALL MODEL WITH CORPORATE PROFITS TAX AT HOME

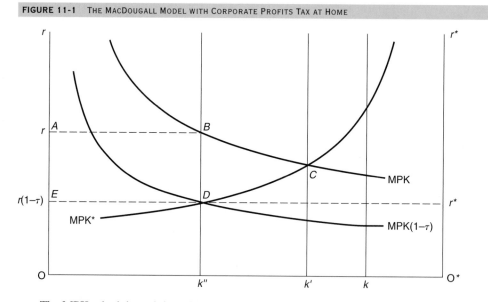

The MPK schedule and the MPK* schedule represent the demands for capital in the home and foreign countries from the origins O and O* respectively. The length of the horizontal axis represents the total quantity of capital available in the two economies and the initial allocation of capital is at k. The optimum allocation of capital is at k', where the marginal products of capital are equalized. When the home country imposes a tax on domestic corporate profits, denoted by τ, the after-tax MPK schedule shifts down to $MPK(1-\tau)$. This result discourages domestic investment and encourages foreign investment, so the new equilibrium is at k'', where the after-tax marginal products of capital are equalized. Too much capital is located abroad, and not enough capital is located at home, so there is a deadweight loss of area BCD.

As long as the home country does not tax income earned abroad, the capital owner can escape the home country's tax by investing abroad. The capital owner will therefore decide where to invest based on after-tax rates of return. At the margin, the after-tax rate of return at home, $r(1 - \tau)$, will equal the rate of return abroad, r^*, in the absence of foreign taxation. Therefore, the pre-tax rate of return must be higher in the home country, at r. As shown in Figure 11-1, the final allocation of capital is at k'', which is clearly suboptimal because the optimum allocation of capital is at k'. The figure demonstrates that there will be over-investment abroad—viewed from the position of global welfare—resulting from the imposition of domestic taxes in the home country. After all, economic returns at home are higher than economic returns abroad, $r > r^*$. In terms of Figure 11-1, the loss of world welfare is given by the triangle BCD. The total tax revenue collected by the home government is area ABDE. This exhibit illustrates that when the home country has a higher tax rate than the foreign country, capital export neutrality does not hold and there is a misallocation of capital.

One way to correct the distortion introduced in Figure 11-1 is for the home country to tax returns on home capital regardless of where the capital is invested. Figure 11-2 demonstrates the same scenario in the previous figure except both domestic and foreign returns are taxed by the home government. This shifts MPK to MPK$(1 - \tau)$ and MPK* to MPK*$(1 - \tau)$. Because both schedules are shifted downward by the same proportion everywhere, the intersection of the after-tax schedules preserves the optimum allocation of capital, k'. At the margin, the after-tax rates of return at home equal the after-tax rates of return abroad, $r(1 - \tau) = r^*(1 - \tau)$, so the pre-tax rate of return at home equals the pre-tax rate of return abroad, $r = r^*$. The total revenue collected by the home-country government is area ABCD, which is larger than area ABDE in Figure 11-1. This exhibit illustrates that if the home country taxes foreign earnings at the same tax rate as domestic earnings, capital export neutrality does hold and there is no misallocation of capital. (However, as will become clear later, this result requires the foreign tax rate to be less than or equal to the home tax rate.)

FIGURE 11-2 THE MACDOUGALL MODEL WITH CORPORATE PROFITS TAX AT HOME, INCLUDING FOREIGN INCOME

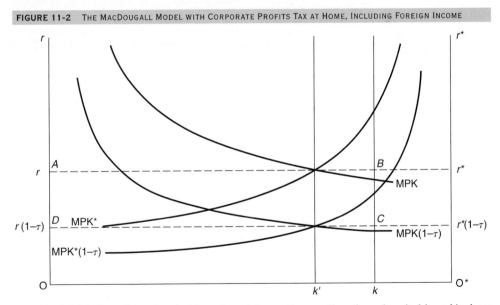

The initial allocation of capital is at k, and the optimum allocation of capital is at k' where the marginal products of capital are equalized. When the home country imposes a tax on domestic corporate profits, denoted by τ, the after-tax MPK schedule shifts down to MPK$(1 - \tau)$. If the home country also imposes the same tax of τ on foreign income, the after-tax marginal product of capital schedule on home-country capital invested abroad shifts down to MPK*$(1 - \tau)$. This tax scheme preserves the optimum allocation of capital because the after-tax marginal products of capital are identical at k'.

Capital Import Neutrality

Capital import neutrality, also known as foreign neutrality, means that taxes do not distort the after-tax returns to domestic and foreign suppliers of capital. In other words, taxation is import neutral if equal before-tax returns to competing supplies of capital translate into equal after-tax returns. This neutrality puts domestic firms and multinational corporations on an equal footing, even with respect to home country taxes.

In Figure 11-1, where export neutrality does not hold, import neutrality does hold. No matter where the capital comes from, it is taxed in the country in which it is invested, and nowhere else, which means that all capital invested in the home country pays only the tax rate τ. Similarly, all capital invested in the foreign country pays no taxes anywhere. Hence, capital import neutrality holds.

In Figure 11-2, however, where export neutrality does hold, import neutrality does not hold because the multinational corporation operating in the host country has a residual tax liability to the home government. This situation means that the multinational corporation is at a competitive disadvantage vis-à-vis domestic firms in the host country. After all, domestic firms have no tax bill whereas multinational firms have a tax liability to their home government. The rate of return on domestic capital invested in the host country is thus r^*, but the rate of return on foreign capital invested in the host country is $r^*(1 - \tau)$. Although there is no distortion in the MacDougall diagram, the tax scheme may be inefficient because there could be production distortions in the host country.

Summary of Tax Neutrality

In analyzing the two types of tax neutrality, capital export neutrality is usually of prime concern because the distortionary effects on the allocation of capital are unambiguous. In this case, the MacDougall model lends itself to analyzing capital export neutrality and global welfare. Capital import neutrality, on the other hand, is likely to be of less concern because the effects of tax disadvantages on international production and competition are not well specified. In other words, it is not obvious how much concern we should attach to the fact that different suppliers of capital receive different after-tax returns. There are distortions to the supply of capital (which are not depicted in the MacDougall model because supply is exogenous). These distortions lead to deadweight losses of welfare if after-tax rates of return to suppliers of capital vary across countries because the origin of the supply (as countries' savings)

is sub-optimal from a global perspective: one country should be supplying more capital and another should be supplying less capital. For more on this, including all the appropriate extensions of the MacDougall model, see Organization for Economic Cooperation and Development (1991), particularly Annex 3.

From the analysis, several points should be evident. In general, either export or import neutrality holds—but not both. In fact, the only perfectly neutral tax system is one in which all countries have the same tax rates (and no double-taxation occurs). This point will become clearer in the next section. Finally, it should also be clear that neutrality depends on who pays the taxes—not on what government collects them.

Figures 11-1 and 11-2 depict two alternative tax philosophies. Currently, the Netherlands, Hong Kong, and France are examples of countries that exempt foreign income from domestic taxation. This practice is sometimes called the *territorial principle* of taxation, in which taxes are levied on equity returns occurring within the territory, regardless of the source of capital, and no attempt is made to tax the foreign income of domestic capital owners. Figure 11-1 depicts the territorial principle. The arrangement of taxing profits earned overseas exists in most home countries, such as the United States, Japan, and the United Kingdom, and is sometimes referred to as the *worldwide principle* of taxation because home governments have a claim on the firm's worldwide profits. Figure 11-2 depicts the worldwide principle.

Global Tax Neutrality and National Welfare

Up to this point, we have been concerned with global welfare and tax neutrality. We will now show that international taxation gives rise to a conflict between global welfare and national welfare because taxation alters the distribution of national gains from international investment. This conflict, in turn, can cause conflicts between home country governments and host country governments, often catching the multinational firm in the middle. Some of the accounting activities of firms discussed in the chapter serve to restore maximum global welfare, but they simultaneously intensify the conflicts between governments and the multinational firm.

We have come to appreciate the significance of a completely neutral tax system in removing distortions from the economy. Figure 11-3 illustrates one such neutral tax system where both the home and host governments impose identical corporate profits taxes. This system has the effect of shifting MPK to MPK$(1 - \tau)$ and MPK* to MPK*$(1 - \tau^*)$. As the

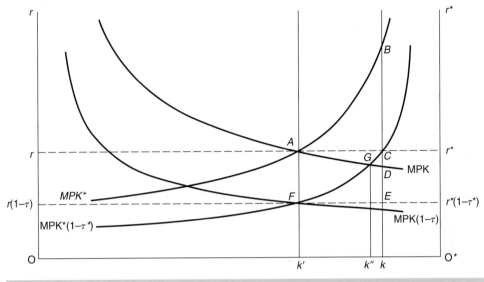

FIGURE 11-3   THE MACDOUGALL MODEL WITH IDENTICAL CORPORATE PROFITS TAXES AT HOME AND ABROAD

The initial allocation of capital is at k, and the optimum allocation of capital is at k' where the marginal products of capital are equalized. When the home country imposes a tax on domestic corporate profits, denoted by τ, the after-tax MPK schedule shifts down to MPK$(1 - \tau)$. When the foreign country imposes the same tax rate, denoted τ^*, corporate income, the after-tax marginal product of capital schedule on all capital invested abroad, shifts down to MPK$^*(1 - \tau^*)$. If the home country gives a full tax credit for foreign income taxes paid, the optimum allocation of capital is preserved because the after-tax marginal products of capital are identical at k'. However, area ACEF represents tax revenue accruing to the foreign country that would otherwise be income to the home country. The optimum welfare for the home country is achieved when it gives a deduction for foreign income taxes paid rather than a full credit, resulting in an allocation of capital at k''.

marginal product of capital schedules shifts in the same proportion, the intersection at the optimum allocation of capital is preserved at k'. There is no misallocation of capital, so capital export neutrality holds. Because all sources of capital are taxed at the same rate, capital import neutrality also holds. There are therefore no deadweight losses to society from the tax scheme.

Because of the first-crack principle, there is a redistribution of welfare that does not occur in the absence of taxation. Before taxation, we know that the increase in the home country's GNP resulting from foreign investment is the triangular area ACD. The increase in the host country's GNP is the triangular area ACB. Because of taxation, however, the host country collects area ACEF in revenue from the returns to the equity capital form of direct foreign investment, and this money stays in the host country.

This revenue increases the welfare of the host country such that the net increase in GNP from foreign investment is the larger area ABEF. As the tax revenue ACEF is no longer brought back into the home country, the net increase in home country GNP is area ACD minus area ACEF. As Figure 11-3 is drawn, there is a net decrease in GNP of area ADEF. The conclusion from Figure 11-3 is that the home country is likely to be a net loser from foreign investment whenever there are taxes imposed abroad.

The point the diagram illustrates is that the tax systems which maximize global welfare are not compatible with those that maximize national welfare. Viewed from the home country, over-investment abroad takes place. Conflicts between governments often arise because of each country's desire to tax multinational corporations' profits. The multinational corporation is sometimes caught in the middle.

National optimum would be reached when pre-tax returns domestically equal the post-tax returns abroad:

$$r = r*(1 - \tau*)$$

because r is the marginal benefit of investment at home and $r*(1 - \tau*)$ is the benefit to the home country of any foreign investment. In Figure 11-3, this equilibrium, $r = r*(1 - \tau*)$, corresponds to point G, for an allocation of capital at k''. The home government should tax both sides so as not to disrupt this marginal choice:

$$r(1 - \tau) = r*(1 - \tau*)(1 - \tau)$$

and it is clear that this equilibrium is achieved using the deduction method examined earlier. Over-investment abroad, as viewed from the home country, will not occur if the home country provides the less-valuable tax deduction rather than a full tax credit. At the same time, however, there will not be under-investment because capital will be free to flow abroad whenever the returns are high enough to compensate for the additional taxes paid. As long as the government preserves the appropriate marginal choice, the optimum amount of investment from the home country's standpoint will be achieved. We reiterate, however, that this solution precludes the global optimum.

Some accounting activities of firms, in seeking to show profits in low-tax countries, serve to restore maximum global welfare at least temporarily. One strategy is to allocate costs to high-tax countries, thereby maximizing the value of expense deductions. Another is to set prices on goods and services traded internally such that subsidiaries in high-tax countries pay high prices or receive low prices for them. The pricing of goods and services traded internally is called *transfer pricing*. In practice, the phrase has acquired negative connotations associated with firms that set prices to shift profits from subsidiaries located in high-tax countries to those in low-tax countries specifically to reduce the total tax burden.

To the extent that cost allocation and transfer pricing strategies are available, profits will indeed spring up in low-tax countries, often called *tax havens*, and disappear from high-tax jurisdictions. The profits of multinational firms are therefore mobile, at least to a certain extent. Economists often assert that cost allocation and transfer pricing strategies are economically efficient because they allow firms to produce where pre-tax returns are highest and then shift profits to low-tax jurisdictions. Production itself is not shifted—just the profits. The insight that production will not be shifted means that there will not be dead-weight losses of global welfare in the MacDougall diagrams examined throughout this chapter whenever companies can effectively ignore the effects of taxation. The result, however, is that the profits transferred to the low-tax jurisdictions must generally be reinvested there. If this action represents over-investment, there will be distortions from the misallocation of capital in future periods. Hence, firms seeking to maximize their global profits serve to maximize global welfare in the current period, but if the reinvestment decisions are suboptimal there will be longer-run distortions to global welfare. For more on this, see Aliber (1985).

Although these accounting strategies can restore maximum global welfare, they don't necessarily remove the conflicts between governments and multinational corporations. In fact, cost allocation and transfer pricing strategies generally accentuate the conflicts between the host and home governments and the multinational corporation. Nearly every country therefore sets guidelines for these accounting activities of multinational firms. Accounting manipulation therefore becomes costly because the use of managerial time and legal fees can be high for any governmental investigation. We will return to these accounting manipulations and governmental regulation in the next chapter dealing with political risk.

TOOLS FOR ANALYSIS II
Mathematics of How Profits Change as a Transfer Price Changes

When there is no residual tax liability to the home government, the profits from transfers from one branch to another can be summarized in a simple equation:

$$Y = [(P - C)(1 - \tau) + (P^*S - P[1 + \tau_d^*] - C^*S)(1 - \tau^*)]Q$$

where:

Y is the income or profit of both branches combined, expressed in the currency of the exporting (producing) country

P is the transfer price

C is the cost of producing the goods

τ is the income tax rate in the exporting country

P^* is the final selling price of the good

S is the exchange rate between the exporting country and the importing country

τ_d^* is the import duty in the importing country

C^* is the cost of selling the goods

τ^* is the income tax rate in the importing country

Q is the quantity of goods sold

From this equation, we are able to take the derivative of income with respect to the transfer price:

$$dY/dP = (1 - \tau) - (1 + \tau_d^*)(1 - \tau^*)$$

and with a little manipulation we determine how the profits of the firm change as the transfer price changes:

$$dY = [\tau^* - \tau - \tau_d^*(1 - \tau^*)]dP.$$

❖ ENDNOTES

1. For further treatment of many of the issues introduced here, see the collections of articles in Razin and Slemrod (1990), Giovannini, Hubbard, and Slemrod (1993), and Feldstein, Hines, and Hubbard (1995a and 1995b).

2. Based on Rick Wartzman, "Foreign Firms' Income in U.S. Is Understated," *The Wall Street Journal,* June 4, 1993, p. A2.

3. See Chowdhry and Coval (1998) for an in-depth treatment of multinational tax policy in an intertemporal setting, as well as implications for financing.

❖ REFERENCES

Aliber, Robert Z. "Transfer Pricing: A Taxonomy of Impacts on Economic Welfare," in *Multinationals and Transfer Pricing,* ed. by Alan M. Rugman and Lorraine Eden, London: Croom Helm, 1985.

Altschuler, Roseanne, T. Scott Newlon, and William C. Randolph. "Do Repatriation Taxes Matter? Evidence from the Tax Returns of U.S. Multinationals," in *Studies in International Taxation,* edited by Alberto Giovannini, R. Glenn Hubbard, and Joel Slemrod, University of Chicago Press, 1995, pp. 77–115.

Ault, Hugh J., and David F. Bradford. "Taxing International Income: An Analysis of the U.S. System and Its Economic Premises," Chapter 1 of *Taxation in the Global Economy,* ed. by Assaf Razin

and Joel Slemrod, University of Chicago Press, 1990, pp. 11–46.

Billings, B. Anthony, Larry Bajor, and Al Gourdji. "Competitive Tax Disadvantages Faced by U.S. Multinationals: How to Address Them," *Columbia Journal of World Business,* Winter 1990, pp. 28 – 39.

Bodner, Paul M. "International Taxation," Chapter 30 of *Handbook of International Accounting,* edited by Frederick D.S. Choi, John Wiley & Sons, 1991.

Caves, Richard E. "Taxation, MNEs' Behavior, and Economic Welfare," Chapter 8 of *Multinational Enterprise and Economic Analysis,* Cambridge University Press, 1982.

Choi, Frederick D. S., and Gerhard G. Mueller. "Transfer Pricing and International Taxation,"

Chapter 11 of *International Accounting,* second edition, Prentice Hall, 1992.

Chowdhry, Bhagwan, and Joshua D. Coval. "Internal Financing of Multinational Subsidiaries: Debt vs. Equity," *Journal of Corporate Finance,* March 1998, pp. 87–106.

Chown, John F. "Tax Structures and Finance," Chapter 11 of *The Handbook of International Financial Management,* ed. by R. Z. Aliber, Dow Jones-Irwin, 1989, pp. 373–407.

Engle, Howard S., and Mark T. Campbell. "Foreign Currency and U.S. Income Taxes," Chapter 20 of *The Handbook of International Financial Management,* ed. by R. Z. Aliber, Dow Jones-Irwin, 1989, pp. 594–637.

Feldstein, Martin, James R. Hines, Jr., and R. Glenn Hubbard, editors. *The Effects of Taxation on Multinational Enterprises,* University of Chicago Press, 1995a.

Feldstein, Martin, James R. Hines, Jr., and R. Glenn Hubbard, editors. *Taxing Multinational Corporations,* University of Chicago Press, 1995b.

Giovannini, Alberto, R. Glenn Hubbard, and Joel Slemrod, editors. *Studies in International Taxation,* University of Chicago Press, 1993.

Grubert, Harry, and John Mutti. "Taxes, Tariffs and Transfer Pricing in Multinational Corporate Decision Making," *Review of Economics and Statistics,* May 1991, pp. 285–293.

Harris, David, Randall Morck, Joel B. Slemrod, and Bernard Yeung. "Income Shifting in U.S. Multi-national Corporations," in *Studies in International Taxation,* edited by Alberto Giovannini, R. Glenn Hubbard, and Joel B. Slemrod, University of Chicago Press, 1993, pp. 277–302.

Hines, James R., and R. Glenn Hubbard. "Coming Home to America: Dividend Repatriations By U.S. Multinationals," in *Taxation in the Global Economy,* ed. by Assaf Razin and Joel Slemrod, University of Chicago Press, 1990, pp. 161–200.

Hines, James R., Jr., and Eric M. Rice. "Fiscal Paradise: Foreign Tax Havens and American Business," *Quarterly Journal of Economics,* February 1994, pp. 149–182.

Kim, Suk Hi, and Seung H. Kim. "International Transfer Pricing," Chapter 22 of *Global Corporate Finance,* Blackwell Publishers, fourth edition, 1999, pp. 538–554.

McDaniel, Paul R. *Introduction to United States International Taxation,* Kluwer Law and Taxation Publishers, 1989.

Organization for Economic Cooperation and Development. *Taxing Profits in a Global Economy: Domestic and International Issues,* 1991.

Razin, Assaf, and Joel Slemrod, editors. *Taxation in the Global Economy,* University of Chicago Press, 1990.

Rugman, Alan, and Lorraine Eden, editors. *Multinationals and Transfer Pricing,* Croom Helm, 1985.

Scholes, Myron S., and Mark A. Wolfson. *Taxes and Business Strategy: A Planning Approach,* Prentice Hall, 1992.

CHAPTER

12

POLITICAL RISK

CHAPTER OBJECTIVES

AFTER READING THIS CHAPTER YOU SHOULD BE ABLE TO:

❖ Describe different kinds of public policies toward multinational corporations and the nature of political risk.

❖ Use conceptual paradigms to understand government policy changes.

❖ Assess the impact of political risk on interest parity theorems.

❖ Identify sources useful for political risk assessment.

❖ Incorporate political risk analysis into capital budgeting decisions.

❖ Propose ways to manage political risk and political incidents.

We begin this chapter by looking at public policy toward multinational corporations and its role in defining the current operating environment for each subsidiary. In the second section, we link the uncertainty over changes in public policy to political risk, and use this link as a basis for examining how multinational corporations should view the effects of policy changes on the value of foreign subsidiaries. In the third section, we make an effort to understand government policy changes through two popular models of government behavior: benefit-cost analysis and bargaining power analysis. Having established the nature of political risk, in the fourth section we analyze its effect on real interest parity, uncovered interest parity, and even covered interest parity. Together, these four sections provide the analytical foundations of political risk that can be used in assessment and management by multinational corporations. The managerial aspects in this chapter begin in the fifth section with an overview of political risk assessment, or the efforts by corporations to estimate the potential for government intervention. We then examine the method of applying this political risk assessment to capital budgeting decisions in the sixth section using several examples. We conclude the chapter with topics on managing political risk in the seventh section and managing political incidents in the eighth section.

12.1   INTRODUCTION

Direct foreign investments are exposed to a multitude of interventions by both host and home governments. Dramatic events such as expropriations and nationalizations grab headlines and most managers' attention, but the cumulative effects of other operating restrictions can be just as devastating. Although most firms focus on government actions that reduce the value of the firm, there are occasionally beneficial government actions that increase the value of the firm. The degree to which a company is affected by political events is known as **political exposure.** As with foreign exchange exposure, it is a measure of what the company has at stake. **Political risk** is defined as the variability in the value of the firm (or subsidiary) that is caused by uncertainty about political or policy changes. As with other types of risk, this risk can be represented by a distribution of the firm's value due to political incidents.

While this chapter develops an analytical approach toward political risk that provides a basic framework for assessment and management by multinational corporations,[1] the chapter is really a short introduction to what is otherwise a vast literature spanning the disciplines of economics and political science.[2] The first half of the chapter is conceptual, focusing on the nature of political risk and its effects on capital flows. The second half is managerial, discussing applications of the conceptual analysis to decision-making in multinational corporations. This chapter builds on several previous chapters by incorporating political risk. Instead of attempting to survey the entire vast literature on political risk, our objective is to draw together many of the concepts presented throughout this book.

Having defined political risk as the variability in the value of the firm caused by uncertainty about political changes (as a parallel to exchange risk), we revisit several interest parity theorems discussed throughout the book: real interest parity, uncovered interest parity, and covered interest parity. Managerial aspects center around capital budgeting analysis in the presence of political risk. To conduct this analysis correctly, the assessment of political risk must involve estimating the probabilities of different political incidents, and managers must consider ways to manage political risk and political incidents.

12.2 PUBLIC POLICY TOWARD MULTINATIONAL CORPORATIONS

Public policy toward multinational corporations determines the environment in which the corporations must operate. Host-country policies are clearly the most important in this regard, but home-country policies are often influential as well. Occasionally, third-country and multilateral policies may even play a role. In this section, we briefly examine these three areas of public policy.

HOST-COUNTRY POLICIES

Host-country policies can be viewed along a continuum, with complete prohibitions on direct foreign investment at one end and enormous incentives on the other. Few countries refuse foreign investment altogether, but most countries have restrictions in at least some sectors. The United States, for example, is generally open to foreign investment. However, there are several areas where the United States places prohibitions and restrictions on foreign investment levels. In particular, any business that can be construed as important to national security is strongly restricted. Foreign ownership in nuclear energy or defense construction is prohibited outright. Similarly, freshwater coastal shipping enterprises, airlines, and broadcasting firms face limitations on foreign ownership.

Some countries have generally restrictive atmospheres. For example, Japan, France, and Korea appear suspicious of any foreign investment, and foreign attempts at ownership generally encounter bureaucratic resistance. At the other end of the spectrum, some countries, particularly those with less developed economies, offer tax cuts and subsidies to foreign investment in an effort to attract industry and increase local employment. For example, Ireland and Singapore have been quite successful in attracting foreign investment by providing substantial reductions in corporate income taxes.

In something of a twist in the analysis, some researchers have pointed out that many government policies that create market imperfections actually induce foreign direct investment; see, in particular, Brewer (1993), and, more generally, Boddewyn (1988). For example, U.S. trade barriers may have spawned direct foreign investment by foreign automobile firms as a means of circumventing the barriers. In general, a host country wants to use foreign investment policies to enhance its domestic welfare. The population generally welcomes any policy that will increase domestic levels of income, employment, exports, research and development, technology, and national security.

HOME-COUNTRY AND THIRD-COUNTRY POLICIES

Home-country policies, while often overlooked as a concern for multinational corporations, are nonetheless quite important in the effective formulation of corporate strategy in dealing with political risk. Home-country policies can also be viewed along a continuum, with restrictions again at one end and incentives at the other. The main restrictions on foreign investment are for foreign policy reasons. Trade and investment embargoes imposed as political weapons are popular with some countries. For example, the United States has maintained an embargo on trade and investment with Cuba for

40 years. Many countries have technology restrictions to protect their national security. The United States used to restrict computer trade and investment with Eastern European countries, and restrictions on weapons trading are also designed to protect national security. There are also many restrictions on capital outflows set up for macroeconomic reasons.

Most countries are concerned with protecting their domestic income, employment, and tax revenues, and may impose a variety of capital controls. An important tool the home country has is its tax treatment of foreign income: it can adjust the tax levels to encourage foreign investment in countries where it sees positive economic, political, or social effects, and discourage investment in those countries where it sees negative economic, political, and social effects. An example of tax incentives for foreign investment is the Caribbean Basin Initiative, in which the United States viewed revitalization of Caribbean countries as economically and politically important both for itself and for the Caribbean.

While generally less important, third-country policies occasionally interfere with direct foreign investment. In other words, policies emanating neither from the host country nor the home country may affect multinational operations. Arab nations, for example, have not only prohibited trade and investment between themselves and Israel, but have also prohibited foreign firms from operating in these nations if the firms trade with or invest in Israel. Evidence suggests that this secondary boycott is fairly effective in influencing operations of multinational corporations, primarily because a boycott office maintains a blacklist of firms which are banned from Arab nations.[3] Hence, public policies in third countries matter: in this example, policies in the Arab countries affect operations in Israel.

MULTILATERAL POLICIES

The final public policy concern to multinational corporations is multilateral policies. Examples of institutions that make multilateral policies include the United Nations Center on Transnational Corporations (UNCTC), the Organization for Economic Cooperation and Development (OECD), and regional organizations such as the European Community that create a level playing field for foreign investment and reduce competition among host countries. The OECD, for example, has developed a voluntary code of conduct for multinational corporations (the 1976 OECD *Guidelines for Multinational Enterprises*) which outlines the benefits of MNCs operating in host countries and provides some forms of protection from political risk. In 1982, the United Nations drafted the *Code of Conduct for Transnational Corporations* covering the following concerns of developing host countries: ethics in international business, political interference by MNCs in national affairs, appropriate technology transfer, and respect for national sovereignty. In addition, the International Labor Organization (ILO) has a (1977) *Declaration of Principles Concerning Multinational Enterprises and Social Policy* dealing with issues of employment and industrial relations. The main weakness of multinational policies is that there is little power to enforce them; therefore, they are generally ineffective as rules and regulations for international investment. They do, however, serve a definite purpose by allowing the parties involved with multinational enterprises to have an understanding of what to expect from each other. In other words, they serve as checklists of mutual privileges and responsibilities. One exception is the European Community's regulation of MNCs, which tends to address specific, legally binding measures, particularly with respect to accounting disclosure and corporate taxation.

12.3   THE NATURE OF POLITICAL RISK

Now that we have examined public policy toward multinational corporations, we can take the prevailing political environment as background and proceed to define political risk as the potential for the value of an investment to change due to changes in government policy. As with the public policies themselves, these possible policy changes can be arranged along a continuum, again decomposed into host- and home-country activities.

For host-country policy changes, the continuum would include expropriation and nationalization at the severe end. At one time, during the 1960s and 1970s, these events constituted the core of the political risk literature. More recently, however, expropriations and nationalizations have waned in importance (see Minor, 1994) and other forms of interventions have moved to the forefront. For example, foreign exchange controls are still important in Latin America and Asia. Tax increases and additional government regulation would be at the mild end of the continuum. Even something apparently minor, such as closer scrutiny of transfer prices, can affect the value of the firm. A wide variety of policies between these two extremes is possible, including currency controls, price controls, export requirements, local content laws, forced joint ventures, and equity dilution requirements, among others.

For home-country policy changes, the continuum would include required divestment and various sanctions at the severe end. In the United States, the former has been of particular concern with respect to investments in South Africa, where public pressure (although not public policy) caused many U.S. multinationals to withdraw from the country; see Kibbe (1988). Licensing requirements and changes in the tax treatment of foreign income would be at the mild end. Even closer scrutiny of transfer prices by the home country can affect the value of the firm. Again, a wide variety of policies between these two extremes is possible.

12.4   UNDERSTANDING GOVERNMENT POLICY CHANGES

Because political risk involves the potential for changes in the value of a foreign investment, managers (and academics) commit substantial resources in attempting to understand the nature of government policy changes. Observers have identified two types of government policy changes: general and selective. General policy changes are not directed at foreign owners; tax increases or changes in government regulation are usually general because they rarely single out foreign owners. A growing body of research, however, indicates that the most costly government policy changes associated with political risk are selective, or directed primarily at foreign owners. Furthermore, they usually select specific industries. One study by Bradley (1977) found that interventions had been predominantly in the oil industry and other resource-extraction industries. For the period 1960–1974, 12 percent of U.S. oil subsidiaries abroad were expropriated and 18 percent of U.S. subsidiaries in resource extraction were expropriated, compared to 4 percent in utilities and transportation, 4 percent in insurance and banking, and 1 percent in manufacturing. Equity dilution requirements are also directed at foreign owners, and again pertain more to some sectors than others.

A more recent study by Encarnation and Vachani (1985) demonstrates that required equity dilution in India was in fact decided on a case-by-case basis, with characteristics of the firm taken into account. In the United States, recent scrutiny of transfer prices has apparently been directed at Japanese firms. The distinction between general and selective government interventions is not always clear. For example, something as general as across-the-board currency controls is usually selectively enforced.

In an attempt to understand government policy changes, this section examines two interpretations of the nature of government behavior: benefit-cost analysis and bargaining strategy analysis. Both of these approaches are able to account for both general and selective interventions. The major point here is that political risk is not based solely on host-country-specific factors, but is also based on industry-specific and even firm-specific factors.

BENEFIT-COST ANALYSIS

A country faces a trade-off when it changes government policies pertaining to direct foreign investment because there are both benefits and costs of government action. One way to understand government policy changes is by examining the benefit-cost analysis that is associated with such changes.

The benefits of intervention are usually obvious. If expropriation occurs, the country receives the firm's assets and all the future cash flows. If price or currency controls are imposed, the country achieves more macroeconomic control. If local content laws or equity dilution laws are enacted, the country gets more employment, job training, and access to technology. If more regulation is introduced, the country receives microeconomic control over the affected industries. If additional taxes are imposed, the country receives additional revenue.

Interventions, of course, rarely come without repercussions. The costs of intervention are generally longer-term and are therefore often undervalued. If expropriation occurs, there will be less investment in the future and even some divestment, which will result in a decline in the economic base, higher unemployment, and less transfer of technology. If macroeconomic controls are imposed, there may be additional unemployment and general stagnation. If local content and equity dilution laws are enacted, there may in fact be less investment and less technology transfer in the long run. If taxes are raised, there will be a loss of the tax base to the extent that firms can locate profits abroad.

If a host country takes steps to encourage foreign investment, the benefits and costs will be reversed. Although increased foreign investment will result in an expansion of the economic base, reduced unemployment, and increased technology transfer, the host country will have to accept fewer microeconomic and macroeconomic controls, or possibly even less tax revenue from foreign investment.

Clearly, the question that remains is what the net benefits of any change in host-government policy are, and how these benefits change over time. The benefit-cost analysis asserts that government policy changes occur when the present value of the benefits from intervention exceeds the present value of the costs of intervention. In such a scenario, the firm can expect policy changes as the benefits net of costs increase. However, estimating the benefits and costs of government intervention is usually very difficult, for both the government and the multinational corporation. Furthermore, governments are not always motivated to weigh benefits against costs. Analysis has therefore expanded into a broader concept of bargaining power discussed in what follows.

It is important to note that this same benefit-cost analysis can be applied to home-country policy decisions. In other words, the analysis follows if the benefits of

---

APPLICATION 12-1

COCA-COLA IN INDIA AND IRAN

Political risk can originate from either the host or the home country, and the foreign operations of The Coca-Cola Company have indeed been affected many times by both the U.S. and foreign governments. Coke's operations in India and Iran provide two high-profile examples of these effects.

In India, The Coca-Cola Company had developed a successful business and Coke became the country's leading soft drink during the 1970s. As part of a new investment policy restricting foreign ownership to less than half of any project, the Indian government required all wholly owned foreign subsidiaries to dilute their equity. (For more on this, see Encarnation and Vachani, 1985.) Recognizing that this requirement may have required that it share its secret formula, Coca-Cola refused to dilute its stake, and instead withdrew from India in 1977. The Indian government's equity dilution requirement clearly reduced the value of Coke's Indian subsidiary. Coke's bottlers, family-owned businesses that bought concentrate and mixed the beverage, were also hurt because they were left without a product.

In Iran, Coke had extensive operations and firmly established relationships with bottlers by the 1970s. A U.S. embargo after the 1979 Islamic Revolution forced Coke to shut down operations in 1980. Coke resumed operations in Iran by the end of the 1980s, but President Clinton reimposed the embargo on Iran in 1995 and Coke was again forced to shut down operations. Clearly, the U.S. government's embargo reduced the value of Coke's Iranian subsidiary. However, a Coke bottler in Tehran, Noushab Manufacturing Co., has continued using Coke bottles to bottle a local cola, and the Coca-Cola Company insists that nongenuine product in genuine bottles damages Coke's brand value. In addition, Noushab is suing Coca-Cola for cutting off shipments of concentrate as a result of following the U.S. sanctions, which thus requires the company to spend money on legal fees to defend itself. As a result, the U.S. embargo has destroyed more value for the Coca-Cola Company than just the value of the Iranian subsidiary.

Returning to India, one of the bottlers left without the Coca-Cola product in 1977, Parle, began bottling a local cola called Thums Up. By the 1990s, Parle brands represented a majority of the soft drink market. The Indian government also began liberalizing restrictions on foreign ownership in the 1990s, and Coca-Cola decided to re-enter the Indian market. In 1993, Coke returned to India by buying Thums Up and other brands from Parle. In this situation, re-entry was somewhat easier because of Coke's earlier presence. However, The Coca-Cola Company is embarrassed by the fact that Thums Up remains more popular than The Real Thing, Coke.

Sources: Nikhil Deogun and Jonathan Karp, "For Coke in India, Thums Up Is the Real Thing," *The Wall Street Journal,* April 29, 1998, p. B1; Daniel Pearl and Nikhil Deogun, "Today's Pop Quiz: Where Is Coca-Cola Not the Real Thing?" *The Wall Street Journal,* July 10, 1998, p. A1.

---

home-country intervention are thought to be political or are associated with enhanced national security, and if the costs are perceived as losses in profits and a blow to the general welfare of the home-country population.

BARGAINING POWER ANALYSIS

Recent studies examining the nature of government policy changes have been successful by examining relative bargaining power. Both the host country and the multinational firm have bargaining power, and the occurrence or severity of incidents often depends on one party's bargaining power vis-à-vis the other. In this section, we focus on the development of the bargaining power literature as presented by Poynter (1985, 1986). [For further development of the bargaining view, along with extensive discussion of all the players involved, see Behrman and Grosse (1990).]

A host country's bargaining power is derived from the size of the market it offers, the wealth of the market, and the abundance of raw materials. The host country is in a relatively strong position when the size and wealth of the markets are big and raw material inputs are abundant. Such a country can effectively play off firms against one another to achieve maximum enhancement of its domestic welfare.

A firm's bargaining power is derived principally from the uniqueness of its product or the technology required to produce it. To a certain extent, the size of both the multinational corporation and its ongoing investments add bargaining power. If the firm is relatively strong, its geographic spread is large, and the product or technology is unique, it can effectively play off countries against one another to attain the highest subsidies and tax breaks possible when making investments. An empirical study by Fagre and Wells (1982) using the extent of foreign ownership of subsidiaries as a measure of bargaining power[4] suggests that the bargaining power of multinationals is related to: (1) the level of technology, (2) the degree to which the multinational attempts to differentiate its products, (3) the extent to which a subsidiary's output is exported to other subsidiaries of the firm, (4) the diversity of products offered, and (5) the degree of competition from other multinationals. Somewhat surprisingly, the Fagre and Wells (1982) study concludes that the bargaining power of multinationals is apparently not related to the size of the investment.

According to the bargaining power literature, incidents of expropriation and nationalization take place when the host country's bargaining power exceeds the multinational firm's bargaining power. To understand incidents, then, analysts must focus on how bargaining power changes over time. When the initial investment is made, the firm's bargaining power is higher than the host country's; otherwise the investment would not have been made. After all, at the inception of the project the firm has a product or technology that the host country does not have, and the country is interested in wooing the firm. As time progresses, the bargaining power of the host country increases. This occurs partially because the size and wealth of the domestic market increase, but also because host-country nationals gradually acquire the skills necessary to operate the project and because competitors to the multinational corporation who are willing to advise the country or operate the project emerge. If the basic project stays the same through time, the firm's bargaining power is stagnant. However, if the operation grows or if exports increase, the firm's bargaining power will increase, but most likely at a slower rate than the host country's bargaining power will grow. This means that the host-country's bargaining power will eventually equal the firm's bargaining power. Beyond this point, intervention is more and more likely to occur.

Sharp changes in the economic environment can shift the bargaining power of the government or firm. For example, a dramatic increase in the value of a natural resource deposited within the country will increase the country's bargaining power; conversely, a decrease in the value of the natural resource will decrease the country's bargaining power. These shifts can respectively hasten or delay intervention.

Moreover, different countries have different levels of bargaining power and acquire additional bargaining power at different rates. Poynter (1985, 1986) particularly compares Bolivia and Brazil. The former is a small country with a relatively low income level and therefore has little bargaining power. The latter, however, is a large country with a relatively high income level and therefore has a high level of bargaining power. Furthermore,

Bolivia is growing very slowly and its population is slow to acquire technological skills. Brazil, however, is growing steadily and its population is quick to acquire technological skills. Although most observers would instinctively pick Bolivia as a riskier country because its future is less certain, bargaining power analysis suggests that Brazil is riskier because its bargaining power is high and growing. This contradiction has led some to conclude that bargaining power analysis is most useful in predicting incidents within a country, but is much less useful in predicting incidents across countries.

12.5   POLITICAL RISK AND INTEREST PARITY THEOREMS

The presence of political risk distorts the allocation of capital in much the same way as market segmentation and taxes distort the allocation of capital.[5] In this section, we examine this misallocation of capital due to political risk and its effect on real interest parity, uncovered interest parity, and covered interest parity.

DEVIATIONS FROM REAL INTEREST PARITY

In a general sense, political risk can be thought of as creating a divergence between the physical returns possible from an investment and the expected value of returns from an investment in a country where there is some degree of political risk. Suppose, for example, the physical returns on an investment amount to 15 percent, and the firm will receive a 15 percent rate of return as long as the project is left alone. If expropriation without compensation is a possibility, however, the rate of return may be -100 percent (where the firm loses everything invested). The expected value of the return will therefore be less than 15 percent to reflect the potential of complete loss. If the probability of expropriation is assessed at 1 percent, the expected return on investment is:

$$(0.99)(15\%) + (0.01)(-100\%) = 13.85\%.$$

Although the physical return is still 15 percent, firms will make decisions based on the expected return of 13.85 percent, and the political risk will thus discourage some direct foreign investment. This concept is developed in further analytical detail in "Tools for Analysis" at the end of this chapter. The model presented there demonstrates that a country with (disadvantageous) political risk has less capital and higher real interest rates than it would otherwise have. In particular, there is an interest differential between the risky country and a home country or the rest of the world: $(r^* - r) > 0$, where r^* is the foreign country's equilibrium real interest rate and r is the home country's equilibrium real interest rate.

Once again, there are two ways to view the political risk described. On one hand, if we think of it as general political risk, the expected returns of all investments in that country will be lower. On the other hand, if only foreign investors face the political risk, the lower expected returns to capital pertain only to direct foreign investment and not to local investors. This distinction is the contrast between general and selective government interventions discussed in the previous section.

The interest differential reflecting political risk, $(r^* - r)$, is best understood in the context of financial markets. For otherwise similar financial assets, such as bonds, the instruments issued in or by a risky locale must carry higher rates of return, which may explain why real interest rates are typically higher in developing countries than in developed ones, or even why not enough capital is going into developing countries in general. It is clear that more investment occurs in the safe countries, which are most likely to be stable, developed market economies.

In fact, the concept of a safe haven is often given as a reason for the large inflow of direct foreign investment into the United States in the 1980s. Note the similarity between exchange risk (discussed in Chapter 1) and political risk: both may explain real interest differentials between countries. However, the difference is that exchange risk relates to the currency of denomination for claims, whereas political risk relates to the jurisdiction in which an investment is made and is separate from the currency denomination. Although the interest differential for political risk is intuitive for financial instruments, political risk for multinational corporations should be viewed as industry-specific, firm-specific, or even home-country specific, and therefore additional analysis will be required for non-financial assets.

DEVIATIONS FROM UNCOVERED INTEREST PARITY

In moving from real interest rates to nominal interest rates, the deviations from real interest parity identified above result in *ex ante* deviations from uncovered interest parity. This is the same step taken in Chapter 2 (see pages 73–74) when examining the *ex ante* deviations from uncovered interest parity due to capital market segmentation or exchange risk. Unfortunately, in empirical analysis of deviations from uncovered interest parity, it is quite difficult to distinguish between political risk and other effects. The relevant comparison for identifying the magnitude of segmentation or exchange risk is between interest rates for the same borrower or lender in the same jurisdiction, but for different currency denominations. In this construction, any *ex ante* deviation from uncovered interest parity is due to market segmentation or is a risk premium for foreign exchange risk. The relevant comparison for identifying the magnitude of political risk is between interest rates for deposits or borrowings in the same currency, but in different jurisdictions. For example, one might compare a deposit rate on dollars in the United States to a deposit rate on dollars in the United Kingdom. In this scenario, there is no currency risk, just political risk.

Unfortunately, the empirical work on deviations from uncovered interest parity must usually deal with different currencies, different jurisdictions, and different borrowers, which bundles together exchange risk, political risk, and even some default or sovereign risk, making it quite difficult to distinguish the individual effects. One exception is a study by Dooley and Isard (1980) which found differences between interest rates on domestic DM deposits and offshore DM deposits for the period 1970 to 1974, which they attributed to capital controls and political risk.[6]

DEVIATIONS FROM COVERED INTEREST PARITY

The deviations from real interest parity and uncovered interest parity attributed to political risk also result in deviations from covered interest parity when the interest rates compared are for instruments in different political jurisdictions. When we discussed the covered interest parity theorem in Chapter 2, we specified that the forward rate is calculated from Eurocurrency deposit rates. These deposits are in the same physical location, usually at the same bank, but simply denominated in different currencies. Hence, there is no political risk in bilateral comparisons, but there is exchange risk. However, covered interest parity holds whether or not there is a risk premium for foreign exchange risk, so covered interest parity holds well when Eurocurrency deposit rates are used because arbitrage is riskless and relatively easy. Deposits in two different locations, however, involve political risk because arbitrage would require exposure to governmental actions.

Because of political risk, covered interest parity does not hold perfectly when interest rates other than Eurocurrency rates are tested. In particular, covered interest arbitrage does not hold when national treasury bill interest rates are used. On the surface, there appear to be riskless arbitrage profits available if a forward contract is available. This is not true, however, because there is political risk associated with the treasury bills that is not associated with the Eurocurrency rates determining the forward rate. To arbitrage, an investor would (for example) have to get money out of his home country, exchange it in the foreign currency market, get the money into another country, purchase the treasury bill and wait until maturity, then get the proceeds out of the country, settle the forward contract, and get the money back into the home country. There is a political risk that this chain will be broken, and this causes a deviation from covered interest parity when treasury bill rates are tested.

The major point here is that deviations from covered interest parity represent a political risk premium. In one of the earliest, seminal studies of deviations from covered interest parity, Aliber (1973) identified approximately a 2 percent risk premium on the U.S. treasury bill interest rate vis-à-vis the U.K. treasury bill for the period 1968 to 1970.

12.6   POLITICAL RISK ASSESSMENT

Now that we have discussed the nature of political risk and its effects on interest parity theorems, we can examine the derivation and assessment of probabilities of incidents. The initial challenge is in determining what data or information we need for analysis. In the assessment of political risk, managers must look at several factors.

Host-country factors are certainly very important. Measures of these country-wide risks can be obtained from commercial assessment firms that formulate indexes of political risk.[7] These data generally represent an aggregation of the subjective assessments of a panel of experts on various economic, social, and political factors. Thus, the index is usually a measure of the entire business climate, rather than just the political environment. Chapter 1 introduced one such general evaluation of country risk by *Euromoney*. Other indexes focus more specifically on political risk. Most of these services also produce in-depth country reports. Political Risk Services in East Syracuse, New York, publishes the *Political Risk Yearbook* annually and the *International Country Risk Guide* (ICRG) monthly, along with country fact sheets and data sets. The Economist Intelligence Unit (EIU), based in London, provides quarterly ratings and individual reports for many countries; EIU's Country Risk Service was formerly an independent company known as Business International. (This report is in fact distinct from the EIU's more general Country Reports series.) DRI/McGraw-Hill, in conjunction with Standard & Poor's, publishes *Country Risk Review* quarterly, which contains a global overview of country risk and country-specific information.

Examining host-country factors is sometimes referred to as the "macro approach" to political risk assessment because it is based on a wide array of economy-wide indicators. Most of the commercial political risk firms specialize in the macro approach. Although this approach might be an important component of planning and operating a direct foreign investment, it cannot be the whole basis for analysis. In fact, most empirical studies even fail to establish a relationship between direct foreign investment and political risk. [One study in this area is Kobrin (1976), which examines various economic, social, and political aspects of the environment.]

Another important set of factors is home-country specific. These represent actions by the home country, and actions by the host country directed specifically at the home country. Here, it is important to look at trade climates, investment attitudes, and the potential for an embargo or forced divestment.

Even more important than country-specific factors are the particular characteristics of an investment project. A firm will gain useful insights by examining industry-specific and firm-specific factors, an activity sometimes referred to as the "micro approach" to political risk assessment. Most observers consider this analysis an integral part of the project's planning and operating process. Schmidt (1986) states that the political risk depends directly on the characteristics of the foreign investment: who owns it, what technology it uses, and to what economic sector it belongs. Assessment then involves a two-sided analysis. On one side, managers should look at their specific industry relative to others, and gain some general understanding of their comparative political risk. On the other side, managers should also analyze competing firms to gain a deeper understanding of their own firm's political risk within that industry. For example, if a multinational has a subsidiary that dominates an industry of mainly domestic competition, it should attach some amount of industry-specific and firm-specific risk to that environment. Clearly, host-country attitudes toward the interests of the subsidiary would be less favorable here than if the industry were composed of many multinational subsidiaries and no domestic firms. These micro factors probably explain the earlier puzzle that empirical research often fails to establish a relationship between direct foreign investment and political risk.

Once information is gathered, the firm needs to make effective use of it. The objective is to generate estimates of the probabilities of different political risks. Most firms rely on subjective judgment based on the body of information they have gathered. However, there are some econometric methods, such as probit and logit analysis, that are capable of substantially formalizing the history of interventions. Unfortunately, the complexity of the task usually makes assessment less active than simply reactive; see Kobrin, Basek, Blank, and LaPalombara (1980), which also discusses a variety of management implications. For more on approaches to the assessment of political risk, as well as a comprehensive, non-technical forecasting model, see de la Torre and Neckar (1988).

12.7   CAPITAL BUDGETING ANALYSIS

When political risk is introduced into the evaluation of an investment project, managers are required to adjust the capital budgeting analysis somehow to arrive at present value estimates that reflect the political risks involved. The preferred approach is to alter the expected cash flows to take account of the probabilities of political interventions.[8] This approach is recommended because it focuses on the specific numerical information required, rather than on vague notions of the future political climate. Precise estimates of the probabilities must be addressed in any effective analysis of political risk. One often-suggested simplification is adjusting the discount rate. The adjustment, however, is usually far too arbitrary. Furthermore, political risk is generally considered unsystematic because it can be diversified internationally, and is assumed not to alter the project's systematic risk. Hence, altering the discount rate from the all-equity cost of capital specified in the Capital Asset Pricing Model is not appropriate.

In terms of the centralization-versus-decentralization paradigm of international capital budgeting, political risk is of little consequence. Although political risk may raise the general level of interest rates in a risky country, thereby increasing that country's cost of capital, political risk analysis in international capital budgeting is more project specific, and must be carried out regardless of which method is used because direct foreign investment simply faces more political risk than financial assets do. As described earlier, a large part of the political risk involved with nonfinancial assets is industry-specific, firm-specific, or home-country specific. Multinationals must therefore analyze more political risk than is reflected in any simple interest differential. While interest differentials hold in the aggregate, there will likely be wide project-specific variation. As a practical matter, the countries which concern us the most with respect to political risk generally do not have developed financial markets or market interest rates anyway. Centralized capital budgeting is, therefore, usually more appropriate.

ANALYSIS OF POTENTIAL EXPROPRIATION

As capital budgeting in the presence of political risk should alter the expected cash flows, our analysis uses the expected value of cash flows given probabilities of political incidents. For a potential expropriation, the relevant capital budgeting formula is:

$$EPV = -CF_0 S_0 + \sum_{t=1}^{T} \prod_{n=0}^{t-1} (1 - p_{t-n}) \frac{E[CF_t S_t]}{(1 + COC)^t}$$

where

$CF_0 S_0$ is the initial investment, a known home-currency cash flow
CF_t is the cash flow in period t denominated in the local currency
COC is the all-equity cost of capital for home-currency cash flows, a constant
p_t is the probability that expropriation will occur in period t, given no previous expropriation
T is the life of the project

Note that, for simplicity, this formula imposes centralized capital budgeting.

We will once again develop the concepts embodied in this formula through an example. Consider Belmont Enterprises, a multinational coffee broker involved in all phases of coffee production from growing the beans to roasting them and distributing a ground product to specialty coffee shops all over the world. Belmont Enterprises is looking at a new investment in a bean-processing plant in a Latin American country with the following cash flows:

Year	US$ Cash Flows
0	−250,000
1	+200,000
2	+300,000

The all-equity cost of capital for the project is assumed to be 20 percent because it is like most other bean-processing plants Belmont operates. The present value of this project is therefore $125,000 based on the straightforward application of centralized capital budgeting developed in Chapter 3.

Experts within the firm know that the project is subject to more political risk than the other projects Belmont currently operates. They think that expropriation without any government compensation is the biggest concern, and they assess the probability of expropriation to be 25 percent in each of the next two years. To find the present value, managers at the headquarters office of Belmont Enterprises write down the expected value of each cash flow:

Year	Expected US$ Cash Flows
0	−$250,000 (a known cash outflow)
1	(.75)(200,000)
2	$(.75)^2(300,000)$.

The managers then calculate the expected present value of the project using the 20 percent discount rate:

$$EPV = -\$250,000 + (.75)(\$200,000)/(1.20) + (.75)^2(\$300,000)/(1.20)^2$$
$$= -\$250,000 + \$125,000 + \$117,187.50$$
$$= -\$7,812.50.$$

The project that looked good before political risk was incorporated now looks like a money-losing proposition. The firm would not want to undertake the project because the expected net present value is negative.

Another approach to the same project analysis is to look at each of the possible outcomes. That is, look at the present value of the cash flow in each possible outcome, and determine the probability associated with that outcome. The analysts would then take the products of each probability and present value of cash flow and sum them to get the expected present value of the project. In the Belmont Enterprises example:

Outcome	Probability	PV of Cash Flows
Expropriation in Year 1	.2500	−250,000
Expropriation in Year 2	.1875	$-250,000 + 200,000/1.20 = -83,333$
No Expropriation	.5625	$-83,333 + 300,000/(1.20)^2 = 125,000$

Taking the product of the probability of the outcome and the present value of the cash flow if that outcome occurs, the expected present value is again −$7,812.50.

One feature of this model is that the method can be used to solve for the break-even value of political risk probabilities. The firm can then decide whether the probability of intervention is greater or less than the break-even value. If the probability of intervention is judged to be less than the break-even value, the firm then expects the project to be profitable. For example, Belmont Enterprises may not know what the probability of expropriation is. Letting p denote the probability of expropriation, however, Belmont knows the probability distribution for the different outcomes as a function of p and knows the present value of the cash flows for each outcome:

Outcome	Probability	PV of Cash Flows
Expropriation in Year 1	p	−250,000
Expropriation in Year 2	$(1-p)p$	−83,333
No Expropriation	$(1-p)(1-p)$	125,000.

The break-even value for p can be determined by setting the expected present value to zero:

$$(p)(-250{,}000) + (1-p)(p)(-83{,}333) + (1-p)(1-p)(125{,}000) = 0$$

and solving for p. The equation can be rewritten as:

$$-250{,}000p - 83{,}333(p - p^2) + 125{,}000(1 - 2p + p^2) = 0$$

or:

$$208{,}333p^2 - 583{,}333p + 125{,}000 = 0$$

and therefore, from the quadratic equation,

$$p = \frac{-(-583{,}333) - \sqrt{(-583{,}000)^2 - 4(208{,}333)(125{,}000)}}{2(208{,}333)} = 0.2338.$$

(Recall that for a quadratic equation of the form $aX^2 + bX + c = 0$, the solution is

$$X = \frac{-b \pm \sqrt{b^2 - 4ac}}{2a}$$

and we restrict probabilities to satisfy $0 \le X \le 1$.)

If Belmont estimates that the probability of expropriation exceeds 0.2338, it should not undertake the project. Alternatively, if Belmont estimates that the probability of expropriation is less than 0.2338, it should undertake the project.

Keep the following points in mind. First, this model only incorporates the level of the probability of intervention. A more complex analysis would account for uncertainty in the estimate of the probability as well. Second, this method can be extended to any type of political risk: potential exchange controls, increased taxation or regulation, and so on. Finally, this method can also be carried over to home country actions. For example, rather than analyzing the probability of expropriation, we can analyze the probability of forced divestment.

ANALYSIS OF POTENTIAL NATIONALIZATION WITH COMPENSATION

We now proceed with capital budgeting analysis but create a situation where there is no longer the risk of all-out loss. Now, the risk is nationalization of the firm's operations, but with some compensation for the loss. The procedure for analyzing the risk is the same, however, specifically by taking the products of the probabilities and the discounted present value of cash flows and then summing. For a potential nationalization, the relevant capital budgeting formula is:

$$EPV = -CF_0 S_0 + \sum_{t=1}^{T} \prod_{n=0}^{t-1}(1 - p_{t-n})\frac{E[CF_t S_t]}{(1 + COC)^t} + \sum_{t=1}^{T} \prod_{n=0}^{t-1}(1 - p_{t-n-1})\frac{p_t C_t S_t}{(1 + COC)^t}$$

where all variables are as defined before, C_t is the compensation received in the event of nationalization, and p_0 is defined to be 0.

Returning to the previous example to demonstrate the use of this formula, Belmont Enterprises estimates that if nationalization occurs, the government will compensate the firm with $100,000. Figure 12-1 presents a tree diagram of the potential outcomes of the project. This tree diagram is similar to the one used in Chapter 5 discussing real options. However, the situation there involved managerial decisions at certain points in time, and here there are no decisions by the firm. Instead, the tree diagram recognizes the exogenous nationalization events. To find the present value of the project, the firm must calculate the probability that the cash flow will occur and the present value of the cash flow if it occurs. Hence:

$$EPV = -250,000 + (.25)(100,000)/1.20 + (.75)(200,000)/1.20$$
$$+ (.75)(.25)(1000,000)/(1.20)^2 + (.75)^2(300,000)/(1.20)^2$$
$$= \$26,041.67$$

and because the expected present value is positive, the firm is likely to undertake the project.

Once again, we can also conduct the analysis by looking at the possible outcomes. The following chart summarizes the present values of the potential outcomes based on the tree diagram in Figure 12-1.

Outcome	Probability	PV of Cash Flows
Expropriation in Year 1	.2500	$-250,000 + 100,000/1.20 = -166,666.67$
Expropriation in Year 2	.1875	$-250,000 + 200,000/1.20 + 100,000/(1.20)^2 = -13,888.89$
No Expropriation	.5625	$-250,000 + 200,000/1.20 + 300,000/(1.20)^2 = 125,000.00$

Taking the products of each outcome's probability and discounted cash flow and then totaling, we get an expected present value of $26,041.67. The expected present value is greater than zero, but note that the project is profitable only if there is no nationalization.

FIGURE 12-1   Tree Diagram of Potential Nationalization with Compensation

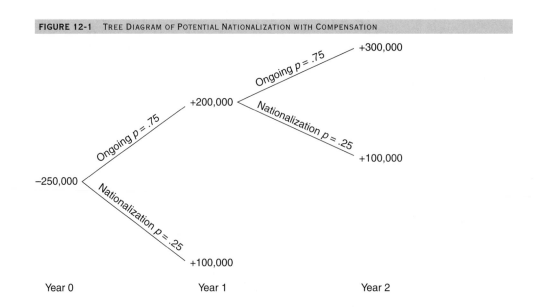

Year 0   Year 1   Year 2

Other forms of compensation can be incorporated into the analysis. For instance, insurance on the subsidiary may pay for part of the loss. In addition, indirect compensation through managerial contracts is frequently available in politically unstable countries. Also, home country tax laws may provide tax deductions associated with extraordinary losses. Finally, the parent may reduce its own liabilities associated with the project through extensive foreign borrowing.

12.8   MANAGING POLITICAL RISK

For a multinational willing to invest in a politically risky environment, a variety of measures are available *ex ante* to help reduce a firm's political exposure and political risk. This section briefly considers four main management strategies. For additional development, see Shapiro (1981).

An obvious strategy is to purchase insurance through one of the various political risk insurance programs, such as the U.S. government's Overseas Private Investment Corporation (OPIC), the World Bank's Multilateral Investment Guarantee Agency (MIGA), or the Lloyds of London private consortium. This insurance usually protects only asset value, however, and not potential cash flows.

Another possibility is to alter the structure of investment to alter the benefits of host-country intervention. For example, a firm should be ready to shift activities through multiple sourcing or segmented production. Otherwise, a firm should control inputs through high levels of imports. Other options, if possible, are to control output markets or even to plan to upgrade investments through time by building in expansion capacity.

A third effective means of reducing the exposure is to borrow extensively in the local currency. Now a component of the debt denomination decision pertains to political risk. While outright default is rare, it is at least a possibility. If the country nationalizes the subsidiary, it also nationalizes debt. Back-to-back loans are sometimes useful if capital controls pose some restrictions. The parent can deposit funds into a major multinational bank, and the bank can then lend money to the subsidiary.

Entering into joint ventures that take on local partners represents another strategy for reducing political risk. The partner obviously must not be in a position to become your competition, and must also be unable to take over the whole operation. Arrangements to somehow share windfall profits with the host country have also been suggested as a possible option, making the host government a joint venture partner. Finally, planned divestment over time that benefits the host country may be a possibility for *ex ante* risk management again using the host government as a joint venture partner.

12.9   MANAGING POLITICAL INCIDENTS

Although multinational corporations do not generally benefit from tightening of host-country restrictions, it is important to understand what options exist for a multinational that finds itself in such a situation. An empirical investigation by Poynter (1982) points out that not all firms experience the same degree of government intervention, an observation which forms the basis of managing political incidents. When a host country increases regulation of foreign investment, at least three options exist *ex post*.

BOUGAINVILLE COPPER LIMITED

CRA Ltd., short for Conzinc Riotinto Australia Ltd., an Australian mining firm, operated a majority-owned subsidiary under the name of Bougainville Copper Ltd. in Papua New Guinea from 1972 to 1989. Papua New Guinea is a nation of 3.5 million people inhabiting a collection of islands north of Australia. It has rich deposits of many different minerals, including copper, gold, and oil. The open-pit Bougainville Copper mine, one of the world's largest copper mines, is located in Panguna on Bougainville Island. Melbourne-based CRA Ltd. (itself 49 percent owned by Britain's RTZ Corporation, P.L.C.) owns 53.6 percent of the mine, and the Government of Papua New Guinea owns 19.1 percent; the rest of the shares are traded on the Australian Stock Exchange. Over the 17 years the mine was operating, copper production totaled 2.8 million metric tons, gold production totaled 285 tons, and silver production totaled 715 tons, valued at nearly $5 billion. The mine also provided revenue to the Government of Papua New Guinea amounting to 17 percent of its total revenue, so political risk appeared small.

Although not threatened by the Government of Papua New Guinea, the Bougainville Copper mine faced a different kind of political risk: direct opposition by the inhabitants of Bougainville Island. Bougainvilleans have always considered themselves different from the people inhabiting the islands of Papua and New Guinea. A group of rebels has been calling for secession of Bougainville Island from Papua New Guinea, and the Bougainville mine became a target in the insurrection. In fact, the secession movement grew out of longstanding native dislike of foreign rule. When Australian officials, who administered the territory under a United Nations mandate, negotiated to acquire the land for the mine in the 1960s, they did not negotiate with the women who were the traditional landowners under the island's matrilineal family system. Hence, when the Bougainville Copper Agreement was signed in 1967, the wrong people signed. When Australia granted independence to Papua New Guinea in 1975, Bougain-

villeans did not want to be part of Papua New Guinea, but Australia recognized that the government of Papua New Guinea needed the revenue from the Bougainville mine.

On several occasions in the latter half of 1988 and the first half of 1989, rebel landowners seeking to close the Bougainville Copper mine attacked property and employees at the mine with bows and arrows, shotguns, and dynamite stolen from the mine itself. In November and December of 1988, saboteurs attacked support facilities (burning buildings, vehicles, and other equipment) and toppled towers supporting power transmission lines. Further attacks on facilities and towers supporting power transmission lines occurred in May 1989, and the company was forced to close the mine. An attempt to reopen the mine in September was aborted following attacks on buses transporting mine personnel, and the mine has not yet reopened. Rebel landowners, discontent with the division of the mine's wealth, demanded $11.5 billion in compensation for environmental and social damages.

The insurrection on Bougainville Island has been successful in shutting down the Bougainville Copper Mine, although not (yet) in accomplishing secession from Papua New Guinea. The copper mine, which had more than $500 million in revenue and $115 million in after-tax profit in 1988, began experiencing losses in 1989. The mine still sits idle, with no immediate plans to reopen. Hence, although the Government of Papua New Guinea supported the Bougainville mine, in what Sterba (1990) refers to as a "textbook example for business schools of how to do things right in a joint venture between a multinational company and a Third World government," political risk arose from local opposition. In fact, the opposition was longstanding and would have been important to evaluate before the mine was established.

To hedge some of the project's risk, CRA Ltd. purchased insurance for property damage—including damage caused by sabotage but not damage caused by "insurrection, rebellion, revolution, civil war, usurped power or action taken by a

APPLICATION 12-2 (cont.)

government to prevent such an occurrence"—and business interruption which results in loss of profits. After a dispute over the terms of the policy, in early 1990 CRA Ltd. collected $78.6 million dollars

for the 1988–1989 policy year, which was substantially less than the $306.6 million claim filed. The insurrection on Bougainville has clearly cost CRA Ltd. quite a lot.

Sources: James P. Sterba, "Chaotic Paradise: An Audacious Rebel in Papua New Guinea Shakes Copper Market," *Wall Street Journal,* January 8, 1990, p. A1.; Tony Patrick and S. Karene Witcher, "Pritzker Weighs Buying CRA Stake in Copper Mine," *Wall Street Journal,* March 26, 1991, p. A18; "The Arrows of Bougainville," *The Economist,* May 23, 1992, p. 37; Kate McIlwaine, "Island Uprising Causes Mine Coverage Dispute," *Business Insurance,* December 4, 1989, p. 3; Kate McIlwaine, "Mining Firm Settles Coverage Dispute," *Business Insurance,* March 5, 1990, p. 23; Kevin D. Mutch, "Claim Involving Captive Raises Issues," *Business Insurance,* July 16, 1990, p. 23.

Simply following the law and altering operations accordingly is a first option. In particular, companies with low-technology product lines, low exports, and low research and development expenditures may find that their relative bargaining position is too weak to negotiate and may find they have no choice but to follow the letter of the law. In the case of expropriation or nationalization, this means surrendering everything and leaving the country. For milder forms of political intervention, this option may be turned into cooperative arrangements. In a study of equity dilution requirements in India, for example, Encarnation and Vachani (1985) found that following the law often meant establishing joint ventures and expanding the company.

Some companies may not find following the law to the letter the best option. Obeying a host country's regulations may have hidden consequences if following the regulation affects the way the host country and other governments view the company. The company may set precedents that other governments will use to regulate other subsidiaries. Years later, the same host country may even perceive that it can successfully change the rules again given the company's earlier response.

If the company views following the regulation as having such consequences, it may consider discontinuing its operations, which is the second option. Of course, the outcome is the same as in the first option discussed above if the political incident is expropriation or nationalization. Poynter (1982) notes that some firms are indeed forced out of the nation. For milder forms of political intervention, however, it is an important voluntary strategy. Encarnation and Vachani (1985) point out that many large multinational corporations, including IBM, chose to discontinue operations in India following the equity dilution requirements rather than alter operations to follow the law.

The third option is to negotiate a settlement, or at least open dialogue with the government. A government generally will lose more than it gains if a company leaves the country. If the company has high-technology product lines, high research and development spending, and high export levels, the country will lose a great deal if the company shuts down operations. Even in the event of expropriation or nationalization, the government may find that operations are less profitable than when the multinational corporation was running them. Usually, companies will find themselves with some power to negotiate a compromise with the host country. In the case of expropriation or nationalization, the settlement might provide for management contracts as well as purchase of assets and technology.[9]

In the case of forced equity dilution, one settlement might be an agreement to allow issuance of fresh equity to local investors rather than simply requiring selling off foreign-owned shares. Sometimes, the company can negotiate benefits for the subsidiary in exchange for following the law. For example, Encarnation and Vachani (1985) point out that a subsidiary may be allowed to expand its product lines by following the equity dilution requirement in India. Clearly, a company should always try to negotiate its best settlement and then weigh the costs and benefits associated with following the settlement against the costs and benefits of discontinuing operations. Austin and Ickis (1986) report that many multinationals have survived, grown, and generated profits in the post-revolution economy in Nicaragua mainly by managing relations with the host government despite a wide range of government policy changes.

❖ SUMMARY OF CHAPTER OBJECTIVES

1. Describe different kinds of public policies toward multinational corporations and the nature of political risk.

Host-country policies toward multinationals can span a continuum from outright prohibition on one end to enormous incentives on the other. Home-country policies regarding outward investment can also span a continuum from outright prohibition to enormous incentives. Political risk is the potential for the value of an investment to change due to changes in government policy, and changes in government policy may be viewed along a continuum. For host-country policy changes, the continuum ranges from expropriations and nationalizations at the extreme to simple tax increases or additional government regulation on the mild end. Home-country policy changes would range from required divestment and various sanctions on the extreme end to tax changes or licensing requirements on the mild end.

2. Use conceptual paradigms to understand government policy changes.

Government policy changes can often be understood in terms of benefit-cost analysis, in which the benefits of any policy change would exceed the costs of the change, or bargaining power analysis, in which policy changes occur when the country's bargaining power is especially high and the firm's bargaining power is low.

3. Assess the impact of political risk on interest parity theorems.

Political risk introduces a deviation from real interest parity because there is a difference between the physical returns possible from an investment and the expected value of returns from an investment in a country where there is some degree of political risk. As a result, the country with (disadvantageous) political risk has higher real interest rates than other countries. The deviation from real interest parity also shows up as a deviation from uncovered interest parity. In fact, political risk also causes deviations from covered interest parity that cannot be arbitraged away because there is a risk that government intervention will prevent future capital flows from occurring.

4. Identify sources useful for political risk assessment.

Information for political risk assessment can be divided into two types: (1) macro information on host-country factors, which is widely available from commercial political risk assessment firms, and some on home-country factors; and (2) micro information on industry-specific and firm-specific factors which is more difficult to collect and must be done by managers within a firm.

   5. Incorporate political risk analysis into capital budgeting decisions.

Political risk is incorporated into capital budgeting decisions not by adjusting the discount rate, but instead by adjusting the cash flows to reflect the effects of potential political incidents in expected cash flows.

   6. Propose ways to manage political risk and political incidents.

Political risk can be managed *ex ante* by purchasing insurance, altering the structure of an investment to reduce the benefits of government intervention, borrowing extensively in the local currency, and forming joint ventures with host-country partners. Political incidents can be managed *ex post* by obeying the intervention, discontinuing operations, or negotiating a settlement.

❖ QUESTIONS FOR REVIEW

1. [Class discussion] Political risk is usually associated with adverse developments in a host country. Why is this perspective incomplete?
2. [Class discussion] You are the chief financial officer of a small U.S. firm thinking of undertaking its first foreign investment. The project is in a developing country, and you are concerned about political risk. How would you go about assessing the political risk? If your firm undertakes the project, how would you manage political risk (before any incidents occur)? If your firm undertakes the project and a political incident occurs, how would you manage the incident?
3. True or False: Indicate whether the statement is true or false and clearly explain why.
   a. When a multinational corporation thinks equity dilution of an investment will soon be forced by the host government, the corporation should withdraw from the country.
   b. Political risk is one possible explanation for observed deviations from uncovered interest parity, but cannot explain deviations from covered interest parity.
4. [Class discussion] According to country risk ratings in *Euromoney* (see Table 1-8 in Chapter 1 on pp. 31–36), where high numbers signify safety, Poland has less political risk (rated 15.99 out of 25) than Papua New Guinea (rated 8.85).
   a. Why do you think Poland is less risky than Papua New Guinea?
   b. If a firm is comparing projects in Papua New Guinea and Poland, how should it take into consideration the different levels of political risk?
5. You are the chief financial officer of Tiger International, a multinational corporation based in Brahma, and you have the opportunity to bid on an investment project in Medalla de Oro. The project is expected to have a net cash flow in two years of 80 million sols, the local currency in Medalla de Oro. (There are no cash flows the first year.) The current exchange rate between the Brahman royal and the Medalla de Oro sol is 230 sols/royal. The Central Bank of Medalla de Oro is offering you a two-year-ahead forward contract on sols at the rate of 350 sols/royal. The nominal risk-free interest rate in Medalla de Oro is 45 percent, and the term structure of interest rates is flat. Tiger's cost of debt is known to be 50 percent in Medalla de Oro. The required return on the world market portfolio in Medalla de Oro is

60 percent. Your capital budgeting department tells you that beta for this project is 1.3. The capital budgeting department also tells you that the all-equity cost of capital in Brahman royals is 33.35 percent. There are no taxes in either Brahma or Medalla de Oro on this project.

  a. What is the all-equity cost of capital in Medalla de Oro for this project? If Tiger centralizes capital budgeting, how much is it willing to bid for this investment project, in royals?

  b. There is a risk that the government of Medalla de Oro will expropriate your investment before the payoff at the end of the two years. Your advisors estimate that there is a 20 percent chance of expropriation without compensation in each of the two years of the project. How much is Tiger willing to bid for this investment project now, in royals?

6. Gizmo, Inc. is a U.S. company contemplating an investment project in Argentina. The dollar cash flows from the project are expected to be $200,000 in each of the next three years. The initial cost of the investment is $300,000, so the present value of the project is $121,296 using a discount rate of 20 percent. One characteristic of Argentina, however, is that temporary exchange controls are often implemented when there is a balance of payments crisis. Your political risk experts estimate that there is a 20 percent chance that Argentina will impose exchange controls next year and a 20 percent chance that it will impose exchange controls in two years. If there are exchange controls in either or both years, you will be unable to remove your funds from Argentina until the exchange controls are lifted. If there are exchange controls, you are also unable to invest the funds, so they sit idle and do not earn interest. By arrangement with the central bank of Argentina, you have the assurance that you will be able to remove funds at the end of the third year when the project is finished.

  a. Carefully and clearly set up the way you are going to analyze this project in the presence of political risk using a tree diagram.

  b. What is the expected value of the project given the possibility of exchange controls? Would you give your approval to this project or not?

7. Suppose Adam Industries of the United States is considering a two-year project in Afghanistan and is worried about expropriation. The company isn't ready to estimate the probability of expropriation, but is interested in knowing the break-even probability. The present values of cash flows for the three possible outcomes are:

Outcome	PV of Cash Flows
Expropriation in Year 1	−500
Expropriation in Year 2	200
No Expropriation	500

where amounts are in thousands of dollars. If the probability of expropriation in Year 1 is the same as the probability of expropriation in Year 2, what is the probability at which this project breaks even?

8. [Class discussion] United Fruit Company (UFC) is worried that its banana plantation in Honduras will be expropriated during the next 12 months. However, UFC knows that compensation of $100 million will be paid at the year's end if the plantation is expropriated. If the expropriation does not occur this year, the plantation will be worth $300 million at the end of the year. A wealthy Honduran has just offered UFC $128 million for the plantation. UFC would have used a discount rate of 22 percent to discount the cash flows from its Honduran operations if the threat of

expropriation were not present. Can you suggest how UFC should evaluate whether or not to sell the plantation now for $128 million?

9. [Class discussion] Given that expropriation and nationalization have declined in relevance since the 1960s, what are the most important sources of political risk currently?

10. [Group project] Extended Exercise: Polydemic-Mexico's Political Risk

You are the chief financial officer of Polydemic Enterprises, a U.S. multinational with operations spread throughout the world. Your capital budgeting department has presented a proposal to you for a five-year resource extraction project in Mexico. The company's strategy for projects like this is to hedge expected cash flows in the forward market. The report therefore analyzes the project by first converting cash flows to U.S. dollars at forward rates and then discounting at the home-country cost of capital. The expected year-end net cash flows are as follows:

Year	Net Cash Flow
1	$100,000
2	200,000
3	300,000
4	300,000
5	250,000

The initial required investment in plant and equipment is $500,000 and the cost of capital is 18 percent. The capital budgeting department concludes that the net present value of the project is $174,986, so the report recommends that the project be undertaken.

a. You notice that the proposal does not include any analysis of political risk, but you are concerned about potential expropriation of the investment. You therefore decide to determine what probability of expropriation will make the expected value of the project (close to) zero. (Hint: use a spreadsheet.) Your estimate is that the probability of expropriation is the same in each of the next five years. What is this break-even point?

b. You decide to call a meeting to discuss political risk. The objective of the meeting is to determine if the probability of expropriation for this type of project is greater than or less than the break-even point determined in your analysis. Who would you invite to this meeting? What information or data would you need? How would you arrive at a probability estimate? Assume that, at the end of the meeting, you decide that the probability of expropriation is between 7 percent and 9 percent. Would you give your approval to this project or not? Given the possibility of expropriation, should the firm hedge the expected cash flows in the forward market as just outlined?

c. One way of managing the political risk inherent in a project is to purchase insurance. Assume that some company or government agency is willing to provide insurance coverage for the amount of the investment in plant and equipment. Under the terms of the policy, a payment will be made to Polydemic at the end of the year for the beginning-of-year book value of the plant and equipment in the event of an expropriation. Depreciation is to be based on the straight-line method, assuming that the plant and equipment have a five-year life and a value of zero at the end of the fifth year. The insurance premium, to be paid at the beginning of each year, is 10 percent of the book value of the plant and equipment. Determine the cash flows associated with the project, taking the possibility of insurance into account. What is the break-even probability of expropriation in the presence of insurance? If you still think that the probability of expropriation is between 7 percent and 9 percent, would you give your approval to the project now or not?

Does the insurance increase the expected value of this project? What is the purpose of insurance? If you are confronted with a choice between two projects involving political risk with the same expected present value (either with or without insurance), how would you decide which one to choose?

d. Aside from the opportunity of buying insurance, what other strategies are there for dealing with political risk before incidents occur? What strategies are there for dealing with political incidents once they occur?

TOOLS FOR ANALYSIS
Political Risk in the MacDougall Model

This section looks at a model of capital flows and political risk based on the MacDougall model developed in "Tools for Analysis I" at the end of Chapter 1. Figure 12-2 presents the situation. Assume that the diagram pertains to all forms of international investment: portfolio investment, intermediated investment, and direct foreign investment. The marginal products of capital at home and abroad are MPK and MPK*, respectively. If

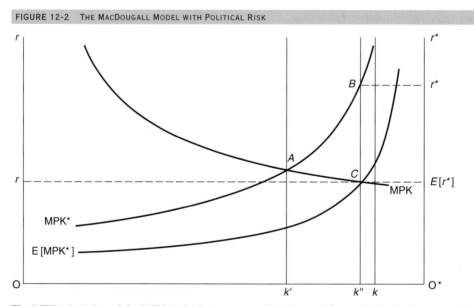

FIGURE 12-2   THE MACDOUGALL MODEL WITH POLITICAL RISK

The MPK schedule and the MPK* schedule represent the demands for capital in the home and foreign countries from the origins O and $O*$ respectively. The initial allocation of capital is at k, and the optimum allocation of capital is at k' where the marginal products of capital are equalized. With political risk in the foreign country, however, the marginal product of capital expected by the home country investors, denoted $E[\text{MPK}*]$, is less than the marginal product of capital physically possible. The equilibrium allocation of capital is at k''. As too much capital remains at home and not enough capital moves abroad, there is a deadweight loss of area ABC.

there is political risk abroad, there is a difference between the physical returns possible from a foreign investment and the expected returns allowing for the possibility of political incidents. The essential feature is that the return in the foreign country is uncertain: the investor may get a high return (shown along MPK*) if no intervention occurs or may lose everything (a negative rate of return) if expropriation occurs.

Taking into account the probability of political incidents, the expected returns from foreign investment are below MPK*, at $E[\text{MPK*}]$, where E denotes the expected value. Domestic capital owners therefore compare the marginal product of capital at home to the expected marginal product of capital abroad. They locate capital abroad until the expected returns abroad are equal to the domestic returns, $r = E[r^*]$. This behavior leads to an allocation of capi-

tal at k'', so if the initial allocation of capital is at k, the amount of foreign investment is the length between k and k''. This distance is less than the optimum allocation of capital, which would be the distance between k and k', because of the foreign political risk. Hence, political risk causes underinvestment abroad and a global deadweight loss shown by triangle ABC. The real interest rate in the source country, r, is below the real interest rate in the foreign country, r^*, and the difference between the two can be interpreted as a risk premium for political risk. The MacDougall model of political risk is fundamentally the same as the MacDougall models of capital market segmentation and exchange risk, and to the models of taxation developed in Chapter 11. All of these models explain why real interest differentials arise, but indicate different reasons.

❖ ENDNOTES

1. For more on defining and assessing political risk, see Kobrin (1979) and Sethi and Luther (1986).
2. Some of the recent, general books on political risk include Kobrin (1982), Kennedy (1987), and Stapenhurst (1992).
3. For more on this, see Sarna (1986).
4. Lecraw (1984) also links percent of equity ownership in subsidiaries to relative bargaining power; in addition, success (profitability) of the subsidiary is linked to relative bargaining power.
5. These were examined in Chapters 1 and 11, respectively.
6. Of course, this is not an examination of deviations from uncovered interest parity but of an-

other interest parity implying that interest rates on the same currency (holding all other characteristics of the asset constant) should be identical across locations, particularly between onshore and offshore markets. Presumably, failure of this interest parity would also lead to the failure of uncovered interest parity.
7. For a survey, see Simon (1982) and Political Risk Services (1998).
8. For further discussion, see Shapiro (1978, 1983).
9. For a discussion of negotiating with a host country after expropriation, see Hoskins (1970).

❖ REFERENCES

Aliber, Robert Z. "The Interest Rate Parity Theorem: A Reinterpretation," *Journal of Political Economy*, November/December 1973, pp. 1451–1459.

Austin, James E., and John C. Ickis. "Managing After the Revolutionaries Have Won," *Harvard Business Review*, May-June 1986, pp. 103–109.

Behrman, Jack N., and Robert E. Grosse. *International Business and Government: Issues and Institutions*, University of South Carolina Press, 1990.

Bradley, David. "Managing Against Expropriation," *Harvard Business Review*, July-August 1977, pp. 75–83.

Brewer, Thomas L. "Government Policies, Market Imperfections, and Foreign Direct Investment," *Journal of International Business Studies*, first quarter 1993, pp. 101–120.

Boddewyn, Jean J. "Political Aspects of MNE Theory," *Journal of International Business Studies*, Fall 1988, pp. 341–363.

de la Torre, José, and David H. Neckar. "Forecasting Political Risks for International Operations," *International Journal of Forecasting*, 1988, pp. 221–241.

Dooley, Michael P., and Peter Isard. "Capital Controls, Political Risk, and Deviations from Interest

Rate Parity," *Journal of Political Economy,* 1980, pp. 370–384.

DRI/McGraw-Hill. *Country Risk Review: A Publication of the Global Risk Service,* fourth quarter 1995.

Encarnation, Dennis J., and Sushil Vachani. "Foreign Ownership: When Hosts Change the Rules," *Harvard Business Review,* September-October 1985, pp. 152–153.

Fagre, Nathan, and Louis T. Wells, Jr. "Bargaining Power of Multinationals and Host Governments," *Journal of International Business Studies,* Fall 1982, pp. 9–23.

Hoskins, William R. "How to Counter Expropriation," *Harvard Business Review,* September-October 1970, pp. 102–112.

Kennedy, Charles R., Jr. *Political Risk Management,* New York: Quorum Books, 1987.

Kibbe, Jennifer. *Leaving South Africa: The Impact of U.S. Corporate Disinvestment,* Investor Responsibility Research Center, 1988.

Kobrin, Stephen J. "The Environmental Determinants of Foreign Direct Manufacturing Investment: An Ex Post Empirical Analysis," *Journal of International Business Studies,* Fall-Winter 1976, pp. 29–42.

Kobrin, Stephen J. "Political Risk: A Review and Reconsideration," *Journal of International Business Studies,* Spring-Summer 1979, pp. 67–80.

Kobrin, Stephen J. *Managing Political Risk Assessment,* Berkeley: University of California Press, 1982.

Kobrin, Stephen J. "Testing the Bargaining Hypothesis in the Manufacturing Sector in Developing Countries," *International Organization,* Autumn 1987, pp. 609–638.

Kobrin, Stephen J., John Basek, Stephen Blank, and Joseph LaPalombara. "The Assessment and Evaluation of Non-Economic Environments by American Firms: A Preliminary Report," *Journal of International Business Studies,* Spring-Summer 1980, pp. 32–48.

Lecraw, Donald J. "Bargaining Power, Ownership, and Profitability of Subsidiaries of Transnational Corporations in Developing Countries," *Journal of International Business Studies,* Spring-Summer 1984, pp. 27–43.

Minor, Michael S. "The Demise of Expropriation as an Instrument of LDC Policy, 1980–1992," *Journal of International Business Studies,* First Quarter 1994, pp. 177–188.

Political Risk Services. *1995 Political Risk Yearbook,* Political Risk Services, 1995.

Political Risk Services. *The Handbook of Country and Political Risk Analysis,* Political Risk Services, second edition, 1998.

Political Risk Services. *International Country Risk Guide,* Political Risk Services, 1995.

Poynter, Thomas A. "Government Intervention in Less-Developed Countries: The Experience of Multinational Companies," *Journal of International Business Studies,* Spring-Summer 1982, pp. 9–25.

Poynter, Thomas A. *Multinational Enterprises and Government Intervention,* London: Croom Helm, 1985.

Poynter, Thomas A. "Managing Government Intervention: A Strategy for Defending the Subsidiary," *Columbia Journal of World Business,* Winter 1986, pp. 55–65.

Sarna, A. J. *Boycott and Blacklist: A History of Arab Economic Warfare Against Israel,* Rowman & Littlefield, 1986.

Schmidt, David A. "Analyzing Political Risk," *Business Horizons,* July-August 1986, pp. 43–50.

Sethi, S. Prakash, and K. A. N. Luther. "Political Risk Analysis and Direct Foreign Investment: Some Problems of Definition and Management," *California Management Review,* Winter 1986, pp. 57–68.

Shapiro, Alan C. "Capital Budgeting for the Multinational Corporation," *Financial Management,* Spring 1978, pp. 7–16.

Shapiro, Alan C. "Managing Political Risk: A Policy Approach," *Columbia Journal of World Business,* Fall 1981, pp. 63–70.

Shapiro, Alan C. "International Capital Budgeting," *Midland Corporate Finance Journal,* Spring 1983, pp. 26–45.

Simon, Jeffrey D. "Political Risk Assessment: Past Trends and Future Prospects," *Columbia Journal of World Business,* Fall 1982, pp. 62–71.

Stapenhurst, Frederick. *Political Risk Analysis Around the North Atlantic,* St. Martin's Press, 1992.

Page numbers followed by f indicate figure. Page numbers followed by t indicate table.

G